Doomed Destroyer

"We're going in but we're not coming out!"

Ron Cope

Clink
Street

London | New York

Published by Clink Street Publishing 2017

Copyright © 2017

First edition.

ISBNs: paperback 978-1-912262-06-9
ebook 978-1-912262-07-6, 6

Doomed Destroyer's Front Cover Image: John Hamilton was acknowledged as one of the world's leading World War Two artists. The paintings do not glorify war, but are a tribute to the courage and endurance of the sailors and marines. With the kind permission of his daughter, Jane Hamilton.

Dedicated to all the NATO Forces, especially those mentioned in this book: Royal Norwegian Navy, Polish Navy, German Navy, Royal Navy and including the British Merchant Navy. These naval forces are now working together to provide our security.

Contents

Acknowledgements

Peter Mitchell, the owner of 'submerged.co.uk' sadly passed away since finishing this book. Without Peter's cooperation and genuine interest, it would have taken a few more years to complete. He was a career Royal Marine and a highly experienced deep-sea diver. We swopped a few interesting stories over the years. Rest in peace, shipmate.

I would like to give a big thankyou to my publisher Clink Street/Authoright and show my appreciation for all the team's professional efforts in once again producing the task set them.

Thank you to the Imperial War Museum (Collections and Research Department). Audio Recordings for their great online assistance and speedy reply to my regular requests. Code Numbers of audio interviews as below:

Marshal Soult 12207; Sam Evens 11335; Cope 11586; Pulford 10610; Bourton 10746; Cheshire 16304; Robinson 11286; Harris 16792

Another thank you: War Diaries of the German Zerstörers [destroyers] involved in the Battles of Narvik. Archives at the Bundesarchiv-Militarachiv (BA-MA) Freiburg, Germany. As seen below.

RM Nos with initials of the ten German Zerstörers for instance GT 94/95 [Georg Thiele], BvA.94/78, WZ.94/78, 94/80, DvR.94/93, HL94/94, WH.94/95, HK94/99, EK.94/72 and AS.94/100. The contents taken from these documents were kindly translated into English by the distinguished Norwegian author Alf Reidar Jacobsen. Alf allowed me to use some of his 'first seen' photographs.

Another distinguished Norwegian author, Geirr Haarr who in the latter stages of writing the book gave me sound advice and also allowed me to use some of his fantastic photographs. Both were indispensable to round off and filling in gaps for the story.

There were many accounts that enhanced the contents of my book, but one stands out which I felt had to be included. This was by Theodor Broch, who at the time of the Battles of Narvik was the Mayor of Narvik and had his experiences published in the book *The Mountains Wait.* I was privileged to be given permission from Theodor's daughter Siri [nee Broch] to include parts of her father's book. I would also like to thank Supreme Judge Lars Oftedal Broch for putting me in contact with his sister, Siri.

My sister-in-law, Jacqueline Vickery for her ongoing dedication, to reproofing and correcting errors. Alison, my wife for her patience over the nine years. She can now have her breakfast room and conservatory back.

John Warburton-Lee, Ralph Brigginshaw, (Norway), Trevor Baker for their fantastic support; now considered friends. Tom Currie, who was there from the beginning when I decided to put pen to paper and for his encouragement. Wikipedia (donations made), Leo Styles (Australia), Frank Hackney (Johannesburg)), Warrant Officer Anthony Royle R.N. Ret'd (grandson of Cyril Cope), Bill and Borg-Anna Sanders, Chris Mitchell at 'submerged. co.uk', Dr Nik Sifferlinger (Austria), Percy. C. Danby and Victor Wallwork. (Canada)

I was greatly thankful to Frank Hackney and ex pat living in Johannesburg who surprised me with his E Mail stating, *"I came across these photos and many more from WW2. I was told the collection belonged to a German who was on 'U-Boats. Are they of interest?* They certainly were because they included shots taken shortly after the Battles of Narvik. The Kriegsmarine was Theo Werner Schettler who had settled in the Transvaal area after the war, he was either an official naval photographer or took them on the opportunites his U-Boat surfaced. My appreciation goes to Theo who would never know that his amazing efforts, seventy seven years later would be honoured in a British book.

A special mention must go to all the families and friends who were prepared to provide the accounts of their loved ones.

Barbara Wakeham and Joan Jowitt (Marshal Soult's family friend and his sister), Carole Knowles (daughter: John Hague), Robin Ward, Claire Scholfield and Louise Nicholas (family of Captain David Nicholas), Christopher Clark (son of Lt Urling Clark), Barbara Roche (daughter of Harold Siddall) Donald Lancaster (nephew of Lt Peter Lancaster), Yasmin 'Yassie' Duckworth (family of Cyril Holehouse), Lesley Hood-Bourton (daughter of Dougy Bourton), Les Smales, Jose Johnson and Ellen Siddall (daughters of Thomas 'Daddy' Norton). Jill List (Billy Bradfield's niece), Norman Bowden (son of Norman Bowden), Shelia and Arthur Horner (Shelia is daughter of Joe Settle), Jim Cook (son of Stan 'Cookie' Cook), John Farrier (nephew of Bill Wallis), Ann Cruistan and Brendan Sheridan (sister and nephew of John Mulhall), David Goodey (son of Albert Goodey), Christine Taylor (Australia – granddaughter of Leslie Oliver), Rob Harry (nephew of Jack Tucker), Terry Flannery (son of Captain Surgeon Albert Flannery), Janet Brown (niece of 'Ginger' Turner), Jim Renshaw (son of 'Stormy' Renshaw), Chris Boylan (son of First Officer Christopher Boylan), Shelley Hutton (granddaughter of Guy Hunter), Pat Duffy (son of Joseph 'Pat' Duffy), Gavin Holt (grandson of Alfred Holt), Chris Lane (grandson of George Lane), Jim MacKenzie (grandson of James Smail), Gordon Lees (family friend of George Sutton), Geoff Webber (nephew of Harold Webber), Danny Beckford (grandson of Daniel Beckford), Tony Blundell (great nephew of Nicholas Blundell), Ged Jackson (great nephew of Billy Feddon), Terry Orford (nephew of Ted Orford), plus additional contributions from Daryl Harries, Mike Stanner, Tore Eggan, Denis Darmanin (Malta) John Mizzi (Malta), Petty Officer Daniel Reardon (HMS *Warspite*) John and Sylvia Cooper, (assisting my book signing events by joining me in their WW2 re-enactment Naval Uniforms). Professor. Robert Moore (University of Liverpool), Bob Lawrence (crewman-Leslie House). Peter Kershaw (son of Stan 'Jake' Kershaw), Nigel Sefton (family member of David Johnson).

Nick Grant at Ian Allan Publishers for giving permission to reproduce quotes from Peter Dickens book.

War and Son.co.uk, warmemories.co.uk, 'www.bluebird-electric.net' 2016, 'Beachcombing's Bizarre History Blog'.

National Archives at Kew and Her Majesties Stationary Office. National Maritime Museum, Greenwich. The Imperial War Museum. The Commonwealth War Graves Commission.

Search iwmcollections.org.uk/civilians learningcurve.gov.uk/homefront. kington.keo.mercurytide.com, news.bbc.co.uk

Neville Chipulina (Gibraltar) 'A History of the Chipulina Family'.

Last but not least, the Polish gentleman who saw me at a book signing event in Telford Town Centre Library, for advising me how much the Polish Navy were involved in the Battles of Narvik and others theatres of war. I hope by chance he gets to know about my book, if so make contact through my publisher. This would put my mind at rest.

If I have forgotten anyone, forgive me but by all means make contact and the error can be corrected at a later date. In the meantime, every effort has been made to trace the copyright holders of photographs and illustrations.

Author's Preface

This book, similar to my first, *Attack at Dawn*, is not intended to mislead readers into thinking it is a comprehensive work of naval history. I leave that to those with far more professional qualifications. However, I believe it should be considered as being the first definitive record of accounts brought together from those who were actually involved in the Battles of Narvik.

I would also like to point out that the actual 'First Battle of Narvik', took place the day before on the 9th of April 1940. This was when the German Navy arrived and was confronted by, two First World War Norwegian coastal defence ships, *Eidsvold* and *Norge*. The ships plight is covered later in the book.

Foreword (1)

My father, Fred Ward, was born in 1919 and is now the last remaining survivor of the HMS *Hunter*, H35.

At ninety-seven-years old Fred has been fighting a long battle with old age and although very weak, he is still able to recount his memories of the fateful day of April 10th 1940.

After leaving Portsmouth, HMS *Hunter* sailed for Narvik, the crew not knowing what lay ahead, were just told to be ready for further orders. They sailed into Ofotfjord and stopped near a lighthouse where a boat was sent to shore for intelligence gathering. When the boat returned, the order was given to prepare for battle.

It was freezing, snowing and visibility was poor with the *Hardy* leading the flotilla as they weaved their way through merchant ships that were docked in Narvik, then all hell broke loose.

The noise from the gun fire and explosions echoed off the side of the mountains. It was like having your head compressed, you could not think, the training just takes over. The *Hunter* was hit, disabling her in the middle of the fjord, unable to move, she was a sitting duck.

The last thing Fred remembers before jumping into the freezing water was seeing his Captain, *Lind*say De Villiers walk back into the bridge. He looked at Fred and nodded, as if to say over you go. A lot of sailors jumped in immediately as they were near fires or other hazardous things, but my father felt safer staying on board. Most of them had already succumbed to the cold, it was snowing and the water was like ice. Fred was now in the water and watched as the *Hunter* sank, taking her Captain and her trapped crew to the bottom of the fjord with her.

There were about fifty Stokers on board and most were probably still alive when she sank; but their exits were buckled from the explosions and they were trapped. This haunts my father to this day.

This book is in memory of Fred's fellow shipmates.

Able Seaman. 'Gunner' Fred Ward.
Cinderford, Gloucestershire. May 2016

Written by Fred's son, Robin Ward.

Prior to sending my manuscript to the publisher, I received a post from Victor Wallwork in Ottawa, Canada. He had been searching websites for information on the Battle of Narvik. In the Falmouth newspaper *The Packet* dated 2010, I was looking to find contacts for my first book. It was a surprise to hear from Victor that his stepfather Percy Danby, known as 'Dan', was a crew member on *Hotspur*. Percy, who was 98 years young, also lived in Ottawa. As you would imagine a lot of post went back and forth over the following weeks, slowly gathering Percy's experience at Narvik. The publishers would have to wait, politely of course.

Percy Danby from Doncaster had joined the Navy in October, 1938, as a 5th Class Engine Room Artificer. His first sea draft was to the battleship *Resolution*.

Foreword (2)

Ron Cope has asked me to provide a few words to introduce his book. I have already provided him a brief account of the details that I recall, and he has weaved these into the reports and stories of others in the pages that follow. I am proud to have served and to have played my part in the action. I have read accounts of the first and second Battles of Narvik. They say that the victory we won there helped the Allies to win back Narvik, even if it was only temporarily. And I have also heard it said that the victory probably helped to delay an invasion of Britain, because the German navy had lost so many of its destroyers at Narvik. During the battle, I wasn't thinking about these things. I had been trained to do important work, and I was so busy trying to do it under difficult conditions that I didn't have time to think about the immediate danger, much less the big picture.

I am grateful to Ron Cope for taking up and carrying on the good work about Narvik that was begun by his late father, Cyril. I had the pleasure of meeting Cyril and going out to dinner with him one evening during a visit to England in 1993. I am sure that he would be proud that his son has taken up the cause with such passion. Without dedicated men like Ron, the testimony and the stories of the men who were there – whether they were lost, wounded, or survived – what became of them, their families, might otherwise be lost to future generations.

Percy C. Danby, Lieutenant (E), C.D. RCN Retired.

Ottawa. March 2017

In Percy's words, "When war was declared in September 1939, *Resolution* was at anchor in Portland Harbour, Dorset. My first serious trip to sea was on *Resolution* to deliver ten tons of gold to Halifax, Nova Scotia. On my return to England, I was drafted to Chatham Naval Depot and a few weeks later to the destroyer HMS *Hotspur* which was refitting in Chatham Dockyard in January 1940. After the completion of the refit, we joined the Home Fleet in Scapa Flow in the Orkneys in northern Scotland, doing escort duties and anti-submarine patrols in the most appalling weather.

"When *Hotspur* went to action stations I was stationed in No.1 Boiler Room, attending an emergency diesel-driven generator and acting as backup Petty Officer in charge of the unit. The engine room received information directly from the Bridge and kept the boiler rooms informed via voice pipe of what was happening."

Percy Danby aged 98 proudly wearing his 2nd Destroyer Flotilla Association of Narvik blazer and awarded medals. [2016]

Prologue

Another Hunter Story – 1968

An intriguing story by Able Seaman Marshal Soult, was amongst his memoires, twenty-eight years after his experience on HMS *Hunter* at the Battle of Narvik. It was his choice for the title and in his own words below. It begins in his county of Cornwall.

Camelford to Bodmin, Bodmin to Fraddon, Fraddon to Ladock, Ladock to Tresillian, Tresillian to Truro, Truro to Perranworthal, Perranarworthal to Penryn. The journey from Tintagel to Falmouth is through country as diverse as the names of villages and towns en route. Even the climate changes, the temperature especially. I had left Tintagel on a cold, grey wintry morning. At Falmouth, early in the afternoon, though the air was balmy, vaguely hinting at spring.

Lucretia Kelly and I sat in a four-sided shelter on Falmouth sea front. Stone steps rose to a wooden bench. Before us stretched Falmouth Bay; a calm, vast, unruffled sheet of water, reminding me that this is the softer, gentler side of Cornwall. It was across this same stretch of water that a journalist Robert Manley sailed his *Tinkerbelle* the last miles of a single-handed voyage from Falmouth, Massachusetts, to Falmouth, Cornwall. It is here too that the 'Tall Ships' race had begun.

Falmouth, sprawling at the mouth of a large inlet of sea has a long nautical history. Sir Walter Raleigh knew the value of this harbour. Falmouth, for many years, was an appointed port for mail boats or packets; they continued to call until 1850. The end of the packets meant a decline in Falmouth's trade, but the authorities responded with vision by building and extending the docks. The docks remain an important factor in the local economy. Falmouth, too assumed a certain importance in the last war as a repair depot and centre for British and American navies, a fact Hitler's bombers did not overlook. In and around the town, British and American troops trained and waited for D-Day.

Lucretia Kelly is a smartly dressed woman with brown eyes. She had sent a photograph of herself, taken more than a quarter of a century ago. I recognised her as soon as she had opened the door of her home twenty minutes ago. That photograph of Penryn Accordion Band and this stone shelter were two threads in a story which had roused my curiosity; and had brought me fifty miles to meet her.

Her story concerned Falmouth in 1940, a year of German conquests in Europe, of Dunkirk and threatened invasion. During the day, Lucretia Kelly [then she was Miss Johns] worked in the book binding department. In the evening, exchanging working clothes for a black and red uniform, black skirt, red blouse, black velvet bolero and red sash; she played the accordion in local dance halls.

Those were nights when dancers were moving to music like 'Roll Out the Barrel', 'Somewhere in France' and 'Boom'. There were seven in the band; four boys and three girls, five with accordions, one at the drums, another at the piano. It was a year in which Cornish cinema audiences saw Dorothy Lamour in *Typhoon*, Dickie Lupino in *Just William* [...] and Shirley Temple in *The Little Princess*.

One spring evening Lucretia Johns had met a special young sailor, Alan. [Lucretia explains] "It was in the dance hall, then named the Winter Gardens Ballroom, but it really was the Polytechnic Hall; when he came up stage to ask for a request tune. He was fair, rather nice looking; he came from up North, he told me, and he had a sister, a hairdresser. He was aboard HMS *Hunter*, then in Falmouth Docks, and after that we had several dates. On March 7th the ship's company held a 'farewell dance' at the Princess Pavilion, and being a naval dance, everybody went to it, so that the other dances were empty. Anyhow, our band had to play in the Winter Gardens and Mr Conyngham, who ran the dances, made us play to an empty hall. But around nine o'clock he had a change of heart, and closed down .... you can guess where I made for!

"The next night – *Hunter*'s last ashore, Alan and I went for a walk and ended up here in this shelter. At one point in our conversation I turned to him to say something, and had all I could do to stop myself from screaming, because Alan had turned into a skeleton. I turned away, and then forced myself to look and speak to him, and when I looked he was quite normal once again. I didn't tell him of my vision, as I didn't want to scare him; but I must have looked queer, because he asked me if I was all right, although I'd done my best to hide it. Alan was just the same after the vision. It seemed to have no effect on him."

Next day HMS *Hunter* set sail from Falmouth, called at Plymouth to store ship before making way to Scapa Flow, Scotland. Then, on the April 10th, on the BBC one o'clock lunchtime news report, came the announcement of *Hunter*'s sinking in a Norwegian fjord. Lucretia Kelly still vividly remembers the horror. "My family and I were sitting at lunch, and I stood up from the table and shouted: 'Alan is dead!' I frightened my mother, and, at the time, she must have thought I had gone out of my mind. However, the truth turned out to be much stranger and not as she expected."

Concluded at the end of the book.

Introduction

Having written my first book *Attack at Dawn* and finishing off the second, I was asked the following question by a newspaper feature writer. "Would you still have gone ahead with the challenge if you had known it would have taken you eight years?" "Probably not." However, now it is finally out into the public domain, and all the dedicated hard work is over, naturally I feel it was all well worth the thousands of hours it has taken in my life.

Second question: "How did the writing of this book come about, one asks?" A long story. (To summarise my 'Introduction' in *Attack at Dawn*.) In the early 1970s my father, Cyril Cope, was the founder member and Honourable Secretary of the '2nd Destroyer Flotilla Association of Narvik,' which quickly grew into over 200 members. He himself was a twenty-one-year-old Torpedoman on HMS *Hardy*, the flotilla leader. Subsequently, with his own experience in the first Royal Naval Battle of Narvik and material gathered from other Association members he was able to build up a relatively historical archive. I myself had joined the Royal Navy in 1964 and by now was halfway through my twenty-three year career, taking a close interest in the Association's developments.

During the 1990s the Association was fast running out of members due to their ages. Cyril decided to write his own book about the epic events occurring on the 10th April 1940. Sadly, Cyril's own age and ill health took over and he was unable to fulfil the task.

Also, in 1990, Cyril was interviewed at his home in Exwick, Exeter by a curator from the Imperial War Museum (IWM) in London. The audio tapes are still in the museum's historical records and are accessible to the public. Cyril passed away three months after my Mam, Edie in 2003. I contacted IWM in 2010 and they kindly sent me CD copies. It had always struck me that at some stage this was 'a story that needed to be told' for future generations. Having retired from the Royal Navy in 1986, I realised that other than the technological advances, it was obvious that there had been few

1

traditional changes. Therefore, I felt I was well placed to carry on the task my father had not been able to complete.

During the nine years of considerable research – as you will see from my list of 'Acknowledgements' – I was able to make contact with a substantial number of people personally associated with the five destroyers, *Hardy*, *Hunter*, *Havock*, *Hotspur* and *Hostile*. In 2014, having been advised to check the number of words. I concluded that I needed to write two books. However, it has turned out to be a welcoming bonus, because whilst the first book was in the public domain, I managed to gather additional material for this book. For example, accounts of the 'battle' by the opposing German forces on land and sea and, equally important, the suffering it caused to the local citizens ashore.

My intentions remain the same, which are rather than just presenting a historical account of the warfare strategies, the book should predominantly focus on narratives provided by those brave sailors and civilians who were present at the time. Most of the armed forces on both sides, were young men and with little experience of life at sea, never mind in war. Equally for those Royal Navy and Merchant Navy seamen who came out of it alive, who with their remarkable efforts were able to survive, until they were finally repatriated back to Britain.

This really is a true story lost in the mist of time.

PART ONE

HMS Hunter's Early Years

HMS Hunter's Short Life Almost Comes to an Abrupt End

On the 13th December 1934 the ship builders Swan & Hunter on the Tyne and Wear were given an order by the Admiralty to build an 'H' Class destroyer to be eventually named HMS *Hunter*. The founder of the company way back in mid-nineteenth century was George Burton Hunter. Coincidence or not? The cost was £253,167 and the company had become to be known as one of the best shipbuilders in the world. In the twentieth century, the company's pedigree included such famous ships as RMS *Mauretania* which held the 'Blue Riband' for the fastest crossing of the Atlantic; and another, RMS *Carpathia* which went on to rescue survivors from RMS *Titanic*.

As you will read, HMS *Hunter* will have a number of survivors needing to be rescued, but under totally different circumstances. The *Hunter* was 323 feet in length with a beam of 33 feet, and displaced 1,370 tons (standard load) and 1,883 tons (deep load). She was powered by steam turbines driving two shafts which developed 34,000 shaft horsepower (25 kilowatts) providing a speed of 36 knots (41 mph). She carried a maximum of 480 tons of fuel oil that gave her a range of 5,530 nautical miles at a steady speed of 15 knots. She was designed for a ship's complement of 137 in peacetime but when the war began she was cramming 158 crewmembers in her decks.

At the time she was a formidable war machine, with an armament of four 4.7 inch single open mounts, for anti-aircraft defence, two 0.5 inch quadruple machine gun mounts, two quadruple torpedo tubes and one depth charge rail with two throwers fitted (port and starboard) for her thirty-five depth charges, with a trained crew ready to match any foe that was capable of making a challenge.

Hunter was launched on the 25 March 1936 and attached to the Devonport base, under the command of Lieutenant Commander Bryan Scurfield. In October 1936, she sailed to join the Mediterranean Fleet, where she would remain for three and a half years.

When I decided to start writing my first book about HMS *Hardy* and her crew members' accounts, I had not expected a substantial number of their families, predominantly of HMS *Hunter*, to make contact with me. In fact it was wonderful to find there were two of *Hunter's* crew still with us, Seaman 'Gunner' Fred Ward and Able Seaman John Hague, both then ninety-one years old. I will refer back to them later.

However, from my father, Cyril's documents, I discovered an account under the heading 'The *Hunter* Story' which did not identify the writer's name. Because of mentions of Able Seaman Marshal Soult; I was correct in presuming, and it appears to be so, that as he was a regular attendee at the '2nd Destroyer Flotilla Association' reunions; it was he who gave it to Cyril in the 1970s. Marshal's address, was on a list of *Hunter* members' addresses, which showed Marshal came from Falmouth. A letter sent to the local newspaper *The Packet*, led to my making contact with his family and friends.

This was a stroke of luck as Marshal's account provides a considerable amount of well written and interesting information.

Marshal Soult during 'New Entry' training circa 1937.
[Barbara Wakeham Collection]

Here Marshal Soult begins his story where he finds himself being sent to more exciting and warmer climes than he could have imagined. "Having completed training at HMS *Wildfire*, we then went on to our bases, mine was Plymouth. After a short time I was put on the reserve list for a draft to the 'Med'. It was by accident that one above me on the list had been thrown off a ride or something at a fun fair in Plymouth. So I was sent with a 'Tiff' to join HMS Active in January 1938." [1]

When Marshal joined *Hunter* he was quickly made aware by his new shipmates of the pride they felt for their ship. Marshal explains, "HMS *Hunter* was commissioned and joined the 2nd Destroyer Flotilla in the Mediterranean Fleet on 30th September 1936. The ship had been involved in the Spanish Civil War."

As you would expect having a crew from many different parts of Britain there was a lot of banter around the ship concerning their favourite football teams. One particular mess had its fair share of Mancunians, so amazingly priority was that of looking after your shipmates rather than causing heated arguments between warring 'United' and 'City' fans. However, in May 1937, that may have changed as Manchester City ran away with the Division One title, with fifty-seven points and a fantastic one hundred and seven goals. Thirty of them scored by their new £10,000 signing Irishman Peter Doherty. However, it would not be long before the euphoria turned back to loyalty to their shipmates.

To expand a little on *Hunter*'s involvement in the Spanish Civil War, the ship was enforcing the edicts of the Non-Intervention Committee, from 1936–37. This included an arms blockade imposed on both sides by Britain and France. Whilst on patrol, between 2 pm and 3 pm on the 13th of May 1937, there was a massive explosion on board the ship. The news of the event was quickly broadcast around the world.

The explosion occurred amidships under the ships galley, Stoker Petty Officers' mess and the Torpedomen's messdecks. It caused the boiler room oil-fuel pipes to burst, releasing floods of oil fuel. Further forward there was sea water flooding, the radio equipment was put out of action and the ship began to list heavily. There was eight of her crew killed and fourteen injured.

---

1   'Tiff' is the nickname for an Artificer. These men have higher education qualifications than other ratings and complete a longer period of trade training. They tend to be promoted much quicker.

As 'Damage Control' trained crewmembers rapidly went to the aid of casualties, many brave acts took place. The ladder down to the boiler room had been blown away. To reach them the rescue party had to jump down eight feet into three foot of oil fuel and on to a deck which might not have been intact. Throughout the rescue attempt the rescue party were in imminent danger of falling through the shattered deck into the water and fuel. Moreover, they were under the impression that the ship was about to founder.

Their exertions to save life consisted in dragging living and dead comrades from under the wreckage and out of the oil fuel and passing them up on deck. The whole operation took between five and ten minutes. Had those rescued been left much longer they were at high risk of swallowing oil fuel and would have undoubtedly have died. As well as those with severe burns who, if immersed in the substance for any prolonged period of time, would have suffered an agonising death.

Initially, it was uncertain as to the cause of the explosion and an official 'Inquiry' began immediately. The story continued to run in the national newspapers, here is just one comprehensive report.

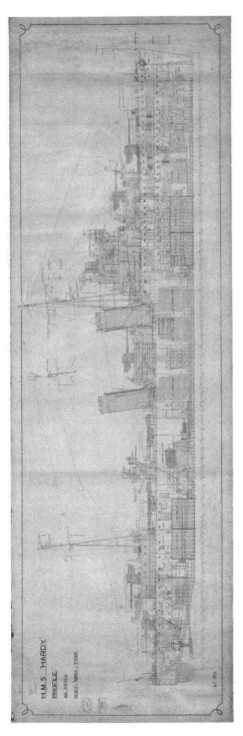

H.M.S. HARDY.
PROFILE
AS FITTED
SCALE ¼INCH= 1 FOOT

Kind Permission of the National
Maritime Museum, Greenwich, London

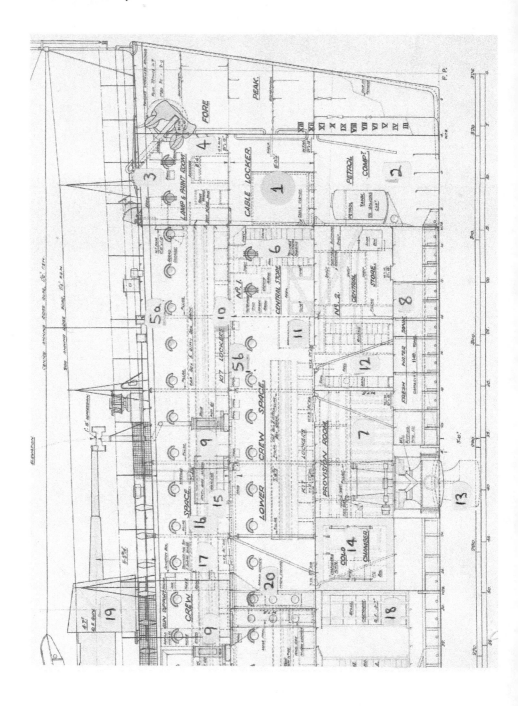

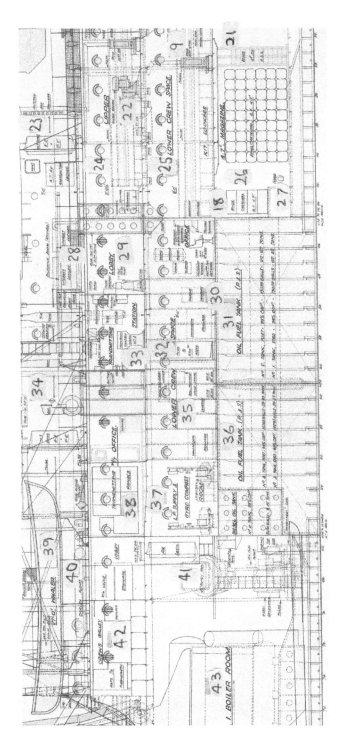

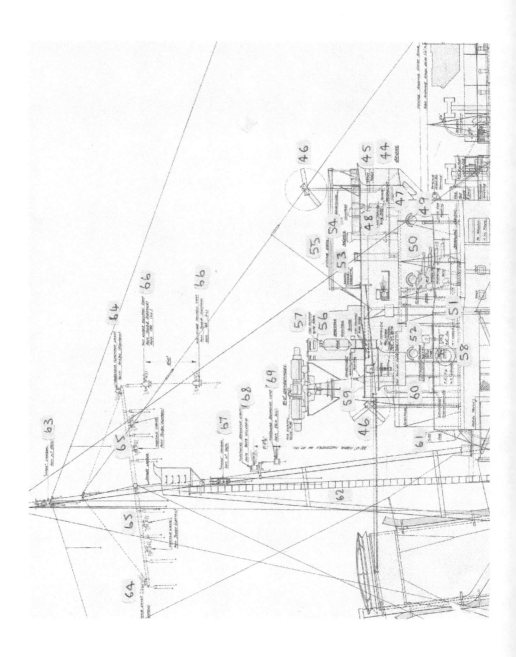

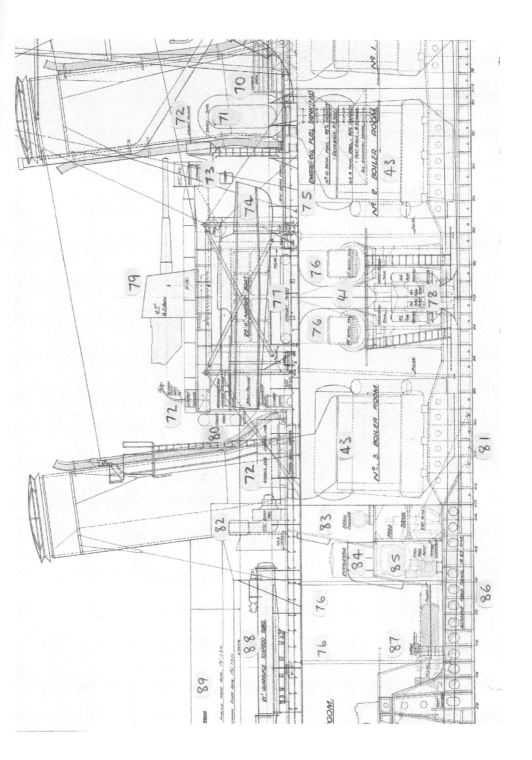

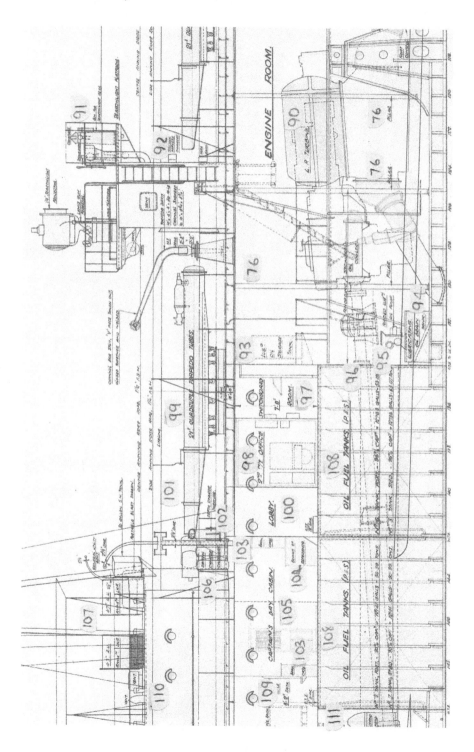

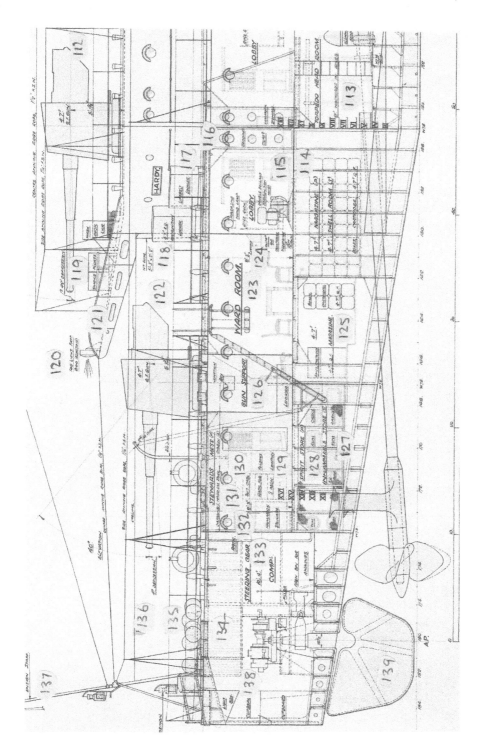

Numerical Key to Sections of Ship's Profile – As Fitted.
(Scale 1/4 inch = 1 Foot)

Section 1. (For'd)

1.   Anchor Cable Locker.
2.   Petrol Compartment.
3.   Lamp and Paint Store.
4.   Cell (temporary use if needed).
5.   a. Stokers Messdeck.
     b. Communications Messdeck.
6.   Central Stores Office.
7.   Provision Room.
8.   Fresh Water Tank.
9.   Stove.
10. Kit Lockers
11. Hammock Storage.
12. Storage Racks.
13. ASDIC type 121 (first production retractable dome).
14. Cold Chamber (freezer compartment).
15. Anti-gas Mask Locker.
16. Cap Boxes and Ditty Box Racks.
17. Stowage for Tea and Sugar Boxes.
18. Boxes Cartridges 4.7-inch.
19. No1 Gun. 4.7-inch QF (All Guns are Open Shield).
20. Bread Locker.

Section 2.

21. Boxes 0.5 Inch Machine Gun Ammunition.
22. 4.7 Inch Shell Ammunition Hoist.
23. Watertight Door from Upper Deck.
24. Chief Petty Officers and Petty Officers' Mess.
25. Seamen's Messdeck.
26. 4.7-inch Shell Magazine.
27. Floodwater Inlet to Magazine.
28. Lifebelt Lockers.
29. Lobby to Canteen Flat.
30. Folding Lavatory.

31. Oil Fuel Tanks. No1 Stbd 15080 galls / No2 Port 15039 galls
32. Door to Stoker Petty Officers' Mess (watch keepers accom).
33. Gun Control Transmitter Station (console suite).
34. Air Flow Vent.
35. Torpedomen's and ASDIC Operators' Messdeck.
36. Oil Fuel Tanks. No3 Stbd 14898 galls / No4 Port 14365 galls
37. Low Power Supply and Gyro Compass Room.
38. Wireless Transmission Office (transmitting panels).
39. 27-foot Whaler.
40. Carley Float.
41. 48-inch Supply Fan.
42. Crew's Galley.
43. Nos 1, 2 and 3 Boiler Rooms.

Section 3.

44. Open bridge.
45. Chart Table.
46. Semaphore Indicator.
47. Remote Controls for W/T and ASDIC.
48. Fire Control Voice Pipes (guns).
49. Wheelhouse.
50. 0.5-inch Machine Guns (pom pom). (Port and Stbd)
51. Signal Deck.
52. 10-inch Signalling Projector / Box Signal Pads.
53. Pelorus Platform.
54. Compass Platform.
55. Awning Ridge – (hot weather / climate).
56. Director Control Tower.
57. Fire Control Voice Pipes.
58. Lifebuoy.
59. Range Finder.
60. Captain's Sea Cabin (Starboard). Navigator's Office (Port).
61. Flag Lockers.
62. Jacobs Ladder.
63. 'Upper' Lanterns.
64. Yardarm Flashing Lamp.
65. Fighting Lamps.

66. 'Not Under Control' Light.
67. Middle Lantern.
68. Masthead Steaming Light (electric).
69. Masthead Steaming Light (oil).

Section 4.

70. Lumber Rack.
71. Carley Float.
72. Lifebelt Locker.
73. No. 3 Gun Ammunition Locker.
74. 25-foot Motor Boat.
75. Emergency Oil Float Tank (Port 2043 galls / Stbd 2057).
76. Pillars.
77. Carley Float.
78. Oil / Fuel Pump / Heaters.
79. No. 3 Gun Q.F. 4.7-inch.
80. Carley Float.
81. Sea Water Inlet.
    43. No. 3 Boiler Room.
82. 17-inch Supply Fan.
83. Drain Cooler.
84. Evaporator.
85. Main Feed Pump /Feed Tank (9.87 tons).
86. Reserve Feed Tank (19.67 tons).
87. Water Extraction Pump.
88. 21-inch Quadruple Torpedo Tubes (For'd).
89. Awning Ridge Rope.

Section 5.

90. Turbine in Engine Room.
91. Compass Telegraph.
92. Torpedo Impulse Chargers.
93. Lubricating Oil Storage.
94. Lubricating Oil Drain Tank.
95. Forced Lubrication Oil Pump.
96. Shaft Tunnel.
97. Switchboard.

98. Second Wireless Transmitting Office.
99. After Quadruple 21-inch Torpedo Tubes.
100. Lobby.
101. Lifeline.
102. Depth Charge Thrower.
103. Book Cases.
104. Book Case for Reference Books.
105. Captain's Day Cabin.
106. Depth Charge Carriers.
107. 4.7 Guns Ammunition Lockers X2.
108. Oil Fuel Tanks (Port 18141 galls) (Stbd 18141 galls).
109. Rifle Racks.
110. Vent.
111. Torpedo Heads.

Section 6. (Aft).

112. No 4 Gun QF 4.7-inch.
113. Torpedo Heads Room.
114. 4.7-inch Shell and Magazine Room (Port and Stbd).
115. Double Bollard Ammunition Hoist.
116. Bedding Cupboard.
117. Lifebelt Locker.
118. 4.7-inch Ammunition Locker.
119. Smoke Floats.
120. Fog Light.
121. Gun Safety Cover. (Also For'd Gun)
122. No 5 Gun QF 4.7-inch.
123. Wardroom.
124. Letter Box / Cupboard for Compasses, Telescopes, Gun Sights.
125. 4.7 inch Cartridges Magazine.
126. Gun Support Circular Trunking. (Same for all the guns.)
127. Inflammable Store.
128. Spirit Store / Rum Casks Racks.
129. Folding Lavatory.
130. Stewards Messdeck.
131. Suit Case Rack.
132. Hammock Stowage.

133. Steering Gear Compartment / Emergency Steering position.
134. Depth Charge Stowage X 20.
135. Depth Charge Racks.
136. Lifeline.
137. Ensign Staff.
138. Stern Cupboards.
139. Rudder.

THE EXPLOSION ON HMS *HUNTER*.

Thought to Have Been Caused by Floating Mine.
The Scotsman. May 15th 1937.

The Admiralty stated last night that a preliminary investigation into the cause of the explosion in HMS *Hunter*, in which eight men were killed and injured, suggests that the ship struck a floating mine [...] Adds that it is unlikely that further details can be available until the vessel has been docked. Arrangements are being made to tow her to Gibraltar [...] Where an examination of her hull has been made.

20-Year Old Glasgow Man Amongst the Killed.

The list of those killed.
BETTRIDGE, Arthur, Leading Seaman, D/JX 135096, Derby.
CRAWFORD, George H, Ordinary Seaman, D/SSX 17152, Glasgow.
GRIFFITHS, John H, Petty Officer Cook, D/MX 48073, Cheshire.
HOUSE, Leslie V, Able Seaman, D/JX 135005, Dorset.
SWIGGS, Wilfrid R, Stoker Petty Officer, D/K 56346, Polperro.
TURNER, Bertie C, Petty Officer Telegraphist, D/J 72652, Somerset.
WAITES, Alfred, Stoker 1c, D/KX 86525, Hull.
WATTERS, William, Leading Seaman, D/JX 130358, Devonport.

Ordinary Seaman George Crawford, was only 20, and died on the fifth anniversary of his father's sudden death while watching a football match. A year ago he joined the Navy to be with his two chums, who are brothers.

Worse Disaster Averted
Help Given by Vessels of Spanish Government

Valencia. May 14. – Further details of explosion aboard HMS *Hunter* off Almeria yesterday reached here today.

Divers have carried out an inspection of the damaged hull of the vessel, following the appointment of a mixed commission of British and Spanish officers to investigate the cause of the explosion while the vessel is still in Spanish waters.

While no official report has yet been communicated to the Press, messages from Almeria are believed to confirm that only the speed with which help arrived saved a much worse disaster, possibly the total loss of the *Hunter*. The destroyer is said to have been getting lower and lower in the water when the Spanish Government destroyer *Lazaga* dashed up at full speed, followed by coastguard vessels, and the sea being calm, towed the *Hunter* by the bows to Almeria, where she was moored to the quayside. [The information I have, which was reported later and probably more accurate is that flotilla sister ship HMS *Hyperion* towed '*Hunter*' to Almeria, accompanied by the *Lazaga*.]

Mixed Commission's Investigation

Almeria. May 14. – It is understood here that the investigation of the Anglo-Spanish Mixed Commission has confirmed that the explosion on the *Hunter* was the result of a floating mine. The two holes are explained by the secondary effects of the explosion, one hole being much smaller than the other. The commission, which began its work at 4 a.m. this morning, was still continuing its inquiries at 3.30 p.m. By that time the slightly injured had been taken from hospital and brought on board HMS *Hyperion* and HMS *Arethusa*. The latter had arrived from Barcelona, and was flying the flag of Rear Admiral Wells, who is presiding over the Commission's inquiry.

Water Rushing In

At 4 p.m. according to one account, water was still rushing in, and the *Hunter* would have sunk where she was if Spanish tugs had not gone alongside and helped to support her by numerous cables, while powerful pumps got to work on the flooded compartments. A squad of divers were able to close a certain number of watertight doors, but are said to have failed to recover four bodies reported to have been trapped in the engine-room. Efforts were made today with blowpipes to cut away the steel plating of the engine-room, it is reported.

The Admiral commanding the Third Cruiser Squadron arrived at Almeria shortly after daybreak. HM. flotilla leader *Hardy* and HMS *Hyperion* reached here from Gibraltar during the night. – Reuter.

A later Reuter message from Valencia states that the *Hunter* is now being towed to Gibraltar by British destroyers, according to the British Embassy.

Three of the Dead Buried at Almeria

The three dead brought ashore yesterday from the destroyer were buried in the British cemetery here this afternoon are; Petty Officer John Griffiths; Leading Seaman William Watters and Ordinary Seaman George Crawford.

The names of the six men still lying in hospital with serious injuries are given as; Cook George Bond, Petty Officer Stoker Ernest Denley, Telegraphist Stephen Cavaghan and Seamen Samuel Thompson, John Oliffe and Edward Anderson, – Reuter.

Sunderland Echo. 15th May 1937. HMS *Hunter* Victims.

The streets of Almeria were crowded when the funeral of the three seamen who lost their lives in the accident to the British destroyer *Hunter* took place yesterday. Wreaths were sent by Spanish Army and Navy units. The coffins were carried respectively, by members of the Spanish Government Air Force, by marines from the destroyer *Lagaza* and marines from *Jaime Primero*.

The procession was followed by the crews of *Arethusa* and other British naval units. Representatives of the Spanish Government, all the notabilities of the province, the local naval authorities, and members of the Consular Corps were also present. Spanish troops in Almeria marching past the coffins with Union Jacks, arrived at the English cemetery.

The next day *Hunter* with a large hole in her side, was towed stern first to Gibraltar by the light cruiser HMS *Arethusa*.

Funeral Procession in Almeira. [Jim Renshaw son of James 'Stormy' Renshaw]

When the *Hunter* arrived in Gibraltar Dockyard work started immediately on releasing the remaining five bodies trapped in her boiler room. The dockyard workmen, under highly emotive and trying conditions did a sterling and successful job of extricating two. The others three bodies were released shortly after.

It was also reported later that there was another crewmember, who during the incident had performed heroic actions.

Hunter towed to Gibraltar by the light cruiser HMS
Arethusa. [John Hague's family collection]

Press Association Release. May 17th 1937
Courageous Navy Officer

The bravery of Lieutenant Commander Scurfield, commander of HMS *Hunter*, following the explosion on board the destroyer last Thursday, was revealed last night by other officers from the vessel.

When the explosion occurred the commander was in his cabin. He rushed out, and as he was passing the galleys he heard loud cries from the boiler room, which is underneath the galleys.

Stopping, he saw Petty Officer Cook Griffiths pinned in the wreckage and half covered in hot oil.

Unhesitatingly, Lieutenant Commander Scurfield jumped into the boiler room through the shattered deck, and managed with great difficulty to drag Griffith from the wreckage.

Later, with superhuman efforts, he pulled the injured man out on to the deck. He himself was up to his waist in hot oil the whole time. [...] The commander, it was added, also succeeded in extricating other ratings from the flooded compartments.

On the 12 November 1937, the *London Gazette* announced "The King has been graciously pleased to approve the Award of the Medal of the Military Division of the Most Excellent Order of the British Empire, to the undermentioned for gallant and distinguished services rendered when HMS *Hunter* was mined off Almeria on the coast of Spain on 13th May 1937."

Lieutenant Patrick Noel Humphries, RN. James Smail, Petty Officer. James Frank Collings, Able Seaman. Ernest Thomas, Able Seaman. Herbert Abrahams, Able Seaman. The commanding officer, Lieutenant Commander Scurfield, received the 'Albert Medal', the highest peace time award. Surgeon Lieutenant Alfred Edward Flannery received a Commendation from the Commander-in Chief of the Mediterranean Fleet. [His great coolness and efficiency in most trying circumstances.]

In July 1937 there were questions in the House of Commons about a claim for compensation from the Spanish government. The then Foreign Secretary Mr Anthony Eden replied, "I understand that as the result of the Court of Inquiry, which was subsequently held into the circumstances in which the incident took place, the Admiralty are now satisfied that a detailed claim for compensation can be presented. As soon as I have received from them the exact figures the necessary steps will be taken without delay." It is said that a bill was presented to the Spanish Government for £70,000 to cover the cost of the damage incurred by *Hunter.*

On a sad note, out of the fourteen crewmembers injured, only one returned back to the ship to fight again. This was Able Seaman Ernie Rothwell from Swinton, near Manchester; tragically almost three years later, Ernie would not be able to escape with his life a second time.

With regards to Surgeon Lieutenant Alfred Flannery, during my early research for possible contacts with crew members of families or friends associated with the 2nd Destroyer Flotilla, I visited Malta in 2010. Whilst there, out of the blue, although in fact at the time I thought this pre-destined, I found information, of Captain Alfred Edward Flannery R.N, the Senior Medical Officer in Malta between 1961 and 1963. More interestingly, it was reported that Alfred had served as the flotilla Medical Officer for 2nd Destroyer Flotilla for almost three years from 1936 to 1939.

It was obvious that Alfred had been highly respected in the Maltese community, especially in the Forces Families Medical Service. However, that was where my research ended, and any suggestion that 'it was meant to be' was blown apart. On my return home Captain Flannery had to be put on my 'must do' list. Eventually, once again I contacted my reliable fact finding sources, Hans Houterman in Holland, whose well organised website continually records the service history of Royal Navy Officers. Captain Flannery was born in Old Castle Co Cavan, Ireland in 1906 the youngest son of Canon William Flannery.

Although it had taken six years, finally fate stepped in unexpectedly when Alfred's youngest son, Terry, living in Florida, made contact. Terry like many families wanted to know more about a family member serving in the Second World War, in this case his father. From Terry's efforts this led him to the 'submerged.co.uk' website.

I will come back to Terry Flannery shortly, but meanwhile continuing with his father's naval service, in 1931, aged twenty-five, Alfred received his commission into the Royal Navy and immediately began a one month course for Medical officers. Within three months he was shipped out to the China Station, where he remained for over two years. Many years later Alfred told his son Terry of an amusing incident, although it was a close call with potential fatalities. "When my father was in China on a riverboat posting, one of the Chinese cooks on board, for some reason became very angry. This led to him dropping a hand grenade down a hatch and then sitting on top. My father said this required him to pick parts of shrapnel from a lot of sailors' backsides for quite some time later."

On Alfred's return to Britain, he had several shore appointments before arriving on board HMS *Hardy* in December 1936, as flotilla Medical Officer. This coincided with his promotion to Surgeon Lieutenant Commander.

Prior to the *Hunter* being mined, Alfred had embarked on the destroyer, as this letter to his then fiancée, Liz Duffy from New York describes. Alfred starts by stating where the ship is when his letter was posted.

(Letter last Thursday sent off via HMS Griffin. The ship that we relieved here)

Saturday May 8th (1937)

"We are supposed to look after the 'Sea end' of 'non-intervention'– that is to board ships going into Almeria and make sure that they are not carrying contraband [...] The 'Griffin' told us that Almeria was bombed the morning we arrived but since our arrival all has been peaceful. We know nothing about the length of our stay here nor shall we till we are relieved [...] Thursday 13th May. We are not leaving now till Saturday morning and are taking about sixty refugees with us so it will be quite late when we get to Gib. [...]"

There is no mention of the tragic mining incident which occurred in the afternoon of the 13th May, perhaps he wrote the letter in the morning to catch the post bag leaving the ship. Or more likely for confidentiality reasons, he could not mention the event. After the mining, as previously mentioned, *Hunter* was initially towed back to Almeria by her flotilla sister ship *Hyperion*. On the 15th May she was once more towed, this time by the light cruiser *Arethusa*, arriving in Gibraltar.

I will come back to Alfred Flannery's letters home and his departure from the 2nd Destroyer Flotilla, in the meantime, the scene is set for HMS *Hunter's* arrival in Gibraltar. She would be carrying the bodies for burial of those killed by the Spanish mine. It would also become an unexpected surprise respite for the ship's company, which would last for another three months.

It was a lovely warm Mediterranean evening as the ship put into Gibraltar late at night and tied up on the outer mole, which in fact doubled up as a breakwater. Those upper deck seamen tying the ship alongside who had never previously had the pleasure to visit Gibraltar, would have been immediately impressed with the gigantic 'Rock' set before them. However, although it was too late for shore leave, a sailor's mind quickly sorts out his priorities, which are chiefly how do you get ashore? It seemed a long walk to the town along the mole and through the dockyard. There wasn't even any 'Dysoes' like Malta! However, next morning their fears were allayed because the main noticeboard explained the ship's daily liberty boat routine for the time it would be in harbour. But the crew had woken to a murky looking sky above, a full transformation from the previous day's weather at sea. [2]

---

2   'Dysoes' are a form of water transport as will be explained shortly.

Gibraltar – Main Street – [from direction of the dockyard gates]
to the Spanish border. [Cyril Cope's collection]

One young seaman turned around to his 'Three-Badged' sea daddy and queried the lack of sun. He was then promptly given a rundown on the climatic weather changes in the 'Gib' area. "You have to remember we're in a subtropical climate there are unreliable winds around these parts. That dense low cloud up there is known as the Levanter. It's a warm east to northeast wind funnelled through the Straits of Gibraltar, mainly from July to October and also in March. But it can occur at any time, where warm, humid air has to rise against the rock; and cools down and condenses. Got that?" The young lad seemed to still be working it out in his head, but nodded anyway.

"Let me tell you a bit of naval history," continued the 'Three-Badge' man. "On the west side of the 'Rock', towards where you're looking, back in the Atlantic there are violent sea currents, which are very dangerous for us sailors. The wind itself blows strongly from time to time in opposing directions; whirling around, making our lives more difficult. As you look out over there, not far away on the seabed is the richest shipwreck in history. Namely, His Majesty's Ship *Sussex*, containing millions of pounds in gold coins; lost about 300 years ago.

"The Admiralty looked into the sinking and the records show that the ship was caught in a Levanter. They described freak winds that threatened to hurl the ship against the rocky Spanish shore. The ship attempted to tack into the wind, and run back around Gibraltar. Within seconds, tens of thousands of gallons of water rushed into the vessel's open gun ports. The end came swiftly, while the Admiral slept. His body was found later clad only in his nightshirt."

The 'Three-Badge' man seemed pleased that he had been able to remember the story after all these years. The young seaman under his charge appeared keen to listen, still looking out to sea. Although his mind was possibly focussed more on putting in a request form to his Divisional Chief to complete the forthcoming 'Divers' course on their return to 'Blighty'. Dreaming of a hoard of gold treasure he rushed down below to impress his mess mates by telling them about the climatic weather up top. [3]

There was still a need to extricate five of their shipmates from the damage below, funerals would have to be arranged with the governor of Gibraltar Office in due course. The substantial sized Royal Naval dockyard would start planning for the *Hunter* to go into dry dock as soon as possible.

---

3   HMS *Sussex* was an 80-gun ship lost in a severe storm on 1 March 1694 off Gibraltar. On board were possibly ten tons of gold coins. This could now be worth more than $500 million, including the bullion and antiquity values, making it one of the most valuable wrecks ever. After a short stopover in Cadiz, the fleet entered the Mediterranean. On 27 February, a violent storm hit the flotilla near the Strait of Gibraltar and in the early morning of the third day, HMS *Sussex* sank. All but two 'Turks' of the 500 crew on board drowned. Due to the extent of the fatalities, it was not possible to establish the exact cause of the disaster, but it has been noted that 'the disaster seemed to confirm suspicions already voiced about the inherent instability of 80-gun ships with only two decks, such as the Sussex, and a third deck would be added for new ships of this armament.' 'www.bluebird-electric.net'

For the moment the crew would be able to enjoy the delights on offer in this famous port of call. Both the exotic daytime shopping in Main Street and the 'alternative' types of entertainment in the evenings. For many sailors arriving finally from their various naval ports in Britain, there is no better place than this peninsular of land where Africa meets Europe. It is not only seen as a part of home but also exemplifies Gibraltar's position as a British fortress since the early eighteenth century. The crew were not to know it yet, but it would become a vital factor in British military strategy for the forthcoming World War Two.

Caption: Hunter in Gibraltar dry dock, background is HMS *Greyhound* HO5 which also went on to participate in the Narvik Campaign. [Jake Kerswell's family collection.]

It was just before midday and the welcomed 'pipe' reverberated throughout the ship – 'Up Spirits'. At that order the Officer of the Day, accompanied by the Duty Petty Officer and a supply department rating, drew the key from the keyboard sentry and duly signed the Key-Book in his presence, for the 'Spirit' storage compartment.

Inside the gloomy space, reeking of stale rum there contained the tools for their task ahead, a long copper pump was placed into the bung-hole of a full rum cask. The rating then drew off into a large copper vessel a quantity of neat rum which in other copper utensils was carefully measured into 'gills'. The amount of 'gills' corresponded with the numbers of the ships company entitled to their daily rum ration. The remainder was poured back and the cask was re-bunged. That completed it just required the vessels to be cleaned and dried before the Spirit storage compartment was locked and the key returned to its positon on the board.

The next task was to place to one side the amount in gills of neat rum required for the Chief and Petty Officers' rations. Then water was added to the remainder to give two parts to one part of rum, known as 'grog'. Waiting expectantly outside was a queue of each mess 'rum boson' with their own rum 'fanny'. Returning to their messes they would find some old salts waiting with mouths open and their tongues to the fore, waiting for their tot of 'Nelson's Blood'. The final event should have been the easiest, drinking it, some doing so in one gulp because they couldn't stand the taste. [4]

Those over twenty having had their tot and lunch were now ready to meet their cousins of Gibraltar. Once transiting the expanse of water by a converted fishing trawler, between the breakwater and the main dockyard gate leading towards a steep incline to the Alameda Gardens and then the Rock Hotel, the men immediately felt relaxed within a safe haven. But for many it was not a scenic climb they needed but a gentle walk to the left and the start of Main Street. Then it was another world to appreciate. The 'Levanter' had gone and the skies were blue, time for a spell of shopping along many retail outlets. Most were like an 'Aladdin's Cave' with colourful, exciting and unexpected goods from around the world. Just about everything and anything was on offer, for the right price.

This is where you needed an experienced member of the mess, to show you the ropes of bartering with the predominantly Indian shopkeepers. "Right lads, follow me don't say a word, let me do the talking," insisted the

---

4   It was known as 'Nelson's Blood', because it was wrongly communicated, that after the Battle of Trafalgar, Nelson's body having been brought ashore in Gibraltar, was immersed in rum for the journey back to Britain. In fact, it was, ironically, French brandy. The amount of rum to each sailor was in fact 74 ml, almost a treble pub measure but not 40% but 60% strength. This would put a man on the threshold for a drink / driving offence.

'Old Salt'. The troop of matelots hovered around whilst the leader spent time looking at the shops contents.

After five minutes, "How much is the ladies dressing gown with the dragon on the back, my friend?" "This has come from China, made as you can see with silk and gold wire, sir." "How much?" "It is forty shillings, sir a very good price for British sailor." "Too much, I'll try somewhere else," replied the now impatient naval bartering expert. "Please sir, I have also British sailor's favourite perfume for lady, popular now, called '4711', I give also at half price with silk dressing gown." At which point it was a wave goodbye and the troop moved out onto the pavement outside. "That was cheap, Hooky [slang for Leading Hand], my girlfriend says that '4711' perfume is all the rage, and costs a guinea at home." "Not to worry, they don't shut for another six hours. I am looking to get the dressing gown and matching silk pyjamas for the same price."

So off they went with one of them saying, "This bartering lark leaves you dead thirsty." There were two renowned beer halls in the vicinity, the 'Trocadero' and the 'Continental' – the latter was popular for obvious reasons as there was a 'Ladies Orchestra' performing. The troop having got through a couple of drinks decided it was time for 'tapas' provided from a local man wandering around with paper cones of salty prawns, for three pence a cone.

Some soon got bored with the lady band, mainly because they were nearly as old as their own mothers. Though that did not seem to worry the many pensionable matelots close to retirement. Next stop at 240 Main Street was the 'Trocadero', a typical 'wild west' type saloon bar complete with swing doors and very popular when the Fleet was in town.

The Trocadero had a resident band that played from opening time to eleven o'clock at night. As the evening wore on, the overworked musicians inevitably began to sound like an old gramophone record that needed rewinding.

Another party of the Stokers decided to wander up the 'Rock' to witness the Barbary Apes, one of them said in a serious manner, "They say that as long as the apes are here, so will the British remain, no wonder they are well looked after." At that moment a larger one jumped on his shoulder and grabbed his cap. "Come here you bastard." This led to an obnoxious smell being left on his 'white front' down to his white shorts, as he retrieved the cap, panicking about how he would have had to explain the loss when returning back on board.

Another Stoker mentioned, "There seems to be lot of construction work going on, with loads of hard core being driven down to the town." Looks like they're digging massive tunnels, it's the Royal Engineers, I think." "Yeh, last time I came to Gib the 'Pongos' took us up the North Front looking over to La Linea on the Spanish side. The tunnels there were excavated during the 'Great Siege' in the eighteenth Century, fantastic, don't know how they did it, other than using a lot of gun powder." The next stop was the summit, where they met a local who told them all about the history of O'Hara's Battery. [5]

Western Daily Press. Tuesday 18th May 1937. Gibraltar, Monday.

A funeral with full naval honours was given in Gibraltar this afternoon to Bertie Turner and Leslie House, whose bodies were extracted yesterday from the boiler-room of HMS *Hunter* when the destroyer was towed back here from Almeria. [...]

Turner was a Petty Officer Telegraphist and his home was in Bridgwater, Somerset.

House was an Able Seaman from Parkstone, Dorset.

The escort firing party and pall bearers were supplied by the Second flotilla. The funeral procession was headed by the Royal Marines band from HMS *Arethusa* and buglers from the King's Own Yorkshire Light Infantry sounded the Last Post at the grave side.

On arrival at the cemetery, four Spanish refugees assisted naval ratings in shouldering the coffins, covered in the Union Jack into the grave. Thousands of townspeople mingled with 200 Spanish refugees as unofficial mourners and a large wreath, bound with red, and blue ribbon, was placed by the Spanish refugees.

---

5   The main excavation of the new tunnels began in earnest between 1939–1944 by the Royal Engineers and a contingent of Canadian Engineers. The Rock is in fact honeycombed with a 32-mile-long network of tunnels excavated from the limestone. Masses of rock were blasted out to build with huge man-made caverns, barracks, offices, and a fully equipped hospital complete with an operating theatre. The public can now visit these fascinating tunnels by organised tours. Whilst doing a two-year tour of duty in Gibraltar [1977–79], I was fortunate to be able to arrange a visit, accompanied by my father, Cyril, to this 'underground town'. I myself worked in the Royal Naval Communications Centre [Comcen] at street level but right in the middle of The Rock.

In the meantime, back to another group of *Hunter* crew, these were the young Seamen 'Gunners'. Not on liberty leave but considered a training session, led by two Leading Gunnery Ratings. They were fortunate, as they could get round Gibraltar quickly in a Royal Naval lorry. First stop, the Napier of Magdala Battery, where they were amazed as they stood before the '100 Ton Gun', a 17.2-inch rifled muzzled-loading gun. A monster compared with the guns on board at 4.7-inch.

The Leading Gunner explained, "As you can see below there is Rosia Bay, that's where we will be going later for our well-earned swim. Even a beer if you keep your mouths shut." The Gunner continued, "There's another one at the Victoria Battery, made in Britain, and both were in service from the 1870s. Fifteen were built mainly for coastal defence, but two were made for the Italian Navy. The Royal Navy turned them down because they were too heavy and costly. The projectile could be fired every four minutes reaching a distance of eight miles and needed a thirty-five man crew." The Leading Gunner shouted out, "There are another two, in Malta, which when we get there and if you are interested can be seen at the Rinella and Cambridge Batteries. Right, any questions, no, good, let's get back to the lorry and next stop it's the King's Bastion and Moorish Castle." At which point the training group couldn't take their eyes off the sight below and the promise of a dip and even more so that cool bottle of beer awaiting them.

Back at the 'Trocadero' the Stoker troopers were enjoying their beers and probably because the place was packed, they were watching an unscheduled performance of a Spanish flamenco dancer. She was dressed in her beautiful-coloured skirt with castanets continuously cracking in the air. The strength of her whole body is directed into her lower legs and feet, providing the unmistakable sound from her blue sturdy solid 'Zapatos' heels hitting the dance floor in rhythm. Whilst, her face remains stern but showing true passion. The 'all male' audience looked on spellbound, until the end, when there was rapturous applause.

As all the sailors got back to serious drinking, with a telling smile and carrying a large brown paper bag, the professional 'barter man' arrived. "I told you chaps, all it needs is patience. I got the lot for forty-five shillings, smell that perfume!" His mess mates were very impressed and looked forward to 'pay day' to put into practice their short introduction into getting one over the shopkeepers in Main Street. Perhaps not realising, although it reduces their profits they never give their goods away at a loss. I know from personal experience when spending a month in 1977 trying to get the right price for a Seiko watch. Once bought, I was chuffed with my own improving bargaining skills. Alas, whilst my wife Alison was doing her shopping I would venture into a different shop only to find that I could have got one cheaper there.

The above mention of 'pay day' would trigger a special evening's entertainment at the Fleet Canteen for the off-duty sailors. It was one of the only times they were able to participate in legal gambling and there was a significant amount of money prizes to be won. The more ships that were in harbour then the bigger the winnings. The evening ended on a high note because the last 'House' was a doubler, twice the winnings! It was very popular and therefore advisable to be sitting with your beer, well before the first house. It was well organised by a mixture of the NAAFI staff and a Fleet Canteen committee made up of a Senior Non-commissioned Officer as Chairman and other representatives from the ranks. A percentage of the takings went to the local Naval Welfare Fund.

The establishments that catered for the Navy's unquenchable thirst would grow ever more vociferous and the melodies less and less coherent as the night wore on. If the door of one of these establishments happened to swing open as you passed by, you were almost overpowered by the stench of cheap beer and stale vomit.

Outside stood the Law. The normal complement was made up of several nasty looking Redcaps and some even nastier looking RAF police. A few civilian coppers, a pair of professional looking thugs from the Naval Depot and a group of rather sheepish ships' police often kept them company. "When closing time came the real action began. The swing doors would open with a crash and out came a raucous melee of uniformed men, some still trying to settle some argument or other. The majority were determined to carry on their singing in the open air without the benefit of music." [Quote from Neville Chipulina – 'History of the Chipulina Family.']

As I have tried to describe the *Hunter* crew had busy 'runs ashore' in the first week. So, to hear they were to stay for at least another three months, caused many smiles, most knew they had to slow down, not only for health reasons but also to watch the pennies. This was especially because soon the Home Fleet would be docking in Gibraltar, when sailors would be meeting up with old shipmates. It was also an opportunity for the ships companies to compete at a variety of sporting pursuits. These finally round off with a fiercely fought 'Regatta' between ship's cutters or whalers.

Once more this was one of the few times when betting was officially allowed, where each ship would hold a tote for the betting odds.

In Surgeon Lieutenant Alfred Flannery's next letter to Liz, dated Thursday 3rd June 1937, is a good example of the complexities of trying to keep the loved ones at home up to date with the ships immediate and future programmes. Of course, when the war came it was against the 'King's Regulations and Orders' to give details of ships positions and plans.

The letterhead shows HMS *Hunter* but it has been crossed out and changed to HMS *Hereward*, a sister ship. So there will be no relaxing in the friendly environment of bars and cafes of Main Street in Gibraltar for the doctor has to do his rounds in the flotilla.

"We went into 'Gib' on Tuesday [1st June 1937] to drop off my case of appendicitis [...] doubt we will get mail before we get back to Malta on the 18th. We go back to 'Gib' on Monday the 7th. Stay there a few days and then go out and patrol off Cadiz till fourteenth when we sail for Malta [...] Let me explain about docking. Normally our ships do two docks a year. One short for about a week and the other a long one or so. We were due to do our short one, just now at 'Gib' and our long one sometime in November and December also in 'Gib'."

Alfred's next letter to Liz from Malta was dated 30th June 1937 and now had an HMS *Active* letterhead. He had now gone full circle and returned once more to providing medical duties for the *Hunter* crew. It is a personal letter and not for public viewing. Suffice to say that around this time arrangements were probably being made for their marriage, which eventually took place in Malta on 16th November 1937. They received a silver cigarette case as a wedding present from the officers on board *Active*.

Now Marshal Soult continues his past memories of the early days of *Hunter* with the Mediterranean Fleet. "The story goes that Rear Admiral Sir James Somerville (Admiral destroyers) was out rowing in his 'skiff' (light rowing boat) in Gibraltar harbour and dressed in civvies, he entered the hole. When he re-emerged, a stoker, leaning over the side of the ship, greeted him with the words, 'Bugger off – that's our bloody hole!' The 2nd Destroyer Flotilla considered itself the doyen of Destroyer Flotilla's. For instance, on one occasion we were sent to another flotilla for an exercise. On leaving harbour in Malta we were very close to the leader ahead. We then received a signal advising us of speeding leaving harbour. Our reply was, "Sorry, 2nd Destroyer Flotilla leaves five knots faster."

Alfred Flannery and Liz Duffy wedding ceremony. [Alfred Flannery's family collection.]

On completion of *Hunter*'s temporary repairs she left Gibraltar on the 18th of August 1937 for permanent repairs in Malta. The ship's company was then transferred to HMS *Active* until 4th of July 1938 before re-joining back in service *Hunter*. The total time out of action was over eighteen months.

Prior to the event in May 1938, the footballing fans on board were taken by surprise to hear from home that Manchester City, having won the title the year before had gone from 'Champs to Chumps'. As English Champions the club's performances had been acclaimed over Europe, with invites to play friendlies during the summer 1937. However, one of these was not to the players liking. In the build-up for the following years' 'World Cup' in France, they had to play against a German Select XI at the Berlin's Olympic Stadium with a crowd of 70,000. Star player, Peter Doherty later wrote, "The whole place was peppered with armed Nazi guards. We were expected to give the Nazi salute at the line-up before the match began, but we decided merely to stand to attention. When the German national anthem was played, only 11 arms went up instead of 22!"

Malta: Back and Ready

The *Hunter* having arrived at Malta, Marshal describes that the whole nucleus of senior and older hands on *Hunter* were a "proud and happy" unit having come through action in the Spanish War. In July 1938 the repairs completed, the ships company were transferred back and *Active* went into the reserve fleet.

HMS *Hunter* for most of the time was berthed opposite Sliema, the smaller harbour to the north west of Valletta which was popular with the sailors for shore leave. In the 1930s the harbour was home to two Destroyer Flotillas, a number of submarines, a hospital ship and a large number of smaller naval craft. The aircraft carriers, battleships and battle cruisers had their moorings in the Grand Harbour and provided a spectacular panorama from the Upper Barrakka Gardens in Valletta.

2nd destroyer Squadrons visit to Venice [circa 1938] [Cyril Cope's collection]

The ship's company on board *Hunter*, possibly because it was a crew from both the Devonport and Chatham Bases, were a mixed variety of men from the Southwest, Geordies, Scottish, Welsh, North West, Irish, Malta, Yorkshire, Lincolnshire, Kent and London. Normally, most ships would come from a specific British region, for instance the Western Region, where the main Naval Base would be Devonport. This region covered Scotland down to the southwest, including Wales and Ireland.

This would result in an interesting messdeck with a possible mix of townies like 'Cockneys' and those from the countryside known as 'Westos'. Both with their own characteristics and quirks. The former cheerful, gregarious and quick witted, whilst the latter can be more reserved, individualistic and suspicious of anyone 'not of their own ilk'. However, not long after joining your first ship if you want a peaceful life, you realise that you have to muck in, cause no 'waves', and make an effort to get on with your newly acquired messmates.

Hunter Ships Company in Malta [circa 1939]. [John Hague's family collection.]

The serving members of the Armed Forces loved Malta. There were four main Army Barracks: St George's, St Andrew's, St David's and St Patrick's. Three barracks were quite close to Sliema, one for the gunners and each of the other two housing an infantry battalion. There were Swordfish and Gladiator biplanes, temporarily at Hal Far airfield while their aircraft-carrier was in port. Often they would fly low along the Sliema seafront, probably hoping to get a glimpse of one of their girlfriends. The crowds would give them a wave and they always waved back.

Many of those serving on the island at the time probably thought that if there was another world war this was probably one of the best place to be stationed. They knew that there was the potential to shelter all the population from air raids. The island's infrastructure was built on an abundance of sandstone, where tunnels could be easily constructed. The majority of the homes were built of limestone with walls over a foot thick. So an enemy bomb dropped there would do a lot less damage than in a British city conurbation. The main focus of any foe would be to put out of action the Naval Base in Valletta Harbour. However, whilst some damage could be done to arms and other miscellaneous fitted equipment, the fort has resisted many sieges over the centuries. It also had a massive tunnel network between all the creeks and it is said to be one of the best shelters in the world. [6]

Between August 1938 and 23rd March 1939, *Hunter* would need to have completed sea trials and have begun a 'Work Up'. Here a Torpedoman describes the rigorous programme necessary for making the ship and the crew into an efficient fighting unit. "When a ship is recommissioned, and you go out to a station, whether it is the Mediterranean or Home Fleet, you do the 'Work-Up' period which lasts two to three months. We started our practice drills as soon as we entered the 'Med': Gunnery, torpedoes, and depth charge exercises for hour after hour. Later on it would be for day in day out, night in night out, never knowing when we would be returning to harbour.

"This was only the prelude. In the late 1930s warships with a new crew were usually only given three weeks of 'Work Up' to attain a high standard of teamwork efficiency in order to enable the ship to take part in any battles with the enemy whenever and whatever time they may take place. It's very hard work for everybody concerned, energy-sapping and soul-destroying because the drills are repeated time after time until the Captain is satisfied that the ship's company is one hundred per cent efficient in all departments. We spent most of the time at sea on exercises, firing guns at targets towed by other ships, and anti-aircraft guns at targets towed by aircraft. The torpedoes would have 'dummy heads' and every time we

---

6   During World War Two the fort again stood the siege with an armament of three Bofor guns which were manned by the Royal Marines and later by the Royal Malta Artillery. In total, the fort suffered sixty-nine direct hits between 1940 and 1943.

fired them in practice, we had to go out in a whaler to pick them up and bring them back to the ship. Then we set to cleaning and polishing them, to prepare them for the next shoot and put them back into the tubes. We did this during the day and the night off Malta, because we could never do enough nor do it right."

There are various methods used on board to break the monotony at sea. So it would not be any different on '*Hunter*' to arrange a 'Beard Growing' competition for the ship's company. Taking into account the low average age of the sailors, many would be too embarrassed to play along with the task. They were known on board as 'Skin'. The Navy unlike the other two services were only allowed to have a 'full set', not moustaches or sideburns alone. There were many incentives, a longer lay-in in the mornings, more time for breakfast, and a protector against the adverse weather or the blazing sun. It could also be a financial asset: a saving on not having to purchase shaving items or a bonus of a daily allowance. The latter was because it would free up time taken for the crew to use the washrooms.

Willing crew members needed to make a request through the Coxswain onto the Captain to grow their beard. Once the facial hair was thick and widely spread sufficiently, it would require an inspection by the Coxswain. His decision would be either, "granted go to the ships office to change your daily rate of pay" or in this case because it was an on board competition with a smirk, "get that f......bum fluff off now!"

Having completed a stint of exercises at sea, those on board *Hunter*, especially the new crew members, would never forget their first re-entry into Malta's Grand Harbour. The 'lower deck' was cleared and other than the 'upper deck' seamen, the rest would be in their best uniforms. A fanfare of bugles echoed around the harbour and on passing other Royal Naval ships the traditional 'piping' between them took place. Depending on the seniority of the two Commanding Officers, the junior of the two first salutes and the more senior then in turn returns the salute. There would be many larger warships in the Grand Harbour, and in *Hunter*'s case she would be the junior ship. However, on this occasion there were interspersed cheering sailors on the other ships moored alongside or anchored out. This was to acknowledge that they were witnessing one of the first ships to have been in action, having sustained damage in the Spanish Civil War.

Malta Harbour [circa 1939] [Cyril Cope's collection.]

Once the traditional 'entering harbour' procedures were over *Hunter*'s crew were stood down and whilst the ship was moored, they milled around taking in the wonderful sights of the Grand Harbour. However, it would not be long, whilst leaning on the guard rails, before they noticed an obnoxious smell. Later on, when finally landing for shore leave they would discover what it was. However, for those lucky ones not on 'duty watch' it was quickly get down below for a body wash from a bucket and hair shampoo with a block of 'pussers hard' (coarse bathing soap also used for cleaning clothes). Not a lot of deodorants in those days for the armpits. "Don't forget your 'Station Card' Jack, otherwise you won't be allowed ashore!" Swiftly he climbs the various ladders and onto the quarterdeck for the next 'Liberty Boat'. All lined up in smart white tropical uniforms, a freshly ironed blue jean collar and silk with lanyard all squared off, black boots polished (white tropical canvas shoes had not yet arrived) and hat – fore and aft (not cocked, well not until out of sight of the ship). Inspection by the Officer of the Day is 'done and dusted' and they are dismissed.

The sailors would have had the choice of waiting for the official liberty boat or to pay out for a 'Dyhajsas' (pronounced 'Dysoes') many of which would already be paddling water alongside the ship waiting for a fare. These taxi vessels were elegant and colourfully built on the same lines as Venetian gondolas and used as a means for a short cut from the dockyard.

Travelling ashore on a Dyso was a formality but coming back could be hazardous for some inebriated sailors returning to their ships late at night. Having spent their Maltese lira, they took to jumping off the vessel to swim the remainder of the journey. The Dyso owners were obviously not at all pleased with losing their fare and over the years this caused a lot of animosity between them and 'Jack'.

Back to that smell and they discovered it was horse manure. The main transport offered by the locals are 'Gharries', a two-passenger carriage drawn by a horse. The manure was kept in piles until it was cleared at the end of the day and duly taken away inland to farms and gardens.

The stinking mess was soon forgotten when those sailors not in a position to pay the fares, came across a box-like lift shaft which twenty of them nervously crammed into. For those who had never previously ventured into this cubical machine, it was a harrowing experience. Clanging up in the lift, the men found it difficult to breathe, this was not helped by the hot summer air outside.

With such a slow ascent, it became a tedious task and there were those who wondered "Is it worth the hassle?" But once the mechanical clang occurred to tell them that they had reached the end of their transit, it was soon all forgotten. Valletta was now their oyster. There were those who ventured to look over the ridge from whence they came [300 feet] and decisions were rapidly made to return to the jetty by an alternative route. Probably by sharing a 'Gharrie', if they had enough money left in their pockets, after their intention to leave nothing spared financially, on their 'run ashore'.

The officers on board had made their own arrangements for an evening's entertainment. One of them on his last visit to Malta had seen the early stages of the building of a premier luxury hotel just outside Valletta's 'Porta Reale'. It was to be called the Hotel Phoenicia, owned by Lord and Lady Strickland and designed by Architect A.M.B. Binnie. Unfortunately, when the officers arrived at the refurbished hotel, they found it was still not open for business. [7]

However, whilst the officers were looking elsewhere for alternative venues, the lower deck sailors knew exactly what to do; follow an 'old salt' from the ship for a guided tour of the well-known dens of 'iniquity' or 'delights'. Although, there was another option where clientele could find an improved ambience for enjoying a drink and on some nights dancing as well. This was the Vernon United Services Club for 'other ranks'. A great venue to get to meet members of the opposite sex predominantly British service and non-service ladies. The story goes that when the Americans joined

---

7   When war broke out the Hotel Phoenicia was not officially open and subsequently requisitioned by the armed services. It was officially opened in 1947, to provide a "cosmopolitan clientele with a standard of comfort and service equalling that of the highest grade hotels in any European capital".

the Allies a certain handsome aircrewman 'Gunner' on Flying Fortresses asked a pretty English 'rose' for a dance. She immediately agreed but when he wanted another dance she refused politely. The man was Clarke Gable at that time in his early forties but still able to 'shake a wicked hoof' on the dance floor. Why, was he refused a second dance? The English rose complained later that his sweat was spoiling her dress. [8]

Back at the Vernon Club, a group from the seamen's mess decided to have a quiet start to the evening, playing darts. "Hey, have you seen whose ship's in port, as well?" shouted one of the 'Two-Badge' men over the noisy crowd around. "Oh hi, the Welsh answer to Charles Atlas himself, Pete Hooson, and I see he's with his mate Rob Thwaites, the 'Geordie Ghost', the Navy winger who leaves fullbacks in his wake." "Yeh! Whatever you do don't ask them to play darts for a bet, they're cracking around the board. They won the flotilla doubles tournament at the Fleet Club in Pompey last year."

During their game, a batch of 'Crabfats' asked if they could join in. It wasn't long before the 'Two-Badge' man's thoughts switched to the possibilities of improving his 'run ashore' finances. A quick negotiation with Mr Atlas and the Geordie, a wager with the 'Crabs' was agreed. "Late night bars here we come," thought the seamen. Of course the 'Crabs' had made the mistake of believing, how do you improve your dart throwing skills on a 'bloody warship!'? [9]

---

8   Clark Gable was a Hollywood star and among the most famous personalities in the world when two events altered his life. First, the Japanese attacked Pearl Harbor on Dec. 7, 1941 hurtling the United States into World War Two. Then, the following month, Gable's beloved wife Carole Lombard was killed in the crash of a DC-3 airliner returning from a war bonds tour. Devastated, patriotic, and at age 40, a bit old for military service, Gable didn't feel that the work he and Lombard had been doing to raise money through war bonds was enough of a contribution. He sent a telegram to President Franklin D. Roosevelt asking for a role in the war effort. The President replied, "STAY WHERE YOU ARE!" Gable didn't. He volunteered for the Army Air Forces, went to the 13-week Officer Candidate School, and was trained as a photographer and aerial gunner.

9   The term 'Crabfat' comes from the colour of RAF uniforms when the Royal Flying Corps amalgamated with the Royal Naval Air Service in 1918. The light blue colour was identical to the greasy mercuric oxide jelly (or crab fat) used at the time for the treatment of body lice – better known as 'crabs'. The word 'Scouse relates to a stew usually made from ship's biscuits and fish called 'lobscouse' frequently eaten by sailors and still eaten in Liverpool.

In the meantime, the darts match as expected was progressing in favour of the senior service, but chatting between the two teams was becoming more of a focal point. "What you lads doing in Malta?", "Oh, we work on a special assignment at Dingli Cliffs," replied the Leading Airman. "Hey, one of our Telegraphists on board went out there today, he said you couldn't get near the place for security and fences." Not getting a reply there was a change of conversation, "Where's all the women?" asked Scouse. "Well dance night is on Saturday's, where because of the lack of women they are allowed in free. But if you mean the local ladies, they lock them away at home." Another AB known as 'Yorkie' enquired, "That's a bit desperate." "Yeah, but Paul over there seems to be doing alright." Paul the Leading Airman hearing his name mentioned came over. It was time for another round of 'Blueys' (local beer) which was going down well and beginning to loosen their tongues.

"Tell him Paul what happened to you mate." "Ah! I have been seeing her since I came here, but it gets a bit complicated." Another messmate has sat down at the table, "Is she a cracker?" "Yep, her name is Patricia." "What's the problem?" "Well, when I first met her, where she was working in a posh shop in Sliema, I gathered up the courage to ask her out, she seemed keen. Her eyes were like blue diamonds with that beautiful 'Med' dark tan." All ears pricked up, waiting in earnest for the rest of his story. "Go on then," said one, in expectation of a fruitful ending. "Well, after a couple of visits to her shop, few weeks later she kept her promise and we met, but she had a so called 'chaperone' with her. I think it was her aunt." "What the bloody hell happened then?" An excited 'Two-Badge' Leading Seaman shouted. Paul now more relaxed having had two 'Bluey's'. "It went ok, other than I didn't feel at all comfortable with 'Miss' all eyes and ears on the other side of the table. I didn't even have a chance to give Patricia a good night kiss, which I was looking forward to."

Paul's audience became quiet, patiently waiting on his next words. "I must have impressed, because I was invited 'up homers', to meet her mum and dad. But I had another surprise, a priest was sitting there. Patricia's parents were welcoming, but the 'Bish' [slang for a 'man of cloth' as in Bishop] looked stern." At this point a few of the crowd went off to the bar for another 'bevvy'.

Paul carried on with his tale of woe, "Anyway it seems they must have thought I was alright, upstanding bloke and all that, because I was allowed to take her out again unchaperoned. However, as long as I never took her to a bar and made sure she was home by nine." There were now only three matelots left to hear the rest.

"She wants to get tied up to me but I am having second thoughts." "Why?" One of them asked. "Well can you imagine what it would be like if we did and when we got back to Blighty the whole family turned up?" At that the 'daddy' of the seaman's mess came over and put his hand on the 'Crabfat's' shoulder, "Take my advice son, you will probably meet a lot more other princesses along the way, but if you do go with your heart, wait until the war is over." Wise words from the 'Three-Badge man' probably a worthwhile sentiment for members of his own mess, which he would have given immediately, had he known what was in store for their ship. So off went the two groups of newly made pals down to the 'Gut' making for the Blue Peter bar. [10] [11] [12]

The officers were lucky in finding a legendary venue at the Malta Union Club within a building on Kingsway in Valletta, when the sixteenth-century 'Auberge de Provence' was open for visitors. Built like many other historical sites from local limestone blocks it had withstood time and wars. Tonight's delights were a classical evening of music from a string quartet and a local well known male opera singer. Accompanied with a 'Vesper Dry Martini', including one measure of 'Kina Lillet', a shot of London Dry gin, shaken well until it is ice-cold and a large slice of Sicilian lemon: served in a deep champagne goblet. As recommended by one of more worldly-wise officers

---

10   In fact at Dingli Cliffs there were secret buildings of the RAF's Radio Direction Finding Station, the first in Malta. Unfortunately, when the second one was added at Dingli after the war had started, it had to be built underground. Including an engine room providing electrical power which needed an exhaust vent shaft to the outside of the cliff face. The word got round quickly that the farmers in the area, seeing fumes emitting into the atmosphere, thought the British were covertly cooking at a time when the Maltese faced rationing. So for those servicemen, like Paul with a local girlfriend and working at the site, it could have put paid to any friendly relationships.

11   I would add that Britain before the war began the development of radar technology was in its infancy. Prior to war being declared, tests were carried out regarding calibration and by the time the war began the primitive radar could read the height of the incoming raiders and their direction. However, the kit that was sent out to Malta, still in its early stages of development was unsuited to the Mediterranean climate. The summer heat caused major problems with the electronic valves, so much so that the radar could only be used for eight hours a day. Also, the antennas fell victim to the naturally strong winds on the Dingli Cliffs and had to be redesigned at the Malta Dockyard

12   'Two- and Three-Badge men' will be explained in another chapter.

in the wardroom mess who remarked to his friends: "Well you never know this maybe the last time we have an opportunity to enjoy a decent evening out for a while." At least the officer was not tempted to request the potent if not lethal cocktail the 'Razzle Dazzle', which the club had had to ban at one stage, after a visiting US Navy cruiser crew had introduced it to their unsuspecting members. It appears the behaviour of many in the bar went downhill fast with heavy heads the next day. [13] [14]

It is perhaps ironic that the surroundings where the officers were rightly enjoying their free time were constructed by Italian stonemasons with their superior skills and the aperitifs they were drinking were predominantly also a product of Italy. Which was then a country ruled by the 'National Nazi Party' led by Benito Mussolini. It would not be long before the dictator would be sending his air force to incessantly bomb the small island of Malta in an attempt to force them into capitulation.

When the war finally really got started the bombs dropped by the Italians which missed their target and landed in the sea, created a good source of stunned or dead fish to go with home grown potatoes and tomatoes. It is also interesting that at this time submariners came in port for a period of respite from the stress of living like sardines in an awful smelling environment. Most were under twenty-five and, having over-indulged, would leave either the Vernon or Union Club's to start horse and cart races, careering round quiet streets of Valletta late at night in gharries at high speeds. Who could blame them for letting off a bit of steam and it appears that the authorities, in proper Nelson fashion, 'turned a blind eye'.

Back to the group of the crew, led by the 'Old Salt'. On first sight they became a little apprehensive but still optimistic of a good night out. First to the renowned 'Gut' or 'Ghut' (Maltese), the nickname for Strait Street

---

13   Kina Lillet was launched in 1895 as an aperitif and tonic and quickly became known as "the aperitif of Bordeaux". In addition to the wine and quinine, it consisted of a blend of fruit liqueurs.

14   In the early twentieth century 'Razzle Dazzle' had been a popular cocktail for many years (for those brave enough) in New York's high society scene. It consisted of one part brandy, one part absinthe herbal liqueur and one part ginger ale, offered in a frozen glass. Although absinthe was referred to as a liqueur, it was a spirit composed of anise, fennel and other culinary herbals. In fact, in 1915 it was banned in America but of course that could have drawn more inquisitive drinkers to wanting to try something different.

[Triq-Id- Dejqa] within the walls of Valletta. This was a narrow lane, down-hill with steep houses and bars on both sides, which for most of the day blocked out the sun, leaving a nice cool environment for an iced cold Cisk or Hop Leaf beer. During which time some shipmates would have resorted to buying 'sticky greens' for their 'pash' [abbreviation for passion, for their latest acquired girlfriend]. Here the older sailors reminisced in making comparisons between the other infamous ports of call: Bugis Street in Singapore, Blood Alley in Shanghai and the Wan Chai District of Hong Kong. The 'greenhorns' would be listening intensely without making a murmur, the knowledge could be useful for future ventures to foreign ports or if not, to impress messmates on their next ship.

Strait Street known to sailors as The Gut. [Unknown contributor.]

As the evening draws in and the sticky greens had left some with a lack of funds, they decided to depart from the top of the street to the lower end for the sleazier entertainment. They would then become fuelled on a cheap, rough and strong red wine. The taste improved by the addition of lemonade or for those who could afford it, drinking the white variety mixed with gin. The choices of bars were many, 'The Lucky Wheel', 'The Piccadilly', 'The Silver Horse' and 'The Carmen Bar'. On this occasion, they decided to go where the resident band with singers were joined by anyone in the audience who wished to go up on the stage. We now call them 'Karaoke Nights'.

The music was belting out a rhythm of sorts and on entering the bar they discovered that the singer was a matelot with a red sweaty but happy face. He had his drunken oppo's arms round him who was grinning gormlessly with his eyes half open. In the corner was a Stoker from another ship in the 2nd Destroyer Flotilla whose nickname on board was 'Grumpy'. "Do you know he would carry two packets of fags with him at all times, one visible, with just one in it and one full packet hidden. So he wouldn't have to give anybody his last one," the 'Three-Badge' man said to the rest of the group.

Next to Grumpy was a second Stoker from his ship well known for falling asleep after a couple of 'John Collins'. "He is at it again, inspecting the inside of his eyelids. I don't believe this we've nearly got the full team in here. He's Sleepy, there's Happy singing on the stage held up by the inebriated Dopey, all we got to do is find out where Bashful, Doc and Sneezy are." They all started laughing and it triggered them to move on to another bar, in a line singing the Walt Disney favourite, "Hi Ho Hi Ho – It's off to work we go...!!" To loud applause. [15]

The next bar was renowned for its secret room at the back of the pub. That is if you were in the know. These men would usually be those who had been visiting Malta for donkey's years. Like the 'Three-Badge man'. "Wait lads, whilst I clear it." Reminding himself that the code to get in was 'Hush' after the name of the bar the 'Hush Hush' [not the real name]. Here was a place to lose the last of your 'ackies' and if you weren't careful one or more of your 'Badges'.

The croupier, for a better term, had a folded green mat on a table which

---

15   I would add that since the war Maltese wines have greatly improved in their quality. Marsovin for instance has won a number of prestigious awards and the island even produces something similar to champagne.

had six symbols: A crown, an anchor, a heart and diamond, a spade and club. It was a dice game and it is said the player would receive back about 92% of his bet and the remainder would go to the house. So, it was very tempting and a straight-forward opportunity for the servicemen to have a chance to reclaim some of their previous outlay for more wine and perhaps also as the night progressed, 'women and song'. Although the banker has a favourable edge over the punter.

The bar had an unsophisticated method that was used as a look out system, none other than a wolf whistle plus a getaway back door leading straight down to the outer walls of Valletta and for those brave enough a leap below into the unknown.

The game originated in the eighteenth century and I believe remains popular for some reason in the Channel Isles and Bermuda. The only legal times Crown and Anchor can be played in these islands are at an annual Jersey agricultural shows (the August 'Battle of Flowers'), and Bermuda's annual cricket 'Cup Match'.

However, the first time I came across the game was in Singapore in 1971, when I was attached to the Australian 18th Signals Regiment. The Aussies enjoy a flutter on any form of gambling but I was not expecting what I witnessed that night. Down an alley in Chinatown there was a group of their sailors betting on a collection of 'Bombay Runners'. These large aggressive cockroaches were separated in a small wooden compound placed on the flag stones. But returning to the Crown and Anchor just outside the Naval Base there was the 'Nelson' Bar, where upstairs a small team of Aussie sailors ran a game. Apparently, when the Military Police arrived the shout went out, "Leg it, the Crushers are here." Bodies could be seen going in all directions, some venturing to leap out of the first-floor windows. [16] [17] [18]

Back to the *Hunter* crew and it was not unusual after a first night run ashore, that the next day the ship's Coxswain would be sorting out the list

---

16   The Naval Patrol from the dominions usually turned a blind eye when finding a sailor '*non compos mentis*', as long as he had shipmates at hand to look after him. Unlike the US 'Shore Patrol', who could be a little heavy handed.

17   'Ackies' is another Royal Naval slang word for foreign loose change, originally on the Mediterranean Fleet Station. Since then over the years it has been adapted to 'ickies', 'klebbies', 'shrapnel' or 'washers'.

18   I would add that Bugis Street many years ago was sanitised, as would be expected in this now thoroughly modern, thriving pearl of the Far East.

of offenders. Some offences would require the Captain having to make contact with written apologises to perhaps bar owners or local dignitaries for the behaviour of the sailor or sailors. At worst the Captain would be summoned to the office of the Flag Officer, in this case Malta. Charges would be placed before the sailor, unless he was in cells ashore, where it could be a civil matter. However, fortunately most are dealt with on board, in this case it was two, who as previously described, tried to avoid paying the 'dysoman' his fare and had to be assisted aboard in a bedraggled state.

The following day they were called for by the Coxswain and told to get their caps immediately and to meet him on the Bridge. The Officer of the Day, "What do you have to say?" A weak excuse was given, claiming his mate had fallen off the 'dyso' accidently and he went in to save his life. The Coxswain ordered both in turn, "Off Cap." Officer of the Day looking stern, "First Lieutenant's report." "On Cap – about turn – quick march." It was over in two minutes. Out of hearing the Coxswain goes over to the two culprits, "Now listen here you two drunken reprobates, you had better have a better reason than that, when you go in front of 'Jimmy the One'."

Justice has to be seen to be done as a deterrent to make sure there were no repeats by any of the ship's company. So next day having been seen by their Divisional Officer, the same procedure was repeated, at the First Lieutenant's 'Table'. The Coxswain's loud voice reverberated around the Bridge, "D/SSX 24823-Able Seaman-Smith-one step forward-salute, Smith did on 16th May, 'recklessly jump off a dyso, returning to the ship to avoid paying the fare'." "Off Cap." The men admitted the charges, apologised for their behaviour, the divisional officer's gave their character reports. "It does not need me to tell you both that your behaviour was disgraceful and could have put not only your own lives at risk but others as well. Fourteen days number 10 A's, and compensation immediately paid to the 'Dyso-Owner'. It is noted: anymore recorded bad behaviour, then these charges will be taken into account. I am going to keep a close eye on you two; Coxswain." "On Caps" – about turn –quick march." [19]

Marshal Soult recalls the occasion when Surgeon Lieutenant Alfred

---

19   They were fortunate, probably because of a previous good character. The punishment given resulted in – no liberty for two weeks, to muster Morning, Afternoon, Dog and First Watches in the rig of the day and they were required to do extra work. And no 'Make and Mend' on Saturday or Sunday as they were required to work.

Flannery disembarked. "We carried the flotilla's doctor and when he was transferred to another position and had to leave our ship, I can remember seeing him in the boat that was taking him away from the ship, standing there with tears running down his face. He had been part of a happy ship's company."

It was now the end of July 1939, Surgeon Lieutenant Alfred Flannery with his wife Liz from New York had enjoyed a long spell in Malta. Prior to Liz leaving America, she had been introduced to a Maltese family; Marie and Arthur Mortimer, Marie's sister was a nun in New York. This led to the families forging a 'lifelong' friendship, and until this day the children of both families remain close friends.

After Alfred left Malta he was given appointments to other ships and shore bases in Britain and he and Liz's family had expanded to four children by the end of the war.

Terry Flannery, Alfred's youngest son relates a war-time story about his father when he was on board HMS *Orion*, a Leander Class cruiser, escorting convoys with much needed cargoes for the desperate Maltese. "My father brought some food and other needed supplies for the Mortimers. He said, they could hear the cheering of the Maltese people miles out at sea." Subsequently, *Orion* supported the army in the invasion of Sicily. [20]

The convoy is also known as the '*Kovvoj ta Santa Marija*' in Malta; the arrival of the last ships of the convoy on 15 August 1942, coincided with the Feast of the Assumption (Santa Marija). The name Santa Marija Convoy and the day's public holiday, in part, honours the arrival of the convoy. The attempt to run fifty ships past bombers, E-boats, minefields and submarines has gone down in military history as one of the most important British strategic victories of WW2. More than 500 Merchant and Royal Navy sailors and airmen were killed and only five of the fourteen merchant ships reached Grand Harbour. The arrival of the remains of the convoy did not break the siege, that continued until the Allied victory after the Second Battle of El Alamein and Operation Torch in November 1942 in the western

---

20 'Operation Pedestal'. To sustain Malta, the United Kingdom had to get convoys through at all costs. Despite serious losses, just enough supplies were delivered for Malta to continue resistance, although it ceased to be an effective offensive base for much of 1942. The operation officially started on 3 August 1942 and the convoy sailed through the Strait of Gibraltar on the night of 9/10 August.

Mediterranean, transformed the strategic situation and enabled land-based aircraft to escort convoys.

Another story that Terry remembers his father telling him, was with regards to Alfred providing treatment to a distinguished patient. "This also took place in Malta. Lord Mountbatten (not sure what rank he was at the time) had been visited by the Iranian Ambassador, who had given Mountbatten a large tin of Iranian caviar. Mountbatten became sick (anecdotally – he was a bit of a hypochondriac) and my father was called. He questioned Mountbatten and asked what he had eaten – caviar! My father said he would take the caviar to the lab to be tested. It is thought that Mountbatten had the 'Maltese Dog', a twenty-four-hour bug, probably due to the terrible water on the island. My father said, that the caviar was bad. Mountbatten got better. My father and some friends finished off the caviar."

I will return to Alfred and Liz Flannery and how their future evolved, including two more additions to their family.

Back to Marshal Soult and his memories in Malta, "The captain, Lieutenant Commander Scurfield, was a real naval type. I think the crew admired him for his actions when the ship was mined; because the big hole in her would fit a double-decker bus."

Marshal relives an uncertain moment for the crew on *Hunter* in March 1939. "A 'Pipe' [a tannoy announcement around the ship] was made that we were to be kept in the 'Med' for another eight to nine months. Some had already been out there for two to three years." Marshal indicates that this led to much discontentment and the morning after receiving the bad news there had been discussions between crew members which could have very easily been looked upon as a 'mutinous' act. At the 0805 'muster of hands' when working parties were detailed off to various parts of the ship, there was a 'spontaneous' reaction. "No one moved." Subsequently, the First Lieutenant relayed to the crew that the captain would see the commander in chief of the Mediterranean Fleet, Admiral Dudley Pound, about their grievances. Then everyone decided to carry on, but there was no 'falling in', they just went to their daily chores.

"It was that night on shore leave that some of the *Hunter*'s crew were asked by other sailors on other ships, 'What was going on with your lot today?' 'Not much, why?' 'Well, all our marines on board were mobilised.' The following day Admiral Dudley Pound came on board *Hunter* to speak to the crew. The lower deck was cleared and the admiral went on to explain that in view of the present international situation he could not spare what was in his estimation the 'finest anti-submarine division in the Fleet'. Therefore, the reason for 'Hunter' and other destroyers being needed in the Mediterranean was because of its new 'ASDIC' equipment in detecting submarines. Then a voice from the back shouted, "We don't want to know about the 'ASDIC', we want to know when we're going home." This was followed by a deathly silence with the officers looking mortified and stretching their necks to see who the culprit was.

"They never found out of course, but I have an idea it was a certain Leading Stoker. Ironically, the admiral was eventually promoted to be the First Sea Lord which required a return to London. As is the tradition when a commander in chief leaves his fleet, all the ships line up, to do a sail pass and the sailors take their caps off and give three 'Hurrahs!'. But, this time there were no cheers from *Hunter*.

"I shall always remember that this was a happy ship. A certain bond existed between the members of the ships company. No doubt this had come to be because of the dangers they had shared. Subsequently, it rubbed off on all who joined us. In the Mediterranean Fleet, we were on 'non-intervention patrols'. We transported five Palestinian Jews to exile in the Seychelles.

"We were due to return to the United Kingdom in March 1939 to 'pay off'. 'Hunter' was a member of the 1st destroyer Squadron when Mussolini invaded Albania. We finally returned home in August 1939 with a long paying off pennant. One of the longest I believe."

In the 1970s, there were a series of features provided by Sam Evens, a Petty Officer Stoker on *Hunter* for the *Plymouth Evening Herald*. In them was his personal account of the Battle of Narvik and his ongoing experiences before managing to escape back to Britain. To complement Sam's account, I was able to access an audio-taped interview he gave to the Imperial War Museum.

Sam was born in 1905 in Devonport, Plymouth. He left school at the age of thirteen. His father was a carpenter on the railways. Initially, Sam worked in a fruit shop earning fifteen shillings a week. "I asked the boss for a rise and he said, 'Don't come in on Monday, as trade was very poor.' So I went home and my father said, 'Best thing to do is to join the Services.' So I joined the Army, then just gone sixteen, but I told them I had just gone eighteen, put my age group up and went into the Royal Field Artillery. I joined at The Citadel on Plymouth Hoe, served three years in Britain, then they said, 'Would you take on another nine years to complete the twelve?' which would mean going to India, because that was where the artillery was stationed most of the time. So I said, 'No way.'

"I came out, left it. I went down to 'New Passage', the recruiting office at the dockyard there. Done an exam, at first they said 'No', if you've been in the Services, you couldn't join the Navy, because I was on a shilling a day 'reserve' pay. So I went home and told my father and he said, 'Try again tomorrow, I know somebody down there and they'll put you through.' I went, they sat me down and did a little test, 'the four simple rules' and when I'd done that they said, 'All right, fall in outside' and we marched down to the barracks and from there I started in the Navy. Very nice, 'cos I was used to routine and the service discipline and it didn't come too hard. It was hard on a lot of people that couldn't stand discipline."

Sam Evens and his father. [Sam Even's collection]

Different approaches to discipline often result in personality clashes, and thus conflicts. Sam remembers how "Many a time they had a fight of an evening and it finished up in the gymnasium; or sometimes back of the yachts' yard where we were stationed just outside St Budeaux, that was the naval training camp outside there. I was on many ships before *Hunter* including HMS *Hood*, the battleship, so I gained much experience as a stoker, as these included coal-burning ships. The boiler room (on *Hunter*) was much easier, everything was cleaner, fans oil pumps, feed pumps were fed from the engine room."

In hot climates, you would imagine the heat to be unbearable in such places as the boiler and engine rooms. In fact, it was the reverse and often the best parts of ship to be on watch. This was because there were large forced draft fans, supplying air for combustion in the boilers, as well as adequate fans to cool the engine room compartment. Compared with the messdecks, where it could become very uncomfortable. Although there was a ventilation trunk throughout the ship. There was also an added bonus for the engineering staff, whilst on watch they could soak their grease and sweat covered overalls in extremely hot water.

Sam, now aged thirty-two, had risen to the rank of Petty Officer. "In 1937, I was sent to St Angelo in Malta to pick up HMS *Active* – we were then transferred from *Active* to *Hunter*. We done two years before going back to Plymouth. There was talk of war [...] then news came that she had to be ready for sea again. We joined up with the rest of the flotilla from Portsmouth and Chatham.

"We went down to Gibraltar, we refuelled there and then we set off on patrol to Sierra Leone, stopping ships and asking nationality and all that. Then from there we went to Bermuda and then to Halifax, Canada for convoys. During the convoys, a ship was cut up into two during the darkness of night, during the change of course, one of the ships was unlucky and rammed by the HMS *Queen Elizabeth*, a cruiser. I don't know if there were any survivors. When you're in a convoy you don't stop. We didn't come across any enemy. We joined the fleet again at Scapa Flow."

On the 22nd of August 1939, Lieutenant Commander *Linds*ay De Villiers became the new commanding officer of *Hunter*. Born in Cape Town, South Africa in 1904, at the age of thirteen he began the same route into the Royal Navy as that of Captain Warburton-Lee, Commander of HMS *Hardy*. De Villiers' first ship as a Midshipman was HMS *Lowestoft* stationed with the 'Africa Station' before joining ships in the Mediterranean Fleet. In 1927, he became First Lieutenant on HMS *Petrel*, a river gun boat on the China station. Between 1930 and 1936 he returned to destroyers moving around from Africa, the Mediterranean and Home Fleets. By this time he had married Pamela and they had a son. His first command came in 1936 with HMS *Amazon* then after tactical courses, HMS *Blanche*. Two weeks before the war broke out he began his appointment on *Hunter*.

Within a week the top command had been changed, as Lieutenant Alex Stuart-Menteth also joined the ship as the First Lieutenant. After the captain, he was the next most senior seaman officer and eight years younger. Alex was born in Merstham, Surrey. He had joined the Royal Navy at the age of fourteen and began his four-year training spell at Dartmouth Naval College. On completion as a Cadet he appears to have been promoted within the normal time span to Lieutenant in December 1934. Before arriving on *Hunter* he had gained a lot of experience having had appointments to various types of ships, though predominantly destroyers.

Was it a coincidence that for whatever reasons, these two officers were given appointments to join *Hunter* a few days before the declaration of war?

War is fast becoming reality...

On the September 1, 1939, the pre-dawn skies lit up over the Baltic Sea as the German battleship Schleswig-Holstein opened fire on a Polish fortress on the Westerplatte Peninsula as assault troops hidden aboard the vessel stormed the shoreline. The venerable ship that had seen action in World War One fired the first salvoes of what would be a second global conflagration. Without a declaration of war, 1.5 million troops stormed Nazi Germany's 1,750-mile border with Poland. They came from the north, south and west by land, by air and by sea in a quest to regain territory lost by Germany in the Treaty of Versailles and colonise its neighbour.

The Nazis overwhelmed the antiquated Polish defences with their blitz-krieg, or 'lightning war', tactics. German tanks steamrolled into the country. The Luftwaffe destroyed airfields, bombed passenger trains and mowed down civilians indiscriminately with machine-gun fire. Incendiary bombs torched Katowice, Krakow and the capital city of Warsaw. By sea, German warships and U-boats attacked the Polish navy. The one-million-man Polish military was undermanned and underequipped. So antiquated were some army units that cavalry horses trotted to the front lines to confront the enemy's mighty armoured tanks.

Prime Minister Chamberlain flew back to Germany, meeting Hitler in Bad Godesberg on the 2nd of September. Hitler decided to discard the proposals of the previous meeting and now he demanded immediate occupation of the Sudetenland and that Polish and Hungarian territorial claims on Czechoslovakia be addressed. Chamberlain objected strenuously, telling Hitler that he had worked hard to bring the French and Czechoslovaks into line with Germany's demands, so much so that he had been accused of giving into dictators. However, Hitler was not interested.

The following day, Hitler sent a five-page letter, outlining the demands he had spoken of the previous day. Chamberlain replied by offering to act as an intermediary with the Czechoslovaks, and suggested that Hitler put his demands in a memorandum which could be circulated to the French and Czechoslovaks

War is declared

It is recorded that, on 3rd of September 1940 when war against Germany was declared, jubilation went round the ships in the fleet and great excitement was felt. Guns were cleared and made ready for action. Ammunition was brought up from the magazines and placed in 'Ready Use' lockers, 4.7-inch shells were stowed in the 'Ready Use' racks around the gun platforms. Two sets of four torpedo tubes midships were drawn and armed with warheads. The 0.5 machine guns were loaded. Already the ASDIC operator would be 'pinging away' with signal waves travelling through the water, optimistically waiting for a reflected return signal from a U-boat.

The war at sea began on the same day and to everybody's surprise in such a violent manner. The 13,500-ton liner *Athenia* was torpedoed without warning off Ireland by a U-boat with the loss of 112 lives, twenty-eight of them American citizens. Two weeks later the aircraft carrier HMS Courageous was also torpedoed off the south-west of Ireland, 518 crew members went down with their ship.

During this period a crew member who joined *Hunter* in Malta was nineteen-year-old Joe Settle. Becoming 'restless' he had wanted to go to sea, so joined the Navy in September 1938. Prior to Joe's draft, whilst the ship was being repaired in Malta, he had served for a short spell on two other destroyers. The experience gained good results with promotion to a Stoker First Class within five months.

Another young seaman who joined at that time was the 'joker' in the pack, James 'Stormy' Renshaw. Here he relates his early experiences, albeit 'tongue in cheek'. "After my six months' training, I was shipped out to the Mediterranean, to join a ship that had just been sunk. This was still actually in peacetime; it was the HMS *Hunter*. She was reputed to have hit a mine, but she sank down to a floating level. I joined her when she had been rebuilt. The first journey that we had was to join the Spanish 'Revolution' that was taking place. We clued up in Barcelona and took out the British

Consul and all of his employees, because Barcelona was being bombed. We had one attack, which was by small Italian fighter planes. Meanwhile, the Germans were practising their bombing technique on the poor Spaniards.

"After that, we did a cruise of the Mediterranean, then came home to Plymouth. Whilst we were back in Plymouth, restoring, threats from Adolf Hitler came along. The ship finished up joining the South Atlantic Fleet to cut off two ships that were going to cut the 'Trans-Atlantic' cable. From that, we started doing convoy duty from Halifax, Nova Scotia in Canada to Bermuda, picking up cargo ships, grouping them in Nova Scotia, for the journey across the North Atlantic. During this, we got into a hurricane and we had to be convoyed ourselves, as we were so damaged.

"Arriving in Plymouth again and being repaired, we went to cruise the North Atlantic again. Whilst we were doing the Iceland and Beyer Island run, we had a signal sent to us to say that the Germans were invading northern Norway; and would we kindly go up there and give them a thrashing? But it didn't work out that way; being a junior member of the ship's company, I was supplied with nothing more than an empty revolver. On querying as to what I was supposed to do with this thing, I was told that I'd be given ammunition when we arrived in Norway. Meanwhile, if I got into any trouble, I was to swing it round my neck. Anyway the boat landing never came."

Whilst in Falmouth there were two major engineering tasks to complete, a defect on a steam pipe and a major routine maintenance check. The work would be overseen by Lieutenant (E) Alick Reid and his two most experienced senior rates, Chief Artificer Edward Gould and Chief Stoker David Moore.

One of the steam pipe flange joints was leaking and if it finally blew, super-heated steam could produce a dangerous situation for the then engine room watchkeepers. The repair work was made more difficult because the flanges had to be pulled apart within a maze of other pipes. This meant these had to be moved first to allow access to complete the task. However, the look on Alick Reid's face as he came into the wardroom for his belated evening meal said it all, 'job done' and it was time for a 'Horse's Neck'. [21]

On board, there was a system which took the sea water and with aid of the copper evaporator tubes and a condenser provided distilled water not

---

21   Brandy and dry ginger, a common drink before the war with a long spiral of lemon peel or zest.

only for the boilers but also for cooking, washing and bathing. Obviously it was a top priority that the system was thoroughly checked, before going to sea as well as for comfort of the sailors.

The next task was the quarterly boiler clean. This had been completed by Chief Stoker David Moore and his team. He was not expecting any major problems for the next stint at sea. It was also a relief to have finished it, because in port it could mean that more of his stokers would be able to join the rest of the 'off watch' ship's company with free time to go ashore, if need be. However, the boilers were now in top-notch condition. All the furring inside the many tubes had been cleaned out. This had required, firstly, dismantling the boiler drums, the baffle and other gear. Then a brush being pushed down each tube individually to clean them out before being 'sighted', to ensure there was nothing left inside them. If there was and had it not been noticed, then the obstruction would result in hot water not being able to circulate, which would subsequently cause incandescence and melt the tube, providing another dangerous situation, this time affecting the boiler-room personnel.

As mentioned the 'sighting' of the boiler was a very important final part of this task and usually had to be completed by a commissioned officer. Nobody would be allowed in the boiler room until the procedure was finished. This procedure was carried out by Alick Reid.

Alick with the assistance of an experienced and reliable stoker, would make their way into the boiler room where the iron watertight hatch would clang shut behind them. Alick would worm his way in with difficulty, lying on his stomach, he would drop ball bearings down the tubes to confirm that there were no obstructions. This would be done in conjunction with a wooden board with holes in it like those used in a solitaire game, holding thirty-six balls altogether. At the bottom of the tubes the Stoker caught them with a small bag and the officer 'chalked' each tube as he dropped a ball down it. Then a pause during which the wooden board was passed down to the lower drum and the Stoker fitted the recovered balls into it. The pause lengthened while he searched for the balls he had failed to catch. Finally the filled board was returned to the officer in the upper drum and the cycle started again. When the check was completed, the officer was the last man to leave the drum, and the boiler-room hatch was bolted in place.

I am sure many an Engineer Officer must have had nightmares. As the last thing to remember was the piece of chalk. One such officer said, "As I watched the hatches being bolted into place after 'sighting', the thought often occurred to me that an unpopular engineer officer might easily vanish without trace!"

Moving forward, on the ship departing from Plymouth, Chief Petty Officer George Sutton, by elimination appears to have been the Coxswain on *Hunter*, in a similar role to a Master-at-Arms on larger warships. He would have been responsible for the overall discipline of the Ratings on board, taking his orders from the First Lieutenant. He would also take the helm when entering or leaving harbour, completing difficult manoeuvres, or when at action stations. He was a highly-experienced seaman, having joined the navy as a 'Boy Sailor' in 1916. Having become an ordinary seaman, during the First World War, he saw service on the battleship HMS *Colossus*.

I was provided with George's service records by Gordon Lees, whose father was a 'mate' of George. Gordon is a member of the 'Oldham Historical Research Group', hence his interest in tracing back George's naval service and personal life.

George Sutton's naval background was intriguing not only because it had spanned over nearly twenty-four years involving two wars, but also because there was some information in his service records but nothing about his private life. So for that I had to rely on what additional information Gordon Lees could bring to the table.

However, for now from George's service records I have been able to deduce, that in the early 1920s he had been moved to the submarine branch. Promoted to petty officer in 1925 and then in 1929 he had extended his engagement for a further ten years. During his time in the branch he moved around substantially with varying submarine depot and repair ships, earning promotion to chief petty officer by 1936. Prior to the beginning of the war he spent a short period on the submarine HMS *Narwhal*, but left because he was coming up to the end of his engagement. So it was in July 1939, doing the last of his time at the submarine base 'Dolphin' in Portsmouth, and with an impending war over the horizon, that this resulted in George being placed on 'active service'.

With his vast naval experience and an exemplary record, he would be a crucial resource and leader to his future Junior Rates. Knowing the man only on paper, I would not be surprised if George did not grumble but relished the ongoing challenge. Alas, it would not be as a submariner, as his age was against him and he had to return back to general service. In January 1940 he was sent to the destroyer HMS *Whitshed* and within a week of joining, the ship was involved in the sinking of U-boat 55.

Two weeks later the British merchant ship *Sultan Star*, having left Buenos Aries seventeen days earlier, carrying 8,000 tons of frozen meat and 1,000 tons of butter, on approaching the English Channel, was sunk by a U-boat. The *Whitshed* was sent immediately to the area and after attacking the U-boat, managed to rescue all seventy-two of the crew from the merchant ship.

Surprisingly, George, after just thirty days, left the *Whitshed* and almost a week later was given a 'pier head jump' to HMS *Hunter* on 1st of March 1940. I wonder whether this was because of his possible experience regarding the newly introduced ASDIC equipment recently fitted on some destroyers. Or was it because *Hunter* was the junior ship in the 2nd Destroyer Flotilla, and it was felt that an experienced helmsmen was needed for what was about to take place. Or, a less dramatic reason, maybe he simply had to relieve another seaman chief petty officer who for whatever reason had to leave the ship. At first his service records left more questions than answers until I was contacted by a local historian in the town of his birth. This will become clearer later. [22]

Another contact I received was from Rob Harry in Perth, Australia. His uncle, Ordinary Seaman Jack Tucker was from Cardiff and on board *Hunter*. Similar to George Sutton there was little information about his personal background and once again more questions than answers. I assume at nineteen years of age he had not yet reached the rank of Able Seaman. Jack had just finished his basic training and been sent onto complete another course. Kindly, Rob sent a copy of a letter that Jack had sent to his mother.

Sun 10th Dec A.C. Tucker

H.M. Signal School
Portsmouth.

Dear Ma,
  Many thanks for your letter which I received just a day ago. Thanks very much for the 10/- note. [ten shillings equal to 50p today] It was very handy. I was stony broke before. As you can see we have shifted from Devonport. When you write again don't forget my new address. Will you send down my flannels and coat and shirts etc., when you can. Have my [looks like greys] been cleaned yet?

---

22   The saying, 'pier head jump' is over a hundred and fifty years old and originates from the Mersey Docks area.

Well Ma I'm afraid I haven't any news for you at present. I am expecting to hear from Jean very soon. It's her birthday on the 12th. I bought Jean a present out of that 10/-.

This is all for now Ma. Give my love to all at home and please write soon.
Your Loving Son
Xxxxxx Jack

So once Jack finished his course in Portsmouth he was quickly drafted to *Hunter.* Maybe not too dissimilar to George Sutton, in that young Jack for whatever reason was sent to *Hunter.* Perhaps another 'pier head jump' but this time unbeknown to Jack, into an early test of action at sea.

Hunter's Crew

For non-nautical readers, I think it would be a good idea to give you a picture of life on board the 'H' type destroyers. But before then, why is it called 'messdeck' or 'mess', used in the other two services and now by police and fire fighting forces? It would be nice to think it came from British shores, but it comes from an old French word, *'mes'* –'portion of food'. I won't go into too much detail but prior to that from the Latin verb *'mittere'* – 'to send', the original sense being 'a course of a meal put on a table'.

"This sense of mess, which appeared in English in the thirteenth century, was often used for cooked or liquid dishes in particular, as in a 'mess of pottage' (porridge or soup). By the fifteenth century, a group of people who ate together were also called a mess and it is in this sense that it persists in the 'mess halls' of the modern military." Source: Wikipedia.

Now back from the history lesson. It is worth noting that the rates of pay for Junior Rates at this time depended on whether they had joined up before 1925, in which case they were on a higher rate. Also for every three years over the age of eighteen Petty Officers and below were awarded a badge (stripe) up to a maximum of three. These badges were worth 3d a day. So 'Three-Badge men' earned 9d a day. There were also extra earnings for those entitled to a daily tot of rum (over twenty years old), but who abstained, this also amounted also to an extra 3d (12d to a shilling – 20 shillings to the £).

Therefore, as an example, the **weekly** pay rates up to Leading Hand were as follows;

Boy Sailors	8 shillings and 9 d (43p) on completion of training.
Ordinary Seaman Rate	14 shillings (70p)
Able Seaman Rate	22 shillings and 02 d (£1.18p) (Joined after 1925)

Able Seaman Rate	25 shillings and 06 d (£1.35p) two badges (Joined after 1925)
Able Seaman Rate	31 shillings and 06 d (£1.60p) two badges (Joined before 1925)
Able Seaman Rate	33 shillin gs and 03 d (£1.66p) three badges (Joined before 1925)

In 1940, the civilian average weekly pay (six days, ten hours a day) for a craftsman was £5 and a labourer £4. Although, service men did receive free food and lodgings, albeit not hotel standard. [23]

Ralph Brigginshaw – to my knowledge, the only surviving crew member of HMS *Hardy* – a signalman, tells me that on joining up at St Vincent (boys' training establishment at Gosport) they were paid every Thursday. This was 1 shilling and 6 pence and a bar of 'pussers' soap. "The balance of the money was put in the Post Office bank for us."

At that time, a pint of beer at today's prices would be 9 pence, a bottle of wine 33 pence, a packet of crisps 1 pence, a gallon of petrol 27 pence, a first class stamp 1 pence, a Ford Popular car £80 and the average house £750.

Now imagine the scene is set at sea; the ships are sailing through gale-force winds and driving rain. The seas are rough and darkness has fallen. The ships company when on operations cannot be at full action stations all the time, so they are stood down to two watches for periods of six hours at a time. The Junior Ratings (Leading Hand and below) accommodation areas are spread around the ship but all are one or two decks below the iron (upper) deck and most are forward. They are numbered, from the bows to aft Mess 1, Mess 2, Mess 3 and so forth. The further you are up for'd the more motion can be felt and on a destroyer the deck can go up and down by well over 25 feet in very rough seas. When the keel hits the bottom of the waves the force causes a violent shudder which oscillates throughout the ships superstructure but and in particular for'd. I can confirm this having served on frigates which were similar in size to the old destroyers.

The ship can be at different degrees of readiness. Let us also imagine presently there is no immediate threat from an enemy so to allow time for rest and meals the crew are in two watches. Because No 2 Gun (for'd) and

---

23 Source www.winksworth.org.uk/A04VALUE.html.

No 3 Gun (aft) were on raised gun decks these were normally the ones kept manned and ready. Therefore, when No 1 Gun crew came on watch they went to No 2 Gun and not their own. The torpedo tubes, depth charge traps and throwers were also manned and ready in a similar manner.

The seven man for'd gun crew are now going off watch and would have to negotiate the journey as you can imagine under difficult conditions. Their haven, if you could call it that, is the seamen's No 5 Mess, two decks down below the fo'c's'le . The 'Gunners' would have to move slowly to a vertical iron ladder down to the open irondeck and walk aft to a screen door just below the Bridge. In mountainous seas this is a treacherous task not helped when dressed in wellington boots over a boiler suit topped by a soaking wet oil skin coat. There would only be guardrails to hold onto, although by doing so they are obviously nearer to the side of the ship where any incoming seawater will be at its most powerful swell.

Having managed the passage so far on the wet slippery irondeck, and having arrived at the steel screen door, this would require one of them to unlock the bulkhead door's heavy latches. Then walk to the starboard side moving for'd down a passageway, not much wider than three feet. There would be various compartments along the passage as they continued walking for'd. These included the transmitting station (TS), then the wireless telegraphy (WT) office and finally the junior ratings washroom with a sliding steel door (no baths). It is here that the 'Gunners' could finally discard most of their wet attire and dry their cold bodies. The compartments deck would have a number of galvanised 'dhoby' buckets scattered around in which to put wet clothes. It maybe that having to go back on watch in six hours' time some of the Gunners would wait for their turn when the next rest period arrives. They would just discard their wet gear, have something to eat and get their heads down

They would now have entered No 5 Mess, which at first glance would not be a welcoming sight. The deck head is low but they would have to stoop even lower to avoid touching the slung hammocks where their mess mates were probably absorbed in deep dreams, some snoring but none in tune. A vision from the story of the 'Black Hole of Calcutta' would come to mind, but at least now they would be feeling warmer if not yet fully dry.

The idea of the naval hammock goes back to the 1590s. It not only allowed extra space during the day but also kept the sleeper well balanced, irrespective of the motion of the warship. A sailor, probably in a previous century, with an innovative mind decided his hammock needed to be more comfortable. He found a two-foot length of wood, cut a 'v' shaped groove both ends, which then held open the second outer strings of the hammock where the head rested. The outer strings was tighter than the rest so that it raised a protective lip along each side to keep out drafts and prevent the sleeper being thrown out. A narrow mattress was also issued.

There would be metal lockers bolted to both of the ship's sides, port and starboard in twos, one on top of the other with a stowage rack above for kit bags or suitcases. Each sailor would have a personal key. Space would be at a premium so the lockers were not large, in fact you could wonder how on earth the sailors might have managed to place all their kit and personal belongings into them. On joining the Navy, the recruits have numerous 'kit musters'. The kit needs to be set out and ironed to the exact same size as that shown in an example provided on a picture hung up in the messdeck. The idea being that this then allows all the kit to smartly fit into the regulation size lockers.

As you would expect, the clothes-cleaning procedure for engine and boiler-room personnel would be an increased onerous task than most of the other crew members. Here a Stoker completing New Entry Training in the 1930s describes crucial parts of the task. "The class instructor took us to the wash place and patiently went through the process to expect at sea. The wash room was locked behind us, and we had to fully strip off. There were wooden troughs and we had a set order for the type of articles to wash, starting with whites and ending with the oiled soiled boiler suit.

"We used what was called 'Pussers Hard' soap and a brush for parts of the uniform that could withstand the friction. We began by washing underwear in our own trough, there was plenty of hot water. The instructor reinforced, "When you go to sea you always strip off in the bathroom and wash all your clothes this way, you will soon get over any embarrassment about being in the 'nud'.

"There was a special skill in not letting the blue from the 'blue jean collar' go into the three white decorative tapes and the blue strip around the 'white front'. We then came to the boiler suit which was without doubt the most strenuous job even with the brush. This was followed by scrubbing the hammock and cover on the 'deck' as the instructor called it. Although it had previously been left to soak in a copious amount of soapy suds. Next job drain and refill the troughs for rinsing the articles in the same order. Finally, we had some fun turning the drum of a centrifugal contraption to extract as much water as possible. Of course, some 'show offs' had to try to outdo the rest of us pretending it was the hand-driven air-raid siren.

"The instructor pointed out that on board ship there would be no problems for Stokers to dry their stuff, there would be plenty of 'cabooses' [hideaway compartments with hot machinery] available, if need be. Pointing to the supplied drying rack trolleys for hanging the wet gear, he asked us to take them next door into the boiler room. Task done, we began frolicking in the same wash troughs, dousing ourselves in the fast running relaxing hot water. Maybe it would be the last time we would enjoy the event in such a way. We were off to our first ships next week." [24]

Superstitions considered lucky for sailors:

For sailors to have tattoos. Throwing an old pair of shoes overboard just after launch. To have a black cat on board. For a child to be born on the ship. For sailors to wear gold hoop earrings. To step aboard using the right foot first.

Unlucky:

To name the boat with a word ending in 'a'. To have the bottle not break when used in the launch ceremony. Changing the name of a boat. Sailing on a Friday. To see rats leaving a ship meant that someone would die on the ship. A ship to cross an area where another ship once sunk. To lose a bucket at sea.

Returning to life on board *Hunter*, a part of the mess would be partially lit for those able to eat their 'scran' or participate in any other nocturnal activities. However, this would be by way of a small lamp masked by blue paint on the deckhead. All 'scuttles' with blast-protected glass and their 'deadlights' are tightly secured, so it would be almost total darkness.

---

24 Tradition says the blue jean collar dates from the times when seamen wore tarred pigtails, not true as the collar was not part of uniform until after pigtails disappeared. The three stripes have nothing to do with Nelson's three victories but was simply standardised to three when the uniform was regulated. Superstition has it that it is considered lucky to touch a sailor's collar. The bell-bottomed trousers were designed so that they could be rolled up easily when scrubbing the decks. Ratings used to have either five or seven horizontal creases and this did not represent the seven seas or five oceans but depended on the length of the sailor's leg. The lanyard was originally used to carry the hornpipe

There would be two scrubbed wooden tables bolted to the deck on both sides and each would constitute a separate mess. The tables were utilised not only for meal times but also writing letters home and playing card or dominoes. Although, unlike at home they could also be used as an additional place for a mess member to sleep, especially if the ship was carrying more than its normal complement. [In fact, all the ships in the 2nd Destroyer Flotilla, when later they were sent into battle, were over-crowded.]

The nearest for'ard messdeck was No 5 Mess and the next No 4 Mess which was the torpedo crews and ASDIC operators' mess. Then came the central circular support of No 1 Gun, and for'd of that structure were Nos 3, 2 and 1 Messes. No 1 Mess being the furthest for'd where the compartment began to narrow towards the bows of the ship.

The stench would be unimaginable, with restricted air flow causing an unpleasant smell which would consist of uncontrolled flatulence, cigarette and pipe smoke, both stale and new. If that wasn't enough, the foul smell of unwashed sweating bodies, plus dirty and wet clothes and of course vomit in buckets, the result of those sailors who had not yet or never would gain their 'sea legs'. Not all food items would have been devoured. Today's 'Cook of the Mess' had managed to make a large 'Manchester Tart', left in a 'dixie' the remnants of which would be going stale by the minute. There would be one bonus though, an ongoing hot water urn to brew a well-earned mug of tea accompanied by a daily tot of 'nectar' from the last remains in the 'rum fanny'.

Naval Terminology:

'**Pusser**' Slang term for anything belonging or attached to the Royal Navy. Originates from the word 'Purser' (continues to be used for an officer title in the Merchant Navy).

'**Dhoby**' comes from those sailors in the past who were deployed in the Far East naval bases. It is a Hindu word sailors adopted for washing clothes. I will not need to explain what the terms 'Dhoby Dust' or 'Dhoby Itch' mean.

'**Scran**' is food.

'**Deadlights**' are hinged metal flaps clamped over the scuttle on the order to 'darken ship'.

'**Cook of the Mess**' would be a mess member from a duty roster. He would be detailed for the week and excused forenoon (0800–1200) work at their normal part of ship.

'**Rum Fanny**', this needs a more in-depth explanation. These were used for holding the mess rum ration, originating from 1867, to provide canned mutton as an alternative to salted meat in a cask. However, sailors took a while to get used to the method because around this time a young girl named (Sweet) Fanny Adams had been murdered and her body dismembered. The sheer coincidence resulted in Fanny's name living on in a completely unintended way.

'**Manchester Tart**' was a 'clacker' or as we would say pastry crust, with a thin layer of jam over a thick layer of lemon flavoured custard. The top of the pie has a sprinkling of desiccated coconut.

The term 'clacker' is now used by men in the public arena when they say, "Wow, look at the legs on that bit of clacker." These are just a small selection of a sailor's extensive slang words, to allow the reader to understand that in the Navy they have their own vocabulary. It can take years before a sailor will become fully conversant with all the content. Some of which need an 'X' rated certificate.

More examples of Naval slang: Do not try too hard working it out as sailors like to keep things simple but encrypted. Here some of the culinary delights on board ship.

Adam and Eve on a raft: Two fried eggs on a piece of toast.
Cow Pat: Country pancake.
Dockyard Tortoise: Cornish pasty.
Deep Sea Steak: Kippers.
Elephants Footprints: Spam fritters immersed in batter and fried.
Frog in a Bog: Toad in the hole.
Italian Teabags: Ravioli.
Neptune's Dandruff: Table salt.
Nuts and Bolts: Mutton stews with small bones in the meat.
Oggie: Cornish pasty; derived from Mr Hogg a pie-seller at the toll gate between Plymouth and Devonport.
Pigskin Pie: A fatty bacon roll.

Worms in Red Lead: Tinned spaghetti
Sea Dust: Cooking salt
Shake and Pigmy: Steak and kidney pie
Hard Tack: Ships biscuit.
Spring Loaded Chicken: Rabbit.
Once you have chosen your grub the sailor would say,
"I could **eat a horse between two hammocks**" [Great hunger]
"What's yer brew?" "**Reindeer Juice**". [Very strong lager]
Then for dessert "**Bathing Beauty**" [Blancmange because it shivers and has such lovely curves]

A conversation in the mess at tea time could sound like this. "I wanted to be a 'sea buffalo' before I joined up but wasn't fit enough, but I put it down to having too many brain cells. Still better than ending up as a 'poultice walloper' or being in the 'dustmen' department." His mate looked at him with a smile, "'Pass the slide' please – cheers matey." "Cor that 'awning' is a bit stale, oh no! Not 'PLM' again, why not a tin of 'Chinese wedding cake' for a change?" A messmate showing concern, "Where's Bill, he's got to see the 'Sin Bosun' tomorrow before he gets married." "He's on 'jankers'," replied another.

Work that lot out, it took me twenty-three years and they still kept on coming. There is a translation at the end of the chapter. [25]

Ralph Brigginshaw, confirms the dining arrangements and the living conditions on the destroyers: "We had no special cold weather clothing and did the best we could. As regards hammocks we were issued with these and took them with us from ship to ship. Fortunately, we managed to find enough hooks to hang them on, even with the extra crew. But it made the messes quite cramped and a job to turn in between the night watches."

The dining arrangements, termed 'Canteen Messing', gave each mess the responsibility for ordering their own weekly issues of tea, sugar, cocoa and milk. Depending on how long the ship had been at sea there was also a daily issue of bread, margarine, potatoes and meat. Although bread would normally only be baked on board when in calm seas and under normal ships routine. (In other words, not cruising or action stations). Otherwise, they would only have bread available in harbour or when alongside a depot ship. If there was no bread then in order to sweep up the gravy or soup it was back

---

25   Rick Jolly's book *Jackspeak*.

to the notorious 'ship's biscuits'. These delights were kneaded cakes of flour, baked with the least quantity of water as possible and then stored below, until such times as required for emergency rations when they would emerge in the company of the wheat eating beetle called the 'weevil'.

As you would imagine, fresh fruit and vegetables would not last long at sea, so the appointed 'cooks of the mess' would have to rely on the tinned source. However, to the hungry sailors this could prove to be an untimely problem. The tins were stored in a locker between the messdecks. Access was from the heavy lid at the bottom of the locker. In times of rough weather the tins could escape and be found floating around in any water that had made its way inboard. This could quickly result in the labels becoming detached from the tins. Thus, this often resulted in a frustrated 'cooks of the mess' trying to make a soup and opening what he thought was a tin of peas only to find it was a tin of rhubarb. It was not long after the war that the idea of labelling was discontinued and the contents were 'branded' on the top of the tins.

Finally, when the day's rota of the 'cooks of the mess' had got together all the ingredients for the next meal, off he would go to the main galley for Petty Officer Cook Richard Richards and assistants Charlie Sadd, James Williams and Bill Wallis to supervise and complete the final task. Of course, all departments on board are ribbed about the job, and it is no different with the galley staff. The story goes that their branch is the most difficult in which to pass exams, because no one has passed the course yet. From my own experience, to provide meals at sea is the same as at home but under more demanding and difficult conditions – it is called cooking. However, when the cook becomes a chef, for example when the chief petty officers are entertaining for a 'Ladies Night' in harbour, when wives, fiancés, girlfriends and women friends are honoured, then there will be an opportunity to see the 'chef's' exceptional skills.

Leading Cook James Williams, aged twenty-four, was from Liskeard, Cornwall and prior to joining the navy was a printer by trade. Cook Bill Wallis was twenty-two, he came from London and previously worked as a baker. I was fortunate that Bill's nephew John Farrier made contact with me. John, a school teacher, who now lives in Bergen, Norway, has been a great help. He became my eyes and ears, providing me with information about both Norway and northern Sweden.

In crammed messdecks on operational duties, there would be little the men could do about tidying up their living quarters, gash (naval term for rubbish) accumulated; cigarette packets, nutty wrappers (toffee papers), crusts of bread, tea leaves and old newspapers or magazines. This would have to wait until calmer weather when it could be 'ditched' over the side. However, when 'dream time' came and they would finally arrive in port or anchor off, as sure as night follows day there would be an immediate order for First Lieutenant's 'rounds' of all the Junior Rates messdecks. Or the more daunting prospect of Captain's rounds. The saying goes in the Navy, "If you can't take a joke, why bother joining up?"

However, they would now have arrived in Shetlands Island 'mainland' harbour. The messdecks cleaned and tidy having had First Lieutenant's rounds. It was the 4th April 1940, a Tuesday evening, the first of two days' rest for the ships companies of the five destroyers. Although, for some it was still 'turn to' such as the watch keepers and those doing crucial repairs or maintenance on weapons or below in the engine and boiler rooms. It was not an easy task working out who would have time off to go ashore. If there were defects they had to be worked on until put right. To do this it was crucial that the task was given to the ratings with those skills needed for the particular equipment. So it meant these experienced men are made available whilst trying not to stop their leave.

One of those having to continue working until repairs are completed is the leading stoker in charge of the boat's maintenance 'part of ship'. Since the ship had recently been stationed abroad he had been having trouble with one of the boat's engines giving up the ghost and now another had to use his own description "gone tits up".

He was complaining to the Coxswain of the boat in question. "They're fine for the small harbours that we have in Blighty, where the water is cleaner and has only short distances to come ashore. But not quite up to it when in some ports like Freetown in West Africa, when the water cooling system were always getting bunged up. In the 'Med' last year, the port whaler's cylinder head cracked and we had no replacement. So it was a massive welding job having to use the galley stove to pre-heat it. The bloody 'Yanks' the small boats on their ships, as you would expect were more rugged though less glamorous. Sugar! I have just hit my fingers with this bleeding hammer." The Coxswain with a sympathetic look, realising he had half an hour to catch the next liberty boat, decided it was time to go.

Unlike the boat's Coxswain, not many men ventured ashore to the desolate landscape of the Shetland Isles, especially at this time of the year. It is a subarctic archipelago of Scotland, fifty miles north east of Orkney and 170 miles southeast of the Faroe Islands. It divides the Atlantic to the west from the North Sea to the east. Those who did decide to go ashore took advantage of the wonderful walks, searching out the fauna and flora or the famous sea-bird nesting sites. The few public bars existing were known for their traditional fiddle style music, but alas there was none tonight.

Here again I will try to put together a scenario showing how those members of the ship's company, off watch, were relaxing whilst believing there was something afoot at command level. As I have explained, the gun crews were in the seamen's No 5 Mess and the torpedo crews and ASDIC operators were adjacent in No 4 Mess. Nearby were the signalmen and radio operators and the stokers' messdecks. Many of the men would be writing what would possibly be their last letters home for a while.

A very important event when reaching harbour is receiving the canvas bags of mail, there are no problems getting volunteers to drag them on board or sort them out in the temporary dual purpose mail office. Receiving mail, like food, rum and 'baccy' are crucial needs to the ships morale. The ships company knowing the mail has arrived on board are waiting expectantly for the high-pitched pipe of the bosun's mate. Then the announcement, "Mail is ready for collection." More often than not it needs two or three men from the mess to haul the bags down the ladders because there are not only letters but boxes of 'goodies' from home

Once delivered there is a deathly silence whilst the mess members start to open their gifts from 'Postie'. Stoker First Class Daniel Percy Beckford from the East End of London was pleased with his letter from his wife Rose, who announced she was "expecting a baby". He had to write back straight away to tell her how happy he was and that he would soon get home on leave. He was aged twenty-three, a fit young man who boxed for the Navy. We will return back to the stokers' mess shortly.

Another happy sailor was the nineteen-year-old Ordinary Seaman Jack Tucker. He received a reply from his "Ma" to the letter he sent last month. Perhaps settling his mind about having his civilian clothes at hand, possibly to go ashore when staying the weekend at the Royal Sailors Rest in Portsmouth. [26]

---

26   The letters sent home were usually mailed from the ship when arriving at the next port of call. This meant that there could be a considerable number of mail bags dispatched containing letters written over a long period of time.

Another of the ship's company had also received a letter from a young lady in Gibraltar. He had met her almost three years previously when the ship had limped in to the port after the 'non-intervention patrol' during the Spanish Civil War. 'Love must have been in the air', because the young seaman visited Gibraltar when *Hunter* came into port again in 1939 on her way to West Africa. The romance blossomed as since then they had written to each other on a regular basis. However, the news was not good as he told his 'oppo', "Rosa says there is a rumour going round the 'Rock' that there's going to be a mass evacuation of non-essential men, women and children. They're all worried because the government are thinking of sending them over the Gib Straits to Morocco, poor kid! It seems like I am never going to catch up with her, until it's too late and she will find someone else." "What will be will be, matey?" replied his 'oppo'.

The 'love sick' sailor will never see Rosa again, and she will not know his grave will be in a Norwegian fjord thousands of miles away. [27] [28]

The seamen and engineering departments were the largest on board *Hunter*, seventy-seven and thirty Junior Rates respectively. Therefore, there would be more than one mess for either departments. First, we look in the

---

27 The following June 1940 some 13,500 Gibraltarians were sent to Casablanca in South Morocco. Unfortunately this coincided with the surrender of France and the establishment of the Vichy Government. It appears the large number of people from a British colony was embarrassing and dangerous. This is especially as Britain had attacked and sunk a number of French ships in French Algeria to keep them from Germans hands, killing many French sailors. Following the evacuation of Dunkirk, the British had agreed to transfer French troops to Morocco and as they disembarked the French, so a decision was taken to evacuate the Gibraltarians. So it was back via Gibraltar before 10,000 were sent to London, 2,000 to Jamaica and a lesser number to Madeira. To conclude, the evacuees started to return in 1944, although the last of them did not make it back until 1951.

28 Translation in the mess conversation:
Sea Buffalo: Royal Marine.
Poultice Walloper: Sickbay attendant.
Dustmen: Stokers.
Pass the slide: Pass the butter.
Awning: Pie crust.
PLM: Pork luncheon meat.
Chinese wedding cake: Rice pudding.
Sin Bosun: The chaplain.
Jankers: Summary punishment carried on in a ship.

seamen's messdeck for an introduction to some of the characters who later play a part in the book.

In the corner, there was a heated discussion going on between a few seamen from both sides of the Pennines. Folk from Lancashire and Yorkshire were fiercely proud of their rugby league teams. Able Seaman John Hague, nineteen years old, nicknamed 'Albert' because of his Oldham accent was a keen player of the sport. But for the war, he could have gone on to reach higher levels in his rugby career.

John's father worked down the coalmines, so it was not unusual in those times that son followed father. John says, "I wanted to join up to get away from the 'pits' but I was turned away at first because I was too young". So when eventually there was no work available, he decided he was going to join the Navy. He walked from Oldham to the recruiting office at Deansgate in Manchester which was approximately thirteen miles. He told me, "I lied about my age to get in and I was accepted but had to go back down the pit until I had to report back to Manchester, for another do. There I was kept overnight in what was a 'flea ridden' doss house near Strangeways Prison. I then had to catch an early morning train with other recruits to Plymouth."

Shortly afterwards, John's sister Annie was sent a letter from the naval training base to say he had joined up and asking her to write to him, as this would make his training easier and show her support. "I did my basic training including a swimming test, where I was able to help others to get through theirs."

The ever-supportive Annie roped in another person to write to John whilst he was at sea. This was a work colleague May Chamberlain. They finally met on John's next home leave, and as his daughter Carole fondly mentions, "The rest as they say is history." Although before John could 'tie the knot', he had a number of crucial hurdles to overcome in the following year. Namely, surviving a German attack and a sinking, becoming a prisoner of war and eventually escaping back to Britain. Not a lot then?

Unfortunately, in those days the Royal Navy only competed in rugby union, which was predominantly an officers' sport. However, temporarily he converted to the different 'rules'. He also recalled with a smile, that when playing for his ship in Bermuda there was a concrete cricket pitch in the middle of the rugby field. He says, "It was hard if you were tackled there!"

One of John Hague's chums was a Plymouthian, Able Seaman Norman 'Jan' Stewart, not yet twenty. He lived with his mother in the Prince Rock district. Whilst his father also serving in the Royal Navy, was away on minesweeping duties. Norman's worried mother now having two involved in the war, recalls that his parting words were, "I must go and we will come through with flying colours." She need not worry as when the going gets tough, her young son's bravery will save an officer's life.

There was another rugby-playing seaman in the mess who was not on board at the time. It had to be a Welshman, in fact from Rhydaman (Ammanford), Carmarthenshire. Here his daughter Wynne Jones explains, "Dad had been posted off the ship some weeks before, to play rugby for the Navy. He had served on *Hunter* from 1939 as an Oerlikon gunner". Unfortunately, Wynne in the comments section on 'submerged. co.uk' did not provide her father's name.

You will have read about the bravery of Able Seaman Ernest Thomas BEM, when *Hunter* was struck by a mine during the Spanish Civil War. He was also from Wales, the Glamorgan town of Trealaw, the son of William and Elizabeth Thomas.

There were two men in the mess from Aberdeen. Able Seaman William Edwards joined the Navy in 1938 and had been home on leave in January. This probably meant his duty watch had been on 'retard leave' and he was required on board for the Christmas period. His older brother was serving in the Royal Artillery in France, whilst his father had served throughout the First World War.

A further two Scottish mess members were from the Naval Base town of Rosyth. Able Seamen Charles Coutts and Guy Hunter were both aged twenty-three and after six years of service were already considered experienced sailors. Especially having served on *Hunter* during the Spanish Civil War. Charles played for the ship's football team and before joining the Navy was an active member of the Scouts movement and the YMCA. I will come back to Guy Hunter later, because after surviving the First Battle of Narvik, he had a lot more trauma along the way managing to get out of the grip of the Nazis and back to Britain.

Able Seaman Robert Hay was described by John Hague as a 'bubbly' character. He was still nineteen and on his last leave at Christmas had become engaged to Ruth Guyan, also from Aberdeen. His brother Thomas was on active service with the Royal Artillery in France. Robert had been in the Navy eighteen months during which time he had served on the cruiser HMS *Edinburgh*. Due to an accident he had a spell in the Royal Naval hospital. Once he was passed fit he was sent to *Hunter*. Maybe, it was bad luck because if he had not injured his foot he would have still been on the cruiser. Although that would have depended on how long he had remained on board. Because in April 1942, *Edinburgh* was sunk by U-boat 456 as she was returning from the USSR with gold bullion to be delivered to USA for the payment of war equipment. The convoy destroyers following were able to pick up 840 of the crew but another fifty-eight were lost. [29]

A number of sailors going on overseas deployment keep a diary of dates of ports visited or events that occurred. Probably as a memoir so that they could show family and friends on their return home. However, if retained by the family, these can become important historical documents for future generations. One which came my way was meticulously compiled by Able Seaman Nicholas Blundell. This evening he is focused on completing the final touches. He began his diary in August 1939 when *Hunter* left Devonport and travelled to the west coast of Africa, on to the Caribbean and Canada.

However, what was unique about Nicholas' recordings was that he also clocked up the nautical mileage and temperatures. I will never know, but it is possible he was the ships Navigator's 'Tanky' and had direct access to the sea going charts and diary. Either way he made a note that until their return to Devonport on the 8th of February 1940 the ship had "travelled 30,500 miles, the highest temperature was 99F (37C) in Trinidad and the lowest was 16F (-9C) in Halifax, Nova Scotia. Out of 153 days away, we have done 116 at sea".

Nicholas was from Fleetwood in Lancashire, a major fishing port. He was the third oldest of nine children and at the age of eight suffered the tragic loss of his mother and two sisters. At school he was a keen footballer and won medals in competitions. Both Nicholas' parents came from fishermen's families and on leaving school he joined his father Robert as a deckhand on one of the local trawlers. So for Nicholas it was a natural progression to continue a career at sea and at the age of seventeen he

---

29   In 1981, the gold bullion was removed from the wreck.

joined the Navy. As did two of his younger brothers, Ron and Eric, later in the war.

Nicholas' first ship was HMS *Active* which as mentioned was involved in the Spanish Civil War, for which he was 'Mentioned in Dispatches'. Later, *Active* went into the reserve fleet in Malta. As covered previously, in 1938 the *Hunter* crew were temporarily transferred to *Active* for accommodation. It seems that rather than send some of the crew of *Active* back home and to another ship, it probably seemed sensible to draft them onto the now repaired *Hunter.*

Able Seaman 'Gunner' David Radcliffe with his fiancée Elizabeth Simpson enjoyed going to the cinema during the times he came home to Bootle. During his last fourteen days' leave, two months ago he had married Elizabeth. They also managed to fit in a trip to see the popular film of the moment *Gone with the Wind*, starring Vivien Leigh as Scarlett and Clark Gable as Rhett. His mess mates were keen to know the storyline over and again.

David had been in the Royal Navy for seven years, previously serving on three ships. He had followed in the footsteps of his father, a merchant seaman, who sadly was lost at sea during World War One. A newspaper article mentions that David initially attended a local school before completing his education at an orphanage "for the children of merchant seamen". Possibly because this was the only option for his mother as she had such a large family to care for.

David was listening to his oppo's woes in the same for'd gun team. He was explaining the effect the war was having on the family 'fruit and veg' market stall. "It's really hit us, just had a letter from my sister Eda. She says, not only have the Sicilian lemons and Jaffa oranges completely gone out of circulation but bananas have now become as extinct as a dodo. Seems like these U-boats in the Med are moving further afield and into the South Atlantic."

'Gunner', Fred Dorward, aged twenty-four was from Dundee, another one of many who hailed from Scotland. He had also been on board during the action in the Spanish Civil War. He had joined at sixteen and previously served on HMS *Rodney*. He had recently married Margaret (nee Stewart). He was regarded as a strong swimmer.

Most messdecks have one or two amusing characters who keep up the spirits of their colleagues. I have already introduced Able Seaman James

'Stormy' Renshaw – I have no doubts that he was one of those in the seamen's mess. Although, he had just finished his training, as you will read Stormy grew into his naval career rather quickly. Here he begins his account in a typical Yorkshireman's straight-talking manner: "I was born in Sheffield. After an uneventful youth, I decided to join the Navy. My brother and I applied through the recruitment office; he failed and I was successful. So I finished up with a ticket to go up to Manchester to join the recruitment group, and I was sent down to Plymouth; in the Royal Navy."

Able Seaman David 'Jonno' Johnson was born in the fishing port of Grimsby [29/02/14] and on leaving school followed his father and older brothers as fishermen. Sadly two of his brothers had previously died at sea. Subsequently, David gave up his job on trawlers as his parents were terrified of losing another son. However, apparently unperturbed in 1935 he joined the Navy. He met Ethel [nee McClean] in Plymouth and they were married in 1939 and in the same year daughter Irene was born. At the time of the manuscript going to the publishers I was contacted by Nigel Sefton, Irene's son in law, who was researching for a 'family tree'. Thanks to Nigel he had been able to obtain David Johnson's service records to supply a late entry and confirm a number of issues, which you will read later.

At one of the mess tables there were three mature members happily playing a friendly game of dominoes called 'fives and threes'. The wager could have been for half a tot of the others rum the following day. You could not bet with money, or in fact officially for another man's daily ration. However, they were well respected and would have been a steady influence on the younger seaman.

One of those 'greenhorns' was Ordinary Seaman Bill Parton from Pontardawe in South Wales. He was twenty-one years old and his first language was Welsh. Prior to enlisting he was a plasterer. He was lucky to survive and under extraordinary circumstances, as you will read later.

Going back to Marshal Soult, who in his comprehensive account on joining stated that he had found a 'happy ship'. Here his family provide some personal background information about this very capable man, who was considered extremely mature for his age of twenty. Shown by the responsible position he had been given when the ship would eventually go into battle. His action station was in the 'gun director' at the centre of the *Hunter*'s Bridge platform. From here he was able to describe the ship's involvement in battle and her tragic end.

Marshal left school at fifteen and worked in a shop for eighteen months before joining the Royal Navy. His father worked in Falmouth Dockyard, but prior to that he was also in the Navy during the First World War; including serving on HMS *Warspite* at the 'Battle of Jutland'. Marshal's brother Peter, now living in Kentucky, USA, says, "Without telling his parents he took a train to Plymouth, when he was quite young and joined the Royal Navy.

"As mentioned, Marshal did his 'Boys' Time' on the training ship HMS *Wildfire* at Sheerness on the Isle of Sheppy. His brother Peter believes that when an 'entry' training staff member asked what his name was, he said, "Marshal Soult." The officer replied, "I don't want to know the name of the ship, I want your name." There remained confusion, even for me, until almost seventy years later, when I discovered that at that time there remained a First World War cruiser of the same name. Hence, from what I thought was my 'eureka' moment, I assumed his father had connections with the cruiser during his own naval service and then decided on giving Marshal his forename. However, Marshal's sister Joan Jowett finally put me right, that in fact the family tree traces back to a Frenchman, Field Marshal Soult, one of Napoleon's senior officers and that is how her brother got his name.

Back to the mess, Marshal looked round at his pal, who had the mess in stiches. "I've heard everything now," said his mate holding a letter. "My brother lives in Leicester and he's saying here that they have started painting black iron railings and kerbstones and fences the colour of white." "Why", enquired one of those listening. "Because of the blackout, it helps people out and about to be able to see where they're going at night in the dark." "You're joking?" "They say, since the blackouts there's been an increase in traffic accidents and crime." At which point those listening shook their heads and went back to reading their letters from home. [30]

---

30 This was a real phenomenon that spread across parts of Britain, and may have genuinely meant well. As in 1941, it was recorded that traffic accidents did increase remarkably, with 9,000 fatalities on British roads. However, the white iron railings saga did not last long, because many were subsequently removed to be melted down for the war effort. It gets worse, unfortunately the iron was not usable and eventually many railings were dumped at sea!

Marshal Soult was probably looked upon as having one of the brightest minds in the mess. So he was able to impart his knowledge to others. Marshal listened intently to his other pal's surprise inclusion in a letter from home. "My aunt in Suffolk reckons they are being asked to collect 'conkers' from horse chestnut trees for the war effort. She remembers, as a child doing the same in the last war, something about 'munitions'. The school kids are loving it, but becoming distracted by having contests rather than concentrating on the job in hand." Marshal, "Sounds like the government are taking no chances and stocking up. Believe it or not 'conkers' hold a very important ingredient in cordite propellant for shells, it's called 'acetone'.

"In the last war, a similar chestnut collection was kept secret, there was even a query made in the House of Commons. The answer given simply stated that they were required for 'certain purposes'. This was for fear that the Germans would discover this ingenious method of acetone production. Even the collection points and storage depots were kept secret. Schools were paid I think about seven shillings per cwt of conkers. No one would have thought that the humble conker would then play a part in the war effort. Not just school pupils and staff were involved but also scout troops, WVS centres and WI groups. The last I heard other types of propellants were more effective and a better quality. However, due to German submarines attacks supplies of acetone from other sources, like maize from America were affected. So it required an alternative supply, probably the Government are taking no chances and want to stay one step ahead in case of emergencies."

All those listening were just glad that they had on board the latest cartridges of cordite ready to be tested against the enemy.

Returning to Able Seaman Guy Hunter, who was an all-round sportsman, both a keen rugby and water polo player. He had also figured in the Mediterranean Finals of the light-heavy-weight boxing championships. Guy had a namesake in the mess, Able Seaman Thomas Hunter. You have to wonder if someone within the drafting organisation in those days had a bizarre sense of humour. By sending both to the same named ship. Sadly, Thomas did not survive the First Battle of Narvik.

Guy joined the Navy at the age of fifteen, in 1929. His granddaughter, Shelley Hutton, informed me that her grandfather had married her grandmother, Maizie Campbell. Maizie was from Edinburgh and was introduced to Guy by one of her brothers, this was when Guy was home on leave. "My gran – Maizie was 'stepping out' with one of Guy's brothers, she had heard all about him but they had never met. He completely turned her head when they did finally meet. Such a handsome man," explains Shelley.

Probably one of the newest recruits on board was Ordinary Seaman Fred Ward, aged twenty, who had joined the Navy five months earlier. He had left his widowed mother and siblings at their home in Cinderford, Gloucestershire, to become a volunteer for active service. Similar to Fred, as indicated Ordinary Seaman Jack Tucker had not had much time to become accustomed to life at sea before he was whisked off to *Hunter*. Probably having to swiftly take all his civilian clothes back home to his mother in Rennie Street Cardiff or find a stowage in the barracks or Aggie Westons the sailors retreat.

Before leaving the seaman's mess, last but not least, there was one able seaman in the mess who trod carefully on board ship. This was a well built, blond Liverpudlian, Cyril Holehouse, aged twenty-five, from Anfield. He had just had his birthday and hoped to live for many more. Cyril had nearly not reached his first birthday when he had been a subject in "all the newspapers". He was not only born with a 'caul' over his face, but became known in the press as the 'Jam Jar Baby'. Apparently, he was born so small he was kept in cotton wool in a shoe box on the mantelpiece. His mother Isabella was working in 'Service' at the time and Cyril was cared for by a nurse. Isabella, later married Timothy Beesley who raised Cyril as his own and taught him to walk when he was four years old.

Cyril had an older brother George, and there were five more siblings with Timothy's surname. In folklore, the story goes that if the skin of a baby's caul is given to a person, it will protect them from drowning. Hence, it would be regarded as a valuable by a sailor. It was such a highly-prized article that medieval women often sold them for large sums of money. Brother George having joined the Navy, suggested that Cyril wanted to follow in his footsteps. However, it appeared that his mother at some stage had sold the 'caul', not difficult when living in Liverpool where so made seamen lived. It seems that when Cyril mooted the idea of enlisting, his mother began "regretting the day she had sold it and this was why she was adamant he should not join". This was explained by Yassie, the wife of Cyril's nephew.

However, this did not stop Cyril and he probably waited until he was eighteen before joining, when he wouldn't need his mother's permission. Possibly he also knew about the 'caul' but bravely took his chances. He may have been born prematurely but helped by life in the Navy, he is remembered as being a tall and a strong swimmer.

He is also remembered for his thoughtfulness towards his younger siblings. One example was towards his baby sister May, now aged seventy-eight, and at the time too young to remember the experience. However, her elder sister Carrie, now in her nineties, does. I leave it to Yassie, May's daughter-in-law, to tell the story. "May was sobbing her heart out and Cyril home on leave asked, 'Why is the baby crying?' He was told that a few of them had gone to the 'pictures' [cinema] and May wanted to go also, but she was too young. Cyril, immediately said, 'C'mon, I'll take you to the pictures.' He tacked a load of pictures around one of the rooms, picked her up and walked her around each picture and told her a story about each one. May was very pleased and truly believed he'd taken her to the pictures."

Returning back to the stokers' messdeck, to a stoker who was one of the 'raw' recruits who joined the ship in Malta, nineteen-year-old Joe Settle. Born in Wigan but later moved with his family over the Pennines to Doncaster. Not too far from 'Stormy' Renshaw's home city. Joe was the youngest of six children born to Stephen and Eliza Jane. Joe's father and two of his brothers worked at the Askern Colliery. On leaving school Joe became a labourer in another part of the colliery, turning coal into a smokeless fuel. However, becoming 'restless' he wanted to go to sea, so joined the Navy in September 1938.

Prior to Joe's draft to *Hunter*, whilst the ship was being repaired in Malta, he had served for a short spell on two other destroyers. The experience gained had resulted in him becoming a stoker first class within five months. Joe's best pal was stoker Tom King from Gainsborough, Lincolnshire. When the going gets tough they would team up to make their escape from the Germans.

Over twice the age of Joe Settle and probably the oldest mess member was Stoker First Class John 'Jack' Hiscock, born 1899 in Watford. He would be regarded as the 'daddy' of the mess and given a lot of respect. Other than the fact that a younger leading stoker would be in charge of the messdeck, Jack would be there to advise on a day to day basis. Initially, having joined as a Boy Sailor in 1915 and trained as a signalman at 'Ganges'. During

World War One he served on the cruisers HMS *Euryalus* in the East Indies Station and on return to Britain HMS *Sapphire*. In 1919, he transferred to the engineering branch. This was probably at his request having previously been employed in the electrical industry. Similar to many other sailors after World War One he did not have to complete his twelve years' engagement and was discharged to Royal Fleet Reserve in 1922.

Jack's service papers showed he had re-engaged in August 1939, I am unsure as to whether he looked forward to this event in his life or not. Either way he was drafted to *Hunter* within two months.

Another mature stoker, although not as old as Jack, was Stoker First Class Harold Smart, aged thirty-two. He came from Derby and before enlisting thirteen years earlier he had worked at the Rolls Royce factory as a 'Miller' on a grinding machine. He had served on the WW1 light cruiser *Comus*, the aircraft carrier *Eagle* which had been converted in 1924, the battlecruiser *Royal Sovereign* and finally back to light cruisers, this time *Ceres*. Between ships he had become married (name of his wife not known but initial 'E') and they had a son and daughter. Interestingly, he joined *Hunter* in Bermuda just before Christmas 1939, when the ship was having defects repairs caused by a hurricane. It would have been unusual to fly ratings out to join a ship unless there was an extraordinary requirement.

Stoker First Class Robert MacKay, age twenty-nine, had joined the Navy relatively late in life four years previously. He was brought up by his grandparents in the quaint old town, 'Royal Burgh of Auchtermuchty' Fife, the title given by King James V in 1517. Whilst *Hunter* was on Atlantic convoy duties, when the ship came into Halifax, he was able to visit his mother, who had moved to Canada. His father had served in the Black Watch in World War One but had been killed.

Stoker First Class John 'Chats' Harris, aged twenty-three, had been in the Navy for five years. He lived at home with his parents and sisters and brothers. He was engaged to Miss Ivy Trout and before leaving home after his leave he had told his fiancée, with bravado, "I'll turn up some day!" Would his prophecy hold true? Coming from Plymouth John had a lot of opportunities for swimming in the sea or the open-air pool on the 'Hoe'. This would be his salvation when he needed to survive a sinking ship. However, 'Chats' family and Ivy would not see him again for another five years.

Two of the stokers were concerned about their mess mate, Bill, who had just read his mail from home and had gone very quiet. "Ok 'oppo', had a 'Dear John'?" "No, problems at home, had a letter from my Mam. I'm the oldest of eight, she's struggling as Dad's not well and he may be laid off at work". The conversation moved on to include others sat round the mess table. Thinking about life at home and the difficulties involved. "It could be worse, my missis has told me the next door neighbours kids had been evacuated to North Wales but they had arrived back home again. Seems the 'phoney war' carries on, people have even stopped wearing their gas masks. Won't be long before we'll have bacon, butter and sugar back on the menu". [These were rationed four months earlier and meat products had just been added to the list.] Another, chipped in, "Our lot at home, because it's a farming area, don't have many problems. We're lucky, the local greengrocer has bought his own lorry, he goes into the country and buys the veg direct from the growers."

This appears to leave the rest of the group dismayed by the look on their faces. The distressed stoker, Bill, appears to get angry, "I suppose you also get as much butter as you want. My Mam told me, the last time she saw butter was two years ago when she had our youngest bairn in hospital. All we have is marge [margarine] and she don't buy meat other than a bit of mince." It appears that those having just joined the discussion felt it was the right time to get on with their five and threes game of dominoes.

Bill and his two mates go up top for some fresh air and a smoke to console him. He continues telling them of the concerns at home. "Before I joined the 'Andrew' [Royal Navy] I earned 14 shillings and nine pennies [74p a week] and that went towards the total family earnings. My Dad was getting £2 17s 6d [£2.87p]. Like you I am now on 22 shillings [£1.18p], so my Mam is wanting to know if I could send more home. I can't blame her as she has now written a list of what she needs to pay out for." Bill gets out his letter from home. The list of weekly outgoings are: Rent 10/6d – Coal 3/6d – Lighting 1/6d – four to five loaves of bread a day, 5d each – marge, six pounds at 5d. I have to laugh every time there is a funeral or wedding the old man gets out his suit, the only one he owns, white collarless shirt with cuff links from a box and the only decent pair of black shoes he has to his name. The only new bit is a collar my Mam goes and buys for the occasion. My Mam laughs that she thinks it is the same attire he wore for my christening, and that was twenty-two years ago." At this juncture, off the three men went back down below laughing, problem not solved but diffused for another day.

It is worth mentioning that many ships had what were termed 'Rubber Barons' ("anyone give me a rub of a tenner" – loan of money) now known as 'Loan Sharks'. These would flourish on a Junior Rates messdeck. He would normally be an old salt, having travelled the five oceans in his career. During which time he had learnt that during voyages some of the crew, would become short of funds before the next pay day. Subsequently, he would become the last resort to approach for a loan with interest. It could be a small amount to cover the cost of basic necessities, for instance razor blades or shaving soap. However, there would be others who had spent heavily in port on 'wine, women and song'. It was these spend-thrifts that the ruthless 'Baron' was looking out for. Although it was considered a serious offence under the 'King's Regulations and Admiralty Instructions' it appears many continued with the behaviour undetected. [31] [32]

Kieran Hosford, the nephew of Stoker Daniel 'Joe' Murphy writes in a website forum for 'World War Two Memories', "My Uncle hailed from the 'Skibbereen' area of County Cork in Ireland and was commonly known as 'Joe'." I will come back later to Joe Murphy, who although he survives the forthcoming battle will see out the rest of the war in a German 'POW' camp.

---

31 Those not aware, by now Britain's cities had more barrage balloons than we now have wind farms, this was to make the Luftwaffe fly higher on bombing raids. Pillar boxes were painted with yellow gas-sensitive paint, 400 million sandbags were placed around the entrances of shops and public buildings. There were 38 million gas-masks circulated in the population. At the beginning of the war [seven months before] every householder had to register their details of all those living at their home. Everyone was issued with a 'Ration Book' and ID card, each person registered with a local supplier from whom their rations would be bought. The coupons were handed to the local shopkeeper for goods purchased. What the Stokers involved in the mess discussion did not foresee was that rationing would increase. In the forthcoming July – tea and marge, March 1941– jam, May 1941 – cheese, June – clothing and eggs, and July – coal. This was due to the increase in miners being called up to serve in the forces.

32 Interestingly, before the war Britain imported 55 million tons of food a month. Once the war had started this dropped rapidly to 12 million. Therefore, rationing began to ensure a fair share of food, otherwise as food became scarce, prices could rise, leaving poorer people unable to afford necessary items. There was also a concern that some selfish people may hoard items, leaving none for others. Rationing did not finally end until 4th July 1954, when restrictions on the sale and purchase of meat and bacon were lifted.

There was another crew member from County Cork, probably in the same mess, this was Stoker William 'Billy' Bradfield, from the village of Timoleague, Bandon. Because of their mutual birthplace, as usually happens, they would have been close shipmates, looking out for each other. Billy was the eldest of four children born to Rose and James. Sadly Rose died in 1935 at the age of thirty-four. At the time Billy was fourteen whilst his sister Dolly was seven and two brothers Thomas and Fred were only aged six and three respectively.

It was Jill List, the daughter of Thomas, who contacted me with the family background. Jill, explains, "The death of their mother hit the family very hard and at the time there was no work in the village. When Billy left school he worked for a local doctor called Dr O'Driscoll, who was a retired Royal Naval 'Surgeon'. Billy carried out odd jobs for him and it was the doctor who influenced Billy to sign up for the Navy; which he did at Cork with several others from the village. [Billy's service records show that he enlisted on the 26th October 1937.]

Finally, but not least, Stoker First Class George Lane born in 1894, aged forty-six and another veteran from the First World War. Between the wars, he had been a postman driver and hailed from Manchester.

In the Communications messdeck there was Leading Signalman William Kessel. He would have the job of supervising his three signalmen. As a group they were known as 'Bunting Tossers', for obvious reasons, manning the flag deck and bridge. There was also a leading telegraphist, Thomas Lawson, in charge of four telegraphists. Their place of duty would be in the Wireless Office, as well another in the Remote Control Office near the bridge. Nineteen-year-old telegraphist Harold Webber's family originated from Penryn in Cornwall but before the war they moved to Falmouth. He had three younger siblings, sisters Marjory and Jo and a brother Keith, just two years old. Telegraphist Rex Brown, aged twenty, came from the 'Pit' village of Wingate, County Durham, where he worked down the mine. The inhabitants never forgot the tragic explosion in 1906 when many miners were killed.

Harold Webber was on 'first' watch [2000 to 2400] in the 'Wireless Office' dealing with any radio signals or messages, that needed immediate attention.. He was joined by Rex Brown, who wanted a quiet space to write a letter home. After half an hour, Harold laughs, "What you doin', writing your memoirs?" Rex smiles but looks to the deckhead. However, it was an ideal place to be able to tune into the ship's spare radio to listen to an alternative station to that being wired around the ship. Tonight there was a special BBC programme featuring Glenn Miller and his band. They had so far gone through some of the favourites, like, 'In the Mood' and now it was time for another foot tapper 'Chattanooga Choo'. It seemed to have given Rex some inspiration as he concentrated back on his writing pad in earnest. [33]

Back in the communications messdeck, the stage was set for an evening of cribbage. Once more totally against the 'King's Regulations and Admiralty Instructions', the overall winner would have the glory of 'sippers' from the losers' next day rum ration. The 'Daddy of the Mess' had to emphasise he would be checking when the deal was done, because last time the winner had sneakily taken a 'gulpers' of one man's tot of 'Nelson's blood'.

On the flotilla's leader, *Hardy* there was a petty officer 'yeoman of the signals' and petty officer telegraphist, unlike the *Hunter* which as the junior destroyer had to rely on leading rates to take charge of the communications department.

However, they would have been backed up by signalmen such as Thomas Norton, who like George Lane, was another veteran of the First World War and also coincidently a postman driver from Moston in Manchester. Thomas was born in July 1897 and on completing his schooling at the age of fourteen became a 'telegram boy'. Just before his sixteenth birthday he joined the Navy as a Boy Signalman. The following year World War One began and it was not long before he was involved in action. This was in February 1915 on HMS *Irresistible* in the 'Gallipoli' landings, known as the Dardanelles Campaign. This would place his age then at seventeen. He was fortunate to survive because not only was *Irresistible* hit by a mine but the ship he was eventually transferred to, HMS *Ocean*, shortly afterwards was also sunk by a mine. So at an early age he had already experienced action at sea.

After the war in 1920 Thomas was discharged at the age of twenty-two, although he returned to a less exhilarating lifestyle it was still a hard-working environment, little did he know that within twenty years he would take

---

33 The newer ships, built in the mid-1930s had their own SRE (Ships Relay Equipment) installed which connected a tannoy system around the ship. This enabled radio programmes to be wired to messdecks which could then be temporarily disabled for command or general ship's announcements. However, BBC News or musical programmes were only available depending on the communications department being able to tune into the appropriate stations.

part in yet more traumatic experiences. On his release, he became a Royal Naval Reservist and as previously pointed out found employment. Thomas' granddaughter Jose explains, "My granddad married Georgina Ellen and they had three children, George, Thomas (Jose's father) and Margaret Mary. They lived in the Wythenshawe part of Manchester."

In September 1938 as a 'Reservist' Thomas was one of those who were quickly conscripted back into the Navy just prior to the outbreak of World War Two. Jose continues, "When granddad re- joined the Navy, after the war started, Gran moved to the Blackley area of Manchester to be with her family."

It was the early days of electronics, unlike after the war the telegraphists were both users and maintainers of their sophisticated equipment. They were usually bright individuals with an interest in keeping up with developments in their field. Tonight the conversation turned from radio communications, whether on board or at home, to the future progress of television technology. It was news to those listening. Both the young telegraphists and particularly the older signalmen were intrigued by one of the telegraphists whose hobby had moved on from making crystal sets to making his own 'valve' radio. He went onto explain that a similar system could be used for sending video signals wireless to their homes in the future. The telegraphist, being a Scotsman, was proud to tell them that one of the early innovators was John Logie Baird from Helensburgh. However, he added that the Americans had taken the technology further and soon the first experimental TV station 'W2XWV' in New York had been allowed a license to transmit programmes.

Sadly, out of the nine mess members only two would eventually return home to their loved ones and, although less important, would never witness the rapid development of modern communications technology. One of those who would have been looked after by both Leading Signalman Kessel and the 'Daddy of the mess' was a young Signalman Edward Bennett Day from Kent. He had already been a lucky survivor from the sinking of HMS Courageous, which was torpedoed and sunk in the opening weeks of the war, going down with more than 500 of her crew. [34]

The Junior Rates attached to the 'Supply' department were probably

---

34 *Courageous* was decommissioned after the First World War, but rebuilt as an aircraft carrier. After recommissioning, she spent most of her career operating off Great Britain and Ireland. She briefly became a training carrier, but reverted to her normal role a few months before the start of the Second World War in September 1939.

accommodated in the after part of the ship. This allowed the officers stewards and cooks to be in easy reach of the officer's quarters and wardroom. Other than Joe Mulligan, the canteen assistant (NAAFI) who was a civilian, the remainder wore what was termed as the 'fore and aft' uniform, similar to Senior Rates. The mess also included, as previously mentioned, the general ships company cooks James Williams and Bill Wallis, sick-berth attendant Frank Maddocks, and a leading supply assistant, Frank Roberts. The officer cooks Mercieca, Aquilina, and Officer Steward Bartolo, all from Malta. These would have been supervised by Leading Steward James Rowe.

This evening most were off duty and had decided to have a mess games night. Not all the men were interested in what was going on at home. It could have been too depressing. So first up would be 'Uckers', a modified game of Ludo, developed over the years by sailors to make it more tactically interesting. The counters can be piled up to become 'blobs' and, depending on the amount piled, will dictate what is needed to challenge to get past the 'blobs'. However, a 'mixey blob' negates the need to have to challenge. [35]

Anthony Bartolo aged eighteen, came from Sliema in Malta. Similar to his countrymen, he was a courageous young man, who at the age of nineteen voluntarily enlisted for service in the Royal Navy at the outbreak of World War Two. Not knowing what the future outcome would be for himself or the allied forces in their fight against Nazism. HMS *Hunter* was his first ship. Obviously, at action stations stewards and cooks would not be required for their normal ship's duties and would normally be part of the for'ard or after Repair Parties, usually medics or alternatively ammunition suppliers. Similarly, not all the stokers would be needed down in either the boiler or engine room, so they would be utilised elsewhere.

In the supply department's mess, from the eight members, only three would survive the sinking of their ship.

In the torpedo and ASDIC ratings mess, one of the tables was being utilised for a very competitive card game called 'euchre', pronounced ju-ker. Most of the other sailors found the 'mind-boggling' rules for this 'trick-taking' game hard to follow. However, three of the two pairs of players

---

35   The Fleet Air Arm had their rules and terminology complicating the game even further. In some messdecks they had manufactured an Uckers board which was built into the surrounding furnishings. The games became very competitive and could end up being very noisy events, with a mixture of so called 'industrial' language.

competing at that time were from either Cornwall or Devon and had been introduced to the game by their forefathers.

The interloper was Torpedoman Alfred Holt, not from the West Country, he came from Salford. He had been around so long, possibly few could beat Alfred and had to rely on him for the full rules of the game. Born in 1896 and now aged forty-three, Alfred joined the navy at sixteen in 1912 and therefore was a veteran who had served in the First World War. In 1936, after twenty-four years naval service, he retired to work as a gas fitter with the Stretford Gas Board. But, with the possibilities of a further war brewing, as he was in the Royal Fleet Reserve, he was one of the first to be called up.

Alfred Holt with baby son. [Alfred Holt's family collection.]

Chief Petty Officers, Petty Officers and Wardroom

Moving to the CPO's and PO's mess you have read about Petty Officer 'Stoker' Sam Evens, a born and bred 'Plymouthian' who left the Army for a more varied and exciting life. He was vastly experienced having been on coal burning ships. He was a happy man now he had a cleaner job on the oil fed engines of *Hunter*. However, at sea he would still be a round the clock watchkeeper with his fellow petty officers Richard Ryman, Pat Duffy, Jake Kerswell, Bill Muddle and John Goold. It could have been on an evening like this, when the ship was in harbour that Pat Duffy told Sam and others in the mess, that he had had a premonition. It was a bit vague because the ships company at that time did not know their next destination. Either way it was a prophesy Sam would never forget. **"We're going in but we're not coming out."**

Joseph 'Pat' Duffy aged forty was also an experienced petty officer stoker with over twenty-one years of service. He had served on the ships *Resolution*, *Warspite* and *Eagle* and if it hadn't been for the war he would have reached the end of his career in December 1940. He was born in County Mayo, Ireland and when asked 'where's that?' he would always quote in Irish, "*Contae Mhaigh Eo* – the plain of the yew trees." However, his family had since moved to Skelmersdale, Lancashire. But because of Pat's many years in the Navy, he and his wife Mabel settled in rented accommodation in Plymouth with their five children. The youngest was named Patrick, aged two, but when Pat went to Narvik, Mabel was expecting their sixth child

Another experienced petty officer stoker, Richard 'Dick' Ryman was thirty-nine years old. The family lived in the village of Bodicote in Oxfordshire. His father served in the Army Service Corps during the First World War. Dick's first employment was as a railway porter. It maybe, that seeing so many WW2 service personnel passing through the station, finally influenced him to join the Navy on his eighteenth birthday. During his early years he served on battleships with the China station. In 1934 he had his first experience of a destroyer, HMS *Kempenfelt* which became involved in the Italian invasion of Abyssinia. Similar to many of his existing crew members he served time on HMS *Active* during the Spanish Civil War. It was during this period that he was promoted to petty officer.

Dick's parents were very proud of their son who spent a lot of time away from home. He was very popular within their circle of family and friends and they looked forward to his home leave, no more so than his sister, Esmee, seventeen years younger. The story goes that in one of Dick's early leaves, he took Esmee out in her pram. Returning home, his mother asked where the baby was. A quick panic occurred as he realised he had left Esmee outside the 'Horse and Jockey'.

Dick married Lily Yates in 1926, although it nearly never happened. He was late turning up and Lily's father suggested that they ought to begin thinking about going back home. Dick and Lily made their home back in Addenbury, the next village from his parents. They had two sons Richard aged seven and Basil aged five.

Four months previously Dick would have reached pensionable age but had to stay on for the duration of the war. On his last leave in February, the family remember him taking Basil and a nephew to Banbury where he bought them both toy horses from Woolworths.

This evening he had just finished writing a letter home to Lily, he was unable to say where he was but did state "We have had some bitter cold weather but still summer will soon be here then I shall be OK."

'Jake' Kerswell born in Ilfracombe, Devon was thirty-seven years old, but for the war he would have been able to retire in little over four years. It appears that initially he joined the Navy in 1918 during the latter stages of the First World War, completing nine years. However, as a leading stoker, a few years later he re-joined, wanting to complete his twenty-two years for a pension. His first wife had died at a young age but eventually he remarried Gladys from Swansea in 1933. They had two daughters, Joan and Margaret and a son Peter. Two of his brothers were in the Army and the youngest brother was in the merchant navy.

Between wars, as you would expect, Jake had served on many warships. He was also on *Hunter* during the Spanish Civil War and after a spell on *Active* re-joined *Hunter*. He was then promoted to acting petty officer stoker. By all accounts with his vast experience he was also regarded as being 'firm but fair' in his dealings with those ratings with whom he came into contact.

Jake Kerswell on the left with arrow pointing to him. [Kerswell family collection.]

Petty Officer Stoker's John Goold and Bill Muddle make up the fifth and sixth watchkeepers in the boiler room. Unfortunately, I have no information on them, other than John was a Royal Fleet Reserve man and possibly served in the First World War.

There were two Engine Room Artificers Fourth Class in the mess (equivalent to Petty Officer), John Farnell and Fredrick Taylor. Normally the two of them would have joined at the age of eighteen and because of their higher educational standards they were provided with an initial two-year engineering apprenticeship. Once they had completed their sea training they were guaranteed advancement to 4th Class. If they showed no problems in their aptitude they would eventually reach the rank of Chief Engine Room Artificer.

However, John Farnell appears to be a member of a unique club in that he joined in early 1938 and two and a half years later became a chief petty officer. This can only be explained by the fact that before volunteering he was an engineer with the Leeds train manufacturing firm 'Greenwood and Batley'. He was also a 'Reservist' in the 'Auxiliary Air Force' at the

Yeadon Aerodrome. (Later to become known as the 'Leeds and Bradford International Airport'.) So he would have been seen as a great prospect when he chose to enlist in the senior service. Of the two ERA Fourth Class, only John Farnell would survive the Battle of Narvik, although only by good fortune as you will learn. Here is the beginning of an article in:

The Yorkshire Post. 17th July 1940

"Chief Petty Officer J. A. Farnell, aged 27, of Tong Road, Leeds, formerly of HMS *Hunter*, one of the British destroyers lost at Narvik [...] is now home on leave after a remarkable series of escapes [...]". The remainder of the news report will follow in a later chapter. Suffice to state, as you can see John originated from Leeds and by this time had been promoted to CPO. He would also go onto have a distinguished career until 1958.

For Senior Rating watchkeepers there would be a special sleeping billet so they would not be disturbed during the day. Although for socialising and mealtimes they would use the CPO's and PO's mess. Tonight there would be a lot of talk surrounding the next move the flotilla would take. Every so often those in discussion would give quick glances in the direction of Chief Stoker David Moore and Chief Engine Room Artificer Edward Gould who were in quiet conversation. What were they talking about? Maybe, mechanical problems down below or as they both had the confidence of their boss, Engineer Lieutenant Alick Reid they would undoubtedly know about any future plans for the flotilla. Especially, David Moore, as the mess president, would have continuous liaison with 'Jimmy the One' (First Lieutenant). All Royal Navy ships survive on 'Buzzes' spreading around the ship and it is even better when an individual is in a position to start one.

I would add that once the survivors are fully accounted for, Chief Stoker David Moore from Plymouth, aged forty-five, would become the senior officer in charge.

Chief Petty Officer James 'Jock' Smail, DSM, had been in the Navy for twenty-five years, during which time he had climbed the ladder of promotion. He had been with *Hunter* for four years since it had been built by Swan and Hunter at the Wallsend Ship Yard. Three and half of those years were spent away with *Hunter* or alongside in Malta. In those days there was no returning home on flights for a period of 'R and R' (Rest and Recuperation) leave. He originated from Galashields but married Jean (nee Morrison) from Dundee where he settled. They had a daughter. James was awarded his Distinguished Service Medal when *Hunter* was involved in the Spanish Civil War. He would go on to do another brave act, certainly out of the ordinary by today's standards, when the ship went down.

Chief Petty Officer George Sutton as I have already explained had a vast amount of experience as a senior rate. By now having been on board over a month he would have become a highly-respected member of the mess. Whilst the Junior Rates would still be working out 'how he ticked'. Nobody wants to get on the wrong side of the ship's Coxswain.

George was born in 1899 the third child of George and Sarah in Werneth, Oldham. He left school at twelve to become a 'metal turner' apprentice. For whatever reasons, at the age of sixteen he joined the navy as a Boy Sailor, despite it being only the second year into World War One. He must have realised that sometime in the near future he would be in active service at sea

Here family friend Gordon Lees (Oldham Historical Research Group) explains, "George married Betsy-Ann North in 1924 at Werneth, I suppose from there they moved elsewhere together. [Naval drafts.] On the 16th February 1929 Betsy-Ann died with complications in 'childbirth' and had cardiac failure, at the age of twenty-seven. Presumably because of the length of time she was in labour. It was very sad for him and family relatives. I therefore wonder, being on a twelve-year period of engagement, if he had re-enlisted when he had got over the grief of that."

To Gordon's credit he never gave up trying to find out more about George and shortly afterwards he came up trumps. As Gordon proudly points out, "The final twist, on 'Ancestry' [Web Site] looking for his will and it went to his widow called May, of Tudor Street, Oldham, the sum of £717. So he did get married again, at the same church as in 1924, to May Deven (born in 1897), on Boxing Day 1939. There were no children recorded."

Although, a First World War veteran and within the last two months having seen action, the question is would George's luck hold out in this war?

Another popular mess member was Charles Falzon, age twenty-six, and another of the ship's company originating from Malta. To be exact, from Cosificua near Valletta where he had started his employment with the NAAFI organisation. He had quickly risen to the position of manager. Although, on board he was known as the NAAFI 'Damager'. In an evening like this in harbour, he could become very handy for unofficially opening his shop for his mess mates, who were desperate for cigarette roll up paper or something for a sweet tooth. It is a shame that ashore in some quarters the NAAFI canteens became renowned for their 'poor quality' of food. Not taking into account they were also subject to war rations, it resulted in calling them by the slang word 'Naff'. Although, from my own experience at sea many years afterwards, their standard was considered exceptional. [36]

On the fo'c's'le , getting a breath of fresh air away from the tobacco smoke, were Engine Room Artificer Albert Stone, Petty Officer Supply William Barrett, Shipwright Second Class Alfred MacDonald and Electrical Artificer Third Class 'Andrew' Black. (Both equivalent to Chief Petty Officers). All had an interest in cars, motor racing and attempts to beat the world motor car speed record. Alfred MacDonald explained that these machines were powered by two aircraft engines. "They weighed over three tonnes and were nearly thirty feet long." William Barrett chipped in, "Yea, and they had problems finding a transmission and tyres that could take the power". "I remember last year in Malta seeing John Cobb's record breaking run on the 'Movitone' at the pictures. What was his speed?" asked Andrew Black. "Oh it was about 370 miles per hour, I think," answered William.

William Barrett was thirty-six and lived in Plymouth which is the only personal information I have about him. Although, as you will read, he was able to give some relevant information about the aftermath of the battle. Whilst Stone and MacDonald's bodies were either never found or buried in an unmarked grave.

Andrew Black's, first name was in fact Albert but it appears he preferred to be called by his second name Andrew. Andrew, an only child and aged twenty-six, lived with his parents in Portsmouth and had joined the Navy at the age of fifteen. He must have passed his Higher Educational Tests at the artificer apprentice training establishment HMS Fisgard. At the time situated in Portsmouth. (It moved to Torpoint, Cornwall in October 1940) Although it would not be for another two years that Andrew's experiences in the remainder of the war, that had caused such anxiety to his parents, would also become a special feature in his local newspaper, the *Portsmouth Evening News*.

---

36   NAAFI, an abbreviation for Navy, Army and Air Force Institutes. It is a non-profit retaining organisation for the lower ranks started by the Government in 1921. Commissioned Officers had their own facilities.

Andrew's part of ship would have been at the electrical generators and his action stations probably one of the 'Repair Parties'. I suggest the latter because it probably saved his life.

Moving on, Chief Petty Officer John Brendan Mulhall was born in 1910 in the fishing village of Ardglass, County Down, Northern Ireland. He was the second child to John and Catherine Mulhall. On the day of his baptism the parish priest decided to include the name Brendan, as on that particular day it happened to be the feast of Saint Brendan, the patron saint of fishermen and sailors, which turned out to be very apt.

Anne Cruistan, John's niece, assisted by the memories of John's sister Elizabeth, has provided some background memories. "From a young age John insisted that as soon as he was old enough he would "Join the GRAVY." As he got older he spent all of his free time at the quayside listening to the fishermen talk about their tales at sea. On one particular day, he decided to join them on board and set sail for the far-off island of the Isle of Man. In reality, about twenty miles, as the crow flies, from Ardglass. My poor grandmother was beside herself with worry and that was the end of his high seas adventures. In the meantime, his enthusiasm for the Navy was fuelled through his friendship with a local naval man, Mr Wait. They would spend hours together talking and discussing life in the Royal Navy.

"In 1922, when John was aged twelve, my grandmother, after a lot of persuasion, signed the papers for John to sit the exam for the Navy. He and my grandfather made the journey to Belfast. Later that day a telegram arrived, it said, 'PASSED EXAM, SAIL TONIGHT'. This was the start of his new life".

If the age of twelve is correct, then this indicated he had joined a naval training school in England.

However, John Brendan Mulhall went on to serve on the following ships: the HMS *Impregnable*, *Hood*, *Furious*, *Defiance*, *Revenge* and then *Hunter*, to name but a few.

I have to say this is a very experienced group of Senior Rates that any Captain of a warship would be proud to command.

The 'wardroom' is where the officers had their meals and spent most of their recreational time in harbour and off watch. There are conflicting views as to where the name 'wardroom' originated. One suggests, that in the far past it was known as the 'wardrobe room'. In fact, the lower deck sailors, similar to 'Cockney' slang, still refer to it as 'wardrobe'. It is said the term was derived from the days when it was where officers kept their spare wearing apparel. More intriguingly, it was also where loot secured from enemy ships, would be stowed. The second suggestion, less likely, was because the wardroom in action stations converted into an emergency sick-bay with an operating table and necessary equipment; hence, 'wardroom'.

The captain was only present in the wardroom by invitation of the president, who was the First Lieutenant. On *Hunter* as previously mentioned this was Alex Stuart-Menteth. He was responsible for overseeing the general running of the wardroom. He appointed other officers to be members of the wardroom committee, delegating them to various responsibilities. These included a 'wine member' to look after bar stocks and officers bar bills. A 'treasurer', to keep the mess accounts. A 'secretary', to be responsible for recording the wardroom mess minutes at meetings and the 'entertainment member' to arrange social functions.

In harbour the officers would be required to wear formal evening dress or 'mess dress' on formal occasions, at either 'white tie' or 'black tie' events. Each evening at dinner, if wine is served, a toast would be made depending on the day of the week. The Navy traditionally makes the loyal toast seated, due to the evident danger of low deckheads on wooden sailing ships. The toasts are typically given by the youngest officer present at the mess dinner.

Monday. Our ships at sea.
Tuesday. Our men.
Wednesday. Ourselves. (Because nobody else is likely to bother)
Thursday. A bloody war or sickly season. (To ensure a quicker promotion) This refers to the desire and likelihood of being promoted when many people die: during war or sickness.
Friday. A willing foe and sea room.
Saturday. Wives and sweethearts (May they never meet)
Sunday. Absent Friends [37] [38]

---

37 The parts in brackets are the 'tongue in cheek' remarks provided by a past Royal Naval officer not serving on HMS *Hunter* or involved in the First Battle of Narvik.

38 Commissioned or non-commissioned officers never clink glasses when they make a toast. The sound is reputed to be too much like the solemn toll of the ship's bell as the body of a sailor was committed to the deep. Thus, it is assumed that the clinking sound will herald the death of a sailor. Silencing a clink that has occurred, or quickly clinking a second time, is thought to confuse the devil enough that he might take a soldier instead.

By 2015 women had been serving at sea in the Royal Navy for over twenty-one years. Therefore, the Ministry of Defence taking into account 'cultural changes', decided that officers at the traditional Saturday evening toast were now required to state 'Our Families'. The Tuesday toast was also changed to 'Our sailors'.

Amongst other families who made contact with me during this period was Helen Maidlow. Her father, John was the identical twin to Lieutenant Richard Maidlow, a seaman officer on *Hunter*. Unfortunately, little more information was divulged. Although, a visit to the National Archives in Kew, provided an interesting letter dated 1941, mentioned later.

It was not unusual that at the outbreak of war the Navy needed to have medical officers on board ships of destroyer size and above. These were qualified doctors from all fields recruited into the Royal Naval Voluntary Reserve. Subsequently, they were then given a short course on the surgical needs at sea, whether in battle or otherwise. As such, it may have been that Horace had been part of the flotilla's medical team required to move from ship to ship when necessary.

On board *Hunter*, Surgeon Lieutenant Horace Garner-Evans, RNVR would have been in that responsible position. Horace's father, Henry had a Saddlers business in Llangollen, Denbighshire, and became an Army private in the First World War. Horace was born in 1909 and when he was eight years old, tragically his father died in hospital during the First World War. Henry was only thirty-five, so this left the burden of bringing up Horace and his younger brother Emlyn, to their mother Margaret.

However, this did not stop Horace excelling at school and then completing a medical degree at Liverpool University at the age of twenty-one. Upon qualifying he became a doctor at the Liverpool Royal Infirmary Hospital and then the Children's Hospital, finally moving onto taking a practice in Wellingborough for five years. During this time, he married Christine Mabel Hollingworth in 1935. At the outbreak of the war Horace volunteered for service in the Naval Medical branch. Further information indicates that in January 1940, his first appointment as surgeon lieutenant for sea service was on HMS *Hotspur* but three weeks before the Battle of Narvik he had been transferred to *Hunter*. Would this save his life?

In another chapter you will read copies of the letters mentioned above, written eight years after the event. Suffice to acknowledge, that for Horace having been in the Navy for no more than six months, his first experience of going into 'Battle' would become an awesome challenge.

As you have read Engineer Lieutenant Alick Reid was a crucial member of the ship, his responsibility for the engineering department was immense. Especially when you compare that on the lead ship *Hardy*, with the same engine and boiler rooms and other mechanical equipment, the department was led by a commander rank. Unlike Lt (E) Reid who would have to rely heavily on his proficient junior officer, Sub Lt (E) Peter Lancaster and his Senior Rates. I do not have much personal information on Alick. What I do have will become clearer later.

Alick Reid's action stations would be in the engine room, where he could directly oversee the efficiency of the equipment and relay any immediate defects back to the captain. Whilst Peter Lancaster's action station would be at one of the 'Repair Party's' positions but available to transfer to either if necessary.

With regards to Sub Lieutenant Peter Lancaster –the following was provided by his nephew Donald Lancaster. Peter was a young man who would have been a natural to receive a commission in the Royal Navy, since his family genealogy shows that on his grandmother's line going back to the sixteenth century is a certain Sir Francis Drake. Also amazingly, his great, great, great grandfather John Cook was the older brother of the other historically famous seafarer, Captain James Cook.

Aged 25, Peter had a public school education at Harrow. His father Major Wilfrid Drake Lancaster headed a family engineering firm started by his grandfather. So it followed that it was also only natural that he went on to complete an engineering degree at Oxford in 1935. On top of that Peter, "loved sailing and was a member of the Treaddur Bay Sailing Club in Anglesey, of which his father was a founder member".

The close-knit family lived at Woldingham village in Surrey. Peter enrolled as a Royal Naval Voluntary Reserve (RNVR) prior to accepting a commission in the Royal Navy. This would have given him an opportunity to become familiar with not only the mechanics in both the engine and boiler compartments, but also most importantly, the overseeing of maintaining the equipment up to a high standard.

Peter's brother, Gordon, two years older, served as a Royal Air Force Reserve from 1935, and having completed an engineering course at Cambridge, at the beginning of the war was commissioned flying Sunderland sea-planes in the RAF.

Peter Lancaster, as a junior officer in the wardroom would have been seen as an ideal choice for the 'entertainments member'. He was young, confident and mature, well spoken, had a good brain and immaculate manners. He would have been told by the First Lieutenant that once the ship finally arrived back in Britain it was his responsibility to organise a 'Dining In' evening. The First Lieutenant had pointed out that because the Captain, (Lieutenant Commander de Villiers) had joined just before the war began (August 1939) there had not been an opportunity for the wardroom to give him the traditional 'welcoming dinner' on board. He went on to add that he had spoken to the chief buffer to make him aware of the intended occasion and that an awning would be required on the quarter-deck. "It will be the first time we have attempted to do this since rationing has been introduced, but I am sure that Petty Officer Cook Richards will be able to wrestle up something extra special", the First Lieutenant, stated optimistically.

As the First Lieutenant was making his way out of Peter's cabin, Peter enquired, "With respect Sir, what is the awning for?" "Oh sorry, I should have mentioned, whilst there is obviously no immediate rush, invitations will need to be sent at a later stage for the wives including the captain's wife Pamela, and other wardroom member's escorts to attend. It is usual to have pre-dinner aperitifs; shall we say at 1900 for 1930 when we go below to the wardroom. Let us not forget the ladies will not have previously met so it is an opportunity for them all to get to know each other and relax. Have a word with Leading Steward Rowe, as he seems well versed in the 'Dining In Routine', I think he actually has an official guidance booklet. Best of luck!"

No doubt Peter would have had to take a deep breath, and begin to think, that over and above his duties in the engineering department, this task could become a daunting challenge; which he could not afford to get wrong. This idea was reinforced the next day when he was able to retrieve the booklet from Leading Steward James Rowe. James helpfully pointed out that when guests arrived and were welcomed with aperitifs on the quarter-deck, Peter would probably become aware of the so called 'doughnut' effect. This was when the guests formed small circular groups to make small talk. He suggested that by passing around a dish of peanuts, he would have an opportunity to break up the groups and introduce them to other invited guests. Especially, in the case of the 'honoured' party. In addition, James also advised he should have handkerchiefs readily available for lady guests. Peter quickly realised that he would need to rely heavily upon James, if the event was to become a success.

In the meantime, Peter began to read through the booklet until the need for a short nap became the main priority. Later out of necessity, he picked up the booklet once more and continued to scrutinise the onerous task. [39]

Peter may not have got through the full details because his thoughts moved onto what he should be doing the next day in the engineering

---

39   For those readers interested, the 'Official Booklet' began, with the term of the 'butler', presumably this would be the leading steward and there were two procedures, if or not a Royal Marine band was present. Make sure guests are fully *au fait* with appropriate dress standards and punctuality, although he was sure his colleagues would not let him down. The 'butler' would report to the president (First Lieutenant) "Dinner is served", who in turn would ask the honoured guest (Captain), if he is ready for dinner. At the table the 'butler' would report to the president "Mess seated, Sir". Napkins should be laid flat on laps out of view. The list went on, 'smokes' must be put away – only appropriate conversation used (i.e. political or controversial, especially wartime issues) – No acting boisterous – Maintain correct posture at the table. By the time he got to silverware and advice on using cutlery from the outside in, he decided to put a line through the lot. However, the next part became interesting. He knew he could pass the responsibility for the wine onto the appropriate mess committee member, it was now time for the procedure:

a.   The President starts each course before anyone else.

b.   After the last course, the table is cleared and the 'butler' reports, "Table cleared Sir". President taps the table, "Grace". If a Chaplain was not present, this would be given by a junior officer. "For what we have received, thank God."

c.   Decanters have been placed. 'Butler' reports, "Wine (port) ready to be passed, Sir."

d.   President and those officers with decanters in front of them, follow the President's motions in removing the stoppers and passing the wine to their left. (Some mess dinners have strict rules that whilst the decanter is passed around it must not touch the table until arriving back at the despatching officer. To do so the offending officer would expect a fine of sorts.)

e.   When the wine has completed the circuit, 'butler' reports to President, "Wine passed, Sir." Officers then replace the stoppers.

f.   President taps the table. President the toast. "Mr Vice, the King".

g.   The vice gives the toast, "Gentlemen and ladies, the King."

h.   All members and guests raise their glasses repeating, "The King."

i.   After the 'King's Health' has been drunk anyone may leave the table without permission. The President gives permission to smoke.

department. "Oh no! I've just remembered, tomorrow I am Officer of the Day." [40] [41] [42] [43]

Unfortunately, as events transpired, Peter Lancaster will not have another opportunity to look at his booklet nor will the lady guests be able to visit the wardroom on HMS *Hunter*.

However, tonight in the wardroom it would have been an informal evening meal. Mr James Henry Coombe, had just been promoted to Acting Warrant Officer 'Gunner' a position usually held by a commissioned officer. This was probably because at this early stage of the war there was a lack of sufficient officers trained in gunnery warfare, resulting in the Admiralty, having to promote from the 'lower deck'. If the truth be known these 'Warrants' in all the branches were excellent in their fields and handy to have around in times of battle.

40　By now Peter would have realised that the passing of the wine procedure as described was only for wardrooms on large warships or ashore. Hence the maximum number including guests he would have to cater for, would be twelve.

41　In a much smaller wardroom there would be no need to be concerned about the procedure not being synchronised. The instructions continued with the possibility of further toasts and passing of the wine. This as many times as the President would wish, therefore the stoppers would not be replaced between each of these rounds. When the wine is no longer required, the stoppers are replaced and this is the sign for wine and gavel to be removed. I would estimate that at this point Peter is overwhelmed with so much to remember and pass onto his wardroom members.

42　Royal Navy Officers and Senior Rates have the privilege of remaining seated when 'Toasting the Sovereign'. Some sources state that this privilege was granted by William IV. A popular story mentions that Charles II was on board his namesake ship *Royal Charles* and had bumped his head on the low overhead of the wardroom when he stood up to reply to a toast that had been drunk to him. He stated that henceforth, naval officers would never again rise to toast a British sovereign. In 1964, Queen Elizabeth II extended the privilege to the Royal Marines in honour of their 300th Anniversary.

43　With regards to dealing with any misconduct at the table, the protocol stipulates, "Should any member or guest misbehave during dinner, before the 'Loyal Toast' has been drunk, the President taps the table, and may warn or fine the offender." (In case of a guest, his host has to pays the fine). This could be a round of port or liqueurs. On the occasions that I attended Mess Dinners, this was taken light heartedly and was an opportunity to wait for a mess member, either a novice or one who had forgotten the routine, to become an unsuspecting offender.

James now twenty-seven, originated from Plymouth before the family moved in 1922 to Alphington, Exeter. At the age of fifteen he set off for Greenwich Naval School to extend his education and become a Boy Sailor. Subsequently, he had made excellent progress both educationally and in seamanship. Along the way he had served in light, heavy and minelaying cruisers and the battleship Malaya. Ideal for learning his profession as a 'Gunner' and by means of steady, conscientious work he gained well-merited promotion.

James was navy through and through. In fact he came from a family of four generations of men giving their services to the country. His grandfather was a Crimean veteran, and his father, Petty Officer J. Coombe, was wounded during the Dardanelles operations. James also had two brothers serving with the forces, one in the Navy and the other with the RAF. If you wanted to know anything about naval history from any country around the world, he was the one to approach.

After completing their main course, as usual Mr Coombe came out with a snippet of information which was new to his fellow diners. "As you know it has been repeatedly stated from our American cousins that we are involved in a 'Phoney War'". Heads nod, not out of boredom but waiting patiently for him to impart another unique piece of knowledge. "However, do you know what our friends in France called it?" All present were waiting in anticipation. "drôle de guerre", the 'Funny War', while the Germans called it, 'Sitzkrieg' the 'Armchair War'," shouted out Mr Coombe. Spoons ready for the dessert, were at once banged on the table, as a way of showing their delight.

What the officers did not know was that moored nearby was the flotilla's leader HMS *Hardy*. Where, Captain Warburton-Lee was completing one of his last letters home to his wife Elizabeth. At the end he stated, **"Don't forget the war is going to start quite soon. I am going to start it."** Not realising just how true those final words would be.

PART TWO

Churchill: "I leave it to you to decide."

Operation Wilfred

It was approximately 0100 hours in the first week of April 1940, time to go back to sea, the ship's company not knowing what to expect. Prior to departing, the engineering department started work before everyone else. Usually in the early hours of the morning. They would be led today, once more by Engineering Officer Alick Reid, the Chief Engineer Artificer and Chief Stoker. Steam machinery has to be warmed-up slowly, so the boilers had to be flashed up and then the steam is introduced gradually to the pipes and turbines, a routine which took two hours or more.

One of the young seaman officers who for familiarity training purposes was observing the procedure, queried, "What happens in an emergency when we have to set sail straight away?" The Chief Artificer had to stop and think about this in order to give the right answer. "Well..., we can light up the boilers and pass steam almost straight through to the turbines. But sudden expansion of all the pipes and machinery, and lack of time to 'bleed off' trapped water, could damage the turbine blades. This could cause steam leaks which would have to be repaired at the first opportunity." Off went the officer, seemingly pleased he had asked the question and received an answer and hoping that the First Lieutenant would be impressed by his eagerness to learn.

The crew members of *Hunter*, similar to their colleagues on the other ships in the flotilla, realised something was afoot because of all the comings and goings of the commanding officers. As usual the 'buzzes' were flying around each ship but the truth probably was at this moment not even the commanding officers other than D2 (commander of the flotilla – Captain Warburton-Lee) knew the forthcoming options.

Marshal Soult begins, "The 2nd Destroyer Flotilla started out on what was supposed to be a simple job, escorting some 'I' class destroyers which had been converted to minelaying ships. The upper decks of these ships were full of deadly weapons of war. Quite a lot of the Hunter's ship's company could remember what damage one of these could do to a ship, having experienced it themselves. Out to sea went the 2nd D.F., five small ships looking after their charges like a mother hen does with her chicks. It would have been a terrible thing if a U-boat had managed to get through the screen and successfully attacked the minelayers, one hit and it would have been goodbye to the ship and all in her.

"As it turned out the little Armada reached its destination, a fjord in Norway, where transport ships carry iron ore, transited to the open sea to wage a war. Our ships were interested only in stopping those of the enemy from reaching home with the vital iron ore so badly needed in Germany. The mines laid would force them to leave Norwegian neutral waters and our submarines and ships could attack them. This was known as 'Operation Wilfred'."

If there was to be an invasion, the German armed forces would need to refuel, restock and have their heavy armour arriving in time for battle and if necessary suppress any challenge from Norwegian resistance.

Anton Schmitt and her ships company. Probably 'Commissioning Day'. [circa 1939]. (A Theo Werner Schettler photograph via Frank Hackney.)

Three store ships left Hamburg on the 3rd of April, two of them that you will read about were *Rauenfels* carrying weapons and ammunition and *Alster* with motor transport and military stores. Two oil tankers departed from Wilhelmshaven on the 4th of April and another from Murmansk on the 6th of April, *Skagerrrak, Kattegat* and *Jan Wellem*. The *Jan Wellem* you will also become familiar with in other chapters. Measures were taken to make the ships appear as innocent as possible, from both external and internal inspection. *Alster* for instance, was given a layer of coke over main cargo.

Narvik was a northern Norwegian port where the protection of its surrounding mountains provided an all year round ice-free transition for cargo ships which included the shipments of iron ore. The high grade iron ore came from the mines at Kiruna and Gallivare in Sweden by round the clock trains straight to the loading quay at Narvik harbour.

Narvik port in peace time. (Geirr Haarr Collection.)

Thousands of tons of iron ore were carried out of Narvik each year. This was the first winter of the war, so no surprise that both the British and Germans were making sure that they had more than their fair share. A foreign observer, at night trying to sleep in his hotel noted that there was a continuous rattle of trains with their ore boulders going into a crushing machine. From which its contents were then transferred by chutes into the holds of cargo ships.

The cranes, derricks and busy wharves remind us that as well as being in an area of great beauty amongst mountains and fjords, it is also a town that relies on its industry. Narvik lies within the Arctic Circle and the Midnight Sun is visible from 26th May to 19th July. The 'Sleeping Queen', an impressive mountain forms an almost perfect profile of Queen Victoria in repose. Looking across to the opposite side of the fjord is a mountain resembling Winston Churchill – also in repose with chin jutting out and looking ruthless.

The iron ore could be brought out by the German cargo ships, free from interception by being within the neutral Norwegian territorial coastal waters. With the route through many off shore islands and channels virtually the whole of the coast was known as the 'Leads'. Once the territorial waters ended at Stavanger the German cargoes would have to venture into the open sea. However, from here they would have the protection of the home based Luftwaffe. The British and French governments finally agreed to the minelaying of the 'Leads' in order to force the German cargoes to seaward where they could be confronted. The allies had warned the Norwegians and Swedish governments that the interpretation of their 'Neutrality Rights' was working in favour of the Germans. [44]

---

44   The next few chapters will have Kreigsmarine ranks attached to German named personnel and other terms, here is a list that readers can refer to.

German.	English.
Kriegsmarine	German Navy.
Zerstörer	Destroyer
Mechikergefreiter	First Class Stoker
Matrosen-obergefreiter	Leading Seaman
Matrosen-matt	Seaman Petty Officer
Bootsmannsmatt	Deck Petty Officer
Ober-matt	Chief Petty Officer
Bootsmann	Boatswain [Bosun's Mate]
Oberbootsmann	Chief Boatswain [Bosun]
Oberfahnrich	Sub-Lieutenant
Leutnant	Lieutenant [Junior]
Oberleutnant	Lieutenant [Senior]
Kapitanleutnant	Lieutenant Commander
Korvettenkapitan	Commander
Hefenkapitan	Harbour Captain [Narvik Harbour]
Fregattenkapitan	Captain [Junior]
Kapitan	Captain
Kommodore	Commodore
KonterAdmiral	Rear Admiral
VizAdmiral	Vice Admiral
Admiral	
GrossAdmiral	Admiral of the Fleet
Bundesmarine	West German Navy [after the World War Two]
Wehrmacht	German Army
Weserubung Nord	The Invasion of Norway
Abwehr German	Military Intelligence.
Fallschirmjager	Paratrooper.

On the 1st of March 1940 Adolf Hitler ordered the invasion of Norway, codenamed 'Operation Weserubung'. This operation would involve most of the Kriegsmarine. Participating units were divided into five groups, which were to occupy six of the main Norwegian ports. It was originally set for 20 March. However, like British operations, various delays postponed the operations and the invasion was finally set for 9 April. The intentions of the Nazis Government was to not only have permanent access to Swedish iron ore but also to occupy the Norwegian ports in order to allow her warships to have easy transit to the North Sea.

On the 6th April two blacked-out trains left Berlin for a ten-hour journey in a northerly direction. General Eduard Dietl and his 3rd Mountain Division had been stationed in the capitals barracks for a month waiting for the order to move. Now the Alpine troops were finally on their way, to where they did not know, but most were pleased.

The two trains continued their course until they reached the North Sea. Coming to a halt at the Columbus Quay, those watching the arrival witnessed the amazing sight of the troopers looking out of the carriage windows into a new world. Many of the young Alpine men had not only never visited northern Germany but neither had they seen the open sea. They appeared to be a smiling bunch looking forward to the next part of their journey.

So it was that the troopers embarked, Group One Force departed to Bremerhaven at 2200 hours, consisting of ten German Zerstörers of the 1934A and 1936 classes, commanded by Kommodore Friedrich Bonte. Each of the warships carried around 200 of 1,900 Alpine Troops from the 139th Mountain Regiment of the 3rd Mountain Division. Oberleutnant Herrman Laugs, the gunnery officer on board *Hans Ludemann* describes the moment, "The sky above us was glassy clear, like a sheet of silk. The stars were out, but all we thought about was going into action."

After a short while Korvettenkapitan Friedrichs made an announcement over the ship's tannoy system: "The task facing us is both great and formidable. The Fuhrer has ordered that Norway must be safeguarded. We are bound for Narvik. We shall execute his order to the best of our ability – secure in the knowledge of how grateful the Fuhrer will be. Long live Adolf Hitler!"

The troop-carrying destroyers were escorted most of the way by the battleships *Scharnhorst* and *Gneisenau*.

Kommodore Bonte was described by one of his officers on board the *Wilhelm Heidkamp* as "a great bear of a man, good looking and possessing many endearing qualities. He made no attempt to downplay the difficulties facing us because of the Royal Navy's supremacy at sea. But at the same time he radiated calm and was optimistic about our ability to achieve our objective. He hoped that the British would be taken by surprise and that luck would be with us." [Albert Bach]

It was well known in the Kriegsmarine officer corps that the forty-three year old Bonte was anti-Nazi, as were a number of other officers under his command. Oberleutnant Karl-Theodor Raeder, on board *Erich Giese*, comments, "Bonte was a torpedo officer and veteran of WW1. He was regarded as resolute and brave, he was held in high esteem by all who knew him." The Korvettenkapitan of *Erich Giese* Karl Smidt adds, "In moral terms he was a first-class man, firm as a rock", Smidt, like Bonte viewed Adolf Hitler with distrust. [45]

Kommodore Friedrich Bonte commanded the Zerstörer flotilla into Narvik. Note the picture in his cabin, irrespective of whether you supported Hitler or not, it appeared an expectation for all Kriegsmarine officers from top to bottom. [Via Alf. R. Jacobsen – scan from Fritz-Otto Busch, Narvik. Vom Heldenkampf deutcher Zerstörers.]

---

45 Oberleutnant Raeder was the son of the Gross Admiral Erich Raeder. He survived the war and rose to the rank of Kapitan in the Bundesmarine and in the 1970s became the Naval Attaché to the West German Embassy in London. He and my father Cyril Cope helped to promote the beginnings of the reunions of the veterans from both sides who fought at Narvik.

General Dietl, aged forty-nine, joined the Army in 1909 and fought in World War One. After the war he joined the German 'Arbeiter' political party, which existed till 1920 and was a precursor to the National Socialist German Workers Party, commonly referred to as the Nazis. In fact Dietl gave Adolf Hitler, then a little known member his first opportunity to make a party public speech. This occurred in a Munich military base, and was a gesture which had it rewards once Hitler eventually became the party leader.

In the meantime, Dietl continued to serve in the German Army, moving quickly through the ranks. He helped organise the 1936 Winter Olympics held in Germany. Remaining a firm Nazi supporter he became one of Hitler's trusted friends and a favourite General.

Here Peter Dickens, in his book *Narvik – Battles in the Fjords*, describes the moment. "When the mountain troops had embarked in the German Zerstörers (destroyers) all had been gay and exciting. But the weather worsened. "The men from Tyrol, Styria, Carinthia and the Voralberg, in the very heart of Europe, met ships and sailors for the first time; their boots clattered on steel decks, they slipped down ladders and fiddled like children with valves and switches to the alarm of their hosts. Where were they going? To Scotland perhaps, there were mountains; yes, it must be Scotland, and why not? Whiskey is good. They were dreadfully overcrowded to be sure, but the voyage would not be long.

"Now, as darkness closed in on the evening of the 7th, they knew they had come to hell. Emasculated by nausea they found themselves hurled from one unyielding bulkhead to another, only to be catapulted back whence they had come; where they sought to put their feet the deck forestalled them by plunging downwards, and they only met it again on the upwards thrust which jarred their ankles but failed to stop their stomachs. There were many broken limbs and countless abrasions, and in their minds fear strove for mastery with resigned despair. No wonder some felt they must breathe fresh air at any cost, even to the extent of disobeying the most rigid order to stay below; and no wonder the swirling, cascading masses of water that were wrenching boats, stores, guns and motorcycles from their lashings, seized them too and swept them into the black void astern."

The ships had to endure the inevitable losses of life that night, but there was not going to be any turning back now. The *Hans Ludemann* had just managed to avoid another ship by feet, and similarly the flotilla leader *Wilhelm Heidkamp* and the *Anton Schmitt* nearly collided. The *Wolfgang Zenker* and *Bernd von Arnim* suffered partial steering failures, and weather damage occurred throughout the flotilla. The more recently built *Diether von Roeder* class ships seemed to fare better. Irrespective of the challenging journey it was an excellent accomplishment. Unlike their enemy the Royal Navy, they were not used to experiencing regularly this type of violent weather at sea. However, this was the task set to them by Gross-Admiral Raeder who had demanded the greatest possible determination and to hold fast throughout, which by the end of the foul journey they had achieved. [46]

Moving forward by approximately a week after the two Battles of Narvik had taken place, the diary of Alpine Trooper Klaus Hauser was found by Theodor Broch, who was then the Mayor of Narvik. Klaus' diary provides a personal account to go with the previous description of the young soldiers travelling for the first time overseas to fight a war in a part of Europe they knew little about.

Theodor Broch begins, "I had hung my jacket over a chair. Some papers peeped out of one of the pockets, the book and photos I had found in the abandoned German quarters at the Seamen's Home. [...] It was a diary, half filled with notes and observations. The German Gothic hand was a little difficult to decipher, but the handwriting was as clear as a pupil's just out of grammar school. The first entry was dated April 7th, 1940. 'On the high seas'.

"From the night's reading I learned that Klaus was a very young man and that, although he was not afraid to fight against the whole world, he preferred to do his fighting on land. [...] his description of the twelve hundred and fifty miles sea voyage from Bremen to Narvik was limited [...] to telling of roaring waves crashing against the deck and the great congestion aboard the destroyer. In addition to crews of two hundred and fifty there were equal numbers of Alpine Troops on his ship. Klaus himself appeared to be an Alpine from Steirmark. He made a comparison between the Norwegian landscape and mountains to his home valley.

"The departure from Bremen was mentioned. There had been neither father, nor mother nor girls, promising to send him letters. But there had been a parade on the evening of April the 6th and speeches by the officers. The men had not been told where they were going but they had heard that they were about to have an opportunity to fight for the 'Fuhrer' in one of the most daring military expeditions of history.

---

46   The other four Zerstörers were *Hermann Kunne, Georg Thiele, Erich Koellner* and *Erich Giese*.

Theodor Broch [circa 1943]. Kind Permission of daughter, Siri Broch.

"They had talked amongst themselves in the hammocks in the narrow corridor of the destroyer about what adventures they were about to experience. Most of them guessed it was to be Scotland. It was not until the 8th of April that they were informed that the expedition was headed for Norway.

"We did not know very much about the country or about the people [...]" Klaus wrote. But a statement about Norway had been posted on the bulletin board, [...] so that they might know everything about the Norwegians before their arrival."

Klaus, "We learned that the people of Norway were honest and Nordic, and they never locked their homes. They were slow, like our peasants in Friesland, and suspicious towards foreigners. They had lagged behind in modern progress and did not know anything worth mentioning about war. Also, they had been misled by British propaganda. Therefore, the German soldiers must behave as nicely as possible, especially toward women. We are going to take over Norway in order to protect the land and the people.

"That evening we all had beer, and one of our officers saluted the 'Fuhrer', who had entrusted us with this crusade. We were to protect our racial brethren and bring the New Order to the Land of the Midnight Sun. We all held on to our chairs and roared 'Sieg Heil'. "

Theodor Broch, "[...] I put the diary underneath the mattress and tried to go to get some sleep."

The contents of the young Alpine Trooper's comments are indicative of how Hitler and his henchmen in the early stages of World War Two had even used their powers to hoodwink their own loyal and young valiant serving personnel. However, I have to take into account that Broch's book, *The Mountains Wait* was published in 1943 and may have been embellished by the Allies for propaganda purposes. Theodor's observations in his story becomes an integral part of the next chapters.

Marshal Soult, "On 8th April 1940 the minefield was laid. HMS *Hunter* being the inside escort, we sent an officer aboard a small Norwegian gunboat, which had come out to protest at our presence. They were given a plan of the minefield and asked to look after it.

"That night during a blinding snowstorm the flotilla leader 'D2' ['*Hardy*'] received a signal that another destroyer [*Glowworm*] on a similar mission was being attacked by heavy German units. Captain 'D2' broke off the patrol of the newly laid minefield and in line ahead, all nine ships went to the aid of *Glowworm*. On arriving, after a terrible rough trip through the raging blizzard the ships could only find the wreckage floating around the area. Some of which proved the *Glowworm* had been sunk. Shortly afterwards the nine destroyers were joined by the battle-cruiser *Renown*, flying the flag of Rear Admiral Whitworth. He immediately assumed command of all units and *Renown* leading *Hardy* and the other destroyers and minelayers, started a search for the German naval units. The search went on through the night during heavy snow storms and rough seas till approximately 0345 hours the next morning."

Glowworm in heavy seas. [S. Bell Great Nephew of Bill
Piper, died on *Glowworm*. Family collection.]

The *Glowworm* had intercepted the German units which were on their way to Narvik. It first sighted *Diether von Roeder* and engaged it with gunfire, hitting it and setting it on fire. This ship broke off the fight and disappeared into the mist. Then the cruiser *Hipper* attacked *Glowworm* hitting her several times. *Glowworm* got in some hits on *Hipper* and finally rammed it.

In Geirr Haarr's well-recommended book, *The German Invasion of Norway – April 1940*, Geirr adds, "*Glowworm* was going down quickly and Lieutenant

Commander Roope gave the order to abandon ship. Legend has it that at the last moment, Lieutenant Commander Roope shook every hand of every man around him. At 10:24 GeT, *Glowworm's* boilers exploded and she slipped under; the abrupt stop of the siren causing an eerie silence in spite of the storm.

"Having searched briefly for 'Mechikergefreiter Ritter' [a crewman who went overboard during the sea battle] and not yet under way, Kapitan zur See Heye felt obliged to assist the British sailors struggling for their lives. He gave the unprecedented order for *'Hipper'* to heave to, downstream of the drifting survivors. In spite of the danger of British ships showing up at any time, he stayed for over an hour rescuing survivors. Lowering of boats was out of the question, but all personnel on deck, including some soldiers, helped to pull the frozen, oil-soaked British sailors up by ropes and ladders. The oily, icy water exhausted the British survivors. Many grabbed the ropes thrown at them but could not hold on and drifted away. Lieutenant Commander Roope was seen in the water helping his men to the ropes. Finally he took hold of a line himself and was pulled some distance up the side of the cruiser. To the horror of British and Germans alike, just before reaching safety he let go and fell back into the water.

"From a crew of 149 on board *Glowworm*, forty men were pulled out of the water. Several were wounded and at least two later died. The rescued men not in need of medical attention were given dry clothes, cigarettes and hot coffee. They were questioned, but only a few were willing to say much. Kapitan Heye learned little more than the name of the destroyer and that she had belonged to a squadron of three more destroyers and possibly one or two larger ships, bound for Lofoten. None of the survivors appeared to have any impression of the larger tactical picture and expressed surprise to have encountered a German cruiser at sea."

The *Hipper* had been so badly damaged by *Glowworm* that it had to return to Germany and took no further part in the Norwegian invasion.

Three of those survivors, Stoker's Bert 'Curly' Harris aged twenty and Bert 'Ginger' Lowman aged nineteen and Able Seaman Duncan Blair also aged nineteen have since provided their accounts on that fateful day and thereafter.

Bert Harris joined the navy with his brother Edwin who was two years older, in February 1938, and both went on to become crew members on *Glowworm*.

Bert begins his account, "It was on 5th April 1940 that the *Glowworm* with three other destroyers made up the escort for HMS *Renown* and steamed across the North Sea, although we never had any idea what the operation was for at that time. It was a rough and very cold journey. All that day rumours kept going around about the German Navy being at sea, and we were hoping it was true so we would get the chance to meet them, as we felt pretty sure of ourselves being with the Renown.

"My Brother and I were both young Stokers on the *Glowworm*. We both lived on the same messdeck and of course we thought a great deal about each other, as we had joined the Navy together and had been together all the time. As we rolled and pitched our way across the North Sea he told me to be very careful whenever I had to go on watch and hang on tight as the sea was washing over us. And so it went on until the morning of 6th April when the alarm went out that a man was washed overboard, he was a torpedo man. A signal was made to Renown. We were told to turn and search for him, it was hopeless in such weather but our skipper turned the *Glowworm* and began the search. That left us all alone as the rest of the group carried on course. We never saw them again. Needless to say the man was never found. We steamed around all that day hoping to make a rendezvous with the *Renown* again, but no luck.

"The following morning on 7th April our luck seemed to be right out when another man was reported over the side. A search found him tangled in ropes which were trailing over the side. When they pulled him in he was badly injured and there was no hope for him. Well, that was a bad omen indeed. For two consecutive mornings, something nasty had happened and we were all asking what the third morning would bring. We were still on our own in the great North Sea, or at least it seemed that way.

"And so I come to the morning of 8th April 1940. I was asleep in my hammock when suddenly the loud ring of alarm bells sounded and all the off-watch men scrambled to their action stations. Mine being in the after part of the ship, in the magazine supplying shells for the gun crews. Not a very nice place to be in.

"As I made my way along the upper deck I saw another destroyer in the distance and wondered who it could be. After a short while I soon found out. Our Captain, Lt Cdr Roope sent a signal asking her nationality as she flew no ensign. The next moment she answered us with a salvo from her guns. Then the fun started. After exchanging round for round with her she turned and steamed away with us in pursuit. After a while we were told we were chasing her into a squadron of our own fleet who could be seen in the distance. However, we soon found out our mistake as it was a German squadron that we were being led into. But instead of turning and running for it, our Captain took the *Glowworm* into action against the German Cruiser *Admiral Von Hipper* and her escort of four destroyers. While we kept hard at it supplying the guns it seemed as if all hell broke loose. The *Hipper* opened up with her big guns and started to knock us about. She seemed to be hitting us hard as we were chasing around in the heavy sea getting into position.

"All our guns were firing, but our torpedoes which we fired missed the *Hipper* although they went very close to her. Our Captain was a good seaman and he knew how to handle his Ship. By now, we were badly damaged but he kept manoeuvring the *Glowworm* so that it was easier for the gun crews but this could not go on much longer as we had a very bad list to the starboard side. Most of the guns were soon out of action. I was still in the magazine when the *Glowworm* gave an extra thrust forward and there was a crash and a shudder. The lights went out, the ship rolled and tossed and suddenly seemed to settle well on her starboard side. Then came the order to abandon ship. We had just made our last big play. Our Captain had done all he could and what was right to the last. He had turned the *Glowworm* and drove her straight at, and rammed the *Hipper*. Causing quite a bit of damage to her.

"By this time I and others had made our way to the upper deck. As I passed the place where my Brother's action station was, I called to him but there was no answer, so I went to look for him. I got to the hatchway and looked down, it was pitch black, water swirled around. I kept calling but had to get out as we were well over on our side by now. I reached the upper deck and was shocked by the mess we were in. The Germans had shot us to pieces and were still doing so. Only one of our guns was firing now and it seemed strange to me as it was the aftermost gun. He must have been a very brave man as the ship was sinking and men were jumping over the side, but he kept that gun going for quite a time.

"As I reached the Upper Deck I got my first look at the *Hipper*. She seemed to be such a huge ship with her Swastika painted on her foremost deck. They were still firing at us with their big guns and machine guns. I crawled on my hands and knees along the deck to a lifebelt locker and was lucky to find some there. I passed some to others and strapped one around me although I was in two minds whether to jump or stay where I was, as it was a big thing to leave the ship and jump in the North Sea. So I waited and talked to a stoker who had his leg blown off. Another young stoker locked himself in the galley.

"One thing struck me as funny at the time, yet another stoker had jumped over and had got washed back again. As he picked himself up he said he would rather stay put as it was too cold in the water.

"I remember a young officer shouting "Open all sea cocks", although we were sinking fast now. I never saw him again. Then the Captain came and told us to get off as soon as we could. That was the last time I saw Lt Cdr Roope. By this time the ship had turned over onto her starboard side and the siren was blowing and smoke was belching from the funnels.

"I scrambled down the port side and then onto the bottom of the *Glowworm*, she turned right over in the water. All the time the Germans were pumping shells into us. At last I decided to take the plunge and jumped into the sea and swam as hard as I could from the sinking ship. After what seemed a long time I stopped swimming and just let the lifebelt keep me afloat. I watched the end of HMS *Glowworm*. The Germans finished her and she began to sink below the waves with men still standing on her.

"I felt lost and just could not realise that my ship had gone. I didn't know what to do next, one minute I was tossed onto the top of a huge wave and the next down into a steep valley of water. I was just drifting, swimming made no difference. Then suddenly right in front of me I saw the German ship. I was being carried towards her. I could see some of our chaps being pulled up the side of her. I swam as fast as I could, because I thought if I never reached her I would be lost forever. It was at this moment that I felt the underwater explosion and a kick like a mule. It must have been some depth charges on the *Glowworm*. I was nearly all in but I managed to look up and see some German sailors who threw a rope. I grabbed it and that was the last I knew for a long time.

"I finally came to my senses to find a group of Germans standing around me. When I moved, one of them gave me a cigarette and asked me if I felt alright. I was under a cradle of electric light bulbs which they had put over me to keep me warm. My first words were for news of my Brother, but there was none. I felt sick and stunned as it was weeks before I could realise that he had gone with all the others. All that was left were twenty nine survivors of that grim and terrible day. The following day only twenty-seven, two having died of oil fuel poisoning. They were buried at sea.

"I must say that they were the best German sailors I ever knew. They looked after us the best they could. The ship's Captain came to us and told us that our Captain had been a very brave man. We were all locked below decks with armed sentries. We were there until the following Friday. The *Hipper* was on her way to Norway where she discharged the troops she was carrying. Her mission completed, she made for the open sea again.

"We had been at sea for quite a time when excitement ran high amongst the Germans. Something was happening and before long came the sound of gun fire. We knew that we were being fired on by the Royal Navy. It gave us all a queer feeling not knowing what would happen as we were shut down below with armed sentries on the hatches. But they told us we would get the chance to get out if anything happened.

"HMS *Renown* was chasing us. However, this was not to be. The *Hipper* got away as she had a good turn of speed and the weather was in her favour.

"We were kept below all that week while the Germans steamed full ahead. On the Friday evening they let us come up on the Upper Deck for fresh air and told us we would soon be put ashore. Later that night we were taken off and handed over to the Army at Wilhelmshaven. It was there I knew that I was going to be a Prisoner of war..

"Much later we learned that Lt Cdr Roope had been awarded the Victoria Cross. It was a proud day for us all."

Glowworm just before the ramming *Hipper*. Photograph taken on board *Hipper* but given to Bert Harris by a German soldier. [Glowworm.org.uk – S. Bell Great Nephew of Bill Piper, died on '*Glowworm*'. Family collection.]

Bert Harris lived in retirement near Weymouth with his wife Joyce. She says, that he still has nightmares where he throws himself out of bed swimming for his life. Many photos of the engagement and the aftermath were given to Bert who got them from a German soldier who photographed the action. Bert kept them hidden all through his years as a prisoner of war.

Bert 'Ginger' Lowman was a nineteen-year-old Stoker mechanic on the *Glowworm*. He was knocked out and badly injured during the fighting. Bert takes up the story on the morning of 8th April 1940.

"At a quarter to eight the alarm bells went for action stations. I was supposed to be on watch at eight o'clock but once you go into action you stay where you are. I went to the Petty Officers' Mess as an ammunition supplier, where the number two gun support was situated. It was those fifteen minutes that saved my life because I know my boiler room got blown out of the ship. If I had been on watch at the time I wouldn't have been here now. I often think of the poor devil that was down where I should have been.

"A shell exploded in the Petty Officers' Mess but luckily it exploded on the other side of the gun support. The concussion knocked me out. When I came to, I found that the back of my left hand was gone and I had shrapnel in my left arm and leg. The floor of the Petty Officers' Mess was covered in blood. It looked like a butcher's shop. I felt the ship listing over. She was going down. I began sliding down with it. I managed to crawl to the other side and up on deck. I remember seeing one of our stokers running along by the lifebelt lockers. He didn't seem to be injured. I didn't know what happened to him but he didn't get picked up.

"Just as I got in the water she heaved right over and I got caught up in ropes and wires underwater. I thought to myself that I've had it now. I struggled and struggled and all of a sudden my head popped out of the water. I could see she was about to go down so I swam as hard as I could to get away from her as I didn't want to get sucked down. I could feel myself being drawn back. Eventually I managed to get away from her. I was swimming with one leg and one arm heading towards the *Hipper*. I was one of the last to leave the *Glowworm*.

"I was lucky that I didn't swallow any oil when I was in the water. There were about three or four inches of oil on the surface of the sea. I know a lot of chaps swallowed it. But as my mouth and nose became blocked with it, I put my head under water below the layer of oil and cleared it. I kept doing this until I got picked up. The Germans put a rope over the side with a loop in it. At first I grabbed it with my good arm but half way up I didn't have enough strength to hang on, so I let go and went back into the water. They put it down again. So this time I put my right arm through the loop and I tucked it under my left armpit. As they pulled me up like that, I could feel my arm coming out from under my armpit. I thought that I would let go again before they could get hold of me. Just at the last minute as I began to let go I could feel hands on me and blacked out.

"The next thing I remember I woke up in a bunk in the German sickbay and there were a couple of German sailors rubbing me down with towels getting all of the oil off of me. They congratulated us on a good fight. I didn't realise we had rammed the *Hipper* until the other chaps told me later on. We must have injured a lot of them in the battle as I looked to another part of the sickbay which was full of German sailors.

"Somebody told me that during the action Captain Roope's dog was sitting between his legs and was killed by shrapnel, but he wasn't touched.

"The next morning I was fast asleep when all of a sudden their guns started firing, which were right outside the sickbay. One of the stewards came in who could speak perfect English. I asked him what was going on. He told me not to worry and that one of our ships had been sighted but it wouldn't give them any trouble. I asked him if he knew which ship? He replied that it was the *Renown*. On hearing this I waited for the whistle of the shells to come over as I knew that the *Renown*'s 15-inch guns had a longer range than the *Hipper*'s. But the *Hipper* managed to escape in the bad weather conditions.

"Back at home my sister was listening to Lord Haw Haw who announced that I was one of the survivors of the *Glowworm* and she went rushing around to tell my Mum and Dad who thought I was dead as they had heard that the *Glowworm* had sunk with all hands.

Duncan Blair was a nineteen-year-old Able Seaman on the *Glowworm*. He lives in retirement in Australia. What you are about to read are his words spoken on tape and sent to Simon Bell the owner of the website dedicated to HMS *Glowworm* Organisation.

"The *Glowworm* was with the *Renown* to screen the minelayers that intended to mine the entrance to Narvik. On the morning of 7th April 1940 we lost a man overboard by the name of Ricky. Able Seaman Ricky, who was a lifebuoy sentry.

Missing In H.M.S. Glowworm

Edwin Harris (23) and right Bert Harris (20).

Bert Lowman back row centre pictured in Stalag 13 as POW. [Glowworm.org. uk – S. Bell Great Nephew of Bill Piper, died on *Glowworm*. Family collection].

"On the morning of 8th April as we were steaming in the hope of picking up the rest of the unit, we came across two German destroyers which we immediately engaged. We were fortunate enough to inflict some damage on one of the destroyers and they both turned and fled immediately back into the squalls that were blowing across the ocean. When we appeared on the other side of the squall, lo and behold in front of us was this bloody great German ship, the *Hipper*. The Captain ordered smoke to be laid so we had a smokescreen, and we turned around and went back into it. When we came back out of it the next thing was to fire torpedoes at her, which was done. But unfortunately none of them found their mark, which may have made a big difference to the whole episode.

"In the meantime, we had received many hits. We had dived back into the smokescreen. When we came out the Captain said 'stand by to ram' and that is what happened. We turned around and we ran straight into the *Hipper* smashing into her side and tearing a gaping hole in her. I believe this was instrumental in disabling her water desalination plant. As we turned away we received many hits some of them very serious. In fact one of them ripped a hole in the engine room in the starboard side of the ship. The Captain, then realising that we were sinking, ordered us to abandon ship.

"I was in the Petty Officers' Mess as an ammunition handler. When the order to abandon ship came I went through onto the starboard side of the fo'c'sle. There was a Carley raft there which was still intact. I believe it was the only one that was left in that condition. But to undo the lashings was impossible as the seawater had tightened the rope up considerably. I could not undo it by hand. There was a young Able Seaman there by the name of Morris, from Bournemouth. I asked him if he had a knife on him because I wasn't allowed to carry a knife being in ammunition supply. He produced a very small penknife that his girlfriend had given him. It had on it 'Souvenir of Bournemouth' or something like that. I managed to cut the Carley raft free from its lashings. Morris and I heaved it over the side. There were two splashes, one as the raft hit the water and one as I hit the water alongside it. I managed to scramble aboard but what happened to Morris I'll never know because from that day to this I never saw him again.

"The raft slid alongside the ship and me and the other men in the water managed to push off so that we weren't carried into the gaping hole in the starboard side. Eventually after we had cleared the ship I turned round and saw the ship sliding under.

"The last person to talk to our Captain was a Petty Officer named Townsend. Both he and the Captain used to play cricket for the flotilla. The Captain said to Townsend: "I don't think we'll be playing cricket for a long time yet." Then he proceeded to go to the wardroom where the sea cocks were situated to open them and sink the ship.

"We were in the water for quite a considerable time before the *Hipper* returned and proceeded to pick up survivors. Among the survivors a few names have come to mind; Petty Officer Townsend; Petty Officer Walter Scott; Leading Seaman Smith from Southampton; Leading Seaman Shergold; Able Seaman Andrew Perry; Able Seaman Edgar Seeward; Able Seaman Bob Rainer; Able Seaman Mallett; Able Seaman Merritt; Petty Officer Gregg and one or two others.

"Eventually I was helped out of the water with a rope. From my waist down I was absolutely frozen. I never felt so cold in all my life and I don't think I've warmed up yet. We were taken to Wilhelmshaven and handed over to the military authorities where they proceeded to interrogate us. Two of our ratings who were ASDIC operators had an immediate change of status by becoming torpedo men. After interrogation we were sent to a prison camp in a place called Spannenburg in Germany where we were registered in an officers' camp of all things. I was given POW number 161. Then we were sent to a naval camp near Bremerhaven. Whilst there I met two Flight Sergeants who had been shot down over Germany on the day war was declared, operating a leaflet drop.

"I finish by saying two of the brightest moments in my life were: the first when I joined Her Majesty's Royal Yacht Victoria and Albert at Portsmouth in 1935 during the Coronation season. I was one of the six boys on the ship who were awarded the Coronation Medal. The other great moment of my life was when I eventually returned home and heard the news that the Captain of *Glowworm*, Lt Cdr Roope had been awarded the Victoria Cross. The very first action of World War Two resulting in the award of the VC."

As reported by Bert Harris earlier, the *Hipper* Kapitan Hellmuth Heye had visited the survivors below decks to tell them how brave they and their Captain had been in the confrontation. Apparently Kapitan Heye did not leave it there, once the *Hipper* returned to Germany he let it be known to the Red Cross of the incident and felt the British should be told of the bravery shown by the *Glowworm* crew led by her Captain.

It was only on the repatriation of the *Glowworm* survivors after the war, when Lieutenant Ramsay was interviewed by the Admiralty, that the order of events came to be known in Britain. As a result Lieutenant Commander Roope was posthumously awarded the Victoria Cross, Lieutenant Ramsey received the Distinguished Service Order and Engine Artificer Gregg, Petty Officer Scott, Petty Officer Thomas and Able Seaman Merritt the Conspicuous Gallantry Medal.

London Gazette dated 6th July 1945, "The Commanding Officer, whilst correctly appreciating the intentions of the enemy, at once gave chase. The Germans heavy cruiser, *Admiral Hipper*, was sighted closing the *Glowworm* at high speed and an enemy report was sent which was received by HMS *Renown*. Because of the heavy sea, the *Glowworm* could not shadow the enemy and the Commanding Officer therefore decided to attack with torpedoes and then to close in order to inflict as much damage as possible. Five torpedoes were fired and later but without success. The *Glowworm* was badly hit; one gun was out of action and her speed was much reduced, but with the other three guns still firing she closed and rammed the *Admiral Hipper*. As the *Glowworm* drew away, she opened fire again and scored one hit at a range of 400 yards. The *Glowworm*, badly damaged, stove in forward and riddled with enemy fire, heeled over to starboard, and the Commanding Officer gave the order to abandon her. Shortly afterwards she capsized and sank. The *Admiral Hipper* spent at least an hour picking up survivors, the loss of life was heavy but some of the *Glowworm*'s complement were saved."

There are several questions about the attack that have never been entirely resolved. Did the *Glowworm* ram the *Hipper* on the orders of Roope, as one survivor claims and which is the preferred narrative? Or could it have been another crew member directing the ship? Or was it just the *Glowworm* itself taking on a life of its own as its steering instruments ceased to function? A pointless aside: Roope was known by his men as 'Rammer Roope' because of a pre-war accident in May 1939.

Another question is whether the sacrifice of *Glowworm* was necessary. It has been suggested, that perhaps Roope should have decided that discretion was the better part of valour and run for the horizon. Although, it has to be said, this is not something that Royal Navy Captains routinely did in the last war. Instead, he chose a fight that he must have known would end in his ship's destruction, hoping against hope that a torpedo would find the *Admiral Hipper*'s side and that the sacrifice of his ship would not be in vain.

Glowworm at Alexandria after colliding with HMS *Grenade* in in May 1939 whilst on night exercises. [S. Bell Great Nephew of Bill Piper, died on *Glowworm*. Family collection.]

One other haunting detail: the *Glowworm's* siren had jammed in the early part of the attack and it was giving off what has been described as a permanent 'banshee' wail for the last minutes of its existence.

The picture was clearly taken from on board the *Hipper*. As mentioned it was given to Bert Harris, by a German soldier and Bert kept it safe for many years before allowing it to be published. It is one of the most remarkable photographs from the war at sea and shows *Glowworm* running hard under smoke in her death dance. At this time most of the British crew were still alive, minutes later the vast majority would be dead.

["2016 Beachcombing's Bizarre History Blog. Tags: HMS *Glowworm*, Royal Navy, WW2."]

Returning to Admiral Hipper, Bert Harris and his shipmates, having finally been landed at Wilhelmshaven, goes on to describe his five years' experience as a Prisoner of War, in an interview for the Imperial War Museum. Bert, "We had been treated very well in the messdecks on board the *Hipper*, and we were given cigarettes, the Germans were very friendly. We arrived in Wilhelmshaven early morning, were taken off and took to the naval barracks. We stayed there for quite a while and were interrogated, being asked simple questions. Like, what speed we were going, how long in the navy. Wanted to know about HMS *Cossack*, they seemed very interested, I don't know what would have happened if I said I had been on her.

Kapitan Heye, oversees the rescue on board the *Hipper*.

Survivors are pulled aboard the *Hipper*. The man in the water is believed to be Bert
Harris. The next shows crew of *Hipper* continuing desperately to rescue the survivors.
[S. Bell Great Nephew of Bill Piper, died on *Glowworm*. Family collection.].

Picked up from a 'Carley Float'. [Alf. R. Jacobsen Collection]

"We were walked around the town – for people to see us, but they were cheering for the German Navy. I presumed my shipmates were transferred to various POW camps. I arrived at Spangenberg Castle [Oflag IX-A. North Eastern town in Hesse Region. 140 miles Wilhelmshaven – as the crow flies] where I worked in a forest. It was hard work and there wasn't much to eat. We kept ourselves busy helping the officers to escape. The Germans didn't allow them out of the camp to work, so we used to swap clothes with them. Quite a few officers escaped this way. On one occasion three of our Mosquito fighters flew over the compound. The guard in the watch tower, although he wasn't supposed to, fired at them. One of them broke off and flew straight at the tower. As if to say to the guard 'so you want to play do you?' The Mosquito pilot aimed and fired his guns killing the guard so that all the bullets landed outside the compound away from us.

"Later, I was moved onto Wiemar to work in a factory on the roads, the camp was full of French and other countries POWs. The Germans were not very good to us, they would come up and hit you with their rifles, just like Bang! *Schnell, Schnell, Schnell* – Englander". [Faster, Faster...] The Germans were looking as if they were on top of the world and could do no wrong."

After approximately twelve months Bert had gone full circle and found himself back at Wilhelmshaven and this time the Marlag Camp. "It was a good camp run by the German Navy, no work we were kept in the camp and it was run on the same lines as a ship."

Bert Harris, "They then decided to transfer us again for working, they took a lot of us out and put us on a train for nearly two weeks and we finished up in Poland." It was difficult to work out Bert's timeline with regards to the camps he resided at. But he went on to explain to the Imperial War Museum interviewer. "I ended up at Oderberg in Poland. Most of the chaps in there were from the Army. I mucked in with a survivor from the armed merchant cruiser the *Rawalpindi*. We were in a small working party, it wasn't too bad really but we always had the German guards at you, they were always there."

The main administrative camp nearby was the notorious Stalag VIIIB, Bert remembers, "It was at Lamsdorf, Upper Silesia, a really big transfer camp. On one side there were Russian prisoners and other nationalities."

I will come back to Marlag du Nord and Stalag VIIIB [later renumbered Stalag 344] camps near the end of the book, as it relates to some of the *Hunter* crewmen. I will also complete Bert Harris' account of his experiences in 1945 when he was involved in the 'Death March' from Oderberg to freedom.

S. Bell whose great uncle, Bill Piper lost his life on *Glowworm* wrote, "Ever since I could remember I had often heard my family mention my great uncle." As a result he researched and made an attempt to find out how Bill died, the ship's history and the events leading up that fateful day. Subsequently, he began his own website. [www.Glowworm.org.uk]

S. Bell continues, "The story of the *Glowworm* captures the very essence of the British Wartime Spirit at that time. I am very proud that my great uncle was one of the men who served on the *Glowworm* and hope that this website honours his memory and all the other men who were on her that day […] I am honoured to have been in the company of heroes." [47]

47　S. Bell also mentions, that in 1969 a Hollywood screenplay writer Larry Forrester got interested in the story of the *Glowworm* and intended to make a film about it. However, when he showed the draft to the survivors, they disagreed with his portrayal of the crew, especially the Captain. He then turned his work into a fictional novel: *The Battle of the April Storm*. The film was never made.

The Trojan Horse Arrives

I will now return to a brief account by various crew members of the 2nd Destroyer Flotilla, after the sinking of the *Glowworm* about the following action when the Royal Navy confronted the German Navy. Here first Marshal Soult: "Just as dawn was breaking and as the morning watches were being piped, two large vessels were spotted far out on the horizon, starboard side. Action alarm stations were sounded but before all stations were fully manned the enemy opened fire. The first salvoes fell ahead of *Hunter* on the port side of *Hardy*, then more salvoes came screaming over, too close for comfort near the leading ships. By this time *Renown* had opened fire in reply and because of her longer range guns was able to keep the enemy at a distance which prevented them from hitting any of our destroyers. It would appear that *Renown* was the main target for the enemy ships, because before they broke off they managed to hit her a couple of times. But did no serious damage or casualties."

The enemy ships were the heavy cruisers, *Scharnhorst* and *Gneisenau*. Here are three of *Hardy*'s crewmen who witnessed the event. Signalman Ralph Brigginshaw, "I happened to be on the middle watch [midnight to 0400] when we met the two German ships. We were bouncing along astern of the *Renown* and I was on the bridge with an 'Aldis' lamp to keep in touch with the destroyers astern of us. We opened fire, which didn't do a lot of good, except that it cheered us up a bit in all the rough weather. It certainly wasn't the sea for torpedoes."

Dougy Bourton: "I was the 'Loading Number' on No 4 Gun and we were firing at such extreme range that the guns were elevated so high that at times I was on my knees forcing the shell and cartridge uphill at an angle of 45 degrees to get it into the breech. The weather was atrocious, so much so that we couldn't fire No 1 Gun [foremost gun], so that we had to bring up their crew aft, with the ammunition parties. But eventually the *Scharnhorst* had been hit several times, and the *Renown* had only suffered very minor damage. The *Scharnhorst* and *Gneisenau* took off and made their escape."

Cyril Cope and the other Torpedomen's efforts were in vain: "We waited and waited but the weather was against us. It was impossible to close the range and the Admiral in *Renown* realising that the destroyers could not maintain the high speed for much longer signalled Captain 'D' (Warburton-Lee) to abandon the chase, leaving *Renown* to carry on alone. We had no misgivings leaving it to the battle cruiser because we knew that she was more than a match for the two German ships. Very soon the ships of 'friend and foe' disappeared from our sight in the thick blanket of snow and mist. The mine laying destroyers left for home escorted by *Hostile*, but we in *Hardy*, having received signals from Admiralty to proceed to Vest fjord, which led to the iron ore port of Narvik, set off with the other three ships."

Cyril goes onto explain about the strategy of destroyers in battle. "When a flotilla goes into battle to make a torpedo attack on the enemy ships, you go in line ahead as fast as you can go. When you get into range you swerve off to port or starboard and fire all your torpedoes. So as we then had five destroyers in the flotilla, that's eight torpedoes on each firing at the enemy. That means there was a chance that one might hit. Not necessarily hit, because that would be lucky. The idea was to make their ships turn away and not be able to fire their guns at your own battleships or cruisers. All of us who manned the tubes were hoping we would be able to get near enough to mount a torpedo attack because five destroyers each with eight torpedoes to fire, going in at high speed towards the enemy would be a wonderful sight. A sight not seen since the 'Fleet Battles of the First World War', and given a certain amount of luck, some of the forty torpedoes might find the target."

In early April, a person who would be of great interest to the Germans arrived in Narvik. This was Giles Romilly who was aged twenty-three and a war correspondent for the *Daily Express*. In 1939, he was covering the early conflicts between Finland and Russia. When it became apparent that the Germans were initialising an invasion of Norway, the newspaper decided to send young Romilly to Bergen. But en route his plans were changed and instead he was sent to Narvik. This was disappointing for him, because he knew that at this time of the year Narvik had less hours of sun than in other parts of the region and was in an isolated area where snow storms still occurred on a regular basis. However, as it happened the diversion put him in a position to witness the German invasion at first hand.

In the meantime, Giles Romilly had booked into the Hotel Royal and whilst waiting for any developments on the war front, with his keen eye he did not waste time and he started to make observations about his surroundings. He had noticed that whilst the Captains of the merchant ships in the harbour went ashore for business reasons, their crews had to stay on board. Their ships were not much more than a ship's length apart. The British vessels had guns mounted on the stern aimed directly at the Germans' ones. Although the local harbour authorities had made sure they had control, so breech-blocks and ammunition were stowed under hatches with a heavy seal.

The town of Narvik on 8th April as would be expected at this time of the year was thick with snow which had been cleared from the roads. The community were looking forward to the May time sun coming to finally melt it away for a few months. Talk was going around about the advancing German Nazis having reached their neighbouring country Denmark. Although the Norwegian Government had been given assurances by the German Foreign Ministry (and thereby Adolf Hitler) that their neutrality would be respected, grave doubts naturally remained.

In the Imperial War Museum I discovered they had a diary in their archives [Private Papers (13097)] which was kept by Merchant Navy Captain D. J. Nicholas. He was the Master of SS *Blythmoor*, a twenty-year-old, 6,600 ton cargo steamer owned by the Runciman Walter and Sons Company in Newcastle upon Tyne. He had recently brought his vessel into Narvik and was anchored just inside the harbour, waiting to load up with iron ore. On completing his diary he would never have thought that seventy years later, it would become an important account to supplement the other documents recording the historical event which was about to unfold on the 9th April.

8 April '40 Monday
7 German 5 British 3 Norwegian 3 Swedish at anchor. Monday evening 1 German cargo vessel (large) deeply laden. 1 Dutch vessel [both] arrived Narvik. Thought to be result of mine laying in Vestfjord

Also on the 8th of April, the Mayor of Narvik, Theodor Broch, was in his office. It was a usual busy Monday, with post and packages being delivered. The next few days were to become even more hectic but out of his control. It started with having to provide a 'sea worthiness certificate' for the Master of SS *Romanby*, which had had some damage in a harbour collision. He was made aware that the Customs Office had noted that there were a total of twenty-five iron ore transport vessels in the harbour.

Mayor Broch recalls, "On the way I had met a friend from the Customs Office. He had worked all night and was on his way home. All had been inspected [cargo ships in port] on arrival and their radio transmitters had been sealed. That morning a huge whaling ship, the *Jan Wellem* had arrived from the north. He had been on board himself. It had exceptionally large food stores from being southward bound. Perhaps it had been chased into harbour by the British. He had not noticed anything unusual. The crew had been polite, but the cigars were bad. I told him that I was going onboard a British ship. "Then you will at least get better cigars," he yawned, and was on his way.

"I was taken to the ship by a ferryman who operated a kind of harbour taxi service. Business was not too bad. Tips were better since there were more British and fewer Germans, but there was not much of the traditional good spirit in the harbour. Everything was secretive. No one knew when the boats arrived or left. On the surface everything was peaceful. The ships lay side by side, flying the Union Jack or the Swastika, but all had secret machines covered up on the foredeck. They kept their cannons under cover. Harbour police were to be seen on every side. There was much talk about spies, yet no one had been arrested [...] So things could not be so bad after all. But it was not pleasant anymore."

Custom Officers had been surprised that although *Jan Wellem* had arrived from Murmansk concerns were raised as to why a ship on a transit south to Germany was carrying so much food cargo. Mayor Broch on leaving SS *Romanby*, having signed the certificate, sat down with the merchant seaman 'Master' and had a farewell discussion about where the war was leading. "When things begin to happen will we be likely to get into trouble?" queried the Mayor. "So far Great Britain has perhaps not done too much land fighting, but still rules the sea. The Nazis might be able to sneak up a freighter or two along your neutral coast to Narvik, but warships which have to go out to sea will not get through. You may rest assured there is no longer danger up here." He could have not been so far from the truth as the 'Master' will find out shortly.

As the Mayor departed from the cargo ship he noticed that the *Jan Wellem* anchored well away from the harbour, had a larger than normal swastika on its foremast and just a little further away were the Norwegian naval coastal defence ships *Norge* and *Eidsvold*.

The two 'panser ships' had arrived on Sunday 7th April, lying at anchor so the off-duty crew were allowed ashore. At the Hotel Royal downstairs in the lounge area a large party was developing. A group of the 'panser ships' crew had been skiing in the mountains near the Swedish border. Leaving their gear and wet clothing outside, sprawled around the bar they were now feeling euphoric as a result of their afternoons exercise. Tragically for many it would be their last opportunity to enjoy the thrills of hurtling down the snowy slopes of the mountain terrain in their beloved country.

Prior to *Norge* arriving, the Captain, Per Askim had been on holiday with his wife Signe. They decided that Signe would follow Per to Narvik and book into the Hotel Royal until the situation became clearer. Early Monday morning the hotel receptionist rang Signe to say there was a phone call for her. She rushed down to take the call, it was Per sounding anxious. "Something very serious has happened. The British have laid mines in the Vestfjord. I have been at it since five this morning [...] I can't keep the phone engaged for long. I'll ring you when I have time."

The locals in Narvik had got wind of the British mining of the 'Leads' and they were obviously very concerned about how this would affect the exporting of the iron ore from their harbour. Their feelings were exacerbated when news came that ships were not permitted to leave the harbour. On the arrival of *Jan Wellem* a local man speaking for his friends at one of the bars in town, commented worryingly to the British clientele, "This is probably the beginning of the Germans taking refuge to avoid your blockade." It would not be long before the man and his compatriots were to find the whaling ship was there for completely different reasons for its own self interests.

Back at the Hotel Royal in the evening, Signe received another phone call from Per. "'Hello, don't ask me anything. Things are becoming serious and if you hear gunfire this evening, it'll be from us. Thank you for all the good times we've had together. Look after yourself. Get yourself off to bed and stay calm.' 'Yes, all right. But Per...' I cried. But he had already put down the phone." Signe continues, "There were a lot of people in the lounge, commercial travellers, foreign journalists and a number of army officers. The last-mentioned didn't seem any more concerned about the situation than usual. I couldn't help being surprised that they should be sitting there carefree when Per was clearly getting ready for battle and firing could start at any moment."

Unknown to the Admiralty and therefore the senior officers at sea, the

German flotilla had managed to nearly complete her voyage to Narvik. It seemed fortune had gone her way as she was not detected by her foe. Dickens writes, "At 2100 on the 8th of April, Kommodore Bonte considered that he should be abreast of Skomvaer and entering Vestfjord. The only positive indication of his position was a single radio beacon, though that was not identified with certainty, and he relied mainly on dead reckoning. Given the highest navigational skill it was still a courageous act to press on into ever more confined waters, and Bonte's heart must have been in his mouth [...] A light was sighted [...] but not identified, then a cliff nearly ahead that caused a violent evasive turn to port; torpedoes were nearly fired as the rocks looked like an enemy ship, which it would have been no surprise to find".

The lighthouse was not operating. This was to be expected as the German forces had been told that the Norwegian Government, uneasy at last, had ordered all navigational lights to be extinguished. It was a half measure that had no effect on events, especially as many lights were unmanned and could not be switched off.

Oberleutnant Albert Bach recalls the transit in the Vestfjord, "I was awoken at half past two [morning] and had a proper shower for the first time since leaving Berlin". On his way to the bridge he noticed dawn breaking. "We were in a kind of dark narrow corridor. On either side mountains thrust their way upwards into low clouds. The fjord was calm and there wasn't a light to be seen ashore. It was snowing a little, I could just make out the other Zerstörers sailing line astern at about thirty km/h, their bows clearing the water to leave a wave of white foam on either side."

The flotilla was now approaching Narvik, the intensity of the crews' excitement into the unknown grew by the minute. Oberleutnant Hans Rohr had assembled his hundred men of No 7 Company on the quarterdeck. "Weapons, equipment and ammunition were brought up from below. As we were to be first to go ashore with the intention of taking Colonel Sundlo [Commander of Norwegian forces in the area] prisoner. I took the precaution of issuing the men with hand grenades." He and his men were exhausted experiencing of seasickness and deficit of sleep. Most being on the upper deck for the first time would have felt intimidated by the sights around them. Although accustomed to mountainous surroundings and snow, there was little escape with skis or by mechanical means.

Back in Narvik the locals had heard the 7 pm news bulletin the evening before, that a wrecked German cargo ship (*Rio de Janeiro*) had drifted onto the coast of Lillesand in Southern Norway. More intriguing was that the locals had found drowned young soldiers bodies, as well as dead horses. Naturally alarm bells started to ring in the minds of those hearing the news and word soon got around. Immediately harbour officials, who were having supper at a local hotel, rushed back to their offices. All leave was cancelled for crew members on the 'ironclads', *Norge* and *Eidsvold*. The senior officer in command Captain Askim on *Norge*, had received a signal via London, that intelligence showed that German attack on Narvik was imminent. Although, Norwegian authorities were of the opinion that this was probably not the case. Either way Askim decided it would be best to go to 'war stations' and ordered the *Eidsvold* away from the crowded harbour and out into the fjord to guard the approaches to Narvik. [48]

Norge and *Eidsvold* 7 April 1940 (Norwegian Resistance Museum)

---

48   The *Rio de Janeiro* had been torpedoed by a Polish submarine *Orzel* which had escaped from Estonia seventeen days after the war had begun. A 150 men and 80 horses drowned, whilst there were 183 survivors.

Per Askim, aged sixty, and Odd Willoch, aged fifty-five, were friends and had a mutual interest in 'cutting edge' technology, mainly wireless communications. Askim made his name in the Lighthouse Authority, whilst Willoch was amongst the nation's fishermen and trappers as the intrepid Commander of Fishing protection. After his death protecting his country, which you will read about shortly, Askim said of his friend, "He was always in a good humour, full of initiative and determined to see that everything went smoothly."

Odd Willoch was the son of chief engineer Einar and his wife Hannah. Willoch's grandfather was a politician and was also born into a family of artists, a physicist, a scientist and a previous nineteenth-century prime minister. On joining the Royal Norwegian Navy he attended the Norwegian Military Academy and studied wireless technology in Britain. He commanded the offshore patrol vessels. He became head of the Technical Section of the Naval Corps, a signals instructor at the Naval College and wrote manuals for 'radio hams'.

In 1940 he had reached the rank of Kommandorkaptein and took command of *Eidsvold*.

Captain Odd Willoch. One of the renowned Norwegian naval officers between the interwar years. [Ingrid Willoch (daughter) Collection.]

Per Askim was promoted to Second Lieutenant in 1901 and was a Captain by 1910. By 1934 he was promoted to the rank of Kommandorkaptein, and he retired from the Navy in 1936.

He was employed at the Ministry of Defence from 1905 to 1907 and lectured at the Norwegian Naval Academy. He worked for the Admiral staff from 1920 and then from 1930 to 1939 was a section leader in the Norwegian Coastal Administration. In 1940 he was recalled to the Navy, given the command of the *Norge* and was in charge of the coastal defence in northern Norway.

Both enjoyed being family men of the 'old school', principled and conscientious, but it appears that after years of the country being indoctrinated by pacifist propaganda, this tended to place them unready to face the viciousness of the Nazi's war machine.

By Captain Odd Willoch facing a horrifying death he would leave behind his wife Marie Kristine and their three children.

Kommordore Bonte must have been a relieved man and praised his luck with which, along with his boldness and determination he had completed his task of arriving at Narvik with his flotilla intact. Just as importantly, he had got there before the British Navy and would now be able to disembark his tired and gaunt looking passengers, with their armaments and stores. However, unknown to him he would have another important task to do before relaxing in his day cabin. The following day, 9th April 1940, would become a sombre occasion in the history of Norway.

Whilst there were snow storms on the last lap of the German flotilla's arrival, Bonte detached his Zerstörers to prearranged tasks. One to patrol the entrance of Ofotfjord at Baroy Narrows, another two to land Alpine troops at Ramnes and Hamnes, three ships to the east to Herjangsfjord and the Norwegian Army camp and depot at Elvegårdsmoen . There the Alpine troops quickly took control. At 0415 Bonte arrived on his flag ship *Wilhelm Heidkamp* and two other Zerstörers off Narvik harbour. The visibility had worsened when the Zerstörer *Bernd von Arnim* (Korvettenkapitan Rechel) received orders to enter the harbour to land the first assault troops at the 'Post Pier'. This she did, first sailing past the *Eidsvold*, and then threading her way between numerous merchant vessels anchored in the harbour.

Although it was early in the morning messages by word of mouth must have rapidly gone around the vessels, because soon sleepy looking crewmen began to emerge from below decks. The *Bernd von Arnim* was greeted with anxious queries in an assortment of languages, "Are you English?" and *"Deutschland uber alles?"* In the meantime, the *Eidsvold* had fired a shell over the bows of *Wilhelm Heidkamp*. Captain Willoch orders were to resist any German attack, whilst Bonte's was, "To present the operation to the Norwegians as a friendly move to protect them from the British, and on no account to fire first."

The *Eidsvold* crew, were ready at war stations, so Willoch allowed Bonte to send a German negotiating officer on board. This was Kapitanleutnant Heinrich Gerlach the Staff Officer Assistant. In fact it quickly became apparent there was never going to be any negotiating, as the German officer demanded an instant and complete surrender. Willoch contacted his superior Captain Askim for further instructions. The reply was to fight. The relatively rapid developments had obviously taken Willoch by surprise. Probably in a state of shock, whilst witnessing the *Heidkamp*'s guns pointing at his ship, a gentleman to the last, he bravely told the German officer of the decision. At that the officer clicked his heels, returned to his boat and when clear of the *Eidsvold* fired a Red Verey light.

On board the *Wilhelm Heidkamp* Kapitanleutnant Hans Erdmenger ordered full speed ahead the moment he saw Gerlach's red flare. He wrote, "The ironclad suddenly increased speed, I assumed that the idea was to ram us. We were in a dangerous position as, in the course of the negotiating we had drifted quite close to the *Eidsvold*."

Oberleutnant Bach recalls, "The force exerted by our engines was absolutely amazing. We leapt forward and the *Eidsvold* receded –100 metres – 300 metres – 500 metres. We all had our eyes glued to the Norwegian ship. Would they open fire? Would they blast off with their heavy guns – and blow our fragile hull to bits."

On board the *Eidsvold* the ships gunnery officer Knut Thorkelsen, receiving Willoch's order, shouted, "Fire!" Unfortunately, the WW1 ironclad took too long for her guns to be brought round to bear, by which time the modern German Zerstörer had moved into a windswept snow screen. Hans Erdmenger, under the testing circumstances, asked for permission to launch their torpedoes.

However, Bonte's conscience came into play and declined the request. It appears his thoughts were honourable, in both avoiding immediately creating significant animosity from the Narvik community as well as not wanting to send a weaker adversary to the bottom of the harbour. But to the astonishment of those on the bridge, General Dietl, Hitler's comrade-in-arms, as 'Commander in Chief' of the occupying force, shouted *"Schiessen!"* [Shoot or fire.] [49]

Oberleutnant Rohr with his Alpine Troops was still on the quarterdeck awaiting orders. "I heard the splash and saw four 'eels' [torpedoes] streaking across through the water towards the ironclad. Before the Norwegians could fire a shot there was a violent explosion. It was like an earthquake! Spurts of flame shot up and a cloud of black smoke rose skywards. Seconds later the ship disappeared beneath the surface."

Back on board *Eidsvold* the violent upheaval was as you would have expected. Petty Officer Holstad in the after turret when he felt the ship move to one side on the first hit. He goes onto describe the moment, "When the next two hit the hull, it was as if the *Eidsvold* simply disintegrated. It was turmoil! There was a great deal of noise and all I could see was smoke." However, he was able to make his way through a maze of twisted metal, until he found himself on top of the turret. At which point the ship turned fully over. He recounts, "I've no idea of how long I was under the water. When I surfaced, I could see the red-painted bottom of the stern some 20 to 30 metres away. I could hear frantic cries for help but couldn't see where they came from."

So it was that the *Eidsvold* sank, bow first. Holstad and the ships Bandmaster Henry Backe found a float onto which they were able to drag themselves. The float drifted towards the shore in the company of two of their fellow survivors who had luckily found a dingy. Heinrich Gerlach returning from the *Eidsvold* in the *Wilhelm Heidkamp* pinnace was able to pick up four more. That was the total sum of survivors and Kommodore Bonte would probably not be feeling victorious as what he feared had happened before his very eyes.

---

49   It is recorded that Kommodore Bonte had intensively disliked his own actions, not just for the negative effects and reactions from the Norwegian resistance but also because he felt it was a great moral indignation of his sense of honour. It is suggested it might also have affected the functioning of his decision making abilities over the next twenty-four hours, before his own death.

On the *Wilhelm Heidkamp* bridge. [Via Alf. R. Jacobsen – scan from Fritz-Otto Busch, Narvik. Vom Heldenkampf deutcher Zerstörers.]

The violent episode had brought confusion to the opposing commanding officers of the *Bernd von Arnim* and *Norge*. Rechel was having problems finding the 'Post Pier' as on his deck there was a mass of Alpine troops waiting to disembark. Whilst binoculars were trained on the *Norge*, Rechel managed to get his bearing through a gap in the snow shower.

Rechel: "I made a 90-degree turn, and suddenly caught sight of the pier, a bare 80 metres away. The off-duty engine room watch had been lined up along the starboard rail to help, if help were needed, and right behind them were crouched the [Alpine] troops, ready to leap ashore the moment we docked. It was then that I saw that the *Norge* was bringing both her guns to bear on us. I immediately gave the gunnery and torpedo officers permission to fire if the Norwegians did."

By now the Norwegian Admiralty and the government had been able to establish who the invaders were and sent a message to the telegraph office in Narvik. The message was short "German warships are to be fired on, British not." The telegraphist in charge Johannes Deisen quickly summoned a taxi to the quay. A launch was already waiting for him. Deisen explains, "I had promised to deliver the message in person, the weather was awful, snow showers and a strong wind blowing. It wasn't long before the *Norge* loomed up in the murk. She had steam up and her guns had been swung into position." Deisen gave the message to a crew member, then at that moment he heard shouts from on board the ship telling him to getaway quick. "As the launch drew away the *Norge* guns blasted off. I saw flames belch from their muzzles and the force of the blast was so strong that I had to huddle down in the boat for cover."

Captain Askim having previously heard the explosions that caused the demise of *Eidsvold*, opened fire with his 21 cm and 15 cm guns from a range of 900 metres. He did not wait for the telegram message. "By then the weather had improved a little, but it was still practically impossible to see anything through the viewfinders," he wrote in his report. To his dismay the first salvo was short resulting in the Germans returning fire with all guns. The *Norge* tried to dodge the enemy's accurate salvos, by hiding behind merchants' vessels. During the engagement Rechel managed to put his ship in a position to allow a landing, not only to his own great relief but I imagine also to the by now weary and traumatised young Alpine troops.

Subsequently, Rechel on *Bernd von Arnim* bridge, saw the *Norge's* first salvo had fallen short, "I immediately gave orders to return fire with every gun available – regardless of the fact that the *Norge* was partly masked by steamers [merchant vessels]. I completed the docking and saw the first of the troops leap ashore and take cover behind the concrete wall of the dock."

In the meantime, Korvettenkapitan Max-Eckart Wolff steered the *Georg Thiele* into the harbour, resulting in the *Norge* having to cope with two Zerstörers firing from both port and starboard sides. Askim, alarmed, "I heard something whistling past. It was probably a shell striking and exploding forward, beneath the bridge. It was impossible to differentiate between explosions, there were so many. Once I saw a column of water rise up close to the quay. But I've no idea if it was a 21 cm shell of ours exploding in the water or on board the Zerstörer."

The engagement lasted ten minutes, none of Norge's shells hit their adversary. As gunnery officer Hans-Georg Buch records, "The lack of effect of our opponent's gunfire was incomprehensible to any gunner."

The *Norge* appearing for seconds between two merchant vessels this finally gave Rechel a chance to launch his torpedoes. The first five missed, even at close range. Although the sixth malfunctioned, the seventh hit the *Norge*. "She turned over on her axis and remained afloat for a short while, keel uppermost. When she went down, one of the propellers was still turning, one minute it was all over," remembers Rechel.

It was a horrific moment, the engine room was flooded, trapping many Norwegian crewmen, some of whom had not been in the Navy very long.

Askim records, "Out of sheer force of habit, I brought the engines to a stop. It didn't help of course, as one of the torpedoes had gone straight into the engine room, with disastrous results. I sounded the siren to summon assistance, then tried to make my way out of the wheelhouse by the port door, but it had been wrenched from its mounting and blocked the exit. I went under where I was, on the bridge.

"Somehow or other the pressure of the water must have propelled me through the doorway – otherwise I would have been caught in there like a rat in a trap. When I reached the surface, the *Norge* was twenty-odd metres away, bottom up. The propellers were still turning slowly, calling to mind an animal in its death throes."

The sixty-year-old Captain Askim, having lost his ship is now needing to save his life, he desperately finds and hangs onto a wooden messdeck bunk. "A man black with oil and soot swam over and grabbed hold of the same bunk. I remember thinking that the least he could have done was to let his Captain have the bunk to himself! He started shouting and wailing in mortal fear, prompting me to tell him to shut up and calm down. He either took offence at what I'd said or saw something better to cling to, as he swam off. That was the last I saw of him.

"In the end I could no longer see any ships or people. It was still dark. I've no idea of how long I lay there. All I remember is that I realised that I was beginning to lose consciousness and that I twice called for help. I recall thinking that my shouts sounded pitifully weak in the watery blackness. After that I remember nothing."

As mentioned there were eight survivors on *Eidsvold* and ninety-seven from the *Norge*, leaving a total of 282 Norwegian sailors killed. [50]

On 8 May 1945 he was the only Norwegian member of the Allied Surrender Commission at Lillehammer when the German General Franz Bohme signed the surrender conditions on behalf of the German troops in Norway.

After the war between May to December 1945 Per Askim headed the Norwegian Naval Command. He then returned to his job in the Norwegian Coastal Administration, where he worked until his retirement in 1952. He died in Oslo in 1963, at the age of 82.

---

50   Per Askim was evacuated to Britain in 1940, and served as naval attaché in Washington from 1940 to 1943. He then served as head of the Planning Section at the Norwegian High Command in London. He was awarded the Norwegian War Cross with Sword for his achievements during the Second World War.

Alpine troops disembarking. [Geirr Haarr Collection].

Returning back ashore, Giles Romilly was awoken by the noise of the gun fire, looking through the window he noticed the usual snowstorm and half-light, neither of night nor dawn. Then two explosions lifted the bedside telephone. "I heard blurred sounds of distress and confusion; the voice of the hall clerk: "Yes. Yes. It is trouble in the river." I dressed and ran downstairs. On the landings, at the door of the bedrooms were officers of the Norwegian garrison, in flowing night shirts [...] The hall was a mass of dressing gowns and tousled heads. Outside, soldiers were tumbling helter-skelter, rifles clutched anyhow, down the steep, slippery slope that led to the harbour."

Captain Nicholas

9 April '40 Tuesday
Awoke about 2.00 am and had a look on deck. Wind rising and heavy snow falling.

3.00 am called Chief Officer and told him to let go second anchor. 3.30 – 4.00 am. Heard two or three other vessel letting go 2nd anchor.

4.30 am Heard anchor let go close to. Had a look on deck to see what vessel it would be. Found it to be Norwegian 'man-of-war' [Norge] close to – swinging round on anchor. Still heavy snow storm, went back to my room again. Soon after heard a shot fired and immediately went on deck where I saw the Norwegian 'man-of-war' firing towards the shore her shell striking the water.

The Norwegian 'man of war' was lying between my ship starboard and a loaded German vessel [M/V Bockhenheim Ore-carrier] which had arrived the evening before.

The Norwegian was using the German as a screen, going astern then firing her guns and then going ahead. I could not see what she was firing at owing to the snow storm. I had the Watchman' call all hands. Then I saw a torpedo miss the Norwegian 'man of war' and pass close ahead of my ship. By this time I supposed there was a submarine in the harbour, but also noticed shots being fired from off our port quarter towards the Norwegian, also shots were fired from towards the shore on our starb'd quarter at the Norwegian. None of these shots apparently hit the Norwegian, but a German cargo vessel which lay on our port bow was hit by one shell.

The action was not long, when I observed the Norwegian 'm.o.w'][Man of War] was hit on her starboard side about the mainmast by a torpedo, the smoke and debris rising higher than the main mast. 'Man of war' turned turtle and sank less than 3 minutes. Heard cries of men in water. In meantime, I had ordered lifeboats to be swung out and lowered to rail. On hearing cries of men in water – ordered boats into water when I observed German destroyer close to, with guns trained on us. I sent out signal 'Proceed into harbour', no wireless used. I ordered all crew into boats and went and destroyed secret papers etc. by burning same in galley stove. Then I went all over vessel to make sure that the crew were in boats and no one left behind – looked over port side to tell the Mate to cast off but he had already done so. Then went down ladder to starb'd boat and left ship.

Weather clearing and stopped snowing. Observed 3 German destroyers. Hailed [to] port boat but they made for Narvik.

Similarly, the Narvik community were awakened by the sounds of gun fire and the shaking of their homes. At first some thought it was the dynamiting in a nearby ironworks but then another explosion told them it was something different, it was from the sea. People gathered together, a soldier ran past, but could not answer their queries, shouting back, "Too much fog." German soldiers appeared with mounted machine guns, swastika flags started to fly from official buildings. The Mayor having reached the City Hall was told by the caretaker that he had witnessed, hundreds of German soldiers marching up from the harbour and jostling with Norwegian soldiers. It became apparent that Colonel Sundlo in charge of the Norwegian Army in the Narvik region had surrendered his troops and had ordered the men to remain in the barracks. However, some officers and men had refused to obey the order and had escaped to the mountains.

The Germans in an attempt to justify their attack started putting up posters and handing out pamphlets. Kindly translated from Norwegian to English by 'Norland Rode Kors Krigsminnemuseum – Narvik.'

"Announcement"
To Norwegian soldiers and Norwegian people."

Against the sincere will of the German people England and France declared war on Germany in September last year.

This is the reason why England has continuously infringed Norwegian and Danish territorial waters.

For lack of pretexts threats have been forwarded that German use of Norwegian and Danish territorial waters no longer will be tolerated. All preparations have been made to take up positions on the Norwegian coast.

The greatest warmonger of this century, Mr. Churchill has openly declared that legal formalities will not stop him. He has prepared the attack on Norwegian and Danish coasts. Some days ago he was appointed Commander-in-Chief of the British forces.

The German government cannot tolerate that a new combat area is being established in accordance with the wishes of English and French warmongers.

The Norwegian and the Danish governments have known these plans for some time, and their attitude is no secret for the German government. They are not willing to, nor capable of rendering effective resistance against an English attack.

Germany has therefore decided to forestall the English attack and to protect Norwegian and Danish neutrality as long as the war lasts.

It is not the intention of the German government to establish strategic positions, but to hinder the development of Scandinavia to a war theatre.

Because of this, big German military forces have from early this morning taken into possession important military targets in Norway and Denmark. Agreement about these precautions are now being discussed between the German and Norwegian governments. These agreements shall secure the maintenance of Norway as kingdom that army and fleet are to be kept, and Norwegian freedom and independence secured.

Until the termination of these negotiations, it is expected that army and fleet show understanding for this, also that people and local authorities show good will and avoid any resistance, passive or active. To use means of force will be useless. All military and county centres are therefore requested to contact the German commandants.

People are requested to continue their daily routine and keep the public peace.

From now on the German army and fleet will take care of the security of the country against English infringement.

The German Commodore
"VON FALKENHORST"

By now the Germans had got wind of the young British journalist Giles Romilly and that he was staying at the Hotel Royal. "German soldiers, humped like tortoises using enormous packs, struggled up the slope, and halted at the hotel. A swastika flag was run up on a nearby post. I watched from the window of my locked bedroom, outside of which stood a soldier who said, pleasantly, '*Das ist pech fur sie*' (This is bad luck for you)".

Per and Signe Askim. [Per Askim's unpublished memoirs.]

Captain Askim's wife, Signe remained at the Hotel Royal awaiting any news of survivors from the sunken ships. She wrote, "I was feverishly packing suitcases, all the lovely dresses of which I was so proud, the silver fox furs [...] I was in a daze. Sometimes I gave way to tears, but I knew from experience that people don't do that in moments of crisis. Later that morning there was a knock on the door and Doctor Waaler came in. 'Have you heard the news?' he asked. 'Yes, I know, *Norge* is gone down.' 'No I don't mean that, your husband's alive! Get yourself up to the hospital and you can see him.' 'He's alive, you mean he's alive?!' I exclaimed, and threw my arms around him. I shall never forget the warmth in his eyes, which were filled with tears."

There was no media announcement in Germany about the sinking but rumours were rife in Wilhelmshaven. Frau Bohme, wife of the *Anton Schmitt*'s Captain, found out what she could from Headquarters and then toured the naval town on her bicycle to confront and reassure the ship's company's families. The interest taken by a Captain's wife for the ship's crew could be a priceless ingredient for morale. Similarly, Irene Courage, wife of the Captain of *Havock* was another such, among many, and a great favourite of officers and men. But there was no bicycling for her; she was ill and would not live to see her men again. Her loss would shake them more than the battle.

It did not take Signe Askim long to put on her coat, and hat in hand, "[...] passed a group of Germans in the foyer and out the door [...] I must have passed a number of Germans, but none of them took any notice of me. There was only one thought in my mind – that my husband was alive."

The Narvik hospital was high above the town, when Signe arrived she was confronted by the corridors being packed with wounded men. "I found myself surrounded by people I knew and loved [...] Tears streamed down my cheeks and every time I saw someone I knew, I exclaimed, Oh, I am so glad! Thank God you're alive too! [...] One of them, his head swathed in bandages, came over to me, and said, "I'm from the *Norge* as well." I gave him a hug too." The doors of the wards were open and she could see that all the beds were full.

Captain Sandved, second in command on the *Norge* came over to her and took her to her husband. "I took out my handkerchief, wiped my tear-stained cheeks and went in. There were two beds occupied by men I didn't know and another one surrounded by a tall screen. I took a cautious look behind it, and there was my husband, deathly pale and with his face all cuts and bruises. His eyes were closed. I hardly dared to breathe. Was he dead after all? Slowly he opened his eyes. I stepped closer. He gazed at me intently and his lips moved in an attempt to speak. I sat down beside him on the bed and laid my cheek against his. 'What did they manage to do ashore?' he asked, his voice barely audible. 'Nothing,' I answered. 'There was nothing they could do.'"

The following day after the demise of *Eidsvold* and the *Norge* and the arrival of the Germans, the heavy clouds mixed with the smoke coming off the smouldering wrecks in the harbour and the bombed houses. It whirled around the town, making its way up towards the surrounding mountains. For Fru Martha Hagen and her son Magne who were sitting in the front room of their white-painted two-storey house, it was a reminder that war had reached their country. [The account of Fru Martha Hagen is recorded in an excellent 1960s book written by Johan Waage which focused on the overall perspective of the 'Narvik Campaign', which is the actual title. Johan provides a very good insight on how the German occupying forces and the battles for their town affected the citizens.]

Here Fru Martha Hagen begins her story, she remembered how six months previously when the war had just begun that whilst doing her shopping she heard the gossip going around about the poor Polish people. The woman behind the counter was saying, "When they bomb a village from the air, they don't know who's living in the houses underneath. Those bombs kill anyone who gets in their sights. There are pictures of Polish villages in the papers – you can see for yourself." Fru Martha retorts, "I don't look at things like that, I've got two children in bed upstairs, a boy and a girl. I've quite enough to worry about as things are." The woman went on, "The worst thing of it is, that the Germans put out those pictures themselves. They glory in their wickedness! They're trying to frighten us out of defending ourselves if they should ever take it into their heads to attack us."

Fru Martha Hagen, later realises how she got it completely wrong when she replied, "We'll never have war here, there isn't a chance of that!"

She was now obviously in a highly nervous state and had begun writing a letter to her daughter, Liv, who lived away. In it she attempted to describe the recent terrifying events:

"Yesterday morning I was awoken by an explosion. Half a sleep as I was, I thought that they were blasting up at the works, and seeing that it was not yet 5 o'clock, I began, still half awake, to wonder whether it was the 1st or the 17th of May. But I realised that these were not ceremonial salutes, so early in the morning. At last it occurred to me that it was no business of mine, and, since I was still very tired, I tried to get some sleep again and not to worry about what might have happened. Then I was almost thrown out of bed by a frightful explosion. I got to my feet and I heard Magne calling to Solveig in her room: 'Take it easy! It's only a bit of shooting down by the harbour.'

I heard Magne get up and go up into the attic. Then he went downstairs, and I heard him talking to people in the street. Afterwards he came up to my room. 'There's been a battle down at the harbour!' he said. 'People are saying that the Germans have captured it!'

I was so flabbergasted that I could only say, 'For pity's sake! We've got a war right outside our door!' I still couldn't realise what had happened to us. I thought that there must have been some fighting and that one side had chased the other all the way into Narvik harbour.

But after Magne had been out again and returned he said, 'It's quite true... they say that the Germans have captured the whole town!'

'You mustn't believe everything you hear,' I answered, and got up. It was half-past five. First of all I went into Solveig to calm her, and then I went down to make some coffee. Magne came in once more. 'Yes, it's perfectly true,' he said. 'We've got German soldiers outside the door now!'

I looked out of the window, and there they were, Heaven help me, four of them, two outside and Maud's door and two outside ours. I rushed up to Solveig to tell her about it in the best way I could, but she thought I was joking. 'It's a pity I'm not fit, otherwise I would go down to have a look at them myself – I expect they're good-looking boys.'

And I must admit they were good-looking boys, one must grant them that, all Austrians. Magne went out and chatted to them and asked whether they had come to shoot us. They replied that of course they did not mean to shoot their 'Norwegian comrades,' and that they had only come to protect us.

'What about when the British come?' Magne asked. 'They won't come – our Air Force will see to that.'

They did not mention that hundreds of 'Norwegian comrades' were already at the bottom of the harbour and off Framnesodden. At the moment the firing ceased, and we had no more of it that day.'

Returning back to 'Operation Wilfred' and Marshal Soult: "The minelaying destroyers having left for home escorted part way by *Hostile*, the four other *H* ships made for Vestfjord which led to the port of Narvik. We arrived there during the forenoon of the 9th April and because of intelligence reports from Admiralty to Captain D2, which told of German units occupying Narvik, it was decided to go up the fjord at noon. Attack the German units and the harbour batteries then land 25 men and one officer from each ship, to take the town. The intelligence reports were so conflicting that Captain 'D2' decided to send his Paymaster Lt Stanning and the torpedo officer, Lt Heppel to the Pilot Station at Tranøy to gather what information they could."

At the sharp end where the crucial decisions were being made we return to '*Hardy*' and Lt Paymaster Geoffrey Stanning who was not a seaman officer, however, he was Captain Warburton-Lee's secretary amongst other duties. He took notes of decisions and orders taken, when an encrypted signal is received or needed to be sent then he had the code books. He would know what was in his Captain's mind before any other officer on board.

Here is part of Stanning's personal account at this moment in time. "[The Captain] sent for me while I was having lunch and said he was thinking of calling at the pilot station at Tranøy to see if that was occupied by the Germans, or whether they had any information that might be useful to us. [...] We decided that I should go in the skimmer, as it might be possible to escape fast in it if the place was occupied by Germans [...] We arrived off Tranøy at about 1600 and clutching a chart I got into the starboard sea boat. Just as I was going, 'Torps' (Torpedo Officer Lt Heppel) came and suggested that he might come too which I was only too glad of for his considerable moral and physical support. We [with a signal man] landed on the nearest point of land and told the boat's Coxswain to go round to the pier which we could see in the little harbour.

"We could see the inhabitants, mostly men, coming down to the pier, but there did not seem to be any Germans as they were all strolling along in the most nonchalant fashion. After getting fairly near to them we found that we were on an island separated from the land by about fifty yards of sea, so we had to call up the boat again and go to the pier in it. We went ashore at the pier and walked up to the crowd of about twenty to thirty men and boys, some of whom spoke English to a certain extent."

One of those present was the assistant lighthouse keeper Erling Andreassen and his thirteen-year-old son Torbjorn. Torbjorn many years later as an adult recounts, "All day Monday and throughout the night into Tuesday 9 April, a fresh to strong wind had been blowing, interspersed with flurries of snow. My father went on duty at two o'clock that night to relieve the other keeper, Ner. At about half past three, in the grey light of dawn, he came and woke my mother and me and beckoned us over to the kitchen window to see something quite extraordinary. Just disappearing into a snow shower was a warship heading up the fjord towards Narvik. My father told us that there had been more ships heading into the fjord at high speed."

Stanning, "We asked them whether they had seen any Germans and they said they had seen five German destroyers going towards Narvik that morning; when asked how large they were they said: 'Larger than that one', pointing to *Hardy*. We suggested one of them might like to come and pilot us to Narvik, but their refusal was definite and unanimous. [...] we drew pictures in the snow of Narvik and its harbour [...] Another man then said he had seen a submarine go up towards Narvik and that he was sure the place was mined. A small boy said he had seen six destroyers not five as the other man had said. It never crossed our minds then that there could have been six and five, making eleven in all. They asked if we intended to attack Narvik and when we gave a non-committal answer, said we ought to go and get some more ships before we tried."

Stanning ordered the signalman to give Warburton-Lee a provisional summing up. It was witnessed by eleven year old Olav Elsbak, "A sailor with two flags walked out onto the edge of the pier and semaphored a message out to the destroyer waiting beyond the light." It was an impressive sight for an eleven-year-old boy who had just learned the alphabet – and a lesson for life.

Stanning, "On our way back I saw we had four ships with us and found that *Hostile* had arrived. When we got on board we explained the situation to 'Wash' and discussed the thing thoroughly in the chart house".

Throughout the 9th of April, signals were sent back and forth between Captain Warburton-Lee, the Admiralty and senior officers at sea in the battle groups. For now it is sufficient to state that the following two significant signals are ones which the crew members would always remember.

Captain Warburton-Lee had sent a signal to the Admiralty, which read, 'Norwegians report Germans holding Narvik in force, also six destroyers and one U-boat are there and channel is possibly mined. Intend attacking at dawn – high water = 1751/9th'. The reply from Mr Churchill, First Lord of the Admiralty, was as follows: 'I leave it to you to decide what action to take. You are the sole judge, but whatever you do, I shall back your decision to the limit'. [51]

Captain Nicholas' diary continues.

Time about 5.30 am. A few survivors of the Norwegian 'man of war' picked up by German boats. Accounts say later about 28? None alive visible while we were in lifeboats. Landed alongside Norwegian ships lifeboat. On landing observed German destroyers come alongside and discharge soldiers, other soldiers discharged by boats from another German destroyer. Town soon taken over by German troops who also took battery and disowned garrison of about 300 men. Put crew up at 'Sailors Home' and took Mate with me to find out what was what. Found Germans in charge of the British Vice Consulate and went to Hotel Royal to see British Consul. Found Germans had established Headquarters there, no sign of Consul. Later in the day went down to the loading quay and tried to go on board the S/S 'Romanby', found German soldiers in charge. So went back to 'Sailors Home'.

Norwegian people seem to be left alone by the Germans, except commandeering motor lorry's etc. Counted 8 German destroyers. As they discharged their soldiers they proceeded outside Narvik.

The two *Hardy* officers having gone over their estimated time at the pilot station returned to brief the Captain D2.

Stanning continues, "It was a most thorny situation. We had been told to attack Narvik and therefore must do so unless there were urgent and very strong reasons against it. Although the Admiralty obviously had no idea how strong the enemy forces were in Narvik, to ask for further instructions would be delaying the operation to an unreasonable extent; and we also had a feeling that possibly our operation at Narvik had been timed to fit in with some other undertaking further down the coast, and any delay on our part might possibly prejudice someone else's success or even safety.

---

51   There was a hidden code for the terminology in signals learnt by naval officers. If the junior ranking officer sent a signal to his superior with the wording 'Intend', unless otherwise 'counter ordered', it would be done; and the Junior Officer is not seeking a reply. Hence, naval custom was, in signals you never state 'Propose' when you can 'Intend', and never request for guidance.

"But whether the Admiralty would consider the extremely grave risk of five modern destroyers justifiable in view of the new information seemed doubtful. On the other hand, our information was not necessarily reliable and as the Admiralty had given us specific information, it was reasonable to suppose they knew better. We already had experience of the unreliability of local information when we were in the South Atlantic; when one day we [*Hardy* and two destroyers] were variously reported as two tankers and a submarine, six destroyers and two cruisers. Someone reminded the Captain of this".

At the time the rest of the flotilla commanding officers were unaware of the ongoing developments. Captain Warburton-Lee had a dilemma, if, as ordered he decided to go onto Narvik and failed in his task, with the loss of part of his flotilla, it could have been seen by his superiors that he was wrong to go in when he knew there was considerable opposition. Alternatively, should he have decided to withdraw, questions would have been asked as to why, on unreliable information from the pilot station (including a boy). Especially when his superiors had given him specific intelligence and he had no reasons to doubt. As Stanning states, "He spent a most unhappy half hour in which, to my mind, he more than earned his VC."

In the meantime, on *Hardy* and the rest of the flotilla, expectant 'Landing Party' platoons were getting themselves sorted out. As explained by a crew member on *Hardy*, "We had finished our packing and only had two more things to do. A last letter home just in case, to be left with a pal, then a cup of neat Navy rum to cheer us on our way. Everybody was ready for the off, we queued at the galley for the rum. I was second [in the queue], I drank mine, but before the next chap could get hold of his cup the 'Officer of the Watch' came in shouting, 'No more rum, Chef, the orders have been changed, the job's off till midnight!' I staggered down to the messdeck with my pack and not having had any sleep for forty-eight hours, got my head down on a mess stool and slept until the next watch, which was the 'First Dog' at 1600 hours, not long really, three-and-a-half hours."

Geoffrey Stanning, with his colleague officers, was in the vicinity of the charthouse: "We all waited about, quite unable to help him as it was a decision which he alone could make and that without encouragement or advice from us. He decided, as we had been hoping, to go on with the operation. I went straight away to cypher a message to the Admiralty. In which he gave the information 'Torps' and I had obtained at Tranøy and said he intended to attack at dawn, high water. The reason for the postponement was partly that we had spent a fair time off Tranøy and though there was still time to get up to Narvik that night, it would be much better to go up before dawn and get there when there was more chance of surprise". [52]

Captain Nicholas' Diary – same day, Tuesday 9th April, in the evening.

About 5.30 pm. Germans visited 'Sailors Home' and informed 'Matron' that German officers from destroyers will be billeted at 'Home'. Had tea at 'Home'. During the day observed German shifting cargo ships from alongside Ore berth to centre of harbour, three destroyers laying behind the merchant ships and using these as a screen in case of attack. I considered all things, our position as Britishers, the Arctic conditions prevailing and came to the conclusion that the best protection I could give my crew, was to put ourselves in the German Commanders care. This I did about 8 pm when it was getting dusk. The Commandant first decided to intern us on board our own vessel but after consultations the German Harbour Master decided to keep us ashore for the night. We were then marched off to a school which had been commandeered. Here we met the crew of the 'Romanby' who informed us that the crew of the 'Riverton' was also in one of the school rooms. We just lay down on the floor and tried to sleep. Mr G. B. Romilly a Daily Express reporter joined us.

Also that evening, Giles Romilly was seen by a German lieutenant in a forage cap [a field cap worn by Wehrmacht and SS, based on the Alpine Troops ski cap] who spoke good English. He had a face that would frighten a lot of people but seemed to have good manners. He ordered coffee and food for Romilly and gave the guard a cup also. The lieutenant began, "I never thought that I should live to see another war between Britain and Germany. I lived in France for ten years I became so fond of it. But I suppose the truth is, a great country like Germany could not be held back forever. [...] We think we know that we are right to fight against the Jewish capital and against plutocracy."

At that Romilly with his overcoat and Swedish fur hat, carrying his suitcase, followed the lieutenant downstairs where the reception area was

---

52   An attack at dawn and high tide would take them over any possible laid mines and the sun would be in the eyes of the enemy at the time of attack.

crowded with German Wehrmacht officers. Described by Romilly, "A sprinkling of majors and colonels, Iron Crosses and monocles, and a dash of claret-collared, hawk-featured general." An 'elegant' and thin looking major was amongst a gang of men in all sorts of strange attire, whilst apparently being confronted by a tall, tired-looking man who seemed to be the leader. The man speaking in slow and precise English did not appear to be getting his message over." The man described was Captain David Nicholas. The lieutenant wearing the forage cap, with Romilly nearby, having heard what the Englishman was saying intervened. In a loud voice, so everybody in the hall could hear, the lieutenant explained to the major, "They are part of the crew of an English steamer. They want to make themselves prisoners, Herr Major."

Of course the lieutenant was playing to the crowd perhaps hoping it would improve his chances of quick promotion, by getting the response he wanted from his superior comrades; most of whom were in raptures of laughter. Although it was not to the liking of the now annoyed looking gang of merchant seaman who had to hold their tongues. The German harbour-captain on his way out of the hall shouted out also laughing, "Part of a crew! Where's the other part?" The Major answered, "They rowed to another district of the town, Herr Hafenkapitan." "Ha! We catch 'em! We shoot 'em and hang them!" However, the harbour-captain's jovial remarks in English seemed to restore the spirits of the captive merchant seaman. It would not be long before Romilly met Captain Nicholas and his crew.

Stanning continues his observations at the command level. "I don't think the operation orders were changed to an appreciable extent, but the ships were given the gist of the situation as it now was and told the new time of the attack.

"This was an ideal time, before returning back down the fjord, for Captain Warburton-Lee to devise his 'Tactical Plan' which would then be passed on to the commanding officers of the other four destroyers. These were sent in separate signals".

Tactical Plan.

1.   Ships are to be at action stations from 0030. When passing Skredneset, *Hardy* will pass close to shore and order a fine line of bearing. Thereafter ships are to maintain narrow quarter line to starboard so that fire from all ships is effective ahead.

2. Germans may have several destroyers and a submarine in vicinity, some probably on patrol. Ships are to engage all ships' targets immediately and keep a particular look out for enemy who may be berthed in inlets. On approaching Narvik, *Hardy*, *Hunter* and *Havock* engage enemy ships or shipping inside harbour with guns and torpedoes.
   Hotspur engage ships to northwest of Framnes, and the Framnes battery if firing. *Hostile* assist on either targets. Prepare to make smoke for cover and to tow disabled ships.

3. If opposition is silenced, landing parties from all ships except *Hotspur* make for Ore Quay unless otherwise ordered. *Hardy*'s First Lieutenant in charge.

4. Details of batteries as in Admiralty message on pp. 42/43.

5. Ships are to operate ASDICs whenever possible and attack any submarine.

6. Additional signal to withdraw will be one Red and one Green Verey light from *Hardy*.

7. Half outfit of torpedoes (four) to be fired unless target warrants more destroyer depth settings to be used. (6 ft and 8 ft, alternate torpedoes.)

8. In order to relieve congestion of movements all ships when turning to fire torpedoes or opening are to keep turning to port if possible. Watch adjacent ships, keep moderate speed.

9. Additional communications. Set watch on:
   • 2800 kc/s on remote control.
   • Fire Control Wave. (For concentrating firing; not used). [53]

These Tactical Orders by Captain Warburton-Lee were later seen as concise, thorough and clear instructions, when taking into account the up to date intelligence available at the time. Although, those highly qualified and well versed in naval warfare strategies may suggest some probable deficiencies were omitted.

Not only Captain Warburton-Lee had issued his Orders, but previously that afternoon Kommandore Bonte had sent a signal to his ten Zerstörers. Here translated into English:

---

53 British destroyers unlike their opponents had not yet been fitted with voice radio. This circuit was operated by a Morse key on the bridge and used for rapid ships manoeuvring and action signals, usually in the form of groups from the Fleet Signal Book.

Captain Warburton-Lee VC. [John Warburton-Lee collection.]

Commander destroyers.   9. of April 1940.

SECRET
To all destroyers.
Short Letter
Order for 9. and 10. of April.

Refuelling in harbour of Narvik in order; 3 D.flotilla, 4. D.flotilla (Oil delivery over the sides of the tanker only.)

Anchor positions through the night:

Harbour of Narvik: "Heidkamp", "Ludemann", "Schmitt", "Roeder", "Kunne".

Ballangen bight: "*Thiele*", "Bernd von *Arnim*".

Elvegard: "Zenker", "Giese", "Koellner".

Positions to be established latest before nightfall.

State of Preparedness:

a. War guard, good watch of fjord entrance for enemy forces and Norwegian submarines.

b. Immediate preparedness, 2 boilers.

All ammunition for rifles, heavy MGs, light MGs, pistols down to 10% of stock to be handed over to the army. Also light MGs if at hand, and hand grenades down to 25% of stock.

Commander destroyers

Back on board Hunter and the other destroyers, having been updated with Captain D2's decision, whilst there must have been anticipation there was also a spreading feeling of excitement. Marshal Soult explains, "We turned away from land and headed out to sea, trying to stooge around until the time came to approach the Vestfjord, for what was to be a surprise attack. The journey up Vestfjord started at midnight with *Hunter* following *Hardy* with the other ships behind [in line ahead]."

During this anxious time Captain Warburton-Lee was pleased to welcome reinforcements by the way of the returning *Hostile* back safely with the flotilla. He turned seawards to await the hour at which he calculated he must turn back to arrive off Narvik at dawn. However, U-boat U-51 had sighted the flotilla on its course away to open sea. As you will read this would be a defining moment, if the venture to challenge the enemy at Narvik is to be successful or not.

Marshal Soult, "It was fortunate that *Hardy* had a good Navigation Officer, Lt Commander Gordon-Smith on board. This was because a trip in total darkness up any of the Norwegian fjords was a very hazardous one, but going up that particular one it was more so. With the added problem of a blinding snowstorm, the uncertainty of whether the fjord was mined and, whether the Germans had taken control of the shore batteries, making it far more dangerous than usual."

On this evening of the 9th April, not only was it a momentous occasion for the Royal Navy but also a few hundred nautical miles south an incident occurred which was to become a crucial part for any later British tactical hopes of success. The previously mentioned German oil tanker *Kattegat* in preparation for her supply mission, after three days of sailing had made it to the pilot station at Kopervik in Western Norway on 6 April. It was scheduled to arrive at Narvik on 9 April. The *Kattegat* and *Jan Wellem* were the two tankers the Germans relied upon to quickly refuel the Zerstörers and then enable them to escape back to Germany before the Royal Navy could trap and sink them. However, the Captain of the *Kattegat* had been warned of a British naval mine field in the Vestfjorden and refused to continue, choosing instead to anchor up in Sandlagbukta, south Norway.

The Royal Norwegian Naval Fishery Protection and Coast Guard vessel *Nordkapp*, during her patrol had had a signal exchange with the *Kattegat*. The pilots who had entered *Nordkapp* into a port mooring reported that the tanker's thirty-nine man crew were all armed and wearing naval uniforms. Hence, the Captain of the *Nordkapp* considered it would be nigh on impossible to make a boarding and seize the ship, especially as his own twenty-man crew had a total of only four rifles amongst them; and even if it was possible, controlling the larger number of German sailors in the port of Bodo while being out gunned would have been far too risky.

Subsequently, the Captain of *Nordkapp*, in view of the 'aggressive' messages received from the *Kattegat* sent a short signal telling the crew to abandon ship within ten minutes or face the consequences. As there was no reaction, a warning shot was fired from *Nordkapp*, then as still no response, four rounds were fired into the enemy's 'waterline'. The German crew having opened the ships valves the *Kattegat* sank quickly. There were no German casualties; thirty-four became POWs, whilst another five managed to escape into the hills.

Of course, the Admiralty in London were not immediately made aware of this incident and if they had been, at this stage they may not have known the significance of the potential advantage for the 2nd Destroyer Flotilla as they went to meet their foe.

Giles Romilly under escort moved out of the Hotel Royal through the snow to a school building and was directed up a staircase where he came face to face with another guard. Pushed into a room and the light switched on he is greeted by deep snores mixed with groans and a number of expletives you would not like your grandmother to hear. When his eyes adjusted he was confronted by a large body of men lying on the wooden floor, utilising parts of their clothing as pillows and blankets. Next to each of them was a suitcase. It was a classroom and all the desks were stowed together on top of one another. Romilly recalls a voice: "'What ship are you off, brother?' I answered that I was a journalist, and the word seemed to mock me. 'Room for you here, Journ'y!'"

As mentioned, U-boat U-51 having witnessed the British flotilla apparently moving back out to open sea, Kapitanleutnant Knorr relayed this back to Kommodore Bonte. It appears this resulted in some complacency. Korvettenkapitan Bohme on *Anton Schmitt* awaiting its turn to refuel, went aft to the warmth of his day cabin. At least he made an attempt to be ready if necessary for action, turning in fully clothed and with his life-jacket over his head. Unlike one junior officer on *Erich Giese* seen putting on his pyjamas and had to be admonished by his senior. Bonte, himself did not set a good example. Although the journey from Germany had taken its toll and night time tends to reduce a persons' mental energy, once he received the signal from U-51, this seems to have led to a false sense of security. So he too went to his bunk, feeling confident his orders to the other Zerstörers had covered every contingency, and quickly went into a deep sleep.

The *Wilhelm Heidkamp* now anchored in the centre of the harbour and hidden behind merchant ships, was seen as bounty for occupying forces. The naval leader now snoring away in a secure bed, was followed by the off watch ships company. The young officer, Karl Raeder had just got into his pyjamas, already feeling 'battle' weary, when the artillery officer sharing his cabin opened the cabin door. "He demanded to know if I was mad. I oughtn't to take off my clothes in case the alarm went. So I dressed again, tumbled into bed and slept the sleep of the dead."

In more comfortable surroundings Leutnant Albert Bach and his fellow staff officers had dined well at the Hotel Royal. It had been a tiring day to say the least, so they retired to their bedrooms, satisfied of how events had gone so far. "I was happy and grateful at having survived the voyage and once again being able to go to sleep in a warm hotel bed."

Back in London the Admiralty staff also had an eventful day with many meetings and were also ready for their beds but feeling more secure than the enemy in Narvik. The private secretary to Churchill said, "I was very worried about Winston, he was knocked out, and I had to manoeuvre him into bed."

Navigating the Vestfjord

Those readers who have already read my first book *Attack at Dawn* will realise that I have had to repeat small parts in this book. The reason being that firstly, some readers will not have read the earlier book and secondly, after the first battle the *Hunter* casualties were such that there were fewer survivors to provide accounts.

The five ships were now entering into literally unknown waters. None of the seaman officers on the bridge of the five ships had ever previously navigated the Vestfjord, let alone under the present weather conditions and darkness. During the hazardous four hours' journey to meet with their enemy, it was crucial the five destroyers kept in contact by wireless telegraphy. In my father's documents, I found a copy of the W/T log recorded on board *Havock*. There was no mention from where the copy came. But it may have been provided by one of the officers or telegraphists on board at the time and my father was given it at one of the Narvik Association's reunions. *Havock* was fourth in line and most of the signals orders were sent by Captain Warburton-Lee (D2). These were to all the four ships identified as D F (Destroyer Flotilla). The Captains of the ships would have relayed their messages or replies in 'Morse Code' via the bridge Telegraphist. What follows are the communications once the flotilla started their journey, deep into the fjord.

0044 (Time) 2nd D F from D2 – Proceed at 12 knots.

Noise was kept down to a minimum but important final tasks had to be completed. One of these would be to make sure secret papers and cryptographic material procedures for disposal are reinforced. For example, to make sure the person responsible for ensuring that the safe aft should be dumped in an oil fuel tank, would be briefed again.

0106 2nd D F from D2 – Proceed at 20 knots.

0146 2nd D F from D2 – Proceed at 12 knots.

At this point, there appeared to be another vessel ahead because *Hardy* went 'hard a starboard'. This resulted in the ships getting out of line in a disorganised manner. Shortly afterwards a ferry lit up like a Christmas tree came out of the fog: *Hostile* had to rapidly veer off. It seemed at the time that she may have had to navigate her own way to Narvik.

Whether on the upper deck or below, no differently than the other ships crew. *Hunter's* crew was feeling tense and not in control of its destiny. In the boiler room the Petty Officer Stoker handled the steam valves and his Leading Stoker the oil fuel valves, as if they were wearing kid gloves. When they went to action stations the Engine Artificer had checked and ran the generator to make sure they had emergency lighting if it was needed. At the 'Repair Parties', firefighting or flooding gear was being checked and rechecked. A Leading Torpedoman, in charge of any electrical equipment and lighting looked over the breaker systems. If there was any damage in action then the power in that part of ship would need to be isolated, as well as redirecting supplies from the 'forward' switch board to other 'after' services still workable. Those responsible for First Aid made sure the contents in their medical bags were topped up.

0215 *Hotspur* from D2 – Are you alright?

0216 D2 from *Hotspur* – Yes, you are just out of sight.

The ships now moving out of line, D2 was particularly concerned about *Hotspur's* repositioning.

0221 2nd D F from D2 – My course and speed 075 degrees, 12 knots.

The fjord was narrow in parts, no shore batteries seen so far. The new ASDIC sets were being used to help in the navigation. These gave soundings off the fjord shore line. For the majority of the transit the ships could not see very far as the snow was now coming down thickly. In fact, visibility, in naval terms, was one and a half cables, equivalent to 300 yards.

0232 *Hotspur* from D2 – I am about to pass Hamnes Holm abeam to starboard.

0233 D2 from *Hotspur* – In touch.

0234 2nd D F from D2 – Turn in succession to 095 degrees.

0239 *Hotspur* from D2 – Are you in touch?

0240 D2 from *Hotspur* – Yes.

0242 2nd D F from D2 – Good luck, let them have it.

0249 D F from D2 – Make your call signs if in touch.

0250 – Call signs.

Another ingenious method to overcome the snowstorms was receiving 'bearings' from the radio stations 'ROST' and 'Bodo'. The snow also provided problems for the guns and torpedoes. Since the snow kept piling up and the breech blocks froze up. If the traversing gear on the tubes got blocked up, this would cause a problem when they came to turn them onto a port or starboard bearing. The Royal Navy still had the older type of torpedo launcher, which could only fire in one position. Therefore ninety degrees outboard from their normal steaming site of fore and aft. However, the more modern German destroyer's tubes were able to be placed in various firing positions.

Onwards the flotilla steamed through the dark, 'Arctic' night, closed up for action stations, huddled around their weaponry. Foremost tubes trained to starboard; after tubes trained to port, firing cartridges inserted but 'ready' pushes withdrawn. No noise, no talking, just the gentle swish of water against the ship's side. Gun's crews, closed up. Described by one sailor "as silent as the grave".

The following is described by a crew member on *Hardy*, although there would have been similar feelings on the other four ships. "Occasionally, a jut of land was sighted, now and then a tiny blue flash of a signal for the next ship astern, otherwise total blackness. A whispered message came through – 'we are fifteen minutes from Narvik'. Nerves were getting tensed up and straining our eyes we could just make out a snow covered shoreline.

"The orders were to sink all ship's targets and needless to say everyone was 'on their toes' the whole time. It was bitterly cold and where we were moving around in a vain effort to keep warm, we were forming circles of ice on the deck. Rum and tea were brought around and did we need it? Generally a quiet atmosphere surrounded the ship as was only to be expected in such a tense situation".

All the ships had an open-top bridge, leaving the officers and men more exposed to the atrocious weather conditions than those in other parts of ship. At the gun turrets, there were still difficulties to cope with such as, having to bring red-hot pokers out of the galley to thaw out the breech blocks. However, the tactics to transit up the fjord as silently as possible, at such a speed as to enable the flotilla to arrive at the entrance of Narvik harbour as the dawn broke, appeared to be working.

During my spell on the staff at Dartmouth Royal Naval College in 1977, I remember the Officer Cadets being emphatically reminded that 'one of the first principles of war is surprise'.

0330 2nd D F from D2 – Turn in succession to 080 degrees.

My father Cyril, in his account mentions, "Dawn in that part of the world came up at approximately 0345. We arrived outside the harbour entrance at 0350, once again on time. Through the swirling mist and snow those of us on the upper deck by now frozen stiff with cold and immobility for nearly four hours, could just see the inside of the harbour."

Peter Dickens (page 56) describes, "Gordon-Smith of *Hardy*, and the navigating officer of the *Diether von Roeder*, both advised their Captains to turn towards Narvik Harbour having calculated that they were in exactly the same position at exactly the same time, 0340. The *Hardy* however, was somewhat to the south and west of her dead-reckoning position, perhaps owing to an over correction for the flood stream and some leeway from the now north easterly wind. The two ships turned course 110 degrees and kept perfect station on one another, at the most one and half miles apart and probably less, totally unaware of the fact."

0342 2nd D F from D2 – Turn in succession to 110 degrees.

0344 2nd D F from D2 – Am steering for entrance of Narvik harbour.

0346 2nd D F from D2 – Form on a line of bearing 280 degrees.

Torpedoman Cyril Cope aged 18 on joining the Navy in 1936. [Ron Cope Collection]

Lt Paymaster Stanning [*Hardy*] in his account observes, "Just as the Pilot (Navigation Officer) was convinced we were there, we saw land on our port bow and more land ahead as we went on but it turned out not to be Narvik but a small inlet to the South West. We turned and went out again and went further up the main fjord, keeping the land on the starboard hand in sight. Up to now we had seen no sign of civilisation at all and what was more extraordinary, no sign at all of Germans as we had thought they would have had a destroyer patrolling the lower part of the fjord or at least a submarine anchored in the channel.

"We thought we had either passed the patrol in bad visibility or else there was none there. Several people even thought, Heppel [*Hardy*'s Torpedo Officer] and I had got hold of the wrong end of the stick at Tranøy and that there really were not many Germans at Narvik and hopes began to revive, of a landing party. But for the fact that just at that moment we saw a fishing boat lying off a small wooden pier on our starboard hand; that looked more promising and a moment later we saw a headland on the port bow which Pilot thought must be the north side of the harbour entrance. It was!"

0350 2nd D F from D2 – Proceed at 6 knots.

0352 2nd D F from D2 – Turn together 20 degrees to starboard.

0356 2nd D F from D2 – *Hostile* in touch.

0359 2nd D F from D2 – Turn together 30 degrees to port.

Stanning starts to feel the tension rising in himself and those around him. "The snow had cleared and it was getting light, we could see where we were. The fjord at this point was very wide and we increased speed a little bit, I didn't see any sign of life ashore. The fjord widened into a sort of bay. Like a hunter approaching the lion's den, we crept warily forward to what was obviously the entrance to the harbour."

0405 2nd D F from D2 – Stop engines.

Having reached their destination this order was given to confirm the correct bearing to proceed.

0406 2nd D F from D2 – Proceed at 10 knots – turn together 40 degrees to port.

0408 2nd D F from D2 – Stop engines.

0410 2nd D F from D2 – Go astern.

0411 2ⁿᵈ D F from D2 – Stop engines.

Another crewman on *Hardy*, Gunner Dougy Bourton looks in awe. "The only thing of any interest at all, as we approached Narvik, was that we went through the wash of a very large ship. We wondered what it was and we rolled quite considerably. So we were all on our toes waiting because we had been standing at action stations all this time. We had been fed soup or hot tea laced with rum, as we got nearer Narvik. This would have been close to four o'clock and the scene was as if you were looking at a stage, curtains were parted and you saw the whole harbour displayed, like a theatrical battle.

"I was the 'loading number' for No 4 Gun. I stood alongside the tray and pushed the tray forward, which contained the shell and cartridge. The cartridge was about three foot long, made of brass, with a base of 6 to 7 inches, narrowing down to 4.7 inches, where it entered the breech behind the shell."

Gunner Geoff Bailey also on *Hardy* explains his role on No 2 Gun, "Our 'faces' set, the 'gunlayer' with his eyes on the gunsights, AB (Jack) Hay ready to shove a round into the breach, the two loading numbers standing by with the second round in their arms and myself with my eyes glued to the range dial, my ears cocked to catch the slightest order from the bridge. We were ready for heaven knows what, the whole German fleet for all we knew."

0412 2ⁿᵈ D F from D2 – Turn together to 010 degrees proceed at 10 knots.

0413 2ⁿᵈ D F from D2 – Point ship to 010 degrees.

0415 2ⁿᵈ D F from D2 – Turn together to 010 degrees proceed at 10 knots.

Through the swirling mist and snow the *Hardy* crew on the upper deck could just see inside the harbour. Engines stopped whilst they waited for the other four ships to catch up. The *Hotspur* and *Hostile* were detached to engage shore batteries at Framnesodden. *Hardy* alone glided silently into the harbour. Both *Hunter* and *Havock* waited outside, across the harbour mouth, just clear of the entrance.

0416 2ⁿᵈ D F from D2 – Proceed at 6 knots.

0418 2nd D F from D2 – Turn together to 90 degrees.

0422 2nd D F from D2 – Am entering south side of harbour.

0423 2nd D F from D2 – Am turning to port follow me round.

A gentle swing to port and they nosed their way further into the harbour. To those able to see they witnessed many ships, a number flying the Nazi swastika. One of *Hardy* crew recounts, "I saw a small sailing boat with a couple of people in it, I felt like shouting to them to scram before they got hurt. I looked through the gun port and lying between them was a German destroyer making a beautiful target for our torpedoes."

0424 2nd D F from D2 – Proceed at 12 knots.

0426 2nd D F from D2 – Alarm bearing 010 degrees.

Another crew member recalls, "There was a large British iron ore ship [RMS Blythmoor]. It was obviously heavily laden, because she was so low in the water. As we came close we were able to look down on her, we could see there were two German sentries, one aft and one for'd, with guns. However, on seeing us glide towards them they scampered down hatches. They didn't fire their guns, didn't raise an alarm, Captain Warburton-Lee brought the *Hardy* alongside the merchant ship with our engines just ticking over. This obviously allowed the Captain and others on the bridge to take a good look into the harbour."

0428 2nd D F from D2 – Am turning to port, standby to fire, torpedoes starboard side.

0429 2nd D F from D2 – Near ship is British.

"There was already one ship run aground on our starboard side as we went in but there were plenty more good ones about for us to sink. Merchant ships were small fry at that moment. We were looking for destroyers and a submarine. All our guns had been unfrozen with hot oil on the way up and were loaded ready for anything. Everything seemed to be still very quiet and peaceful but that was all changed a few minutes later when we suddenly sighted a destroyer's bows, showing from behind a large whaling ship."

Dickens (page 60): "All peered intently, and none more than Heppel (Torpedo Officer) who knew that his torpedoes would be called upon the moment a target was sighted. He had trained his forward tubes to starboard and the after mounting to port so that his reaction could be instantaneous; enemy speed zero, safety pins out of the whiskered pistols, impulse cartridges inserted, stop valves open. Someone breathed, 'There they are!' and the Chief Yeoman broke out the battle ensigns already furled at the two mastheads."

Marshal Soult in the guns' director tower above the bridge, continues. "On arrival at the entrance to the harbour Captain 'D' signalled the final orders, *Hunter* then *Havock* to follow him [*Hardy*] into the harbour. The other two [*Hotspur* and *Hostile*] to keep watch outside for any intervention from ships in other parts of the fjord, and to take care of the shore batteries.

The men on the torpedo deck of *Hardy* swiftly forgot about the icy conditions and started to realise they were fast approaching their first experience of battle with the enemy. The Communications Number who had his headphones clutched tightly to his ears was gripped with excitement. The foremost tubes are waiting for further orders. "On our starboard side we saw a wonderful sight, especially to a trained gunner and torpedoman. An array of merchant ships of many nations, all taken over by the Germans by this time. Not that we stopped to ask mind you. In line with the sights on my tubes I could see two merchant ships, bow to stern, with just enough gaps in between to see an oil tanker with a German destroyer tied up to her, with fuelling pipe lines still attached. I looked to my right to see two more German destroyers, about 500 to 600 yards apart.

"The order came over the headphones; 'Cut the guard rails.' Completed and confirmed to the bridge. Then, next order, 'Stand By to open fire on foremost tubes'. Forget what else, but the 'oiler' (*Jan Wellem*) and destroyer (*Wilhelm Heidkamp*) first, then any of the other ships. The Captain had decided not to fire the guns, but to keep it as a surprise attack with torpedoes only.

"On the *Hardy* bridge. The Torpedo Officer asked permission to fire torpedoes at two destroyers which we could see alongside each other in the middle of the harbour with their bows towards the town."

Back to the foremost tubes, "Away goes the first torpedo, it passed between the two merchant ships. There is a big flash and bang, up went the destroyer (*Wilhelm Heidkamp*). No time to cheer, away go the other three torpedoes, you could clearly see them making their way through the same gap. They were also direct hits, thinking that's part of the job done. The only destroyers at that time not hit were the two being refuelled (*Hermann Kunne* and *Hans Ludemann*)."

One of the for'd *Hardy* Gun Crew becomes excited, "I heard the swish of the D.C. tin fish as it left the tube, for a second I saw its wake and then a terrific roar as the German destroyer blew up. She had been hit in the magazine, pieces blew hundreds of feet in the air and then we opened up with our guns. It was like hell let loose."

Another eyewitness account, "After the first large explosion there were many more which showed that magazines must have been hit and what must have been thousands of rounds of ammunition began to explode in the air which made a proper fireworks display. That was good beyond all expectation but even at that moment we could not help thinking with horror of the loss of life we must have caused for they were large destroyers, though we could not identify them precisely."

Peter Dickens (page 61) in researching for his book, interviewed both Lt George Heppel and Cyril Cope. He states: "Never fire torpedoes in penny numbers, was a principle well imbued in Heppel and although it was theoretically impossible to miss a stopped ship at such a ridiculously short range he launched three in a narrow fan. On the foremost tubes, Torpedoman Cope's duty was to ensure that the drill went without a hitch, which he did; but being a man of acute awareness of his surroundings he also saw the targets.

"With regard to torpedoes Nos 2 and 3 they in turn were sent on their way. It appears No 2 hit the German destroyer *Anton Schmitt* directly in a compartment adjacent to her main magazine. Cyril vividly recalls "It just blew up and the concussion and shock waves put out of action a third destroyer nearby (*Hermann Kunne*)."

Marshal Soult continues describing the action from *Hunter*. "In one of these destroyers was the Commodore of the German Naval units at Narvik, Commodore Bonte, he was killed when the torpedoes from *Hardy* blew the ship apart. This was the *Wilhelm Heidkamp*. As *Hardy* moved away after firing her torpedoes, *Hunter* took over firing hers and opened up with all guns. As the crew of a German merchant ship ran along the deck to man their guns, a little cockney called 'Charlie Gower' opened fire with the port wing Lewis gun, mowing them down as they ran".

Korvettenkapitan Erdmenger had been awakened by a shout which was put down to someone hearing a shot, but nothing could be seen. "The men were alerted by the clamour of the alarm bells", he noted. A few seconds later one of *Hardy*'s torpedoes tore through the steel plating of the hull and exploded in the aft magazine. This was followed by further explosions resulting in widespread destruction. The stern broke away and the three 15-ton guns were wrenched from their mountings and tossed into the dawn sky.

Anton Schmitt. [Theo Werner Schetller via Frank Hackney Collection]

Wilhelm Heidkamp [Tore Eggan Collection]

Paymaster Lieutenant Stanning in shock and awe recalls, "Thousands of ammunition exploded in the air, making for one enormous firework. The result far exceeded our expectations. But at the same time, we could not help thinking with horror about the loss of human life that we had caused."

Alf Jacobsen in his brilliantly researched book *Death at Dawn* states, "It seemed that the nemesis had caught up with the high ranking German officers who had so cold-bloodedly slaughtered the *Eidsvold* young sailors. Kommodore Friedrich Bonte and First Staff Officer Rudolf Heyke were both killed outright, and the man who had fired the signal pistol, Second Staff Officer Heinrich Gerlach, was severely wounded. Below deck carnage reigned. In a matter of minutes, eighty-one men died and dozens were injured [...] The ship was shrouded in suffocating smoke and sinking fast," Erdmenger wrote. [54]

As *Hardy* retreated, it was *Hunter*'s turn to attack with her guns blazing, she fired between four or eight of her torpedoes into the crowded harbour causing total chaos. Part of which was on the badly damaged *Anton Schmitt*, where the crew hearing the explosions, were awakened by what they thought was gunfire. It is recorded by the Germans that when the crew arrived on deck they thought they were being attacked from the air. Then their own ship received a salvo from *Hunter*.

Thirty-three years later, Korvettenkapitan Fritz Bohme, commanding officer of *Anton Schmitt*, would explain his experiences of those moments to the 2nd Destroyer Flotilla's veterans. Bohme had explained he had had little sleep for the previous two days, finally resting on his bunk he had managed just an hour and half of a deep sleep. He describes what happens next. "Even the *Wilhelm Heidkamp*'s devastation and outside gunfire had failed to wake me, but the hit on my ship shook me more. Springing up from my bunk, a torpedo hit the first turbine room, this caused my cabin door to jam. I was trapped."

Prior to this a member of the *Hardy* on the foremost tubes would never forget the moment. "At 0420 Narvik ceased to be a little unknown town in Norway and suddenly burst out into history of the world; because here one almighty explosion occurred. The first torpedo struck the after part of the first German destroyer, it struck the after magazine. We saw the after gun

---

54   Heinrich Gerlach not only survived his injuries but after the war eventually rose to become the Commander in Chief of the West German 'Bundesmarine'.

leave the ship altogether, curling through the air, it did a complete U-turn and landed on the fo'c'sle of its own ship. Another torpedo struck her and the ship went down."

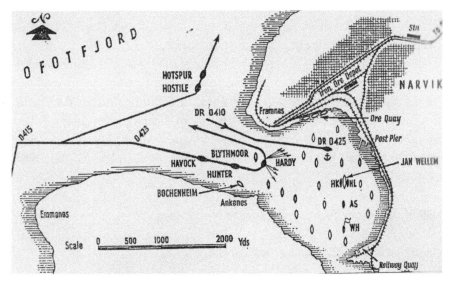

Caption: Map of first attack. [Cyril Cope Collection]

However, *Hardy's* aftermost tubes were having problems, here the Leading Torpedoman explains, "Suddenly, the order from the bridge, 'All tubes, ready starboard'. Our four 'Training Numbers' were struggling desperately to get the tubes around 180 degrees [port beam to starboard beam]. At the same time the foremost tubes were firing and all their torpedoes gone. With that all hell broke loose, as our five 4.7-inch guns opened up on targets that became visible. With our Communications Number screaming his head off, 'Ready Starboard! – Ready Starboard!' I felt completely helpless; but then the men from the other tubes saw our predicament and quickly set to pushing like hell to get those obstinate tubes into position."

The problem was due to the hard packed snow and ice on the traversing gear, they were finding it hard going time was passing. "A split second before they locked into position and I was knocking in the 'ready pushes', the Torpedo Officer in the 'torpedo control unit' had his fingers on the firing switch and the first torpedo shot out, causing the tubes to whip and the 'fish' to slightly graze the protecting stanchion. Then the tubes locked and two more missiles followed."

As one of those from the foremost tubes crew says, "Goodness knows what would have happened if it had pushed the opposite way. One target hit was a large railway jetty used for iron ore wagons to unload into ships' holds. Up went the wooden trestle logs, sleepers, train lines, wagons and iron ore. Oh, what a mess! You've never seen anything like it, we really started to cheer then, we acted like children at a pantomime."

Another eyewitness, "There was a terrible explosion together with a vivid semi-circular white flash of stars twinkling around the edge. If one could forget what that explosion contained, it could be described as being extremely beautiful. But when one thinks of sleeping men being killed outright – then it's different – perhaps though, even if they were enemy. Simultaneously with the explosions we gathered speed and opened fire with the guns."

0439 2nd D F from D2 – Am turning to Northward.

0441 *Havock* from D2 – Come fire Torpedoes.

After ten minutes the *Hunter* followed the *Hardy* out of the harbour undamaged; but the enemy's fire was beginning to kindle and De Villiers decided to use smoke to cover his withdrawal. The *Havock*, was just quarter of an hour behind *Hardy* and followed the same track round the Blythmoor. The natural visibility was no better than it had been, and now it was further reduced artificially by cordite, high explosive, and funnel smoke. Although it hampered the ship in her task it also protected her.

Lieutenant Commander Courage saw first a series of gun flashes, and then made out that they came from a destroyer alongside a merchant ship. In the harbour there was chaos, the *Hermann Kunne* moored to the port side of *Jan Wellem* had taken on 200 tons of oil. Courage decided to open fire, but for whatever reason, bad luck or bad management, no hits were scored on either of the two. When the silence of the night erupted in successive explosions Korvettenkapitan Friedrich Kothe deep in sleep hurried to the open bridge confused, not realising what had happened. "I saw numerous hits on the ships in the harbour, several of them were blown apart by explosions, while others were on fire and enveloping the surroundings in black smoke. It took several minutes for me to grasp that the shells were coming from light forces somewhere in the harbour entrance."

At this moment Kothe, was at last told that steam was on the main engines and rang down for astern power. Desperate to get under way, he ignored the oil hoses and wires. The Torpedo Gunner, Mr Leslie Millns, on *Havock* saw this happen from his action station at the tubes, and as he then received the order, 'Ready starboard', from the bridge he naturally assumed that the *Hermann Kunne* was the target. But Courage had sighted the *Anton Schmitt*, which seemed through the haze to be floating normally, and directed his Torpedo Control Officer, Lieutenant John Burfield, to sink her.

Korvettenkapitan of Anton Schmitt, Fritz Bohme. [Cyril Cope Collection] – Cyril points out, "My wife and I visited his home in 1979, he lived in Hamburg. We returned their hospitality in 1985 after attending our Association Reunion in Birmingham."]

We would say today that Burfield's triple salvo was cost affective. One torpedo hit a merchant ship; another, following the firsts track, was displaced by the explosion so that it neatly dodged the stricken ship and hit beyond her; and the third, though they were not necessarily in that order, took the *Anton Schmitt* in her second turbine room.

Bohme trapped was desperate to escape from his cabin, "I had wrenched the door open and ran to the after end of the iron deck, the ship was listing, as I was running up the slope to the port side the second torpedo arrived. I was blown over into the water but my life-jacket saved me. I saw my ship break in two and sink within a minute. I managed to swim to the Railway Quay with some of my crew." Sixty-three of the crew were killed. His wife would need her bicycle again!

Havock now had a one hundred per cent hit rate, three out of three, but she was living up to her name, there was yet more to come. The *Hermann Kunne* had dropped swiftly astern of *Jan Wellem* and only forty yards from *Anton Schmitt*, at the time Bohme remembered she had received the second hit. The explosion had jarred the *Hermann Kunne* from stem to transom and the engines seized. The *Anton Schmitt* rolled over, laying her mast gently on to the *Hermann Kunne*'s deck. Thoughtfully, a crew member took down the Captain's pendant, where later, at a convenient moment, he presented it to Bohme.

Courage held back his remaining torpedoes, to use his own words, "because the *Hunter* had hit everything in sight. As the enemy gunfire was getting hot and they had the advantage of the light, I increased speed and cleared out."

The guns on *Hardy* were firing heavily at targets. Cyril Cope at the foremost tubes, "Too close it was impossible to miss, but we were not getting anything back from the enemy. So we started our engines and slipped out of the harbour, telling other ships to go in and have a crack. This they did, firing their guns and torpedoes – then out again."

0442 D2 from *Hotspur* – Nothing to Northward.

As mentioned, *Hotspur* and *Hostile* were initially detached to engage any possible shore batteries and cover their three sister ships making their attack. At this stage the whole brave mission was carried out with the strength of the enemy unknown. Hence, because of the damage inflicted, and due to an unsuccessful response battle plans had to be rapidly modified.

A Gunner on '*Hardy's*' after gun, "We fired at everything which flew a German flag or 'Red Ensign' (British Merchants), everything then was a German ship and we did a colossal amount of damage."

There were signs that the Germans were beginning to wake up as they were beginning to fire out of the harbour, "but it seemed to be only small stuff; as it was tracer we could see it coming". Guns on the Nazi merchant ships opened fire, but it was ineffective. "We had turned around until we faced the mouth of the harbour. We came out of the harbour and swung around and slowed down for a breather."

Officer on *Hardy's* bridge: "The two ships sent up to Rombaksfjord had come back by this time and reported that there was nothing there so this time there were five ships to do the attack. We wanted to keep close to the entrance to make sure that nothing came out."

0444 *Hotspur* from D2 – Fire your torpedoes into the harbour.

Let us not forget those brave young men down below. One Stoker describes the action, "You felt more secure with the company and it helped to calm the nerves. Although at action stations nothing at first seemed to happen out of the ordinary. We were shut in the bottom of the ship, you don't know what is happening above you. The only idea you get is from the bridge wanting more steam to go faster, to go slower or to stop. Suddenly, it all changed and we knew that something was happening. We got busy doing our job. The telegraph to the Petty Officer was clanging orders. The Captain up on the bridge seemed to be manoeuvring the ship all over the place".

By the time the first three ships had moved out of the harbour, *Hostile*, was already sending salvoes at the enemy. Dickens (page 66) describes their determination and ingenuity to get their targets. *Hostile* stopped engines. "The gun-direction telescopes were opaque with snow that could not be wiped clear fast enough, but over open sights it was hardly any easier to aim. Spotting fall of shot was almost impossible so 'blind ladders' were used, groups of three salvoes fired rapidly, with an 'up' 400-yard correction between each; then the same with a 'down' correction and so on. Steady nerves and good drill resulted in the *Diether von Roeder* being hit twice, seriously, while the *Hostile* remained unscathed."

Korettenkapitan Erich Holtorf recorded: "Shortly after the alarm sounded, we took two hits in the oil tank of No 2 boiler room, a fierce fire broke out, there was a lot of smoke and flames were coming out of the gash in the hull." There was other serious damage, a shell exploded on the upper deck where an ammunition locker was hit and the contents ignited nine men lost their lives. A salvo had hit a messdeck and started a fire for'd, a number of sailors were killed. An injured man rushed on to the upper deck covered in flames and luckily survived. He had been spotted by an officer who pushed him over the ship's side, the officer then jumped in himself and pulled the man out.

0448 *Hotspur* from D2 – Stop making smoke.

As set out in Captain Warburton-Lee's 'Tactical Plan': "Prepare to make smoke for cover and to tow disabled ships." This was cover for *Hardy*, *Hunter* and *Havock* on retreating from the harbour. Thankfully, there had been no need for *Hotspur* to tow any of her sister ships. After the *Hotspur* had cleared her funnels with smoke, Captain Warburton-Lee told Commander Layman to fire torpedoes into the harbour.

0456 2nd D F from D2 – Report number of torpedoes fired.
    D2 from *Hotspur* – Four.
    D2 from Hunter – Eight.
    D2 from *Havock* – Five. [In fact it was three.]

0459 D2 from *Hostile* – None.

In the meantime, the five destroyers had formed a disorderly circle continuing to engage the enemy as each moved into position at the harbour entrance. There were naturally feelings of jubilation which echoed around the ships especially for those sailors on the upper deck able to witness the success of their endeavours. However, it soon became short lived as visibility had got very bad again. You cannot blame my father Cyril at this point saying to himself. "I thought Oh God, we have done it – it's over for us!" Another young sailor concurs, "We were in high spirits, and not one of our ships had a scratch. When the last of our ships came out, we increased speed and with guns blazing went back into the harbour, which by now looked to me like a harbour of sinking ships."

In a matter of minutes the ships were clear and out into the open fjord.

It was a chance to assess any damage the *Hardy* had received. Leading Torpedoman Bert Mason explains, "There were no casualties as far as we knew, but we noticed a few shell holes in the after funnel. 'Tansy' Lee, one of our number, picked up a small shell lying nearby. He quickly dropped it and kicked it over the ships side, as it was 'red hot'. For us, the Torpedomen, we thought it was all over as we retreated down to the entrance of the fjord. [...] It was not to be!"

Lieutenant Paymaster Geoffrey Stanning was on the bridge. "A fair amount of small stuff was being fired at us [...] We circled in front of the harbour, again firing guns at the enemy flashes, when we saw them. The enemy by this time was firing heavier stuff which we knew must come from the damaged destroyers and we were anxious to know what damage had been done; as we had heard a good many more heavy explosions but could see nothing of the result."

0501 2nd D F from D2 – Report damage to enemy seen.

0503 D2 from *Hotspur* – Two merchant ships sinking.

0504 D2 from *Hostile* – Merchant ship and destroyer observed to be hit by 4.7 shell.

0505 D2 from Hunter – Five torpedoes hit, damage to enemy destroyer not observed.

0506 D2 from *Havock* – Destroyer hit by 4.7 shell.

Peter Dickens (page 68): "To these reports could be added the *Hardy*'s torpedoing of a destroyer and a merchant ship, but the combined reports do not begin to convey an impression of the havoc actually wrought. It is no wonder that the action was continued, and that Warburton-Lee told the *Hostile*:

"0507 *Hostile* from D2 – If you can find suitable warship target, send four torpedoes in.

"It is fairly clear from this signal and his own actions that in spite of the

Admiralty's order to sink German merchant ships, Warburton-Lee considered their warships to have first priority."

The other four destroyer Captains were under no obligation to follow the Admiralty's order as it had not been made specific in Captain Warburton-Lee's 'Tactical Plan'. The outcome therefore was that *Hostile* followed *Hardy* by prioritising the German warships. *Hotspur* and *Hunter* treated all cargo vessels as legitimate targets if no enemy warship was in their sights, whilst *Havock* was known to have avoided British cargo vessels.

0509 2nd D F from D2 – Look out for torpedo tracks.

By now *Diether von Roeder* was a defeated foe and her part in the battle was nearly over. Her demise came when a compartment near to the after magazine received a direct hit which required the magazine to be rapidly flooded. Finally, she lost her main electrical power supply, and because of the heat and smoke in the for'd part of the ship, it was impossible to cut the anchor chain. Holtorf records, "The ship was blazing like a torch. Although the remaining guns were still firing away for all they were worth, I feared the ship was in danger of sinking, so I gave the order to fire all eight torpedoes."

Commander Wright, the Captain of *Hostile*, must have been frustrated waiting for the right opportunity to release the torpedoes. He probably wanted to finish off with another attack on *Diether von Roeder*, but unknown to Commander Wright, he was not aware that his salvos had caused so much damage below her decks. Just before 0500 the disabled *Diether von Roeder* and the *Hans Ludemann*, which had barely managed to extricate herself from the *Jan Wellem*, together released twelve torpedoes in the direction of their adversaries.

Torpedo Officer George Heppel, just over two weeks after the battle, wrote a report giving his professional opinion, on the battle strategy which was a fair assessment. "After a time, the ships in the harbour started ineffectively to return the fire and *Hardy* withdrew outside the entrance followed by Hunter and *Havock* who had fired torpedoes after *Hardy*. *Hotspur* then attacked with torpedoes from just outside the harbour entrance and all six ships were engaging the harbour and a small battery on Franmnesodden with their maximum power.

"During this period a number of torpedoes, possibly a dozen, were fired at us from the harbour and our ships did their utmost to avoid them. Two, however, ran under *Hardy* and the escape must have been due to the success of the D.G. (degaussing) equipment, or possibility that contact torpedoes were set too deep in the confusion."

The enemy torpedo caused the Captain on *Havock*, Lieutenant Commander Rafe Courage to crouch down beside the binnacle and told those around him, "Sorry lads. There's no more I can do. Here it comes!" Everyone held their breath but relieved when it was seen by a signalman to come out on the other side of the ship. This was to give those on the bridge and later the crew to feel they were 'invincible'.

The German Navy had two models of torpedoes, a battery driven type on their U-boats, and an 'internal combustion' version on destroyers. Both types utilised a 'magnetic pistol' to detonate the warhead. It was designed to explode below their target, causing an increased level of damage. However, at Narvik, as the Germans were later to discover, their innovative device became inoperative, as it was affected by the earth's magnetic field. Especially at the higher latitudes in that part of the world.

This was a stroke of luck for the 2nd Destroyer Flotilla. Fortunately, the Royal Navy had previously discovered these problems and decided to keep to the substantially tested and trusted 'impact pistol' torpedo. The ineffective German torpedo proved to be an obvious advantage to the 2nd Destroyer Flotilla. Whilst the Royal Navy's Mark IX torpedo, of a simpler design, was to prove up to the job. So much so, that probably because of its success at Narvik, it not only remained an effective weapon during the Second World War, but was also used by the Submarine Service for another thirty years. This was probably down to the Royal Navy, unlike their adversaries, having previously spent a long period completing development trials. Especially having been thoroughly tested in areas of high altitude. There is a suggestion that the German Navy's usual efficiency on this occasion was hampered by the pressure from high command, to make sure their torpedo development programme was kept secret.

Korvettenkapitan Holtorf had managed, with serviceable engines, to manoeuvre *Diether von Roeder* to another mooring, the 'Post Pier'. Securing her aft with the bows anchored facing directly out to the harbour entrance. A clever move if his intentions were to make his ship a smaller target should the enemy decide to make another attack.

Back on board *Hardy* the jubilation came abruptly to an end. The Communications Number stated, "Then over my headphones came a message from the Captain. 'We have just done a good job but I think we should go back and do a bit more – perhaps this time we can stay.' Both our tubes crew by this time had trained them fore and aft, there was still one more torpedo left in the after tubes. Having done this, we were free to join our Repair Parties."

0514 2nd D F from D2 – Stand by to follow round again, keep a sharp lookout for torpedoes.

0515 2nd D F from D2 – Stop making smoke.

0520 *Hostile* from D2 – Have you fired any torpedoes yet.

0521 2nd D F from D2 – Proceed at 20 knots.

0522 D2 from *Hostile* – Intend to fire torpedoes when going round this time.

Commander Wright not knowing that the *Diether von Roeder* had changed her position was still optimistic that *Hostile* would be able to send her torpedoes in to finish the job. However, irrespective of moving out of line from the sister ships, his search was in vain.

Diether von Roeder hit three times by shell fire. The stern is secured to Narvik jetty by hawser, while anchor holds her bow off at an angle.
[Theodor Werner Schettler photograph via Frank Hackney]

Diether von Roeder torpedo tubes pointing out to the entrance of the harbour.
[Theodor Werner Schettler photograph via Frank Hackney]

Close up of damage midships. [A German Propaganda Photograph, the book
states, "Technicians quickly clear away and repair the damage, and the fighting
power of the destroyer remained intact." [Cyril Cope Collection]

It appears, as seen in the signal below, that at this stage Captain Warburton-Lee was becoming impatient with his fellow officer.

0530 *Hostile* from D2 – Follow round, don't go the wrong way each time.

Cyril Cope described the 'Second Run' as he saw it: "We approached for our second attack at a fair speed, entered the harbour, rounded the merchant ship which we had not sunk yet – in case it blocked the entrance. We opened fire with all guns at the shore batteries and at any shipping left afloat. The other four ships followed us in doing the same. By this time the Germans were well awake and doing a lot of firing. But they were firing skywards. I was stood next to the First Lieutenant (Lt Commander Mansell). I thought 'this is funny they are not firing at us'. I said to the First Lieutenant, 'They think it's a bloody air raid, sir'. Everybody laughed, including Jimmy the One." (Royal Navy jargon for the First Lieutenant.)

Les Smales', messenger on *Hardy*'s bridge observations were slightly different. "We re-entered the harbour; they were ready for us. I should say, some of them were firing H.A. and other L.A. (High Angle / Low Angle elevation). The Germans didn't know if they were under surface or air attack. It was a crazy sight which greeted us this time round. With stems, sterns, funnels and masts sticking up all over the harbour, making the graveyard of the ships sunk in the first battle. But for the grimness of the situation it was almost an amusing sight. There was more gunfire from what appeared to be shore batteries and they were firing ammunition fitted with tracer. So that you could see it coming towards you – sometimes it exploded in flight, while others went off on contact with the water."

It had been almost an hour since the action had begun and it occurred to Captain Warburton-Lee that due to poor visibility (unlike the first attack) there was little more to gain; so he decided to withdraw his flotilla back into the fjord.

It appears that about this time a long overdue signal was sent to warn the remaining German destroyers not in Narvik that they were under attack. This was sent from the *Hans Ludemann*, which when the action began was being refuelled and had managed to slip away from the *Jan Wellem*.

Marshal Soult picks up the situation in *Hunter*'s Gun director tower. "Once again the five ships reformed outside the harbour. But this time they had to dodge about ten torpedoes which came from inside the harbour; from enemy destroyers, that were not completely wrecked or from the U-boat believed to be in the vicinity. The 'Yeoman of Signals' in *Hunter* spotted one torpedo approaching. He shouted, 'Torpedo on Starboard bow, sir.' The Captain gave the order 'Hard a starboard', the torpedo passed down the ship's side about six feet away."

Mayor Theodor Broch and his family were sleeping "like logs that night and were still dazed when we were awakened by the first gun shots the next morning. They came the same hour as on the day before with heavy detonations". Theodor's young daughter Siri, is awakened by the noise of the salvoes and queries, "Isn't it Christmas today either?" "No it is war". "Is war nice?" "No war is not nice, but it's undeniably exciting."

When Mayor Broch drew back the curtains from the windows he saw what he described as 'fiery tongues' all over the harbour. The clouds hung low but the fog was not quite as thick as on the previous day. He heard thunder coming from the fjord and the harbour replying with fire. Siri asked her father, "Who is firing out there now?" "I don't know who it is. They are friends, and their aim is excellent," he replied.

The family saw direct hits on several of the ships in the harbour. The flames were so intense that the metal itself seemed to be burning. Shells rained upon the harbour and debris from the mail pier sailed through the air and whistled above their home. For a time they were forced to shelter in the basement. "It was a bit cold down there and we were in night clothes." Mayor Broch ran upstairs for some heavier clothing for his wife and daughter but was fascinated by the sight he saw from the windows. One of the German destroyers was on fire from stem to stern. Its engines were still operating but it circled aimlessly without direction or plan. [...] There was nothing to be seen but smoky fog. The cannonading was withdrawing to the outer fjord.

Here Peter Dickens in his own words adequately introduces Mayor Broch, whom I presume Dickens had interviewed for his book. "Rudely awakened on the second morning in succession, Mayor Broch surveyed the collapse of much that had raised his beloved town from a minor fishing village into – what? – an important factor in world strategy. The mainspring of his life as he had lived it so far had also apparently snapped. As a progressive socialist with no interest in war, no comprehension of it, and certainly no premonition that it might ever engulf him, however much outer barbarians might indulge in it to satisfy their brutish lusts, his life until yesterday had been devoted to the peaceful progress and fulfilment of ordinary people. But he did not despair; 24 hours of tyranny had shown him that great ideals must be defended, if necessary at great sacrifice, and the new revelation that his country and his cause had powerful friends became more important than the horror, and he watched with grim satisfaction."

At the school, Romilly with his newly found incarcerated colleagues appreciated the early daylight coming through the huge windows. Then unsuspectingly they were woken by gunfire which slowly became louder until the building began to shake. The men clambered to look out to see what was happening and were not disappointed, there was smoke and flames, even some of the water in the harbour was on fire. There was devastation and sinking ships, but it would have been difficult to pick out who the ships belonged to. Until some of men started one by one picking out the ore-ships *Romanby, Blythmoor, Mersington Court,* "over there look *North Cornwall* and that's *Riverton.*" All a mass of flames and two totally sunk leaving only their funnels to still see. Another upended almost perpendicular, with her bows protruding out of the water. Romilly noticed, "The *Jan Wellem,* that sinister whaling-ship, had moved out from her retirement; alongside her lay two German destroyers which she was feeding with oil."

"Confidence in the power of the Royal Navy was unlimited, some of the seamen put their coats and hats on, their suitcases by their sides. We listened hard for the rifle and machine gun fire which would mean a landing. But suddenly silence."

Kapitanleutnant Sohler of U-46 had no idea that the British destroyers had passed up the fjord some time earlier and his boat was still surfaced at the Narrows, charging its batteries. [U-46 and U- 25 heard gunfire from the direction of Narvik at dawn but never realised what it signified]

Having come back out of the harbour after the second attack you could not blame the relatively young officers, flushed with success, from feeling invincible. However, it was now time to take stock of the situation to allow Captain Warburton-Lee to make an informed decision. Once more, as on the occasion of entering the fjord the day before, there were discussions with his officers. Stanning again seems to be more specific about how the decision to re-enter or not was decided. Probably, this was because it was one of his responsibilities, on behalf of the Captain, to take notes as an official record of battle events.

However, there appears to be an unreliability in the different accounts after such a fast-paced, adrenalin-fuelled event, when the memory is never one hundred per cent efficient.

Stanning in his account writes, 'Wash' then said that he thought perhaps we ought to withdraw and asked us what we thought. The answer was unanimously in favour of going in again and for the following reasons:

1. We did not know what damage we had done nor what forces of the enemy were left. As all guns had ceased firing very early into the second attack it was possible that all opposition had been silenced. It would be ridiculous to withdraw in the face of no opposition at all and if there were any enemy forces left we ought to try and estimate their weight and report it.

2. At the same time 'Wash' was anxious that no one should get torpedoed but it was pointed out that so many torpedoes had been fired at us already that there could not be many more to fire.

3. *Hostile* had fired no torpedoes at all so far and 'Wash' wanted to let her have a turn.

George Heppel recorded, "Visibility closed down again and after this part of the engagement ships withdrew. Torpedoes remaining were signalled to Captain (D2), together with the report of damage, which was nil. The situation was then reviewed. We had five good ships, *Hostile* with her full outfit remaining. This meant that on our most unfavourable intelligence of the enemy strength that we would have to fight one or possibly two ships on patrol on the way out.

"Opinion was divided but the Gunnery Officer and myself were in favour of a last attack with *Hostile's* torpedoes. The reasoning being that we should have to meet the patrol in any case and our success up till then still held out the possibility of our attack being more than a raid by gaining permanent control of the fjord. Captain (D2) decided on the attack and ships were formed in a loose line ahead and steamed up past Ankenes again. Each ship opening fire in turn and *Hostile* firing torpedoes."

Communications Number on *Hardy's* foremost tubes: "Out we came again, still undamaged and feeling on top of the world. We steamed down the fjord about the same distance again, when over the headphones came a similar message as before. The Captain announced, we did more damage, but we are going back in again, but this time we are staying. 'Landing Parties' get prepared."

Gunner Dougy Bourton, on *Hardy* after Gun, "From the two attacks we went through, the only thing we had was a two-inch hole in the after funnel, a piece of paint flew off and it cut my 'Gun Layer' and made a tiny cut on the side of his nose. We were laughing like hell, to say he had been wounded in action. This was a source of great amusement to us."

0544 2nd D F from D2 – Proceed at 20 knots.

The German officers staying at the Hotel Royal, awakened by the explosions looked through the windows in their bedroom to see flames and smoke in the harbour. Leutnant Bach recounts, "Then I heard General Deitl voice in the corridor outside my room [...] He immediately ordered me to get down to the harbour." On his way at a fast rate of knots, he noticed it had snowed through the night but soon his attention was taken away to a more horrendous sight. There he saw a collection of wounded and dazed sailors, looking as though they had been pulled out of the harbour soaked not only in blood-stained uniforms. Bach, "Some explosions sounded like heavy bombs going off, others were more like bursts of light shells. I also heard the muffed and frightening sound of steam escaping from boilers, a sure sign that ships were on the verge of sinking."

The ships were initially in line but Captain Warburton-Lee, in an attempt to be more fruitful in engaging the enemy, allowed the ships to zig-zag at will. The enemy were in a better position to see their targets than the five destroyers, with the harbour still full of smoke and the dense mist having re-appeared. As previously mentioned by Lt Heppel, *Hostile* was able to finally fire her torpedoes. *Hostile* at the end of the line fired four torpedoes into the 'unknown' but received a hit herself.

Les Smale remains on *Hardy*'s bridge, "We were all quite happy and very pleased with our work, but when the Captain ordered yet another attack we weren't quite so keen. It was getting very hot in the harbour and they were ready for us this time, but if the Captain went, we went. For the third time we entered the harbour and they were more than ready. After seeing the effect of our own torpedoes, I know, there was no one not anxious to see the effect of one of theirs on us. Each time one came towards us 'Full Speed Ahead' was ordered and we turned towards it, to present as small a target as possible. On one occasion we had just evaded one, only to run into the path of another.

"I honestly believed that my heart stopped beating as I held my breath, together with everyone else; as we waited helplessly for the explosion to occur. But it never came despite the fact that it passed right under us and the general belief that the German torpedoes were all fitted with 'magnetic heads'. If they were, then we owe our lives to our 'degaussing' gear."

On board the *Hotspur*, Engine Room Artificer Percy Danby was busy in No 1 Boiler Room, attending to the boilers and monitoring the emergency diesel-driven generator. Although his ship was away from the action, they were able to hear gunfire and those above decks could see smoke in the distance. Percy and his shipmates were desperate to return back to their colleagues on the other three ships not knowing fully which way the battle was going. But they soon found it was looking good for their flotilla inside the harbour. "When we reached Narvik Harbour, *Hotspur* and *Havock* were ordered to search the upper reaches of the fjord for German ships. We returned about an hour later to re-join the other ships at Narvik. We stayed there for about an hour, circling firing our guns without receiving any return fire. I felt quite relieved when we were told that we were retiring and we went to full speed."

Escape to Open Sea

"I always thought that war was not one for democracy, but for survival –
and from start to finish I regarded it as that."
John Cook Montague. Army Officer (S.O.E)

The ships at full speed now were hoping to make for the open sea. However, it was Captain Warburton-Lee who suddenly sighted what looked like a cruiser and two destroyers coming towards them from the direction of Rombaksfjord. It soon became obvious they were enemy ships and the order was given to open fire. Almost simultaneously they returned fire. As Stanning states, "Whether it did us good or harm that the visibility increased just at that moment I don't know but if it had kept down for few minutes longer we might even have collided with them."

These were *Wolfgang Zenker, Erich Koellner* and *Erich Giese*, which originally were sent to Herjangsfjord, at anchor awaiting their turn to be refuelled by *Jan Wellem*. They had mustered as much speed as was possible to catch up with their adversaries.

For some unknown reasons, it took nearly an hour for the three Zerstörers to be made aware of the attack in Narvik. Korvettenkapitan Smidt, commanding *Erich Giese* records, "At 0530, the destroyer was lying at anchor off Bjerkvik, less than fifteen minutes' steaming away from Narvik. Shortly afterwards a signal was received in clear reading: British attacking Narvik!" All three Zerstörers weigh anchor, *Erich Giese* was an impressively armed warship but unfortunately for Smidt and his intentions, there was insufficient fuel on board. This only allowed two boilers to be fired.

Karl Smidt was described as tall with a cool head who came from a family of Free Church theologians in the Frisian Islands. This background gave him a knowledge of other languages, including Latin, Greek, French and

English. Similar to Bonte, although he was not a follower of Nazism, he still felt his duties as a naval officer was with the Kriegsmarine. [55]

0553 2ⁿᵈ D F from D2 – Withdraw.

Stanning continues, "The Captain ordered the signal to withdraw red 'Very light' and thirty knots; Clark (Lt Gunnery) protested that we were hitting them and wanted to stay and have another crack at them. But just at that moment two more ships appeared ahead and Cross (Lt Signals) said '*Birmingham*'. The distance was about four miles, I should think. I looked at them through glasses and caught sight of hoods on the funnels and knew they were not *Birmingham's* whatever else they were. We had 'Jane's' on the bridge, so I looked it up in that, found they were large German destroyers and convinced the Captain. It looked as if we were in a tight corner."

Hardy made smoke, fire was returned from the enemy's foremost guns but *Hardy* was not hit.

0556 2ⁿᵈ D F from D2 – Keep on engaging enemy. [56]

All the ships were steaming westward at thirty knots when the two large ships were sighted coming out of the thinning snow ahead. This was at a range of five or six thousand yards. It was thought possible that they were some support, possibly including *Penelope*.

The two German destroyers ahead were the *Bernd von Arnim* and *Georg Thiele* anchored in the Ballangen Bay also previously awaiting their turn to be refuelled.

0558 D2 from *Hostile* – Three destroyers leaving harbour.

0559 – Signal passed in by Hunter. No reply from *Hardy*.
– Only *Hostile* and *Havock* making call signs.

Stanning: "The two Germans ahead turned to port and opened fire and we

---

55 The Evangelical Confessional Church in Germany "worked against the Nazi system from within."

56 This was the last signal made by Captain D2.

engaged them, leaving the other three to our rear ships. I think it must have been at this moment, when we were taking on the two ahead and 'Wash' wanted the others to go on with the other three, that he made his last signal: 'Keep on engaging the enemy', but I don't remember it being made. We also had an enemy report. We were being hit by then and evidently doing them some damage, but they were uncomfortably accurate and I felt several hits forward. Then there was a tremendous explosion on the bridge."

The explosion on the *Hardy* bridge left behind a carnage, but there were some survivors, including a Leading Telegraphist. In my first book, I accounted for all those on the bridge, dead or alive, with the exception of the communications man. [Page 185] Nine years after beginning, just as I was about to complete this book, I received a post from Ged Jackson. "My son has been carrying out a school project about the Second World War. As part of his project I've been researching my dad's uncle, Billy Feddon, who survived the sinking of the *Hardy*. I am led to believe from newspaper reports that he remained on the bridge for some time and carried on with his duties in spite of the shrapnel wound he received. I don't have much information as Billy died when his ship HMS *Dorsetshire* was sunk; he was aged 23. He came from Wigton in Cumbria."

Out of respect I felt that another brave sailor, Billy Feddon, who was lucky to survive one battle but not the next, should finally be memorialised. [57]

Gunnery Officer Lieutenant Clark and Signals Officer Lieutenant Charles Cross were two of those badly wounded, lying prostrate on the deck of *Hardy*'s bridge. Edward Clark, aged twenty-nine, was recently married with a one-month-old son. He was an attentive and diligent officer, who loved the music of Bach and books by the twentieth-century French novelist Marcel Proust. The younger of the two, Charles Cross was also newly married, and an award winner for new ideas and methods in wireless technology. Both died of their wounds before the crew were able to get them ashore. They were highly regarded as officers with the potential of going far

---

[57] In March 1942, *Dorsetshire* was transferred to the Eastern Fleet to support British forces in the Pacific war. At the end of the month, the Japanese fast carrier task force on 5 April, one of her aircraft spotted *Dorsetshire* and her sister *Cornwall* while en route to Colombo. A force of dive bombers then attacked the two ships and sank them. More than 1,100 men were rescued the next day, out of a combined crew of over 1,500.

in the Navy. I will come back to Edward Clark and the family he left behind in a later chapter. [58]

It is from here on that the book now focuses mainly on the events that affected HMS *Hunter* and her crew, some of the names of which I have already introduced in the previous chapters. With regards to the outcome of HMS *Hardy* and her crew, this was the main feature of my first book, *Attack at Dawn*.

Petty Officer 'Jake' Kerswell gives his version at that moment, "This time we were met by enemy destroyers coming out of different fjords; and then it was we who were hit seriously for the first time, getting a salvo in the engine room, putting the starboard turbine out of action."

Sam Evens: "At this point we were ordered by Captain (D) to withdraw at full speed under a smokescreen. All hell was let loose and we were struck by gunfire; as a result our steering motors were put out of action. Then came a terrific crash as *Hotspur* collided with us amidships. The impact was mainly taken in the starboard engine room, killing all hands on watch because of the leaking main steam pipe.

"It's hard to say who was responsible, some of the people said that the steering motors were put out of action and we stopped, then the *Hotspur* ran into us doing twenty-eight to thirty knots. About this time I saw that *Hardy* was on fire around the bridge. She was under heavy enemy fire and was making a run for the beach. Aboard our ship we were given the order to 'Abandon Ship!' as when *Hotspur* drew away from us she left a gaping hole in our side which was rapidly filling with water. It was impossible to get on a boat as they were all severely damaged by shell splinters.

"Then our other destroyers were ordered to leave the fjord, abandon everything and get out as soon as possible under a smokescreen. I could see three of our destroyers disappearing down one of the fjords, under a heavy smokescreen and some German destroyers in pursuit. I really felt this was the end for me as there was just no room on the Carley float and the beach was too far to swim for it".

Jake Kerswell: "Along with the other hits we had received we started to sink, upon which we were given orders to abandon ship. But owing to all

---

58   Marcel Proust, French novelist, best known for his 3000-page masterpiece *À la recherché du temps perdu* (*Remembrance of Things Past* or *In Search of Lost Time*), a quasi-autobiographical novel told mostly in a stream-of-consciousness style.

the boats being smashed we only had the Carley floats and a few improvised rafts to use. The time was about 0600 and everyone got over the side and were clinging to rafts and floats; but owing to the coldness of the water, men were dropping off the rafts and floats at regular intervals. Altogether we were in the water for over an hour, when we were picked up by German destroyers; who did everything they could to bring some life into us, as nearly everyone had lost consciousness when picked up. Just before leaving the ship, I was hit in the head with a piece of shrapnel, which put me out for about five minutes."

Marshal Soult recalls those moments in the final attack. "Suddenly from out of the mist and falling snow three ships appeared, they looked like light cruisers but were in fact large German destroyers. They immediately opened fire, and the British ships replied. Although the odds were 5 to 3 in favour of the British, the difference in size and number of guns the enemy ships had, put the balance slightly in their favour. At this point, however, two more large ships approached from dead ahead and in a position which blocked the route of escape for the British ships. These new arrivals soon got into the battle by letting go with full salvoes, concentrating on *Hardy* the leader. They soon registered hits on her causing terrible damage on her bridge, then *Hunter* started to take punishment, but before she was mortally hit the crew on the upper deck saw *Hardy* take many salvoes then veer away towards the shore.

"No sooner had *Hardy* been put out of the fight than it was *Hunter*'s turn. As she fired salvoes into one of the enemy ships she herself was severely hit, forward she was badly holed. The steering gear was put out of action, and then the engine room received a direct hit putting out of action the starboard engine. With the port engine going at full speed the ship slewed around to port. The *Hotspur* next in line, which also had damaged steering, rammed into *Hunter* amidships carrying half way through, killing all the engine room crew. The two ships were locked together; the *Hotspur*, both engines going full astern pulled away leaving a gaping hole in the stricken *Hunter*'s engine room which rapidly filled with water. The Captain, Lt Commander *Lind*say de Villiers gave the order to abandon ship, this was approximately 0600 hours. The order was carried out in a calm and orderly manner considering we were still under devastating fire from the enemy, they poured salvo after salvo into the two crippled ships".

The First Lieutenant, Stuart-Menteth: "I saw *Hotspur* coming towards us at great speed, she hit us at an angle of 45 degrees, right next to me."

One man, who would have probably been too busy on the flag deck to think about danger, was another veteran from the First World War, forty-two-year-old Signalman Thomas Norton, a 'reservist', who was quickly re-engaged back into the Navy. During the *Hunter's* demise it is without doubt that Thomas would have been leading from the front, standing firm and providing encouragement to the younger Signalmen. One of the reasons that Thomas earned the nickname "Daddy" Norton.

Sam Evens continues his account of those dramatic moments. "There was one Carley float in the water and there were a few swimming around trying to get into it, the ones who couldn't swim. Well, I went down to the boiler room, told those on watch that it's 'Abandon Ship' and 'To Get Out' as soon as possible. Then I went around to find a lifebelt, and went over the side myself. I just slid down off the decks into the water, kicked my shoes off and then just paddled to get away from the ship. It was terrible the cold, that's what killed a lot of them and the cold weather. The only time I felt scared was when I found the ships aerials around me feet.

"It was still blowing and rough. I kept away from the Carley floats, there were too many survivors, catching hold of them. Eventually it tipped and righted itself again, then during this spell the depth charges went off on the ship, they weren't put at 'Safety'. There was a big underwater explosion. That could have affected somebody that was near the ship, but I was too far away to receive anything from the explosion. The ship was leaning over on her beam side; gradually her bulkheads were giving way under the pressure of water. Then eventually she came upright again and disappeared. I thought 'everything is lost now' because there were no other ships to pick us up. The German ships were chasing the other ones out of the fjord."

Dickens writes, "The Engineering Officer, Alick Reid, was just emerging from his engine room hatch to investigate the loss of steam, and was confronted by the *Hotspur's* bow cutting through the metal towards him. Stuart-Menteth, the First Lieutenant, was also there starting to plug the hole made by the shell that had ignited No 3 boiler room. They will neither of them ever forget that moment."

A question mark arises as to whether *Hunter* was sunk by the ramming of *Hotspur* or a torpedo launched by the *Georg Thiele*. Here I include the official reports from the commanding officers of *Georg Thiele* and *Havock*, but first, here is the opinion of naval history author Peter Dickens.

His research shows, "Transformed in a few moments into a flaming wreck, her forward funnel incandescent, the *Hunter* lost all power and control, turned involuntarily towards the enemy and stopped instantly, like a speed-boat coming off the plane. Few of those on board can have had any clear idea of what had hit her, and fewer still survived their wounds and the icy water to tell their story. **The only contemporary report, an unofficial one, states that she was badly holed forward; that and the extreme suddenness of total disaster makes a torpedo hit at least possible,** and the *Georg Thiele* had fired a salvo of three as she passed, claiming a visible hit abreast the bridge." (Dickens, page 86)

From Nikolas Sifferlinger and his co-author Wolfgang Harnack's methodically researched book, *Zerstörer Z2 Georg Thiele*, Nikolas translated the following official report made by Korvettenkapitan Max-Eckart Wolff [*Thiele*]. It gives the account from a German perspective of the furious battle taking place in the fjord – who better a witness than Wolff? It describes how the battle and damage caused was by no means all one-sided.

"At 0657 [gmt 0557] *GEORG THIELE* turns […] to bring all guns into the firing position and at the same time to block the way to the west for the enemy. The firing of all guns was opened at a range of approximately 4,000 metres on the passing engagement to […] of the leading destroyer *HARDY*, who alone comes out of the clearing smoke. Also, *BERND VON ARNIM* opens fire. *THIELE'S* third salvo is on target and fire ignition is seen on *HARDY*. After about ten rapid salvoes she disappears with high flames midships in a dense smoke. When the smoke clears, the burning destroyer is seen to slow down, turns out of line and falls behind. She later goes aground on the rocks south side of the fjord.

"The next destroyer in the enemy line [*HUNTER*] was put under fire by *THIELE* and *VON ARNIM*, as the following three destroyers were still obscured by smoke. These salvoes soon found their mark. In order to prevent the enemy going too far to the west before our 4th Destroyers Flotilla arrived, the course was changed into the other direction. In this phase of the battle *THIELE* did not receive any hits. The distance of fighting was between 2,500 and 3,500 metres and the anti-aircraft automatic guns in the engagement were successful. Two torpedoes had been launched but both missed their target.

"Two single torpedoes launched by the enemy were avoided and detonated on the north shore of the fjord. The turn of direction had led to the battle continuing […] and again our salvoes soon found their targets.

Another destroyer (*HUNTER*) was hit hard by the salvoes of the two German Zerstörers and slow down and was burning. The line of the enemy destroyers broke up but the remaining three [*HOTSPUR, HAVOCK* and *HOSTILE*] changed their courses. They tried to support their comrades and the crippled ship, by laying a smokescreen and concentrated their salvoes. Again, an enemy triple and single torpedoes are launched and had to be avoided.

"A hit was taken on the portside [*THIELE*] and exploded in the [water] tank V11.3.2 [No 1 boiler room] and caused a leakage. Splinters entered the boiler room, destroying the K-Fan 11 and caused leakage to the tank V11.3.1. [No 1] boiler room because of oil leaks was shut down due to fire risk. [This resulted in effecting the sea water used for firefighting and domestic distilled water supplies.] A further hit on the portside passes through the bulkhead and explodes in the after double chamber and there was a lot of splinter damage. There was a minor fire with heavy smoke leaving the ammunition chamber in danger [of exploding]. But can only be flooded by a natural flow of water as the main cooling pump had already failed on 7th April during the transit to Narvik.

"During the next phase of the battle a single torpedo was fired [from *THIELE*] but no effect was seen on the enemy. As the enemy manoeuvred in the area of their crippled destroyer [*HUNTER*] our own course was reversed with hard rudder to starboard to continue the battle. During this change of course, a hit was received on the pivot of Gun No 1 [behind the shield of the forward gun], which was already aiming to starboard. The crew and the ammunition carriers were killed (nine dead), only two survived. The gun was put out of operation. Splinters started a fire at the ammunition hoist which causes heavy smoke in the surrounding compartments. A further hit [...] passed the forward funnel and exploded behind the signal deck. Splinters holed the motor boat, steam pipes, deck above and there was damage to the port side of the bridge. The crew [bridge] were moved to the starboard side, a NCO and a sailor were wounded.

"Another hit entered [...] there is an explosion in the Stokers' Messdeck causing fire ignition. Heavy splinters entered the central weaponry [large and small guns midships] killing or wounding all the crew. As well as damaging the guns and torpedo controls and associated cabling. Further splinters penetrated the bulkhead to the other boiler room, which has to be temporarily shut down because of gas escaping from the firefighting system.

The bilge pump was put out of operation. The guns were able to continue firing by setting the height and directions by telephone.

"At this moment, an English destroyer turned towards *THIELE*, and was running with top speed either for a torpedo launch or an incoming ramming. Our own anti-aircraft guns hit him with a high rate of fire into the bridge and conning area, so that he turned away (1700 m). No torpedoes or launches are seen. A hit entered the starboard side below the rear control stand and doctor compartment. Splinters destroyed the rear gun control and caused a leakage just below the waterline. **A salvo of three torpedoes were launched at a distance of 2800 metres. The right-hand side one hit the enemy destroyer [in line] with the bridge, with a high water and detonation cloud. The destroyer sank immediately. According to reports from WOLFGANG ZENKER who rescued some English sailors it was the English destroyer** *HUNTER*. [As Plan Drawings show 'in line with the bridge' are the 'Oil Fuel Tanks' – although No 1 Boiler Room is next aft.]

"A torpedo from an enemy destroyer missed its target, a further salvo of three torpedoes could only be avoided with difficulty, they passed close behind *THIELE*. In the meantime, the three Zerstörers of the 4th Zerstörer Flotilla from Herjangsbay came in sight, and the *WOLFGANG ZENKER* in front soon joined the battle soon. With black smokescreen, the remaining English destroyers disengaged from the fight and tried with high speed to escape to the west.

"At 0725 [GMT 0625] the firing [of weapons] was ceased by *THIELE* on the enemy, who were now chased by the Zerstörers of the 4th Flotilla. The fires [on board *THIELE*] caused thick smoke around the ship making it necessary to flood the forward and after ammunition chambers. This was because the out of action equipment did not allow a concentrated firefighting. Also the firefighting equipment on board *VON ARNIM*, who came alongside was unable to put out the fires immediately. Only by the total blocking of air access could the fire be extinguished after two hours. However, the ammunition chambers were pumped again and the ammunition was saved.

"Our losses were: Dead – three NCOs and twelve sailors. Wounded – one officer, five NCOs and seventeen sailors. The artillery did perform very well against the enemy artillery of the same calibre. [Incorrect, the Germans large guns calibre were 5 inch to the British 4.7 inch.] Lieutenant Fuchs did a very good job in training and leading the firefighting during the battle. At close distance the automatic anti-aircraft weapons could be used with good effect against the destroyers. It looked as though during the fight the English destroyers did not use their 'pom pom' automatic guns"

The signed report of the proceedings by Korvettenkapitan Max-Eckart Wolff. (To be concluded in the Second Battle)

Nik Sifferlinger also advised me that when researching for his book he was in contact with Matrosen-obergefreiter Alfred Eichholz, a crew member on *Georg Thiele*. He was at the 'distance measurement' control and had the enemy in his sights. Alfred confirmed that he saw how a destroyer was hit by the torpedo. Also, on board *Thiele* was the 1st Zerstörer Flotilla's Senior Officer, (Captain D) Fregattenkapitan F. Berger. He reported, "Passing battle with a little over 2,000 metres distance the destroyers coming from the east are recognized as 4th Zerstörer Flotilla. *GEORG THIELE* gets hit in the artillery control room, the firing is slowed down after this it becomes irregular. **An enemy destroyer disappears in an explosion cloud, obviously a torpedo hit.**

So it appears to be the conclusion by the Germans that *Hunter* was torpedoed. Here another respected author, a specialist on the 'Battles of Narvik' agrees with Peter Dickens version albeit using the word 'likelihood' rather than Dickens' 'possible'.

Geirr Haarr, in his more recent comprehensively researched book provides (page 347) an updated version of this part of the battle [...] "*Hunter* was hit several times in succession and turned into an inferno within a few minutes [...] **In all likelihood, she was also hit by one of three torpedoes fired by *Thiele* at this stage.** *Hunter*'s speed dropped rapidly and *Hotspur*, herself under heavy fire and temporarily out of control from two hits, rammed her from behind. While locked together, the two ships received the full attention of both *Arnim* and *Thiele*."

Dickens continues his description of events, "Hit after hit slammed into the two ships; the *Hotspur*'s engines continued to push the *Hunter* over with a thrust of 34,000 horse-powers and Layman (Commanding Officer of *Hotspur*) was powerless to stop them. He left the bridge and as he did so a shell hit the range finder and killed nearly everyone there; he half slid, half jumped down the ladders to the iron deck, sprinted aft, and shouted down the engine room hatch to the nearest Stoker who in turn took a message to the Engineer Officer, Johnny Osborne. At long last the engines were put to full astern and *Hotspur* drew clear.

"The *Hunter*'s distress will never be known in detail, even the cause and time of her Captain's death is not recorded. The *Hotspur* was hit seven times in all, that she was not destroyed was remarkable, and the factors that saved her were human ones."

Commander H.F. Layman and Lieutenant Commander R. E. Courage, the commanding officers of HMS *Hotspur* and HMS *Havock*, respectively, as was protocol had to present reports of the events involving their ships in the 1st Battle of Narvik. This was sent to the next chain of command, Rear Admiral Halifax (D) Home Fleet. Subsequently, the Admiral referred the report on to the Lord Commissioners of the Admiralty dated the 25th of April 1940. However, it was not until the 3rd of July 1040 that the report was finally published in the London Gazette.

These are the relevant parts of the reports, the first by Commander Layman (Paragraph 22) referred to the collision between his ship, *Hotspur* and *Hunter*. However, it is noticeable that to Commander Layman's honourable credit he did not praise himself regarding his brave actions in saving his ship and crew from further disaster.

"Shortly after *HARDY* had been hit, *HUNTER* was seen to be on fire and her forward torpedo tubes were missing, indicating some explosion. She was seen to lose steam just ahead of *HOTSPUR* at the same moment as the latter's steering and all bridge communications were put out of action. Whilst not under control, *HOTSPUR* collided with the damaged *HUNTER* and these two ships, locked together drew all the enemy's fire. By means of verbal orders to the engine room and tiller flat, given from 'X' gun deck (No 3 gun aft), *HOTSPUR* was able to extricate herself from this predicament but the combined effects of the collision and the damage done by the enemy caused *HUNTER* to sink".

It is important to note that Commander Layman had already trained his crew to a high degree of efficiency. Everyone knew their job and were able to perform their duties without needing additional orders. During the aftermath of the collision, Layman himself rushed to the stern gundeck to enable him to see ahead. He then established two chains of men first to the engine room and secondly the tiller flat, the latter contained the steering engine and rudder head. Hence, he was able to regain control of the ship, albeit with reduced accuracy.

Whatever control there was came down to the foresight of Engineer Officer Johnny Osborne, who, totally against all the ships engineering standards, decided to use sea water in the boilers. Whilst this could cause serious damage to the boilers it could also be effective, when an emergency situation arose, as this obviously was. In fact, he had previously trained his engineering staff to the controversial procedures. Although now all feed distilled water was quickly lost through a shattered pipe in No 2 boiler room, it did the job and the ship maintained its steam power.

I have to mention Marine Donald Thomas, who had been drafted on board *Hotspur* for the previous minelaying operations. He was able to see the Captain's desperate needs immediately. As recorded, "He rushed to and fro with great zeal, while not forgetting to hand a shell up to the gun every time he passed it."

Commander Layman also saw that the two after guns were keeping up a rapid fire in group control at the enemy in the rear. A twenty-year-old Sub Lieutenant Leo Tillie was the officer controlling these guns, which his Captain noted was "calmly and effectively". His actions on the day would probably have made the enemy think twice before closing in for the kill.

Meantime, Leading Seaman Watling on the for'd gun, even after the collision, found it still in working condition. He too went about his duties in a calm manner. On realising snow was not allowing the breech to close properly, he sent for boiling water from the galley. He poured this over the rounds before loading which allowed him to maintain rapid fire over open sights. At a recorded range of 2,000 yards it is assessed that the *Bernd von Arnim* received five hits, resulting in her and *Georg Thiele* being put out of the battle.

Terry Orford having read my first book, wrote to me about his Uncle Ted Orford from Leyton East London, who was a Stoker on *Hotspur*. "Like you, Narvik has always been imprinted on my mind for as long as I can remember. I first learnt about it from my grandparents who had a plaque of *Hotspur* on the wall, that's how I first became aware of the Battle of Narvik. My Uncle told me that he was the last out of the wheelhouse, before it received a direct hit. At the time he wrote to my grandparents to say 'It was hot work'." An understatement or what? I will come back to Ted Orford again.

Engine Room Artificer Percy Danby's version outlines a more comprehensive story, you cannot get information any better than from the man on the spot. "Suddenly, the ship was hit by two or three mighty blows. The lights in the boiler room went out and we listed to starboard. It was at this time that *Hotspur* rammed the *Hunter* amidships. The boiler burners began spluttering. A shell had hit just for'd of the boiler room on the starboard side. Shrapnel had destroyed the main switchboard and the hydraulic lines to the steering gear. It also holed the deck, allowing seawater into the fuel tank below. Seawater mixing with the fuel was causing the burners to malfunction. The Stoker Petty Officer guessed correctly what was happening and changed over to another fuel tank, curing the problem with the burners. I have always believed that his quick thinking saved the ship.

"At about this time we received a 'full astern' order as the Captain was trying to get *Hotspur* disengaged from *Hunter*, which was on fire amidships and apparently sinking. The PO Stoker was an unsung hero."

Victor Wallwork, Percy's stepson, took notes during his meeting with Percy. "Percy was there as the burners threatened to splutter out and he knew what that would mean. He is a technical guy and he recognised when someone knew what they were doing (and when they didn't!). When he told me about this, he said that he, Percy, had been a very lucky fellow, in other words, he had lived to tell the tale because the PO Stoker had had the knowledge and experience to diagnose and fix the problem. Percy knew and liked Engineer Lt. Johnny Osborne, and he feels that he deserved the credit he got for his part in the action. He also thought that Captain Layman was a good Captain and that he deserved his DSO. After all, he said, the Captain had overall responsibility for the ship and for all of us – if it had ended badly, he would have been the one to wear that too."

Back to Percy, "We were then hit by another shell, which blew away the No 2 Boiler Room escape hatch. Shrapnel from this shell damaged steam pipes and the feed water ring main that supplied feed water to all three boiler rooms. The ship would go nowhere without steam! Number 2 Boiler was put out of action. Initially, the Engine Room tried filling the main feed water tank using fire main sea hoses. This was insufficient so No 1 and No 3 boilers used their auxiliary feed pumps to supply feed water directly from the sea to the boilers.

"During this entire time, we were still trying to disengage from *Hunter*. *Havock* and *Hostile* saw that we were in serious trouble. They returned and laid a smokescreen around us. Eventually, after maybe ten minutes, we cleared from *Hunter*. We were then able to steam slowly back down the fjord. The bow had been damaged in the collision and it was acting like a rudder, making it difficult to steer the ship. The German gunnery firing at almost point blank range was poor – further damage was only superficial.

"I was ordered to the Engine Room. I tried to open the boiler room exit hatch but a heavy weight on top prevented me. I was able gradually to shift the weight aside, push the hatch open and escape. It turned out that the weight on top was the dead body of one of my shipmates.

"My next job was to try to control salt depositing in the lower drums of the boilers because this would affect the production of steam. This required connecting a flexible copper hose to the starboard lower boiler drum valve and then to a sea cock valve on the ship's hull. By opening the boiler 'blow down' valve, then the 'sea cock' valve I could let the boiler steam pressure blow the salt deposits to sea for two or three minutes. This procedure had to be carried out continuously for several hours, alternating back and forth between No 1 Boiler on the port and starboard water drums and No 3 boiler port and starboard drums.

"Before we had cleared the fjord, the cruiser *Penelope* came alongside *Hotspur* and took off seamen who were not now required to work the damaged ship. Eventually, we cleared West Fjord and in the open sea we committed our dead in a proper naval service manner to the depths of the Arctic Ocean."

Commander Layman, in his report went onto describe his ship's escape down the fjord with the assistance of the two other flotilla destroyers. "The enemy, however, must have received considerable punishment. One destroyer appeared to have been struck by a torpedo and seemed aground whilst others had been hit by gunfire. *HOTSPUR* and *HOSTILE* had fired torpedoes at the enemy who had replied with four, which passed close down *HOTSPUR'S* side." (Paragraph 23)

This is the only part of the report by Commander Layman that mentions enemy torpedoes being launched but nothing to indicate even a possible hit.

Commander Layman continues his report, "When withdrawing after her collision *HOTSPUR* was still under fire from at least four enemy ships. *HOSTILE* and *HAVOCK* had got clear to the westward practically undamaged. Quickly taking in the situation, they immediately turned back into the fjord and covered *HOTSPUR'S* retirement. This was a bold move, skilfully executed in narrow waters and it probably persuaded the enemy from following up his advantage". (Paragraph 24)

The second report by Lieutenant Commander Courage, to summarise, describes what was witnessed by his ship *HAVOCK* at the moment both *HARDY* and *HUNTER* were in trouble. "Just before *HAVOCK* fired torpedoes, enemy torpedoes were seen approaching on the surface and easily avoided by combing the tracks. *HARDY*, however, who was steering more to port appeared to be hit by one as there was a high column of smoke from her after boiler room and much flame from the funnel. Actually, from accounts afterwards this was a salvo of shell, and she rapidly lost way and passed astern. (Paragraph 15)

"As I was now at the head of the line and no enemy appeared to be westward of us, I turned to starboard 180 degrees and closed the enemy astern, opening fire at 10,000 yards. During this run I passed *HUNTER* who was on fire and losing speed and *HOTSPUR* whose steering gear seemed to be out of action. Unfortunately, the order to open fire could not be complied with, as both foremost guns were out of action, and having no torpedoes I decided that it would be folly to close the range any further, and turned to starboard passing close astern of *HOSTILE* who was making smoke. (Paragraphs 16, 17, 18).

"At this moment the two leading enemy appeared not to be hit and were firing well placed salvoes, while two in the rear were very ragged. *HAVOCK* was again straddled but not hit except by splinters. While withdrawing the after group continued the engagement, until the enemy was lost in smoke. (Paragraph 19)

"While running to the west *HOTSPUR* was observed to collide with *HUNTER* who appeared to be in a bad way, but the former got clear. Once clear of the smoke I drew up alongside *HOSTILE* and both foremost guns being reported again in use, followed her back into action to relieve the pressure on *HOTSPUR*. Fire was opened at 10,000 yards and continued until *HOTSPUR* was out of range when all ships withdrew. The leading enemy appeared to be untouched and were straddling effectively while we were turning. They made no attempt however to close the range, after we had slowed to *HOTSPUR*'S speed. (Paragraphs 20–21)

Lieutenant Commander Courage also makes no mention of a torpedo hit. In all of the *Hunter* crew's accounts there is no suggestion that the ship was even possibly sunk by a torpedo. However, could it be that all those with their own opinions were possibly right, if not the complete answer, in that it was a combination of both? Subsequent to the ramming the sea water rushing into the *Hunter* boiler / engine rooms would naturally cause her waterline to lower. Then the crippled ship was hit by *Thiele*'s torpedo irrespective of any defects it may have had with its magnetic pistol.

I put this possibility to both Nik Sifferlinger and Geirr Haarr. Nik remains adamant that it was the other way round, 'torpedoed then rammed'. Geirr Haarr explains, it maybe the torpedo officer on *Thiele* actually remembered to set his torpedoes for a shallower approach to its target "He was an extraordinary guy. Six torpedoes were fired during the melee and that they all missed on the relatively short distance in question is very unlikely. As well as, those torpedoes that previously went underneath the British destroyers only missed by inches."

Who am I to argue their points of view? How important is it anyway, when so many brave sailors from both sides steadfastly did their duty and many lost their lives in the first epic sea battle of World War Two.

Geirr Haar once more provides a comprehensive description of the rescue attempts of *Hotspur* and surrounding events concerning the Germans reactions. "*Havock* and *Hostile* boldly turned back, *Havock* for the second time fighting the Zerstörers off '*Hotspur*'. '*Hotspur*' regained some speed and under smokescreen from *Hostile* escaped the claws of *Arnim* and *Thiele* which were compelled to pull back, licking their wounds. In particular *Thiele* was severely hit with multiple fires and flooded magazines. Grudgingly, Fregattenkapitan Berger [flotilla commander on *Thiele*] had to leave the rest of the business to Bey [...] He however, lobbed a few shots at the retiring destroyers before turning back, pounding the wreck of *Hardy* instead. Fregattenkapitan Schulze-Hinrichs let Koellner follow as far as Djupvik before also turning back. [Wreckage was later found near Tjeldsund, some of which was marked with *Hotspur*, leading the Germans to believe that also she had been sunk in addition to *Hardy*, *Hunter* and *Hostile*] *Hotspur* and *Havock* continued down the fjord as fast as *Hotspur* could make it."

Stoker Albert Goodey, then aged twenty-one on *Havock*, many years later held the view that his ship achieved thirty-six knots when withdrawing, "being very low on fuel, shells and torpedoes and very high on adrenalin".

A slight deviation before continuing the events after the battle, I would like to take you forward thirty nine years, to Bremerhaven in Germany. It was an emotional event when the Kriegsmarine Narvik veterans returned an invite to their former Royal Naval adversaries from the 2nd Destroyer Flotilla Association of the Battles of Narvik. I have mentioned nineteen-year-old Dougy Bourton. DSM, a Gunner on *Hardy*, who was now a Lieutenant Commander in the Naval Sea Cadet Corps. It was 1979 and Dougy recalls meeting Korvettenkapitan Max-Eckart Wolff, now a retired Admiral. "I remember having a conversation with Max. He heard about me firing *Hardy*'s gun. He said, "Dougy you were firing at me and I was firing at you." I said, "That's correct Max." He replied, "It's a good thing we were bloody bad shots." Which I thought, just about shows the idiocy and the futility of the whole thing we were engaged in." [There are more stories about the Reunions in my first book.]

Back to the *Hunter* crew's predicament whilst their ship is being manoeuvred around the fjord, making desperate attempts to avoid total annihilation, 'Stormy' Renshaw was becoming frustrated. "My ship, having learners aboard, was having a bit of difficulty with the smokescreen. There will be no record of this anywhere, not even the Admiralty will admit it, but we had quite a few greenhorns [newly trained] with us, and they were given responsible jobs such as setting off the smokescreens. Now, there were three smokescreens on the destroyer, one was on deck, one was below deck and the other was the funnels themselves. This young lad lit a large canister the size of a dustbin, but he didn't have the strength to push it overboard, thereby ending the smokescreen.

"So now we are trailing around Ofotfjord with our smokescreen coming behind us. Smokescreens are produced to go into and out of, and our following destroyer went in and out of ours. But in coming out, it plunged into the *Hunter*, virtually cutting her in two. I was down in the shell room supplying the ammunition, when all of a sudden; a shout went out, 'ABANDON SHIP!!' I was very cautious of abandoning ship in twelve degrees below freezing. Because Narvik is an ice-free harbour, the tide is so strong that ice cannot form. Anyway, I got into a life raft, and that was the last I could remember."

Able Seaman Fred Ward was part of 'No 1 Gun' crew and the following is Fred's account as recorded by his son Robin Ward. "The noise from the gun fire and explosions echoed off the side of the mountains. It was like having your head compressed, you could not think, the training just takes over. One of Fred's mates came up to him and asked to borrow his [seamen's] knife as he had lost his own. Fred took his knife out of the sheath and handed it to him. A few moments later there was an explosion, Fred looked over and his friend had gone. This was when he knew the *Hunter* had to go down, the Germans were not going to stop until she was beneath the waves. Running out of ammunition Fred was sat on the deck looking at the freezing water, when the order to 'abandon' ship came.

"Fred could already see bodies floating in front of him, their heads blackened from smoke and fire. He recalled, 'It was as seeing black heads bobbing around everywhere'. A lot of sailors jumped in immediately as they were near fires or other hazardous things, but my father felt safer staying on board. Most of them had already succumbed to the cold, it was snowing and the water was like ice.

"Something made Fred look behind as the Captain, *Lind*say De Villiers was walking past. He looked at Fred and nodded, as if to say over you go. The Captain then disappeared back inside the ship and was not seen again. Fred took his boots off and jumped in. There were about fifty Stokers on board and most were probably still alive when she sank; but their exits were buckled from the explosions and they were trapped. This haunts my father to this day."

The engine room is the biggest compartment on a destroyer, so if it receives a direct hit it causes rapid flooding to ensue. Hence, why in an earlier chapter I suggested, Electrical Artificer Andrew Black, being a member of a 'Repair Party' rather than as usual looking after the ship's generators, survived. However, he had another challenge to negotiate – the near freezing waters of the fjord and safely arrive ashore.

Returning to Engineer Artificer John Farnell, interviewed for **the Yorkshire Post** (17th July 1940),

"Actually, on April 10th normally I would have been in the engine room, but as duties were, I was forward on repair work. We certainly gave Jerry what for before being rammed. However, in quick succession our ship torpedoed a big German ship carrying explosives, five iron ore ships and two destroyers by shell fire".

The remainder of the news report will be shown later,

As previously indicated, Able Seaman Marshal Soult had a bird's eye view of the whole action. "Only Carley floats were intact on *Hunter* and these were thrown over the side as the crew carried out the order to abandon ship. The operation took about fifteen minutes. I left the 'Director Tower' and made my way to the bridge, men were already swimming away from the ship. I was wearing a pair of leather sea boots which were difficult to remove. Seeing my struggles the Warrant Torpedo Officer J. H. Coomb came to the rescue and pulled them off for me. I left the bridge and went to the port side of the upper deck. The only men left on the ship were those who had been killed during the action and a few who were reluctant to jump into the icy cold water. It can be presumed that these few were non-swimmers".

Marshal Soult, thirty years later, received a letter from James Smail's sister, Mrs G. Watson, enquiring about her brother's death. She asked, "His destroyer went down, but we have never had any right word about whether he was drowned or any burial place. I would just like to know if any of your chums knew him". At that time, Marshal was not aware that there were various burial sites but as Mrs Watson describes in a further letter to my Dad, Cyril, "He (Marshal) knew James very well, they just called him 'Jock' [...]

he was a very well-liked [...] James was giving all the chaps rum before they jumped into the water. It seems a fair mystery, I just sit and think what came over him, for he was a very strong swimmer, unless he was hit when swimming, it was hard lines after twenty-five years in the Navy".

It appears from accounts that James 'Jock' Smail remained on board as long as possible because of his concerns about those being left behind, who for whatever reasons were unable to jump into the water. (Although, probably most were 'non-swimmers' who somehow had managed to get through their basic training without completing the mandatory swimming tests.) To give them the necessary extra courage to do so he thought a tot of rum would be the answer. Not recommended by today's standards but in times of desperation a strategy which James thought would help his fellow shipmates.

It seems that Chief Petty Officer James Smail, having eventually jumped into the water was possibly found alive by a German destroyer. However, his death recorded on 23rd April 1940 showed that he 'Died of Wounds'. His body, with thirty-three others from *Hunter*, was probably buried at 'Harvik' (rather than Narvik) cemetery.

Marshal continues, "I thought it would be unwise to enter the water not wearing an inflatable life jacket, so I went to a locker amidships where the life jackets were stored. These I issued to members of the crew as they passed by, keeping the last one for myself. By this time the ship was listing to starboard so after donning the life jacket I decided to leave the ship. The water was freezing cold; the air temperature was 18 degrees below freezing. This no doubt was the reason for so many lives being lost.

"I jumped into the icy water from the upper deck, and after recovering from the initial shock of immersion in water that was nearly freezing, I swam away from the ship's side. A salvo of enemy shells hit the water some 500 yards ahead of me, I stopped swimming but decided to continue, presuming and hoping that the next salvo would go over me. Luckily this proved correct and it did.

"I then swam parallel with the ship towards the stern. I sighted a Carley float and swam towards it, but on reaching it I found that it was already full of survivors and many more were hanging on to the lanyards of the float. I looked back at the ship and saw that she was listing more and more to starboard, she then rolled over and sank stern first; this was at about approximately 0630 hours, just fifteen minutes after the ship had been abandoned. I saw about twenty men still walking on the ship's bottom apparently unwilling to jump into the water. I presume they went down with the ship. Shortly after the ship had disappeared there was an explosion below water sending out a shock wave; this squeezed one's body in a most unpleasant manner and lifted it partly out of the water. I then spotted an empty Carley float which seemed too good to be true, but it was not quite 250 yards away.

"However, I decided that there was no future in staying where I was so I set out to swim for it. After swimming about a hundred yards I came to another Carley float loaded with survivors and many more hanging on to the lanyards. I took a paddle from Chief Stoker Moore and continued swimming to the empty Carley float pushing the oar in front of me. My intention was to get on the float and paddle it back to pick up survivors from the water. The spirit was willing, but the flesh was getting too weak to carry this out.

"On reaching the float I had to abandon the oar, as I had not sufficient strength to climb aboard the float. My legs were now beginning to feel numb, so I hooked my arm through the life line and proceeded to swim back with the float. I succeeded in reaching the other float and men began to clamber aboard my float. By this time the spreading numbness had reached my waist and I felt that I could hold on no longer; so I put both arms on the float and said, 'I'm going'. Able Seaman Stanley Cook and Chief Electrical Artificer Albert Black each grabbed an arm and hauled me aboard. I collapsed unconscious in the bottom of the float."

Marshal Soult goes on to describe the dramatic and valiant attempts to save lives, by both the crew of *Hunter* and their adversaries. "The survivors from *Hunter* were in the icy water for just over an hour, many succumbed to the very cold conditions, losing consciousness and sinking to the deep depths of the fjord. Many brave deeds had been enacted that morning by the crew of *Hunter*, before abandoning ship."

One of those brave sailors was Able Seaman Norman Stewart, known as 'Jan'. [a short version for the nickname 'Janner' used to refer to many of those from the West Country] As mentioned, the First Lieutenant, Stuart-Menteth, was on the upper deck at the point where *Hotspur* rammed at 'great speed'. The collision ripped off a davit, which pinned Stuart-Menteth to the deck, Stewart spotted the incident. Rather than save himself first, he stayed and extricated the officer and "propelled him into a life raft". On reviving from the frightening experience, Stuart-Menteth must have felt, one good turn deserves another. Finding the raft "a bit crowded", he went over, "with his broken leg and dislocated shoulder, to make space for others in even worse case. He clung to a piece of wreckage and then passed out".

Norman Stewart was awarded the Distinguished Service Medal for his brave actions on that day.

Marshal states, "In another incident Petty Officer Tim Cunningham was seen in the water carrying a Stoker Petty Officer, a non-swimmer, on his back. Despite the courageous efforts of Tim Cunningham, neither he nor the Stoker P.O. survived the terrible conditions in which the men from *Hunter* found themselves that morning; conditions which accounted for most of the casualties. Another unfortunate aspect was the fact that *Hunter* went down in the middle of the fjord which at that point was very deep and too far away from either shore for the survivors to swim to."

Stoker Joe Settle, still only twenty years old, at his action station in the boiler room, recalls, "I was lucky to get off the ship as I had to help to close down the boilers or they would have blown up – me as well! After that I jumped into the sea and swam to a Carley float. The first was full of men but they had been in the water which was freezing. It was also snowing so they were frozen to death. I don't know how long I was in the water." Joe's daughter, Sheila says, "It was only because he was one of the last off the ship, he spent least time in the freezing water before being rescued." Joe continues, "The battle was still going on, then the shore batteries started firing so our ships withdrew. Then a German destroyer came and picked up survivors that were still alive."

There was another Stoker who was down below, who also made his way to the upper deck and found it totally "desolate". This was John Hague who, as highlighted in the previous chapter, enjoyed his sport as a proficient rugby league player and had left his girlfriend May Chamberlain at home in Manchester, in order to go back to sea again

When the guns stopped firing, John Hague and his two shipmates, were still at their 'action stations' as ammunition suppliers for No 2 Gun. This would have been three decks below the iron deck. Obviously, during the Battle he heard the loud bangs and felt the violent reverberations throughout the ships super structure; as the enemy's salvoes came in board. However, John and his two shipmates were unaware of the order to 'Abandon Ship'; although an eerie silence descended upon them. Being in the depths of the ship and out of touch with the command, he naturally became anxious about the situation above.

John describes what happened next, "The first we knew it was bad was when we started to tilt, we went up to the deck where we were struck by the chilling winds but there was nobody about, no life rafts or aids. I remember seeing a lot of devastation, in fact No 2 Gun was on top of No 1 Gun spread out over the fo'c's'le." Sixty-eight years later, a BBC reporter referring to the weather asked him what it was like, John retorted: "What's it like being in a freezer? We knew we had no choice but to get off the ship."

John continues and tells me at his home, "I don't know how long we were in the water I tried not to think about the cold and tried to keep moving to keep warm and stay afloat. Soon afterwards a ship came along, they, turned out to be Germans, and threw a ladder over the side. I had difficulty clambering up it, as it was very cold. But after what seemed like hours but must have been minutes really, I was grabbed on board by German sailors. Then they swilled me down with clean water to get off all the muck and oil and gave me dry clothes to put on. The Germans were alright but I didn't have time to be afraid, it all happened quickly."

Stoker Joe Murphy also survived but like many coming back from the horrendous events in the war, he kept his own counsel. Nephew, Kieran Hosford explains, "Joe never really talked about his experiences during the war and the information we have is sketchy. According to my mother's recollections of his story, when the *Hunter* was stricken, Joe and others below decks managed to make their way up on deck to find it relatively desolate. Knowing the ship was doomed; they followed their comrades and jumped overboard."

Robin Ward goes on to relate his father Fred's experience whilst in the water. "Fred his senses numbed and with the other unfortunate men floating nearby, started to tread water, waiting to either be picked up or die. He turned to face *Hunter* which was on its end, sinking. Every ship has a name and a number, the *Hunter* was H35 and Fred was watching this slowly make its way towards the waterline. Fred remembers that because of the sheer bulk of the *Hunter*, it looked as if it was sinking slowly, but as H35 reached the waterline it disappeared very quickly and within a few seconds she was gone. There was a swell in the water and then nothing; it was as if she was never there."

Three German destroyers, having broken off the action against the three retreating British destroyers started to pick up *Hunter* survivors. Many of them were now unconscious in the water, with only their life jackets keeping them afloat. When the men regained consciousness they found themselves on bunks in the German destroyers. They were being well looked after by the German sailors, who massaged their legs and arms bringing back the circulation. They were given coffee and cigarettes, wrapped in blankets, and many of the British sailors owed their lives to the ministrations of their opponents in the battle.

However, some survivors did not find such a welcoming party awaiting them.

Sam Evens, "Eventually the German ships came back and started picking up survivors. We went up the 'Jacob's Ladder', the wooden ladder they put over the side. It was very awkward to get up one of them, especially when you're leaking wet with your coat and trousers on. There was such a rush by everyone to get to the ladder, I was nowhere near first. However, I finally made it up and there was a German officer with a revolver, asking 'Name of ship?!' I didn't say anything and just passed out. We were taken down to the messes, where we were given hot coffee and canvas suits to place over our sodden clothes. Some were very seriously injured. The Germans must have picked them up from the water and a few that came back that were injured they put them in the hospital ashore."

German crew attempting to revive 'Hunter' survivor.

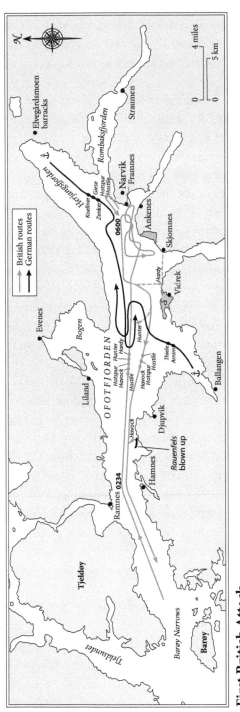

First British Attack

Map of First Battle. [Geirr
Haarr Collection]

Alex Stuart-Menteth recalls, "I vaguely remember being hauled out of the water, but must have passed out and when I came to, I was lying on the deck in the German destroyer's wardroom. I remember seeing a picture of Hitler on the wall facing me."

Joe Settle now safely on board the enemy ship tells us, "I was dried off and laid on a bunk bed until we tied up. We were ashore! I had no clothes or shoes just a blanket. I was a prisoner of war."

Marshal Soult, "I woke up on a German destroyer. I couldn't move my legs. I was in a bunk, a young German gave me a cigarette and coffee, I believe. I couldn't feel my feet or my legs they were suddenly dead. I pointed to him; he set about rubbing them which he did for about ten minutes. The pain was flaming awful but the circulation got back. Apparently our clothes froze on us as we got out of the water and they just cut them off. We were there for a while and then informed that all 'English Gentlemen' would be put ashore at 1000. They came with a pair of German jackboots and put them on my feet, and a blanket – no clothes. Taken on deck and I was just about to go down when this German, who had done my feet, gave me another blanket. Down we went, there was fourteen of us and we were taken ashore in Narvik to a hut in the dockyard".

Robin Ward continues, "Just as Fred thought he would not make it, he was picked up by a German ship. He was pulled out of the water and remembers a German sailor walking towards him with a knife; this is when he passed out. On regaining consciousness he was naked in a bunk with only a blanket covering him. A German guard offered him some bread which he took. He was marched on deck and watched as the remains of 'War' smouldered in the fjord. He was freezing, in shock and did not know what lay ahead for him. He was taken to shore as a prisoner along with other survivors. The war had just started and Fred found himself in the hands of the enemy. But this would not be the last time he would be captured by the Germans."

There was another interesting account of a surviving *Hunter* crew member, that of Seaman Bill Parton. Many years later, he told his daughter Christina, that he had been picked up by a German U-boat. He said he had been given brandy and was well looked after.

From the information I had, this was of interest, as it was the first time a U-boat had been mentioned in picking up any *Hunter* survivors. At the time of the battle there had been at least five U-boats in the vicinity U-25, U-46, U-48, U-51 and U-64. Guessing the number of U-boats concerned, it could have been

U-46 as this was the nearest to *Hunter* when she sank. This submarine had been ordered into Narvik harbour at 2235, when it would have been able to off load Bill Parton and any others to the custody of the German military ashore.

As a matter of interest out of the five U-boats in the area for both battles, U-48 went on to become the most successful German U-boat during the rest of the war. The submarine went on thirteen patrols, sunk fifty-one ships (306,874 tons) and three ships damaged (20,480 tons).

John Hague, by now, was feeling extremely grateful to his German counterparts, but he still had more traumatic memories to share. In the meantime, we will continue with Marshal Soult's account. "As the survivors were being ferried ashore in the German pinnace [doubled banked engine driven boat] they noticed that the enemy were already hard at work fitting plates to the shell damaged destroyers. They saw for the first time the amount of damage that had been done to the enemy ships, the merchant ships and the docks."

It is suggested by medical professionals that a man could survive approximately twenty minutes in the fjord in the temperature at that time. It appears from accounts that most of the *Hunter* crew before being picked up by the German destroyers were around forty-five minutes in the water if not more. It would explain why at least six frozen bodies were found later. One of those was probably Warrant Officer Coomb mentioned by Marshal Soult, along with Able Seamen Robert Blower and Nicholas Blundell, Stokers Harold Smart, Samuel Mann and Chief Petty Officer James Smail.

Captain Nicholas writes in his diary:

10 April 40 Wed. First Battle begins.
After more or less a sleepless night we were promptly awaken by the sound of loud explosions and gunfire. This went on for some time – at last died away. Our thoughts were at once of the Navy. A while later some German sailors arrived wet through and carrying lifejackets. We were all herded to another classroom. Here we could see the havoc done by the British destroyers to get at the Germans. They had sunk nearly everything in the harbour. One of the first to go was an ammunition ship. Of my own ship only the top of the masts and the funnel was showing. One German destroyer was made fast to a Swedish vessel to prevent her from sinking and one lay each side of the German Whaler, both damaged. One destroyer lay alongside the quay apparently undamaged.
I was thankful that none of my crew were on board my vessel. When I asked

the Germans what about something to eat for the crew, I was told that the English had sunk their stores ship so they had no food to give us. However, later we asked to be allowed into town to see what we could get ourselves. The Captains of the 'Romanby' and 'Riverton' and myself along with one or two to carry the stuff if we could get anything, set out under armed guards. We tried a few places and found them shut, so we went to 'Olaf Lanson's' and helped ourselves to bread, marmalade, sausage, sugar and coffee.

This was split into three parts for the three crews. We had a drink of coffee – sliced bread and sliced sausage. We were all then marched to the Café Iris and interned in one room there, where I found 3 Indian firemen from my vessel who had left in the Mate's boat. They informed me that they had been taken prisoner but that the rest of the crew were still at large in Ankenes. Including myself, the crew with me now numbered 23, 19 still in Ankenes.

In the Café Iris were also 14 men, survivors of HMS Hunter, *a destroyer which had been sunk in the morning action. These men were naked except for a blanket each. They had been taken out of the water by the Germans. As their clothes were full of oil and water, they had taken these clothes from them and given them a blanket each. The total number of men in the room was 109. The room was approximately 70 feet by 20 feet and had plenty of large windows, where we could see the harbour and railway etc. We shared our bread etc. with the Hunter's men and our three firemen.*

The office staff at Narvik's City Hall returned to work again. The bombardment went on for hours, even in the late morning they could hear violent explosions from the outer fjord. But this time they knew what was happening, since the first of the German wounded had told the story at the hospital. British destroyers had entered the harbour opening fire before the Germans had discovered them. This time the British had let go first. The leader of the German destroyers was blown up and a Commodore Bonte had been killed. Several wounded Germans had talked of his loss as a terrible catastrophe, and the Mayor later found out just what an important personage he was in terms of the war effort.

Despite the welcome news, the situation in the town continued to be difficult. People insisted on leaving. Most of the rowing boats disappeared during the morning. Families in sports dress and with knapsacks could be seen everywhere going towards the water front and to the north of the town. The Mayor and the Committee were naturally worried about this impromptu evacuation on several counts. Namely, it might prove difficult for small boats to get through to the unoccupied territories, as even the south side, called Ankenesstrand had been taken over by the Germans, who had also confiscated the ferries. The evacuation needed to be stopped and panic prevented. The officials at City Hall told the people that they also had wives and that they would be among the last to leave the area. This seemed to calm down the situation somewhat.

It is Tuesday the 9th of April, and Fru Martha Hagen was attempting to get on with daily life, but still at the back of her mind was the safety and wellbeing of her children. "During the morning Magne went over to Lise, who was alone with the baby, to find out how she was getting on. She had taken it all quite calmly and said that she was going with her landlord to their new holiday chalet near Skjomnes. That is the last we have heard of her.

"People have begun to leave the town as best they could. Those who had holiday huts around Oyjord and Beisfjord went that way, and some went over to Stromsnes. One or two went all the way into Sweden by train, but there were not many of them. Some simply ran away without any idea of where they were going.

"Magne thought that we should get out to Ballangen. I had little or no wish to go, seeing that Solveig was ill in bed, but I helped him to pack a few bags. He said that he would see to getting passes and other formalities. He tried to do this, but he had bitten off more than he could chew, and by the time he had coped with all the queues it was so late before he got everything fixed that the boat to Ballangen had already gone. And I must say I was glad of it, in my heart of hearts.

"That evening an announcer said over the radio that those who wished to leave town would be able to do so next day. They could go by boat to Ballangen, Sklomen, Liland and several other places. He advised people not to take to their heels without having proper plans. But Man proposes and God disposes.

"Next morning we were again woken up at five o'clock by gun fire. I christened it 'Hitler's morning greeting', but this time it wasn't only Hitler's – it came from the British too. The English were here in spite of 'our Air Force'. [Referring back to the optimism spoken by the young Austrian soldier.]

"For one whole frightful hour or so everything trembled and quaked, and then it was quiet again. I don't know what the result was. There must have been losses on both sides, but nothing decisive. As far as we were concerned, though, the result was that all the ways out of Narvik were blocked."

Destroyed wagons on the iron ore quay. [Cyril Cope Collection]

Jan Wellem alongside on the left. [Theo Werner Schettler via Frank Hackney Collection]

"What appeared to be a funnel going into orbit!"

So far, the earlier chapters have mainly focused on the *Hunter* crew's experiences. Before returning to these events, I will now mention the other three ships in the flotilla and their escape down the fjord. HMS *Hostile* initially was not with her four sister ships of the flotilla. She had been despatched with HMS *Birmingham* to search for German fishing trawlers. However, now having returned to the fold, she had played her part in the Battle of Narvik. As mentioned below by Commander Layman, *Hostile* had another crucial role to play before returning to open sea.

Here is the end of Commander Layman's report to the Admiralty. "As *HOTSPUR* was being conned [controlled] from aft and had no signalling arrangements, *HOSTILE* took charge and escorted her to Skjel Fjord. When about 18 miles west of Narvik, the German ammunition ship *RAUENFELS* was steaming up the fjord. Mistaking us for German destroyers she continued her course and was then stopped and blown up by *HAVOCK*. (Paragraph 25)"

Lieutenant Commander Courage the commanding officer on *HAVOCK* reports, "On the way down the fjord a merchant ship was sighted which proved to be the German SS *RAUENFELS*, and *HOSTILE* stopped her with a shot and ordered me to examine her. I fired another round into her bow and she stopped and her crew hurriedly abandoned ship. I stopped and picked them up while the ship slowly drifted to the beach. I sent an armed boat over but she was burning furiously and I was uncertain as to whether she had used W/T to call her friends. I decided not to risk the loss of my party and ordered their return.

"When the boat was hoisted I fired two H.E. [High Explosives] into her to hasten the fire and went ahead. The result was certainly startling, as the German literally erupted and a column of flame and debris rose to over 3000 feet, as testified both by *HOSTILE* and *HARDY'S* survivors to the west who saw it over the mountains at that height. Fortunately no casualties were sustained in *HAVOCK* but some damage to the hull was done. Judging from the fragments picked up she contained all the reserve ammunition and torpedoes for the Destroyer Flotilla, and also minefield". (Paragraph 22)

My friend Bill Sanders in Exeter, whose wife Anna Borg comes from the area, informs me that debris can still be found high up in the surrounding mountains. On *Hostile*, which had moved around to another part of the fjord, the crew witnessed what appeared to be a funnel going into orbit. Initially concerns were raised as to whether this was *Havock* being torpedoed by a U-boat.

In 1990, during the 50th Anniversary at Narvik, I had the pleasure of meeting up with Bill Brown who was a crew member of *Hostile*. He had a larger than life personality with a magnificent theatrical moustache and many interesting sea stories. He also still liked his tot of rum and, on this particular occasion, I had no choice but to join him in a tipple.

Bill went on to tell me about what he remembered of the events leading up to and the action in the first battle. His account was similar to that given to a Norwegian reporter during the Anniversary. "*Hostile* came ill-prepared; we did not have enough food on board and the personal ammunition left a lot to be desired. We only had old 'Lee Enfield' guns and would not have stood a chance had the ship been bombed and we had had to fight the Germans on land.

"We were hit by two shells, which failed to cause serious damage. One hit the potato store, midships, which was empty at the time, as we did not have the time to take any provisions before leaving for Narvik from the base at Scapa Flow".

Apparently, Bill was the only casualty on *Hostile*, the result of when part of one of the ships boats came loose and landed on his head. It is interesting to note that *Hostile*, probably because she had left earlier than the other four ships in the flotilla, had not been fully provisioned. If as had been initially planned, the landing parties had gone into Narvik to free the town, in Bill's opinion the weaponry would not have borne well against the enemy. This of course could have proved a disastrous situation.

The other shell mentioned by Bill hit the 'paint locker' which obviously being inflammable started a fire. However, this was quickly extinguished as told by Signalman Alan Martin. At the time Alan would have been on the 'flagdeck' where he was in a position to see most of the action, unlike his fellow shipmates down below. Here Signalman Martin describes the frightening moments when *Hostile* was leaving Narvik harbour for the last time.

"There were tracer bullets from guns ashore; they were coming whistling over your heads. We had two torpedoes stuck in the tubes. Three torpedoes went under the ship all at once. The Captain didn't know which way to turn; there was not much option but to brace ourselves. Ready for the ship to blow up, I went to the other side [of the ship] and they had gone.

"After the *Hostile* had joined the other ships outside of the harbour the radio phone message from *Hardy* said, 'Engage and hoist the Battle Ensign.' This was on the mainmast [the one aft of the two masts] and a bit strange as we were in dense black smoke. Just as I was about to do this, Smithy, a Signalman older than me, grabbed hold of it and said, 'Not on your life.'"

This was understandable, as a large Battle Ensign, predominantly white with the 'red cross' and one quarter with the Union Jack high on the mast coming in and out of black smoke would be like a beacon for the enemy to target their guns.

As indicated by Commander Layman, he had handed over command to *Hostile*'s Captain, Commander Wright, who quickly faced another challenge. Continuing to go west up the fjord the three escaping destroyers came across a merchant vessel going east. Commander Wright ordered the ship to halt, but she carried on, at which point it was identified as *Rauenfels*. Two shells were fired at her, which had the intended effect.

Hostile then went off to escort *Hotspur* to Skjel Fjord in search of a safe haven to assess the full extent of damage to *Hotspur* and consider the possibilities of re- fuelling and replenishing victuals for both ships.

Apparently, even the German destroyers on their way back to Narvik saw a column of white smoke but unlike *Hostile* probably had more optimistic thoughts that one of their U-boats had sunk a British destroyer. It would be a while before news reached the Germans that their main hope of replenishment for their destroyers, already extremely depleted of fuel and ammunition had been blown up into the sky. The effect of removing *Rauenfels* and the day before the oil tanker *Kattegat* from the Germans' supply chain was devastating, the Zerstörers at Narvik would now continue being refuelled two at a time, instead of the original intentions of four. Also *Jan Wellem* did not hold enough fuel for all ten of the German destroyers. **This had left the German command with a major dilemma about eventually making an escape to open sea.** [59]

---

59   With regards to the artillery lost on *Rauenfels*, this amounted to all the Germans battery and flak guns and ammunition.

It is understandable that, after such a ferocious battle, where it appeared that the Royal Navy destroyers had won the day, that all those of the non-occupying force in Narvik, were frustrated that there had not been any more positive developments. I do not want to be part of the 'if only' or 'why didn't' debate. However, right from the beginning, when Warburton-Lee made the brave decision to attack up and till there was no immediate follow up from the fleet out in the North Sea, decisions could be put down to uncertainty caused by a lack of necessary intelligence. Resulting in those higher up in the command chain rightly or wrongly, not being prepared to take risks. This was probably not helped by Admiral Whitworth who was in command at sea, apparently on previous occasions being 'bypassed' by the Admiralty.

Havock, *Hostile* and *Hotspur* rendezvoused with the destroyer *Greyhound* off Tranøy at 0930. Admiral Whitworth then finally decided to put further caution to one side and ordered the cruiser *Penelope* and a screen of destroyers into Vestfjorden. This was to support the three escaping ships, then establish a patrol off the minefield, with the object of preventing enemy forces reaching Narvik. As well as continuing towards Narvik to make sure none of the German ships, including submarines, could escape from the Ofotfjord. His first objective was completed having met up with the three *H* destroyers at 1100. This time Captain Yates had information that the enemy forces' strength in Narvik was one cruiser, five Zerstörers and a submarine, that other support ships carrying troops could be on their way. As you have read this was not exactly correct.

The commanding officers of *Hostile* and *Havock* wanted to go back to Narvik to end what they had started, and give themselves an opportunity to search for possible survivors. Their request was turned down by Captain Yates, who, later in the evening of 10th April had had a signal from the Admiralty (bypassing Admiral Whitworth), asking him to consider an attack on Narvik, that night or the following day. To summarise, his reply was to emphasise that he could not do three tasks at once. He also felt that he needed more reinforcements advising a delay till the morning of the 12th April.

The Admiralty agreed with Yates' proposal, by sending the following signal. "As enemy is now established at Narvik recapture of that place takes priority over operations against Bergen and Trondhjem. Expedition is being prepared as quickly as possible [...] It is of primary importance to prevent Narvik being reinforced by sea. [The possibility to seize] and hold a temporary base near Narvik with small military force is under urgent examination. In the meantime, you will presumably arrange temporary refuelling anchorage in the North. As Narvik must also be of primary importance to the Germans, it seems possible that battle cruisers may turn up there."

So, unbeknown to those frustrated friends waiting in Narvik, it was going to be another two days at least before a second front began. Or could it be longer? In the meantime, Skjelfjord on the south side of Lofoton Islands was rapidly established as a refuelling anchorage and a much needed repair facility for any arriving damaged naval ships. It became known affectionately as 'Cripples Creek' and a special man to oversee the work was known as 'Snowdrop'. Namely, Hartvig Sverdrup, mentioned in my first book, who became a friend of my father, Cyril.

'Snowdrop' was then a civilian and in charge of a ship repair yard in Norway. Over the following years of the war, Hartvig and his skilled shipyard men became well respected by Captains and crews of the Allies warships. 'Snowdrop' also employed four divers who worked from 0400 to 1800 for days on end, a remarkable feat of endurance.

All the chasing Zerstörers are now back in the Narvik area with a new Commander, Fregattenkapitan Bey, taking over from the deceased Bonte. At 1300 Bey receives his orders from the Admiral at the Group 'West', to get as many of Bey's ships back into battle-readiness. Bey's Zerstörers commanders sent their damage assessments and causalities. Wilhelm Heidkamp had eighty-one dead but usable weapons and ammunition which was removed and used elsewhere. She would capsize in the harbour and sink the following day. Both *Hans Ludemann* and *Diether von Roeder* would need substantial repairs before becoming seaworthy. *Roeder* had thirteen crew killed and temporarily gave up her on board communications equipment to be utilised ashore at the Narvik Wehrmacht Operations Centre.

Anton Schmitt's hull was broken in two and had over fifty casualties, similar to *Heidkamp*, she had been put out of any future plans. *Hermann Kunne* had nine dead and needed work on her engines which had been put out of action by the shock wave caused by the torpedoes that had sunk *Schmitt*. *Erich Koellner* had suffered no hits but because of engine defects had to shut down her boilers. Similarly, *Wolfgang Zenker* and *Erich Giese* had no major hits and went straight to *Jan Wellem* to begin fuelling. However, overall it seemed that significant amounts of ammunition had been expended and few magazines were more than half full.

All crew members of the sunken or out of action Zerstörers and those not needed for essential repairs on the others were sent ashore to relieve Alpine Troops in carrying out their trained duties. At 1400, another order came to Bey, for all seaworthy Zerstörers to depart that evening and join up with the battle-group in the North Sea; for a return to Wilhelmshaven. Bey replied by explaining that only *Wolfgang Zenker* and *Erich Giese* would be able to sail. So it was that at 1940, twelve hours since the first battle, Bey left with the two Zerstörers. As you would expect the crews were apprehensive and not optimistic of eventually making it to open sea. However their fears were shortly alleviated, in the Zerstörers, as it was not long before the patrolling *Penelope* group was seen in the distance. Bey ordered his ship to return to Narvik. The Group 'West' having received Bey's decision, replied telling him that in any future breakout made, "Any ruse of war may be applied." This included utilising copies of the British naval flags which were always kept in the Kriegsmarine's flag lockers.

Another early arrival at 'Cripples Creek' was a towed HMS *Penelope* who had ran aground near Bodo, on the 11th April. She was searching for reported German transports in that area. This time again incorrect intelligence was provided.

In Cyril's documents, there is a letter written by 'Snowdrop' about his experience in getting the *Penelope* back to seaworthiness in order to enable her to return to British waters. 'Snowdrop' mentions that upon initially going on board the *Penelope* he knew nothing about warships. "As I landed, [Lofoton Island] my brother-in-law was on the telephone and I asked him what a ship was called that was larger than a destroyer, but not as big as a battleship?"

To 'Snowdrop' and his company's credit, from when the first casualty *Hotspur* arrived, followed by *Penelope* and then many more after, there was not any thought of payment or salvage money. They just wanted to assist the war effort against the Nazis. It was not until 1946 that his company was finally paid for the work done.

He received an award for his services from King George VI and during the war he became a Naval Commander in the Royal Norwegian Navy. It was to my advantage that in the documentation I have mentioned above, he had neatly placed photographs that he had taken during those dark days in 'Cripples Creek'.

Lofoton Islands also became a sea grave for many Royal Navy men including those lives lost on *Hotspur*. The hospitals at Graval and Reine would soon receive wounded survivors from *Hardy* who were given exceptional skilled surgery and care. As did some of the local population who took into their homes sailors for their rehabilitation and secondary care. I have already mentioned Signalman Ralph Brigginshaw as he was one of those fortunate survivors. [60]

Hotspur moored at 'Cripples Creek'. [Commander Hartvig Sverdrup, Royal Norwegian Navy Reserve Collection. Known affectionately as 'Snowdrop'. Via Cyril Cope]

At 1640, approximately twelve hours after the beginning of the First Battle of Narvik, *Hostile* and the limping *Hotspur* finally arrived at Skjeldfjord in the Outer Lofotens.

Returning back to Signalman Alan Martin, when *Hostile* and *Hotspur* finally reached Skjel Fjord, there remained urgent decisions to be made. "We had had two tons of oil but it had all gone, there were no provisions left, and the canteen only had bars of soap. There was nothing to eat; we had fired all our ammunition, so we couldn't go anywhere. We dropped the anchor to take stock and a cruiser (*Penelope*) came along and gave us some fuel. *Hotspur* thought it was going to sink, so we had their crew on our ship. Some were in our mess, they spoke of blood splattered all over the bulkhead and looked still in a state of shock and subdued."

---

60   Finally, 'Snowdrop' was a main supporter in influencing the Norwegian Government to convince the British authorities to allow the 'Norwegian War Medal' to be awarded to all the crew members of the 2nd Destroyer Flotilla. A saga which will be explained at the end of the book.

One of those was Petty Officer Supply Ernest Symes. However, there was another 'Symes' on board whether they were related or not I do not know but it is an uncommon name. [61]

Percy Danby and the *Hotspur* crew, having completed the sea burial for their shipmates, are starting to feel less battle stressed. "We limped into Skel Fjord that evening, escorted all the way by *HOSTILE* and "*HAVOCK*". Shrapnel holes in the ship's motorboat were patched and it was used to transport those not working in the machinery spaces to *HOSTILE* and *HAVOCK*. Two torpedoes which had malfunctioned and had become stuck in the tubes. These were transferred to the other ships. Only about ten of us remained aboard. The ship was searched and inspected for safety reasons, to make sure that there were no smouldering fires or unreported damage. By this time, she was listing so heavily to starboard that it was feared that she might sink overnight. It was decided that the ten of us remaining would spend the night aboard *HOSTILE* and the angle of the list would be assessed by monitoring any change in the boat falls hanging vertically to the surface of the fjord. The next morning, to our great relief, the list had not changed so we returned aboard.

"Our fresh water tanks were topped up by other ships. The galley was got working but any food not in tins had been ruined by the smoke of the battle. The ship stank of smoke and had to be cleaned throughout."

As an afterthought, Percy Danby also advises that the collision between *Hunter* and *Hotspur* almost certainly caused some fatalities in *Hunter's* boiler room at the point of impact. Whilst he believes that most of the deaths on *Hotspur* were caused by shells. He says this because a number of men appeared to have been concussed; they were dead but did not have a mark on them.

In the early stages of gathering information for my two books, I had a post from Christine Taylor living in Newcastle, New South Wales, Australia. Her grandfather was Able Seaman Leslie Oliver who was one of those killed on *Hotspur*. Leslie was aged twenty-nine and came from Bexleyheath, Kent. He was married to Edith and they had two sons Cliff (6) and David (4). Leslie joined the Navy in 1925, aged fifteen. He was an experienced destroyer crew

---

61   I am advised by Percy Danby with regards to Alan Martin's comments above, that the two tons of oil would have been diesel oil for the emergency diesel-driven generator and for the galley. Adding as fuel oil would never have been as low as two tons.

member having previously served on the 'B' and 'C' Class destroyers, *Keith* and *Comet* respectively. Both ships were attached to the Mediterranean Station.

Leslie was a very good sportsman, particularly at boxing in which he represented his ships. He was also selected for a Navy rugby team, and was a strong swimmer and water polo player.

His son Cliff remembers the day the family received the telegram notifying them of his father's death. At the time they were living with Edith's father. Edith's sisters were also there and Cliff recalls, "There was lots of crying and being told to take my little brother to play outside until we were allowed back in." The family were told he was buried at sea and this is what they still believe to this day.

Granddaughter Christine explains, "My Uncle Cliff followed in his father's footsteps and joined the Navy in 1951. One of the first ships he served on was HMS *Dampier* in 1952. Uncle Cliff had gone ashore and came back adrift. The Petty Officer had taken Cliff's 'station' card and ordered him to report to him in the morning. The next morning the P.O. asked Cliff what the letter 'L' for his middle name stood for and Cliff replied, 'Leslie.' 'Thought so,' said the P.O.

"It turns out that the Petty Officer on board 'Dampier' at the time had served with my grandfather Leslie Oliver during the Battle of Narvik aboard HMS *Hotspur*. The P.O. told Cliff that if he was half the man his father was, he'd never let this happen again – and Cliff took the advice and never did. He also told Cliff that he was with Leslie when he died and told him that 'he was one of the best'. Cliff regrets he never asked more about his father and he couldn't remember the Petty Officer's name.

"My father, Dave went onto join the Merchant Navy at the age of sixteen in 1952, serving for six years. However, once he and my Mum, Greta, had their first child, he decided it was important to be with his family.

"In the few letters we have that granddad wrote to Edith, it is very clear he dearly loved his little family and always signed off. 'With love and kisses for his two boys' as well as declaring his love for his wife, Edith." [62]

---

62   Edith having remarried, moved to Australia in the 60s, as did Cliff and his wife Dot. A couple of years later they were followed by Dave and Greta with their two young children. In later years two more children were born to them. Edith passed away in 2001, aged eighty nine.

Killed.
Ordinary Seaman P. Baldwin
Leading Seaman G. Barrington
Able Seaman R. Church
Able Seaman W. Groves
Petty Officer C. Harrison
Petty Officer G. Holmes
Able Seaman K. Jones
Stoker T. Moysey
Leading Seaman S. Murton
Able Seaman L. Oliver
Stoker J. Saville
Able Seaman B. Scalley
Able Seaman C. Spall
Mr C. Mifsud [Canteen manager]

Died of Wounds.
Petty Officer (Supply) E. Symes
Able Seaman J. Tattersall

Signalman Martin went on to describe how eventually assistance for their needs arrived. "The ship still had stocks of rum left on board and we hailed a Norwegian fishing boat and we gave them rum for a supply of cod. Later we were given the news that we on *Hostile* were going to Aberdeen. The crew were then in high spirits with the thoughts of finally going home." What Martin did not know was how close he and his shipmates were to returning back to Narvik.

It is only appropriate that Engine Room Artificer Percy Danby, now aged ninety-eight, should be given the last words on the repairs carried out on *Hotspur* before returning back to Britain. "Norwegian workmen plated over the hole in the ship's side (which was big enough for a short person to walk through upright!). I remember that every time a German aircraft flew over threateningly, these workmen would stand off from the ship in their own small boat and return when the threat had gone.

"The Engine Room Department set to work readying the ship for the trip back to Scapa Flow. No 1 and No 2 Boilers were badly contaminated with sea salt and had to be thoroughly cleaned. All valve stem packing and pumps packing had to be removed and replaced. Other ships now using the fjord from the Second Battle of Narvik helped this work. I helped a senior artificer to remove hydraulic steering lines that had been damaged in the action. We then removed undamaged lines port side aft and joined them to starboard lines for'd of the steering position, filled the lines with a 50:50 mixture of water and glycerine, pressure tested to 900 psi, and then creep tested satisfactory. These repairs to the steering system took about two weeks to accomplish. It enabled the ship to be steered normally. During this time *Penelope* returned the ship's crew and provided the *Hotspur* with provisions and fuel.

"We were in Skel Fjord for about three weeks altogether doing repairs. I did not learn until later that I was unaccounted for back home during this entire time; my newlywed wife and our families knew only that I was missing.

"Eventually, by the end of April, we steamed to Scapa Flow, where further repairs were carried out, sufficient to enable the ship to steam down the west coast of Britain, up the channel to Chatham Dockyard on 10 May, 1940. Once back in Chatham I was given three weeks of survivor leave and I made my way to Doncaster to see my wife and family. I was given a local hero's welcome."

Doncaster Chronicle, Thursday 2nd May 1940.

WOUNDED SAILOR PLAYED MOUTH-ORGAN
Doncaster Man Tells of British Spirit at Narvik

A hearty welcome awaited Engine Room Artificer Percy Danby of HMS *Hotspur* [...] when he returned to Doncaster on Tuesday [...] confetti was thrown over him on his arrival. A sign bearing the words "Welcome Home" was fixed over the doorway of his father-law's house [...] where he will spend his three weeks' survivors leave. Most of the neighbours turned out to greet him. [...]

"As we emerged from the fjord-in fine weather now – one of our flotilla sank a German supply ship after taking off the crew. The blowing up of that ship was a wonderful sight. One of the funnels rocketed sky-high, and we saw it turning over and over in the clouds.

"The spirit of the men was very fine. The wounded were singing, and one who had shrapnel in his back played a mouth-organ and cheered us all up. In the boiler room, there was a stoker who kept on sticking up his thumb, and remarking, "It's a snip!"

Ends.

Percy recalls *Hotspurs'* next task, "When all the repairs, tests and trials were completed on *Hotspur* and she was once again ready for active service, we were ordered to Gibraltar to join Force "H". We arrived there in early August, 1940."

Commander Layman at Buckingham Palace to be awarded the DCO for his achievement as Captain of 'Hotspur'. [Cyril Cope Collection]

BBC World Service 10th April at 6 pm.

"Mr Chamberlain announced the British achievements. He said, 'I do not propose today to make any general statement on the naval aspect of the war as I hope it will be possible for one to be made by the First Lord of the Admiralty tomorrow. But the House will probably wish to hear an account I have just received of the fierce action fought by British destroyers against the German forces in Narvik. Five British destroyers steamed up the Fjord and engaged six German destroyers of the latest and largest type, which were also supported by shore guns and batteries with newly mounted guns.' The Prime Minister said, that HMS *HUNTER* was sunk and *HARDY* was so severely injured that she had to be run ashore and became a wreck. The *HUNTER* a 1300-ton destroyer, has a normal complement of one hundred and forty-five. That *HARDY*, the flotilla leader, is slightly larger and normally carried a crew of one hundred and seventy-five.

"The Prime Minister continued: 'After a most determined action against a superior force, and larger and more modern ships, and in face of gun-fire from the shore, the damaged *HOTSPUR* withdrew, covered by the two destroyers. The enemy appeared in no condition to attempt pursuit. A 1600-ton German destroyer was torpedoed and believed sunk, and three were left heavily hit and burning.'

"In the House of Lords, Earl Stanhope made a statement similar to that of Mr. Chamberlain. He said that the British action at Narvik was brilliantly executed, and carried out against overwhelming odds. The tradition of the British Navy had been upheld most fully."

I felt I needed to finish this chapter by relating the apparent lack of emergency procedures in the early stages of World War Two. I have to thank an Engineering Officer during the war who produced a very descriptive account of his experiences, warts and all. His name was Eric R. Wilkinson, and he wrote it in 1992, from his diaries. "We were very well instructed in 'Damage Control'. Recent incidents, particularly the sinking of *Ark Royal* in the Med, has alerted the Admiralty to the importance of damage control, and how much could be done by proper discipline in controlling watertight compartments. My Lords were clever, knowing the infinite capacity of naval personnel to avoid going on apparently boring courses in remote locations, they organised a damage control course in Baron's Court, London, from Monday to Friday. Thus people going on this course could get two free weekends, to go home or spend in London, according to choice.

"It was a well-presented course. There were ship models with water-tight compartments and I remember vividly a demonstration of the sinking of the *Ark Royal* showing how it could have been prevented if good water-tight discipline had been observed.

"I don't remember any drill in procedures for escaping from the engine room or abandoning ship. All training was directed to the more positive subject of saving the ship. I suppose this was good psychology – it is extraordinary, in retrospect, how one lived one's life down in the engine rooms or boiler rooms, surrounded by all that superheated steam – and heavy machinery revolving at high speed – with little thought of what would happen if a bomb or torpedo hit us.

"At action stations, we had damage control duties, but most of these were standby. We were kept informed of what was going on by one of the bridge officers., through the tannoy. But because while anything was actually happening they were all very busy, we didn't hear about it until sometime afterwards. We would sit there, at our action stations, hearing bangs and explosions and bumps, followed by silence, and then, eventually, over the tannoy, the Gunnery Officer, 'What happened then was ...'"

If the courses, mentioned above had been introduced in 1939 or earlier it would not have saved HMS *Hunter* from sinking but with improved water-tight compartments, some lives on board *Hunter* and other ships, may have been spared. [63]

---

63 On 13 November 1941 HMS *Ark Royal* by the German U-boat 81 was hit and sank the following day. Her sinking was the subject of several inquiries; investigators were keen to know how the carrier was lost, in spite of efforts to save the ship and tow her to the Gibraltar naval base. They found that several design flaws contributed to the loss, which were rectified in the new British carriers.

The Captured Survivors brought Ashore to Narvik

Upon being rescued by the German Navy, the *Hunter* survivors were understandably confused and in a state of shock, also they were not aware of the full extent of their causalities. At this stage they were uncertain as to how many of their comrades had survived or lost their lives. Although, they were naturally feeling very relieved at having been given the chance to live for another day. Here we carry on with the accounts of the fortunate survivors. As they were picked up by more than one enemy vessel, they were split into two groups when they landed ashore.

Erich Giese's barkass *Hunter* survivors transported to shore. Provided with German sailor's summer rig 'white duck suits'. [Jim Renshaw Collection]

In my father's documents there was another account, mysteriously signed 'W.H.B.' Gunnarn 4.5.40'. Gunnarn is a small town in Northern Sweden. From a list of survivors I had obtained I was able to confirm that the only initials that matched were that of Petty Officer Supply 'Will' Harold Barrett. Possibly, because he was only one of the few surviving Senior Ratings, the responsibility fell to him to provide an immediate and accurate catalogue of the events relating to *Hunter*'s eventual demise and events thereafter.

Shortly after the battle, Petty Officer Barrett recorded. "The ship was abandoned within approximately fifteen minutes and completely disappeared from view at about 0630. All of the crew, except those killed during action, abandoned ship and after swimming for the best part of an hour, we were eventually rescued by three German destroyers. It is interesting at this point to mention that the water was twelve degrees below freezing point, and this must have accounted for a very large number of our casualties. Out of which [of the original 158 [eight officers and 148 ratings], only forty-eight have survived. Of the survivors, one officer still remains a prisoner of war, one officer and three ratings are in hospital. [64]

"It is unanimously agreed by all survivors that the treatment and attention we received from the Germans was of the very highest, everything possible being done for our comfort and wellbeing. Besides being given brandy and other spirits to revive us, we were bathed and clothed except for sixteen ratings who had been picked up separately. At 1000 all survivors were landed, thirty being put on board the German whaling ship *Jan Wellem* and fourteen in the Café Iris".

Able Seaman 'Stormy' Renshaw was back with the living, on board the *Jan Wellem*. "I lost every possession I had, including my bankbook, all my kit, everything went, and I ended up with what I'd finish up in? I was naked when I woke up. I was in a bunk with the Chief Stoker [Moore] nursing me and I managed to scrounge a pair of canvas trousers and a jersey of sorts. In the next cabin to me was a civilian [...] I became friendly with him and all of a sudden, he disappeared and left his cabin open; he left a pair of fisherman's Wellington's, so I nabbed them, but they were much too big."

Able Seaman 'Gunner' Fred Ward recalls that he and his shipmates were marched through the town with only their blankets for comfort until they reached a cafe called 'Iris'.

John Hague mentions that the German sailors brought the dead *Hunter* crewmen that they had picked up to shore. The survivors then carried the bodies, put them on a lorry and they were taken away for burial. In my records there are a number of *Hunter* graves in the Narvik area and some are unmarked. In addition, other records I have shown whether they survived

---

64   My calculations are as follows: HMS *Hunter's* total crew on leaving Britain 158 – Survivors forty-seven [one officer POW / three in Narvik hospital]. It will become clearer in later chapters the suggested deaths of casualties.

or were killed and if the latter, then the date of death was certified. As expected the majority were dated 10th of April 1940, namely the day the ship was sunk.

One of those graves at Narvik (No A3) belongs to nineteen-year-old Seaman Jack Tucker. Within months of joining the Navy from his home town of Cardiff, he had witnessed more sea action than most others of his generation. A few weeks later Jack's parents received a letter from 'Buckingham Palace':

The Queen and I offer you our heartfelt sympathy in your sorrow. We pray that your country's gratitude for a life so nobly given in its service may bring you some measure of consolation.

George. R.I.

In Jack's local newspaper under the title 'On Active Service'.

On April 10th, at Narvik, Jack, age nineteen years, of HMS *Hunter*, dearly loved only son of Mr and Mrs Charles Tucker and brother of Marjorie.

"Let me feel the wind on my temples.
When I answer the last Great Call:
Let my spirit go out in a wind storm.
Clean, pure, on my last ride of all."

I have to thank nephew Rob Harry, Perth, Australia for sending the family's memorabilia. Here Rob adds, "After hearing the news of Jack's death, my grandfather Charles Tucker died not long after of a heart attack. It was a very sad time for the family." [65]

To recap, at this stage the *Hunter* survivors were picked up by three German ships. Initially one group of thirty were incarcerated on the *Jan Wellem*. They were then disembarked to the Railway Waiting Room in Narvik. Another group of fourteen were picked up by a different ship and

---

65   There are thirteen other marked Hunter graves at Narvik Cemetery. As well as nine either marked "Sailor-Known Only Unto God" or not marked at all, some of which are likely to be Hunter crew.
J.S. Rowe, K.B.P. Pearson, F.J. Taylor, T.R. Howell, R. Craft, F.P. Dorward, L.A.C. Lawton, W.H.J. Edwards, E.C. Payne, F.A. Gilbert, W.M. Muddle, A. Holt. (One from Hardy, H.M. Mantle)

placed in the Café Iris. Here Petty Officer William Barrett recalls the conditions in the Schoolroom. "The treatment whilst at the school left a lot to be desired, conditions were very bad. Accommodation was cramped and everyone had to sleep on the floor. Food was very scarce and was served at varying times. A really good days meals was as follows:

Breakfast: ¼ pint of coffee and one piece of bread and jam.
Dinner: ½ pint of soup and one piece of bread.
Supper: ¼ pint of coffee and one piece of bread and jam.

No utensils were available, both coffee and soup having to be eaten from tins. We were allowed a daily exercise of a half an hour each morning and evening."

At the City Hall in Narvik the situation began to move in a fairly orderly fashion. The Rationing Board was working under heavy pressure. Ration cards had been printed and amounts fixed. The system was so devised that any further reductions that might become necessary could be effected without printing new cards. There was enough flour and canned goods to feed everyone for a long time. There were huge stores of fish but these were waiting to be exported to Germany in peacetime. Ironically the German customers had now put in a personal appearance! There was no ice available so the Norwegians had to salt the fish which meant it soon started to smell. The result was not all that could be desired, even though the fish did taste better than it smelled. This was to be their stable diet for the following two months of the war.

The merchant seamen in the school house were wondering why there had been no landing party sent by the Royal Navy. In the afternoon they were ordered out and had to muster outside with their belongings. They obviously began to worry about where their future lay. Tired and in shabby clothes they were told to form three columns and addressed by a German sergeant who obviously enjoyed watching Western movies. "Now you guys, I am giving you a warning, if anyone tries to push off, we shoot." The group were led off in an orderly fashion into another part of town when they came to a square used as a covered market. On the corner was a café, looking up to the first floor they saw gazing down at them what appeared to be a number of men unwashed and partly undressed, waving to them.

Before long they were in the company of the same men. Romilly describes the encounter, "We found ourselves in the presence of fourteen huddling shivering men, wrapped in blankets without a stitch of clothing, their faces whitish-blue with cold. These men, of whom only two were not very young, comprised seamen, stokers, one cook, and one Chief Petty Officer of a destroyer *Hunter*, sunk in the dawn engagement." They went on to tell their story to Romilly and the merchant seamen of the previous few days leading up to the epic battle.

That night the two groups of captives mingled and swapped stories as you would expect. However, it was evident that the much younger Royal Navy ratings had had a far more traumatic experience. They had no idea if there were any more survivors some of whom were their close friends. The men finally exhausted tried to sleep in a place far removed from what you could home.

Romilly once more using his skills as a journalist describes a poignant moment. "Near to me that night on the floor of the Café Iris was a young Welshman, one of the *Hunter* survivors, wearing a boiler-suit and muffler given him by a merchant seaman. Drunk with weariness he fell asleep still rambling through his memories of the battle. 'Actions Stations, see boyo? Feeding the forward starboard gun I was.' He sung out, 'Let 'em have it lads. *Hunter* was ahead. Ay, in the Stokers' Messdeck. I unhooked the Carley float and I kicked it overboard, see. Next thing I know, it is crowded with bloody stokers. Pushing away like hell they were, man. Twice I was sucked back ...' The young *Hunter* survivor unconsciously put his nightmare to one side and went back to snoring, probably dreaming of home and loved ones." Although for many of the survivors, these kind of nightmares would be with them for a long time into the future. [66]

All lives that are lost in battle are tragic stories, but particularly poignant for families like that of the East Ender and Navy boxer, twenty-three-year-old Stoker Daniel Percy Beckford. Danny would not be coming home to re-join his young wife, Rose or be able to enjoy seeing their baby son growing up together. Rose called their son after Daniel and the name is still passed on in the family.

---

66   On the list of the survivor's names, ages and address, there are two of the survivors that fit the description of the young Welshman. These were Stanley Swales (23) from Newport and Frank Youd (21) from Wrexham, both seamen and possibly 'gunners'.

Café Iris, on the corner with the ladder. In more peaceful times.
[Cyril Cope Collection]

Danny Beckford, Daniel's grandson wrote to me, "I do have a few photos of him, I would love to find out more, I was told about him by my Nan Rose who died four years ago aged ninety-two. She used to tell me lots of stories about my Granddad. She had my Dad also called Daniel Percy. My Nan sent my Granddad a letter telling him she was expecting a baby. He wrote back and said he was happy and he would get home on leave. But the day never came for him to see his son. I feel it is my duty to find out everything I can about my Granddad. She [Nan] lived all her life on the hope that he would one day walk through the door and that was right up until the day that she passed away."

A Stoker who survived was the forty-one-year-old veteran from the First World War, namely Jack Hiscock. It appeared his luck was holding out. I presume he would not have been in the engine or boiler room and was probably an 'ammunition supplier' or attached to one of the 'Repair Parties'.

It was not long before provincial newspapers were providing information about the missing men in their area. The *Evening Telegraph* dated 14th of April 1940:

DUNDEE MEN ON HMS *HUNTER*

"The families of two Dundee men who were serving on HMS *Hunter* when she was sunk at Narvik have received information from the Admiralty that they are missing. The letters state there is insufficient evidence whether they may still be alive or not, but that every effort will be made to obtain accurate information. The men are Chief Petty Officer J. Smail, Pebble Street and Gunner Fred Dorward, Craigie Street. C.P.O. Smail has been attached to *Hunter* since the vessel was commissioned.

A double tragedy: James Smail, had been away from his wife Jean and their daughter, as well as the rest of his family for three and half years. He had managed a brief spell of leave before he gave his life in the name of duty to his country. He was very close to reaching his pensionable age. Fred Dorward was not the only crew member to have recently married before having his young life taken away. At least he had a named grave where eventually the British War Graves Commission was able to register its position. Unlike, as you will have read, James, whose body would be buried in an unknown plot. His sister Mrs Watson thirty years later would still be worrying herself as to whether he had drowned, and if so where was he laid to rest.

There are a number of the crew whose deaths were recorded as the 23rd of April 1940. Those that I have already mentioned in a previous chapter were Warrant Officer (Gunnery) James Henry Coombe, Chief Petty Officer James Smail, Able Seaman Samuel Mann, Able Seaman Nicholas Blundell, Able Seaman Robert Blower and Stoker Harold Smart. For some unknown reason, Harold Smart's death, unlike the others, was registered on the 16th of April, 1940. It could have been that these were the unfortunates whose bodies were either found in the water or later died after being landed in Narvik. Incidentally, Harold Smart's family did not get confirmation of his death until more than three months later.

One family searching for clarification were Judy and Tom Mann in Canada. Tom's Uncle was Samuel Mann. They had initially obtained the 'Certified Copy of an Entry in the Marine Register", stating that his death was recorded as the 23rd of April 1940 as 'Died of Wounds'. Confusingly, my source showed that like most of the crew men, he was recorded as 'Missing Presumed Killed' on the 10th of April 1940.

I passed on a letter sent to my father in 1971 from Samuel's sister, Ivy. I understand Tom and Judy are continuing their search to find Samuel's grave. A determined family of another generation wanting to show their formal respect to a relative they never knew.

In the 1970s my father Cyril Cope had met a number of German veterans from the Battle of Narvik at arranged 'Reunions' in both London and Bremerhaven. They were from all ranks and one of them was none other than Korvettenkapitan Karl Smidt who you have already read about, in command of *Erich Giese*. These past adversaries were now friends and mementoes were exchanged. Amongst many gifts and mementoes presented to my father, as the Honourable Secretary, was a log, kept by Karl Smidt, of the events leading up to and during the battle. Here is the beginning of Karl's log translated into English. Other parts will be interspersed in following chapters.

Karl Smidt

APRIL 10 1940. AT 0500 ENGLISH DESTROYERS BROKE THROUGH ALARMING THE GERMAN DESTROYERS IN NARVIK HARBOUR 2 GERMAN DESTROYERS WERE OUT OF ACTION. THE REST OF THE GERMANS JOINED ACTION WITH THE BRITISH. THE BRITISH DESTROYERS *HARDY* AND *HUNTER* WERE PUT OUT OF ACTION; *HARDY* ENDED UP ON THE REEFS OF NARVIK HARBOUR. *HUNTER* WAS SUNK. THE REMAINING 3 BRITISH DESTROYERS ESCAPED BADLY DAMAGED. *GIESE* RESCUED SURVIVORS FROM THE *HUNTER*, THEY WERE FOUND SWIMMING IN THE FJORD. 16 SEAMEN WERE PUT ONBOARD THE BARKASS, 8 OF THEM DIED FROM EXPOSURE.

AT 2040 HOURS AN ESCAPE ATTEMPT WAS MADE BY 2 BATTLE READY DESTROYERS *WOLFGANG ZENKER* AND *ERICH GIESE*. NEAR BARO A BRITISH DESTROYER AND 1 CRUISER WERE SIGHTED. ESCAPE ATTEMPT WAS HOPELESS. NEAR RÜCKKEHR ON RETURN IT WAS NOTICED THAT THE BOILER OF THE *GIESE* WAS LEAKING SALT IN THE CONDENSER!

It is interesting to note, if Karl Smidt's figures are correct, that this is evidence of the *Giese* picking up *Hunter* survivors, (which I already knew), but I was not aware that eight had died onboard of "exposure". However, a photograph taken by the German crew shows more than eight men in the Barkass. This raises the question, did Karl Smidt mean there were sixteen who survived and a further eight died?

My father Cyril was in correspondence with a number Kriegsmarine veterans for the purpose of arranging joint 'Reunions'. Here, relevant to the above, Walter Zimmermann also a crewmember of *Erich Giese* writes [September 1971].

"I can still vividly remember the battle phase [...] when the destroyer Hunter *caught fire by shells and presumably collided with destroyer* Hotspur *while manoeuvring and later sank. Our destroyer* Eric Giese *received the order to pick up all survivors of the* Hunter *immediately, after the battle was over. We were also joined by the destroyer* Wolfgang Zenker, *who also participated in the rescue. As far as I can remember we must have rescued 15 to 20 sailors, two or three of them died later, one of the survivors was from Glasgow.*

"They were handed over after arrival at Narvik to a merchant steamer, after we had provided them on board with rum, cigarettes and other things. The communication with the rescued of the Hunter *was very bad and difficult. They had all suffered from the last events and were excited, and the uncertainty as to how everything would go on, has also led to this.*

"In June 1964 my wife and I, as well as a comrade from the destroyer Erich Giese *visited the cemetery at Narvik and also spent some time at the graves of our comrades from the* Hardy *and* Hunter. *The cemetery is beautifully laid out and the graves are very well looked after."*

Of course, there may have been others picked up elsewhere who also were either found dead or alternatively, still alive and taken to the hospital at Narvik where they later died. For some unknown reason, although their names were registered, they were buried in unmarked graves. This was probably because the Germans were still in a chaotic and shocked state and just felt they needed to bury them as soon as possible after they had died. Hence there are eight graves, 'Not Marked' or 'Sailor – Known only to God' at the Narvik cemetery, where I presume they would have been buried. This would support Karl Smidt's calculations in his diary.

Able Seaman Cyril Holehouse, who at birth became known as the 'Jam Jar Baby' was born with a 'caul', the sailor's lucky charm. Sadly, Cyril, a strong swimmer, was not a survivor but left this world a man who had taken his chances by fighting for the freedom of his country. The family having received the news of *Hunter's* sinking, still wanted to believe he had not died and expectantly was "living life to the full and happy somewhere". After the war, the family had made contact with a number of *Hunter* survivors, who told them that Cyril was helping others off the ship onto a raft that a few of them had made. It was with regret that I had to confirm to the family that Cyril was on the list of casualties and that he could have been buried in one of those unmarked graves at Narvik.

It was also told to me by Yassie, daughter in law of Cyril's youngest sister May, that another sister, Carrie described a further example of Cyril's love for his siblings. Carrie recounts a story when one Christmas morning she woke up to find, instead of a tangerine in her stocking there was a "stinking old tyre" as a replacement for her bike. Cyril asked her why she was so gloomy.

When she told him, she had wanted a whole new bike. Cyril said, "Never mind, maybe you will get one next time." Sure enough, next spell of leave, he took Carrie to the bike shop and bought her a new shiny bike. She was over the moon.

As mentioned, Cyril's brother, George was also in the Navy, but captured by the Japanese in the Pacific. Thankfully for the family he managed to survive. George was able tell the family on his return home, that he had met a friend who had been on *Hunter* and remembered Cyril on that fateful day. The friend had last seen Cyril going back to help someone trapped, because he later saw the man who was trapped, he automatically thought Cyril had survived. Maybe, that is the reason why the family for many years after the sinking hung on to the belief that he was still alive.

Nicholas Blundell, the man who kept a unique diary of the ship's travels. During my research I had contact with two separate members of Nicholas' family. These were Nick and Kath Blundell, Nick being Nicholas' nephew and Tony Blundell, a great nephew. Tony's dad, Geoff, being Nicholas' brother, was six years old at the time. So Geoff predominantly remembers what he had been told by members of his family, during the years after the war. Nicholas' family first heard the news of *Hunter*'s sinking from the radio news announcement. This obviously left the family in despair and frantically searching for answers regarding his survival. During the next week, the *Fleetwood Chronicle* continued to follow up on the story. The initial headline was, 'FLEETWOOD MAN IN H.M.S *HUNTER*', the article pointing out that the family had not received any news of his well-being. The next headline was, 'RADIO NEWS IS CLIMAX TO WEEK OF DREAD', mentioning the family had for a week waited for a telegram from the Admiralty, "that one of their number was lost in HMS *Hunter*, [.....] then on Friday night, came the radio announcement, that it was feared all the crew were dead."

The family continued to have some hope that Nicholas was still alive. His sister, Hilda serving in the WRNS, travelled to Liverpool when it was heard that a ship of survivors from Narvik had arrived. There were also rumours that Nicholas was amongst a group of survivors from *Hunter* to have been taken to a hospital, and that these men were stated, as having 'Died of Wounds' on the 23rd of April.

I would point out that, regarding the survivors of HMS *Hardy*, the hospital ship *Atlantis* did return to Liverpool with survivors but this was on the 4th of June 1940. Although I do know that Lieutenant Stuart-Menteth, having broken his leg, as described in an earlier chapter, was hospitalised by the Germans. However, once the German soldiers retreated as the Narvik Campaign got under way, Stuart-Menteth was rescued by the Allied troops.

I have already mentioned the Stoker called 'Bill', the eldest of eight, where money at home was tight, and as a single man, he needed to send more money home. I am sure this would not be too dissimilar to a number of ratings from deprived backgrounds. Where they received emotive requests from home and relied upon his pals for solace. Should he have died in action then I would add that the 'Death in Service' grant to his parents would not have gone anywhere near enough to compensate for his possible ongoing financial contributions to his family.

General Dietl would be sitting in his makeshift office, having heard that one of his supply ships *Rauenfels* had been sunk. He was now waiting for news about the second one, *Alster*, also bringing supplies and ammunition. However, he would be disappointed.

Dietl was not aware that earlier on the 11th April, as he was about to make enquiries about the ships whereabouts, *Alster* had been challenged by the Norwegian patrol vessel *Syrian*, but the master of the *Alster* had defied an order to go into Bodo port, and made off back into the open sea. Captain Kaaveland on the patrol vessel *Svalbard 11* was off Bodo, and thought it would not be advisable to engage with his crew of eighteen and a few rifles. Therefore, he decided to alert British ships in the area.

The luckless *Alster* having made it to the Vestfjord approach to Narvik, was spotted by the destroyer *Icarus*. Once more she ignored the destroyers signal and ordered the sea-cocks to be opened. *Icarus* at full rate of knots came alongside the vessel. A machine gun was brought to bear, and while tracer bullets whistled around the bridge and wheelhouse, the *Icarus* boarding party sprang aboard and overwhelmed the crew. They closed the sea-cocks and a 'prize' crew was put aboard, who then raised the Royal Navy ensign. The course was set for Tromsø, and the Captain, Lieutenant Commander Maud, who was renowned for looking daunt-ingly like a latter-day buccaneer, was heard to say, "We could do with some supplies too."

When General Dietl had received the news of *Alster*, no doubt his feel-ings of gloom would have increased. Whilst his arrival in Narvik had been positive, the net was closing in around his isolated forces. The Norwegians were mobilising, reports from France stated that French mountain troops and units of the Foreign Legion were on their way. To add to that, incoming intelligence indicated that a large British fleet was in the North Sea making for Narvik. At least there was one personal high for him to cling on to, namely a signal congratulating him for the "energetic and effective manner in which you have occupied Narvik." Sent by no less a person than Adolf Hitler himself.

The Germans had also suffered a massive human loss, Mayor Broch recounts, "From the hospital came an emergency call for extra help and trucks. The dead were now lying up the cellar stairs. 'We haven't sufficient trucks.' 'Make the Germans haul them away' was suggested. The Norwegian Red Cross had more than enough work to look after its own people. The dedicated ladies who had sewed and knitted for the benefit of the cause through the years were of little help now. Young men were needed who were willing to go out when shots were heard and knew how to use shovels and tarpaulins."

In fact Narvik hospital was full with wounded and a makeshift emer-gency station had to be organised at the 'Seamen's House'. Norwegian doc-tors and nurses worked side by side with German medical personnel as naval merchant and civilian casualties were brought in. Smoke hung heavily over the town in the growing daylight and there was a strong smell of fire, cord-ite and oil all over the area.

In 2012, Kirsten Amundsen, who lives in Norway made contact to tell me her great aunt Ingeborg Sandsvik had been the head nurse at the hospital in Ballangen. Sometime after the War Ingeborg was given a gold finger ring. Her story is told in *Attack at Dawn*.

However, the saga became even more interesting. From her great Aunt's belongings she found just one of a two-page letter.

Mr. J.A. Farnell
15, Mellor Crescent,
etc.

Dear Matron,
You will no doubt be very surprised to receive this letter.
I was at the first Battle of Narvik on the 10th April 1940, on board HMS
Hunter. *We were sunk about two miles down the fjord from Narvik in the*
engagement with the German destroyers and was picked up by them, after being
in the water an hour and taken to hospital in Narvik with three others. All of us
had shrapnel wounds and were suffering from exposure and would have died if
it hadn't been for you and your staff.
I have a few days holiday to come and would like to visit you and see Narvik
again [...]

This is evidence that there was another survivor, none other than Engineer
Artificer John Farnell, who was hospitalised in Narvik. Also, when the
First Battle of Narvik began Ingeborg possibly had responsibilities for both
Narvik hospital and the smaller one at Ballangen. However, what is still
unclear, were the *Hunter* wounded segregated from their foes. In my first
book, *Attack at Dawn*, I included HMS *Hardy* survivor Fred Evans account,
where he had been hospitalised in Ballangen. Fortunately, having witnessed
German personnel arriving at the hospital he managed, with the help of the
nurses to be evacuated back to his fellow survivors. (In fact, I was told later
by Geirr Haarr, the Norwegian author, that the Germans were the crew and
Alpine Troops from the Erich Koellner.)

Returning to Farnell's interview with the *Yorkshire Post* (17th July 1940),
from the previous chapter.

[...] "The Germans left us floating in the water which was four degrees
above freezing point for one hour after we sank. We had rescued their
men straightaway. Mr Farnell [...] with shrapnel wounds in the head and
ankle [...] Many of our chaps died from the shock of the icy water. Our
doctor died in my arms while we were hanging on to a float. Mr Farnell
was taken prisoner by a German destroyer and put in hospital at Narvik.
There he had pneumonia in addition to his wounds. When the Germans
evacuated Narvik they left him and others behind in the care of Norwegian
civil authorities [...] He was taken away from Narvik in a British ship, and

survived bombing by German aeroplanes at sea before reaching this country and going to hospital again in Scotland."

Therefore, Farnell and presumably Petty Officer Thomas Marks having also been hospitalised in Narvik, then accompanied Lieutenant Stuart-Menteth to being repatriated back to Britain, possibly on a hospital ship which experienced a hazardous voyage.

Back to the Town Committee's ongoing dilemmas. The German occupation force called frequently at the City Hall for keys to the Prayer House, Public Schools, and other institutions which they had requisitioned for quarters and military hospitals. They told the Norwegians that they did not like to break into the buildings. The Town Committee called upon their teachers in the high schools to serve as interpreters and tried to get as much as possible in writing. They knew that it made little difference just how the Germans stole their property, but felt that they should have some kind of paperwork for the transactions. In order to lessen any panic, they hoped that the use of written documents would help bolster their self-respect in the face of the Germans 'lawlessness'.

Back at the Café Iris, the men were getting used to their new and unusual surroundings. This makeshift abode was quite substantial in size, about twenty-six yards long and seven yards wide, but not large enough when accommodating so many men, included were a number of tables and chairs. The large windows looked over the town square and beyond to the harbour. After rearranging things around all the important items were collected together. These essentials included a much-sharpened pencil, matches, cigarettes, 'Pussers' or duty free tobacco, a toilet roll, a lock knife and a bar of soap. (The toilet roll was to be utilised as writing paper.)

The fair distribution system was controlled by Captain Nicholas, here described once more by Giles Romilly. "Captain Nicholas, bony and thin in a navy-blue suit, picked with long fingers at the throat-collar of his slate-grey jersey, while his low-pitched, soft-needled voice solved intricate distributive puzzles; [In his distinctive accent] 'Let me see now. Aye. There's 'woon' packet of papers to eighteen men, 'woon' of tobacco to twelve men, those as don't want tobacco can take five cigarettes, and who wants pipe tobacco, now?'

"This was the Captain; at forty-five, he had thinnish greying hair, a stoup, a fastidious manner, and a persistent sense of responsibility. To everyone he was a good angel. Nobody questioned the authority which he never claimed."

There were a number of families on Sunday 14th April still waiting for news about their loved ones. Today it was different for Captain Warburton-Lee's wife Elizabeth, she like others remained positive. But sadly it turned out a day she would never forget, nor Bernard's family at Broad Oak, in Flintshire. The telegram from the Admiralty read,

'Deeply regret to inform you that your husband Captain B.A.W. Warburton-Lee of HMS *Hardy* was killed in action off Narvik on 10th April 1940.'

The following day Winston Churchill wrote personally to Elizabeth;

"The engagement was of his own conception and in view of the great risks involved he was given full discretion by their Lordships to attack or refrain from attack. His decision, immediately taken, led directly to the subsequent destruction of the enemy and may well prove to be of major importance in the progress of the war."

Returning to the family of Nicholas Blundell, they finally had to accept that he had been a casualty at Narvik but were none the wiser as to when or how he had died or where he had been buried. Sadly, there was yet another emotional event that the family had to endure. This was when Nicholas' younger brother Ron, aged nineteen serving on HMS *Mahratta* in 1944 was one of 200 crew members who died in action (seventeen survivors) when the ship as part of a Russian convoy (JW57) was torpedoed by a German U-boat (U-990).

I leave Tony Blundell to close the family's story of Nicholas Blundell. "The family never found out where Nicholas was buried despite attempts by his sister, Hilda. We can only assume that Nicholas is in one of the unmarked graves in Narvik."

The nephew of Able Seaman Robert Blower, Chris Cameron-Wilton wrote, "My mother Margaret did not know her brother, as she was only one when he died. There was not a lot said about him." Until Chris did some research, his mother had been under the impression that Robert had died in the Atlantic or Pacific. She also did not know which ship he was on. However, for Chris, having found his uncle's name on the Plymouth Memorial, it all became much clearer. With the date that he died being 23rd of April 1940, he realised his uncle must have made it off the ship.

Chris: "When I did my research in early 2000 there was little to go on and initially I wondered if he had died on the 'march' to Sweden. I assumed because his name was on the Plymouth Memorial, that his grave would be at Narvik and possibly marked the same."

Chris applied for his Uncle Robert's service records from the Ministry of Defence. But it appears that Able Seaman Robert Blower was probably one of the eight casualties picked up by the German destroyer *Erich Giese*, and now rests, as previously mentioned in either an 'Unmarked Grave' or "Sailor – Known Only To God". Probably buried at 'Harvik' with thirty-three other *Hunter* crewmembers

Peter Lancaster, the RNVR officer who had given up the opportunities arising from his degree at Oxford University in return for a commission in the Royal Navy, was another brave man to lose his life. His body was also one of those, most probably found in the cold waters of the fjord. Whether he died trying to swim to safety or not, his register of death was recorded on the 10th April 1940. He was laid to rest at the Ballangen cemetery.

Losing a son or daughter in war is a tragedy in itself but for Mr and Mrs Lancaster it is hard to imagine their shock when hearing a second son Gordon had lost his life. This occurred four and a half years after Peter's death. Gordon had risen in the ranks to Squadron Leader and been awarded the Distinguished Flying Cross (DFC) and Bar. He was highly regarded as a pilot, so much so that he was given the responsibility of flying Air Chief Marshall Sir Trafford Leigh-Mallory, accompanied by his wife, to Ceylon (Sri Lanka). The Air Chief Marshall was to take over as Air Commander in Chief of South East Asia. Regardless of the pilot's warning, the aircraft left England on 14th November 1944 and flew into 'appalling' weather conditions in the French Alps on the way to a stopover in Italy. The aircraft went missing and the wreckage was not found until nearly seven months later.

Donald Lancaster, the nephew who never got to know his uncles explains, "My grandparents lost two sons in the war, Peter at the beginning and Gordon at the end, it was a great blow. In consequence, they saw a need, very personally felt, to help rebuild communities after the war. To commemorate their sons lives and in hope of peace as an outcome of their losses, my grandparents donated a Village Hall, known as 'The Woldingham Peace Centre' to their little part of Surrey. The centre remains there to this day".

There was another Chief Petty Officer 'Missing – Presumed Drowned', for whom the Admiralty telegram would have gone to his newlywed wife May in his home town of Oldham. This was George Sutton the ex-submariner who would never have the pleasure of drawing his naval pension in the future. Although, had his luck not run out at the Battle of Narvik, it would have three months later. As previously pointed out, George would have seen out his submarine service on *Narwhal*. The vessel left Blyth on 22nd of July 1940 to lay mines off Norway but never returned. Subsequently, it was thought she had been attacked by the Luftwaffe with all lives lost.

Torpedoman Alfred Holt, from Salford, not too far away from where George lived, was another veteran who served his country in both world wars, and also lost his life. Alfred's grandson, Gavin, tells of the tragic events that followed. "He was recalled to the colours in April 1939. He was forty-three when he lost his life, leaving behind a wife and three children. My father was the youngest at nine months old [...] I only have one photo of my Grandfather and I have read his military records.

"I am hoping to travel to his grave in Narvik in the near future to pay my respects. My father, unfortunately never made it due to his ill health. I am so proud to have my Grandfather's name mentioned in your book and can hardly wait to show my son, who is currently studying World War Two in his history class. It would be a salute to a man I saw as a childhood hero."

Gavin Holt's need to show respect to his grandfather is just one of the many family contacts I have received in the last three years. These have included copies of letters to loved ones, desperate for news from senior officers, who were trying to keep families aware of the latest developments. With regards to Alfred Holt's wife, interestingly all the sequence of letters she received were kept within the family. These three letters have provided an insight into the emotional uncertainties that the family's had to endure from the time that *Hunter* was known to have been sunk, to over three months later when Mrs Holt finally had his death confirmed. I will come back to these letters sent by the Admiralty later. Similar letters were also received by a number of other crew member's families.

Lieutenant Richard Maidlow was another who never came home. His niece, Helen explains, "My father chose not to speak about his twin's death." I replied with as much detail as I had gathered at the time, including the photograph of HMS *Hunter's* ships company taken in Malta and the web site addresses from where she might find more details about her Uncle Richard.

However, on coming to the end of my research on a visit to the National Archives at Kew I came across a letter in a well-thumbed file (ADM 358/47).

Admiralty.

'G' Coy, 8th Rifle Brigade, C/O Postmaster,
Rawdon, Nr Leeds,
14/March 1941

Sir's,

My twin brother Lieut H.R.M. Maidlow was accounted "missing presumed lost", when HMS *Hunter* sank at Narvik nearly a year ago.

As so many months have elapsed since then, could you oblige me by putting me in touch with a survivor who might be able to give some definite first hand news.

Trusting this letter will receive due consideration in spite of numerous similarly applications.

I remain Sir's
Your obedient servant.
Captain J. Maidlow.

I am glad to say that an apparently frustrated John Maidlow finally received a reply and was advised to communicate with Lieutenant Alexander Stuart-Menteth, by then appointed to HMS *Somali* as First Lieutenant. I have no doubts that Alex would have made sure John received the information he required as swiftly as the General Post Office could deliver it.

In the same file there were letters relating to Pamela De Villiers the wife of the Captain of *Hunter*, who also lost his life. The correspondence was ongoing up to October 1940, between various parties including the Admiralty and, on behalf of Mrs De Villiers, Barclays Bank. It appears that within six months of losing her husband there had still not been a 'Death Certificate' issued. Until this was done she had problems releasing monies for normal everyday living for not only herself but also her son. In addition, it had delayed her receiving a 'Widow's War Pension'. The Admiralty's response had been, that they hoped it would quickly be resolved and a pension was 'under consideration'.

Joe Settle's parents also received the dreaded telegram. "The Admiralty offered its condolences, saying Joe was missing presumed dead. They then proceeded to have a memorial service in the local church," says his daughter Sheila. However, as it was for all the survivors, it took a while before the Admiralty were able to confirm the official, full extent of the casualty list.

But when it finally came through there were families like Joe's who were obviously overjoyed and relieved; whilst for the majority of others, all hope had gone.

I return to the unnamed 'Oerlikon' gunner who had left the ship to play rugby for the Navy. His daughter Wynne Jones explains. "My grandmother had a telegram to advise that her son (Wynne's father) was posted missing, presumed dead, following the First Battle". I am unsure whether Wynne's father would have been elsewhere at sea, but just receiving such a telegram must have been an initial shock. Wynne goes on to explain further, "He served the rest of the war on HMS *Albrighton*. He didn't speak much about what had happened but often regaled us with stories of the men he had served alongside on *Hunter*, Captained by a gentleman called Villiers."

By pure coincidence the unnamed 'Oerlikon gunner' finally settled back into civilian life at an address in Ammanford – namely, Villiers Road, coincidence or not.

Nineteen-year-old Telegraphist Harold Webber was described as 'Missing'. It could be that he was one of the bodies found and buried alongside a substantial number of shipmates at Harvik village cemetery. Their graves were marked "Sailor –Known Only Unto God" but incorrectly from HMS *Hardy*.

It appears Harold's death and service to his country had a knock-on effect as his then two-year-old brother Keith eventually followed in his footsteps. As did Keith's son Geoff, who contacted me providing the family background. Geoff served in submarines and retired as a Chief Petty Officer Engine Room Artificer and is justly proud of his naval lineage

Able Seaman 'Gunner' David Radcliffe, who not only served his country at war like his father in World War One but also followed him to a grave at sea. David's wife of two months Elizabeth tragic loss three months later was featured in a local Bootle newspaper:

Lost in Narvik Battle: Widow Hears From Admiralty

Mr Radcliffe was reported missing after the *Hunter* had sunk in Narvik. "With reference to my letter of the 14th April 1940, I deeply regret to inform you that it has now been officially presumed that your husband [....] lost his life on war service [...] Please allow me to express sincere sympathy with you in your bereavement, on behalf of the officers and men of the Royal Navy [...] In a letter dated July 25th, addressed to his widow, Commodore. V. Critchley, of the Royal Naval Barracks, Devonport, also writes: "high traditions of which your husband has helped to maintain".

There were similar letters from senior officers expressing their condolences that I have respectively received from families and other sources. However, it appears to me that on this occasion the Commodore of the Barracks, had been made aware of David's recent marriage and his father's same fate in World War One. Let us also not forget the effect on David's mother and his possible siblings

Back to the survivors ongoing experiences – as Jake Kerswell recounts. "At 1100 we were taken into the harbour and transferred to a German whaling ship; where we were all treated well by the merchant seamen crew aboard. But the German guards were not so good and our Engineer Officer [Lt Reid] was treated worse than the rest. After two days of this we were transferred to a railway hut on the dockside. During the two days on the *Jan Wellem*, I was given very good medical treatment by the ships doctors who removed three pieces of shrapnel from my hand and x-rayed me."

Obviously the first enemy captives to be questioned would be the commissioned officers, hence in this case Lt Alick Reid, as they may be aware of more important overall information of the ship and her plans. It appears that usually the German Naval Interrogation Officer would start with questions like for instance: port from which your ship departed; the number of torpedoes, depth charges carried; your views politically and on the war; and then subtly a query about the degaussing system and ASDIC equipment, both having been recently fitted in the dockyard. At this early stage of the war they would also be interested in an opinion whether "the United States was expected to enter the war". These are a general collection of questions I discovered after reading a substantial number of reports in the 'Evaders and Escapers' file at the National Archives. I will return to this file later where I found Naval Intelligence reports on four of Hunter's crew when repatriated.

The *Hunter* survivors now separated into two groups. As mentioned by Korvettenkapitan Karl Smidt, his ship *Erich Giese* off-loaded sixteen '*Hunter*' survivors. These were taken to the Café Iris and kept under guard until such time as the Germans decided on an alternative option. These survivors did not know that another thirty of their comrades had been picked up by various other vessels and temporarily accommodated on the German transport *Jan Wellem*. As previously pointed out, she was the main fuel tanker also carrying vital naval stores for the enemy destroyers. The men were put in cabins, about six men to each. Whilst they were guarded, their personal details were taken. The general opinion, as confirmed by Jake Kerswell, was that they were "well received by the Captain and crew". The men sat round discussing the battle and the fate of their comrades. They also did not know how many had survived either the battle or the terrible ordeal in the water.

Both groups were also not aware that four others had been taken into Narvik hospital. On the 12th of April, they would be transferred to a railway waiting room on the dockside. Here they would meet some of the crew of the *Mersington Court* and one or two members of the *Riverton* and *North Cornwall* crews.

As things developed the Germans 'Wehrmacht' did not have much time to spend on the Norwegians during the first few days. "The first British attack has been victoriously repulsed, but is not beyond the cowardly British to return," a strutting little German orderly told the Mayor and those in his presence. This man was kept constantly running back and forth between hotels and the City Hall with requisitions and announcements. "We called him 'Sauerkraut'." Meanwhile the Germans kept up an incessant transport of heavy logs and rails out to Framnes peninsula and to the shores beyond in case the "cowardly British" returned.

Marshal Soult's first observations on reaching Narvik docks, "The Germans were already welding on plates over the holes on the destroyers, making good what had been done a few hours or so ago. We were bungled into a small hut on the dockside, and guarded by German troops, who did not seem to know what to do with us. Sometime later in the day we left the docks and marched up the street. I was naked except for the blankets. We were stopped outside a ladies' dress shop and taken in by a side door which led upstairs to the Café Iris, commandeered by the Germans.

"It was occupied by ninety-four prisoners, the crews of the four British merchant ships. These were *Blythmoor, Riverton, Romanby* and *North Cornwall*. All had called in there for cargoes of iron ore. These men had been captured by the Germans as soon as the enemy took over the port and all the ships in it. Their ships had probably been sunk during our attack, so it was just as well they were safe on shore."

Korvettenkapitan Smidt is determined to have *Erich Giese* repaired and back in action again.

APRIL 11 1940. ENTERED NARVIK ON REMAINING GOOD ENGINE. OBTAINED TECHNICAL HELP FROM THE TANKER *Jan Wellem* WHICH WAS THERE AND REPAIRS WERE MADE.

On returning to Mayor Bloch it seems he had to bite his tongue when confronted by the 'Ortskommandant' [City Commandant] in charge of Narvik [...] "The new chief was Major Hauzel. One glance at him sufficed: he was no good. The type is well known, dominating and brutal, self-satisfied and condescending, with peculiar, calculating suspicion which covers a secret feeling of inferiority. The type dominates the New Germany [...] Not all the German officers are of the Major Hauzel type [...] The majority of them are brilliant technicians trained to severe discipline, and they now follow Hitler as they once followed the Kaiser." Hauzel gave his orders in numbers:

Ein: Quarters must be provided for British sailors taken prisoners [...] They need not be too good. The British prisoners had been incarcerated in Public School, together with the group of Norwegian soldiers [...] but now the Germans needed more room, since the stay was likely to be long.

Zwei: Quarters must be arranged for German sailors of the merchant marine.

Drei: The Major himself needed a new uniform for use in milder weather. Spring would, one hoped, arrive, even in these latitudes.

Mayor Bloch: "The Committee had to explain that there were no more quarters available. All public buildings had already been requisitioned except the City Hall and the hospital. As for the uniform, we carried none in stock. They suggested the Major might try a tailor."

Mayor Broch wished to prevent as long as possible the taking over of private homes, so he found a restaurant in which to house the British prisoners. As already indicated, this was the Café Iris. "There was, however, no building that would take care of the German sailors. They numbered about 500. Finally we had to open the beautiful new church in the park at Frydenlund."

Captain Nicholas continues his diary. He is now the senior ranked captive and has overall responsibility for care of all in the Café Iris, whether Royal Navy or Merchant Navy.

Thurs 11 Apl 40
Made coffee and had slice of bread and marmalade – shared with Hunter's crew.
About 1 pm. A large German plane arrived overhead – dropped supplies by parachute. A cup of barley soup was issued us by the Germans. Nothing exciting

happened. Everybody is keyed up as to when the fleet will arrive. The Norwegian people give us a friendly wave as they pass along.

BBC World Service, Thursday 11th April at 6.00 pm.

"Here is an Extract from Mr Churchill's statement: Off Narvik on Tuesday morning the battle-cruiser *Renown* saw *Scharnhorst* and a ten-thousand ton *Hipper* class cruiser. Our battle-cruiser opened fire at 18-thousand yards and after three minutes, the enemy replied. The enemy almost immediately turned away and after nine minutes the *Renown* observed hits on the forward structure of the German battlecruiser. Thereafter, her armaments stopped firing and later her after turret began firing on local control.

On Tuesday night, he continued, orders were given to our destroyers blockading the West Fjord leading to Narvik to attack the enemy. But after a submarine had reported the presence of six destroyers, the Admiralty thought the operation so hazardous that they told the Captain of the destroyer flotilla that he must be the sole judge of whether to attack and he would be supported whatever he did and whatever happened. The five destroyers entered and attacked the six enemy. The fighting was worthy of any British Naval records."

During the 11th April, *Erich Koellner* and *Hermann Kunne* had completed their repairs and were refuelling. Subsequently, *Hermann Kunne* was sent to search the wreck of *Hardy*. She had floated off during the high tide in the afternoon, drifting across the bay, grounding again in the evening at Skjomnes where she keeled over. Would the Germans find anything of importance?

In the meantime, the *Hans Ludemann* also reported ready and the men sent ashore were recalled.

That night it once more became foggy and Fregattenkapitan Bey was still not prepared to chance a break out. However, the flotilla's fortunes got worse. Firstly, *Erich Koellner* was sent on picket-duty to Ballangen Bay, when at midnight she ran aground. This led to flooding in several compartments and 'tail between her legs' she returned to Narvik the following morning. To add salt to the wound, *Wolfgang Zenker*, whilst at anchor during the night, had scraped her hull on the bottom, causing damage to one of her propellers. Her speed would now be restricted to twenty knots.

Further problems, the Kriegsmarine torpedoes were increasingly proving useless. This time when U-48 had confronted part of the British fleet at Vestfjorden, four torpedoes had exploded prematurely and the remaining two had missed. This was not what you would expect from the usual efficient German craftsmanship. This meant that since the submarines engagement with the enemy, that of the twelve torpedoes fired over half had ended with the same outcome. Obviously this was causing grave concern back at the command centre in Kiel. Although experts had been called in by Donitz the commander-in-chief of U-boats, it was to no avail. [Therefore it was decided to try a mix of contact and magnetic pistols]

On board *Erich Giese* work on the repairs continued at a fast rate whilst also having to contend with other immediate matters.

The BBC Overseas Service, particularly in wartime was very popular and in some parts of the globe was essential listening picked up not only on land but also at sea. News bulletins in Danish and Norwegian began on the days the two countries were invaded; the service in Dutch began a month after Holland was occupied.

Here it is picked up by the radio station WSM in Nashville, Tennessee. To my knowledge this was the only overseas station who for historical reasons decided to record all programmes relating to the war. Even today you can still recover them on line from their vast recording library.

WSM News Report for CST 1940-04-11. 10 pm

"This is London calling in the Overseas Service of the British Broadcasting Service. Before I read the news broadcast an important message to Masters of Norwegian and Danish ships, from the British Government.

The message to Norwegian ships is as follows: a message that has been broadcast from Oslo, telling Norwegian ships to proceed to neutral ports should of course be disregarded.

Oslo is in the hands of the Germans and the Norwegian Government is conducting a national resistance from another temporary capital. The message therefore is sent by the Germans. It does not come from the Norwegian Government or owners and would be contrary to their wishes. Norwegian ships should call at the nearest British or French port for advice. This will now be repeated in Norwegian.

The message addressed by the British Government, to Masters of all Danish ships, is to make to other ports from Copenhagen. Italy, Spain or other neutral ports are under German dictation and therefore should be disregarded. Here is the message in Danish.

By the end of 1940, the BBC was broadcasting in thirty-four languages. Each day seventy-eight news bulletins were broadcast, amounting to 250,000 words.

Smidt's diary:

APRIL 12 1940. AIR RAID BY BRITISH PLANES; *GIESE* SUSTAINED NO DAMAGE.

Captain Nicholas

Fri 12 Apl 40
There is a kitchen in the Café Iris and we are to do our own cooking. We had coffee for breakfast and a plate of soup at 3 pm and again today at 7 pm. Not bad. The plane flew over again today at noon and dropped some more supplies. Towards evening several British bi-planes flew over Narvik and hundreds of machine guns went into action. I don't think any of the planes were hit, a couple of the planes bombed parts of the harbour front where some machine gun's nests were. Later we saw wounded and dead Germans being carried up the road. Also sailors with their gear and concluded that one of the German destroyers had gone west as well. The air-raid over bucked everybody up and we lay down in great hopes of the Navy coming.

It is reported that on this day the forage-capped German Lieutenant came to the Café to interview the *Hunter* survivors and as mentioned by Captain Nicholas there was a British air attack by planes from an aircraft carrier. Marshal Soult describes a nervous moment, "A bomb fell close to the Café and was observed by the men. During this time the lieutenant having just completed an interview with one of the *Hunter* survivors, a Petty Officer went into a little sarcastic banter when the Lieutenant remarked, 'I hope they don't drop a bomb on you people.' The Lieutenant waited for someone to be triggered into a reply, appearing to be enjoying the game. The Lieutenant continued, 'Not very heroic, sinking your own ships, was it?' This was referring to the ore-carriers in the harbour. The brave P.O. fell for it and was unable to hold his tongue, 'We had to get at your destroyers, which were hiding behind!' 'Oh yes, they were inside. You British are so much under the influences of Jewish money. You have got rid of all your good men.'

"The P.O. was not going to stop now, the men standing around them began to wince but no one felt they were able to intervene. 'You had a good man once called Niemoller?' 'Ah Niemoller, yes ...' Subject over, but would there be any consequences? The P.O. moved back to the window and was heard by his shipmates say under his breath, 'God knows how I managed to think of that bastard.'" [67]

Irrespective of significant pressure from his superiors, Fregattenkapitan Bey had given up all hope of a breakout. At 0044 on the 13th April he had received a signal urgently pointing out that a 'large' warship with seven or eight destroyers had been sighted by a Luftwaffe aircraft. To increase his dismay, the fleet had rendezvoused in Vestfjorden. By now Bey must have become a desperate man, possibly wondering what the higher command, even 'The Fuhrer' himself, would be thinking of him.

Bey, believing that a second attack would be similar to the first, decided to send *Erich Koellner* [now back in Narvik] to a position off Ramnes, basically as an all-night watchman with a gunnery emplacement. Her escapade in Ballagen Bay resulted in her not being much use for anything else. Because the waters there were too shallow, her torpedoes were despatched jointly to *Georg Thiele* and *Bernd von Arnim*. Thankfully, taking into account what was about to come, ninety of her crew were put ashore; once navigated to her ordered position, the majority of the engine room personnel were also taken back to Narvik. As described in Geirr Haarr's book, "Few doubted this was a suicide mission or 'Himmelfahrtskommando' that would mean the end of Z-13 *ERICH KOELLNER*. When she left harbour, escorted by *KUNNE*, the other destroyers' crews manned the rails and cheered."

At approximately 0830, Fregattenkapitan Bey's thoughts were probably "can this get any worse?" A signal from Wilhelmshaven, "Expect enemy

---

67   Martin Niemoller came from a very conservative background, his father a Lutheran pastor. In the First World War he was in the German Imperial Navy and served in U-boats and was responsible for sinking British troopships. During this time he was awarded the Iron Cross First Class and after the war became a preacher in the Evangelical church. Subsequently, similar to most Protestant pastors he was a national conservative, thus welcomed Hitler's accession to power in 1933, believing it would bring national survival

attack this afternoon. *REPULSE, WARSPITE,* 5 Tribals, 4 destroyers and probably a carrier." Bey ordered his remaining Zerstörers to be ready at 1300. [68]

Admiral Forbes Commander-in Chief of the Home Fleet ordered Vice Admiral Whitworth to strike in the afternoon of the 13th April with a force of the battleship *Warspite* and nine others screening and submarine detection. His orders: "destruction of German warships, merchant ships and defences in Narvik area." The German intelligence report was close in their estimation, but there was only one battleship. Whitworth transferred his flag to *Warspite* and with eight of his escorts sailed that evening for Vestfortforden. *Eskimo* would join them later as she was sent to patrol Tranøy during the night to secure the entrance to Ofotfjorden. [69]

As is normal procedure in the Royal Navy, when a Captain is about to send his ships company into a potentially dangerous situation, he would have the Coxswain or, for bigger ships, like *Warspite*, the Master-at-Arms would pipe 'Clear Lower Deck'. This evening, would be an exception because of the extremely cold weather on the upper deck, so Captain Crutchley was able to explain the situation on the ship's tannoy system. He informed his ships company, that intentions were to proceed to Narvik and he made it clear that there were potential dangers from minefields, U-boats and torpedoes.

Mayor Broch relates how they received an announcement from the King of Norway on what was to be the first weekend after they had entered the war, Saturday 13th of April. "It was destined to become 'Our Day'. Our front sector was, after all, not forgotten or neglected. [This refers to the local 'Resistance' in the mountains near the Swedish border trying to link up with the Norwegian force]. In the morning we heard the King broadcast a strong personal appeal to all Norwegians. He could not reveal where he was, but he was with the Crown Prince and the Government. They had all escaped a murderous bombing attack. He had seen defenceless cities bombed by Germans. He encouraged his people to continue resistance and to fight."

---

68   Extracted from Geirr Haarr's book: 'Kunne' fully operational, *Arnim* fair shape, *Ludemann* relatively good shape, *Giese* and *Zenker* still under intense repair, *Thiele* not combat ready for several days and *Roeder* would be week or more before she might become mobile.

69   From Geirr Haarr's research, it is worth mentioning that the Germans had intercepted the above signal, "But missed the vital part, stating where the attack would be aimed. This was not decoded and reported until later on the 13th, when it was too late."

Gun Crews to 'Set Fuses'

Petty Officer Daniel Reardon was the gunner's mate of 'A' turret on the battleship *Warspite*. Here he describes the build up to the second Battle of Narvik. "It is one of those dark nights when men have to be very careful changing watch, for the deck is frozen and one false move and it's over the side and nobody knows. So the guns' crews prefer to remain at their action stations and sneak a few minutes' sleep there [...] The news soon spreads – an Admiral has come on aboard. Next a messenger calls to tell all us gunner's mates to report to the gunnery officer. His orders are short and sweet – we are going up to Narvik tomorrow and everything must be on a split yarn. Back to our stations, and plenty to do now. Fuses to be set to non-delay (means only light enemy ships believed there), first-aid gear checked, fresh water provided and all the thousand and one other little things that can make or mar good shooting.

"There is very little sleep left in us now; everyone is wondering what tomorrow will bring. At last it is daylight, and the watch is being called to 'day defence stations'. One young seaman puts his head out of the top of a manhole and soon bobs down again. 'Looks as though we are in the money – you ought to see the destroyers we have with us.' So out we troop and have a look. Nine destroyers. Someone must be making a fuss of us."

The ship's company, having heard the Captain's address the night before, arranged a 'Special Holy Communion' service for 0800, perhaps not surprising the congregation turnout exceeded all expectations. [The diary of Commander P.D. Hoare, suggests that "on a regular Sunday mass, about twenty would normally turn up."]

Around this time *Havock* was patrolling Skjelfjord when she met up with *Warspite* and her fleet. As a respectful jester, the Vice Admiral allowed *Havock* to lead the warships into the approaches towards Narvik. The fleet eventually passed *Havock* on their way, whilst she took up position off Narvik harbour for her task of listening out for submarines with her newly installed

ASDIC set. It is to the crew members of *Havock*'s credit that they continued to withstand the traumatic pace after all they had achieved only three days before. There was little of this brave act acknowledged in future historical records. Hence why I made sure it is documented here.

Petty Officer ' Gunners' Mate' Daniel Reardon continues describing the preparations before going into action. "We have our breakfast and carry on with the usual routine, cleaning and preparing. We are passing some land now, and it looks very snow-covered and forbidding. An early dinner today, before going to action stations [At 1130 consisting of hard boiled eggs and thick corn beef sandwiches]. My own crew are on the fo'c's'le for a smoke, some wag rolls a snow ball and one of 'B' turret's crew gets it in the neck. This is the general signal for a snow fight between the two turrets, when action stations sounds ..."

Action Stations now closed up on all the ships as they pass Tranøy lighthouse at twenty-two knots. The weather could have been worse. The mine sweeping ships are well ahead with their para-vanes in play. [70]

Mechanical sweeps are devices designed to cut the anchoring cables of moored mines, and preferably attach a tag to help the subsequent localization and neutralization. They are towed behind the minesweeper, and use a towed body (e.g. para-vane,) to maintain the sweep at the desired depth and position. Influence sweeps are equipment, often towed, that emulate a particular ship signature, thereby causing a mine to detonate. The most common such sweeps are magnetic and acoustic generators.

Prior to the battle beginning *Warspite* had catapulted her Swordfish seaplane to scout ahead of the fleet. Vice Admiral Whitworth would write later, "I doubt if ever a ship-borne aircraft has been used to such good purposes."

As you are aware there was another Royal Naval destroyer which never got back to Britain, HMS *Hardy*, run aground off Vidrek on the southern shore of Ofotfjord. Now, three days later, the 177 crew members who survived the battle, and having managed to avoid capture had made it to the village of Ballangen. From there they had a good view of the fjord below on the 13th April.

---

70   The destroyers were fitted with ASDIC (sonar) and the ability to use the Two-speed Destroyer Sweep (TSDS). Minesweepers are equipped with mechanical or electrical devices, known as 'sweeps', for disabling mines. They are designed to reduce the chances of it detonating mines itself; it is soundproofed to reduce its acoustic signature and often constructed using wood, fibreglass or non-ferrous metal or is degaussed to reduce its magnetic signature.

Battle Cruiser *Warspite*. [Cyril Cope Collection]

Leading Torpedoman Bill Pulford provides his version of that fateful day. "We were all now dressed like Norwegians best we could. So we went out to the roads and helped clear the snow. We were in the main road, if you could call it that, which came from the fjord to Ballangen. We were clearing the snow when one of the 'lookouts' called out, 'There's a Stingbag.' [Swordfish flown from aircraft carrier] We all looked round and thought he's wrong because we couldn't see any aircraft. But we could hear them, so naturally we thought it was an aircraft we had seen earlier in the day from the German base. We called him all the names under creation and someone said, 'What the hell would a "Swordfish" be doing flying around Ballangen at that time of the morning?' But he persisted it was a 'Stingbag' and then we heard gun fire, first, the whip cracker of 4.7-inch then the rumble of a 15-inch. We thought that must be *Renown* which was in action with us four days ago."

Around this time, plans were made to evacuate the *Hardy*'s wounded by fishermen's boats to a hospital at Gravdal Skyehus. Amongst those sent were nineteen-year-old Signalmen Ralph Brigginshaw and twenty-year-old 'Ginger' Turner, known to his family as Jack. As you will have read in my first book they were close friends (pages 337 and 389). Ginger was born in Fence Houses, Durham and his sister Doris was in the Wrens also based at Plymouth, whilst his younger brother, Henry worked at an ammunitions factory. Their father, Cuthbert fought on the Somme, badly injured and gassed, he was lucky to survive. Sadly he died in 1934 from his wounds.

By July 1940, Ralph had lost touch with his shipmate 'Ginger' Turner. So he decided to write to him. Ralph received a reply from Ginger's mother to say that a week before his discharge from hospital he had died in a tragic accident. Here, Ginger's niece, Janet Down explains, "My uncle went out in a rowing boat with a nurse, they lost an oar and Jack jumped in the water and swam after it. Unfortunately, the wind picked up and the boat drifted further away from him, the current was just too strong and he was dragged under. It didn't help that he had a shoulder and arm injury."

Ginger, was not the first crew member of either *Hardy* or *Hunter* to be able to survive a fiercely fought battle, only to find his luck finally ran out at a later date.

I mention this because one of the satisfactions from writing both books, has been that it has brought many families together. In the case of Ginger, Janet from Exeter having contacted me, with the above information, led to both her and Gill O'Rourke, the daughter of Signalman Bernard Kennedy, another survivor on *Hardy*, making direct contact with Ralph Brigginshaw.

Captain Nicholas Diary.

Sat 13 Apl 40.
This forenoon became aware of heavy firing in the distance and was sure the Navy was on its way. At noon the supply plane flew overhead and dropped its usual supply.

About 1 pm the concussion from the gunfire was shaking the windows and the walls at the Café. We assumed that the German destroyers and the battery which was in German hands were being wiped out. A German destroyer which was in the harbour went out with her guns in action, but by what I heard later she did not last long.

On the morning of the 13th April the population of Narvik and the surrounding villages could hear the sounds of bombardments in the Ofotfjord. It was like distant thunder when a storm is getting nearer. The men in the Café Iris were looking down at them in the square and smiles with 'thumbs up' signs were exchanged. Whilst the German soldiers marching or driving inside their vehicles were looking extremely worried, the people of Narvik appeared to accept the consequences with a smile, even though for most it was an anxious one. Especially when the thunderstorm finally arrived and overhead there were the whistles of naval shells. It was for them to find shelter.

The men watching from the window, according to them, were unsure whether to cheer or feel regretful, "When the chaos appeared to reach its crescendo a German destroyer, damaged in the first battle, took its chance and guns firing, bravely made her way towards the enemy. Where there was surely no escape."

The Zerstörer, as you have read was *Erich Koellner* on her 'suicide mission', escorted 200 yards ahead by *Hermann Kunne*. At 1200 the two ships saw the *Warspite's* Swordfish, piloted by Petty Officer Frederick 'Ben' Rice, the observer, Lieutenant Commander W. 'Bruno' Brown and the gunner Leading Airman Maurice Pacey. Off Baroy, *Hermann Kunne* having increased knots, soon sighted the multitude of Royal Navy destroyers, turned and headed back to Narvik, signalling Bey. As the radio office on *Warspite* had tuned into *Hermann Kunne's* plain language communications, *Warspite* bided her time for now.

Back to the Swordfish, when reaching Narvik they saw that none of the Zerstörers had left the harbour, which they duly reported back to the fleet. On their return to *Warspite* they spotted *Erich Koellner* and reported this to *Warspite*. The Captain had been unable to reach his chosen position and had returned to Djupvik. By this time the Royal Naval fleet had advanced and visually spotted *Erich Koellner's* masthead. Three Tribal ships, *Bedouin, Punjabi* and *Eskimo* rounded the shoreline and the result was a short engagement. *Erich Koellner* and her brave crew tried to put up a fight, but the Tribal ship's pom-poms were no match for them. These were followed shortly after by *Warspite*, whose 15-inch shells hit "like express train coaches". Thirty-one men were killed and any survivors were detained by Norwegian forces.

Fregattenkapitan Bey, having expected an afternoon attack had not yet ordered his Zerstörers to their battle positions in the adjacent fjords. Late being better than never, this he decided to do now. Unfortunately, his U-boats for a variety of reasons were not ready to move. U-51, thinking the alarm was similar to the previous day's air attack, cast off from refuelling with *Jan Wellem* and dived to the bottom of the harbour, where it remained. In the meantime, Petty Officer Rice, under instructions from his observer, Lt Commander Brown, was navigating around the side fjords, when they came across the anchored U-64 in Herjangsfjord.

As researched by Geirr Haarr, "Rice put his lumbering double-decker into a daunting dive-bombing attack. Two 50 kg anti-submarine bombs were dropped from about 100 metres on the unprepared boat. One hit the bows, the second exploded close to the side of the boat between the bows and the conning tower. The combined effect of the bombs cracked the hull open and water poured in; U-64 started to sink. The majority of the crew managed to escape and swam through icy water to be rescued by Jagers (Alpine Troops) at Bjerkvik, but eight men perished. Leading Airman Pacey opened fire with the rear gun as the Swordfish pulled away, striking the conning tower. One of the lookouts replied with his own gun, hitting the tail plane of the Swordfish, making her controls sluggish. The extent of the damage could not be seen, but Rice considered it would be safe to continue, provided he 'flew slowly and manoeuvred gently'. Brown agreed and they stayed in the air".

Petty Officer Ben Rice would say later, "Flying in the fjords, particularly in narrow ones – resembled flying in a tunnel between steep sides of the fjords and low cloud ceiling." [71]

Gunner's mate Daniel Reardon describes the moment on *Warspite*. "Our gun-house crew is soon correct and so are the shell-room and magazine

---

71 (RM98/155). Some of the survivors of U-64 were trapped inside the sunken boat and had to escape through a free-ascent to the surface (three casualties occurred during this). The crew was employed for a while as gaolers and ammunition handlers before repatriation to Germany by railroad through Sweden.

crews. We report to control and turret officer tells me I can load. We hear the order repeated to the men down below, the cages come up with a thud, and out go the rammers. We can feel that we have increased speed as the ship has begun to vibrate. Heavy explosions shake the ship, and we hear that the destroyers are attacking a submarine. Suddenly comes the order 'Salvoes' and the right gun comes to ready. Then 'Enemy in sight' and the sight-setters chant the ranges. It is just like a practice shoot. Our guns are nearly horizontal, so the range must be short. Then the 'ding-ding' of the fire gong, the right gun moves a little, comes steady then there is a 'Woof' which rocks the turret." [72]

Reardon: "The left gun is now at the ready, and fires while the right gun is reloading. 'B' turret, firing over our heads, blows away our 'blast bags' and the turret fills with smoke – like London on a November night. The turret officer calls out, 'Tell the crew we have hit a destroyer and she is burning nicely. Good work, boys keep it going. Steady firing now.' Then the trainer reports, 'Blimey, another one has got it,' and the news is passed to the men below. You can hear the cheer. Down in the machinery space the OA (Ordnance Artificer), his face covered with oil and sweat, grins and holds up his thumb. Hydraulic pressure is ok."

Back to Geirr Haarr's highly respected researched book, which now focused on the beginning of the second battle. "Meanwhile, Fregattenkapitan Bey hoisted the red standard 'Z' on *ZENKER* and led *ARNIM* out of Narvik at 12:45. [The red standard Z 'an den Feind' – 'advance on the enemy' was a traditional signal used by German destroyers and torpedo boats going into battle.] *LUDEMANN* was already a mile ahead. *THIELE* followed a while later, but *GIESE* had not worked up sufficient steam and stayed behind. Korvettenkapitan Kothe saw the other Zerstörers leaving the harbour and turning *KUNNE* back on a westerly course, intensified efforts to lay a smokescreen to hide them as long as possible. Coming out of the Narrows, Force B [Royal Naval ships] spread out on a solid front ahead and abeam of *WARSPITE*, but had limited room to manoeuvre. The German destroyers, on the other hand, were in the wider part of the fjord and by zigzagging in

---

72   As *Warspite's* forward turrets were facing almost dead ahead, the blast from 'B' turret damaged the blast bags of 'A' turret ['A' turret foremost] covering the points where the guns protrude from the armour. 'A' turret thus filled with choking cordite smoke adding to the discomfort of the turret crew from having the 'B' gun's blasting deafeningly just above their heads. (ADM 199/473)

broad sweeps managed to use their broadsides to a maximum effect in spite of being seriously outgunned."

During the battle firing distances varied from six to fourteen miles but the Royal Naval destroyers fired a shorter distance. Although the weather improved, gunfire smoke did not help the gun control. Initially, the Zerstörers got the better of their enemy, receiving no hits, whilst the Royal Navy ships were straddled by accurate salvoes. However, overall the battle having gone on for an hour, there were no major hits for either of the opposing ships.

Marshal Soult recalls. "On Saturday the 13th of April at approximately twelve noon, the survivors from *Hunter* heard the thunder of large guns, then the explosions of the shells as they landed in the docks. Realising that an attack by their countrymen was under way the men rushed to the windows of the café. They could see shells dropping in the docks and among the few ships still afloat in the harbour. As the action continued, buildings in the dock area were reduced to rubble. A lorry loaded with German wounded came from the direction of the docks. It passed the café, turned left crossing a bridge over the railway. The guns of one of the destroyers opened up on the bridge hitting the parapet and narrowly missing the lorry. The attack lasted all afternoon. The damage sustained by the enemy in this second attack coupled with that of the first, broke the back of the whole German Naval force at Narvik."

Romilly saw another German lorry, "Packed with ammunition it approached the railway bridge from the square. The destroyer put a shell behind it. Accelerating for his life, the man at the wheel leapt the bridge like a kangaroo, skidded, and stuck fast askew in snow-slush. The destroyer circled, fired no more shots. Then she went out astern."

The locals who ventured from their shelters were able to see the chaos for themselves. German soldiers, including the young Alpine troops dressed in their white skiing tunics, on skis or with them strapped to their backs, were being organised for escape to the mountains. The men in the Café Iris could see Red Cross flags being stretched over roofs. By now singing could be heard from the Café.

It's a long way to Tipperary
it's a long way to go
It's a long way to Tipperary

to the sweetest gal I know
farewell to Piccadilly
so long Leicester Square
It's a long way to Tipperary
but my heart lies there

Followed by "Pack up your troubles in your old kit bag ..." and many more. As described by Giles Romilly, "Bellowed in tuneless triumph to a tuneless piano."

As you would imagine *Warspite* as a battleship was a heavy and clumsy vessel built to fire at long distances at other similar large ponderous warships. Designed to engage by keeping an approximately steady course between salvoes. The revolving mass of one twin turret weighed 750 tons, each gun 100 tons, and a shell nearly one ton. This would require powerful hydraulic machinery to operate every movement. Here Dickens describes the process, "To load, a three-tiered caged [lift] rushed upwards from the depths [magazine] behind the gaping maw [mouth] of each breech. Then a huge chain uncurled itself to ram the shell firmly into the rifling and then withdrew; the cage shifted up a notch and the first half-charge was rammed, then the second; down went the cage, the breech closed, and the gun was free to return to its firing elevation. The maximum rate of fire of two rounds per minute may be thought remarkably fast under these conditions, but to a destroyer it gave time to dodge."

Geirr Haarr explains, "Target holding was made difficult for the British destroyers by the German ships criss-crossing, but there is little doubt that the German gunnery control was superior on this day." [73]

HMS *Hardy*'s Torpedoman Cyril Cope: "As we looked down from our vantage point high above the fjord we saw German destroyers coming at full speed from the direction of Narvik. Their guns were blazing at targets which at that moment we still could not see. The scene changed very rapidly. The enemy ships were backing away. Some began to take punishment. Then into our view came the most wonderful sight that any of us could have wished for, two lines of destroyers in 'V' formation with the good old

---

73   The Royal Navy ships, as pointed out earlier, were mainly utilising SAP [semi-automatic piercing] shells. Whilst, the Kriegsmarine depended on their HE [high explosive] shells, exploding on impact with the water, causing splinters to strike the enemy.

Warspite in the centre. The destroyers were *Hero, Forester, Eskimo, Bedouin, Foxhound, Kimberley, Icarus, Punjabi* and *Cossack*.

"The enemy destroyer which lay below us at the entrance to the inlet had by now turned broadside on to the fjord, with its torpedo tubes facing the direction from which *Warspite* and her attendant destroyer screen would come. The enemy's intention was plain to see; a torpedo attack without warning. Because of the curve in the coastline, our ships would not see this lurking destroyer until after the torpedoes were fired."

Royal Navy ships going into action in the Second Battle
13th April 1940. [Geirr Haarr Collection]

Wolfgang Zenker made a torpedo attack on *Warspite* but to no avail and was driven off by the guns of the battleship and the screening destroyers. *Bernd von Arnim* also fired her torpedoes but *Cossack, Kimberley* and *Forester* was able to avoid these unharmed. By now U-25 had resurfaced and fired two torpedoes at the screening destroyers. But the Captain probably realising his U-boat was not having much of an effect on the battle, decided to track back to Ramnes, where he might be able to pick off any Royal Navy ships returning to open sea.

Warspite, needing to keep in confined waters and within her screen, could only bring to bear her two forward guns. But her own gun smoke and the screening destroyers together affected gun fire control, resulting in her only firing two rounds a minute. Geirr Haarr best describes the scene, "No hits were scored in this part of the engagement, but the metre-long muzzle flame from the big gun and the howling of the heavy shells in almost flat trajectory low over the fjord made for a terrifying spectacle. The noise echoing between the cliffs and shells exploding on land created avalanches of rocks and snow tumbling down the mountainside."

HMS *Hunter* survivor Petty Officer William Barrett records that about 1300 on the 13th April because of the "heavy bombardment of Narvik by the British Fleet and Air Force", all the prisoners incarcerated in the Railway Waiting Room were transferred to schoolroom in Narvik.

At 1330 the Royal Navy Fleet Air Arm were given the opportunity to become involved in the melee. Nine Swordfish from *Furious* dived down on the Zerstörers, dropping bombs but to no effect and two aircraft were lost. By now as a result of the previous battle on the 10th April, this had left the Zerstörers almost out of ammunition. Fregattenkapitan Bey [pronounced Buy] ordered his ships by 'voice radio' to retire to Rombaksfjord, in a desperate attempt to shelter from *Warspite*'s gunfire.

In the afternoon locals heard heavy gunfire again from the outer fjords and "increasing in violence". The German-occupied sectors of the town were evacuated. The 'Alpine Troops' marched out towards the north side, leaving behind some to defend the harbour and to hold the Telegraph Office. One young local fellow came running from the direction of Framnes and reported that the whole fjord was swarming with ships including many British warships, one of which was a colossus of a warship.

Although the sailors on *Hermann Kunne* at the time would not realise it, they were fortunate that the signal for whatever reason was not received. Hence, her commanding officer Kovettenkapitan Kothe headed for Herjangsfjord, where his ship with empty magazines was grounded, he had even used up all the high explosive, practice and star shells. Prior to the crew being evacuated, he ordered depth charges to be primed with explosives. Ironically, throughout the battles other than the engines requiring repairs *Hermann Kunne* had received no damage or casualties. In the meantime, unbeknown to Kothe, his ship had been tracked by *Eskimo* and *Forester*. This was the end as *Eskimo* launched a torpedo into the grounded *Hermann Kunne*, blowing off her stern.

Hermann Kunne. When warmer weather arrived. [Theo Werner Schettler via Frank Hackney Collection]

As the five Zerstörers were being pressed into Herjangsfjord with the Royal Navy ships following behind they must have realised they were defeated. Ammunition running low they knew there was no hope. The British would acknowledge their adversaries had fought well, but would then return to the reality. As ships in turn passed the wreck of their sister ship *Hardy*, there would have been revengeful feelings among the crew. The Germans had brought this on themselves, acting like an uncivilised and barbaric race, occupying smaller defenceless neighbouring countries. Of course the Royal Navy men at this moment, would not have known that a greater loss of life had occurred, no more than a few miles away from them in the fjord; namely the sunken HMS *Hunter*.

However, in later years, for naval historians, the question was, "had the battle been won or lost?" Over the last one hour and twenty minutes, enemy ships had fired many hundreds of rounds at each other and disregarding the *Erich Koellner* incident when the range was point blank, not one single hit had been scored by either side.

There was no blame to either side, as Peter Dickens points out. "The weapon-systems were just not up to their designed task despite the research, development and money that had been lavished on them; and those ships were the elite of the two navies, built in peace and manned by highly trained regulars [...] Had the British Home Fleet contained more carriers than battleships, and had they been equipped with strike aircraft and weapons expressly designed to replace the gun as the Fleet's main offensive power, the two naval battles would hardly have been needed. And had the German establishment admitted to itself that destroyers' guns were virtually useless at ranges of over 5,000 yards it would probably never have mounted the Narvik operation unless it could have found some means of providing local air power. The German torpedo failure was of course even more disastrous because it was one-sided."

APRIL 13 1940. SMIDT – *Erich Giese*. AT 1215 HOURS ALARM! BREAKTHROUGH OF 1 HEAVY BRITISH DESTROYER UNDER THE COMMAND OF *WARSPITE*. AT 1352 HOURS TRIED TO START UP THE *GIESE*, BUT 12 KNOTS WAS THE MAXIMUM SPEED. IN THE MEANTIME, THE REST OF THE GERMAN DESTROYERS JOINED THE BATTLE. FINALLY *GIESE* LEFT NARVIK HARBOUR, WAS ATTACKED BY ONE BRITISH AIRCRAFT AT THE ENTRANCE BUT IT WAS SHOT DOWN INTO THE SEA 100 METRES IN FRONT OF THE *GIESE* IN OFOTEN-FJORD, 5 OR 6 BRITISH DESTROYERS WERE SIGHTED. THE *GIESE* CAME UNDER FIRE.

Erich Giese was now repaired and ready to join her sister ships, but at the harbour mouth her port engines failed and prevented her turning. The fjord appeared to be full of British ships other than *Hermann Kunne* and she was retreating rapidly up Herjangsfjord. *Bedouin* and *Punjabi* launched five torpedoes but they missed *Erich Giese*. Korvettenkapitan Smidt pointed his guns on *Punjabi*, hitting her with rapid fire of six shells. Several exploded causing fires and damage, gun control systems, main steam pipe and the wireless office. Seven men were killed and fourteen injured. The Captain of *Punjabi*, Commander Lean had no options but to withdraw, sending a signal to his sister ships, "Am damned sorry I have got to come out of it, main steam pipe and guns out of action."

Because *Punjabi* crew were obviously well trained with their 'Damage Control' procedures, they got their ship back in action almost an hour later.

Likewise, *Erich Giese*'s engineers worked frantically and the ship was fit for sea even quicker. Once more she left the harbour, but this time to an unwelcoming reception. Smidt, having received signals from his sister ships, knew they had left the area and was heading towards Rombaksfjord, leaving him and his crew to face the Royal Navy alone.

Later, Smidt acknowledged his fate, "[...] the proper duty of an officer [...] is to inflict as much damage on the enemy as possible [...] We had ten minutes' worth of ammunition and all torpedoes, so we could fight. But I had no hope that we would ever reach port again."

Erich Giese was confronted head on by five smaller enemy destroyers, like hounds catching up with the fox. The Royal Navy ships were led by Commander McCoy, on *Bedouin*. At point-blank range *Erich Giese* was hit hard. Smidt and his crew fought bravely, launching their torpedoes and firing their guns until depleted, making one hit. That is with exception of three shells found by Gunnery Artificer Piening, who assisted by Seaman Gangelhoff in stubborn defiance was able to discharged them.

But the *Bedouin*'s salvoes and possibly a torpedo, had left the *Erich Giese* a 'blazing inferno'. Her Gunnery Officer, Ian Garnett, had trained his gunnery crews to high level of efficiency. This probably had resulted in the ship receiving no hits, other than splinter holes from near misses. The *Erich Giese* now out of control, finally without power and taking in water, stopped. Smidt feeling that his duty was done, gave the order to 'Abandon Ship'. However, it was too late for eighty-three of her crew members who perished.

Korvettenkapitan Smidt's Diary:

THE BATTLE OF THE *GIESE* AGAINST OVERWHELMING ODDS LASTED 15 MINUTES. THE BATTLE PICTURE CHANGED RAPIDLY. THE REMAINDER OF THE AMMUNITION WAS RAPIDLY USED UP, AS WELL AS THE TORPEDOES. ONE BRITISH DESTROYER *PUNJABI* HAD TO WITHDRAW FROM ACTION BECAUSE OF DAMAGE.

DURING THE SHORT BATTLE THE *GIESE* WAS HIT 22 TIMES. ENGINES AND ELECTRICAL INSTRUMENTS WERE PUT OUT OF ORDER. LAST BATTLE DISTANCE WAS 1000 METRES. COMMANDER ORDERED EVERYONE TO ABANDON SHIP.

ALL SURVIVORS WERE GIVEN THE CHOICE OF RESCUE AT LAND OR TO GIVE THEMSELVES UP AS PRISONERS. WITH THE AID OF LIFEJACKETS THEY REACHED LAND. MOST MEN SURVIVED AFTER DIFFICULTIES WITH THE COLD 3 DEGREE WATER. NINE MEN WERE TAKEN PRISONER.

The crippled *Erich Giese* whose crew had fought bravely but
could not save their ship. [Geirr Haarr Collection]

The *Foxhound* came along and rescued eleven in the ice-cold waters, in the
meantime, the rest of the surviving crew scrambled ashore. It would be a
further ten hours before the burning vessel sank in the fjord.

German sources later held persistently that British ships had used
machine guns on the *Erich Giese* sailors in the water. [ADM 199/473 and
IWM 95/3/1]

Captain Nicholas

Sat 13 Apl 40
Soon afterwards [afternoon] a British destroyer came into the harbour and came
alongside the quay. He was greeted by machine gun fire. He then lay off the quay
and placed a few shells in the quay side buildings where the machine gun bullets
came from. Later we saw wounded Germans being taken to hospital.

Returning to the fate of *Diether von Roeder* still moored to the 'Post Quay'. In
defiance, she had fired her two forward guns at any target sighted. *Warspite*
received one hit on the bridge but only caused superficial damage. The commanding officer of *Diether von Roeder*, Korvettenkapitan Holtorf had made
use of a tunnel nearby in the docks so he could give instructions to his gunnery team left on board.

A wireless transmission from the Swordfish piloted by Petty Officer Ben Rice indicated a German destroyer [*Diether von Roeder*] alongside a jetty. This led to *Cossack* and *Kimberley* going to scout out the situation. The Captain of *Cossack*, Commander Sherbrooke having found his foe, opened fire; like a wounded beast, *Diether von Roeder* fought back with her own salvoes. *Cossack* received shell holes on the waterline and splinter damage to the main steam pipe, both boiler rooms and fires broke out in the lower messdecks. As a precaution one of the magazines had to be flooded. However, all measures taken did not stop *Cossack* going aground at Ankenes, but with her aft guns still firing.

Dickens provides his version, "*Diether von Roeder* hit her [*Cossack*] in the gun fire control room [...] More hits slammed home, the nose-fused German shells opening huge, four-foot diameter holes in her side and sending jagged fragments tearing inwards to kill and wound men, wreck compartments, and perforate steam-pipes and hydraulic leads to guns and steering engine. It became clear that the tactical factor which really mattered was the *Cossack's* exposed beam as opposed to *Diether von Roeder's* narrow end-on silhouette. The British guns fired rapidly and evidently scored some hits, though not near the two guns which was the only place that mattered."

The *Diether von Roeder* was now on fire aft but her guns also kept on firing salvoes until the last shell had gone. *Kimberley* who had stayed outside the harbour came to support *Cossack*, whilst one of *Warspite's* massive shells fell on the lame *Diether von Roeder*. The twenty-five Gunners left on board, who had caused all the chaos, had nothing more they could do. There had been no casualties. Finally they abandoned ship, leapt on to the jetty, scurrying down the tunnel, no doubt to receive a much back slapping welcome from their Kapitan, Holtorf and other crew members. In the meantime, three Gunners remained on board to attach demolition charge fuses. I will return to the final minutes of *Diether von Roeder* shortly.

No Escape for the Zerstörers

Hans Ludemann, Wolfgang Zenker, Bernd von Arnim and *Georg Thiele* having entered Rombaksfjord, relatively unscathed, knew time was running out. *Wolfgang Zenker* and *Bernd von Arnim* with no more ammunition realised they could not carry on the fight. Both Captains decided to take their Zerstörers further into the fjord through the narrow sound at Straumen and onto shallower parts known as the Rombaksbotten sandbanks. *Georg Thiele'* and *Hans Ludemann* with their remaining ammunition, including torpedoes, prepared an ambush inside Straumen for any following enemy ships. [74]

As you would imagine there was immense tension in Narvik town but the local populace were still keeping an eye on proceedings both in the fjords and around the town. They could not see much of what was taking place out at sea, but they were aware that the sea battle was getting nearer to them. Shells came in over the harbour and naturally caused heavy damage in the town, people ran into the streets. They hid behind the walls and buildings, they could hear shell splinters whine through the air. As a normal precaution women and children were a priority, and places of safety had been sorted out. Cellars and basements of properties, a subway, not yet fully constructed was also utilised and assessed to be able to accommodate a thousand people. It quickly became a popular safe haven.

Mayor Broch: "Our destiny was being decided in the fjord. The shooting never seemed to come to an end [...] We could distinguish the heavy shots; these must have come from the largest guns. The mountains hurled the sound like a ball back and forth among themselves. Once we counted the echoes up to seven."

---

74   In 1979 Cyril and Edith, at the invitation of the German veterans, was visiting Germany when news came in that Gottfried had pass away. Cyril on behalf of the 2nd Destroyer Association, attended his funeral. Gottfried's wife was so pleased he was able to attend, she presented Cyril with a framed painting of the *Wolfgang Zenker*.

Fregattenkappitan Gottfried Ponitz of the *Wolfgang Zenker* [Cyril Cope Collection]

The effects of the deafening noise and devastation were having an effect on the Wehrmacht and surviving Kriegsmarines. There was an explosion in the harbour, which brought locals out into the streets. They witnessed enemy soldiers coming from the direction of Framnes forest, wet bedraggled souls, having despatched their weapons. German sailors appeared to have been psychologically affected, with "stone-like stares, some laughing half-delirious"; moving down the street singing, stopping to talk to locals. They told us that it was the British battleship which was out in the fjords with many other ships. When the locals suggested the end was in sight, they smiled forlornly, muttering "Kamerad" [comrade].

The *Warspite* stayed in Herjangsfjord, whilst *Forester, Hero, Icarus, Eskimo* followed by the command ship *Bedouin*, moved on. They had had an initial report from Ben Rice's Swordfish that there were two enemy ships in Rombaksfjord, which was later changed to three ships. The promontory at Straumen and the steep sides of the fjord hid the waiting Zerstörers from the Royal Navy ships. It was now 1445 when the Captain of *Eskimo*, Commander Micklethwait, was the first to negotiate his ship through the entrance. Followed by *Forester*, whilst *Hero* waited at the sound, and *Bedouin* and *Icarus* remained outside.

As the British came in sight, *Hans Ludemann*, having transferred all her ammunition to the three after guns, opened fire from a distance of three miles. All her last four torpedoes were also launched towards Straumen, more in the hope of hitting her target rather than being efficiently controlled. One of the torpedoes went under *Forester*'s bow section. *Eskimo* fired her guns which hit *Hans Ludemann* aft – not only finishing off two guns but also killing their gun teams. The third gun was damaged. The Captain Korvettenkapitan Friedrichs, knew that whatever fight there had been it was now over. He decided to head for the Rombaksbotten sandbanks to join his two sister ships aground.

Bernd Arnim and *Wolfgang Zenker* beached. [Geirr Haarr]

Looking down into Rombaksbotten the *Hans Ludemann* and *Wolfgang Zenker* beached
– taken from a passing train. [Theo Werner Schettler via Frank Hackney.]

In the meantime, *Georg Thiele*, hidden behind a smokescreen, had lost her gun-fire system so had to rely on local control. It was Korvettenkapitan Wolff's intentions, with his remaining torpedoes, to delay the British ships allowing his fellow Captains to scuttle their ships and save the crews lives.

It was now *Georg Thiele*'s turn to face the violent storm ahead. Commander Micklethwait [*Eskimo*] wanted to resolve the issue quickly to enable him to chase the other Zerstörers down the fjord, so that their involvement in the battle was now finally over. However, Micklethwait would find the task not as easy as he first thought. As he positioned *Eskimo* for a broadside torpedo attack, *Georg Thiele* received a number of hits causing several casualties. But perhaps the Captain of *Eskimo* had not been made aware of the boldness of Korvettenkapitan Max-Eckart Wolff from the First Battle.

Micklethwait in a later report, "When the total destruction of the enemy could not be obtained without running a certain risk, I went straight through the narrow entry to the Rombaksfjord and was prepared for the danger of being torpedoed by the enemy just inside."

He was about to manoeuvre his ship in the narrow part of the fjord when he saw three torpedoes which *Hans Ludemann* had launched. Ordering "Full Ahead – all", instantly 44,000 horse-power thrust her ahead of the torpedoes which missed close by. He was still not out of trouble as *Eskimo* was fast approaching the shoreline, and he ordered, "Full Astern". Dickens describes the heart-fluttering moments, "Reversing the engines and their braking effect was equally positive; shaking every rivet she pulled up as the rocks vanished under the forecastle when viewed from the bridge, for her engine-room department was as efficient as her gunnery."

The Captain of *Hero*, Commander Biggs brought her up to the entrance of Straumen, but decided to halt as he felt there was insufficient room for three ships. Although *Hero* continued firing her foremost guns. Just at this moment a surreal event took place, a local man in a rowing boat pulled over to the ship and asked the gun crews, "You sink the enemy?" "Yes," they replied. "Good!" he said. He was the schoolmaster and on the shore, the crews could see the children skiing home. No doubt being able to witness such a dramatic sight meant that they would have a great story to tell their grandchildren in the future.

Back on board *Georg Thiele* the fight carried on as best she could. The highly resourceful Torpedo Officer, Oberleutnant Sommer was given the freedom by Wolff to launch his torpedoes once the British were sighted. Sommer had stationed himself with the tubes crew waiting patiently for the right moment. That moment arrived when *Eskimo* was going through the 'Full Ahead / Full Astern' manoeuvres and Sommer sighted the *Eskimo* 'beam on' and was stopped dead in the fjord. The final torpedo was launched, the other having been fired accidentally when a torpedo crewman fell wounded onto the firing lever, so that it ran out of control exploding on the shore. But Sommer and his crew probably groaned as they saw the second torpedo running on the surface. Another failing from a familiar fault, one must ask?

Above in the skies Lieutenant Commander Bruno Brown in the Swordfish saw the torpedo track and attempted to contact *Eskimo* by radio, to no avail, so the code 'T-T-T-T', [torpedo approaching] was flashed.

However, at least the torpedo was running straight and the *Georg Thiele* tube's crew's dismay soon turned to euphoria, as it 'slammed' into *Eskimo*, just below the No 1 turret. This left the turret hanging vertically over the bow section. Fifteen men were killed instantly in the turret (or thrown into the water), the shell room and magazine compartment, and ten were wounded (two mortally). Heroically, the nearby No 2 turret crew having taken thirty seconds to regain their composure then carried on firing.

Micklethwait, certain that his ship would soon sink, fired his last torpedo which missed its target. With the after turrets also continuing to fire, he headed his ship, stern first, back towards the Narvik area. Fortunately, the many hours of 'Damage Control' training exercises had paid off. Bulkheads had been shored up, hanging electrical cables and anchor chains, with now redundant heavy equipment were all jettisoned. Finally the forlorn looking destroyer although with a brave and proud crew, was now back under control. [75]

HMS *Eskimo* with her gun turret hanging vertically.

---

75   The crew on *Georg Thiele* who witnessed the damage her torpedoes had done, took it for granted that they had sunk the enemy destroyer. In fact they mistakenly thought the *Eskimo* was *Cossack*. Subsequently, the Zerstörer signalled this incorrect information back to Germany. The following day, similar to all warring nations the Nazis for propaganda purposes took advantage and the story was broadcast around the world.

The devastation looking from the jetty. [Hartvig Sverdrup Collection]

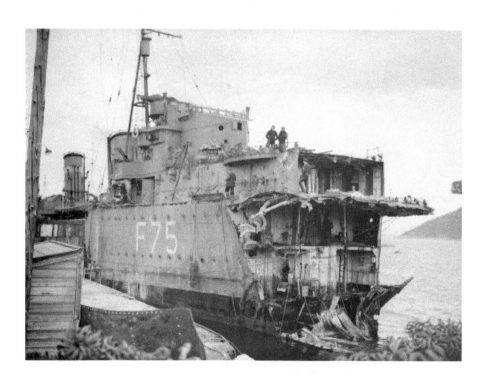

In the meantime, *Hero* and *Icarus* went ahead to catch up with the three unaccountable Zerstörers. They entered Rombaksbotten in no rush being wary of a repeated ambush. Unknown to the destroyers, the enemy were now out of the equation having grounded themselves on a sandy beach.

The *Diether von Roeder*, had three Gunners left on board, with their demolition charges at the ready, and her Captain, Holtorf and other crew members hidden in a nearby tunnel. But the German ship had unwanted company, albeit on the opposite side of the harbour, the grounded *Cossack*. *Diether von Roeder* from an immobile position had caused massive damage to *Cossack*. Commander Sherbrooke, on viewing the silent and deserted *Diether von Roeder* from across the harbour thought she looked worryingly in 'good shape'. Something had to be done about her and ordered Lieutenant Commander Peters, Captain of *Foxhound* to investigate. Although the fire aft on '*Diether von Roeder*' had now died down, the *Foxhound* still made a cautious approach, deciding to do a run alongside the German ship. "Hands to boarding stations" was piped and two lots of landing parties mustered on the quarterdeck, fully equipped with webbing, cutlasses, rifles and gaiters. [76]

Holtorf from his tunnel was particularly impressed by the gaiters, and who could not blame him? But it was also what he saw next. The British sailor's uncontrollable urge to make a joke of any out of routine event, and so they tumbled up from below dressed as swarthy, kerchiefed [piece of cloth worn over the head or neck] pirates with knives between their teeth. [77]

It was clear to the Germans who realised that their last chance had come to inflict damage on the enemy, and Matrosen-matt Tietke [Seaman Petty Officer] in charge of the demolition squad was ordered to light the

---

76 Torpedomen always had 'scabbards and cutlasses' normally tied by lanyards to the funnel where they were at the ready. My father Cyril said, "This was something we practised when doing our 'work up' in the 'Med', in case we were needed for boarding other ships. Goodness knows what we were supposed to do with them; I could never envisage having to use one. 'Gospel Truth.'"

77 British sailors loved pretending to be pirates, in fact I think half of them were in a previous life. In the 60s to 80s I was on board ships [including the aircraft carrier *Ark Royal*] when at sea for weeks we had "Pirates' day". I could never fathom out where so many of the lads were able to conjure up eyepatches [probably the sick bay had a big call] or plastic cutlasses and knives. I even think they were part of their belongings brought on board in their kitbags, almost in anticipation of the great event. They say, sailors never quite grow up but it was fun to let your hair down.

nine-minute delay fuses to the two carefully placed depth charges. To Peters, there was something sinister about this silent foe, not least in the fact, as he could now see, that she appeared to be completely without blemish (all damage in the first battle had been on the far, port side) and perfectly capable of rounding on him murderously. He ordered the teeming upper deck to be cleared, though that was not easily achieved, and then fired two or three 4.7-inch rounds which of course triggered no response.

"Holtorf willed Peters to come on. He did so, but when the *Foxhound* was only fifty yards clear, Tietke and his two men jumped from their ship and ran for their lives, necessarily in full view. Peters stopped, and at once to Holtorf's dismay a hot rifle and machine gun fire from houses along the waterfront raked the *Foxhound*'s decks, the soldiers and sailors responsible not having been told of the plot. The *Foxhound* was lucky to lose only one man killed, because, Peters immediately ordered 'Full Astern' both to get clear of the firing and because it had quite convinced him that a trap was about to be sprung. The water churned, the ship gathered sternway, and then two colossal explosions rent the last of the German destroyers. When Peter's eyes had adjusted to normal after the blinding flashes and the smoke had drifted away, the *Diether von Roeder* was just not there."

Mayor Theodor Broch witnessed the above events from the Post Pier. "The harbour itself was a ship's graveyard with wreckage wherever one looked. Flocks of frightened sea gulls screamed in the air. Occasionally they dived hurriedly into the waters to nip at some of the strange objects that floated in the oily sea. [..] The new pier was torn apart. The huge concrete block at the end had been cut in two as by a huge axe. [...] Whole parts of warships lay silent testimony to the terrific force of naval artillery fire. The whole inside of a warship seemed strewn around. It was the strangest sight I had ever witnessed [...] it was like a gigantic jigsaw puzzle which had been left unfinished. One could, however, somehow guess that, if the parts were brought logically together again, they would make up a warship or, more accurately, one of those German destroyers which brought to Narvik the chaos of the New Order."

Broch had also witnessed the Germans observation post in the tunnel and *Cossack* entering the harbour, slowly to Ankenes, where the sea bottom was even. Although he did not actually know the name of the ship, he had kept watch on the destroyer which was less than a mile away which was sending shells over the harbour in order to put out a machine gun nest under the iron ore pier. He kept hoping that the ship would eventually raise itself off the bottom, but realised if he remained any longer watching from his vantage point that he could be mistaken for a German. As he walked away back to his office past the shelled-out warehouses, he ran into a German Naval officer with a revolver in his hand. "His face was tense, his jaw jutted forward." "I had you at dead aim all the time," he said. "If you had attempted to contact the gentlemen across the water, you would have been a dead man. I can assure you of one thing, and that is that your friends the British will never come!"

In the meantime, *Cossack* had nine killed and twenty-one wounded. She was stuck solidly and Sherbrooke felt he needed to have a thorough under-water examination before attempting to re-float her. Later in the afternoon the *Foxhound* returned to *Cossack* because Lieutenant Commander Peters was concerned *Cossack* "seemed to be stuck in the most unhealthy position". Sherbrooke, assured Peters, he was not ready yet, but accepted his offer of receiving *Foxhound*'s doctor aboard. Subsequently, Peters took *Foxhound* out of the harbour to pick up survivors from the *Erich Giese*, as ordered by the Admiral.

After all the drama of the battle in the Straumen Narrows, *Georg Thiele* crew did not have time to celebrate their 'kill'; fires had to be brought under control. Oberleutnant Fuchs, the Gunnery Officer, was able to control the after guns by telephone line, but had to shout orders to No 2 gun over the front of the bridge. Numbers 3 and 4 were firing intermittently because the ammunition hoist had been demolished. Then a shell hit near the bridge resulting in severe casualties, both there and at the No 2 gun. The Second in Command, Kapitanleutnant von Lepel, was mortally wounded, losing both legs and an arm. Fuchs recovered sufficiently from concussion and was able to make his final report to Wolff, himself lying face downwards streaming with blood. *"Ich bekomme keine Munition mehr in die batterie."* ["I have no more ammunition for the guns."]

Dickens writes, "Heroics now would have been false ones. The wheel had turned full circle, for what *Georg Thiele* had done to the *Hardy*'s bridge had now been done to hers. Himself wounded and virtually alone among the dead and unconscious, Wolff decided like Stanning to put his ship ashore and save what lives remained. Like him he gave the necessary orders and similarly there was no response, for the Telegraphsman was dead, so he carried them out himself. Full ahead; and the remaining boilers delivered such a surge of power that the bow was lifted high over the narrow ledge at the waterside, while the forefoot crumpled inwards on the jagged rocks; the time was 1500."

The grounding was at Sildvik, the cost of delaying the British chasing her sister Zerstörers resulted in fourteen killed and twenty-eight wounded. Whilst a number of the surviving crew went over the side of the ship, others lowered themselves over the forecastle directly on to the shore. Wolff, like Stanning made sure the secret material was thrown over the stern into deep water and followed his men. Sea cocks were opened, depth charges fired and ship listing was drawn down to the sandy flats. Wolf was amazed, also as Stanning to find so many of his men still alive. Those crew members who were fit were able to make their way up the almost 1,000-feet steep climb to the top of the fjord face. Eventually transport was sent to bring them back to Narvik. It was a tribute to Korvettenkapitan Max-Eckart Wolff and his crews fighting spirit that even when the British guns fell silent, it was not for another forty minutes before they began to negotiate the journey down the rest of the fjord. [78]

The Georg *Thiele'* grounded and her hulk was left there as a reminder of the fierce battles. [Geirr Haarr Collection]

---

78   Kovettenkapitan Max-Eckart Wolff, similar to Karl Smidt, held firmly that many of his men had been killed or wounded after they had come ashore by British guns.

The wreck is remains there to this day. This photograph
was taken in 2001. [Nik Sifferlinger Collection]

HMS *Hardy* initially grounded at Vidrek by 13th April 1940 had drifted to Skjommes,
where she remained until after the mid-1950s. [Ron Cope Collection]

Wolff, at the time was not aware he had given the other three Zerstörers crews time to evacuate. But, he had also provided sufficient space to get the wounded ashore, as well as essential supplies, including guns, food and any handy equipment. So *Hero* and *Icarus* on arrival found the Zerstörers unattended which allowed search parties to board immediately the only one not to have keeled over. This was *Hans Ludemann*. The search party found little of significance, there were papers now reduced to cinders on the bridge and souvenirs, such as swastika flags, and binoculars. However, what stuck out most was the ships interior which was 'extremely smart and well fitted out', more like an ocean-going yacht than a warship on active service.

The retreating *Warspite* and a number of her destroyer screen, with the disabled *Eskimo*, were feeling relaxed now the enemy had been taken care of. There had been no Luftwaffe air strikes and no major concerns about U-boat attacks. Even the sun had come out for the first time in over a week. It was 1600 and tea time in His Majesty's Navy; boiled eggs, thick bread and something to take the place of butter. If you wanted another option you could not go wrong with 'corned dog' (naval slang for tinned corned beef) instead of eggs. In the meantime, a whaler was dispatched with medical personnel to *Eskimo*.

Back on board '*Warspite*' the day's work was almost done for the gun crews. Petty Officer 'Gunners' Mate' Daniel Reardon describes the elated atmosphere, "Sixteen rounds from each gun so far. The salvoes now aren't going so fast, because the different targets are sunk or blown up. After a while 'Check fire' is ordered and the ship seems to be stopping. 'Crews may go on top of turrets,' and up there it is a sight – burning and sinking enemy ships all around us, and our own destroyers searching into every little corner that might hide something ... 'We return to our action stations, and the turret officer and I make out our report as we steam down the fjord. Nothing special in it – just that everyone did their job from the youngest to the oldest. Thirty-two rounds fired by each gun, no salvoes missed. One of the crew in the turret cabinet had a tea-kettle on the electric radiator and every time the fire gong went he lifted it off to stop it being spilt.

"Wounded from the destroyers are next brought aboard; some are beyond help and are buried at sea that night. Now we *Warspite's* know we shall carry on as we started."

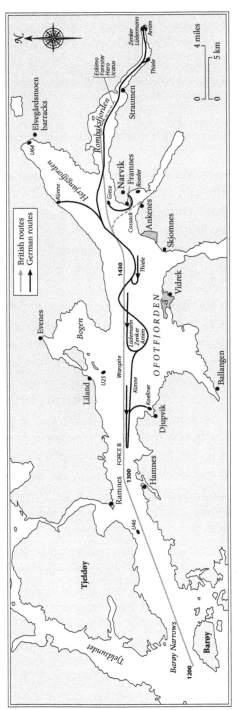

Second British Attack

MAP OF SECOND BATTLE.
[Geirr Haarr Collection]

Ben Rice's Swordfish was still out and about providing crucial on information, completing a last surveillance of Rombaksfjord he sighted the grounded *Georg Thiele*. This allowed him to dispatch the last of his bombs before rendezvousing with *Warspite*, where the aircraft was craned back on board from the still cold waters of the fjord. [79]

Back in Narvik town Mayor Broch was with a fire brigade team driven round in a classic car provided by the Iron Ore Director. By now the old car was in a bad state of repair having previously been utilised by the Red Cross. The town was deadly quiet, the gun fire had almost stopped, with the odd explosion from the direction of Rombaksfjord. Swastikas were still blowing in the wind on top of Public Service buildings, in particular the Telegraph Office. It was then that an idea came to Broch, which he hoped might assist the likely British landing by causing confusion among the remaining German forces.

Stopping outside the office, which had been taken over by the Germans to transmit telegraph and telephone connections, Broch went inside and approached the Wehrmacht Corporal in charge. He was obviously a worried man having heard the consistent gunfire and witnessed the panic that had set in on his fellow compatriots. Broch made it clear the game was up and the town was now back in Norwegian control. Adding that they expected the British to arrive at any moment. The look on the Corporal's face said it all, as he looked out of the window and saw the deserted street. On the expected defensive, he immediately blurted out in Danish, "Ach, but I am not a combatant, I am a telephone watchman." It was then pointed out to him, "But you carry a weapon." Clicking his heels, he handed over his pistol and declared himself to now be Broch's personal prisoner. The Corporal and his comrades, who did not offer their weapons went off marching up the mountain.

The story goes that they did not get far before meeting another platoon coming down. After stopping for a discussion, they all came running down back to the Telegraph Office. Broch, "We jumped in the car and drove off. They fired at us. The right window was smashed, but we escaped in the dignified old car cutting the corners so fast that the curtains flew."

---

79   Lieutenant Commander W. Bruno Brown was awarded the Distinguished Service Cross, Petty Officer 'Pilot' Ben Rice, the Distinguished Service Medal and Leading Airman Gunner Maurice Pacey was 'Mentioned in Dispatches'.

That would not be the end of the matter as Broch would be looking at the death penalty.

Commander Sherbrooke, taking a chance, decided his ship *Cossack* should remain overnight until the next tide, whilst still precariously close to where the occupying force were present. As a precaution secret material was incinerated and anything with weight not needed thrown overboard. The wounded men given immediate attention and shoring up damaged parts of the ship. It was not until later that it became known the Germans, 'racked their brains' to think of a way of getting back at *Cossack*, if not just for propaganda purposes. The enemy were still smarting from the armed forces finding and eventually *Cossack* recovering allied seamen from the re-adapted German prison ship, *Altmark*. (See below)

Commander Sherbrooke's wife recalled a very worrying time when she heard a broadcast by Lord Haw-Haw, "We said we would get the *Cossack* and we have. She is lying a blazing wreck in Narvik harbour and her Captain is dead on the bridge." Was this a separate broadcast to the one already mentioned in the footnote regarding the mistaken identity of *Eskimo* for, once more, *Cossack*? If so, it shows how desperate the German propaganda machine was to place the now world renowned destroyer as both defeated and sent to the bottom of the sea. As it happened both *Cossack* and *Eskimo* survived to fight another day.

So it was not long before the German army tried to take advantage of *Cossack's* misfortune with snipers taking pot shots and a field howitzer firing from close range. Although the First Lieutenant Peter Gretton thought it was more likely a heavy mortar attack fired deliberately from somewhere up in the mountains at 1700 hours. However, the *Cossack* crew were up to the challenge, with their 4.7-inch guns and pom poms. It then eventually became a relatively quiet evening. [80]

Once *Bedouin* had rendezvoused at Rombaksbotten with *Hero* and 'Icarus', Commander McCoy carried out Admiral Whitworth's orders, to destroy the German ships immediately. It was now almost 1700 when *Hero* launched

---

80 *Altmark* was a German oil tanker and supply vessel supporting the 'pocket-battleship' Admiral Graff Spee, in the South Atlantic. Allied surviving seamen were transferred from *Graf Spee* to *Altmark*. After the *Graf Spee* was scuttled by her crew in the River Plate action, December 1939, *Altmark* attempted to return to Germany. She was spotted by RAF aircraft in the North Sea, within Norwegian territorial waters and pursued by several Royal Navy destroyers led by *Cossack*

a torpedo, cutting short the ship life of the *Hans Ludemann*. Whilst, gun fire finished off her two other wrecked sister ships.

PART THREE

Hunter's *Survivors Fate is decided*

"That makes a perfect score"

At 1742, a satisfied Admiral Whitworth sent a signal to Admiral Forbes, Commander-in-Chief Home Fleet, to report all German ships and a U-boat had been sunk. It was now time for Whitworth to decide his next move. He had given thought to ordering a landing party to relieve Narvik, especially as the occupying residents had seemed to have gone quiet. However, the Admiral later recorded, "With the force available only a small party could be landed, and to guard against the inevitable counterattack, it would be necessary to keep the force concentrated, close to the water front, and to provide strong covering gunfire. In fact I considered it would be necessary to keep *Warspite* off Narvik." So it would be to the dismay of the Narvik community, and of course, the captured British sailors that Admiral Whitworth decided against a landing, because he had "insufficient forces available to take on possibly at least 2,000 highly trained German soldiers stationed in the town." In fact, on the 13th April there were no more than a few hundred Alpine Troops actually in Narvik, 800 had been dispersed along the fjord and in to the mountains.

What the Admiral also did not know was that many soldiers and stranded sailors had fled in fear of the shells hitting the town. At one stage there was almost a panic situation as the occupying forces took off in a disorderly straggle along the railway line or into the mountains, in an attempt to escape the expected British landing. However, the Admiral had other considerations, as intelligence reports came his way. *Foxhound* had a German officer rescued from the *Erich Giese* who confided with his captors that "the disposition of *Warspite* is not safe because of U-boats". Added to this a Luftwaffe squadron arrived in the area which finally persuaded the Admiral it would be wise not to remain too long in the fjord. [81]

---

81 Admiral Whitworth having ordered *Foxhound* to pick up any survivors from *Erich Giese*, [most of whom had swum half a mile in the ice-cold fjord]. That *Foxhound's* whaler intercepted a life raft, where two officers and nine men were rescued.

At 1830 having made his decision, not to recapture Narvik, Whitworth ordered *Foxhound, Icarus, Forester,* and *Hero* to rendezvous with *Warspite,* whilst, *Punjabi* who took on board the wounded men from *Cossack* and *Eskimo* because the ship needed further repairs, went into Skjelfjord. The *Warspite* and her flotilla on her way down the fjord was attacked by U-25 but missed. *Foxhound* had an ASDIC response, although her throwers misfired, it was enough to make the U-boat Captain to go deeper. [82]

In the afternoon watch *Ivanhoe* and *Hostile* had returned to the fjord and been ordered to join their sister ships *Kimberley* and *Bedouin* who were to assist *Eskimo* and *Cossack*. Later, *Eskimo* having transferred her wounded, despatched any redundant men and with seventy-six crew left on board, escorted by *Bedouin,* stern first began a precarious attempt to reach Skjelfjord. At 0450 it required *Bedouin* to eventually take *Eskimo* in tow, and was another twenty-four hours before they successfully reached their goal.

With regards to 'Cripples Creek', I have already introduced you to the Norwegian 'hero' Hartvig Sverdrup, was known affectionately by men of the Royal Navy has 'Snowdrop' for his leadership in repairing their ships at Skejelfjord (Cripples Creek). 'Snowdrop' wrote an obituary for St John Aldrich Micklethait in the newspaper *Lofoton Posten* in August 1977, by then a retired Admiral. *"There is not a single person who took part in this War in 1940 who does not remember how the* Eskimo *with her stern first crawled out to Skejelfjord in Lofoten; where the vessel – under constant air attacks – was patched up so much that she – still with her stern first managed to get back to Britain.*

During the repairs in Skjelfjord [...] I went on board nearly every day. I therefore got first-hand experience as to how a real British Naval Officer of the 'Hornblower' type, mastered his wrecked vessel during the air attacks. His crew adored him, and for me personally he was my first and greatest experience during the War. I shall always remember him with deep gratitude for the example he has been for us all. May he rest in peace."

Returning back to further 'Task Force' movements, prior to around midnight *Warspite* and her Destroyer Flotilla had returned to Narvik to collect more wounded to be transferred to the destroyers in turn. As the sun was rising over the mountains, the task completed, the ships, minus *Forester,*

---

82 It was not until many years later before it that the British had not adequately taken into account the possible submarine threat when sending *Warspite* into narrow waters of the fjords. In fact she had passed within striking distance of U-boats on fourteen occasions, and attacked four times without ever being aware of it.

sailed out of Ofotfjorden to Vestfjorden. There had been a total of twenty-eight sailors killed and fifty-five wounded, although the numbers of dead would increase over the following days.

BBC World Service, Saturday 13th April at 9.00 pm

British destroyers sank altogether three German destroyers in the Battle of Narvik Fjord on Wednesday morning, according to the crew of the Swedish steamer *BODEN*, which was in the Narvik Roads at the time. They have now reached Sweden, and they state that fifteen cargo boats belonging to Britain, Sweden, Norway and Germany were sunk during the battle. They described the scene in Narvik harbour as one of complete chaos. When the British destroyers made their daring attack the Germans took possession of the *BODEN*, which was sinking, and launched the boats to rescue survivors of the three sinking German destroyers. One of the German destroyers had been cut in half.

At the Town Hall, the Committee members waited patiently for any news of a landing. Maybe they thought that in order to surprise the occupying force, the British would leave it till darkness fell. In the meantime, intermittent reports came in but in the early hours the landing did not happen, although hope continued for the next day. During the night the lights went out, evidently because the power station at Rombakken had been hit. Two boys from Beidsfjord gave a witness account of the violent sea battle. They were certain four German destroyers had been driven in to the fjord, one had laid itself crosswise, blocking the whole fjord. Whilst the other three had sailed into the 'foot' and had beached, saving the crews [...] Then the British had forced the blockade [...] Finally, the last German had been beached, whereupon the Germans blew up all their ships.

The Committee straightaway began accounting for all ten German destroyers. "Two were sunk in the harbour on 10th April ... several were hit, one of them capsized at the pier. That makes three, and today's harvest was four more in Rombaksfjord." "And another sank outside Framnes," said one of the boys. "And we saw one go into Herjangen that went smack bang ashore on the rocks and blew to bits. That makes minus six today, and I myself had seen the remains of one down at the pier this afternoon." added

Broch. "That makes a perfect score!" There was an excited applause, then they broke out into the only English song they knew off by heart, 'Tipperary' – except for 'My Wild Irish Rose', which did not seem to fit the occasion.

Mayor Broch and his fellow Committee are very happy after their analysis of the German's sea battles defeat. But imminently this would change to despair. The German enquiries will continue to find the major culprit at the Telegraph Office incident.

The events over the last few days had obviously made a resounding and patriotic effect on not only the Norwegian civilians but also those serving in the armed forces. During the night of the 13th April, *Havock* received a visitor, Kaptein Brekke of the Norwegian submarine B3. *Havock* was to rendezvous with Admiral Forbes in the Lofoten Islands. It was an opportunity for Brekke to make a formal request to take part in the Allies next moves in his country's fight against the occupying force. However, he was ordered to take his submarine off Andoya, so as not to be mistaken by the allies for a German submarine. The same precautions were also laid out for the British submarines, as anything under the surface was to be considered the enemy. At least Brekke must have felt that he had been of some benefit as he was able to provide a lot of information and maps of the area.

Deviating slightly back to one of the *Hardy* survivors, Petty Officer Supply Fred Evans who had developed severe frostbite and probably because Ballangen Hospital was almost full on 13th April he was transferred to a quickly prepared emergency hospital. Obviously the medical services were expecting more patients, but Fred strangely found himself on his own.

Many years later, at 2nd Destroyer Association Reunion, Fred was unable to confirm that none of his fellow members had known about this extra hospital facility. In 1973 Fred even wrote to the Mayor of Ballangen to see if he could confirm, but to no avail. I found a copy of his letter in my father Cyril's documents. Fred's full story of his spell at the emergency hospital is in my first book. However, since including the account more has come to light about his experience of being joined in the hospital by a large number of unexpected patients. Here is a summarised version of Fred's letter to the Mayor and a final explanation which unfortunately he is not here today to hear and so be able to put his mind at rest.

Fred begins, *"I developed severe frostbite and was being treated by the doctor. As I could not walk unaided I was taken to an emergency hospital [...] None of the*

British sailors knew anything of this emergency hospital, and in order that you may be able to identify it, I have drawn a sketch of its interior separately. It was built at a fairly large hall with a stage at one end and main entrance at the opposite left end corner. The whole floor space being filled with freshly prepared beds, with not one occupant. There were only Red Cross nurses, apparently waiting to receive expected casualties. I did not know then of the second Narvik battle which was taking place about that time. [...]

"A few seconds after I got undressed and into bed I saw through the windows, a procession of wounded men in uniform [...] carrying their rifles. ["] Some were blinded, some had body injuries [...] I felt quite fit in comparison [...]. It was like watching scenes from films [...] When they began to reach the entrance to the hall at the left-hand corner of the stage [...] I suddenly realised that they were all Germans. I could not decide what to do, being undressed in bed and not aware of another exit. I could not seek advice from one of the nurses because the Germans would not enter the hall and were becoming congested around the entrance.

"I then realised that the delay was being caused by nurses trying to relieve the men of their rifles which they would not relinquish. Naturally the nurses felt that hospital patient should not be armed while the men wished to retain their ability to defend themselves against the danger of attack by the British. It appeared there could be no solution to the impasse, with the congestion outside increasing as the wounded men were still walking around past the windows.

"Suddenly, a middle-aged, largish Norwegian appeared through the doorway. I think I understood later that he would have been the 'Burgo-master'. He took immediate action by shouting in a commanding German voice to the wounded Germans. All I recognised were the words "Deutsch Reich", and finally "Heil Hitler". It seemed obvious that he had assumed the authority of a German commanding officer and ordered the men to 'ground arms', because immediately there was the rattle of rifles hitting the cemented floor, and the men commenced trooping into the hall. I happened to catch the word 'sailors' by one of the nurses and so I quite believed that they were men from one of the sunken or damaged German ships." [...]

In the meantime, the rest of the *Hardy* survivors were still anticipating either a landing or at least communications reaching one of the retiring ships to rescue them. HMS *Hardy*'s Bill Pulford describes those moments. "Well, we just all grouped up together about a hundred of us and as we watched this lot, we couldn't say a word. I had a rock in my throat as big as Gibraltar, no one mentioned anything, I am sure everyone felt the same. My eyes were really wet with tears – 'At last relief.'"

Cyril Cope, "We spent the rest of the afternoon looking out over the fjord, hoping and praying that our comrades in the little armada would find out somehow that we were ashore awaiting rescue. We were delighted to see the lines of victorious ships coming back down the fjord from Narvik. Once again we clapped and cheered [...] Our cheers turned to near tears as we sadly watched them disappear from our sight round the bend in the fjord's coastline. At that moment we gave up all hope of getting out of Norway. We were feeling very despondent as we all went back to the school, to then sit around and talk about our chances of escape."

Returning back to Fred Evans' predicament as lost soul amongst a large number of the enemy, he looked for solutions. "By this time I had managed to gain attention of one of the nurses, explaining that as I was British I didn't think that I should be there. She quite agreed with me and immediately helped me out of bed, and after helping me to dress in some fashion, I was bundled out through another door. [...]

"Dusk was falling by this time and I do not remember the direction I took, I may have been supported on foot or on some form of wheeled chair. For the first time since my arrival at Ballangen I came into contact with other of my shipmates. I think it was a school building and I was put to lie down with others slightly wounded on an upstairs floor. [...]

"Later that night, the 'Burgo-master', appeared amongst us. I recognised him mainly by his voice. He was not speaking to me, but to a group a few yards away. He was describing how he had had to pretend that he had received orders from the German 'High Command' that the men entering the hospital in Norway were to hand over their arms and ammunition. [...]

"The British Narvik veterans were guests of the Germans Narvik veterans at Kiel [1973] and I thought it would be a wonderful opportunity for me to confirm the story. But to my immense dismay, from over one hundred German veterans I could obtain not the slightest verification. Indeed 'Captain Kurt Rechel practically convinced me that the Germans that I saw with rifles were not the German Navy. [...]" [83]

---

83   Rechel was commanding officer of the Zerstörer *Bernd von Arnim*.

Fred Evans later hoped that the Ballangen Mayor, through those in the community who were there at the time, would remember the event. For those who are interested, as I have already mentioned, the full text of his letter is in my first book.

Suffice to say that Fred's assumption was correct because the wounded Germans were from the Zerstörer *Erich Koellner*. As you will remember she was on the receiving end of a battering from *Warspite's* 15-inch guns and put out of action at Djupvik. [See map] Probably most of those having made their way to the emergency hospital were Alpine Troops. Later they would be placed in the custody of Norwegian soldiers.

However, there are two crucial points here. Firstly, although Fred did not know it, if he had not made his move at that precise moment it could have meant that he was not accounted for by the *Hardy* crew and missed that night's escape with his shipmates. Secondly, the distance between the *Hardy* survivors and the emergency hospital was close. Should the Germans have known that the enemy who sunk their ship was nearby, those rifles would have come in very handy. Goodness knows what the outcome would have been then.

There was to be more excitement and twists and turns yet to come for the *Hardy* survivors as told in *Attack at Dawn*. Suffice to say some survivors were despatched to various sister destroyers. Although these destroyers after the 13th April remained in the region, at least for now they had escaped capture by the enemy on land. However, Leading Torpedoman Bill Pulford, Able Seamen Stan Robinson, Charles Cheshire and Les Smale, had been transferred to HMS *Hero*, whilst Able Seaman 'Gunner' Dougy Bourton had been sent to HMS *Havock*.

The following day, the 14th April a signal was sent from the Commander in Chief with the good news that eleven destroyers, including *Havock*, were to escort the battleships *Rodney*, *Renown* and *Valiant* to Scapa Flow. On the 15th April, Admiral Whitworth met with the C in C, it having become clear there was to be no imminent landing. Whitworth took up a supportive role with *Warspite* and was screened by *Havock*, *Hostile* and *Foxhound*. There they remained in the Narvik area until 24th April, so an early return home for some of *Hardy's* crew was not to be.

BBC World Service, Saturday 13th April 10.15 pm.

Here is the official Admiralty Communiqué for which you have been waiting: since the attack upon the German destroyers in Narvik on Wednesday by the second Destroyer Flotilla, this flotilla with reinforcements has been blockading the enemy in the Narvik Fjord.

This morning at about noon, HMS *Warspite*, accompanied by a strong force of destroyers, using mine sweeping and other appliances, advanced up the Fjord to attack the German destroyers, some of which were already injured, which were sheltering in the harbour and also to engage any shore batteries which might have been erected. According to reports which have been received from the Commander-in-Chief, Vice Admiral Whitworth hoisting his flag in the *Warspite*, commanded the attack which was extremely successful.

The enemy opposition was not found to be remarkably severe. A field howitzer which had been mounted ashore was put out of action by the fire of HMS *Cossack*. Four German destroyers were shattered and sunk in Narvik Bay. Three others fled up Rombaks Fjord, a small inlet eight or nine miles long behind Narvik town. These were also pursued, engaged and destroyed. At the moment of issuing this communiqué, the Admiralty is not precisely informed as to the conditions in Narvik Town. Parties of men, possibly German soldiers, have been escaping from it over the hills and further details are awaited.

This destruction of seven of the enemy's destroyers was not achieved without loss. Three British destroyers were damaged in the fight, but not seriously and the British loss of life is believed to have been very small. No estimate can be made at present of the German losses in personnel, but the seven destroyers must have contained over a thousand men. The Admiralty has signalled their congratulations to the Commander-in-Chief Admiral Sir Charles Forbes, to Vice Admiral Whitworth and to the officers and men engaged in this vigorous, daring and skilful attack still proceeding.

Back to *Cossack* and her difficulties – at 0315, because of her damaged engines, she was only able to transit stern first, but escorted by *Forester*, she finally made it to Skjelfjord, thirty-six hours later.

The German command was not impressed with the apparent

indecisiveness of the Royal Navy, to not immediately follow up their success with a recapture of Narvik. Even though the British had overwhelming superiority. Neither was the First Sea Lord, Winston Churchill impressed. He urged the C-in-C, Admiral Forbes to consider occupying Narvik so as to ensure a later landing would be unopposed. It is not recorded if this signal was received by Whitworth. However, he was aware that a substantial expedition of allied forces were on its way and that it should be diverted to Narvik. He signalled the C-in-C and Admiralty:

"My impression is that enemy forces in Narvik were thoroughly frightened as a result of today's action, and that the presence of *WARSPITE* was the chief cause of this. I recommend that the town be occupied without delay by the main landing force. I intend to visit Narvik again tomorrow Sunday in order to maintain the moral effect of the presence of *WARSPITE* and accept the air and submarine menace involved by this course of action."

It appears, that a number of naval historians had little doubt that had Whitworth's proposal been actioned, in the weeks to come the situation would have been different, and many more lives saved.

The following day the Admiralty requested an assessment of the strength of the occupying force at Narvik. Whitworth replied [Monday 14th]: "Information from Norwegians sources estimates 1,500 to 2,000 troops in Narvik. German Naval Officer prisoner states that there are many more than this, but I think this statement was made with intent to deceive [...] but *Cossack*, aground in Narvik Bay for twelve hours yesterday, was not seriously molested. I am convinced that Narvik can be taken by direct assault without fear of meeting serious opposition on landing. [...]" [84]

Back to Mayor Broch, who was about to walk into considerable trouble. He left his colleagues at the Town Hall and with one of the firemen walked to the Hotel Royal. On arrival, the reception area was full of soldiers, who

---

84 I have to make a special thank you to Geirr Haarr for giving his permission to use the meticulously researched parts of his book, *The German Invasion of Norway – 1940* regarding the Second Battle of Narvik. I sometimes thought that he had his own bunks in both the National Archives and Imperial War Museum! However, if any reader wishes to have a more comprehensive account of the second battle, or the Norwegian campaign then I thoroughly recommend his book." (ISBN 978 1 84832 0321)

then surrounded the two men and gun barrels were shoved into their backs. One soldier shouted, "This is the fellow who had made Wiedener give up his weapons." Finally, Corporal Wiedener confronted Broch, who replied, "Yes, I was that fellow." The fireman explained that he had been on duty at the fire station all afternoon. This was confirmed by Wiedener and the fireman was allowed to go. Broch, his identity established, was marched off by a German Army Captain, whose title was 'Chief of Espionage and Military Intelligence Officer'. The Captain was accommodated at the hotel and so it was that Broch was placed under arrest and detained in one of the top bedrooms. A sentry was stationed outside and Broch awaited his fate.

After the second battle, due to the heavy bombardment, the *Hunter* and merchant seamen in the railway waiting room were moved to a school room. Joe Settle recounts, "We were loaded onto a lorry. I was given a pair of trousers and a shirt, with a large pair of boots from a merchant seaman who was a prisoner. It was horrible in the camp [railway waiting room], not much food, no tea or coffee. One day we got a drop of schnapps and a cigarette – it was Hitler's birthday [20th April]. To pass the time we played cards or Ludo."

One of the group was Signalman Thomas Norton who later explained that someone had covertly obtained a torch. Subsequently he was the obvious choice to make use of it, should the time come to try and make contact with their comrades on other ships. In the meantime, the torch was hidden in the school's guttering. The opportunity to use it quickly came. However, on trying to retrieve the torch, it was accidentally knocked down the drain pipe.

This waiting room was probably the same place that was occupied by the other group before being transferred to the Café Iris. In addition to the thirty *Hunter* survivors there were "between fifty and sixty merchant navy men and they all slept on the floor in very cramped quarters". The food for this group was not much better than for those at the Café Iris: coffee, bread and jam for breakfast and supper; soup, bread and jam for lunch. They were allowed half an hour's exercise in the morning and evening under the watchful eyes of their guards.

The consequence of the second battle which saw all the German destroyers sunk or run aground, so that they were of no further use, was the affect that this had on the occupying forces morale. No more so as witnessed in the Café Iris, where their guards needed reassurance that they had treated their captives well. Querying if it was the same for prisoners of war in Britain, Captain Nicholas did his best to give assurances, probably to quell any possible immediate retributions. Either way it seemed to work as the guards appeared relieved and became increasingly friendlier.

However, it is recorded that the Café Iris still had cupboards topped up with grocery rations and a fully equipped kitchen, as you would expect for a place where the public came to eat and drink coffee. The Café owners' family cooked their meals first, followed by the guards. It was not easy for the prisoners who could smell all kinds of culinary delights, which never crossed their tables.

Mayor Broch's time had come, he was escorted downstairs by the sentries, given something pretending to be coffee, probably thinking that this might be his last and if so then he would not miss it. He had waited in the lobby, where he had made friends with his sentry, who showed him a photograph of his 'sweetheart' in Germany. The German military lawyer arrived, who did not appear to be officer trained, and made notes of Broch's explanation for his actions. Broch admitted the facts, but in mitigation said that he genuinely believed that the British were about to land. Unfortunately, not surprisingly to save his own skin Wiedener had embroidered his account, stating that Broch's behaviour was far more threatening than was actually the case. Once both aspects of the mitigating and aggravating evidence had been concluded, a report was sent to General Dietl for his decision on sentencing.

The Germans had set up an English language propaganda radio programme on different frequencies, which could reach far and wide, including America. These regular transmissions went on throughout the remaining five years of the war and the presenter had a precise and immaculate English gentleman's accent. He called himself Lord Haw. Namely, William Joyce, aged thirty-four, who was born in Brooklyn, America, from Irish and Anglican parents. Shortly after his birth the family returned to Ireland. He later became involved in the British Fascist Party.

'Germany Calling, Germany Calling, Germany Calling'.

This is an announcement, the operation to occupy the Denmark and Norway coast has proceeded as according to plan. On marching onto and landing on Danish territory, no incidents occurred anywhere. No significant resistance was offered along the coast of Norway, except Oslo. Resistance there was broken during the afternoon and Oslo itself was occupied. The German Minister for Norway, received representations from the Norwegian Press today and informed them of a new upheaval, which is best for the Norwegian Government.

"Recalling this morning's upheaval, I wish once more to draw the attention of the Norwegian Government to the facts:

That any resistance to Germany's actions, will be completely senseless and would only lead to an aggravation of Norway's position. I repeat that I have measures that Germany, does not intend to infringe the integrity or political independence, of the Kingdom of Norway, either now or in the future".

William Joyce was eventually convicted of treason and hanged in Wandsworth Prison, London in 1946.

I would add that in Britain, it was not considered an offence to tune into and listen to these programmes but was not advised. As you will read, the drip feeding of partial announcements to the *Hunter* and merchant seamen survivors had an adverse effect. They were left feeling uncertain about the campaign's progress, especially as a defeat meant them spending a long time in a German prisoner of war camp.

The Hotel Royal's smoking room had a fireplace, it was an ideal place to sit and learn the latest information, as occupying officers walked through to the dining-room. This was where Broch sat whilst waiting for a verdict. A number of groups of officers passed by in conversation, Broch learnt that the battleship was *Warspite*. That the destroyer beached at Ankenes was probably *Cossack*, which had now re-floated at dawn. Broch had also been given the general impression that the level of morale had been raised, during the night as the situation had gone quiet. However, he realised the Germans were very angry about those *schwein* the British who had been firing at German sailors whilst scrambling ashore. This appeared to Broch as hypocritical, "They, of course, would have waited until the enemy had finished taking their position."

The prosecutor nervously reappeared. He was to the point, informing Broch that General Deitl had found him guilty of 'violating Section 36 of the German Military Law having to do with sabotage of communications'. As Broch came from a lawyer's background, the prosecutor smiled grimly.

"I take it you understand?" Broch nodded. The prosecutor left Broch sitting in his chair. Only then did he realise it was serious, although surreal, as it was in the well-known setting of the hotel. So was this to be his last day? "If I could be spared seeing anybody I could stand it. I must not think of those who would left behind. Now there was not much that I could do for them anyhow."

Kriegsmarines take over from Alpine Troops

The aftermath of the defeated Kriegsmarine, away from the Narvik harbour was soon to show itself.

Officers, NCOs and sailors from the sunken Zerstörers looking like a defeated force, made for shore in whatever uniforms or overalls they had been wearing in the battle, soaked in seawater and some blackened with oil and looking very exhausted. However, it was not long before they became efficiently organised. They seemed to manage to find suitable attire and were formed into platoons for various tasks. It became apparent that once they were sorted out it allowed the Austrian *Gebirgsjäger* – (Alpine troops) to move out of Narvik to do the job they were trained for in the mountains.

Note this is the same jetty shown previously when the Alpine Troops arrived. Probably when they were eventually required to leave either to the mountains. [Theo Werner Schettler via Frank Hackney Collection]

There were in fact 2,600 German sailors who suddenly found themselves on land, initially with nowhere to go. However, they were a welcomed sight for General Dietl. His forces were more than doubled. Dietl later wrote, "The carrying out of the task of holding Narvik was, I can say, only possible with the employment of such a strong naval force ashore."

Caption: General Dietl with one of the Kriegsmarine sailors who were utilised for duties ashore. [Cyril Cope Collection]

In the meantime, there were lots of funeral parties to be arranged, and care for their wounded comrades. But eventually the sailors were placed under the command of Fregattenkapitan Berger, who had been Senior Officer for the First Destroyer Flotilla on board *Georg Thiele*. Amongst their tasks, they were used to secure the railway to Sweden, with the naval engineers maintaining the railway tracks and rolling stock. Korvettenkapitan Kothe and the crew members of *Hermann Kunne* together with Korvettenkapitan Erdmenger commanding officer of *Wilhelm Heidkamp*, were attached to the Austrian Geirgsjager Regiment.

The remainder of the sailors were detailed for guard and security tasks in Narvik. It is recorded that some of these equipped with army uniforms and suitable armament, adapted so well to life on land that they later took part in the fighting.

Captain Nicholas Diary

Sun 14 Apl 40 8.30 am. German bombers flew over town and out towards fjord before flying away. No supplies seen to fall from it. These supplies are eagerly watched for by the crews of the ships interned. As the food question is serious. We get very little to eat and I have complained often of the conditions and quality of food. 109 men living and sleeping in the one room, but the Germans say it's the best they can do, as they have no food themselves, also the Norwegian people are rationed. We have had several loaves of bread, packets of biscuits and cigarettes thrown up to the window by the Norwegians people. The German guards are furious about it.

A lieutenant [crewman on Erich Giese*] came into the room and told me we would get into trouble if we opened the window and got food from the Norwegians. He said someone would think we were hungry and were starving on what they gave us. He said, "Remember you are prisoners of war." He said, "The English had machine gunned the Germans in the water." I said, "I did not believe him." He said, "Remember you are a prisoner of war."*

Anyway the food supply has improved a bit. Heard Pom Pom fire this evening.

The lack of food was also affecting the civilians, as previously mentioned many had already left the town. It became apparent to General Dietl that because the remaining inhabitants had come to the conclusion there was not going to be an immediate return of Allied forces, there would be a continued presence of the Germans. If more were to leave, it would disrupt the German plans to avoid an imminent British army land force arriving.

Hence, Dietl ordered his subordinates to immediately halt the potential exodus, which in his mind would be of benefit to them. The Germans at that time had little if any artillery, whereas the British with their heavy naval guns could raise the town to rubble. By keeping the 5,000 or so Norwegian civilians in the area, the British might think twice of such a bombardment. In fact, as history shows the commander in charge of the landing force, General Mackesy, having left Britain on the 12th April, had already indicated this was not a course of action he would want to take. However, it is also worth mentioning that many military experts subscribed to the view that if the landing force had left one day earlier, there would have been a strong possibility of Narvik being recaptured.

Subsequently, the Norwegian authorities were ordered to halt the evacuation.

BBC World Service', Sunday 14th April 9.00 am.

Yesterday's was the second raid on Narvik made by the Second destroyer flotilla. Listeners will remember that earlier in the week five British destroyers of the flotilla were led up the narrow fjord by their commander Captain Warburton-Lee to engage superior German forces which were supported by shore batteries. The exploit was one of the bravest in naval history. Two of our destroyers were lost, but the British force left the fjord with three German destroyers on fire and one torpedoed and believed sunk.

The second attack on Narvik by a larger Royal Naval force and the increased destruction inflicted on the Germans, although it gave the *Hunter* survivors euphoric feelings, must have left them apprehensive about possible retribution. They were now prisoners with insufficient clothing and food and obviously extremely concerned about whether their captors would overreact. These concerns were reinforced by further incidents.

However, whilst appreciating how the survivors must have been feeling, it was all too real for Mayor Broch, as he waited for his fate to be finalised. In the late morning the prosecutor returned, explaining that he had conferred again with the General and his officers. Because of a plea by the Town

Council, who had sent an appeal on the basis that the Mayor spoke German and was considered indispensable to the civil administration, it had been proposed that Herr Broch be pardoned. The General gave his consent, but insisted that Herr Broch must give his word of honour to report to Captain Muller every day at 12 noon and at 6 pm. To which the relieved Mayor duly promised.

Three hours after the previous BBC radio announcement, probably to uplift the nations' morale, the Admiralty felt another update on the situation in Narvik was necessary.

BBC World Service, Sunday 14th April at Midnight

The British Navy's entry into Narvik Fjord yesterday, and the sinking of the seven German destroyers, was front-page news in all the Paris newspapers today. French gratification has been expressed in many ways, notably by M. Reynaud, the French Prime Minister, who has sent a telegram to Mr Chamberlain saying "The French nation shares Britain's feelings of admiration and gratitude for the Royal Navy, which has added a page of glory to its records, and has inflicted on the enemy a wound that will never heal".

It is estimated this morning by an official of the French War Office that as a result of the action, at least a third and probably half of the German Navy is at the bottom of the sea. He pointed out that the victory would have an enormous lead to interesting military developments. For Germany it was a bitter blow.

An Admiralty casualty list issued tonight shows that Captain Warburton-Lee, commander of HMS *HARDY* lost his life during the gallant action at Narvik Fjord last Wednesday. Another officer and fourteen ratings of the destroyer were also killed and three officers seriously wounded. Two ratings, listed as missing, are believed to have been drowned, and six are seriously injured. Captain Warburton-Lee, who, had spent most of his thirty-two years' service in destroyers, led his flotilla into Narvik against overwhelming odds. Knowing that superior enemy forces were in the Fjord, he sent a radio message to the Admiralty, asking: "Shall I go in?" As Mr Churchill has since told the House of Commons, the Admiralty replied that he must be the sole judge. Back came the message: "Going into action!"

Marshal Soult goes on to describe the feelings of fear as the guards are changed from Alpine troops to Naval. "As soon as they took over the Petty Officer in charge went into the room where the *Hunter* survivors were and asked which prisoners are Royal Navy. On being told, he said that he and the rest of the guards were the sole survivors of one of the destroyers sunk in the battle. The hearts of the *Hunter* men sank when they heard this, fearing reprisals, but they need not have feared; he only wanted to shake the hand of every survivor, which he did, much to the relief of the men." However, as you will read, not all the Kriegsmarine personnel were as friendly.

The men's incarceration did not only develop into uncertainty and boredom, there were humorous moments, as they had a saviour in the shape of a young Norwegian girl. She would pass by the open window every day and never failed to throw a packet of cigarettes or a loaf of bread up to the men looking out of the window. One man, Marshal Soult, had the job of catching whatever was thrown. He never missed. Marshal, "The men looked forward to her daily visit. She was dressed in ski pants, boots, jacket and pork pie hat, and was a typical Norwegian, a blonde, lovely looking girl. At one time the German guards told the men that she had been told not to continue the practice of throwing the food to the prisoners but to give it to them to hand over. She ignored the order and carried on as usual."

At the Town Hall the staff were happy to have a relatively quiet spell to allow them to bring records up to date. All major incidents and decisions taken were catalogued with witness statements. It was good news to hear that the "dominating and obnoxious" Kommandant, Major Hauzel was going to follow his predecessors by moving from Narvik, up the railway line. However, before moving he sent his last order by his Orderly, known as 'Sauerkraut'. Hauzel wanted a pair of "first class soft bedroom slippers with stiff toe-caps and low heels". The staff politely explained they did not store slippers in the Town Hall. Off went Sauerkrat having been given a cigarette and told it was impossible to purchase slippers on the Sabbath.

It was not long before a Oberleutnant with a guard of soldiers arrived. "Herr Ortskommandant wishes, first, to inform you that the ordered articles must be delivered; secondly, that he must have them before 1 pm." The guard clicked all its heels. That was all! The staff just looked at each other, not knowing whether to laugh or cry. They had taken the banks, the schools, and the church. And now the slippers on Sunday!

One of the staff had an uncle with a shoe shop. He remembered that for advertising purposes, there was a huge pair of slippers in the shop window. They were finally delivered by the janitor's seven-year-old daughter. It was great fun for her to drag them all the way to the Kommandant's residence. It was not long before the Oberleutnant came back, stating that the slippers did not fit, they were too big. The Kommanant wanted to exchange them for a pair many sizes smaller, he could not work out why such a pair had been sent. The tongue in cheek answer was that they were very sorry, but they did not know what size he wore. Perhaps the Oberlneutant's feet could exchange them since he had more knowledge of the Kommanant. Off went the Oberleutnant with the giant slippers under his arm.

Captain Nicholas.

Mon 15 Apl 40. Heard gunfire during the night. Had breakfast – two slices of bread and cups of coffee, first breakfast supplied by Germans. Coffee made from burnt wheat. About 1 pm 'Air Raid' warning given and British bi-planes seen, a few bursts of machine gunfire from the ground but nothing much. 4.30 PM British destroyers came into harbour and fired 3 rounds at machine gun nests and went out again, later heard distant gunfire.

One of the casualties of the sea attack resulted in the '*Jan Wellem*' being hit by a 4.7-inch shell. This required a speedy task of getting her supplies ashore. As Giles Romilly wittily suggests, "Loaded with food as well as oil, the whaling ship had been an important part of the invasion plan, and we just felt pleased with the Germans for their thoroughness."

The Narvik community were still waiting for any further news about the British movements. "Every morning we said to ourselves, today something will happen, but as the days passed we became more patient. Nothing this week. All right. But next week we shall be free again."

Many of the locals were getting used to the fighting, their resilience and bravery was an indication of how quickly those under immense threat can adapt. Fru Martha Hagen sums up the situation adequately, "The sound of gun-fire and the whistle of shells and splinters and projectiles, or whatever they call all these murderous weapons, has now become our daily music. Finally, we got so accustomed to it that we didn't bother to take shelter in the cellar except when it really got bad. We put our beds in corners on the ground floor and took refuge under them. The house shook so dreadfully that it seemed a miracle that it could hold together.

"The farms out at Framnessasen, Vassvik and Taraldvik had the worst of it. Apart from some of Frydenlund and Oscarsburg many farm houses were set on fire by shells and others damaged in one way or another. Several families gathered together wherever it seemed safe. As far as we were concerned we had good reason to stay where we were.

"Sometimes we got news from Finland, Sweden or Tromso on Magne's radio. One day as I was listening to the news from Oslo on my own set, and holding my breath so as not to miss anything, I heard, among other things, that Narvik had been shelled by British on Friday afternoon [12th April] and that if the German commandant had not ensured the safety of the civilian population... Actually, I never heard what would have happened in that case because I switched the radio off. It was just too much for me. The truth was, as I had already heard from Tromso, that the British Navy had told people to clear out of Vassvik and the surrounding area as they intended to shell it. It was up to them, of course, to make up their minds where to go to. But that evening the German commandant announced, over the Radio Narvik, 'No one is allowed to move!' and so on and so on, just a lot of fine words which meant nothing."

On the 15th April it became clear that a landing in Narvik was not imminent and Admiral Whitworth had a meeting with the Commander in Chief Admiral Forbes. We will never know if the Royal Navy had decided to land, and it had been a success, would it have changed the outcome of the Norwegian campaign. The Kriegsmarine could ill afford to have lost so many ships at all, but to lose them within three days was a terrible blow. Similarly, it appears that many risks were taken in carrying out the 'Operation Weserubung' including the Zerstörers being placed in an impossible situation of having 'no easy way out' should it go wrong.

In addition to that, if Fregattenkapitan Bey, having taken over command, on the 10th April, had been bolder in his decision making, a number of his Zerstörers could have escaped back to Germany. On the night of the 11th and 12th the weather had closed in, so there had been another opportunity. It has been questioned as to why he did not even consider the escape route through the Tjeldsundet (see map) rather than taking the direct route to open sea. In which case, there would have been a stronger possibility that the Zerstörers would have avoided being confronted by the enemy. Once into open sea, the speed and firepower of the Zerstörers would have had an advantage over most Royal Naval vessels.

Tues 16 Apl 40.
A plane appeared over the harbour this afternoon and dropped a couple of bombs. Don't know if anything was hit, can see the smoke of British Pom Pom fire and concluded plane was German.

There were many offers of help in the community, a seamstress offered to make British flags. They could be useful if there was a celebration in the town in the near future. It was fortunate that they did not know the truth, that it would be a very long time before they could be unfurled out of the windows.

Narvik Town reduced to rubble. [Cyril Cope Collection]

Wed 17 Apl 40
The guard was changed and sailors from the sunken destroyers relieved the soldiers. They were in the charge of the Lieutenant who told me to remember I was a prisoner.

At the Hospital the staff were doing a sterling job with the predominantly German wounded. The Head Surgeon was often required to be at the operating table for the whole day. His expertise was held in high esteem by the Germans, showing up their own apparently inferior doctors. It was noticeable that the dying soldiers did not make confessions or reveal military secrets, but they did become more human as they neared the threshold of death themselves.

In the hospital, also noticeable, was a pretty young blonde nurse with her hair braided around her head, a real fairy-tale princess. She spoke reasonable German and so was able to communicate with her patients. She received many proposals, but only gave them some hope, by saying she would think it over, once she knew they were soon to die. Apparently one young officer became seriously infatuated, he would talk to her about philosophy and quoted the romantic poet with radical political views, Christian Heinrich Heine. Possibly this one for Grete and his cold surroundings:

A single fir-tree, lonely,
A northern mountain height,
Sleeps in a white blanket,
Draped in snow and ice.
His dreams are of a palm-tree,
Who, far in eastern lands,
Weeps, all alone and silent,
Among the burning sands.

He told Grete he had been a medical student and within two years he would be able to practise in a small Bavarian village where his parents owned a farm. But he would never come round to admit that Germany could ever commit a wrong. He talked of the 'New Order', beautiful well-formed children. Blond men and women with strong wills would dominate the world. "But what of the rest of the world?" asked Grete, "Besides I have a sister who is a brunette," she quickly added. "Even the others will become happy, since they were born to obey. Yes, all will be truly happy in this life, the only life there is. So happy." replied the young officer, and died.

The survivors from *Hunter* were unaware at the time of the extent of the damage done by the attacking British ships.

Marshal explains the two opposing views of the guards. Here the first continued to be affable. "On many occasions during the days of imprisonment in the café the same Petty Officer would enter the room looking for men to do some work. He would point and say, 'You, you and you but not you, you're Navy.' He treated the men from *Hunter* with courtesy and respect, and did what he could to make their captivity as easy to bear as he possibly could, under the circumstances.

"But one day a young German Naval Officer who was in charge of the guards went into the Café Iris to have a look round. The men from *Hunter* asked if they could have some clothes. They had received none since leaving the enemy destroyer and only had blankets to cover themselves. He replied: You machine-gunned my men in the water' repeating it over and over again, there was no hope of getting any clothes from him. However, some of the men did manage to get items of clothes one way or another.

"One chap helped himself to a pair of grey flannel trousers, a shirt, a sleeveless pullover, and a pair of socks from a parcel delivered to the café from a laundry. Up to that time he had had only a blanket to cover himself, and a pair of boots, two sizes too small for him. When he took the boots off, his feet swelled to twice the normal size. He later exchanged the boots for a pair of canvas shoes which one of his mates had; these had been two sizes too large for his mate. So it was a very advantageous exchange to both the men, up to a point that is, because later on those canvas shoes were not much good for walking many miles in deep snow".

It appears that the survivors were being given information by their guards that Germany was winning the campaign in the occupation of Norway, including Narvik. It may be that the guards were only telling them what they themselves were told by their High Command. However, as you have read, Korvettenkapitan Karl Smidt, *Erich Giese* would certainly not have had that opinion.

Deviating slightly – you will remember Wynne Jones' father missing the ship departure because of his commitment to playing rugby for the Navy.

There was another occasion where a crew member was reported a casualty. The *Western Morning News* dated 17th of April 1940 took up this extraordinary story, with the headline:

WENT TO SYMPATHIZE

"When a welfare visitor called on Mrs O'Brien, of St Levan Road, Devonport, to console her for the loss of her husband, A.B. John O'Brien, in the destroyer HMS *Hunter*, which was sunk in Narvik Fjord last week. A.B. O'Brien himself appeared from the bathroom with a lather-covered face and vigorously denied that he was dead.

A.B. O'Brien was a member of the destroyer's crew for three and half years, but three hours before HMS *Hunter* left port for Norway, he was sent to a specialist, who ordered him to hospital for a week.

He is a footballer, and has been Captain of the Mediterranean Fleet team. Sometime ago he received a kick just above his eye and has since suffered from severe headaches. He is at present home on leave."

Giles Romilly's future became more uncertain as he was told to pack and then led away to the Hotel Royal. He was met by the 'forage' capped lieutenant who enquired about Romilly's health. "Fairly well, thank you," he replied. With a mischievous look the Lieutenant asked, "What will your uncle say, Mr Romilly, when he hears what has happened to you?" Romilly probably thinking he had finally been rumbled, "I don't think it will affect his polices." Lieutenant, "You have an uncle who is a high personality in English politics, haven't you?" "Yes, Mr Churchill." replied Romilly. "Oh, is it so?" Said the Lieutenant looking vague as he smoked his cigarette, pushing his head forward "like a baby bird reaching for food". He stood up clicked his heels and was gone.

Romilly was kept in the hotel lounge under guard until sunset. Left pondering his future, he even had optimistic thoughts that having been told to bring his suitcase he would be freed. Whilst waiting he was able to read a German daily news bulletin which mentioned the Norwegians were fighting in many places and 'the enemy' had landed troops on the island of Hinnoy, thirty-five miles northwest of Narvik. Then the 'forage cap' appeared again, "All right, Mr Romilly. You can go home tonight to sleep." So he returned to the Café Iris, to a "derisive cheer". His optimism for release now gone, at least he was able to give fellow prisoners the good news about the fighting and landings.

Captain Nicholas Diary.

Thurs 18 Apl 40
A quiet day on the whole. Everyone wishing that some sort of action will take place. Plenty of grumbling about the quality of food. Most of the soldiers appear to be leaving town, as we saw lorries of them.

By now serious consideration had been given to dealing with the bodies of both Norwegians and Germans who had lost their lives in action. Mass graves were dug, but not until the frozen ground had to be blown up with dynamite. Today, the 18th of April, the burials took place, with a Norwegian priest giving the sermon. General Dietl and a German senior naval officer gave speeches. Although it was felt the ceremony was used for propaganda purposes, and those from the occupying force attending, by now knew the feelings of the town people towards them.

Fri 19 Apl 40
Heard from Romilly who had got hold of a small handbill printed in German that British soldiers had landed at Tranoy Island and were making a base at Harstad. German seaplane flew over Narvik and landed in harbour..
Noon. The supply plane flew over town and dropped several boxes, but not by parachute. These burst open on hitting the ground.
About 8.45 pm. A bi-plane flew over and was fired at with machine guns. She dropped some bombs about a mile away.

On 19th April, the Kommandant and Mayor Broch visited the Café Iris. After the second battle various Kommandants moved on "farther up the railway line" away from Narvik. At this time, the new Kommandant thrown into the front line, was none other than the commanding officer of *Anton Schmitt* which was put out of action in the first battle. Here Broch describes their visit, "This time the Kommandant was no more than a Captain, Korvettenkapitan Bohme. But even so the change was far better. He was more a sailor than a politician, and, also, he was one rank lower than his predecessor, a fact which we construed as a happy omen. The Germans evidently did not wish to be defeated under such a fine creature as a Major.

"Kapitan Bohme gave us permission to visit the English prisoners. Their chief complaints were about the 'ersatz' coffee and the 'news' that the

Germans were giving them. As for coffee, I knew about that, but what kind of news was being circulated? That the Norwegians resented English intervention and that nowhere in Norway was there any fighting going on."

On his visits, Mayor Broch outlined the true picture of the situation. He had been able to talk with Giles Romilly, who he felt had been in "excellent humour but had looked considerably thin [...]". However, the Mayor had not been able to see him again, as Romilly had been unable to restrain himself and rejected with contempt at the news reports brought to him by the sentry later that evening. The next day the Mayor was accused of talking politics with the prisoners, and further visits were denied to him.

Moving forward thirty years, Welshman Dougy Bourton DSM, a nineteen-year-old Able Seaman 'Gunner', at a joint reunion of veterans in Bremerhaven forged a remarkable friendship. Here Dougy tells the story: "The Captain of the *Anton Schmitt* Fritz Bohme [now full Captain rank, Retired] told me himself, that it was the first time he had taken his clothes off for the best part of a week. He had turned in when he heard this mighty roar, when the torpedo hit them. He then ran up the companion way and the sea came in to meet him and washed him down again through the opening in the deck leading to the staircase to the cabins. He got away with it. Fritz Bohme was a very nice man and a fine sailor and good company. He and his wife Tilly became good friends of ours".

The 19th of April was an important day for two of the 2nd Destroyer Flotilla, when *Hostile* escorted her sister ship the badly damaged *Hotspur* back home for repairs at Chatham Dockyard. It appears that when the ship was 'taken in hand' by the dockyard, some of the crew after their survivor's leave were temporarily drafted for service on vessels required for the Dunkirk evacuations. One of these was the already mentioned modest man, Stoker Ted Orford from East London. His nephew, Terry Orford explains, "My uncle went on to spend most of his time serving on *Hotspur*, he was later involved in the 'Battle of Cape Matapan' and the Crete Evacuations. I have a certificate awarded to him for his time at Dunkirk.

"I learnt that during the war *Hotspur* was adopted by the people of Tottenham. Uncle Ted married Lou after the war, who sadly died in her 40s, so he spent most of his time bringing up their two teenage daughters. He became a delivery driver and lived in a two up two down in Leyton with outside toilet and a tin bath. I looked out for Ted, I wrote to the local council, his MP and his doctor in an effort to get him rehoused. I mentioned that he was a 'war hero' (Narvik, Matapan, etc.). Eventually they rehoused him in a flat in Walthamstow. I visited him in hospital the night he died, it was very sad. I was very disappointed that Ted gave all his war medals to one of his work colleagues before he died in 1984, aged 67."

Captain Nicholas.

Sat 20 Apl 40.
The bread sent in today consisted of 3 cases of mouldy bread. I complained very hard about it and they took one case away and send us a number of loaves of brown bread. The reason I complain is because I am in charge of the camp and the food is not enough for the number of men. Heard the sound of guns and saw one or more destroyers in the north fjord.

This evening the Red Cross people (3) paid us a visit. A doctor to see to our health, and some books and chocolate etc. Also, a bit of news of the outside world. Heard that the Germans had gone across the north fjord and been fired on by destroyers.

Sun 21 Apl 40.
The German Commander came to the conclusion, which we knew for some time, that we were overcrowded and three small bedrooms are given over to Capts, Officer Eng and P.O. [Looks like] Which gives us a bit more room all round. The Red Cross has promised us beds and blankets. So that will be a change from sleeping on the floor. I have managed a wipe down a few mornings about 3.00 am. But only a few of us have done that. Heard also that a number of men from other British ship, are interned in the school. Complained about other two cases of bread and pointed out that it was not fit to eat. Also if they have no bread to give, why not give us flour and let us make our own bread. Flour is to be given us, so we shall be alright for bread.

Mon 22 Apl 40.
10.30 am. Heavy bombardment by our ships, some shells passing overhead until after noon. During afternoon Germans blowing up quayside and places along waterfront.

Marshal Soult, "On many occasions a little light relief was afforded to the prisoners in the form of attacks by 'Swordfish' aircraft from the Fleet Air

Arm on the railway and docks. Many bombs were dropped and as worthwhile hits were registered on suitable targets, the prisoners gave a loud cheer. These planes came in very low to make their attacking run and they must have borne charmed lives; because all the time they were at the café watching the attacks, the prisoners never saw one plane shot down. It is quite possible that the 'Swordfish' were from the aircraft carrier *Furious* whose planes had taken part in the Second Battle of Narvik; two planes were lost in that battle.

"One day the '*Hunter*' prisoners were being interrogated by a German Army Officer [Forage-capped Lieutenant] who was asking how many aircraft carriers Britain had. One man said, 'We can't have any now, Lord Haw has claimed that they have all been sunk.' The interrogation came to an abrupt end with the arrival of a Fleet Air Arm plane on a bombing raid. The interrogation didn't continue."

The merchant seamen and Giles Romilly were spending their fourteenth night in custody, would it be Romilly's last in Norway? There was the usual snoring and probably a few men talking in their sleep when a guard shook Romilly and told him to dress and pack. He went outside where the harbour-captain, who Romilly remembered making jokes in Hotel Royal lounge two weeks before, was shuffling around to keep warm. He pointed to a car with a guard in the back and told him to get in, whilst he sat at the front. The car sped off wheels slightly screeching in snow. Having negotiated the harbour road, they came to a narrow lane "running parallel with, and fifty feet above an inland finger of the fjord. The end of this road, as I knew, was a tiny village beyond which were nothing but mountains".

The car having reached its destination found there was a wooden landing-stage. Sentries dressed in white uniforms could be seen amongst the surrounding trees. A motor boat had arrived whilst a "large grey sea-plane" had also just arrived. In the meantime, during the boat cruise the harbour-captain struck up a conversation by asking him what department of the government he worked for. Romilly said, "For none. I'm a journalist." "Journalist! Ha. Ha! We know very well what that means." […] "You're a spy aren't you?" […] "You will have to tell that to other people. You will find it more difficult then […]

As it happens Romilly was going nowhere, at least not yet, as the aircraft had engine problems. On the boat's return, Romilly observed the "wide scene of momentous, terrifying desolation. Twenty-nine ships, warships and merchant-men, lay with many drowned sailors, under those cold blue waters." With loss of sleep, Romilly was returned to the Café Iris.

Captain Nicholas Diary.

Tues 23 Apl 40.
Heard heavy explosions at 2.30 am, which shook the building. The Germans had blown up the Ore Quay. No 3 berth has been quite demolished.

At 3.00 am. The guard came and took Romilly away, they said he was to go to Germany by air, as he is Churchill's nephew. He came back at 8.00 am and said they could not start the plane. At 10.00 am. The Commander came and told us that we would have to march to Sweden. 60 men would leave at 1.00 pm and 60 would leave at 2.00 pm. At 1.00 pm the crews of Riverton and Romanby set out. Also Romilly was taken back to the plane which I believe got off alright. The men from HMS Hunter *were removed to the school, they are not to go with us. We managed a meal of sorts before 2.00 pm. At 2.00pm my crew joined up with the crew of the 'Mersington Court', also most of the crew who had been missing since we left the Blythmoor. My crew now numbers 28, 14 still missing, left them.*

Captain David Nicholas' diary pauses but continues at end of the march to Sweden.

Captain Nicholas was on his way to Sweden, hence would not have known, the final outcome of Giles Romilly's fate. Here Romilly recounts the moment that he left his newly found comrades from different backgrounds and thereby life experiences, from whom he sincerely felt he had learnt so much. "A short, fat officer came in beaming, and proclaimed: 'All de men from de steamah will today go free. We do not want civil prisoners in Narvik. You must be ready to leave in two parties, one at 12.30 de other 1.30. You will be escorted along de Erzbahn to de Swedish frontier. A nice walk maybe two days. If one try to leave de party he will be shoot. First give away all your knives to de guards.' There was a wild shout of pleasure and joy.

"Still beaming, the German called my name. 'You must stay.' I said good-byes, shook hands with everybody. Then I was taken out."

Ceremonial Sword found

I was pleased to receive from Jose Johnson the granddaughter of Thomas 'Daddy' Norton, his diary written from the time he and his colleagues were incarcerated till two and half months later. Some of the contents slightly contradict others accounts, but this diary is important because it was recorded as the events progressed.

The Norton Diary.

Thurs 11th April. Names taken for sending home. Learned that we had sunk 2 destroyers and damaged one, also 11 merchant ships.

Fri 12th   *Transferred to railway hut on jetty and joined company of Merchant seamen captured from British ships in harbour. Air raid followed, hits were made and a good barrage was put up.*

Sat 13th   *Transferred to school in town heavy fighting at sea. Big sea battle, British ships entered Narvik. Hopes raised. [Sunk] all German ships (13) and 2 subs. Very poor food and rations given, hungry, not much sleep, room crowded (63) sleep on the floor, 1 blanket each. Our ships have left harbour.*

Tues 16th   *Same conditions ½ hour walk in fresh air, taken.*

Wed 17th   *½ hour morning / evening walk, conditions same. Hopes still high*

Fri 19th   *German planes drop food and ammunition by parachute, learnt that British troops had landed 27 miles away, food running short. Our planes over, land batteries open fire, barrage not as effective kept locked in all day. Germans easily frightened. Commandant*

> *and Narvik Mayor came to see us, learnt our names not forwarded handed them in again.*

Sat 20th   *Extra bread, usual walk allowed. Hitler's Birthday, allowed ½ glass of beer to each man.*

Sun 21st   *No bread in the camp. Things quiet for time. Later gunfire heard. Possible attack on Batteries. Wondering if things are OK at home.*

Mon 22nd   *More bread arrives, fires started in harbour, more RAF attacks. Germans blowing up pier and ships.*

This is the first mention of a visit by the German Commandant and the Narvik Mayor, Theodor Broch to the *Hunter* survivors. It appears the original list of survivors taken by the Germans had gone amiss, probably not surprising due to the chaos in Narvik town before and after the second attack by the Royal Navy. I have a copy of this list, although obviously not written by a person fluent in English. It provided confirmation of the names of those survivors held in captivity at Narvik.

Another observation is that none of those captured would have been celebrating Hitler's birthday but the beer would have been welcomed. The *Hunter* survivors probably had thoughts in their minds of wanting to substitute it for a tot of rum, 'Nelson's blood', with the toast, "God Save the King".

In Joe Settle's account, he mentioned he had managed to escape during a Royal Navy Fleet Air Arm bombing. "Tom King, a friend from Gainsborough and I set off to walk to Sweden, which was a thirty-mile walk, by following the electric wires over the mountains. It was a walk in deep snow which sometimes came up to our chests, I was only wearing a shirt, trousers and oversized boots which kept filling up with snow. It was bitterly cold and we kept having to rub snow onto our ears to prevent them from getting frost bite. We had no food or water so we had to put snow in our mouths for a drink. We came across several empty farmhouses where we could take shelter."

One of the Mayor Broch's special messengers reported that the British prisoners had been ordered to prepare to leave. They were under heavy guard, and it appeared that they were to be marched into the mountains. As they marched past, the Mayor was able to wave to the Captain of the SS *Romanby* and he waved back.

A few days later Norwegian prisoners were also taken away from Narvik along the same railway line on which they had been brought down.

Mayor Broch, "One of the British destroyers accompanied this last prisoners' march by steaming in close to the shores of southern Rombaksfjord. Shells rained in from the fjord and the prisoners had to run for cover. Two Norwegian officers grasped the opportunity, jumped down the slope and ran at high speed towards the shore, where they were picked up by a boat lowered from the destroyer. We learned, too, that Major Omdahl had also escaped during a snowstorm in the mountains and had reached the Norwegian forces in the North. That evening I and his friends 'skaled' for Major Omdahl with German beer.

"The city had prohibition, but since it was only beer and stolen from German stores, they let the law sleep for one evening. Meanwhile all the best whiskey was sent to the hospital as the Germans raised their requisitions, at an inverse proportion to the number of troops stationed in the town. At first, they had asked for only the best brandy; but, later on, as nothing but younger officers stayed in town, the stars on the bottles also decreased in number."

Referring to Major Omdahl, having put together a detachment of locally stationed soldiers he had managed to get them out of Narvik on the 9th April. Unfortunately they had a crushing defeat earlier and the German Alpine troops had continued to pursue them into the mountains. This eventually resulted in a fierce battle at Norddalsenden, and the Norwegian mountain fighters being driven towards Bjornefjell. On the 16th April, the enemy took them by surprise, many were killed or taken prisoner but the majority were then driven across the Swedish border. However, small parties of them had regrouped and were by now wandering about in the mountains hoping to meet up with other Norwegian detachments or escape into Sweden.

The situation in Norway was obviously not going the way the Germans wanted, so another appeal had to be made by the German Commander-in-Chief, 'von Falkenhorst'.

"Announcement"

I have been given the task of protecting the land of Norway against attacks from the Western powers. The Norwegian government has refused several offers of co-operation. The Norwegian people must now themselves decide over the destiny of their country. If the announcement is complied with, such as it was with great understanding by the Danish people in the same situation, Norway will be spared from the horrors of war.

If resistance should be offered, and the hand offered in peaceful intention should be refused, I shall be forced to proceed with the sharpest and most ruthless means to break the resistance.

Anyone who supports the issued mobilization order of the fled former government or spreads false rumours will be court-martialled.

Every civilian caught with weapon in hand will be SHOT.

Anyone destroying constructions serving the traffic and military intelligence municipal devices will be SHOT.

Anyone using weapons contrary to international law (dum-dum) will be SHOT.

The German army, victorious in many battles, the greatest and powerful air force and navy will see to that my announcement will be carried through.

The German Commander-in-Chief

Von FALKENHORST

Infantry General

Copy supplied by 'Norland Rode Kors Krigsminnemuseum Narvik.'

As the Royal Navy salvoes from the fjord increased in intensity, it seemed to have a detrimental effect on the occupying force where the Germans troops became more inebriated by the day. Once again the 'Ortskommandant' [Commandant] rank descended this time to Oberleutnant (Lieutenant). This was a twenty-nine-year-old engineer trained Oberleutnant Poetsch. Although appearing as a pompous soldier at least he had a sense of humour and all around it was agreed, "Him we were going to keep."

Marshal Soult's account of the move out of the Café Iris. "On Tuesday 23rd of April, at 1300 hours all the merchant navy prisoners from the café and those from the schoolroom were collected together by the guards and informed that they were going to be marched to the Norwegian–Swedish border; and that the *Hunter* prisoners and Mr Romilly would leave later. The men realised that the Germans were preparing to get rid of them because they were becoming a burden on them. No doubt two factors were responsible for this. First, the food situation was becoming desperate for the enemy as well as the prisoners; secondly at this time the Germans knew that an allied assault on Norway and Narvik in particular, was imminent. They did not have the food to feed the prisoners, and they could not afford to waste men for guard duties if the attack by the Allies should materialise.

"So they decided to send the prisoners to Sweden to be interned. On hearing that they were to move out later, the *Hunter* men searched the kitchen of the café for grub. They found two large tins of jam and two loaves of bread. These they put in a sack and later that day when they were transferred to the school the sack went with them. At the school they were reunited with the thirty members of the *Hunter* ship's company who had survived. In two rooms below the one occupied by the men from *Hunter*, some Norwegian troops were billeted. They too were told to prepare for a long march."

When the Germans were retreating, there were bands of beaten Germans continually drifting through the town and up Fragernes Mountains. One of the locals describes the moment, "Laboriously they trampled a path for themselves, zigzagging their way up the steep slope. Their dark rows stood out against the snow like curving snakes. An old woman came down the hill with her mattress on a sled. She owned a little cabin up on the ridge, but now it was packed with Germans." She had pointed skywards when asked by the Germans which was the route to Sweden.

Moving away for a while from the *Hunter*'s survivors and Giles Romilly's dramatic situation; coincidently, at the time I was writing these chapters I was visited by a very interesting gentleman for whom I had been searching for over six years. I will come to him shortly. At some time since the first battle a German officer had come across an abandoned Royal Naval officer's ceremonial sword.

It has been reported by sources that after the first battle, the Zerstörer *Hermann Kunne* was sent to examine *Hardy* where she had finally settled at Skomnes in the afternoon. It was said "boarding her was no problem, but the fore part was still on fire and could not be approached; her No 1 boiler room and stern were burnt out and she seemed to be hard aground forward. She was certainly no use to the Germans; though in her Captain's coat pocket were some interesting documents: the orders for the operation, several signals with coded and clear versions, a short gunnery manual and orders for formation steaming. Other trophies included some Long Service and Good Conduct Medals awaiting presentation when a pause in operations should allow." The question is, was the officer's ceremonial sword found at the same time?

Alternatively, that the finder was a German Naval /Army officer who had been detailed off to make a more thorough search on the grounded *Hardy* for any signs of other secret material left behind by mistake or details of newly installed equipment. Especially the degaussing gear, or the ASDIC system. I would add that I discussed the disposing of the secret material when the order came on *Hardy* for abandoning ship in my first book.

But now back to the intriguing story of the ceremonial sword. As previously pointed out most of the able survivors on the German ships had re-grouped back in Narvik, coming under the command of the German Army General Deitl. The Officer took his newly found 'Battle Trophy' back to his temporary billet, possibly hoping future improvements in his countries dire situation would allow him to take it back to the 'homeland'. However, as the German command began to retreat away from Narvik to the mountains, so it was that the Officer had to leave the sword behind.

Subsequently, the sword was found by a Mr and Mrs Roman when they were able to return to their home, after being evacuated. They in turn gave it to their son Karl, as a memento, Karl had been a Norwegian Army Lieutenant during the war.

Twenty-five years later, Karl Roman, recognising it as a 'Wilkinson' ceremonial sword, for refurbishing purposes took it to the company's representative in Norway. Wilkinson's in Britain had kept records for nearly 100 years and the swords had been given a serial number. From that it was confirmed that the sword was a prize presented to 'The best Sub-Lieutenant for the year 1931–32, presented to E.K.U. Clark'.

At the age of twenty-nine, Lieutenant 'Gunnery' Edward Keats Urling Clark was killed when a salvo hit HMS *Hardy*'s bridge. He left a widow, Lorna and their five-week-old baby son. Whilst the company now had a name they did not know the whereabouts of the family. That is until the story appeared in the *Daily Telegraph* and was noticed by Commander Colville, none other than the Queen's Press Secretary. Amazingly, the Clark's knew the Colville's who lived near each other. This led to the arranging of a special presentation ceremony at the Wilkinson Sword, Pall Mall showrooms.

The *Shepherds Bush Gazette* in June 1965 featured the story, "Remarkable Story of 'Clark' sword".

Karl Roman commented, "I am extremely pleased to be in England for this occasion […] I promised when I found it that I would one day return it if I ever could. In those days it was an offence in Norway to even have a knife!" Then he presented the sword once again splendid and shining to Mrs

Lorna Winchester, who was Lieutenant Clark's wife by her first marriage. "I am absolutely thrilled to have it back in the family," she said. "I have often wondered what became of it. Thanks to the generous nature of Wilkinson's it is now with us again." And Wilkinson's generosity went even further. To compensate Mr Roman for parting with the sword [...] he was presented with an exact replica.

Moving on fifty years to 2015, during a 'book signing' event for my first book at Whitchurch (incidentally the town nearest to where Captain Warburton-Lee was born), the son of Urling Clark unexpectedly came to meet up with me. Christopher, now seventy-five years of age, a retired civil engineer, lives in the village of Malpas, Cheshire. Christopher points out, "The only means of identification on the sword was the heavily stamped number, with characteristic modesty my father had not had it engraved with his name or description of the prize." There was an additional surprise from the Sword Presentation event, as explained in the newspaper feature. An unexpected announcement came from Mr Roman [...] "On behalf of the Norwegian Air Force I would like to take this opportunity of inviting you as our guest to Norway to see your father's grave." Adding later, "Truth is stranger than fiction."

Mr Roman was as true as his word. Returning to Christopher, "I was flown to Oslo six weeks later, then onwards as a guest of Scandinavian Airlines [...] Mr Roman met me in Tromsø, which is just inside the Arctic Circle, seven hundred miles North of Oslo." Christopher stayed four days and was welcomed as a special guest, being shown around various sights. I leave the last words to Christopher when he was taken to see his father's grave. "We drove to Narvik. Ballangen village where my father and his comrades are buried was about twenty miles south [...] The rusted remains of *Hardy*, still visible above the water, can be seen near the shore of the fjord, only thirty yards or so from the water's edge.

"We reached Ballangen at about nine o'clock that evening. My personal feelings on that occasion must remain private but I would mention I felt very grateful that after so many years the graves were still well cared for."

Thanks to the German Naval Officer, whose finding of the sword enabled it eventually to be returned to the young Gunnery Officer's family. [85]

---

[85] At Dartmouth Urling Clark immediately impressed the training staff. He was top of his term in examinations and was rewarded by becoming 'Chief Cadet Captain' and then awarded the 'King's Dirk'. He was described as "having a brilliant brain and a zest for athletics and a priceless gift of leadership qualities".

It was not just the naval sword that was found on *Hardy*. As you see a Norwegian fisherman had found *Hardy*'s lifebuoy and steel insignia.

The insignia seen here on the starboard side on the main deck below the No4 Gun [Aft]. [Cyril Cope Collection] or see it on 'In board' Ship's Drawings.

Returning back to Giles Romilly, who naturally is extremely worried about his future. The Germans, who probably from their covert sources in Britain would have discovered that Romilly was related to Winston Churchill, felt that he would be an important catch. There was another opportunity to fly out Romilly but once more the seaplane failed to take off. Thus the harbour-captain made arrangements for Romilly to stay at the chalet which accommodated the German sentries seen wandering around the trees near the landing stage. Finally, as dawn broke he was off in "a drenching roar" to the first port of call, Trondjheim, which was a stage post for German seaplanes. Off again, this time Oslo and the "olive-green coasts and pastel fields" of Denmark. "As the sun was setting, the seaplane spiralled, and I saw far below a welter of blue, dancing lights, guide-lights. Travemunde in Germany."

From now on Giles Romilly would be categorised as a 'Promintente' prisoner of war, in fact the first, followed by others including, Viscount Lascelles, cousin to the then Princess Elizabeth and the son of Earl Haig, the British World War One commander. They would be incarcerated in 'Oflag IV-C, or what is now better known as 'Colditz Castle'.

Intriguingly although Romilly never mentioned it in his memoirs which were written some ten years later, in Geirr Haarr's book it is mentioned that there was more to this flight than has been fully told. The fact that so many of the Kriegsmarine ships had been destroyed, which at these early stages of the war they could not afford to lose, meant that there were 'Questions asked in the Reich Chancellery'. Subsequently, "Hitler wanted to hear first-hand what had happened in Narvik and sent a special courier (Fuhrerkurier) to interview (General) Dietl and other key officers in Narvik.

"He (the courier) arrived in a Dornier Do 24 flying boat on the 22nd April. When he left on the 24th, Erich Bey and Leutnant zur See, Gerd Alberts, Bey's adjutant, were on board the *Donier*. Also on board were two British prisoners captured in Narvik. One of them was Giles Romilly [...]." It appears, perhaps the second 'British' prisoner was Lieutenant (E) Alick Reid.

Upon returning to Germany, Bey was confirmed as Kommodore destroyers and C-in-C of the 6th Destroyer Flotilla [...]. The Nazi's propaganda machine, once more got into action because there was no outcome allowed to be acknowledged as a defeat. They made the best of turning the historical event into leading the German public to believe that their sailors had fought bravely, which they had, but against a superior force. Nothing was mentioned about the risks initially taken by the high command or the later sea battle mistakes made by an apparent incompetent leader. If Bey had been held accountable for the losses this could have also had a significant effect on the morale within the Kriegsmarine, at the early stages of the war.

Either way, Bey must have impressed the Führer, because he was promoted again this time to Admiral and became commander for the North Norway Naval Squadron. He perished on board Scharnhorst at Nordkapp on Boxing Day 1943. Subsequent to his death he was described, "An impressive man and an excellent officer, whose main interest was technical; he had the bad luck to be given the wrong employment, and perhaps that came about partly as a result of a slightly unbalanced tradition."

All the surviving Kapitans went onto command other Zerstörers or even flotillas, Smidt and Wolff, deservingly rose to the rank of Admiral. A special medal of 'great glory' was struck for all the Kriegsmarine crew members on the ten Zerstörers. This was in contrast to the Royal Navy's lower deck sailors whose attendance in battle was not acknowledged by a special award. But that is another story. All the future replacement Zerstörers were honoured by being named as the Type 36A, 'Narvik' class.

However, we should not take away the fighting spirit and bravery of the Kreigsmarine during those epic days in April 1940. In 1972, Captain Peter Dickens. RN. Rtd, for the purpose of research for his book, was in contact with Fleet Admiral Max-Eckart. Wolff. Rtd. Here is a copy of Dickens' correspondence:

'Narvik Files': "May I say that the picture that reveals itself in my mind is that you, in *GEORG THIELE*, were the outstanding German Leader in these battles. Through sheer courage and determination to attack, you, with only two ships, sized a momentary advantage of surprise and overwhelmed a greatly superior force; and actually destroyed both *HARDY* and *HUNTER*, yourself. In the second battle, after fighting hard for Narvik harbour, you were the last to retire into Rombaksfjord, and then came your gallant stand. […]"

However, it was not all plain sailing for the High Command in the Royal Navy. The knives were out for those who made the decision about sending the *Warspite* into the confined waters of the fjords. The First

Lord of the Admiralty, Winston Churchill, faced his critics in the House of Commons; "The craven and inept authorities at the Admiralty (laughter) took the risk and were very much relieved to find that there were no special traps of one kind or another in the fjords [...] What would have been said if she had been sunk? 'Who was the madman who sent one of our most valuable ships into congested waters where she could easily fall a prey?' If you dare and fail it is murder of your sailors. If you are prudent you are craven, cowardly, inept and timid."

Once the sea battles appeared to be over, at least for the time being, the population of Narvik were able to venture out from their homes. Those making it out for the first time would have seen an unbelievable sight of debris everywhere and flotsam in an oily harbour. The fragments of sunken cargo ships pointing out above the water, masts, bows and funnels. Houses that were familiar to local people, gone and turned into rubble or more likely burnt to the ground. The church had suffered damage from a 4.7-inch shell, fired by a Royal Navy destroyer, but miraculously did not catch fire.

The only German vessel still accessible was the *Jan Wellem*, on grounding, her sea cocks had been opened but the ship remained undamaged. Once the Royal Navy had left the immediate vicinity she was re-floated. There still remained a significant amount of crucial stores left on board which could be put to good use later by the occupying force. The costs in casualties were high, 200 civilians killed, 570 Norwegian soldiers and 435 sailors, most during April 1940. Those wounded numbered almost a thousand, some of them were seriously wounded with life changing disabilities. In the First Battle, the Royal Navy losses were 147, the Kriegsmarine 176, whilst in the Second Battle, the Royal Navy 41, Kriegsmarine 140. Not to be forgotten there were also 110 Fleet Air Arm crewmen lost at sea or over Norway and Denmark between 7th and 13th April.

It could be that the German Army may have had a substantial number of men killed and wounded on board ships which were not reported at the time by the Nazis. In the 1970s, the 2nd Destroyer Flotilla Association members attended a joint reunion in Kiel. It was a well-organised weekend event and a welcoming occasion by the hosts. Here *Hardy*'s Bill Pulford explains, "It was not until I went to Kiel, that we understood that a torpedo hit what was considered to have been a merchant ship but in fact it was a 'troop transport' with 3,000 German 'Alpine Troops', all of whom went down with the ship." Of course, to my knowledge this has never been officially confirmed.

Returning to 23rd of April and those *Hardy* survivors still in the war theatre on *Havock, Hero, Hostile* and probably those on the other destroyers too, whose dreams of home leave and a hero's welcome back, were diminishing rapidly. Their ships supported Admiral of the Fleet, Lord Cork, with *Warspite* and *Effingham, Aurora, Enterprise* and *Zulu* to shell Narvik. In the meantime, British troops on *Vindictive* were unable to land. The force was screened against U-boats in Vestfjord and Ofotfjord, including *Havock, Hero, Hostile* and the Polish destroyers *Grom* and *Blyskawica*. All this time the *Hardy* men did not realise that on occasions they were transiting over their sunken sister ship *Hunter*. Nor, at this stage, were they aware how many of their comrades had perished with her.

At a signing session for my first book I got into a discussion with a Polish gentleman now living in the UK. He mentioned there were two Polish destroyers the *Grom* and *Blyskawica*, involved in the Battles of Narvik. He seemed frustrated that this fact had never been brought to light in past publications. I promised him I would make sure it was included in my next book.

In September 1939, the Polish Navy became attached to the Royal Navy under the British Admiralty command. They were assigned six destroyers, three submarines, two cruisers and six motor torpedo boats, under a lease scheme. Fortunately, just before Britain declared war on Germany, the Polish mercantile fleet were ordered to remain outside the Baltic Sea and therefore only 9% were lost.

Both *Grom* and *Blyskawica's* involvement in the Norwegian campaign at Narvik was to engage coastal batteries. Sadly *Grom* was sunk in Romaksfjord on 4th May 1940. *Blyskawica* went on to have an illustrious war record. First, providing cover for troop withdrawal from the beaches of Dunkirk, Then British landings at Ouistreham. She was attached to the 10th Destroyer Flotilla as leader. On the night of 9th June 1944 whilst the flotilla was off Ushant, a large German fleet was sighted, which was attempting to disrupt the supply lines to the Normandy beaches. After a decisive battle, in which the Polish Navy made a significant contribution, the allies crippled the last attempts by the German Navy to put to sea again

Over 400 Polish men gave their lives for the defence of Britain and Europe. ['polandinexile.com 2008'.]

You would think they had had enough excitement amid the trauma of war, but even when *Hero* eventually made its journey back home, the nightmares returned. Les Smale describes the event: "Here we were, still out in the North Sea, somewhere. Just twenty minutes after this announcement, the *Hero* turned about and once more made a heading for the Narvik area; where we arrived on Sunday 21st April, in the afternoon. I can't express how we felt but anyone who reads this may well imagine. Hardly had we dropped anchor then along came three German planes and dropped bombs. Fifteen minutes later, back they came to drop more and shortly after, this was followed by yet another attack. No damage was suffered in any of the raids.

"That is until another fearful event occurred, a reminder of two weeks before on *Hardy*. That same night, we, the *Hardy* survivors, were transferred to the troopship *Franconia*, [a 'Cunard' liner] who also re-embarked 600 troops, whom it seemed she had transported to Norway earlier. We sailed again for home at 0800 on Tuesday the 23rd April. We had one escort for a little way and then were left to proceed on our own.

"All went well until 0200 on Friday morning when we were all awakened by a terrific explosion. I was out and had my lifebelt on in no time, and then there was another explosion. I just stood there in the cabin, and well, I was quite surprised when the ship didn't heel over or feel as though she may be sinking. We made our way up toward the upper decks but were stopped by the Master-at-Arms. He had worked it out that we had been met by an escort during the night and they had been dropping depth charges. The explanation sounded feasible, so we made our way back down to our bunks and sleep again. The next morning, the Captain passed a message to us all saying that during the night we had been attacked by torpedoes from a submarine; and that they had exploded either in the ship's wake or at the end of the run."

Charles Cheshire was also in *Hero*: "Eventually, we went back into Norway, where there were a few 'Liners' berthed. I went on one called *Franconia*. There were a number of captured German sailors (prisoners of war) on board. The Captain said, all sailors, it didn't matter if they were German or not, had cabins and the troops; were down in the hold somewhere. I know they didn't go much on it. We set off for Greenock; I suppose we must have been about 24 hours out, early in the morning, when there were two or three loud explosions. Of course there was panic amongst these soldiers; we didn't know what it was. It turned out to be torpedoes which exploded prior to hitting the ship, they had magnetic heads on, so either they didn't go off or were some way away."

Bill Pulford, also on *Hero* recalls, "On our last day out we came into harbour, where the *Franconia* was berthed. On board were all the soldiers who had been evacuated from Norway, which it had been decided was 'too big a project'. We had thirty there, plus some of the wounded from other ships who had survived the Second Battle of Narvik and were being sent home.

"I and one other Leading Hand, being in good health, apart from a shrapnel wound to my leg, were put in charge of the German naval prisoners. There were quite a number of them. The 'codes' (protocol) was that Navy looked after Navy and so forth. I don't know whether it was a matter of revenge, because they were all in uniform and I was dressed in 'God knows what'; Norwegian ski cap, old jacket which was far too big, trousers that looked like 'plus fours' down to my shins and an oversized pair of ski boots.

"Anyhow, they were nice chaps and of course 'Jack', me included, never finished ribbing their backs about Narvik. Where they had ten destroyers and we only had five. They didn't take the ribbing very well, still thinking they had won at Narvik, but we managed to convince them that they hadn't. But not one of them admitted to being a 'Nazi', they were all German 'Kriegmarines'! Even after that, throughout the war I never met a self-confessed 'Nazi'.

"When we got to Greenock, they were the first taken off, they shook hands with us and we gave them a couple of cigarettes each. After all was said and done, they were Navy as we were. We parted in the best of spirits. It was only later on in the war that we met the 'Gestapo' and the 'bully boys' of the German people. You have to bear in mind that at the beginning of the war we didn't have any 'Hostilities Only' men on board and they didn't have the 'SS Gestapo'. We were all seamen and treated each other as such. It was just the unfortunate part of it that made us fight each other."

Dougy Bourton now started to feel it was time to go home. "The next morning, we were split up amongst the fleet. I was unlucky! Some went on board the *Forester,* which was almost out of ammunition and fuel, just enough to get home. But I was sent to the *Havock,* which was part of the old flotilla. I wasn't unhappy about that, it was commanded by Commander

Courage, tremendous man, a fine fighter and quite a character. We did a seven-day patrol with the fleet, whilst others went home. This we weren't pleased about.

"The *Havock* was very low on provisions, although we had food, we only had what they could manage. Don't forget by now we had been at sea for several weeks. Eventually, our patrol was finished and we were taken to Harstad and put on the *Franconia*.

"They took us into the dining room, now don't forget we were literally starving. We must have looked a right bunch, because we were dressed in all sorts. We went straight into the saloon, in amongst all of the troops there. The tables were prepared for six with the knives and forks set out. The 'dish of the night' was 'Cod à la Española', it was unforgettable, consisting of steamed cod, slices of tomatoes and onions. I'm sure that in *Franconia*, which was one of the Cunard Cruise Liners, it was the first time the dish had ever been eaten without waiting, with fingers stuffed in sailors' mouths. We just attacked it, well not polite at all, but we were hungry so that's my excuse."

It was not until three weeks after the First Battle of Narvik that *Havock* returned home to Rosyth in Scotland. The heroic achievements, beyond the call of duty, of the ships company, at the time was not accorded the same welcome home as that of the others in the 2nd Destroyer Flotilla. I hope that my books will now help rectify this exclusion.

To rub salt into the wound, the crew were given just 'two watch' leave of seventy-two hours each. Subsequently, *Havock* moved up the Forth Estuary to Leith for repairs, and shortly afterwards was ready for further action at sea.

Whilst I am on the subject of *Havock*, I have already mentioned Albert Goody who was a Stoker on board. Albert, from Brentwood in Essex, like so many sailors I have written about, came from a humble background. On leaving school he became a locomotive fireman on the Liverpool Street railway route. At the age of twenty, he tired of this type of work and enlisted in the Navy in 1938.

Albert, having completed his basic and engineering branch training at Chatham, joined his first ship *Havock* in September 1938. He would not for one moment have imagined where his first experience at sea would lead him. Albert's son David Goody explains, "*Havock* spent little time in harbour unless under repair. She ran and ran [...] Wherever, she went invariably she met danger and suffered considerable damage, and casualties some of these inflicted whilst taking her toll on the enemy. Her crew were equal to any. When she was wrecked in April 1942, the national newspapers reported the loss with the words; '*HAVOCK*! One of the Navy's most famous destroyers, a ship which survived bombs, torpedoes and full scale battles, has been wrecked.' (This was off the coast of Tunisia). In two and half years, *Havock* was awarded a staggering total of eleven battle honours

In 2003 Albert Goodey at the age of 85 was given the honour, amongst many dignitaries from Norway, Britain, France and Poland, to unveil a monument in Ofotfjord, at Skjomnes, for those who fought in the 'Battle of Narvik'. Albert died in 2006 a proud man, and made his family proud as well.

Approximately, two weeks after Giles Romilly had flown to Germany his father, Bertram passed away. Giles' mother, known in the family as Nellie, was not only grieving for her husband but now she had received word that Giles her youngest son was now a Prisoner of War in Germany. It was not reported at the time that Nellie had contacted her sister Clementine asking if she could come at her time of distress. Clementine had tried to be with her husband Winston, at all times throughout those early years of the war, but with his blessing, it was agreed Clementine should go.

This is the end of Giles Romilly's very informative and sometimes witty account that he witnessed at the time he was in Narvik. For those wishing to learn more about how Giles managed to survive the war I recommend his 1954 book, listed in the 'Bibliography' section. Here is a summarised version of his personal background. He was born in 1916, the son of Colonel Bertram Romilly and Margaret [nee Hozier]. He was educated at Wellington College in Berkshire and Oxford University, and then became a correspondent for the *Daily Express*. Becoming the first to be known as a 'Promintente' prisoner, he eventually arrived at 'Oflag IV-C, or what is now better known as 'Colditz Castle'. I shall come back to this episode later.

The new Ortskommandant, Lieutenant Poetsch, twenty-nine years old, although an engineer by profession, was also a trained soldier, having had continuous military training since boyhood. But he was not without humour, nor gave the impression of being overly the master of his domain. Although, once the subject of the righteousness of the German cause was broached, he tended to get on his 'high horse' to justify his fatherland's advance throughout Europe. However, he also appeared to be a fair-minded man, allowing passes to appropriate persons to venture into 'out of bounds' areas and took little action when he discovered activities taking place of which he did not approve. When a Royal Naval shell blew up the Kommandant's office, he would still arrive daily at the Town Hall to issue military passes.

Poetsch, was always correct and with a smile, even one of the typists commented, she thought he was "quite a nice person", adding he had to act under orders. Until a colleague pointed out, "Don't forget that even a tiger has white teeth and isn't the less dangerous for that." "Well, I don't mean that he shouldn't be shot even though he is a nice man," she replied. One morning Poetsch sent for Mayor Bloch and the Chief of Police to come to his office. "Gentlemen, I have been ordered to inform you that during the night, shots were fired in the streets at German soldiers. The perpetrators escaped. They were Norwegian civilians." "But you took all weapons from us on the day of the invasion," they answered. "What does that matter. The case is closed."

Initially the two men thought that the Lieutenant was joking at their expense. That is until the Kommandant got up from his chair, with an unfeeling smile, "I think the gentlemen do not quite understand the situation," he said, "the case is not open for discussion. I have orders from headquarters to submit a list of hostages who will vouch with their lives for the peace and order of the town. You may name five citizens. I must have their names immediately. Otherwise we must select them ourselves."

Not an easy task but the Mayor and Police Chief put forward their own names and thinking between themselves came up with three more, the City Engineer, the Head Surgeon at the hospital and the Norwegian Manager of the Swedish Iron Ore Company. They left to go, but the Kommandant had not finished, he wanted their names announced on posters in various parts of the town. Poetsch's mannerisms reminded the two men of Major Hauzel, "Weren't we through with that devil yet?" It was agreed, that the City Hall should arrange the public announcements to be posted in prominent places in the town. However, the Kommandant found the phrasing of the announcements not forceful enough and he wrote replacements. Since the Head Surgeon was held in such high regard by the Germans because of his 'marvellous medical feats' with their wounded soldiers, his name was later deleted from the list of five hostages.

Here Theodor Broch describes the emotional end of his and his young family's ten-year stay in Narvik. "I remembered that it was almost ten years to the day since we – Ellen and I – had come up here to build a life together. The time had passed rapidly, although much had happened in these years."

It is now June 1940. "The mountains had closed behind us. After a night of strenuous climbing we had reached the plains between the snow-capped peaks and the last of winter ice slowly melting in the shadows behind them. The Laplander boy who was guiding me through the mountains to Sweden said we could take a breath now. There was no longer any danger of being overtaken.

"We had come from ravaged and looted land. We had seen our country invaded and occupied by hordes of men in green uniforms. The last front in northern Norway where the Germans had suffered their first defeat of the war had been given up. Narvik had been evacuated by the British and our other Allied friends. They were on their way to France to try to stop the deluge before the gates of Paris. We had left behind burning cities and a confused people.

"Three days before from Harstad, a little town on Norway's largest island, our little family of three, the youngest lady three years old, had sailed into the fjords in a small craft manned by an old fisherman and his young son. I was being sought by the Germans throughout northern Norway. The sheriffs of the district and the German patrols had been ordered to return me to Narvik. I was said to be a British spy.

"As Mayor of occupied Narvik, I had negotiated with the Germans. We had not always agreed too well. I sent information to the British warships, and their heavy guns had silenced the Germans positions. Norwegian and Allied troops had recaptured the city and had held it for a week, but had been forced to give it up. Now the Germans were in control of all of Norway.

"In a little cabin, deep in a fjord farm near the Swedish border I had been forced to leave my wife and daughter with friends, and had to go on alone with a Lap guide into the mountains towards Sweden. Now we stood beside a cairn on a mountain crag. The cairn marked the Swedish border. We threw down our knapsacks and took a brief rest. Before going

I looked for a long time on what I could yet see of Norway. The ocean was no longer visible. Mountains stretched on all sides, with snow and green moss scattered between. Mountain streams shone like silver ribbons. The lakes were open, but ice bordered the shores. The wild heather had already coloured its small hard flowers, and but for them the dominating tone was grey.

"It was harsh land we had, but never had it been so delightful, so desirable as now. Our leading men had already been driven abroad. Our ships had been sunk or had sailed away. All along the border were young men like myself. Thousands more would follow. We had to leave to learn the one craft we had neglected. We had built good homes in the mountains, but we had neglected to fence them properly. Now strangers had taken over our land. They would loot and pluck it clean before we returned. But the country itself they could not spoil. The sea and the fjord and the mountains would wait for us."

My gratitude goes to Siri Broch who was Theodor's three-year-old daughter mentioned above, for giving her permission to include parts of Theodor's book.

Peter Broch was born in 1904 and he became a lawyer by profession as well as a politician for the Norwegian Labour Party. He enrolled as a student in 1922. He participated in the Left Communist Youth League's military strike action of 1924. However, his involvement resulted in him receiving three probation orders. He graduated with honours in 1928, and initially worked as an attorney in Oslo. From 1930 to 1940 and 1945 to 1950 he worked as an attorney in Narvik.

As you have read, Broch made his escape from Narvik and was exiled to the United States and United Kingdom but still participated in World War Two. For his extraordinary service, he was awarded the Norwegian Defence Medal – 1940–1945, the Légion d'Honneur in 1946 and the Order of the British Empire in 1975. It was whilst in the United States that Broch was elected to the Norwegian Parliament in 1945. He was then appointed chief administrative officer in Tønsberg, staying in that position until 1973. He then became the lawyer for so-called 'alien workers' in Oslo.

Peter Theodor Broch an honest man dedicated to assisting others less fortunate, was in the right place if not the wrong time being at Narvik in 1940. Without his negotiating skills and leadership abilities there may have been more lives lost. He died in April 1998.

Two families of *Hunter* crew men who made contact with me were from both sides of the Irish border. As mentioned, Stoker William 'Billy' Bradfield from County Cork, Ireland; and Chief Petty Officer John Brendan Mulhall from the fishing village of Ardglass, County Down, Northern Ireland. Both lost their lives on *Hunter*. Similar to many of the crewmen on that day, it is uncertain whether the bodies of Billy or John were ever recovered. If found, then as previously outlined, their graves like many others would be marked 'Sailor – Known Only To God'.

I return back to Billy's niece, Jill List, to explain further. "We don't believe Billy had a girlfriend in the village, as most of the girls were Catholic and he had been brought up in the Church of Ireland. In those days the two could not mix. We believe he had met a girl on his travels and she was wealthy. She had offered to buy him out of the Navy but he had signed up to do a job and he stuck to that! He was home on leave just weeks before he lost his life, when his father told him he didn't have to go back. But he said he was "No coward" and returned. My Dad, Thomas (then aged eleven) clearly remembers the afternoon the teacher heard over the radio that the ship had been hit. The teacher sent him and his brother straight home. My Dad also remembers a letter arriving some days after. I attach a later letter received which my Dad also remembers, confirming Billy had died. Billy's father, my Grandfather, could never accept the loss of his wife and son. He died aged seventy-nine. Billy's name was added to the family grave".

The death of Billy Bradfield was recorded as 'Missing Presumed Killed', six weeks before his twenty-first birthday.

With regards to the family memories of Chief Petty Officer John Mulhall, there were some similarities to that of Billy Bradfield, although from opposite sides of the religious divide.

John's nephew (who was named after him), Brendan Sheridan tells me, "My Uncle wanted to join the navy, he was an altar boy and served mass every day in the village church. The local priest and schoolmaster, who was a 'Republican', tried to stop him. But my Uncle was given support by a Protestant neighbour, who was an ex-Royal Navy man". Brendan, similar to Gavin Holt, is planning in the near future to go to Norway to see for himself the site of the battle.

Anne Cruistan, Brendan's sister adds, "John rose up the ranks and just before he set sail on the HMS *Hunter*, on what was to be his final voyage, word arrived in Ardglass that he had been made up to Chief Petty Officer.

Unlike other stories in your book I am not in a position to contribute to accounts on board the HMS *Hunter* prior to the 10th April 1940 or after the Battle of Narvik. Unfortunately, my Uncle, John Brendan Mulhall, was one of the souls to have met his death in the cold waters of the Arctic. However, my mother, Elizabeth Sheridan, his sister, now aged ninety-six, is delighted that his story is to be included.

"The next word that the family received was on the 10th of April 1940, to say that the HMS *Hunter* went down in the Ofotfjord, outside the Arctic port of Narvik during a battle between the British and the Nazis. Unfortunately, his remains were never found but he lives on in the hearts of his family and my writing this piece in his memory has given my mother closure. Rest in Peace".

Sadly, another casualty, whose body was later retrieved was that of Surgeon Lieutenant Horace Garner Evans, who had shown remarkable courage and been a credit to his profession. Here is part of Horace's obituary in a newspaper at his home town of Llangollen, on the 19th of July 1940.

Llangollen Doctor's Courage and Devotion to Duty
DRESSED WOUND AS SHIP SANK

"On the outbreak of war Dr Evans volunteered for service in the Navy, and was gazetted to HM destroyer *Hotspur* in January of this year with the rank of Surgeon-Lieutenant. Later he was transferred to the *Hunter*. A Petty Officer in HMS *Hunter* has written to his widow, stating that he had a wound in the head at Narvik, and that Dr Evans was dressing the wound, but could not finish as the ship was sinking fast. He and Dr Evans were the last to leave the ship and were in the water for three hours, holding on to a float.

"Dr Evans was unwounded, but collapsed and died from exhaustion and the bitter cold. Only ten minutes later, help arrived and the Petty Officer was rescued. Dr Evans had continued to do his duty to the very last, with no thought for his own safety."

John Lawton, working voluntarily at the provincial museum explained, "I believe that Horace was suffering from an abdominal wound at the time of battle, yet he still carried on treating as well as he could. These wounds combined with the cold of the water finished him off."

As you have read, the Petty Officer was Engineer Artificer John Farnell, whom after being repatriated back to Britain, was then able to write his letter to Horace's wife Christine.

Returning to the letters found in my father's documents, the first one dated 17th of January 1948, was from Christine, the wife of Horace. The copies of the two following letters provide the story behind Christine's successful attempt to find out more about her husband's death and also those who assisted him before his final passing away. Almost eight years after the battle, Christine writes to thank one of the Norwegian men as follows.

> *Step Cottage*
> *Whitchampton*
> *Nr Wimbourne*
> *Dorset*
> *Jan 17th 1948*

Dear Mr Kongsbakk,
> *[...] I heard from the British Admiralty that the body of my late husband Surg. Lt. H. Garner-Evans was buried in Ballangen Civil Cemetery. [...] I wish to tender my heartfelt thanks to you and your son for the way you attended to my husband's body, and accorded him the burial he would have wished for. [...] I hope to visit my husband's grave and shall make a point of coming to see you both and thank you personally.*
> *Yours sincerely*
> *Christine Garner- Evans*

Reply: Vidrek 19th February 1948

Dear Mrs Evans.

I thank you very much for your letter [...] Your husband was severely injured. I and my son and my neighbour Bjorgvin Overvag carried him many hundred yards from the sea and got him into a house where there was a doctor.

You will be happy to learn that your man mentioned you many times before he died. He wanted us to take care of letters from home and also a picture of the family which he had in one of his jacket pockets.

I hope that you have got these things back again, I also hope that a gold watch belonging to one of the fallen sailors has come back again to the giver one. Sue, who had given this to her lovely husband in 1939.

But what we did that day was only our duty.

Yours

Mr Kongsbakk

However, unlike Surgeon Lieutenant Arthur Waind, RNVR, on *Hardy* who went onto have a distinguished medical career, Surgeon Lieutenant Horace Garner-Evans' career potential was cruelly cut short in the line of duty, at the early age of twenty-nine. His grave in Ballangen Cemetery is next to another brave man, the flotilla commander, Captain Warburton-Lee, VC.

As you have read, the BBC were very proficient at providing updated radio announcements worldwide. Although it was also used as a propaganda and misinformation tool, it was not long before their success was recognised and the Service became known by advertising by being included in published war time books.

Britain calls the World

Men, women, even children, risk imprisonment and death to hear broadcasts from London. They are the inhabitants of the occupied countries of Europe. They do so because they have learned that the British broadcasts tell them the truth. All over the world, and in many languages, you can listen to the truth from London. The British radio sticks to the facts – giving the latest, most authentic news as soon as it is known.

In addition to news, the BBC brings to you every night it's world-famous 'Radio Newsreel'. It brings you talks from leaders of the Allies, stories from people in every walk of life, from war workers, from men in the forces at Home and Overseas; and programmes of music and entertainment.

Full details of all the programmes in English, are broadcast from London in Morse [code] every Sunday, and are available to the Press, almost everywhere, a week in Advance.

FROM LONDON COMES THE VOICE OF BRITAIN . . .
THE VOICE OF FREEDOM

Survivors' March over the Mountains

Marshal Soult begins the accounts of the survivors' march into Sweden and the unknown. "On the Tuesday the 23rd of April, at approximately 2100 hours the *Hunter* survivors started their long walk which was to take them to a tourist station on the Norwegian–Swedish frontier. It was called the Bjornfell which pre-war had been a skiing resort. The weather that night was bitterly cold and for the British sailors the going was very rough because they were ill-equipped for such a journey. Lack of food and adequate clothing soon began to tell on the weary men, many of whom were only youngsters. Their route took them via the railway lines which were covered with hard packed snow and as long as they kept to the track between the lines they could walk fairly comfortably. But if they stepped off the track they soon found themselves knee deep in snow, and this made walking very hard."

Forty-six-year-old veteran, Stoker George Lane, remembers the instructions given to them by the German Officer. "All prisoners were to prepare for a long march and to take with them the bare necessities. We had bugger all to take. No mention of our destination was made."

Sam Evens recalls, "This German Commander said, 'Everybody outside: you are going to march out of Narvik.' They had all the Norwegian soldiers, they marched first, then we trailed behind them. We were warned by the German sailors, who were in charge of the patrol, that, 'if anyone "fell out" they would be shot.'

Marshal describes their experience along what appeared to be a never-ending railway track, "At one point it was exposed to the fjord in which British destroyers still patrolled. The Germans had fixed up a very ingenious method of finding out if the lookouts on the destroyers were watching that part of the railway with the idea of firing at anything that moved on it. They had set up a type of sledge with wire cables tied to each end; this could be pulled back and forth over the exposed part of the railway and if there was no response from the guns of the destroyers it was safe to cross.

"As the *Hunter* prisoners waited to carry on with their march the sledge was duly paraded, but as there was no gunfire from the ships below they were told to run across as quickly as they could. Apparently the merchant navy prisoners had not been as fortunate. They had been spotted by the destroyers crews and fired at. Some of their suitcases were lying around in the snow abandoned in the rush to dodge the shells fired by their own countrymen, who of course had mistaken them for German troops on the move."

Sam Evens, "It was a nightmare. Some of the men had to help each other."

John Hague recalls, "We hardly saw any Germans after they got us ashore, I felt we were really in the way and they wanted rid of us as soon as they could. They gave us a little push to hurry us up. 'Jake' Kerswell had been asked who he wanted to help him, as he was hurt and struggling along the way. He asked them to send Albert [John's nickname]. So we were always the last to reach the stages in the march."

Stoker George Lane mentioned that another *Hunter* crew member, Leading Seaman Minstrell, who was also suffering on the journey.

Marshal Soult, "At 0310 hours, Wednesday, [24th April] a halt was called at a junction on the railway track. The *Hunter* prisoners were put in a large wooden building with a contingent of Norwegian troops, who had been marching ahead of them. They were all herded into a loft over a restaurant. The doors were locked, and they were left alone for the rest of the night without food or drink from their guards. The chap who had arranged to pinch the bread and jam from the Café Iris brought them out of the sack and shared the bread out among his shipmates. They opened one tin of jam and dipped pieces of bread into it. Then with all the bread eaten and still some jam in the tin, they dipped their fingers into it; then sucked the jam off. The other tin of jam they gave to the Norwegian soldiers who soon polished it off, but they had no bread to eat with it.

"The prisoners were roused early after a very uncomfortable night of sleeping packed like sardines on the floor. They were given a cup of coffee and a handful of hard biscuits for breakfast. Then at 0800 hours they took to the road once more. They were walking now in snow which was always ankle deep, sometimes knee deep. It was intensely cold and they began to feel weaker with every step they took; it was a struggle to carry on. One big hazard was walking through the railway tunnels in pitch darkness. An unexpected turn in the tunnel, or an uneven piece of ground and it was quite easy to catch a foot in the rail, and fall headlong in the deep slush, all this added to the discomfort of the prisoners.

"One advantage of the very many tunnels was the relief they afforded the prisoners from the bitterly cold winds; but once outside the tunnels the biting wind would force them to wrap their blankets more tightly round their near frozen bodies. Holding the blankets on with one hand would cause that hand to freeze and the fingers would have to be prised open before changing hands and thrusting the frozen hand under the blanket to get warm again.

"On reaching a bridge which spanned the Rombaksfjord, the prisoners could see far below two German destroyers wrecked on the shoreline. [*Wolfgang Zenker* and *Hans Ludemann*, as previously outlined in the Second Battle]. They had obviously been beached during the second battle, and from such a high viewpoint looked like rowing boats. The bridge was covered in ice and there was a very high howling wind blowing down the fjord. This made the crossing of the bridge very dangerous indeed.

"Clutching the icy rail, the men started to cross very slowly, now and again somebody would slip on the treacherous surface. Only by leaving go of their blankets and clutching the rail with both hands saved them from going over the side of the bridge into the icy water of the fjord. This would have meant certain death for anyone unlucky enough to lose their grip on the rail. The last twenty-five feet of the bridge had been demolished by either gunfire or bombs, and the only means of completing the crossing was along a narrow plank which was so thin and weak, only one man at a time could cross by it. That part of the journey was a terrifying experience for the prisoners and it was a great relief when the last man reached the safety of the other side."

Probably, at about this time Joe Settle and Tom King would have realised their journey's end was nigh. "It took three nights. We had to go through a tunnel, at the other end there were two German soldiers with a machine gun. Oh! We've had it now. At the command 'Halt!' we stopped. They couldn't speak English. We couldn't speak German or Swedish. We were no good to them. They couldn't feed us or keep us there, so they let us past, shouting 'Schnell'. A few hundred yards further on, we met the Swedish Army – good. They made us welcome. Took us to some place like a station where it was warm. They brought soup and bread and gave us some warm clothing. Then they brought us a meal but I couldn't eat any more. It was also very cold in Sweden, but as we were almost in Lapland, it was even colder".

Marshal Soult describes his groups determined efforts. "At noon, another halt was called at yet another railway junction; this time the prisoners were herded into a cattle truck, forty four men in one truck. The conditions were appalling but they had to stay there until 1600 hours. By this time they were exhausted but they had to march about a mile where they were put into a hut; the guards telling them that they would be there for the night. Although feeling very tired and almost done in, the men managed to light a fire to dry their blankets and what bits of clothing they possessed."

The Norton Diary:

No water – using snow, or sugar and six small hard biscuits, 2 mugs used. On the march again and arrived at another railway station about 7 miles away. Halted at 12:20. Locked in railway enclosed truck 2-45 [pm] given 1/1 can of soup, 5 cans used and ½ can of cold water. 4:30 pm set off again for about 4 miles arrived about 6:30 told to get some sleep. Housed in small bungalow [hut] lit fire and had some supper, 2 tins of soup each man getting 2 teaspoon full. Each then settled down for sleep 9 pm woke up and suddenly told to get off on march again quickly. Joined up with Norwegians and set off again conditions terrible.

Sam Evens: "Conditions in the truck were terrible. We were given nothing to eat for a whole day. The next evening the guards came and let us out of the truck and into a large hut. For food we were given, one tin of meat and one of vegetables; this was to share between approximately forty men. I remember a Supply Petty Officer, named Barrett who gave us each an extra spoonful of meat and vegetables. By this time we were too tired and cold to complain about anything. All we wanted was to get warm and try and get some sleep."

Captain Nicholas and his fellow merchant seamen ahead of the other group have completed their arduous march but it has taken its toll, especially on the older crew members. Nicholas himself was forty-three. Here he continues his diary.

Wed 24 April
We reached the border about 5.20 pm and were assisted by the Swedish soldiers to their barracks. Here we were given every attention and kindness. Food was placed before us, but I think everyone was too exhausted to eat much. The doctors examined us all and those who were frost bitten were given first aid.

I was just exhausted and suffered some awful pain in the groin and legs, and could no longer walk. Some managed to get into beds, camp beds etc. I lay down and found was thankful to lay quiet.

In the meantime, the *Hunter* crew were still on their travels but they were under a more oppressive and watchful armed guard. Marshal describes their feelings, "At 2200 hours the guards rudely awakened them saying: 'All English men get up; tonight you walk to Sweden.' The men were in no fit state to walk anywhere at that time of night, they had no option but to comply. As they wearily dragged themselves out into the cold, dark night, one of them said to the guard: 'We can't go on like this.' The guard drew out his bayonet and replied: 'If you fall by the wayside you get this, if I fall I get it.' They struggled along, so tired and cold that the brain became numb, it was only capable of directing one foot in front of the other, on and on, until at long last they reached journey's end.

"At 0220 hours on Thursday 25th April, they arrived at Bjornfell. This tourist station was a very well-known skiing resort and a big hotel was the main building. The prisoners were put into the hotel. The Norwegian Army prisoners occupied the lounge and the British took over the restaurant, using the wooden floor for sleeping on, which by that time they were quite used to doing. The journey which all the prisoners had undertaken was a distance of twenty-eight miles, and it had taken thirty hours to complete. This was due to the terrible conditions under which they had had to march, and the weakened condition of the men due to lack of food."

Sam: "Many times whilst the coffee was brewing we were ordered outside in the snow which was at that time six feet deep, to muster and when we returned almost every time half the coffee had disappeared".

Stormy Renshaw explains his survival techniques. "It was a posh ski resort. I decided that whilst we were in this hotel, we make the most of what we could, so I ventures into the bowels of the hotel, the basement. Of all things, I found a box with about a gross of unusually shaped chocolate bars. A chocolate bar in Norway and Sweden in those days was finger shaped, not a slab. Anyway, I finished up with these bars and two oranges. I took 'em up to what we were using as sleeping quarters and I was forced to give them out to the ship's company. This led to me becoming the 'urchin' of the gang."

The Norton Diary:

02.35 Halted at deserted café [Bjornfell Tourist Station] and about a few miles from Swedish boarder. Falling asleep stood up. Housed in café including the guard. Soon asleep, wet clothes, sleeping 4 on a bunk. Transferred below, to sleep on floor, a bit more food. Housed with Norwegian prisoners, cooking our own food, some concoction I can tell you, not enough food though.

Marshal: "It did not take the *Hunter* men long to start exploring the hotel. They found a staircase which led down to a basement. In the basement they found many cupboards with locked doors; gentle persuasion on the doors soon had them open, and what a wonderful sight met the eyes of the hungry sailors. There was flour, cooking fat, oranges, chocolates and a box of cigars. What luxuries and what a boost to the moral of the prisoners. They soon got a fire going, and using a milk churn they got a meat stew on the boil, using melted snow, tinned meat and thickened with flour.

"The prisoners stood around with their tongues hanging out, waiting for the stew to be served out. The cook had made some pastry with the flour and fat and the first batch was eaten and enjoyed; but before the second batch was ready the German guards marched the *Hunter* men away to see a doctor at the sick quarters. He decided he did not want to see them, so they were marched back again. When they arrived back at the hotel they found the second batch of pastry had been taken by the Norwegian prisoners; but realising that the Norwegians had also been very hungry the *Hunter* men kept quiet about the loss of the pastry."

It is interesting to note that there were only two cooks amongst the survivors, those already mentioned, James Williams and Bill Wallis.

Returning to Marshal, "The toilet facilities for the prisoners consisted of a large sloping tunnel dug out of the snow to a depth of twelve feet. When the prisoners were ready to move on, the tunnel would be filled in. The latrines were about fifty yards from the billet, and Germans guarded the route. The look of amazement on the guards' faces when they saw the *Hunter* men saunter out of the hotel smoking large cigars to go to the latrine was well worth seeing. It gave the *Hunter* men something to laugh about, and lord knows they needed cheering up. The prisoners stayed at the tourist station for three days, any work that wanted doing was done by the Norwegians, so the British prisoners just lounged around the hotel resting, and waiting for the next move."

The Norton Diary:

No cigs, to be sent into Sweden, still hoping British troops will come and rescue us, being treated pretty fair, all fed up. Germans are frightened. Weather conditions a bit better, improvement in amount of food. [Swede's will take us but not Germans.]

The advanced group of merchant seamen had been getting used to their freedom away from not only the enemy but also the raging war.

Captain Nicholas Diary:

Thurs 25 Apl 40.
6 am. Had coffee and boarded a train. I was carried and I could not seem to be able to use my legs. 6.45 am left for Gallivare [Lapland North Sweden] 12.50 pm arrived Gallivare, where we had dinner on the station and those able to walk, given a little exercise on the platform. Teatime, the same as dinner time, but I had my meals this time in the train.

Fri 26 Apl 40.
Still in the train at Gallivare Station. Don't seem to know what to do with us. Also some talk of some more crews joining us. People very kind, gave us cigarettes, chocolate, books etc. Food given us in Station Booking Hall where forms and tables laid out.

Sat 27 Apl 40.
Spent most of day in Gallivare Station and had food as before. 6.30 pm. The train moved on again.

Nicholas mentions "talk about some more crews joining us". It appears not to have happened and if did, it certainly was not the *Hunter* crew as they would shortly be travelling on another train in a different direction.

Marshal: "The British prisoners were taken in groups to an office where they were asked to sign a document. A German Naval Officer explained what the document was about and the men duly signed. Declaration reads:

'On my being sent into Sweden I will not take up arms against Germany or her Allies during the continuation of the present war. Should I do so, and in the event

of again being taken prisoner I shall be subject to such conditions as are provided under the Death Penalty Act.'

"The prisoners were then marched through a long tunnel, half way along which was the border with Sweden. This made the total numbers of tunnels passed through by them since leaving Narvik as twenty-one. [Seems like Marshal, to keep focus on the march chose to count the number of tunnels.] The officer in charge of the German guards approached 'no man's land'. The Swedish Army Officer met him, formalities were exchanged then the prisoners were passed through being counted as they went. At the other end of the tunnel they were relieved to find a train which they boarded and sank down into the seats in the compartments. What a comfort to sit on such soft seats, and to feel a sense of partial freedom. I say partial, because they were going into internment, but at least they were out of the clutches of the Germans, so there would be no POW Camp in Germany for them." Sadly for some this eventually became their final destination.

The Norton Diary.

Sun 28th Three days rations given, during afternoon compelled to sign a paper, Undertaking not to take up arms against Germans or Allies, if they do so and are caught, they will be shot. Told we were going to Sweden, 5:15 pm left under armed guard for Swedish border. 5:55 pm crossed the Swedish border after being handed over to the Swedish soldiers by German armed guard. What a relief, train is waiting for us. Half of Norwegian soldiers and all officers . [...] Given some cigs and bread, a hearty welcome. travelled all night.

It was reported later to the British Legation Office in Stockholm by Merchant Navy crew and a week later as a British Press Release. "The men as they marched along the railway to Sweden from Narvik [...] said they saw boxes of dynamite packed in them, indicating that the Germans intended to blow up the railway before leaving. There was enough dynamite there to blow down the sides of the mountains,' remarked one of the [Merchant Seamen] Captains."

Joe Settle appears to have finally met up with the remainder of the *Hunter* group. "Later we were put on a train with all the windows blacked out. We didn't know where we were going. Finally we arrived at a little village called

Gunnarn where we were interned. We were put in a hut type building surrounded by wire, guarded by the Army, but no guns. We were given hot
water for washing etc., which was a luxury that we hadn't experienced for
some time. People from the village gave us clothes, cigarettes and chocolate
and others came from miles around to see us behind the wire."

Marshal: "During the train journey the prisoners were interrogated
by officers of the Swedish Military Intelligence Service, then the train
stopped at a station, here at last the men received the first decent meal they
had had for quite a long time. It was served to them by charming Swedish
ladies, who belonged to a similar organisation to our Women's Voluntary
Service. The meal they gave the prisoners consisted of hot soup, sausages,
potatoes, bread, and chocolate. They also gave them cigarettes. The men
thoroughly enjoyed their meal, and a smoke; they could not thank their
benefactors enough.

"Onward went the train away from the border, then it pulled into a siding
for the night. The men slept soundly in the comfort of the train compartments, on this their first night away from the Germans. They realised that
the worst was over and their plight would surely improve now they were in
a neutral country. The train continued its journey after breakfast the following morning, a stop was made for lunch, then the journey ended at a
place called Gunnarn. This was at 1600 hours on the 28th of April."

Stormy Renshaw. "Finally on the train with the 'Land Storm' from
Sweden [WVS] they gave us tea, cigarettes and other things. We were
locked in railway coaches for a journey across Sweden. Various tactics were
used to find out in which direction we were going. For example, 'If the sun is
over here, the shadows will be over there, so early morning, we were heading eastwards.'

"After all this lot they came the next day and took us to another tourist
station, which was evacuated and they left us there to recuperate for a while
because they couldn't get no transport, no aircraft or anything into feed us.
We could see the Swedish border in the distance. It was daylight there, day
and night, you couldn't escape, no way. We eventually arrived at a railway
station, when a 'Red Cross' train came and took us to the North of Sweden.
We were in a very bad condition by now and we were just glad to get on
board this train, because there were doctors and nurses who treated us. We
stopped at many stations on our way north where they fed us."

Captain Nicholas Diary:

Sun 28 Apl 40.
1.00 am Arrived at the village of 'Jorn' and given food on platform. We then marched to S.A. Citadel [either Swedish Army or Salvation Army Citadel] where we had straw beds and pillows and a blanket. It was good to get our clothes off and we slept like logs. Some were taken to hospital for frostbite.
11.30 am. Marched down to outside of Station and given food again at 6.00 pm. Everybody ate plenty. Then fill in the evening until bedtime by lying down.

Mon 29 Apl 40.
Morning spent waiting for 1130 am. When we get fed and again at 6.00 pm. Heard today that some of the missing crews had got home. Consul arrived and hopes of going home shortly.

Tues 30 Apl 40.
Meals now issued in local cinema in case of rain. It's only a short walk from our billet.

At this point it is worth looking at Sweden's stance of 'neutrality' when war broke out in September 1939. It had declared its neutrality as it had in every European conflict since 1814. However, in World War Two, they had in fact opened their borders to those at risk of capture and imprisonment by the Nazis. They had sheltered almost 8,000 Jewish refugees in 1943, protected 44,000 Norwegians fleeing from German occupation. While Swedish citizens took pride in their humanitarian efforts, most of them did not know that their government was also providing important resources to the Nazis.

Sweden remained neutral when the Germans invaded Denmark and Norway and it had resisted Germany's request to allow its troops to travel along the Swedish railways. Although, this resolve became less as the war progressed and the Nazis appeared unstoppable in their conquests through Europe. Hence, in June 1941 the Swedish government began to permit Wehrmacht troops to travel along its railways. A whole division with howitzers, tanks and ammunition were allowed to be transported from Norway to Finland for its intended invasion of the Soviet Union. German soldiers traveling on leave between Norway and Germany were allowed passage through Sweden — the so-called *permittenttrafik*.

Sweden's cooperation extended to the transportation for a third of the Nazis iron ore to manufacture their weapons. They also gave bank credits to the Germans, who repaid their debt in gold. Thirteen tons of this came from Belgium and the Netherlands, stolen when Nazis occupied their countries. However, Sweden did share intelligence with the Allies and helped to train soldiers made up of refugees from Denmark and Norway, to be used in the liberation of their home countries. Sweden's support continued until an Allied victory was inevitable. When it allowed the Allies to utilise Swedish military airbases between 1944 and 1945. Although, in the early years of the war, as you will now read, it appears that decisions were taken by the Swedish government, not all of which concurred with the wishes of their brave and caring population.

Hospitality in Sweden

The Norton Diary.

Mon 29th Stopped at railway station for breakfast. 06:45, a good meal, then con-
tinued our train journey. Later stopped at another station and had dinner in the
station and railway lines, another good meal. Cigs arriving at destination. About
16:10 marched in to our camp, a church about a mile from station, a nice place
and very well received. Three of us took on job of assisting in the cook house, a
good meal was soon provided for us. Waited on by ladies of the S L K, everything
done for our comfort.

Thankfully, now away from the enemy, Marshal Soult describes the survivors' entrance into Sweden: "Gunnarn was a village in central Sweden, 300
miles south of the place where they had crossed the border. It stood beside a
lake, in beautiful surroundings with a river running alongside. Pine forests
were all around and at the time the prisoners reached there, the snow which
covered the place was beginning to thaw. The village consisted of farms, a
few houses, a school, telephone exchange and of course the railway station.
A really delightful place to the eyes of the *Hunter* men, who had expected to
end up in a POW. camp in Germany. They were going to have plenty of time
to explore this haven of tranquillity, and to get to know the very friendly
people who lived there.

"When they alighted from the train they were unwashed, unshaven and
wearing a motley assortment of clothing. They walked about three-quarters
of a mile to a chapel which was to be their billet during the time of internment at Gunnarn. This chapel had been fitted out with bunks, the catering
was done by the equivalent of our W VS and the job of guarding the prisoners was undertaken by Swedish Army Reservists. The first thing the men
did after picking their bunk was to have a good wash and shave.

"By this time the local people had started to take an interest in them.

They handed out cigarettes, fruit, sweets, and even provided a radio set. They could not do enough for the unfortunate sailors who had been thrust upon them by the aftermath of battle. The grounds of the chapel were about 300 yards square, full of trees which had barbed wire stretched between them up to a height of ten feet. The road from the village ran alongside two sides of the chapel, and the Swedish guards patrolled the grounds and the road outside."

Sam Evens recalls the moment, "They put us in a place called 'Gunnarn'. There we were looked after and put in a guarded camp. It was funny the Swedish soldiers had these peculiar hats like olden time soldiers. There was a big church, not a church really, like a big hall, with beds fitted up with straw in and blankets and this was where we slept. There was a kitchen, attended by the 'Red Cross' people. But we were behind barbed wire fences so we couldn't get out anywhere, until they got used to us being there.

The friendly guards in their tricorn hats and obsolete
rifles. [John Hague Family Collection]

"It got a bit more relaxed and they allowed us to go to work on the farms. We worked for the farmers quite a while, until we started to eat them out of 'house and home'. We were eating too much I think, because it was hard living, especially in that part of Sweden. Anyway, they were very nice and treated us well. I wasn't superstitious but in the camp we talked about Pat Duffy's, **'We're going in and we're not coming out!'"**

Others, like Thomas Norton, worked in nearby forests. Young John Hague remembers with fondness the man now referred to as 'Daddy' Norton: "A smashing little fellow, he helped us a lot".

Norton, Hague and Bowden. [John Hague Family Collection]

At this stage the men did not know if loved ones at home had been informed of those who had survived or were casualties. In Thomas Norton's case he also did not realise the effect that the recent events had had on his wife Georgina Ellen. Here, Jose Johnson, Thomas' granddaughter explains; "Gran first heard that the *Hunter* had been sunk and all hands were feared lost on the BBC 1 pm news. She became very ill, with what was more than likely shock and a nervous breakdown. My Auntie says she took to her bed and her hair went grey and fell out overnight. She was ill for some time. It was about forty-eight hours after the sinking of the *Hunter* when Gran received a telegram saying that all hands had been lost at sea. It was some weeks later that the family were informed by telegram that he was in Sweden."

Stormy Renshaw did not lose any time getting to know the local populace. "We arrived at a little church in a village called 'Gunnarn'. I became friendly with a girl from outside of the barbed wire. She wished to learn English and I wanted to learn Swedish, so between the two of us, we managed to make something of it. I learnt quite a lot. We were then kept in one block; the Merchant Navy men all disappeared, we didn't know where they went.

"Meanwhile, the British Consulate decided that we couldn't run around like this, we'd have to be more suitably dressed. Being Englishmen, we were brought under the spotlight by the newspapers, and we were to be more suitably dressed. He never mentioned the fact that the supplies in our camp were the remnants of the 1914–18 situation. You can imagine a 'Chief Stoker' riding on the back of a horse, with an umbrella up and a bowler hat on; I personally had a velvet suit. But they decided that we should be measured and supplied with the necessary kit, so we all in turn received two grey shirts, a pair of grey trousers, shoes we had to provide ourselves; but we got this kit and we were beginning to look a little bit smart. That wasn't the end of it; we knew there was something behind it."

Marshal, "After a week in the village the prisoners had a visit from a retired British Naval Captain from Stockholm, who had been a Consulate in Norway. He had moved out just before the Germans had arrived in the town where he lived. The officer arranged for clothing and pay to be sent to the men. He also arranged a canteen for them. These two acts of service by this gentleman enabled the prisoners to enjoy substantial meals and live a more comfortable life in captivity. Each man received a suit, pyjamas, shirts, underwear, socks, shoes, ties, mac, pullover and a suitcase; in fact, they were completely kitted out.

Returning to Marshal Soult, "On the 30th of April an event took place which none of the men would ever forget. It was the 'Eve of May Revels', an event celebrated by the local population. On this occasion in honour of the prisoners, and to enable them to take part, the celebrations were held in the grounds of the chapel. In the evening, an old rowing boat was placed in one corner of the grounds. It stood with its bow in the air, supported by two poles, and piles of wood were laid around the base. It was the start of an ancient custom carried out every year on the 'Eve of May'. It reminded the West Countrymen among the prisoners of the celebration of Midsummer's Eve in parts of Devon and Cornwall.

Hunter survivors group photograph. [John Hague family Collection]

Back Row	1	2	3	4	5	6	7	8	9
	William Parton	X	Charles Coutts	Joe Murphy	James Williams	Anthony Bartolo	John Hague	/	/
	Norman Bowden	X	Rex Brown	Thomas Grady	Bill Wallis	Frank Caton	Charles Falzon	William Barrett	Harry Clark
	Stan Kerswell	Thomas Norton	Robert Hay	John Harris	Sam Evens	David Moore	X	Guy Hunter	Andrew Black
Front Row	Joe Settle	X	Fred Butcher	Norman Stewart	John Steel	Jim Renshaw	X	/	/

X Denotes – Not Identified.

"When it became dark the villagers assembled outside the grounds and one of the guards set fire to the wood. Everybody sang songs and hymns in Swedish and English, more gifts were showered on the men. Then the villagers held a collection among themselves and gave the proceeds to the sailors. The kindness of these peaceful village folk to men, who they had never seen before in their lives, was surely unsurpassed by any other peoples of the free world towards British Servicemen; who had found themselves in the unenviable position of internees or prisoners of war, in countries far from their homeland".

The Norton Diary:

Tues 30th April *Weather very warm, comfortable camp, made welcome. Villagers called to see us. Usual bonfire lit in our ground. All villagers around the camp, we sang, were heartily clapped. Villagers also sang to us. Apples, pears, cigs, a very enjoyable evening.*

Wed 1st May *Still plenty of visitors, nice weather, good food, holiday here.*

Thurs 2nd *Given clothes, shaving gear, etc. outlook pleasant. Given wireless by villagers (8 valve)*

Fri 3rd *Heard on wireless that 34 men and 2 officers had been found in Sweden from the* Hunter, *mentioned as dead. Hope our names had already been sent out.*

Sat 4th *Swedish officer visited camp, paid each man 10 Krona's each. Asked if we wanted anything.*

To those unfamiliar with communications technology at that time, radios used electronic valves. The reception and amplification, with a suitable aerial, was improved by increasing the number of valves installed in the circuitry. 'Daddy' Norton was impressed with this present from the locals.

By now information was filtering back to Britain to confirm the safety of those *Hunter* crew members who had survived the sinking of their ship. This led to their family's euphoria spreading rapidly around their communities and local newspapers wanting to report the story.

"The seamen had been released from Narvik owing to the food shortage there, but since their arrival at Gunnarn they have been made much of by the villagers. Yesterday the seamen were taken out on pleasure trips and invited to May Day celebrations. In a 'whip round' the Swedes collected about £12 to buy cigarettes and provided the sailors with a wireless set", writes the Aberdeen *Press and Journal*.

Marshal, "The weather began to get warmer, and the prisoners were allowed out for a walk every Sunday afternoon. They were accompanied by two guards who were much older than their charges, so it was not surprising that at the end of the long walk, the prisoners would be carrying the rifles of the guards; by this gesture trust was established between prisoners and guards. It was not long before five of the *Hunter* men were playing in the local football team, this cemented friendships and made trust much stronger".

Sam Evens, "We would come out of an evening and sing to them all the British songs we knew like 'Roll out the Barrel'. Then the British Consulate got in touch with us. He started bringing clothes and shoes. I got a barbering outfit from him and used to cut their hair for a rolled-up fag at the time".

The family obviously knew 'Stormy' Renshaw better than did his shipmates. Here six weeks after the battle this article appeared in the Sheffield newspaper, *The Star*.

The family of James Renshaw a sailor from HMS *Hunter* have received news that he is safe in Sweden. Their joy is heightened by the news that *Hunter* men in Sweden may be able to return home soon. The telegram that brought joy to his family stated briefly: "I am pleased to inform you that information has now been received that your son is safe in Sweden. Letter follows". Stormy's sister, Mrs Fountain, of Stonecliffe Close, whose husband is also serving in the Navy; told 'The Star' today that when the telegram arrived they thought it contained bad news. "We had been informed that he was missing when the *Hunter* was sunk in the First Battle of Narvik, and I am afraid we had all given up hope," she said. "We were so excited that we could not read the message. The telegram boy had to read it for us. As soon as she heard it my mother ran outside to tell all the neighbours. We were so happy that none of us could sleep last night".

"We've always said he has nine lives," said his sister. "He always seems to come out on top. He once fell from the roof of a house when going after a ball, as a boy. He dropped on a bracket lamp sticking from a wall, and that broke his fall. He was as well as ever in a day or two. When he went to join up first, he went with a broken arm, caused in a cycling accident. They would not have him, but as soon as it was better, he went again. Now my mother says she is going to trim the house with red, white and blue for his homecoming. What makes it better is that another brother in the Army is coming home on leave soon."

Along with bad news of the losses of men there was also further good news coming in for the anxious families of survivors. In the **Exeter** *Express and Echo* **4th of May 1940:**

A NEWTON [ABBOT] SURVIVOR

"News has been received by his wife today […] that Able Seaman Norman Bowden, age 28 […] is one of the survivors […] who it was feared, had been lost in the Narvik action with all hands. What his family did not know, as you are about to read is that Norman will not be wasting his time feeling sorry for himself but busy trying to find a way of getting back home."

"In the meantime, one family in Exeter were still anxiously waiting news of Warrant Officer James Coombe."

Another family desperate for news was that of George Lane. His grandson Chris Lane sent me two letters that were receive by his grandmother from the Admiralty.

Royal Navy Barracks, Devonport. 6th May 1940.

Dear Madam,

With reference to my telegram of today, I have to inform you that your husband, George Lane (Stoker 1, RFR B.8202) is interned at Gunnarn in VASTERBOTTEN, SWEDEN. He is well cared for. Further information as to how to address letters to him will be forwarded to you as soon as known.

Yours faithfully', DRAFTING COMMANDER for Admiral.

Mrs F. Lane, Manchester.

There was also a lot of interest around the world, especially in the 'Dominions'. Here is one report from Australia.

Sydney Morning Herald. 4th May 1940.
LONDON, MAY 3 (AAF)

The *Daily Mail* correspondent in North Sweden mentions that he has found two officers and 45 men of the British destroyer *Hunter* in the village of Gunnarn, on the Norwegian frontier. The villagers are treating them with the warmest hospitality and clothing has been provided from the British Consulate [Legation] in Stockholm. The men will be interned for the duration of the war.

A hundred and fifty British seamen [merchant and Royal Navy] have reached Sweden. They include 36 men of HMS *Hunter*. The merchant seamen will be interned for the present, and the naval men for the duration of the war. The seamen were released from Narvik as a result of the food shortage and are from the following ships: *Mersington* (5141 tons), *North Cornwall* (4304), *Romanby* (4887), *Riverton* (5378) and *Blythmoor* (6582).

The Norton Diary.

Sun 5th May   *Nice weather, wrote a letter first allowed or able to send. Another Swedish officer visited us. Arranged for us to request visit of British Consul, addresses the camp very nice.*

Mon 6th   *Great news informed by British Consul we are not interned. Names again given in, awaiting arrangements for passages to England.*

Tues 7th   *Consul approves at 6:30 pm and took down all particulars. Very nice gentleman, confirmed phone message that we are not interned only awaiting passes.*

Wed 8th   *Consul came again at 10:39 spoke a few words and obtained all the further particulars, all the news we could re Narvik etc. Did not know we had arrived until phone message sent on the Sunday. Paid us another 10 Kronas. Took away list of all articles we required.*

Relief finally comes for the families of two sailors from Scotland by way of the *Courier And Advertiser*. **Dated 8th of May 1940.**

ROSYTH MOTHERS GET HAPPY NEWS

Four weeks of anxiety for two Rosyth mothers have ended happily with the news that their sons, ratings of HMS *Hunter* [...] are safe. The men are A.B. Charles Coutts and A.B. Guy Hunter [...] Relatives of both men are overjoyed at their escape. The good news was conveyed by telegrams, which read: "Am pleased to inform you that information has been received that your son is safe in Sweden. Letter follows."

The Norton Diary:

Thurs 9th May *Conditions still very nice. Guards not so keen as they were. Allowed walk across to the farm opposite also lads help farmers nearby. Everybody been good especially Uncle Sam who runs to the village for us, Speaks English very well.*

Sat 11th *Received news from British Consul we may only be here a week.*

Sun 12th *Our new clothes arrived, everybody satisfied, snowed all day.*

Mon 13th *Whit Monday. Little snow, wore our new clothes, allowed out for game of football. Allowed out later with invitation to coffee and cakes from a local café prop. In the evening allowed to go to station to meet nurse returning from visiting home, 8 pm all allowed out again for an hour or so.*

British Press acknowledged a possible early release of the survivors. Dated: 7th May 1940. "The Swedish Foreign Office confirmed that these men will be released, as against the original intention to intern them, because the Germans had originally set them free at Narvik".

Another Press Release at the same time:

Hitler Pledge to Swede King

Summarised: "The secret letters between King Gustav of Sweden and Hitler during the latter half of last month was disclosed last night by Berlin and the Swedish Foreign Minister added that the Reich Chancellor gave the King an assurance that Sweden's neutrality would be respected".

I will now return to the uncertainties experienced by one of the survivors' families back in Britain.

Namely Mrs Holt the wife of Able Seaman Alfred Holt born in Salford and a veteran from the First World War. Here are summarised copies of the three letters Mrs Holt received from the Admiralty, the first of which is dated the 18th of April, 1940.

[...] "It appears very unlikely that there are any survivors" [...] Whilst, giving some hope, "There is some possibility that a small number were taken prisoner by the enemy" [...] The second letter dated the 2nd of May 1940 informs [...] "From a press source, two officers and forty four ratings have arrived at a town in North Sweden".[...] The last letter in July 1940 came as a devastating blow, putting to rest any optimistic outcome for Alfred's wife and their children. [...] "I very much regret to state that information has now been received that his body was washed ashore at Ornesvika on 19th April 1940 and was buried at Narvik. His identity disc is forwarded herewith". [...]

The *Manchester Evening News* did not take long before they caught up with the emotional story in July 1940, with the headlines;

'Daddy Gone – But Sylvia Can Be Happy'

There will be sadness behind a party held in a house in Northenden, Manchester, tonight. Sometime ago Mrs E. Holt of Royal Oak Road, promised that on the first birthday of her baby son, Derek, she would give a party for her four-year-old adopted daughter Sylvia.

Now Mrs. Holt has received official notification that the body of her husband Able Seaman Alfred Holt of HMS *Hunter* has been washed ashore on the Norwegian coast and buried in Narvik. But the party will go on. "The kiddies don't understand and I promised Sylvia her party". Mrs. Holt told the paper today. "I can't disappoint her now. I shall just pretend to enjoy it".

The newspaper reporter went on to further quote Mrs. Holt, "The last time I heard from Alf was April 1st, but I know he was in the battle at Narvik on April 10th. His particular chum in the same ship was saved and is now interned in Sweden. I have hoped against hope that I would receive similar news about my husband. We were married only two years ago, and he has only seen Derek twice – the last time when he was a month old". In addition to Derek and Sylvia, Mrs. Holt has also to bring up her twin step-children, Jack and Margaret, aged nine. They know of their father's death".

I was able to send a photograph of Alfred's grave to Gavin. Before moving on with the story of the *Hunter* survivors, I leave the last words to Grandson, Gavin Holt. "Thank you so much for the picture. It meant a lot to be able to see my Grandfather's grave. I have all his naval records of service, in fact one of the last remarks made was a recommendation to make him a Leading Torpedo Operator."

For Able Seaman Ernest Thomas, BEM, who in 1937 was in the rescue party that placed him in a life threatening incident in which he was able to save his comrades, unfortunately this time there was nobody to rescue him. He was one of the poor souls who went down with his ship. To quote a military journal, "Thomas was a crew member aboard HMS *Hunter*, a seaman and ship both destined to rest in eternity on the freezing Norwegian seabed."

News: Home and Abroad

By the 16th May 1940, as you would expect, Adolf Hitler's led advance in Europe had become the big news story. Here are extracts from newspapers from around the world at that time, featured in the *North Devon Journal* under the headline:

Foreign Comments on the War.

TURKEY

The Turkish paper *Tan* comments: "The German offensive is not a sign of strength but is prompted by the need to shorten the war." *Cumhuriyet* says: "The German conduct is comparable to, but worse than, the conduct of wild beasts in the African forests." While the Ankara paper *Ulus* states,

"The pretext for aggression not only mocks but is a positive insult to world opinion."

SWEDEN

"Norway May be Allied Gain." – the *Goteburgsposten* declares: "It is possible that the British manoeuvre in Norway will eventually be an Allied gain. Germans in the last war won continual successes but everything collapsed before the opponents' concentrated strength. Now, German troops and material are tied in Norway and the Nazis fleet has been immensely weakened. Another disadvantage for the Germans is that their actions will produce a determined war spirit in England."

SWITZERLAND

The *Gazette De Lausanne* writes: "Germany's complete occupation of Southern Norway seems inevitable, but it does not modify the general situation, while the ultimate success of the adventure is still problematic. Only a month ago Germany was sheltered by the neutrals and she alone profited by the use of their territorial waters and benefitted by all that Denmark and Norway could supply. Now she has the thankless task of maintaining the domination of two blockaded territories. The occupation so dearly bought by the German Navy may present momentary economic advantages, but it is doubtful whether it can compensate for the loss of all the benefits which the Reich derive from their neutrality."

U.S.A.

"The Gangsters of the Air". In an editorial, the *New York Times* writes: "The story of air warfare on open towns has been retold in Ethiopia, Spain, Poland, Finland and Norway. It is not an accidental 'atrocity' needing a Commission to prove or disprove it. It is an attested, studied and boasted method of attack. These are the gangsters of the air. Maybe they gain a temporary military advantage. To gain it they are building up a world-wide horror and contempt, which, some day, be it late or soon, will plough them under."

In the meantime, the news in Britain, as you would expect, was changing at a fast pace and becoming more dramatic by the day. It was difficult for the *Hunter* survivors, in the rural regions of Northern Sweden to keep up with all the news back home.

Proclamation

It was on Thursday that a new proclamation calling up all men from nineteen to thirty-six was signed by the King : It affects all those who have reached the age of nineteen, but have not reached thirty-seven – in other words all men born between May 10th 1903 and May 9th 1921, both dates inclusive.

The Invasion

Very soon after Germany invaded Holland, Belgium and Luxemburg in the early hours of Friday morning. Herr Hitler addressed a message to the German forces on the Western Front, saying: "The hour of most decisive struggle for the future of the German nation has come." – An appeal to Britain for help was sent by Holland and Belgium, and this had the effect of Anglo-French troops marching to Belgium, over which Allied bombers were also quickly in action. Meanwhile, to ensure the security of Iceland, British troops were landed.

Biggest in History

"We are going forward to the biggest battle in history," said the official spokesman of the French War Ministry in Paris on Saturday. It was also on Saturday that French troops were reported to have made contact with the German advance guards in the Luxemburg sector. Britain's mechanised army moved steadily eastwards.

Alien Round-up

On Sunday, up and down the East Coast of England, police working quietly and swiftly, began making Britain's greatest round up of Germans and Austrians. By evening 3,000 of them had been interned, every other alien – about 11,000 of them in a huge banned area had become liable to a daily curfew from 8 pm to 6 am.

German planes were reported to have bombed eighteen towns in France and violated Swiss territory many times in flying to France. Brussels had a succession of air raid alarms. Heavy civilian casualties were reported from the bombing of Belgium towns, while it was officially stated that more than 100 people, including women and children, were killed or injured in Friday's raids on France. Amsterdam had two air raids. Allied units landed in the Dutch West Indies islands of Curacao and Aruba, to prevent possible sabotage by Germans of the oil refineries there.

An Appeal
Mr Anthony Eden, the new War Minister, broadcasting an appeal for men chiefly in small town and villages, to join the local Defence Volunteers, said that it would be a spare time job. Volunteers will not be required to leave their work, or live away from home, and they will not be paid, but will have a uniform and will be armed. "We want large numbers of such men between the ages of 17 and 65 to come forward now," he declared.

Dutch Lay Down Arms
It was stated on Tuesday that the CIC of the Dutch Forces had laid down arms in parts of Holland.

The Norton Diary:

Wed 15th May	*Played football for camp against Swedish team, lost.*
Thurs 16th	*In bed with rash stayed there 3 days. Painted all over.*
Fri 17th	*Weather glorious.*
Sun 19th	*Got up from bed, football match with Swedish team, weather glorious.*
Wed 22nd	*General Douglas visited the camp, very nice gentleman.*
Thurs 23rd	*Restriction removed re having guard taking us around, leave the grounds when we like,*
Fri 24th	*The three of us had a day off from cook house, the girls lent us bikes, and we travelled well into the country, very nice.*
Sat 25th	*Took boats and went rowing on the lake, also went for a walk in the woods, soldiers left the camp.*
Sun 26th	*Raining, football match.*
Tues 28th	*Plenty of time on the river and in the woods.*

Wed 29th	*Told about going home in a few days.*
Thurs 30th	*Ward [Fred] goes sick with scarlet fever. All put in quarantine till Sunday.*

It was not all bad news for the families back home. Around this time another survivor was about to have his birthday. This was John 'Chats' Harris who had made a prophecy to his fiancée. Unknown to him, celebrations had already started, albeit for another reason. A local newspaper reported with the headline;

STOKER'S PROPHECY FULFILLED

"I'll turn up some day," First Class Stoker John Harris, of Parr Street, Plymouth, told his fiancée Miss Ivy Trout, when he left home seven weeks ago to join HMS *Hunter*. After Miss Trout had believed him lost, she heard late last night that his prophecy would probably come true".

HMS *Hunter* was a Devonport based ship, so the local paper, the **Western Morning News** on the 7th and 8th of April 1940, did not waste time in informing the residents of Plymouth that 'Chats' Harris, Norman Stewart, David Moore and Pat Duffy were alive.

JOY IN CITY HOMES

There was jubilation in Parr Street, Sutton Road last night. Early in the evening a telegraph messenger had turned his bicycle into this cul-de-sac, where reside at No 10, the father, mother and young sisters and brothers of First Class Stoker Edwin John Harris [...] Ever since receiving the Admiralty message that he was missing his mother has not for one moment lost her faith that he would turn up again, and her mother love and hope were rewarded; when the telegraph messenger knocked at her door.

He was the bearer of glad tidings – brief message to say Stoker Harris was safe in Sweden. This joy was intensified later when the radio broadcasted the news announcing that the survivors were on their way home.

LAUGHED AND CRIED
"Life Seemed To Be All Sunshine Again"

"How did you feel when the telegram arrive?" asked the *Western Morning News* representative, when he called to congratulate the once-more happy family. "I just didn't know what to say. When the messenger came into the passage, I said to him: 'Don't you bring me any bad news.' And I felt I simply could not open the telegram. I made him open it, and read it. It just gave the name and number, and said: 'Your son safe in Sweden'.

"I didn't know whether to laugh or cry. I did both. I felt I could have flung my arms around anyone. Life seemed to be all sunshine again. It was exactly a month ago today that the battle took place and three weeks ago that we were informed he was missing. But I have never given up hope. I knew if there was a hole to get out he would do so. I have told them all along he was alive. I knew it."

GOOD SWIMMER

"He is twenty-four, and been in the Navy five years [...] and was always a good swimmer. Perhaps that is what helped him to escape [...] In the letters we had from him before they went to Narvik he was very happy. He was in another ship but he scalded his foot, and when he came out of hospital he had missed his ship, and so was sent to the *Hunter* [...] Of course, we do not know any details. Time enough for them when he gets home. [...] Last night there were many neighbourly calls on the Harris family. Their joy was shared by the whole street, for young Harris is popular with everyone".

Unfortunately, whilst Chats prophecy was spot on, what his fiancée, family and friends were not to know is it would take another five years before he stepped back on British soil.

Continuing the *Western Morning News* article:

TEARS OF HAPPINESS

After a month of suspense and anguish Mrs B. Stewart [...] received last night what will be to her the most precious souvenir of the war, a telegram announcing that her son, Able Seaman Norman Stewart [...] is safe in Sweden. "I knew he was alright all along," she confided to her younger son, amid tears of happiness when she received the telegram about seven o'clock.

Her first act, after receiving the congratulations and good wishes of friends was to send a telegram to her husband, who is in the minesweeping service, and also to her mother announcing the good news [...] A.B. Stewart, a Plymouth lad, who is nineteen years of age, has been in the Navy since he was seventeen. "He was a good swimmer, you know. We always believed he was well," said his brother.

MOTHERS OPTIMISM

Amid her anxiety, Mrs Stewart was as optimistic as ever at the weekend. "I shall not give up hope until the very last. Just before he left he told me not to worry," [...] As the Germans are said to have put them out to Norway [...] the newspaper feature finally ends, "It is likely their internment in Sweden will be lifted and that the British authorities will try to get them sent home to England."

About the same time the parents of Norman Stewart were informed he was alive and safe; they were not aware their son had performed an act of bravery by rescuing the First Lieutenant. At a relatively young age he was to be awarded the Distinguished Service Medal. Unfortunately, Norman's mother's optimism would be worn out over the next months or years, as he is one of the few survivors that I have been unable to establish how and when he managed to return home. However, I do know that he did get home in the end because he is on my father Cyril Cope's 1970s list of members for the 2nd Destroyer Flotilla Association.

I have provided a list of survivors whom I have been unable to track down in a later chapter. Perhaps this will result in families or friends making contact with more information.

Returning to the **Western Morning News** feature dated 8th May 1940, here is one survivor I was able to track down but in order to gather further information I had to make a visit to the National Archives at Kew.

WELCOME NEWS FOR FURTHER CITY FAMILIES

"Mrs D.H. Moore, of [...] Mutley, Plymouth, yesterday received confirmation [...] that her husband had survived the sinking of HMS *Hunter* [...] she received the following telegram: 'I am pleased to inform you that information has now been received that your husband, Chief Stoker. D.H. Moore, is interned in Sweden. Letter follows.'"

THEIR PRAYERS FOR DADDY WERE ANSWERED.—" Please God, give us back our daddy "—that has been the daily prayer of Joyce (left) and Hazel Duffy in a little church at Keyham, near Plymouth, since their father was reported missing in H.M.S. Hunter. Now their prayers have brought daddy back from the dead. For Stoker Petty Officer Joseph Duffy is among the Hunter men safe in Sweden.

Newspaper picture of the Joseph Duffey's young daughters.
[Joseph Duffy's son Patrick's Collection]

The newspaper goes on to name another crew member. "In yet another Plymouth home despair has been turned to joy by the news that the head of the family is safe [...] and being well cared for. This at North Down Crescent, Swilly, where Mrs. Duffy and five young children have been overjoyed by the official intimation that husband and father, Stoker Petty Officer

Joseph Patrick Duffy, is among the survivors of *Hunter*." In fact, as previously informed, Pat's wife, Mabel, was expecting their sixth child. Pat's premonition proved to be correct, **"We're going in and we're not coming out."** But would he survive other ordeals coming his way to be able to come home to his large family?

The two Able Seamen who had gone home to Aberdeen on separate leave dates, featured in their local paper the 'Press and Journal' with mixed news. There was heartache for the parents of William Edwards presumed missing and drowned. Whilst Robert Hay, recently engaged was a survivor but like Ivy Trout, Robert's fiancée Ruth Guyan would also be left uncertain as to when he would finally be back home in Scotland.

Another young seaman who would not now be considered as an 'Ordinary Seaman', was front page news in the provincial newspaper the **Gloucestershire Echo,** Dated 21st of May 1940.

FAMILY DISCARD MOURNING
FOREST SEAMAN IS SAFE

It was officially confirmed that Ordinary Seaman Fredrick. H. Ward (20), who was believed drowned in the sinking of HMS *Hunter*, is alive and safe in Sweden. Seaman Ward, who enlisted in the Navy last December, is among a small party who survived the sinking. He was reported by the Admiralty to have been lost, and on receipt of this news, Mrs. E. Ward, his widowed mother, and other members of the family went into mourning. Then came the Admiralty announcement that a number of *Hunter* survivors were thought to be safe in Sweden.

The family have now discarded their mourning and are looking forward to the welcome home that they intend to give Seaman Ward – when he is released from internment.

It seems in life, that those that are persistent in gathering crucial information tend to be noticed and that this triggers a reaction. Irrespective of that I am sure that by now most, if not all of the survivors' families at home, had been made aware of their whereabouts.

I can only recount details of those families who were appropriately informed. Here I return to the second letter received by Mrs Lane concerning her husband George. This is the summarised version.

24th May, 1940.
Dear Madam,
    Further to my letter [...] I have to inform you that should you wish to commu-
nicate with your husband you should address your letters to:
    George Lane, Stoker 1 R.F.R,. Faltpost 800, Litto, Stockholm, 5.

It would be another nineteen months before George is reunited with his family. He was fortunate because many of his shipmate survivors, as you will read, had to wait a lot longer.

One family, as already mentioned finally received the confirmation they did not want. As reported in the Exeter, ***Express and Echo,*** dated 28th of May 1940.

ALPHINGTON MAN DIES OF WOUNDS

"News has been received by the widowed mother of Warrant Officer James Henry Coombe that he has died of wounds received while serving on HMS *Hunter* off Narvik on April 10th [...] His mother, Mrs. M. K. Coombe, resides at Shillingford Road, Alphington, and to her and her family the sympathy of many friends is extended in their bereavement."

Marshal Soult, "By June the weather had got really beautiful, sunny and hot. The men were now allowed out until 12 pm without a guard, and much time was spent at the lake; fishing, swimming and boating. Nearby was a little general store and a café; where they would have coffee and cakes, in between their various hobbies at the lakeside. They were also allowed to attend the local church, and enjoyed the service; especially as one Swedish person took the service in both Swedish and English. The village hall had such a peaceful atmosphere, the people were so friendly they invited the men into their homes. The scars of war were healing very quickly; and the food and good weather soon restored the men to good health".

John Hague, looking back at his time in Gunnarn, believes the local community "kept themselves to themselves at first until they became used to us, then most became friendly". John, in his opinion, felt they were 'mixed' as to which side they supported in the war. "Some sympathised with us and others saw us as a threat. But on the whole, they were friendly and helpful. They could not believe these mad Englishmen diving off a bridge into the water, but they soon joined in."

Apparently, the 'bridge diving' by the towns' youngsters, continued well into the future.

By now the sailors, especially the young and unattached, were well settled into their new environment. They could be forgiven, for momentarily, putting to one side their traumatic experiences in April and the ongoing war. Marshal goes on to relive those lovely innocent times, once more as the third person. "At the dances in the village we were warmly welcomed, especially by the girls, and quite a few romances blossomed out. At one dance the men introduced the 'Valeta'. When the band started playing 'Daisy, Daisy', it caught on and became all the rage in the area. Soon they were borrowing cycles and went on trips to other villages to attend dances with their young Swedish friends.

"Although the prisoners were leading a relatively idyllic life of comparative freedom in a safe community, they still had a yearning desire for home. They listened every evening to the six o'clock news from the BBC. This was their link with home, and their only source of information about what was happening in the war. They were very sad to hear during one of these broadcasts of the loss of the HMS *Ardent* which had been commanded by Lt. Commander Barker, a former First Lieutenant of *Hunter*: later they were to learn that he had lost his life".

HMS Hunter survivors with their Swedish cooking staff
at Gunnarn. [John Hague Family Collection]

The survivors, whilst feeling secure and readily accepted in their new environment, would have been made aware of the ongoing situation in the war against their foe. Especially, between 27th May and 4th June 1940, when large numbers of Belgian, British, and French troops were cut off and surrounded by the German army. In a speech to the House of Commons, Prime Minister Winston Churchill called the events in France "a colossal military disaster", saying "the whole root and core and brain of the British Army had been stranded at Dunkirk and seemed about to perish or be captured".

This had led to the Dunkirk evacuation, code-named Operation Dynamo, an attempt to return the Allied soldiers from the beaches and harbour of Dunkirk in France back to the English coast by any means. Throughout all the welcome frivolities in Gunnarn, the survivors would have been anxious for news. In Churchill's speech ["We will fight on the beaches"] on 4 June, he hailed their rescue as a "miracle of deliverance".

In 1990 for the 50th Anniversary of the 'Battle of Narvik', there was a memorial service at the graves of the men from *Hardy* and *Hunter*. The then Secretary of State for Defence, Tom King, gave a speech in which he acknowledged the fact that there may not have been an evacuation, if the ten German destroyers had not been sunk at Narvik.

However, what the survivors did not know until fifty years later was that some of their HMS *Hardy* comrades who had also lost their ship a month before, had quickly been returned to active service. One of those was Stoker First Class Harry Rogers, twenty-three years old, from Redcar. Although he had suffered a shrapnel wound at Narvik, because it was lodged close to his heart it was decided not to remove the piece. Subsequently, he was still deemed fit to continue his naval duties. The rest of Harry Rogers' amazing story is in my first book. Most sailors in the Royal Navy have a nickname, it would not surprise me if Harry was known as 'Houdini' after the famous escapologist.

Time to Move on

The Norton Diary:

Mon 3rd June   *A Major visited camp, informed us a mistake had been made, Norwegians leaving camp and not us. All very disappointed.*

Thurs 6th   *Finished working in the kitchen. started helping farmer.*

Fri 7th   *Still with farmer, felling and cutting trees. Heard about Capt getting VC. Bad award, strong comments by men at the camp.*

Fri 13th   *Captain Raynor from Stockholm came to see us, no hope of getting home just yet, arranged for telegram to our people, by the Admiralty, and asked for reply to be sent to us. 26 Norwegian women and children arrived at our camp.*

Sat 16th   *Captain came again, weather glorious.*

Sun 17th   *4 letters arrived from England. Heard in letter of Stewart getting DSM. 22 of us had bikes, rode out to football match with football team to Askville, 9 miles away. Very good time, won 5-0 arrived back at camp 6 pm.*

Mon 24th   *No news yet, change in the weather in last few days. Not much change in the conditions*

Tues 2nd July   *Received two letters from home.*

As mentioned by Thomas Norton in early May, the Consulate had led the survivors to believe they were not now to be considered as 'Internees'. That the change in status would result in their freedom and allow them an early return back to Britain. So obviously the news of the mistake must have left them very despondent. Whilst these were the last notes put into the diary, Thomas Norton has a lot more interesting experiences as you will read.

Here is also the end of Captain Nicholas' Diary, in which as expected, now that he and his fellow marchers are finally feeling more secure, the entries have become increasingly sporadic. However, it is not all good news.

Wed 1st May.
We now have coffee and biscuits at 8.30 am. Which helps to pass the morning, the rest of our meals are dinner at 11.30 am. And tea at 5.00 pm. The river which runs through 'Jorn' was frozen solid when we arrived and the place covered with snow.

But the snow is disappearing quickly and the river is melting. We are having very decent weather. I am able to walk about again but to go easy.

Thurs 2 May 40 – 11th May 40. LOUISE (DAUGHTER) BORN 7TH MAY 40
The days pass away much alike. On the whole we have decent weather and the men are quickly getting well. Quite a number of men have been doing odd jobs for the local people and earning a few kronas. This helps them towards smokes etc.

Sat 11 May 40.
The other 3 Captains and myself were guests at dinner at the Hotel of Ryllthen [looks like]. Then we went to the village to see the dancing. After that we came back to our new billets. The three Captains and myself are now living at the 'Pensionat'. At least we sleep there on camp beds which are a treat after the straw mattresses on the floor. We still have our meals at the cinema.

8th to 10th June.
British Consul visited us and goods distributed to needy ones in crew. Heard of evacuation of Norway and Italy's coming into war, and expect this means we are here for the duration.

Similar to the *Hunter* crew there are clearly problems making arrangements for them to be repatriated back to Britain. If the Swedish authorities are not prepared to breach their neutrality by allowing non-combatant seamen the means to leave, what chance have the sailors from HMS *Hunter*.

Captain David Nicholas was liked and respected by his crew and the other men sharing their captivity. He appeared to be an 'Uncle' figure to them, calm and trustworthy, to the point that the men felt if anyone would be able to free them of their predicament it would be him.

David Nicholas was born in Holyhead, Anglesey, a major port since the early nineteenth century when Thomas Telford built a new road to connect North Wales with London. He met his wife ... in South Shields, where she was born, they had three children, Louise, David and Eveline. The family moved to Hexham, thirty-five miles inland.

Prior to the war, having been with the Runciman, Walter and Sons Company for a number of years, David had been given a prize job of being the 'Skipper' of the Lord Runciman's private yacht moored in Southampton. As you have read in his diary, his daughter Louise was born in May 1940. Here Louise mentions a very important day in her life. "Unfortunately, I can't say the exact date of his return though I remember meeting him at Newcastle Central Railway station and sitting on his knee on the train to Hexham which is where we lived (too much destruction in Southampton). At Hexham we got a taxi home [unheard of before!!] I then ran to tell a neighbour, Mrs Silk, "I do have a Daddy and if you don't believe me come and see him." This was the summer of 1945 after VE Day.

Granddaughter, Margaret MacDonald, informs, "My grandad died in 1967, never mentioning what he had been involved in. We believed that he had been in a camp in Sweden for the full duration of the war. So thank you for letting me know another side to the story."

There was another crewmember on M/V's *Blythmoor*, Deck Officer Charles Boylan. Charles went through the same experience at Narvik as that of his Captain. However, later on he became involved in the secret operation of assisting a Norwegian cargo vessel *John Bakke* to breach a blockade and managing to get the vessel to Britain. You will read more about this secret operation later.

Charles went on to become an officer on another merchant navy vessel which was also sunk. Here his son Chris describes the after effect on his father during the war. "My father suffered from malaria for the rest of his life. The war drained him both physically and mentally to the extent that through health problems he left the Merchant Navy. To help his recovery he took on the task as an instructor on HMS Calliope at Newcastle. Subsequently, in 1943-44 he became a lecturer at South Shields Marine

School, later known as South Shields Marine and Technical College. He eventually rose to Head of Department for Radar and Navigation. He retired in 1978. He would not talk about his war experiences, unless he felt like it, and that was the way he remained."

A proud Chris Boylan says, "Afterwards, my Dad was awarded the MBE and later he was invested with the St Olaf's Medal with Oak Leaves by King Haakon for services rendered to Norway."

It was now three months since the *Hunter's* crewmen's ordeal of surviving the demise of their ship and more importantly the tragic loss of so many of their comrades in the deep cold Norwegian fjord. Even now families were still having to accept that their loved ones would not be coming home. One family was that of Petty Officer Stoker Dick Ryman, but for the war he would now be seven months into his retirement putting his skills to use with a civilian company.

Jayne Ryman, the granddaughter Dick would never see, on behalf of the family relates some of their memories. "[...] local families appeared in regional newspapers, such as the *Banbury Advertiser* [...] Wednesday, 17th April it reports that an Adderbury man is "missing, believed drowned". A letter from the Admiralty dated 18th April leads wife Lily to believe there is still hope and she is moved to write [...] for them to correct the article. Although the letter from Devonport states, "very unlikely that there are any survivors of the loss of HMS *Hunter* [...] there is, however, a possibility, that a small number were taken prisoner by the enemy."

On the 2nd May the Rear Admiral writes from Devonport Naval Barracks, quoting unconfirmed information [...] that two officers and forty-four ratings of HMS *Hunter* have arrived at a town in North Sweden. It was not until the arrival of a final letter dated 25th July [...] that Lily received the confirmation which by this time she must have been expecting; it was officially presumed that Dick had lost his life on active service".

"Please allow me to express sincere sympathy with you in your bereavement on behalf of the officers and men of the Royal Navy, the high traditions of which your husband has helped to maintain."

Perhaps here Jayne's sentiments show how the men who lost their lives were never forgotten by their families over the following years. "Although my grandfather died more than twenty years before my birth, he was always alive to me. Gran Lily's living room was almost a shrine to her beloved husband. There were two photos of him looking handsome, dressed in naval uniform [...] a brown leather frame, which always had [...] a poppy tucked into the right-hand corner, stood on the tiled mantelpiece. Hanging on the wall, the framed scroll from the King stated that 'Stoker Petty Officer Richard David Sutton Ryman fought for King and Country to save mankind from tyranny'. I knew those words off by heart."

Marshal, "When the Battle of Britain [July 1940] started, it became very distressing to the *Hunter* men to listen to news of the air raids on their country. Not knowing how their relatives were faring in the air raids; wondering if they would ever see them again. It tended to depress them because there was nothing they could do but hope for the best".

In 2012, from a source in Sweden, I received a copy of a message sent from the British Legation to the Swedish Authorities requesting six of the *Hunter* survivors to be allowed to leave Gunnarn for employment purposes with the Legation in Stockholm. The names put forward were Rex Brown, Norman Bowden, Thomas Norton, Thomas King, Will Barrett, Jack Hiscock and Albert (Andrew) Black. It remains a mystery to this day as to why these six were recommended above the rest of the survivors.

I did discover from another source, that there were at least fifteen given an opportunity to escape directly back to Britain. The route would be conducted under clandestine circumstances.

Surprisingly, for both the survivors and probably the British Legation staff, permission was granted. I have a copy of the telegram dated 17th July 1940 sent from the Swedish Military Department to the *'Chefen for Internierungslager'*. (Chief Officer for Internees) in Gunnarn which shows them to be allowed to travel. This improved the lifestyle for such crewmen as Thomas Norton and Norman Bowden. It also gave them some hope of an early return home.

Thomas Norton had been approved for a 'drivers' job in Stockholm, this is possibly because of his previous driving experience with the Post Office in Manchester. However, in anticipation of the move, the men had two priorities. Firstly, they had to say goodbye to their friends, such as 'Yank', some of whom had been employed on his farm. The second priority for those leaving was arranging a 'farewell party', which apparently went on until 4 am resulting in the men having "terrible bad heads".

Unfortunately, there was a delay in the men's departure, so work carried on as normal, until 16th July when they were told they were to leave the following day. "So there was another farewell party and sing-song." Finally, they left Gunnarn for Stockholm, with a good send off by some of the ladies who had initially attended to them when they first had arrived on Swedish soil. On arrival, they were met by Lieutenant Gibson Harris RNVR, and taken by taxi to the British Legation.

The six sailors were dispersed between various members of the local British community in Stockholm. I can confirm that Norton and Bowden were provided with accommodation by a British couple Mr and Mrs Waring at their bungalow. The next morning the men (presumably all six) attended an interview with Captain Denham the Naval Attaché, which was positive, after which they were permitted to go shopping.

Marshal Soult describes the emotional moment, when the time came for the remaining survivors to leave Gunnarn, albeit probably against most of the sailors' wishes. "One day in August, the men were informed that they would be leaving Gunnarn, to go to a prepared internment camp further south. On the day of departure all of the people in the village assembled at the railway station to see them off. The scene was very touching, with sad farewells being exchanged all round. Before the train rolled out the British and Swedish national anthems were sung, a last handshake, a burst of hand clapping, and away went the train carrying the British sailors. Away from the wonderful friendly people who had done so much to ease the burden of captivity.

Send off at Gunnarn Train Station. [John Hague Family Collection]

"On arrival at the new camp which was near a place called 'Bollnas', the *Hunter* men were surprised to find themselves once more in the company of the Merchant Navy men, who had shared their prison quarters in Narvik. Both groups exchanged details of experiences undergone in the few months since their last meeting."

Next Internment Camp at Langmora, Sweden.

Whilst my book at this point is focused on the *Hunter* survivors' internment, I am conscious that other than Captain Nicholas of *Blythmoor* writing in his diary, the crew members of the merchant vessels were also in a position of uncertainty about their own future prospects. They too had a brave part to play the in the Battles of Narvik. Therefore I felt it important that two of the seamen's accounts should be told.

Prior to and after the First Battle at Narvik. RC Sheriff was a crew member on the *Mersington Court*. "Our ship was torpedoed at Narvik and we were taken prisoner by the Germans. When our troops broke their defences the Germans realised we were an embarrassment to them. They marched us thirty miles over mountainous country and bundled us over the Swedish frontier."

W.H. Martin, then aged 25 from Grangetown, Cardiff was an Acting Third Mate. He describes the demise of his ship at Narvik. "My ship the

8,000-ton Cardiff steamer *Romanby* was berthed in Narvik harbour when the Germans invaded Norway. It like other British ships was sunk by the Germans to block the harbour. On the march to Sweden, we had to go through blizzards, living on hard biscuits and at times up to our chests in snow drifts. The German guards covered us with their rifles all the way."

Back to the *Hunter* survivors' adventures and their attempts to improve their lifestyles. In Sweden, during the war there were three camps in the neighbourhood of 'Bollnas', which is just outside the city of Sunnerstaholm. One was for German and Norwegian sympathisers. Between, 1942 to 1945 Regnsjo was for civilian foreigners and Hälsingmo was where the British were kept. The distance from Bollnas to Stockholm is 200 km and from Stockholm to Gunnarn is 770 km.

'Stormy' Renshaw describes how he manages to get on at the next camp. "The next move was that the church authority decided we had been there long enough. It was a brand-new church, it wasn't blessed or anything. We had to go to a camp down in Hälsingmo, which is another prison camp. Now there, I met up with a young lady, a headmistress of a local school who wished to learn English. Now, some of the features of this cooperation were quite unique. I was taken in, and the family that took me in, clothed and fed me to a standard that was way above that which my shipmates were receiving."

In the meantime, the six *Hunter* survivors were managing to reintegrate themselves in 'City' life in Stockholm. During July 1940, they were provided with other unexpected privileges, including sightseeing trips and to quote, "We went to the pictures, two Kroners and seven Ores to see *Balalaika*, starring Nelson Eddy and Jeanette MacDonald." Thomas Norton became the driver for Captain Denham, as well as looking after the Captain's yacht. They were invited to a reception at the French Legation and visited an English rector and his wife for tea at their home. On each occasion they were well received by their hosts.

It appears families at home were still receiving news of their sons or fathers to confirm they had lost their lives. Here the **Dover Express** on 9th of August 1940 reports:

"Mrs Day, of Clarendon Street, now evacuated to Kettering, writes that her son, Signalman Edward Day, has been officially presumed killed in action whilst serving on HMS *Hunter* in the first Battle of Narvik on the 10th April 1940. It will be remembered that Signalman E. B. Day was a survivor of the *Courageous*."

By August 1940, Thomas Norton's efforts having worked diligently for his employer, including making repairs to his yacht, earned him perks by allowing him to accompany Captain Denham on sailing trips. On another occasion, some of the men were given a 'special film show' of the Gaumont Pathé newsreel of the Battle of Narvik. Shortly after for whatever reasons, Jack Hiscock and Albert Black had to return to the camp at Bollnas. No doubt they were given a good send off by their fellow shipmates.

During this period the remainder of the men were able to enjoy the night life in Stockholm, although they found some of the establishment's 'low dives'. Not all went well, Norton, whilst removing a spirit stove at his accommodation, badly burnt his hand which required regular hospital treatment. He found the hospital "Lovely and clean, all spoke English." On his recovery, he was reappointed to the position of 'Full Valet' to Captain Denham.

This required Norton to do duties which would normally fall to a Royal Naval Steward's part of ship, although Denham was a relatively senior officer. It required him to start the day by making breakfast for his master, followed by general duties and serving at 'Lunch and Cocktail Parties'. From a Signalman to a temporary Naval Steward, Thomas Norton apparently did well in his new role. His proficient manner must have got around the British community quickly and it was not long before he had roped in Norman Bowden to assist him.

It appears that initially they took on a 'Cocktail' party for sixty which was recorded as 'successful'. This led to another success when their adoptive compatriots Mr and Mrs Waring left the full arrangements to Norton and his assistant Bowden. It is said that as usual at the end of these events lots of food and alcohol would be left over. Probably, in true naval fashion, little would be wasted, especially the alcohol and no doubt the leftovers would be made use of elsewhere to the satisfaction of the naval ratings.

About this time, Jack Hiscock returned to Stockholm with Norman Stewart DSM and Petty Officer Stoker 'Jake' Kerswell for a spell of leave. However, the three were well received by Norton and Bowden, who held a party in their honour, probably with the benefit of the above proceeds.

'Jake' Kerswell provides an account of his arrival at 'Bollnas' where he met a representative from the British Legation. "After five months in Gunnarn we were shifted to a camp in the South of Sweden where the Swedish government found us work at road making. On the 20th of September, a Captain who had looked after our interests asked if I would like to try to reach England; going through Russia, Turkey, Syria, Palestine and Egypt with three other ratings, posing as civilians. We all said we would try and were then sent to Stockholm to get passports and called at the different Legations to obtain necessary visas for the countries through which we had to travel."

The Captain mentioned above was probably Captain Denham the Naval Attaché. It appears the Captain Denham had a comfortable lifestyle during these early days of the war. However, in fact throughout the war he was very actively involved in not only befriending significant persons in Sweden but also in gathering secret information. All of which he communicated back to the Admiralty in London.

By now, Norton was issued with 'full dress' attire and continued providing apparent expertise in organising 'Dining In' evenings and cocktail parties. These included a Captain Achans, presumably a Swedish naval officer and a Mr Ross and his wife, a 'Second Secretary' at the British Legation. However, as the saying goes 'work hard, play hard' which seemed to be the case for those *Hunter* survivors spending their time in Stockholm. There were late nights out on the town, returning back to their abodes in the early hours. But no doubt in the back of their minds, frivolities were secondary to the need of eventually finding a way back to their real home.

Christmas 1940 was now approaching, it has been eight months since the *Hunter* men had survived the sinking of their ship. It would obviously have been an emotional time with thoughts of home, particularly for those married with children. At least by now their families would have known that they were alive and, through the Red Cross, they were able to receive parcels of food and other necessary items. Survivor Pat Duffy's son, Patrick, was then aged three; he remembers that with his other brothers and sisters he helped their mother, pack the parcels with homemade treats. There would also have been ongoing contact and assistance offered by the British Legation in Stockholm for the men.

Let us now return to the young sailor representing the Royal Navy, 'Stormy' Renshaw, to see how he fared with his adopters. This was probably better than he had expected. "I was accepted into the family. The reason being, that whilst we in England had turkey for Christmas, they in Sweden purchased a suckling pig. A huge van comes round, selling these suckling pigs, and the pigs are fed on table scraps until Christmas. Come Christmas, it gets the chop!

"They were all leaning over the sty where the pig is kept and the owner of the pig was crying his eyes out. 'The pig is dying, pig is dying,' was all I could get out of him. The pig was over here, then over there, and it was shivering and they couldn't figure out why. I found the answer, I shoved my hand into the straw and found that it was wet. So, we took out the wet straw and replaced it with dry straw, in goes the pig and there goes another medal for me. I was the hero of the village at the time. I was beginning to learn how to ski and all those things rich people do. I was becoming a local figure, in so much as when we had our next move to a nearer camp, I was taken away for a holiday back to the first camp."

In the meantime, volunteers were requested to man Norwegian cargo ships moored in Gothenburg, one of the volunteers had been 'Jake' Kerswell. Maybe, that because of the long delays in carrying through the Gothenburg option, and given the chance to go home sooner, he quickly accepted an alternative escape offer. I can only presume that Jake being a Petty Officer Stoker was one of the first chosen because he was an experienced senior rating possessing trained skills that were much needed back home.

By now, Kerswell had been to Stockholm and visited the foreign Legations to receive the necessary visas for the alternative option. Understandably Jake was possibly feeling apprehensive about the impending venture, travelling around Eastern Europe and the Mediterranean. He indicates that he was accompanied by others. These may have been Able Seaman Norman Stewart and Stoker Jack Hiscock who you will remember came to Stockholm in September, possibly also to collect visas.

Jake describes his long journey to freedom but does not mention his co-travellers. It is unfortunate that later in life he had not added these to his account. *"All was ready for us to leave Sweden on the 25th of September and on Friday the 26th at 0800 we left Stockholm by plane for Moscow, arriving at 1830 that night. The trip was very good. At 2340 that night we left Moscow by train for Odessa where we arrived at 1600 on the 28th after a very uncomfortable trip in a train, the state of which was beyond description. We stayed in Odessa for twenty-four hours and were taken for a tour around Odessa, but the only thing we were shown were a lot of new schools. Everything else we saw was dirty and in a poor state of repair, which seemed to be the same everywhere on our journey through Russia.*

402

"The trip from Odessa to Istanbul was very good, we stopped at Varna [Bulgaria] where we saw troops being embarked in a transport. We arrived at Istanbul on the 1st of November, leaving for [document unreadable] on the 3rd and arriving on the 4th. Here we went on board a Polish refugee ship where we stayed for a week before arriving at Haifa on the 12th of November. We arrived at Alexandria at 0530 on the 13th of November. We left Alexandria on the 21st of November on HMS Ramilles. *The warship called at Crete, Malta and finally Gibraltar, arriving on the 28th of November".*

It appears the only eventful moment of the voyage was when Jake and may be the other crew members, met part of the Italian navy. Jake says, "They immediately turned away and ran to their nearest port. I left the *Ramilles* for the Gibraltar base and became an armed guard on a French ship. On the 8th of December I saw the maintenance Commander of the base, to find out my chances of getting to England. After explaining my case to him, he said he would get me away as soon as possible. On 9th December [1940] I left the base to join HMS *Deptford* for passage to UK. Arriving in a British port safely with a convoy of ten ships on Christmas Eve".

Not only for Jake but also for his wife Gladys and their children, this was the long-awaited end to a dramatic eight months. During which Gladys had initially had to endure formal letters from the Admiralty, first stating that Jake was 'Missing Presumed Dead' and later confirming that he had been 'Killed in Action'. Then finally, being told that he was a captive in Sweden

But given no indication as to when he would be home.

Within a month of completion of 'survivors' leave' Jake was drafted to the Coastal Service vessel HMS *Skirmisher*. He was promoted from Acting to Petty Officer Stoker in June 1941. Probably because of the form he had signed on the orders of the Germans, 'Not to take up active service [...]' he was discharged from the Navy two years later. Happily, this would have coincided with his pensionable time served which was his original intention for signing up for a second engagement. Something he must have thought was never going to happen, once the war started.

Returning back to Marshal and his own apparent frustrations to escape from captivity. "It was whilst in this camp that some of the *Hunter* men volunteered to sail to England in some Norwegian ships which had been held in Swedish ports. All these ships were filled with cargoes of essential war materials. If they could be taken through the German blockade in the 'Skagerrak' and safely across the North Sea, it would be a wonderful feat.

"The Swedish authorities relaxed the restrictions for the Royal Navy prisoners, allowing them to take jobs; two of us went to Stockholm and were attached to the press department of the British Legation. In November we returned to the camp at Bollnas to await the results of our applications for visas." On December the 27th they were issued with passports and allowed to apply for visas. This they did for the following countries: Sweden, USSR, Turkey, Syria, Palestine and Egypt."

The other Able Seaman who Marshal refers to as working with him at the British Legation was Fred Butcher. It appears that during this time the Swedish officer in charge of the camp would issue visas to one or two of the sailors each week. This implies that to some extent the Swedish authorities were colluding by assisting the naval men to make good their escape back to Britain. They were also given inoculations in preparation for their trip. Subsequently, Marshal and presumably Fred Butcher, were cleared to go to Stockholm to receive passports and visas. However, for whatever reason the two men did not depart together.

It was fortunate that Marshal's family had kept a copy of his account. This part, Marshal had decided to call, 'My Journey Home' which his devoted wife Kay had hand written for him.

On the 12.12.1940 I went by bus to Stockholm Airport at 6.30 am I was seen off by Jimmie Watson and boarded a Russian Air Liner. It was a freezing day and I found that all the plane windows were frozen over. The engine started and the plane began to warm up, so I decided to clear the ice from my window in order to see the take off. This was so smooth that by the time I had cleared a patch the plane was about 2000 feet above Stockholm – and I was unaware that we had even left the ground. Our first stop was at Riga in Latvia where we refuelled. We then proceeded to Velikije Luki where we refuelled again and the next stop was Moscow Airport.

Here I was met by a Thomas Cook Agent, a short stocky Russian who spoke with an American accent. We went by taxi to the Hotel Metropole in Moscow along a road which I especially recall as it was dead straight. I enjoyed a splendid dinner at the hotel: A generous helping of caviar, soup, meat and a wonderful ice cream. This was followed by coffee, pastries and vodka, splendid by most standards, but after Narvik, doubly so. A twenty-piece orchestra churned out classical music (not exactly my cup of tea), as I feasted. After dinner I walked inevitably around the Red Square, I saw St Basil's Cathedral. It was so vast that it made me feel even more alone than I was.

I left Moscow at midnight on the train, travelling 'Soft Class' (the other was 'Hard Class'). The compartment was altogether bigger and grandiose in style than its British equivalent. It was furnished ornately and the whole effect was one of faded grandeur. Each compartment accommodated four passengers and at night was converted into four bunks. The padded backs of each side were swung up to form two bunks, whilst the seats formed the other two. Sheets, blankets, quilts and pillows were provided so it was very comfortable. Each carriage was looked after by a male and female attendant.

My travelling companions were a Russian Army Officer, a black-uniformed Commissar and a civilian whom I suspect was an Italian; but not a word was spoken throughout the journey. Two's 'King's Messengers' and their escorts were in the same carriage so I was able to talk to them, and I did so from time to time in the corridor. We travelled through that night, all next day and night and the next day until 6 pm, about 42 hours in all. A large hamper of food had been supplied to me by the hotel, whilst tea and beer were available on the train. A thick blanket of snow covered the countryside and it was bitterly cold.

14.12.40
Finally, I reached Odessa where I stayed in a hotel which must have been very grand in its day.

My bedroom had a private bathroom but no hot water- this was carried up in pails! I left Odessa next day in a Russian steamer. It was still bitterly cold and we sailed to Varna in Bulgaria and then on to Istanbul arriving here on the 18.12.40. On this steamer there were 40 German Jewish children, their ages ranging from 6 months to 17 years. They had been in a Refugee Camp in Finland and were going to Palestine. I remember playing chess with one young lad – his parents were still in Germany and he and his sister could speak good English.

I disembarked at Istanbul and went to the British Embassy where I saw the Naval Attaché'. Here I was told of a change of plans, instead of travelling by train through Syria and Palestine, leaving Haifa by boat for Port Said, I was offered a passage on SS Mandalay, *a British Merchant ship to Port Said, Itself. This proved a most enjoyable trip. There was a 'Lascar' crew and the officers were mostly Scots, who made me exceptionally welcome during the month I spent with them.*

After leaving Istanbul we called at Smyrna, Piraeus the port of Athens and then went on to Port Said. The food was excellent and the two things that stick in my memory were enjoying a different curry dish each day and delicious rice cakes covered with syrup, served at breakfast. I spent a wonderful Christmas with my Mandalay friends. Hogmanay was celebrated as only Scots know how.

We arrived in Port Said on 18.1.41. A launch with a Royal Marine on board came and escorted me from the ship, then took me to a hotel. The Captain of the Mandalay put in a request that I should return to England on the Mandalay (I was helping the gun's crew, so he found me useful). I would have liked this but the request was refused as the orders were to get me home as soon as possible. I stayed in Port Said three weeks waiting for transport. This was pleasant as I was able to meet my friends from the Mandalay and enjoyed sight-seeing. During my stay I was interviewed by an Intelligence Officer who proved to be Lieutenant Commander Astor, a son of Lady Astor.

I finally left Port Said on a Dutch liner, the Christian Huygens, carrying troops. The Mediterranean Sea was closed to all except essential traffic, after the sinking of the cruiser 'Southampton'. So we had to go via the Suez Canal to the Red Sea. Half way down we had to tie up for three days because German planes had dropped mines in the canal. During this time we saw a small mine-sweeping launch blown to pieces about 100 yards from our ship.

We proceeded to Aden, then to Mombasa and on to Durban. The ship docked here for three weeks for repairs. Here I stayed with Mr and Mrs Ramsay. She was secretary of the Navy League and their son was serving in England in the British Navy.

Whilst there I was invited by our Captain's mother-in-law to her home for dinner. [Lieutenant Commander Lindsay De Villiers went down with Hunter.] I met his father who was a doctor serving on Army troop ships. I also met the Captain's five-year-old son.

We left Durban, called at Cape Town and then joined in a convoy en route for England. The SS Mandalay was in the next column, so I had saved no time! Other than a few U-boat scares the voyage was uneventful and we arrived safely at Liverpool.

I travelled by train to Plymouth, arriving on the night of 24.4.1941 to find that Plymouth had just endured three nights of Blitz. A car met me and took me to Devonport Barracks. Normally a fifteen-minute journey, this little trip took nearly two hours spent avoiding unexploded bombs, exploding bombs, diversions and sealed off streets. After an uneasy night in Barracks, next morning I went *through the Doctor and Dentist routine. I was then told that all leave had been cancelled owing to the Blitz but I was granted survivors leave. I was instructed to get a new uniform and these were being issued in the gymnasium.*

The P.O.'s Block (Petty Officer's accommodation building) had received a direct hit in a previous night's Blitz, and I was horrified on entering the Gymnasium to see rows of coffins – about 90 P.O.s had been killed. There were also large numbers of C.P.O.s and P.O.s all waiting hopefully to be kitted out. Some were clad only in pyjamas and others in various states of undress. Realising that their need was greater than mine and that I had little hope of being issued with uniform, I requested to see Commander Harry R.N.B. (Executive Officer Royal Naval Barracks) I was taken before him and asked permission to proceed on leave in civilian clothes. He asked the name of my ship, as soon as I mentioned Hunter *he said, "Permission certainly granted and see that this man gets on leave as soon as possible".*

After a week I was to apply to him and he promised to see about the rest of my leave.

Accordingly, I set out from St Budeaux Station on the last leg of my long journey and arrived, thankfully at my parent's home in Falmouth on 25.4.1941. My trip had taken four and half months". [86] [87]

Jake Kerswell and Marshal Soult have now safely reached home. As recorded in the *Hunter Story*, in the conclusion, Marshal gives an emotional response to his experiences during the previous year. "I realised that my period of

---

86   Lascars were seamen from the Indian subcontinent, mainly Bengal, who served on British ships under what was called 'Lascar Agreements'. This allowed ship owners to employ the sailors under normal agreed service contracts. It meant the seamen could be transferred from ship to ship and retain their service up to three years. At the end of World War One there were 50,000 Lascars living in Britain.

87   Thomas Cook is now a large and popular travel agency most of us at some time will have used. But even in the 1930s the company had grown into an international concern from 1841 when the cabinet-maker Thomas Cook started the business. He began by organising railway trips for anti-alcohol campaigners for one shilling. The first for passengers from Leicester to Loughborough. In 1872 he was his own 'rep' leading a 222-day, 2500 mile overseas tour. In 1886 Thomas' son, John launched a fleet of luxury Nile steamers. So by the time the Second World War came they had offices in major cities around the world, very handy for Britain's war effort.

peaceful coexistence had ended; here once again was the war in all its ugliness. It brought back memories of the shambles on *Hunter* during the battle of Narvik. The dead and the dying, but this time it was civilians who could not hit back as the ships of the 2nd Destroyer Flotilla had done."

So, after a voyage of four and a half months, through three continents and over many oceans and seas; meeting hundreds of people, making many new found friends, Marshal Soult went home to his native town of Falmouth. Here he enjoyed a well-earned leave before continuing war service from which he was finally discharged in 1942.

Operation 'Rubble' – Escape Plans

John Hague, still only twenty years old, had spent most of his initial days in Sweden working on a farm. He explained to me that on moving to Bollnas, Chief Stoker David Moore, the most senior in rank was looking for volunteers. Word had got round that plans were being made to escape by commandeering five (impounded) Norwegian ships which had originally been bound for Britain. Their cargo was much needed war supplies and were now moored alongside in Gothenburg.

John Hague was one of the five ratings who had volunteered, along with Able Seamen 'Nellie' Hunter, 'Jonno' Johnson and 'Jock' Steel. They were left in no doubt that this was a life or death mission, as the German consulate was watching all shipping movements from the harbour closely. John said, "We wanted to make a bid for freedom and home so were prepared to go along with the plan."

Having received instructions, the volunteers waited for a suitable opportunity to become involved in the rightful return of the ships and an early opportunity to return back home.

As you will read shortly there was one of *Hunter*'s crew on the *Ranja* able to give his account. In the meantime, the mastermind behind the operation to crew up and get the ships away was George Binney. The plan was to be called 'Operation Rubble'. George who had been an adventurous person in his younger days, showed himself to be a natural organiser. In his time, as a student at Oxford University, he was known for arranging exploration projects to the Arctic. He also led the way to utilising seaplanes for surveying the Arctic regions. Having been employed by the Hudson Bay Company in the late 1920s, he then moved onto building up exports for a major steel company. At the outbreak of the war, now aged thirty-nine, it appears he was 'head hunted' by the Ministry of Supply, to work within the Iron and Steel Control department. His role included achieving contracts for purchasing necessary items, including machine tools, aircraft parts, steel, guns and steel ball bearings.

In 1940, George Binney was still in neutral Sweden working for the war effort at home. He either came up with the idea himself or it was introduced to him by somebody else higher up the chain of command, to crew up the stagnating Norwegian merchant ships and get them to Britain. He set himself about the task industriously with a determined and inspiring effort. It appears that another incentive was to make sure the cargoes did not eventually fall into German hands. This was a bold and daring move which could have gone drastically wrong.

Whilst the ships had crews on board, predominantly Norwegian, it seems they were not up to full complement. To complete the task there needed to be more reliable volunteers showing enthusiasm towards the planned objective. George Binney, being aware of the captured and interned Royal Navy and the Merchant seamen on his door step – albeit officially prisoners of war – covertly started his recruitment. The added bonus of the availability of the *Hunter*'s sailors was that they were not only trained for tight situations in confronting the enemy but also some had relevant engineering and weapon skills. The latter being a necessity should they become attacked by either air or sea.

It is worth noting here that George Binney's chances of finding reliable volunteers was hampered when the Vice Consulate at the Legation had become ill. It had been his task to secure a suitable team of Norwegian engineers to work on the chosen ships in Gothenburg harbour. However, Binney's luck changed when in his network of contacts, Captain Ivar Blucker, the Chief of the Gothenburg Harbour Police, agreed to offer his clandestine help. He eventually proved himself to be a clandestine supporter of the British war effort and as you can imagine, became a valuable asset to Binney.

As Chief of the Police, Blucker had the privilege of unlimited access within the port area with the power to inspect at will any suspicious items. He could also report back to Binney if he believed somebody was assisting the Germans. As a servant of the Swedish Government he was taking a significant risk by not strictly enforcing the neutrality within Swedish waters.

Blucker patrolled the port making sure the Germans were not making any attempts of sabotage and detailed his security team to guard the ships around the clock. There were also occasions when known Nazi agents were caught. These included two Swedish naval officers found providing information to the Germans, and eventually were given prison sentences.

It was important that Binney was able to have access to Swedish meteorological reports for the cargo vessels dash across the Skagerrak. Unfortunately, Binney was unable to find a way, but Blucker could. The well-placed Blucker was able to find a way to have access to weather reports and coordinate them with British reports to produce a detailed picture of the forthcoming weather.

Blucker even picked out a fjord he felt would prove to be a good hiding place for the ships before they made their dash across the Skagerrak. Making trips along the coast which were forbidden to foreigners and to confirm the weather was favourable for their operation. He even secretly sent a message to Britain, via Gothenburg, that the attempt was about to take place and the Royal Navy should be ready at the other end of the Skagerrak. To conclude his efforts, he cut the phone lines for long distance calls from Lysekil, so no news of the ships' departures from Gothenburg could be transmitted easily to the Germans.

Meanwhile, John Hague and his three shipmates were still waiting patiently for the nod that they were on their way. Finally on the 20th of January 1941 their moment came. At around 1400, the escape plan was put into action. Travelling down to the harbour in civvies, they boarded the ships. Even the weather was in the escapees' favour, as a heavy fog hung over the water and it was a moonless night. One of the cargo vessels sailed first, acting as a decoy, keeping close to the Swedish shore. This was the *Ranja*, John Hague's delegated ship. The other four then left Gothenburg harbour in turn.

As the ships were coming out of the Skagerrak they joined up with a German convoy by mistake. John Hague could see the German guns but fortunately they didn't open fire, probably because the ships were flying Norwegian flags. A ploy used by the German navy itself. Once the Germans realised that part of their convoy had turned and were sailing in a different direction from the main body, they began firing at the ships. They then had the Luftwaffe to contend with by strafing the decks and trying their best to blow the ships out of the water. As if this was not enough there were also minefields to negotiate.

When the minefields had been cleared, it was every ship for herself. John Hague's ship kept up a speed of ten knots, going flat out up until dawn. By then they had reached the North Sea; no one had had any rest and John and his comrades had been on duty for over twenty-four hours, before they sighted a British destroyer and were escorted home.

The **Manchester Evening Chronicle** dated Friday the 1st of December 1944 printed the story. This was nearly four years after the event, probably for security reasons, or to protect certain individuals involved in the 'Operation', as prior to that a lot of secret allied activity was going on in Sweden and Norway between 1940 and 1944, which included the involvement of the remaining *Hunter* survivors.

The headlines of the newspaper:

"Prisoners of War Stole Five Ships, Sailed Home".

Manned by escaped prisoners of war, five grey ships sailed into the Clyde from Sweden, laden with valuable war material. So ended one of the greatest sea adventures of the war. It happened nearly four years ago in January 1941. But the story of how 200 seamen, including 160 British stole these ships from under the noses of the Nazis could not be told until this morning [...]

Some of the sailors who brought the ships to Britain had fought in the first Battle of Narvik. Some of these said that after a drink in a hotel, in which the detailed plans were discussed they then sailed quite openly from Gothenburg [...]

Dornier aircraft circled for two hours over the ships, which were flying the Norwegian flag – a common dodge of the Nazis with captured ships. Off Denmark the convoy was sighted by four Messerschmitts, which made an attack. One bomb a near miss, fell near the decoy ship *Ranja*, wounding the Chief Mate".

Another crew member on *Ranga* was merchant seaman R.C. Sheriff: "She kept close to the Swedish shore in the Kattegat and then we made for the Norwegian coast on the Skagerrak. As we ploughed along we saw the German batteries on the coast, but they did not fire. Perhaps they thought we were E-Boats. Until dawn we kept up a good speed. Suddenly they began to realise that the ships were going the wrong way and in fact making for Britain." (Ends)

Another merchant seaman, W.H. Martin, recounts, "After sighting the British destroyers we made our way to the *Clyde* in thirty hours. We cheered every tug and tramp ship we saw until we were hoarse". Another sailor said, "Providence saved us from minefields, the enemy's bad shooting saved us from his bombs".

There was another survivor of the attack in Narvik harbour, Deck Officer Charles Boylan, a crew member on *Blythmoor*. Here his son Chris explains, "Unfortunately, my Dad did not keep a written record about being a POW at Narvik."

However, Charles also volunteered to participate in 'Operation Rubble' even though he had suffered from malaria since 1937. He was sent to the *John Baake* which on its voyage to Scotland had a similar experience to that of John Hague's ship the *Ranga*. After all these traumatic experiences, you would have thought he had had enough excitement for one war. However, later in the war on board a merchant steamer he experienced another confrontation with enemy resulting in having to abandon ship.

However, as previously mentioned in one of the earlier chapters David 'Jonno' Johnson's family member, Nigel Sefton had contacted me late in the day, to confirm David had accompanied John Hague on 'M/V Ranga'.

Returning back to other *Hunter* survivors, as mentioned by John Hague, regarding Guy Hunter, David Johnson and John Steel, I am uncertain as to whether Johnson or Steel finally took part in 'Operation Rubble'. But I can say for certain that Guy Hunter did not, as you will read later. Although I do know from the service papers of Jack Hiscock, that he was 'Released from Service' on 18th March 1941.

However, as previously mentioned in one of the earlier chapters David 'Jonno' Johnson's family member, Nigel Sefton had contacted me late in the day, to confirm David had accompanied Joh Hague on M/V Ranga'.

This confirms that Jack, probably accompanied Jake Kerwell, escaped via a trip around Europe. They were in the same Stokers branch and around the same age and probably teamed up together. Other than these records I have no further information about Jack but at least the 'veteran', having safely gone through the First World War, had also survived the Second. If he did accompany Jake then it is also a near certainty the brave and much younger Norman Stewart DSM went with them.

However, for those who did participate they received a telegram from the Admiralty; congratulating them on their "spirited and courageous conduct which enabled five merchant vessels to reach this country". John Hague for his involvement was subsequently awarded the British Empire Medal.

George Binney was now back in Britain and as you would imagine highly acclaimed by all he came into contact with, whether politicians or military. He was awarded a knighthood by King George VI. This led to him receiving a personal invite to Buckingham Palace. The King had been fascinated by Binney's adventures and requested to see the full report. Amongst other personal acts of bravery, the King had been touched by the story of the 'valiant' Ivar Blucker. Especially, because as the Chief of Police his involvement had to remain top secret until at least the end of the war.

The story goes that the King, deep in thought, asked Binney, "Would Mr Blucker accept a pair of cufflinks with the Royal Cypher in recognition of his actions?" Binney confirmed that without doubt Mr Blucker would be honoured. Quietly the King removed the cufflinks he was wearing and said, "I hope he will not mind a second-hand pair."

Moving away from the 'Blockade Busting' adventures for a moment to the whereabouts of Lieutenant (E) Alick Reid, I found a letter dated 18th March 1941 in a file at the National Archives titled 'Evaders and Escapers'. I finally got confirmation of the whereabouts of the now promoted to Lieutenant Commander (E) Alick Reid. As you have read he had been transported out of Narvik in a German plane and eventually arrived at an Officers POW Camp at Spangenberg Castle. Here is a letter written by his wife Gutun.

Returning back to other Hunter survivors, as mentioned by John Hague, regarding Guy Hunter and John Steel, I am uncertain as to whether Steel finally took part in 'Operation Rubble'. But I can say for certain that Guy Hunter did not, as you will read later. Although I do know from the service papers of Jack Hiscock, that he was 'Released from Service' on 18th March 1941.

However, as previously mentioned in one of the earlier chapters David 'Jonno' Johnson's family member, Nigel Sefton had contacted me late in the day, to confirm David had accompanied John Hague on 'M/V Ranga'.

> *Oakland Guest House, Waterlooville,*
> *Nr Portsmouth*
> *March 18th 1941*

Sir,

I beg to inform you that I have received a letter dated February 1st this year from my husband,

Lieutenant Commander (E) Alexander Gordon Reid RN, British POW No 1222,

saying he has been moved from Oflag IX A to Stalag X B, Marine Lagan, Germany.

> *Yours truly,*
>
> *Gutun Reid.*

To the Secretary of the Admiralty, Whitehall, London.

Oflag IX A in north eastern Hesse, Germany housed air force officers from Britain and France. The camp was closed in February 1941 this may have been because too many escapes were occurring. The POWs were sent to Stalag X B in lower Saxony which was divided into several sub-camps, one of which was Marinelager (Marlag) controlled by the Kriegsmarine holding British sailors, marines and officers. In the fall of 1941, this part of the camp was moved to Westertimke, which will be referred to later.

Stormy Renshaw, even after his 'claim to fame' within his closely 'knit' circle of Swedish friends, having just seen his shipmates leave, was now naturally wondering when it would be his turn. "I couldn't get home, there was no outlet. I was given a job of testing, by a firm called Trellyborne Gummy Fabriek which is Swedish for Trellyborne Rubber Factory.

"They'd invented a survival suit. Now this survival suit consists of a boiler suit in rubber, with gloves welded on, feet welded on and a double zip up the front, one in brass followed by another one that closed two rubber grommets together. I had to test these, so we blasted a hole in the ice, whilst we were alongside, and had the job of getting in and testing the suits. They were remarkably good, but extremely bulky, and they had a hood. When it came to personal use, you had to take your arm out of the sleeve; if you could get your arm out of the sleeve you could get it into your trouser pockets, and you'd have a kidney shape flask. [...] It was designed to facilitate urination.

"I finished up having to take six Lascars [Indian seamen] as passengers. Now of the six Lascars in that day, five would be workmen, one would be the boss man of the other five. He'd be collecting their wages and sharing out, and providing for their religious beliefs and all that. I had to train them how to put the suits on in an emergency."

Once Norway had become occupied by Germany, a lot of political and legal manoeuvres were initiated regarding the outcome of the stranded cargo vessels. This involved all parties with an obvious interest, including the Norwegians, Britons, Germans and of course Swedes. They were all, for various reasons, determined to have their way in getting control of the requisitioned ships. Some of the ships were considerable assets to their owners, especially the oil tankers. They contained valuable cargoes that had been in the process of being exported from Swedish industrial plants. The British, desperately needed them for the 'war effort', but the blockade meant they could not travel the usual routes.

Germany put a significant amount of pressure on the Norwegian ship owners. It appears their ploy to obtain control of the remaining ships on behalf of the Norwegians was for the Swedish Government to 'seize' the ships. However, the Swedish Government's view was that it had to go through the legal process in a court of law. With regards to the Norwegian ship owners' consent, it seems that at the time some of them were in prison, so it would appear that their signatures were obtained under threat.

The successful outcome of the 'Rubble' operation under the leadership of Sir George Binney, led to him planning another operation which became known as 'Operation Performance'. However, it did not take long before the Germans realised what was happening. Subsequently, they put more pressure on the Swedish Government, who for economic reasons did not want the Germans to halt their export trade. Equally they also needed to receive vital imported commodities and goods. I will come back to 'Operation Performance' shortly.

An Alternative Escape

I'd tried to account for the remaining *Hunter'* survivors' whereabouts, and to determine if they managed to get back to Britain, ascertaining their means of transport. It was then that Trevor Baker, living in Leamington Spa, contacted me. Trevor has an interest in World War Two aviation memorabilia, and in his collection he had purchased an interesting item, namely a 'Visitors Book'. Here Trevor explains, "The book was kept in the officer's mess at RAF Leuchars between 1938 and 1966. It contained approximately 3,500 signatures, many of which are from people who were flown from 'Bromma Airport' in Stockholm".

As a result of my correspondence with Trevor this led to contacting Bob Pearson, a schoolmaster living in Suffolk. Bob had already written one book [*Red Gullet*] and was in the course of writing another. His subject matter concerned espionage activity during World War Two in Norway and Sweden. During ongoing research for his next book, he found various memorandums in the Special Operations Executive file reference HS2-257 'Operation Airplane History of the Stockholm–Scotland Air Service'.

These memorandums were sent from the British Legation in Stockholm to the relevant Ministries in London. The first, dated the 21st of June 1940, related to the concerns raised about the wartime Air Service between Bromma and Leuchars.

To summarise, the memorandum discussing the 'canny attitude' of the commercial pilots stationed in Stockholm appeared to be the overriding issue. Such 'peacetime prejudice' (mainly in regards to air safety measures) caused clashes between the martial expectancies of the British Legation and actual practice. One of the main 'margins of safety' which caused dispute was the inclusion of – quite unnecessary and extremely heavy – parachutes during flights back to Britain.

The author of the correspondence is quick to point out that "there appears to be no real effort to economise in the gear varied on the machine to enable the maximum account of freight to be carried"; as such, valuable freight capacity was being wasted on redundant safety measures. Indeed, "neither the crew nor the passengers wear the parachutes, nor would there be any advantage in their doing so, as the machine would only be attacked over the sea." This leads the author to give the somewhat damning conclusion that the current system "lacks DRIVE commensurate with the needs of the War effort".

This would confirm why there had been delays in arranging for the *Hunter* survivors to be repatriated back to Britain by this route. Although, there were other reasons for the delays.

The second was an appendix to the minutes recorded in a meeting at the Air Ministry dated the 24th of August 1942. This appendix provided a list of the groups or individuals waiting for repatriation or travelling en route elsewhere. Including, 'Fighting' French, Soviet Technicians, Polish, Dutch, and Czechoslovakians – I presume also 'fighting'? However, what was also interesting, that on the list were fifteen "Ratings from HMS *Hunter*".

The third memorandum was dated the 28th of September 1942, once more, to summarise, it was much the same as the memorandum of 1941; there appear to be 'fundamental' issues in regards to the inefficiency of flights between the UK and Sweden. Dubbed by the local populace as "a mere 'fleabite' in the vast scheme of air operations", the Stockholm Air Service's shortfalls appear to stem from the "very inadequate number of planes operating and the almost total absence of suitable machines". In turn, an extensive list of groups of individuals is provided, evidencing those who were still waiting to be repatriated, with some having been waiting for as long as two and a half years.

Much of this problem stemmed from the fact that the aircraft were not only few in numbers, but unable to carry a substantial number of passengers (only four at a time), and not during the autumn and winter months. In order to reinforce the severity of 'this travesty of Air Service', the author states that, "If the situation cannot be resolved quickly, it would be valuable to bring it to the attention of the Prime Minister: It may seem of lesser import in a world war but it is undoubtedly vital to the war effort." Undoubtedly, the inadequacies of the Stockholm Air Service were having wider, detrimental effects by this date. (All three memorandums are condensed versions.)

According to Trevor Baker's 'Visitors Book', in the first batch from *Hunter* to travel, the first name on the list was Thomas Norton. Also, that the flight log showed that his fellow passengers were a number of British Foreign Office officials, Swedish and Norwegian Legation staff in London and including a name you will recognise, that of Captain Denham RN, the Naval Attaché. So Signalman Thomas Norton was amongst some high level travellers for company.

Between September 1941 and March 1942, there was additional correspondence between the British Government and their Legation in Stockholm. The list of British citizens awaiting possible flights back home was growing. The Foreign Office approved a proposal for a 'Repatriation Scheme', but wanted priority given to the *Hunter* crewmen first, and then the merchant seamen.

However, a telegram to the Legation states,

"I have asked the Air Ministry to do all they can to assist but have reason to fear that the demands on cargo space may make it extremely difficult to provide anything like adequate passenger accommodation."

The requests for flights over the following months increased. Some of these were foreign nationals and their wives. The British Legation representative replies, "[...] I had no intention of recommending her for a seat in priority over fighting Englishmen [...] I really begin to see red on this subject. Why does His Majesty's Government do nothing [...] why don't they realise that one good Briton is worth two foreigners?"

Finally, there remained concerns over the growing numbers waiting for potential flights to Britain. "[...] When, I say that we can do no more than scratch the surface of this problem by means of the Air Service, I have in mind the 3,000 Norwegian refugees in Sweden [...]"

With regards to wives accompanying their husbands on flights, it is evident, in these encrypted telegrams that priority was actually given to some Norwegian women. "[...] These women were not transported either because their husbands languished for a sight of them, or by what you describe as back-door methods. They were brought over partly because information was required [...] in connection with secret work in Norway [...]" [88]

What has not been mentioned in the discussions between the two departments is the fact that the British Air Service was accompanied by the Royal Norwegian Air Force in the providing flights. The total number of passengers flown to Britain in 1941 were, 79 British, 144 Norwegians and 80 other nationals. Whilst the numbers for 1942, increased dramatically to, 188 British 546 Norwegians and 175 other nationals. [89]

However, Thomas Norton's wait for a vacant seat was not without stressful moments. On the 23rd of August 1941, there had been no further news but two days later his optimism was raised and he packed his bags. Only to hear there was no aircraft available. He went back to his accommodation then returned to Bromma airport the next day to once more be given the bad news 'No Flight'. However, the following day he was given the all clear. Finally, on the 28th of August he was able to have his final farewell get together with his shipmates and the friends he had made whilst in Stockholm. In my view, it was not a coincidence that his 'Master' was on the same flight and had probably made it available for him to fly out also.

Norton was followed two days later by Petty Officer 'Supply' Will Barrett. It was not till December 1941 that the next crewman left, Stoker George Lane. Then there was another lull for over five months, when Norton's pal, Able Seaman Norman Bowden secured a seat on a flight. There was another gap till October 1942, when swiftly over the following two months another fourteen crewmen were provided with flights. I have listed the outcome of all the *Hunter* survivors in the latter stages of this book.

---

88   Source: Secretary of State for Foreign Affairs: File No K.10162/4818/256 (CYPHER) Pages 2A, 14A and 23A.

89   Statistics from 'www.luftfartshistorie.no'.

PART FOUR

Blockade Busting Attempts Continues

Operation 'Performance'

Throughout 1941 and early 1942 the legal issues regarding the stranded cargo vessels continued throughout the Swedish courts, with many twists and turns. There were appeals and protests between Britain and Germany, which became known in the Nordic newspapers, as 'The Kvarstad Comedy". However, during the protracted legal process, Sir George Binney's planning continued. This included the smuggling of weapons on board the ships, albeit World War One Lewis guns and explosives. The latter in case there was a need to scuttle any of the ships should they be attacked or approached by enemy warships. All this was conducted under great secrecy.

After the War, it was recorded that the Germans occupying Denmark had requisitioned a number of Danish trawlers and whaling boats and armed them. These were made ready to go at early notice with sufficient supplies to remain at sea for long periods. In March 1942, there was also an increased amount of German aircraft reconnaissance patrols around the Kattegat and Skagerrak areas. It was not a coincidence that a German vessel *Ingrid Trabe* came into Gothenburg harbour, mooring across some of the cargo ships that were being made ready for their 'illegal' departure. It was said that uniformed sailors were seen snooping around, taking notice of the anti-aircraft guns placed on the upper decks.

To Sir George Binney's credit, rather than expecting others to carry out his plans he felt he should be leading from the front. He decided to sail with *Dicto* – the British Captain being none other than Captain David Nicholas. Whether that was because Captain Nicholas was a trusted senior 'Master' I do not know.

The Swedish authorities had an inkling that the British were up to something, as by this time all available Swedish naval ships were out at sea, patrolling along the coasts. Orders were given to Captains of the cargo vessels that crew members were not to be allowed ashore. In addition, Swedish military guards and police officers patrolled the dockyard area. Captains also had to confiscate cameras and radios from their crews.

The crew men began to get excited that their departure was nigh. A date was fixed for the 31st of March 1942, when it had been forecast that the coast would experience 'foggy' conditions. George Binney held a final meeting. He gave each of the representative British Captains their sealed final orders. For some unknown reasons the Norwegian Captains were not present at the final conference nor privy to the sailing orders. The plan was for the British skippers to take the cargo ships out of the harbour, handing over command to their counterparts once the territorial line had been crossed.

The Captains were given a number of latitude / longitude positions to reach, but were able to make their own choices as to which course they wanted to set. It appears that this took into account having to negotiate through any known German minefields. On a final rendezvous point, having completed two thirds of the journey, they then had to keep a straight course to their destination, namely the Firth of Forth in Scotland. Their escorts would be six Royal Navy destroyers. There were also contingency plans should their journey continue to be affected by foggy weather.

The Swedish naval vessels were in place, ready to leave. They were given orders that should any of the cargo vessels anchor up in their territorial waters, they were to arrest them and escort them back to port. These vessels had their navigation lights on, in order to show any German ships scouting around, that they were the Swedish Fleet and were on guard, ready to intervene if their neutrality came under threat. The Germans had eleven requisitioned and now armed Danish trawlers waiting for their prey to appear. If that was insufficient, then the next hurdle would be provided by the Luftwaffe's planes based on Norwegian soil. The Skagerrak was blocked by additional armed trawlers, German escort vessels and if needed, three German fast torpedo boats, three S-boats; and three U-boats.

An original copy of the 'Order of the Day' in English [there were other versions for the Norwegian crews] was kindly supplied by Joe Settle's family. This was sent to all ten cargo vessels and composed by Sir George Binney.

To the Masters, Officers, Crews and other Volunteers aboard:
From Sir George Binney.
ORDER OF THE DAY.
Today at long last we are going to England determined, come what may, to render a staunch account of our voyage as befits Norwegian and British seamen. Indeed we run a risk, but what of it? If we succeed, these

splendid ships will serve the allied cause and with their cargoes we shall aid the task of war supplies.

To sink our ships and cargoes rather than to see them captured by the enemy is of course our Duty, and on your behalf I have taken such measures as you would wish.

Should we encounter misfortune at sea, remember that in our homes and among our countrymen it will be said with simple truth that we have done our best for the honour and freedom of Norway and Britain; but I, for one, have never held with this blockade and look once more to our success, believing that before two days have passed your laughter will resound within a British port.

So let us Merchant Seaman – 400 strong – shape a westerly course in good heart counting it as an excellent privilege that we have been chosen by Providence to man these ships in the immortal cause of freedom. God speed our ships upon the venture.

Long Live King George. Long Live King Haakon.

For those readers not familiar with the Scandinavian map, the Kattegat is the sea between Denmark to the West and Southern Sweden to the East. This is a major sea lane from the Baltic Sea connecting the ports of Eastern European countries as well as Germany and the Scandinavian countries. The Skagerrak follows the Kattegat into the North Sea.

The cargo ships left the port in the following order. The number of British crew members is in the first brackets, the second bracket is the approximate *Hunter* crew on board. A list of *Hunter* crew names is given in a later chapter.

Charente	(23)	(5) Left at 2000 31st March 1942
Buccaneer	(50)	(2)
Lionel	(1)	(1) possibly
Storsten	(1)	(0)
Dicto (Flagship – with George Binney)	(31)	(4)
Gudvang	(12)	(0)
Rigmor	(4)	(0)
Skytteren	(15)	(3)
Lind	(2)	(1)
B.P. Newton	(5)	(2)

B.P. Newton left at 2315, this was due to ice in the harbour which in turn slowed down the sequence of departures.

Stormy Renshaw describes what he remembers of his part in the operation. "Came the day that we had to sail, there were ten ships [...] Sir George Binney [...] organised all these ships to come together, off from Gothenburg, and sailed together behind the icepack. But the big ships went in first, breaking the ice. Three of the ships did manage to make it to Newcastle. The one I was on, which carried George Binney, was the M/V *Dicto*.

"Several of the ships, I still have the names of them. We had a wine carrier a *Charente*, which is a district in France; *B.P. Newton*, which was an oil tanker. The one I was on *Dicto*, was a 'one-passage' ship, she made one passage to South America, and they'd loaded the fuel carrying cargo 'holds' with wheat, so there was wheat everywhere. There was no room at all for oil. She was imprisoned in a port much further up the harbour, in the Baltic. Anyway, we all gathered together and at four o'clock, we had the orders to sail."

Stoker Joe Settle had not wasted his time interned in Sweden, "During the summer we helped the farmers on the land and in return we received some good food and a few Kroners to spend. In winter we passed our time learning to ski which I became good at. After about two years in the camp the British Consulate asked us to volunteer to take a ship that was tied up in Gothenburg, to England. He said we did not have much chance of getting home because we had to sail through the Kattegat Sea and the Skagerrak Sea which were under German control and we would have no escort.

"After loading the ship – M/V *B.P. Newton* – with blue steel and ball bearings which were desperately needed as war materials in Britain, and getting the ship sea worthy, we still had to wait for the weather report. We were waiting for a misty or foggy day for cover."

Petty Officer Stoker Sam Evens, recalls, as recorded by the Imperial War Museum, "We were interned in Sweden for two years. We tried hard to get visas to go overland through Russia to Turkey and back through the Mediterranean to England. But we were let down by Russia who would not grant any visas. [Between the first batch of *Hunter* crewmen making good their escape, up until 1942, for some reason the Russians did not want to continue cooperating.]

"At this time, April 1942, there were a large number of Norwegian ships tied up in Gothenburg harbour, with only a few Norwegians aboard them. The British Consul at Stockholm came to our camp and asked for volunteers to go aboard these ships and take the risk of trying to bring them back safely to England. He stressed that only volunteers need apply. George Binney got about twenty volunteers of which I was one. We were then brought down to Gothenburg in twos and threes and put aboard the ship.

"But I was lucky; I had got to Stockholm and I worked in the 'British Legation' there, doing the newsprint for English people in Sweden, the *Daily News*, getting it all ready, giving it to the English people in Stockholm. They printed it out, we put the addresses on the envelopes and it was posted on to them. While I was there I lived in the Faslingham Hotel, which was the Salvation Army. Then the time came for getting on board these ships down in Gothenburg. The only one I knew was Sir George Binney, he was the one doing all the traffic for us".

Another *Hunter* crew member given employment at the British Legation was Stoker George Lane. In a previous chapter, I pointed out that George's account was made, as stated by him, eighteen months after the sinking of the *Hunter*. It was obvious that George had been given a copy of Petty Officer Will Barrett's initial report, dated the 4th of May 1940. To which he added in parts, his own recollections of events. However, George's account was also shown to be counter signed by Will Barrett. I suggest it could be that both George and Will were together working at the 'Legation' or if not George still had some form of contact with Will Barrett. However, from Trevor Baker's 'Flight Log' details we now know that both were flown home from Bromma airport, Will Barrett was second to go on the 31st of August 1941 [third Thomas King – 06/12/41] and then George Lane 30th of December 1941.

The pilots disembarking left the ten blacked out ships to their own devices. *Dicto* found M/V *Storsten* anchored with engine problems. They were warned that if they did not get under way they would be escorted back to Gothenburg and interned for the rest of the war. Fortunately. *Storsten* engineers managed to repair the fault and they continued on their journey. In the early hours of the morning on the 1st of April 1942, after initial concerns for the lack of the forecasted fog, thankfully snow appeared to provide cover. This gave some of the Captains confidence to head out. These ships were *Storsten, Buccaneer, Lionel, Rigmor* and *Lind*.

However, just outside the Swedish territorial waters a German armed trawler ordered them to halt. Both *Lionel* and *Buccaneer* tried to turn back to territorial waters, but the enemy fired their guns. *Buccaneer*, the slower of the two, received the main attention of the trawler. Fortunately for *Lionel*, it allowed her to escape. In the meantime, *B.P. Newton* with 5000 tons of ball bearings and steel, having been ordered out to sea, was followed by the Swedish patrol vessel. The ship had no option but to move out of territorial waters. Subsequently, she had to escape from a German escort warship in the Kattegat and later on when in the Skagerrak she was fired upon by enemy trawlers only 100 metres away.

This led to an interesting situation where the gunfire from the enemy was substantial and the Captain of *B.P. Newton* had to send out a SOS signal. Under normal procedure in such situations it is the duty of the Captain to scuttle the ship. Instead of giving the order to stop engines his Second Mate ordered full steam ahead. A blatant disregard of an order given to him by a senior officer; made even more serious when it was from the commanding officer, and punishable with severe consequences. However, in this case the Second Mate saved the ship and the following October, for his brave actions he was commended by King George VI.

Although the *B.P. Newton* was subsequently attacked on three occasions by German aircraft, she was finally able to make her way up the North Sea. On the 2nd of April at 0640 three warships were spotted and to the crew's relief they turned out to be British World War One destroyers which took her into the port of Methil, Dunbartonshire. Where I am sure the ball bearings were quickly taken ashore to be utilised.

Many years later Joe Settle recalls, "After a few hours at sea the weather improved and we were attacked by aircraft. They dropped bombs very close but we were lucky – just a few machine gun bullets – no one got hurt. After thirty-eight hours *B.P Newton* arrived into Leith, Edinburgh and everyone congratulated us. From Scotland I went home first to see my parents and friends. They were pleased to see me as I had been reported missing. Then I went to Devonport RN Barracks and I was posted to Granby [Barracks] for the duration."

Because of Joe's internment he had accumulated a number of weeks leave, which included 'survivor's leave'. During this period, what should have been a joyous occasion was saddened by the death of his eldest brother Stephen aged thirty-eight. However, whilst on leave there was a happy occurrence. Joe's daughter Sheila explains what happened next, "whilst my father was on leave he attended a dance at Pontefract Army Barracks, which during the war was being used by the A.T.S. as a training base. During the evening he met Evelyn Lax, a twenty-one-year-old girl from County Durham who was stationed at the Barracks doing her six weeks training. Well it must have been love at first sight, as three months later, on the 11th of July 1942 they were married in Evelyn's home town of Horden."

Returning to the fate of the other cargo ships, the *Buccaneer* was not so lucky, being a slower vessel. When confronted by another German armed trawler, Captain Smail ordered the ship to be scuttled. The Germans, in an attempt to prevent this occurring, fired their guns across the *Buccaneer*'s life-boat deck. However, it was too late, there was one almighty explosion and the men were then allowed by the enemy to man the lifeboats. Unfortunately the Captain, on boarding one of the lifeboats, lost his grip and hit the side of the ship on his way into the water. His neck broken, he died on the German trawler on its way with her prisoners (of which there were two women) to the Danish port of Fredrikshaven; where he was buried. The story does not end there because before the ship sank the German sailors managed to board her. They were able to find, amongst other spoils, George Binney's orders, and less importantly a picture of Churchill.

Stoker Joe Murphy, from County Cork, another of the *Hunter* volunteers was on board the *Skyterren*. He later told his family, "There was heavy fog as the ship left the harbour, but the fog then lifted." His nephew Keiran continues, "They ran straight into the path of German forces. Rather than let the iron ore fall into enemy hands, the Captain scuttled the ship". Also on board with Joe, was the young seaman Fred Ward and two other *Hunter* shipmates.

At 0630 on the 1st April the *Skyterren* was warned by the *Rigmor* Captain to get away because the Germans were in the vicinity. Unfortunately, she had ongoing steering gear defects, which caused her to attempt a repair. A German trawler appeared, and after repeatedly ordering her to stop, the trawler fired a shell, which hit her below the bridge. The Norwegian Captain decided to scuttle the ship. Subsequently, after the war, at a Maritime Inquiry the Norwegian Captain in his evidence stated, that the British Captain had caused the detonation of the explosives too quickly, before some of the crew had been warned. This had resulted in one death and many more injured. What followed was a chaotic scene with the crew attempting to get into the lifeboats.

There were four boats lowered with some survivors already in them, whilst others jumped over board or hung onto the davit ropes. They had to get the many injured into the boats and also the stragglers who were last to arrive on the upper deck. One of the boats was motorised but nobody knew how to mobilise it, hence they started rowing away from the sinking ship. It is recorded that many of those on board had escaped from Norway and were wanted by the Gestapo. Two of the lifeboats managed to get away and found the ice pack. They were then convinced that they were in Swedish territorial waters. Unfortunately, they were unable to penetrate the ice and like the other two boats were apprehended.

The German trawler then towed all the lifeboats back to the *Skyterren* and their captives were placed below decks. During the journey the Swedish ship *Gota Lejon* came close to the trawler and the *Skyterren* seamen were brought up top. A number of signals were rapidly sent back and forth between the two vessels, the contents of which were not clear. However, shortly afterwards the Swedish ship headed out to open sea. As one can imagine this left the captured seamen, feeling abandoned and extremely apprehensive as to what the future now held for them. Especially, as a number of the crew were certain that they had only been one mile from the Swedish shore and therefore anticipated the Swedish ship would have demanded that they be handed over into their custody. With regards to *Skyterren*'s demise – at approximately noon on the 1st of April she finally sank, going down in flames.

Joe Murphy, Fred Ward, Stoker Frank Caton and NAAFI Manager Charles Falzon, were so close to returning to Sweden to face the tune, but were now Prisoners of War. We have not heard the last of Joe and Fred as they will finally be once more at the mercy of the enemy, as it must have reminded them of the 'Declaration' they had signed back in two years previously.

Well so far, there are two out of four cargo vessels that have made it back to Britain. Is this a sign that the operation is going to end in disaster or success? Could it result in more seamen being killed or captured by the Germans? Would any more ships be sunk and what effect would this have on the war effort at home?

The *Charente*, with at least five of *Hunter*'s sailors on board, at approximately 1330 (1st of April) was also confronted by two German armed trawlers and a warning shot was delivered. The trawlers quickly raised a 'Stop' flag signal. As already explained, the British Captains were required to take control until reaching Swedish territorial waters. However, for some reason

Captain James Donald still had command. He realised there was now no way of escape, that he needed time to allow the crew to man the lifeboats, prior to scuttling the ship. Therefore, in response to the German trawlers original 'Flag' signal, he tried to give the impression he did not comprehend the message. Captain Donald gave the order to stop engines. He then attempted to activate the detonator, to scuttle the ship. But there was no response.

By now the enemy had launched a boat. As they boarded the ship, Captain Donald made another attempt to set off the explosives and this time he was successful. A Norwegian crew member recalls, "It felt as if so many explosives had been used that the whole bottom must have been blown to pieces." Fortunately, there were no fatalities and only two of the crew were injured, although not seriously. However, two lifeboats were put out of action, resulting in all the crew cramming into the remaining two. Once more the German trawler took them into Fredrikshaven.

Rigmor in the meantime, was making her way towards the North Sea, but it was not long before the enemy appeared by way of a bomber aircraft. The ship sustained some damage from bombs and some missed. The crew used their Lewis gun consistently, until the bomber decided, as darkness fell, to return to his base in Norway. On the morning of the next day, the 2nd of April, the crew got ready for another attack, but to their relief the approaching two aircraft were British Beaufighters from their base at Dyce.

The remaining flotilla of destroyers which had come out to assist the *B.P. Newton*, under the command of Captain Gilling, in anticipation of the other cargoes needing assistance, continued sailing to the east. Two British Blenheim aircraft found *Rigmo*. One stayed to provide some cover, whilst the other went off towards the Destroyer Flotilla, to give the *Rigmo*'s position. Although the Blenheims spotted a German reconnaissance aircraft later, they had reached their range limit and reluctantly had to return to base.

Rigmor was now only 180 miles from its goal of the Scottish coast, but the destroyers were still fifty miles away, north-west. The Luftwaffe had obviously been made aware by the reconnaissance aircraft of *Rigmor*'s position, as well as her course and speed. At 1230 *Rigmor* crew spotted an aircraft and prayed that as before it was British. Unfortunately, it was not, and the ship received gun fire across her upper deck, followed by two bombs. Whilst these missed their target, *Rigmor* sent a SOS, which was received by the destroyers.

Then two more German bombers arrived, discharging their bomb load and strafing the ship with guns. It was inevitable that one would land on the ship. This happened and caused a large hole in the ships side. There was also other damage to crucial machinery, which affected the ship's manoeuvrability. The enemy attacked again with her machine guns, hitting the bridge and the radio office below. During this attack, Captain Gilling was injured and the Lewis gun put out of action.

At 1315 another SOS was sent, apparently the first had given their position incorrectly. The destroyer commander Captain Moncrieff ordered his flotilla to increase speed to twenty-four knots. The Norwegian Captain Monsen ordered the crew to abandon ship. As the lifeboats were being manned, the Germans stopped strafing the ship, but they had not yet finished their objective. Shortly afterwards, two German seaplanes joined their comrades and dropped their torpedoes. As the British destroyers arrived, *Rigmor* was hit by one of the torpedoes amidships. Like vultures waiting for their prey to breathe its last breath, the enemy continued to circle above the ship.

Ironically, one of the British destroyers in the advancing flotilla was none other than HMS *Eskimo*, which you will remember had been badly damaged in the second 'Battle of Narvik'. So perhaps it was only right that by chance she was on station to rescue the *Rigmor* crew in their lifeboats. It appears that because of the valuable cargo being transported by *Rigmor*, Captain Monsen convinced their saviours to make an attempt to tow the stricken vessel. Volunteers were called for, which included both Norwegian and British crew members, to make an attempt to re-board the *Rigmor*. However, it was to no avail, the seas were too rough and the ship by now was listing heavily.

But the exciting episode was not yet quite over. It seems the Norwegian Second Mate, Wessel Borg, on *Rigmor*, who had already escaped from the German invaders in his country to Sweden, had been left stranded alone on one of the lifeboats during the last air strike. Understandably, at this point his thoughts may well have wandered off to "is this the final end for me?" Fortunately, *Eskimo* came along and plucked him out of his desperation. At approximately 1700 on the 2nd of April, HMS *Faulknor*, the flotilla's lead destroyer, shelled and sank the *Rigmor*. The valuable cargo was lost, but more importantly, all of the brave crew, unlike some of their seafaring colleagues on the other ships, were now in safe hands.

It appears that George Binney's initial sailing plan for *Dicto*, was to stay close to the northern coast from Gothenburg, as far as Marstrand (twenty-five miles). However, the ship met a thick and moving ice pack, so a change of course was necessary. They travelled west until they arrived at the end of the Swedish territorial waters. Was it a coincidence that at this point they encountered a German armed trawler? The enemy suddenly switched on their signal lamp, the beam was utilised as a searchlight, then they opened with rapid gun fire.

In response *Dicto* quickly altered course, in an attempt to return from whence she came, before other shots were fired from the trawler. Although none of the gun fire connected with the target, *Dicto* headed back towards the ice pack, followed by the predator. The ice was about two feet thick but *Dicto* went into it at a full rate of knots. This immediate contact with the ice caused ruptures to her hull and the ship started taking on water.

At this point it seems it became a 'stand-off' between *Dicto* and the trawler. The trawler was waiting for an improvement in the weather. Simultaneously, George Binney had no knowledge of how the other ships were faring or their whereabouts. It is worth mentioning that the Admiralty, prior to sailing, had sent a meteorologist to advise on weather forecasts from Britain by listening into the Gothenburg Radio Station. Initially, his task had been to analyse the best time to sail, but then, as he had sailed in *Dicto*, he was unable to give weather updates. Apparently, unknown at the time, there were problems with *Dicto*'s 'sender' system. Hence, there remained uncertainty as to whether the signals were actually transmitted. The forecasts unfortunately showed fog in the Skagerrak slowly disappearing. Subsequently, George Binney decided to break radio silence in an attempt to warn the other ships. Alas, this was too late for some of the ships, *Buccaneer* and *Skyterren* had already been scuttled.

I would add that in Ralph Barker's book *The Blockade Busters* (page 115), he mentions another *Hunter* survivor, Telegraphist Rex Brown on *Dicto*. Ralph Barker: "To his signal Binney received no answer, and he did not expect to; as it was a broadcast message to all ships. But by an extraordinary mischance, the message went out on the wrong wavelength. The Marconi engineer who had checked the sets, a Dane, was thoroughly trustworthy, as was Binney's radio operator, a rating from HM *Hunter* named Brown. Brown checked his aerial current during transmission and was satisfied that the message had gone out."

Dicto later took on a Swedish pilot. Due to the fog the pilot instructed the Captain to lay anchor. However, the Swedish destroyer *Psilander* approached and ordered, that unless the ship accompanied her back to Gothenburg, weapons would be used. Therefore, at approximately midday on the 1st of April *Dicto* returned back into the port from whence she came.

'Stormy' Renshaw on board the M/V *Dicto*: "The unfortunate part about it was that the pilot who was to take us to sea, had bought a local newspaper, and that paper had reported the fact that the English ships were sailing. So all the Germans had to do was to come out and wait for us behind the ice. The one I was on, because it had the 'Chief' (George Binney) on it, turned around in the ice, being a big ship, and finished up back in Gothenburg. The following day, there was a ruckus in the paper. 'Why let these ships go?' I was called up, with a friend of mine, to go to the Consul's office."

At 0800 on the 1st of April, *Lind* at the time was in the company of *Rigmor*, *Charente*, *Gudvang* and *Lionel* when they were also approached by *Psilander* and a sister ship; ordering them out to sea. Nearby were also a number of armed vessels. By now the weather had improved, so they were apprehensive of returning into the Skagerrak. The *Lind* received a warning shot, just as the crew spotted a signal flag hoisted – ordering 'Stop Immediately'. A Swedish vessel came alongside, repeating the initial order, to head out to sea; advising, that should they not, this would result in her forfeiting her right to leave Swedish waters.

Apparently, at that moment '*Lind*' was on the territorial line. The Swedish vessel moved directly into the course '*Lind*' was taking, and tried to push her into a westerly direction. The Norwegian Captain Trovik took over from the British Captain Nicol and ordered full speed on a course towards the North Sea. Sailing through the rest of that day and night there were no incidents. On the morning of the 2nd of April, the Captain had to negotiate his ship through the German mines.

At midday the sun was out and so the crew were probably feeling more optimistic about their chances of reaching Britain: Then the enemy arrived by way of a Heinkel aircraft with its torpedo load. The *Lind* crew responded immediately by firing the Lewis gun, which was a decent challenge, but were unable to stop the enemy pilot discharging his torpedoes from close range. Fortunately, they did not make their target. Then a British Beaufighter appeared which led to an aerial battle, whilst *Lind* continued her voyage. It appears the confrontation continued until the Beaufighter had to return, being on the limits of its range. It was reported that the *Lind* had managed to hit the *Heinkel* and the pilots SOS was picked up by British coastal stations.

On the morning of 3rd of April: by now *B.P. Newton* had reached port, and the *Lind* had finally made the position that had been set out in the initial 'Sailing Orders'; but there was no escort to greet them. In fact, British aircraft from Wick, Kinloss and Dyce had been searching for *Lind* that morning. Eventually, around midday, a 'Hudson' aircraft from Kinloss radioed back to base that they had spotted a 'small tanker'. Subsequently, that evening the crewmen on the *Lind* were extremely relieved to see a destroyer arrive to see them through the minefield. Thus she came into Methil port the following day having completed an eighty-hour voyage.

Here is Petty Officer Stoker Sam Evens version as told to a Plymouth newspaper in 1970. "I was sent on board a '10,000 tonner' [*Dicto*] and then after a while transferred to a small 800-ton boat namely the motor vessel M /V *Lind*. This boat was to act as a lifesaver in the event of any large ship being sunk or badly damaged." Sam went on to explain, "About the middle of March we were told to standby to leave Gothenburg, as this time the harbour was frozen over and no ships could move at all. At about eight o'clock one morning an ice breaker came into the harbour and started breaking up the ice; this was the signal to get ready. We quietly slipped moorings and were away.

"I was the only Englishman on board this particular boat. Before sailing I had managed to smuggle a machine gun on board, given by the 'British Legation' and I rigged it up on the bridge as soon as we left Gothenburg harbour. After steaming for about twelve hours out into the Skagerrak we were attacked by German E-boats. Some of our convoy were sunk and scattered in all directions.

"The weather that time was bad; foggy and falling snow. Later we were approached by a Swedish warship that ordered us back to harbour. As we turned back the warship disappeared into the fog and our Captain said, 'We'll try and get out again,' so we steamed off the Skagerrak into the North Sea. We were soon spotted by a German seaplane, which when he saw us came down to have a good look. I immediately ran and got the machine gun ready and as soon as he was in my sights, fired at him as he made his run past us. He retaliated with cannon fire straight down the port side and then up the starboard. This severely damaged our lifeboats and smashed the bridge and wheelhouse. He flew off and I thought to myself, 'He's gone off to get help or to inform any German ship that may be in the area.'

"But no! He came at us again and as I watched him I saw two large objects being dropped from the plane. I realised that they were torpedoes. Immediately I ran to the bridge and told the Captain what I had seen and he altered course. I saw one torpedo go right under the ship and held my breath but nothing happened. The other one completely missed us. Then the aircraft turned and flew towards the coastline. I went to the Captain again and warned him that they would probably be back with more planes later. From then on, we kept a continuous look out and prayed for darkness to fall. Our luck held and as darkness fell we steamed on towards England.

"Just before dark, we were spotted by one of our own aircraft. At this time we were flying a white flag from the mainmast; we were advised to do this on approaching England as it was a special sign for spotter aircraft to look for. The plane signalled us to stay where we were and that we would soon be picked up by a British warship. A short while later HMS *Cossack* arrived and escorted us into Leith, Scotland.

"On tying up at Leith I was summoned to 'Naval Intelligence' to give an account of what had happened since leaving Sweden. After this, all I wanted to do was to contact my wife and family and tell them that I was in Scotland and would soon be safely home. I went up to 'Naval Intelligence' and explained the story because we were flying a white flag. They could recognise us because they knew I suppose from Sweden, that we had gone out.

"The debriefing officer wanted to know about the aircraft, what it was like. They gave me three days to get to Plymouth from Leith. I had a big dinner at the Princess Royal, a railway station hotel there, sausage and mash. It was a treat really. I had to break my journey at Macclesfield because the wife was there. She'd lost the house down there in Plymouth and was living with her sister. So I stopped off and then I came back to HMS *Drake*.

"The Navy said to me 'You can't go out on a Navy ship again, you signed this agreement when you were taken prisoner, so you can't go aboard a fighting ship again, you have to stop in the harbour.' I had a diesel diving boat to train divers, taking them out to do their lessons and all that. I was then called back to the barracks to do a fire fighting course which was a very serious thing then, especially oil fuel fires."

Petty Officer Stoker Sam Evens, for his voluntary involvement and brave actions, was presented with the Norwegian War Medal accompanied by a Diploma from King Haakon. He was also 'Mentioned in Dispatches', published in the *London Gazette* dated the August 25th, 1942.

Although Sam Evens believes he was the only *Hunter* crew member on board the *Lind*, it may be that there were two others unknown to him who also sailed with the ship, including Cook Bill Wallis, aged twenty-three from London.

Returning back to the general overview of the excellently researched article 'Kvarstad Ships and Men', I am able to provide a summary for the final outcome of the ships and their crew. However, I will focus predominantly on the six ships of which the *Hunter* survivors were crew members.

As previously mentioned, *Lionel* was with four of the ships, including *Lind* at 0800 on the 1st of April. Once more the Swedish destroyer *Psilander* continued playing her part in being authoritative. *Psilander* with a Swedish armed trawler also confronted *Lionel*, ordering her to go west. The *Lionel* made a request to be able to stay in Swedish waters, until the weather improved and also queried as to whether she could go back to Gothenburg. Although she received an affirmative reply, the last part of the signal pointed out "But if you do, you'll never get out again."

The Captain decided to make an attempt to return, but this resulted in a warning shot from the shore. It took a while to receive an answer to his request from the Naval Base. This was indicative of the request having to go to a higher authority to grant permission. It appears their main objective was to either get the ships out of Swedish waters or if not return back to Gothenburg. The Captain decided to take the latter choice and the *Lionel* lived for another day and later joined *Dicto* for another attempt on breaking the blockade. This was to be called 'Operation Bridford'.

The *Gudvang* Captain, before making a decision to return back to Gothenburg, brought his crew together to give them a chance to offer their views on the situation. Finally, he decided to go west and back out to sea. The weather was in their favour which allowed the Captain to come up to maximum knots. Then at 2000 hours two German armed trawlers, signalled her to 'Stop'. However, the order was ignored and the *Gudvang* continued on her course, causing the enemy to send up flares ready to fire their guns. The Captain then ordered engines to stop and his crew were called to come on the deck. The starboard lifeboat, which was on the opposite side to the enemy vessels, was made ready to be manned; when the ship was hit by a series of gunfire. There was some superficial damage and in the confusion the steam whistle became permanently stuck.

The ship was now in a position, where night was falling rapidly and the scene became chaotic. The starboard boat was launched but quickly became overcrowded. The remaining crew managed to man the port lifeboat. The Captain detonated the scuttling charges before the boats started to row away. The intention was to make for the Norwegian coast, somewhat overly optimistic, as the German vessel quickly caught up with them. They were taken on board and once more another batch of prisoners were taken to Fredrikshaven. On landing, they met up with their seafaring comrades from the *Skyterren, Buccaneer* and *Charente.*

I have left the story concerning the outcome of the last Norwegian cargo ship the *Storsten* until the end. Whilst there were none of the *Hunter* survivors on board, it is another story of escaping the enemy that is worth recording.

The *Storsten* was on her own in open waters. However, at 1000 on the 1st of April she was approached by three vessels one of them sending salvo. The ship was not hit and the Captain managed to hide in the fog bank but once this cleared it left the ship vulnerable to attack from German aircraft stationed in Norway. Subsequently, in the afternoon a mine believed to have been dropped by an enemy aircraft caused a massive explosion. This resulted in a water tank exploding and sending water up over the bridge. The steering system was immobilised and a lifeboat completely taken out of service; as well as casualties in the vicinity of the bridge.

The Norwegian Captain ordered a SOS signal but just before doing so the aircraft used a line and hook to take down the radio aerial. The aircraft remained close by firing her guns which put paid to the possibility of rigging an emergency antenna. Then, for those who witnessed it, their heart rates must have increased rapidly, as a bomb was dropped but did not detonate and rolled through the boatswain's legs and went over the side.

Despite the valiant efforts of the crew to defend themselves from the enemy aircraft by firing their Lewis gun, a German trawler firing her guns approached. It was then that the crew realised the game was up and the usable lifeboats were manned. At the inquiry the Radio Operator stated, that he was left to activate the charges to scuttle the ship. The Norwegian Captain, with some of the crew on the motorboat, towed the other two lifeboats with the majority of the remaining crew on board, and managed to slip away unseen.

The next few hours were crucial if they were going to come through unscathed. But as you can imagine the atmosphere on the three boats would have been extremely tense and uncomfortable. Probably exacerbated by the fact there were two women on board the *Storsten*, including the First Mate's wife, who was pregnant. To summarise, the boats were seen by RAF aircraft, recognised by the survivors waving Norwegian flags.

As night fell the motor on the lead boat stopped, the survivors on the third trailing boat moved onto the second which then took over the towing by sail. The third was allowed to drift away. One of the women, married to an Able Seaman, "became hysterical, thinking that those in her boat were trying to kill her". Her husband also became stressed and made attempts to jump over the side. In view of the wind becoming stronger it was decided to 'heave to' for the night.

The following day, Good Friday, there were differences of opinion as to which course to take. Hence, the survivors on the motor boat using the oars, rowed westwards, although still 240 nautical miles away from the Scottish coast. This was in anticipation of meeting up with the rescuing Royal Naval vessels. The survivors on the boat with the sails, knowing the Norwegian coast was much nearer, an estimated thirty nautical miles, felt their chances of survival would be better by heading for Norway and subsequently departed from their comrades.

This group of thirty-two, having found clear and sunny weather, on eventually sighting land, planned that at night they would sink the boat and disperse in smaller numbers. Unfortunately, their intentions did not quite work out, and twenty-three were captured by the Germans. However, it appears most of the others managed to make well their escape back to Sweden. Amongst them was the First Mate. Although he and his wife had lost contact with each other, she finally gave birth in a Norwegian hospital. To relieve readers of the suspense, they were finally reconciled in Trondheim in 1945.

There was another crew member of the *Storsten* who had a remarkable escape purely by cheekily bluffing his way back to freedom. This was the ship's carpenter who sought refuge at a farm, where he and two shipmates were given food and clothing. Obviously, by now they were in need of a good rest but were awoken by the farmer, who informed them that the Germans were looking for them. At the same time three other shipmates also arrived at the farm.

This led to the six seamen being hidden upstairs in a wardrobe in order to leave the farmer to speak with the Germans downstairs. The farmer was very astute, by way of giving the Germans food so that they forgot to check the second floor. Equipped with skis, food and money, after a number of set-backs, the seamen finally got a bus into Kristiansand. However, the bus was stopped at a German checkpoint.

In anticipation of what was about to occur the 'carpenter' nonchalantly walked past the Germans soldiers and off the bus. He then saw his shipmates being taken into a building by their captors. Later on in his travels he was stopped by another German soldier, wanting to know what he was doing out at night. He explained he had just been 'paid off' from his ship and could not find hotel accommodation. At which point the soldier kindly took him to a 'Seamen's Hostel' making sure he was given a room for the night.

The following day because the 'carpenter' had no official documents the hostel advised him to go to the local police station. He kept to his story about being 'paid off' from a ship, but added that he had stayed at a friend's home in Kristiansand and had left his papers there. Subsequently, he requested a temporary pass for Oslo which he was duly given, but was required to report to the police authorities in Oslo.

On arrival in Oslo, he used the same story, asking for a border pass to his home town of Rendal in Sweden. However, when the interviewing police officer seemed suspicious the 'carpenter' suggested he rang the police in Rendal. This the police officer did, and resulted in another pass being issued. What this police officer did not know was that the 'carpenter' personally knew the police staff in Rendal. Soon he was back in Sweden.

With regards to the remaining escapees, it is believed they were eventually flown to Britian, where they joined the Norwegian armed forces. The seventeen of *Storsten's* survivors aboard the motor boat which had hoped to reach Britain, were seen on the morning of the 4th of April by a RAF 'Lockheed Hudson' aircraft ninety miles off Lindesnes on the Norwegian coast. They circled the vessel but then left the area, before being ordered back to the vicinity until another aircraft could take its place. The aircraft having taken forty-five minutes to return to the area was unable to spot the vessel. This resulted in swift action at the base in Scotland and a 'Sutherland' sea boat with an escort of Beaufighter's was ordered to go to the recorded position, in an attempt to hopefully rescue the survivors.

Unfortunately, the weather became increasingly worse which led to the sea boat losing contact with her fighter escort and having to return back to its base, along with the fighters. The following day the weather conditions had not improved and it was assumed the motor boat had been sunk in the storms. At a later enquiry, it was stated the motor boat did not have a mast or sails or a radio transmitter. A valiant attempt by the survivors came to a sad end. Ironically, in hindsight, if they had followed the route of the other vessel they also may have managed to escape to Britain. Which hopefully would have given them an opportunity to fight for another day against the enemy who had brutally taken control of their country, Norway.

There are conflicting statistics regarding the final outcome of those involved in 'Operation Performance'. However, the following is a close approximation. The total number of men and women involved on the blockade busting ships was 471 out of whom nineteen died (*Storsten* accounted for seventeen). Although, 234 were taken prisoner (eight of them women and children), forty-three died whilst in imprisonment, or were executed. There were ninety-nine British seamen, most sent to Milag or Marlag camps in Germany and others to Poland. Of those returned to Sweden, (*Dicto* and *Lionel*) thirty-two out of the eighty-five were British. On a positive note 124 crew members made it back to Britain.

In addition, the blockade busting operations 'Rubble', 'Performance' and subsequent ones brought supplies crucial for the war effort. For example, 100 tons of ball bearings would be enough for the needs of three quarters of the 'Lancaster' squadrons, amounting to 1,200 aircraft; as well as two-thirds of the 1,600 'Mosquito' fleet of aircraft. Whilst during the war a large amount of ball bearings were exported to Britain by aircraft from Sweden, forty aircraft loads could be taken in one small cargo ship. The next attempt 'Operation Bridford' was also successful, by not only bringing more ball bearings and products but also essential equipment needed for the new steel factory that at the time was being built in Britain. This eventually gave Britain the ability to produce their own ball bearings and meant there was no further need to risk future attempts in breakouts from Sweden.

As was expected the partial success of 'Performance' caused a diplomatic row between all parties. The Germans were obviously not happy with the outcome and the Swedish Government made attempts to appear not to have any knowledge of the British 'Operation'. As can be seen below by the Swedish Press release in amongst other world news that was happening at the time.

Swedish Press Summary No 93 of Friday April 24th 1942.

This morning's newspapers publish a W.T. report to the effect that the English Captains of the two ships which returned to Gothenburg, have been summoned for contravention of Swedish export and arms regulations. It appears that the two ships concerned were found on their return to Gothenburg to have been equipped with machine guns. About twenty light machine guns of an old English pattern are said to have been smuggled on to the ships by British officials. The newspapers report that a Swedish protest has been lodged in London and that Sir George Binney has already left Sweden.

A Reuter message of the 7th April, [1942] had stated that sailors, who had reached England, had revealed that their ships had repulsed German attacks with machine gun fire. This report caused considerable surprise as the Swedish authorities had stringently enforced the regulations. No application had been made for the export of arms, nor could such an application have been granted. DNB issued a report on the 8th April [1942] to the effect that the *B.P. Newton* had been armed.

It is also reported that the Germans informed Sweden through diplomatic channels that the captured seamen had revealed that all the ten ships were armed – a circumstance which the Germans found highly remarkable and protested against. It is expressly stated in the newspapers that the British officials, who are alleged to have been responsible for the smuggling of the guns, enjoyed diplomatic immunity. The whole matter is given a most sensational set up in Stockholm – Tidningen. Press comment is strong.

Sir George Binney did in fact leave Sweden in April 1942. However, this was not until he had been brought before the court, and found guilty of weapon smuggling. He must have been relieved with the result; rather than a possible custodial sentence, he only received a financial penalty. Captain Nicholas was also fortunate to receive a financial penalty. Both probably paid by the British Government via the Legation in Stockholm.

With regards to the Court appearance for Captain Nicholas the newspapers in Britain reported the case, here the **Daily Mail Wednesday May 6 1942** provides a summary of the defence of Captain Nicholas. [I presume it was the same defence for Sir George.]

"It was pleased that the attempt to reach Britain and the arming of vessels was on the order of the British Government. If the vessels were to make the voyage they had to be armed against the attack that was certain to come from the Germans.

"'Without arms, crews and ships would certainly have been lost,' counsel said. He maintained that the whole affair was the result of the embargo placed on the movement of the ships during the winter. If they had been able to put to sea on some nights no machine guns would have been necessary."

The four *Hunter* interned crewmen, Renshaw, Brown, Cook and Bowden, for their part on board *Dicto* it was agreed by the British Legation, they had to be put on a flight back to Britain. For some unknown reason Bowden and Brown [numbers five and six] were flown out on 17th May, whilst Cook and Renshaw [seven and eight] had to wait another five months.

8th of October 1942.

I will let 'Stormy Renshaw explain, as only he can, his last moments of Internment. "Now we were living in the Salvation Army in Stockholm and we had to turn up every day to see the Consul. I'd ran out, having only two shirts and only two collars, so I ended up wearing a silk scarf. The Consul called us in one at a time, and queried, 'Why are you wearing a scarf, where's your collar and tie?' I explained to him that I had one collar in the wash, and the other was dirty. 'Well,' he said, this won't do y'know, you are representing England. Get that muffler off, and be available at six o'clock tonight.

"I'd had over two and half years in Sweden by now, no sign or sight of anybody doing anything for me. Cookie and I waited until six o'clock, then suddenly there's a knock on the door. So we opened the door and there was a fellow in a chauffeur's uniform. We gathered what belongings we had; I was in a trilby hat, burgundy raincoat, silk scarf and collars in my pocket, any toiletries that I had. He said, 'Jump in the car.' So we jumped into the car. It was absolutely black, we didn't know where we were, we didn't know where we were going, all we knew was that we were in a taxi.

"We finally pulled up outside a door, so we rushed in and when we got in, there were two Norwegian gentlemen, young seamen, and we all got chatting. We didn't know what we were there for. The fellow came back again and said, 'Right, go in there and sit yourself down.' Now, in there was a pilot's dressing room. There was everything from helmets to flying boots to jackets. So, what do you do with all that? Well, we got rigged up in all this lot and his last words were, 'Watch out there, and when you see a flashing light, run like you have never run before.'

"We're all sitting around waiting, and all of a sudden, a light flashed, and we all rushed across the tarmac, and came to a Wellington Bomber with its side door open. We were virtually pulled in by an airman, and he said, 'Sit there, sit there. That's your seat and that's your toilet, there's a pack of sandwiches and there's your coffee. When I go like this pull your masks down and put them on.' So, we're all sitting there, locked in, not knowing what to do. I wasn't going to move off my seat for that toilet anyway.

"We could hear a rumbling and we knew we were under way; we knew we were going north. We flew up and finally climbed above the height of the German fighter planes from northern Norway, up towards the North Pole and came down into Scotland, where we landed. In the meantime, I was 'took short', because cold weather is a natural laxative. Anyway, we arrived at an airport in Scotland, and I jumped out and opened my bowels right there on Scottish soil."

I am advised that it is unlikely a Wellington Bomber was the aircraft which took them back home. At the time, various aircraft that were used between 'Bromma' and 'Leuchars' were mainly Lockheed Hudsons, Lodestars, Douglas Dakotas and Mosquitoes. The way 'Stormy' Renshaw described his flight it is apparent that the flight was conducted in military fashion. Not all the flights went smoothly, due to poor weather conditions, not all returned to' Leuchars' but were diverted to other bases.

'Stormy' Renshaw and Stanley Cook were now relieved to find themselves back on home ground, but to their surprise they still had further hurdles to negotiate. Stormy continues his account. "We were then shepherded again, this time into the Officer's mess, but they couldn't accommodate us lying down, but we could use the lounge. Come next morning, someone decided we should have breakfast.

"Now, we found it very peculiar that a fighter pilot should have to pay for his breakfast; all the pilots from the fighter squad had to go in and buy their food. Anyway, we had a jolly good breakfast, y' know, we had not seen eggs and anything like that. So a young fellow came round and wanted money. We'd no money, we'd just been in Sweden. So he said, 'Somebody will have to sign for it'. So I signed my name for four breakfasts and four railway tickets from Scotland.

"By dawn, we'd both decided, Stanley and I, that we'd both go back and report to the Navy. We were kept incarcerated for a couple of hours until the big Navy boss came. He took me to one side and he said, 'Who won the cricket match at Lords this year?' We had been in contact with nothing, absolutely nothing. 'Who won the "Cup" then? Who won the Derby race meeting?' I said, 'I know nothing about any of that.' 'Alright,' he said, 'who's that other bloke outside?' I said, 'That's my mate, Stanley Cook, a seaman wi' me. He's been wi' me for the last two and half years.' 'Ok,' he said, 'now you go out through that door there'. So I went out through the door there, then he called Stanley in and asked him the same questions, the final one being, 'Who's that bloke in that room there? 'That's Jim Renshaw,' he said, '"been with him for two and a half years.' So they finally decided that, yes, we are English, yes, we are Navy men. 'Oh, by the way.' he said, 'don't forget to report back to barracks'.

"Now we'd got to go from Scotland, on a wartime train down to Plymouth. It took us twenty-four hours to get to Plymouth. I obviously went to my fiancée's house, much to her surprise. Well, we decided that we'd report in at nine o'clock in the morning. So I went to see this bloke. He said, 'Who are you?' I said, 'I'm Jim Renshaw'. 'What's ye'r number?' I gave him my number, my service number. 'What ship?' and I told him. 'Are you sure?' 'Yes!' 'Who's that fella out there?' I said, 'That's Stanley Cook. He's been wi' me for the last two and half years.' 'Alright,' he said. 'Oh,' he said. 'Before you go, come back Monday,' he said. 'And have ye'r bloody hair cut.' That was my greeting, and Stanley had to go through the whole lot too."

One week later to the day that 'Stormy' landed it became national news:

ESCAPED FROM THE GERMANS
Will Marry a Plymouth Girl

"On Saturday week, Miss Audrey Williams, third daughter of Mr and Mrs. H.E. Williams of Neath Road, Plymouth, will be married to Mr James Renshaw, Sheffield, a naval man who escaped from German captivity [...] Later they crossed into Sweden after signing a paper swearing never to fight against Germany or her Allies. Fingerprints were taken, and they were warned that if caught breaking their parole they would be shot. Mr Renshaw tried to escape in a Norwegian ship through the Skagerrak, but had to return to Gothenburg. Eventually, however, he succeeded in reaching Britain."

The newspaper report ended with a final quote from 'Stormy' which as you would expect was in his usual straight talking and tongue in cheek manner. "Mr Renshaw considers that food rationing on the Continent is "five times worse than in England – half a pound of meat has to last three weeks. Some of the Nazi rankers, said Mr Renshaw, were decent; but he was disgusted with the German officers."

The architect of the 'Blockade Busting' operations, Sir George Binney, although having suffered a heart attack during the latter stages of the War, did not consider peace an excuse to slow down. After a spell back with the firm 'United Steel', who had loaned him to Sweden in the early days of the conflict, he returned to a life of traveling widely. He was encouraged to write his memoirs, he himself believed he could write at least three books and a film, but alas he left his stories to telling them over dinner with his guests.

In 1955, Sir George married Sonia and settled down to a quiet life in Jersey spending his time gardening and his love of antiques. He died in 1972, when one of his requests was fulfilled at his funeral. The flag he had flown when greeting the British destroyers after he had successfully crossed the Skagerrak during 'Operation Rubble' was draped over his coffin.

The last five *Hunter* survivors returned to Britain at the end of November 1942. One of these was Chief Stoker David Moore, of whom I have had little personal information. However, on my visit to the National Archives, I found a debrief report to the Intelligence Service M19 in a file title 'Evaders and Escapers', with a security level, 'Most Secret'. This was dated 28th Nov 1942, written by an Intelligence Officer, two days after David's eventual arrival back in Britain. As the senior ranking survivor, his debrief was obviously seen as containing potentially important information.

M19 28 Nov 1942, S/P.G (NORWAY) 987

Chief Petty Officer (Stoker). **David Moore.** RN Service since 1913.
Interned. SWEDEN 28 April 1940 Private Address.
Left. STOCKHOLM 26 November 1942 Standray Ave
Arrived. ABERDEEN 26th November 1942 PLYMOUTH.

On the 27th April 1940 we were all assembled along with a number of Norwegian soldiers and were taken singly before a German Naval Lieutenant, who produced a document and said, "Read this and sign it". The document was an understanding that, if we were sent to SWEDEN, we would not take up arms during the present hostilities against GERMANY or her allies.

We signed the document in duplicate, and were instructed to put the print of the small finger of our right hand on each copy. 43 Naval Ratings from HMS *Hunter* signed the declaration.

About 1700 hours we were marched with about 100 Norwegian Soldiers under armed guard to the border, about half a mile away. The actual border at this point is in the middle of a tunnel and there we were put into a train for Gunnarn in the Swedish province of VASTRBOTTEN, where we were lodged in church from 28th April to July when we were moved to HALSINGMO in the province of GALLEBORG.

At HALSINGMO we lived along with merchant sailors in wooden huts and were free to move about. Around Christmas 1940 I went to STOCKHOLM to take over a job under the Legation, visiting Internment camps. Owing to sickness I was unable to take up duty and was sent to a sanatorium at UTTRAN near STOCKHOLM. In October 1941 I took up duty at the Legation in STOCKHOLM as a messenger and night watchman and worked there until my repatriation on 26 November 1942. [90]

Ord Seaman. Watson .T. Previously: Fish Worker. From: Wilson Terrace, Whitehills Scotland. Service: 3 years.
October 1940. Work at British Legation, STOCKHOLM.
October 1941. Gothenburg served on Norwegian ship.
March 1942. Back to HALSINGMO before boats set out to run the German Baltic Blockade.
June 1942. Back to British Legation, STOCKHOLM. [Repatriated 28 Nov 1942]

Able Seaman. Coutts. C. S. Previously: Royal Navy. From: Portside Street, Rosyth, Scotland. Served: 8 years and 3 months.
12 November 1940. Left HALSINGMO to live at GUNNARN with Swedish friends for about 6 months.
May 1941. Back to HALSINGMO
December 1941. Employed at British Legation till repatriated 28 November 1942.

---

90   Other debriefs were provided at the same time:

Stoker (1st Class). Broom. D.B.T. Previously: Agricultural Worker. From: Longmoor Road, Sutton Cold Field. Service: 5 years 8 months.

December 1940. GUNNARN.
May 1941. Returned to HALSINGMO.
December 1941. Worked at British Legation in STOCKHOLM. [Repatriated 28 November 1942].

Five days later, to my knowledge the last *Hunter* survivor to be flown home was Leading Cook James Williams.

MOST SECRET. MI9 9/5/P.G. (Norway) 1027.
Leading Cook. J.W. Williams. Previously: Printer. From: Park View, Liskeard. Service: 9 years.
Interned. SWEDEN 28 April 1940.
Left. STOCKHOLM 3 December 1942.
Arrived. ABERDEEN 3 December 1942.

I was interned in GUNNARN and then HALSINGMO. May 1941 I was taken to STOCKHOLM, and from then until my departure from Sweden, I was employed at the British Legation as a messenger and night watchman. For the last months I also assisted in taking micro-photographs. (Previous employment was a Printer).

At this stage, as you will have read, out of the forty-seven *'Hunter'* survivors, three were hospitalised, one officer was taken away by the Germans and forty-three were interned in Sweden. From the latter, four managed to return to Britain respectively in ships involved in the Operations 'Rubble' and 'Performance', possibly another four via Russia and other means of transport and at least twenty in RAF flights from Bromma to Leuchars. As you will see from the list below, approximately ten were captured by the Germans in 'Operation Performance' sailing out of Gothenburg. This tentatively accounted for thirty-eight.

The *Hunter* survivors, or at least those who were not taken as prisoners of war to Germany, became a problem for the Royal Navy. Having signed the 'Declaration', this had led to them being given non-combatant duties. Here we return to Stormy Renshaw to explain, in a way that only he can, the type of employment that was found for some of the sailors. "The job was cleaning out female gas masks. Of course, females used gas masks as handbags as well, and what we turned out of those handbags was nobody's business. A lot of rude stuff there was. We were there for weeks, following the same routine, doing nothing, because we'd signed the treaty, they'd taken our fingerprints and if we were caught again, we'd be shot".

Sam Evens believed there were about twenty *Hunter* survivors that volunteered to participate in 'Operation Performance'. So far from my research I have only been able to account for seventeen. Nor is it known exactly how many made it back to Britain or were captured by the Germans. Here is a list of the cargo vessels, names of the *Hunter* sailors with their ranks, ages and the area of UK or Malta from which they came.

Charente;
Anthony Bartolo *1 Officers Steward 22 Sliema, Malta POW
Andrew Black *2 Electrical Artificer 29 Sheffield POW
Joseph 'Pat' Duffy *2 Petty Officer Stoker 43 Skelmesdale. POW
John 'Chats' Harris *2 Stoker 25 Plymouth. POW No 619
Guy *Hunter* *2 Able Seaman 23 Rosyth. POW

Buccaneer;
Leslie Clayton *1 Able Seaman 28 Leeds. POW No 607

Dicto;
Norman Bowden Able Seaman 30 Newton Abbott (later flight 17/05/42)
James Renshaw Able Seaman 23 Sheffield (later flight 08/10/42)
Stanley Cook Able Seaman 28 Plymouth (later flight 08/10/42)
Rex Brown Telegraphist 22 Durham (later flight 17/05/42)

Lind;
Sam Evens Petty Officer Stoker 36 Plymouth (Arrived in Britain on *Lind*)

Skytterren;
Frank Caton *1 Stoker 23 Morecambe POW No 555
Charles Falzon *2 NAAFI Manager 28 Cospicua Malta POW No 554
Fred Ward. *1 Ordinary Seaman. 22 Cinderford. Glos POW.
Daniel Murphy *3 Stoker 29 County Cork. POW No 608

BP Newton;
Joseph Settle Stoker 20 Doncaster.
Thomas King Stoker 20 Gainsborough.

There is another name that was possibly of a crew member of one of the above vessels;

John Minstrell Leading Seaman 32 Hamrun, Malta [91]

Initially, there were some doubts as to whether Thomas King came home on board *B.P. Newton* with Joe Settle. As I have indicated the RAF Leuchars Visitor's Book lists a Thomas King on a flight from Bromma, arriving at RAF Leuchars on the 6th of December 1941. However, they were both mentioned in the 'Supplement' to the *London Gazette* on the 1st of August 1944' **"The KING has been graciously pleased to give unrestricted permission for the wearing of the following decorations bestowed by King Haakon of Norway for services to Norway – The Norwegian War Medal."** Therefore, unless there is another explanation, then Thomas King came back aboard *B.P. Newton*.

Returning to the captured crew members of the 'Blockade Busters', in 'Kvarstad Ships and Men', it is explained that the captured seamen and the ten (or possibly more) *Hunter* survivors from *Buccaneer*, *Charente* and *Skytteren* were quickly moved on from Fredrikshavn by their German captors. They were transported through Flensburg and Hamburg before arriving at Bremen late in the evening of 6th of April 1942; where they were taken to the Marlag and Milag Nord camp by truck. Although the two injured from *Skytteren's* crew, were not in good health, the remainder, taking into account their survival experience, were well. It was not long before their thoughts must have turned to looking for ways to escape. One Norwegian crew member was escorted by a guard to the train's toilet, where he managed to squeeze through a small window. His reward was entry into England via Sweden.

---

91 *1 Stalag 344 in Lamsdorf, Poland.
    *2 Marlag (Ing Milag Nord Westertimke. (Tarmstedt). Germany.
    *3 Stalag 3A in Luckenwalde, Germany.

Frying Pan into the Fire

"No man has ever lived until he has utterly starved and felt lice crawling over the body." – James Hilton. Prisoner of War. World War Two.

If it was any consolation for the *Hunter* or merchant seamen, they could have been sent immediately to the Stalag XB, only forty three kilometres from Bremen. Although, I am uncertain as to whether any did actually end up there at some stage. At the very beginning of the war this was an overcrowded and poorly run camp; between 1939 and 1945 several hundred thousand POWs from fifty-five nations passed through the camp. Due to the bad conditions in which they were housed, thousands died there of hunger, disease, or were killed by the guards. Estimates of the number of dead range from 8,000 to 50,000.

One unfortunate resident who found himself in Stalag XB was nineteen-year-old Patrick Brady from Salford. As a teenager on leaving De La Salle College Patrick worked for Marconi which was developing wireless telegraphy equipment. However, the war now in its second year he decided to join the Merchant Navy as a Radio Officer. On the 4th of November 1940, aboard M/V *Port Hobart* he sailed out of Liverpool as part of a convoy bound for New Zealand. Twenty days later the vessel left the convoy. Now on her own and in the Caribbean seas, she unluckily ran into the German pocket battleship *Admiral Scheer*. The passengers and crew were taken off before charges were set and the ship finally sunk.

After three months of being transferred from one ship to another, Patrick and his fellow crew members arrived in Bordeaux and were placed in a transit camp at Saint-Médard-en-Jalles. Crew members described the conditions there as "terrible with a lack of adequate food, clothing and sanitation". The men were crowded into rough wooden huts, with one hundred bunks but only four forms and no tables to eat meals. Approximately a month later, initially pleased to hear they were to be moved on, they found themselves herded into cattle trucks followed by an uncomfortable five-day journey then an eleven kilometre march. Finally, arriving at the infamous Stalag XB, where conditions were even worse, the food was appalling, clothing issued consisted of dirty garments previously worn by other prisoners, sanitary conditions were bad and medical supplies poor.

There was a clear hierarchy among prisoners. At the top were British and American POWs, generally treated correctly according to the Geneva Convention. Prisoners from Western Europe (French, Belgians) were also treated as POWs but received less outside help and were not as well-nourished. Italians, who came to Stalag XB after September 1943, were deemed traitors by the German guards, they were ill-fed and used as forced labour. The Soviet POWs were the lowest in the hierarchy being denied POW status, they received no outside food, and were not allowed access to international observers. Guards had a special shoot-to-kill policy for them.

Fortunately, for Patrick Brady and his fellow crew members they only had to endure a year, when in mid-1942 they were transferred to the Marlag und Milag Nord camp. [92]

In my search for crew members or their families of the five destroyers, especially later, those on *Hunter* who had become POWs, I was fortunate to have contact with Peter Siddall. His father Harold from Devonport was a Stoker 1st Class and Harold's close cousin Stanley Stephens was a *Hardy* survivor. Although Peter knew little of Stanley's experiences at Narvik, interestingly he mentioned his father Harold had been a POW when serving on a 'Motor Launch' in Crete. Harold was captured by the Germans on 26th May 1941.

Peter Siddall and Harold's daughter, Barbara Roche, took steps towards making sure their father's story would be left for future generations. Sadly, Peter passed away in 2011, however Barbara has allowed me to include parts of her father's story.

Subsequent to Harold's capture his life thereafter as a POW saw him being moved around in different camps and various parts of Germany and occupied countries. Including Stalag VIIIB where many if not all *Hunter* survivors at times we kept. Thus, Harold Siddall's memoirs will greatly enhance the following chapters, highlighting his fellow sailors fight to survive in the camps.

---

92   As a result of the ill-treatment of the Soviets and a lack of shelter, several epidemics broke out among them. Thousands of them died from disease, starvation and brutal treatment by guards. They were buried in mass graves in the camp graveyard, today a war cemetery.

"The worst days of my life."

From June 1941, the 20,000 Allied prisoners [which included 5,000 Australian and New Zealand troops] captured in Greece, were transported to Germany. They were taken by rail in closed goods wagons on a journey of up to a week. One prisoner wrote in his diary as "the worst days of my life". Another described the ordeal: "A week in cattle trucks in the height of sweltering summer ... No seats or other amenities. All of us weak and suffering from diarrhoea, many with bleeding bowels and no sanitary arrangements whatsoever."

Stalag VIIA

Although, Harold eventually ended up at Stalag VIIIB, here I have edited his observations of life in his first camp Stalag VIIA, at Moosburg, near Munich. The camp induction procedure would be similar to that which the *Hunter* men would have had to endure. Here begins excerpts of Stoker 1st Class Harold Siddall experiences.

The men after a long train journey through southern Germany crammed together in wagons, were naturally anxious about what to expect. They were first taken into what could only be described as a sheep-shearing shed where French POWs were wielding hand-operated clippers. After the procedure, Harold would stand out as the only one with his hair shorn but with a beard. They were then ushered to another building where they would find several deep circular containers of a thick, yellow, sulphurous liquid. Stripped off they had to bathe in these containers whilst scrubbing one another's backs. They had evidently been deloused, "thank goodness!" said Harold.

Now deloused, on the floor were heaps of various uniforms. They were issued with "something like cotton underpants which were secured with a drawstring, and a shirt of rather coarse material". Harold finished up with a Highland regiment jacket and something worn by another Scottish soldier as a dress jacket. The only trousers he could find to fit were a pair of Yugoslav soldier's jodhpurs, which ended just below his knees. Harold joked, "So picture, if you can, a British sailor, with a white bald head, a beard which had gone to seed, outwardly clad in a jacket which nearly fitted, a pair of something or other acting as trousers, socks and boots."

The French POWs took down their particulars, and they had to give a thumb print. Next they were given a rectangular aluminium identity disc to be worn around the neck, stamped in two places 'Stalag VIIA: Number 5850'. Harold and his colleagues could only imagine that should they die whilst in captivity, one half of the aluminium disc would be sent to the International Red Cross. Presumably the other half would go with them to the grave.

It was now time for the necessary inoculations and it quickly became apparent that the same syringe was used for all. The inoculation was in the left breast, "which went in like a thump from a heavyweight boxer". The men then formed up outside and proceeded down the road, which was their first opportunity to see what a prisoner of war camp looked like. On each side of that road were walls of barbed wire as high as fifteen feet, with similar walls branching off at right angles to form compounds. Initially Stalag VIIA had been a camp for French POWs and Harold's group were the first British contingent to enter. Confined to their compounds the French threw Gauloises cigarettes to them, together with matches. Those that smoked soon found the cigarettes were made of strong black tobacco and some fell to their knees when they inhaled the smoke.

On reaching their compound they began choosing their bunks out of a three-tier set, on which lay a mattress with a minimum amount of straw, resting on seven strips of wood. On the mattress there was a thin, dark grey blanket and a piece of cloth to serve as a towel. They were surprised to find that an evening meal had already been prepared by French cooks. The cooks had saved rations as they had been expecting the group the day before. The meal of fish soup was ladled into their own aluminium dishes and would have been devoured with few comments, joking or otherwise.

Beside the huts, which formed a square, there was a lavatory without running water, serving for dual needs – everything expended into a huge crater. Unfortunately, someone had forgotten the toilet paper. In the meantime, they took their food dish and with cold water cleansed it and themselves. Each hut was in the form of semi-detached accommodation, divided by a wash-place consisting of cement troughs into which cold water could run. The windows had wooden shutters, hinged on the outside; come lock-up time these were shut and barred by the guards, who also locked the door, effectively sealing them in. A couple of Alsatian dogs were let loose in the compound, searchlights from the watchtowers swept the area frequently; Harold's thoughts sarcastically were "all this to ensure that nobody could do us harm during the night, I presume!"

The first morning the men had no problems sleeping after their long arduous journey in the railway wagons. However, the men woke up itching caused by fleas, which bred themselves in the straw mattress. For the remainder of their time at Stalag VIIA there would be only a few good night's sleep.

It took a few days before the men were released from isolation in their compound. Then, one morning after roll-call the gates were opened and they were free to wander into the other compounds. These were all occupied by French POWs who had been there since the French capitulation, about a year before. The British servicemen were made welcome and their Allied comrades soon wanted to know the latest developments in the war. One of the huts accommodated French soldiers captured at the 'Maginot Line'. They were fortunate, having walked out with all their kit, so their hut was like home from home. In addition, every month they received "thick, hard, unsweetened biscuits" from their Government. These went a long way to supplementing their daily ration of food.

Each morning the prisoners received a ladle of mint tea and a seventh of a loaf of bread, described as "dark brown stuff, said to contain sawdust for bulk". In the late afternoon the food consisted of a ladle of soup; sometimes cabbage or turnip and, very occasionally, fish soup. Harold recalls that the French had told them that they used dandelion leaves to complement their menu. So it was not long before raiding parties were sent out to the edge of the compounds, carefully avoiding the 'trip wires'. Although the men found the leaves, dust and all, it was bitter food. Apparently, it was not long before stocks became unsustainable.

The prisoner of War camp currency, first used by Harold Siddall
in 1941. [Barbara Roch [nee Siddall] Collection.]

Then one day to their surprise they were each given a pre-printed post-card, with the following four sentences: 'I am well. I am not well. I am wounded. I am not wounded.' They then went about the task of deleting that which did not apply to them, any additions would cancel the card.

Harold Siddall's postcard arrived home months later, in care of the International Red Cross.

Stating: I am a Prisoner of War.
                     I am well.
                     I am not wounded.

At least there was one other positive result, the first being that his father [mother had died in 1936] had been made aware of his welfare and where-abouts, secondly that the postcard triggered them to take it to the Naval Barracks. As having previously been posted, 'Missing in Action', Harold felt assured, "the Powers that Be could put me back on the pay register!"

Occasionally, there would be an issue of boiled potatoes, which worked out at about three each. This resulted in a complicated procedure to make sure each man received equal amounts. First, the potatoes were placed on a clear part of the stone floor, then shared by size into the number of rows for each man in the hut. "Talk about microscopic eyesight!" recounted Harold. Then the senior member of the hut had the difficult task of sorting the pota-toes in a fair distribution, according to size. The men's mouths were proba-bly drooling and once issued, the spuds would have been devoured instantly, skins and all. Shame for those who received a part rotten spud, they may have been luckier next time.

By now Harold had volunteered for employment at a labour camp in Munich, the incentive was to receive the same amounts of food as the civil-ian workers. The work involved repairing railway tracks, but required a total eight miles march to their work place and back in the evening. It was difficult to keep up their energy levels and hold back their breakfast bread ration for the small dish of cabbage soup. Harold recalls, "A favourite meal for the civilian workers was a piece of fat bacon toasted in front of a brazier, as the fat melted it would be rubbed onto the piece of bread and eaten. That smell used to drive us crazy."

One evening on return to the camp, the men got a surprise; they were given a POW postcard, this was their first opportunity to write home. Harold explains, "We were told that we could ask for parcels to be sent, but that the weight limit was ten kilogrammes. Like the others, all I could think about was food and it was farcical as we prompted one another with suggestions, expecting that the parcels would be delivered in a week or two. They never came."

In October 1942, the weather becoming colder, the men found it difficult to deal with the long stretches of railway track in inadequate clothing. They agreed that this issue had to be raised with the German authority. Shortly after, Harold and his comrades received a surprise, "Blow me if one Sunday, large bundles of British Army uniforms arrived in the canteen. These were all parts of captured uniforms which had been deloused. I finished up with a forage cap, brown pullover, an early-issue Army overcoat, a somewhat-modern issue pair of trousers with leg pouch pockets and a British Army greatcoat." They were also issued with a pair of mittens, so on this occasion their complaints had paid off.

Harold Siddall with pal Andy Andrews at Stalag VIIA. First
winter December 1941. [Barbara Roche Collection.]

Other improvements occurred when an Australian Sergeant Major came to be the camp leader, and a doctor from the British Medical Corps and an Army bandsman became their medical orderly. However, to officially confirm a prisoner was too ill for work a German Naval doctor was attached to the camp. Although to be granted 'unfit' status was almost unobtainable.

Harold Siddall points out that by now it became apparent to the camp residents that the German Army fighting on the Russian Front was having a detrimental effect. Each day another civilian was missing from the track work. Enquiring to their comrades, "When is it your turn to go?" the reply would be, "*Ich Weiss nicht*". [Used in colloquial language – to express uncertainty, and usually when asked an opinion on something – "I don't know."] When marching to work they could see posters appealing for gifts of warm clothing for the soldiers on the Eastern Front.

Harold also explained that because of working on the rail tracks in cold winds many of the men suffered from badly cracked lips. When the men asked for ointment, the answer came back, "Be like the gallant German soldiers on the Eastern Front, who used the wax from their ears to rub on their lips."

In September 1943, the Allied forces had begun the invasion of Italy, resulting in an increased influx of POWs into Germany. Subsequently, the overcrowding with the additional merchant seamen from various countries captured in the Mediterranean war zone, meant residents at Stalag VIIA had to move on. The news soon got round the camp; but the question was where? No information was being released, until Harold Siddall and his fellow captives having been contained in their compounds were herded onto cattle trucks and transported to a train station well outside Munich. The men were issued with a loaf of bread and small tin of meat for a few days journey with a small number of stops. Finally, arriving at the town of Freiburg in Upper Silesia, which was almost on the Polish border. Harold recalls, "Unloaded and counted and counted again, we waited until at last we moved off to Stalag VIIIB."

Moving ahead, the liberation of Stalag VIIA came on 29th April 1945 when the American Army arrived, and the Germans requested an armistice. This was rejected leading to a short and one sided victory with American tanks chasing the retreating German soldiers. Subsequently, many Germans surrendered as did the 240 camp guards, German records show that in January 1945 they had catered for over 76,000 prisons in the camp. The camp was eventually turned into a Civilian Internment Camp for 12,000 German men and women suspected of criminal activity for the Nazi regime.

I will return to Harold Siddall; in the meantime, back to the *Hunter* POWs initial experience in captivity.

Marlag und Milag Nord.

The German Navy originally operated a 'Transit' camp in Wilhelmshaven, where newly arrived prisoners were processed before being sent to other camps. The camp was located between the Marlag and Milag camps. After the Allied bombing raids on Wilhelmshaven in February 1942 this facility was located around the village of Westertimke, about nineteen miles north-east of Bremen. Marlag was used for Royal Navy men, whilst Milag was for Merchant Navy men [93]

Fred Ward (right) and two of his fellow POWs in Stalag VIIIB. However, they were attached to the Forced Labour Camp E538 which was the Graff Renard Colliery. (Fred Ward Collection via son Robin).

---

93   Confirmed List of the HMS *Hunter* crewmembers who were taken as Prisoners of War to Germany.
Caton. POW No 555 Stalag VIIIB / 344 Lamsdorf. [Now called Wroclaw, Poland]
Clayton. POW No 607. Stalag VIIIB / 344 Lamsdorf.
Bartolo. POW No unknown. Stalag VIIIB / 344 Lamsdorf,
Falzon. POW No 554. Marlag. Ing Milag Nord, [Westertimke, Nr Bremen, Germany]
Duffy. POW No unknown. Marlag. Ing Milag Nord.
Harris. POW No 619 Marlag. Ing Milag Nord.
Black. POW No unknown. Marlag. Ing Milag Nord.
Ward. POW No unknown Stalag VIIIA [Poland]
Murphy. POW No 608 Stalag. 3A Luckenwalde, [Nr Berlin, Germany]
Hunter POW No unknown Marlag. Ing Milag Nord.
Reid. POW No 1222 Marlag. Ing Milag Nord (Commissioned Officers Billet)

The Marlag and Milag camp guards were 'Kriegsmarines'. Whilst the British POW's remained there for a while the Norwegian women with their children were released. However, the Norwegian men were subjected to 'War Trials'. This resulted in them being sent to other German prisons where the regime was much more authoritarian. It appears that during their incarceration forty-five died.

Subsequently, as you can see from the above list, five *Hunter* men were moved on to other camps in Southern Germany and Poland. As previously mentioned Stalag VIIIB camp was the administrative centre for detailing POW's to other 'Sub Camps' where they were employed in various types of manual work for the ongoing Nazis war effort. In 1943 Stalag VIIIB was changed to Stalag 344.

There was a separate section at Marlag for Non Commissioned Officers. This camp was 330 yards from the Milag camp and the area between contained a prison block, hospital, guard house and a shower block for the men of both camps.

Each camp contained a number of single-storey wooden huts; twenty-nine in Marlag and thirty-six in Milag. Most of them were barracks, while the others contained kitchens, dining rooms, washrooms, guard barracks, storehouses, a post office, and other administrative buildings. The barracks were divided into several rooms each accommodating fourteen to eighteen men who slept in two- and three-tiered bunks.

Usually both camps together contained a total of 5,300 occupants and as mentioned were guarded by German naval personnel. Although later, as the war dragged on, they were replaced by Wehrmacht reservists.

It was obviously important that the POWs were kept occupied not just for their own benefit but also that of the camp staff. In Marlag there was a theatre where the POWs performed regular concerts and plays. They had a sports field and a library with around 3,000 books, sports equipment and textbooks being provided by the Red Cross. Prisoners ran their own various courses in languages, mathematics, and commercial, vocational, economic, and scientific subjects. They were allowed to send two letters and four postcards each month but no restrictions on the number of letters received. Although, as you would expect, all incoming and outgoing mail was censored. A popular entertainment night was on a Saturday provided by the 'Milag Jockey Club' which held race meetings. The 'horses' were wooden models that raced on a 36-foot track, controlled by dice.

The POWs bet on the races, and the money raised was donated to the Red Cross.

There were 5,000 Allied merchant seamen captured by the Germans during the war, most were held at Milag. As civilian non-combatants, according to the '1907 Hague Conventions' merchant seamen "[...] are not made prisoners of war, on condition that they make a formal promise in writing, not to undertake, while hostilities last, any service connected with the operations of the war." However, the Germans always treated Merchant Navy seamen as POWs. In fact, from 1942 the British did the same. In 1943, the Germans suggested an exchange of equal numbers of Merchant Navy prisoners, but the offer was immediately turned down by the Admiralty. This was on the grounds that such an agreement would be far more to the Germans advantage, as it would provide them with a large number of men suitable for use as U-boat crews, of which they were desperately short.

You will remember the headlines from the ***Portsmouth Evening News*** in a previous chapter. **"Twice Feared Dead – Safe"** which referred to the family's joy for Andrew Black. He had a sailed with the *Charente* and was one of those POWs now at Marlag Nord camp. Here is a summary of the newspaper feature:

"A member of HMS *Hunter*, he was first reported missing in [...] 11th of April 1940 when the destroyer was sunk. After four weeks anxiety, the Admiralty announced that he was one of 45 survivors Interned in Sweden [...] While in Sweden he was in communication with his parents and told them that he was given his parole, but often hinted that he would be home "As soon as he could get there". He met a Portsmouth man whose home was in Sweden, and he then mentioned that he was planning to escape at the earliest possible moment.

"Two years and a day after his first adventure [...] he was once again reported to his parents as missing. It was known that he had got away from Gothenburg in an attempt to reach this country, but that the ship had been lost following action by the Germans. For the second time his parents were torn by anxiety, but early in May there was a ray of hope. They learned through a neutral source that it was possible he had been saved.

"No further news was received until yesterday, when Mr and Mrs Black were overjoyed to see their son's handwriting on a postcard from a prison camp in Germany. The postcard was prefaced with the words, "I am now residing in Germany as a prisoner of war". On the card Electrical Artificer

Black says that they get Red Cross parcels regularly but that he would be pleased to receive "as many cigarettes as you like, with chocolate and shoes if possible." As the card was dated 12th July 1942 he had apparently spent his 29th birthday (July 7) in the camp."

Whilst in the camp, Andrew Black and his fellow POWs were pleased to learn that they had become the recipients of a bonus, which was awarded to men who had volunteered for the 'Blockade Busting' operations.

Several escape tunnels were dug from Milag. The first was about 12 m (40 ft) long, built from March to August 1943. Twelve prisoners escaped, though all were recaptured within two weeks. A second tunnel, about 40 m (130 ft) long, was built from April to August 1944. Five men escaped, but again were soon recaptured. Another tunnel built by Norwegian prisoners was discovered before its completion. In addition, another tunnel was dug to store contraband.

Lieutenant John Worsley R.N., was captured in November 1943 during a landing on Lussinpiccolo. Also an official war artist, Worsley painted several portraits of his fellow POWs, and made sketches of the camp, as well as creating "Albert R.N.", [named after a popular 1950s cinema film] a life-sized dummy, that ensured that any escaper would not be missed in the daily head-counts.

There were two other officers; Lieutenant Denis Kelleher RNVR, and Lieutenant Stewart Campbell, Fleet Air Arm, who escaped from Marlag in early 1944, wearing blue overalls to cover their uniforms, and managed to reach England within twenty-two days, first having been smuggled to neutral Sweden on a ship from Bremen.

Another successful escapee from Marlag was Lieutenant David James David, RNVR. In December 1943 James slipped out of the shower block, but was arrested at the port of Lubeck. In late 1944 he escaped again and this time made it to Sweden.

This brings me to a perplexing end to the story of one of the *Hunter* POWs who was incarcerated at the Marlag camp. Able Seaman Guy Hunter, you will remember, was from Rosyth, married to Maizie and an all-round sportsman. Shelley Hutton, Guy's granddaughter informed me that whilst her mother Valerie was born in 1945, her uncle, also called Guy was born in 1943. Obviously this would indicate that Guy Hunter had returned back to Britain, earlier, unlike the other *Hunter* POWs, who were only released at the end of the war. As you will read, there was an arrangement between both sides to exchange the seriously wounded, escorted by fit POWs, although mainly those medically trained. I am sure to get out by the backdoor, so to speak, some shrewd captives would have taken the opportunity.

I will come back to this intriguing episode later but before then here is a possible clue to Guy Hunter's escape, in an account by Reverend Ernest Ball, SSM, a fellow prisoner of war. Reverend Ball provides an excellent description of how life was for the '*Hunter*' crewmen imprisoned in the Malag and Milag camps. '*anglicanhistory.org/religious/ball/war.*'

"In our section were some of other nationalities who had been serving on British ships, and a few like myself, had been passengers [...] Many of the prisoners in the camp had been brought from other places and more arrived from time to time.

"There was a hospital in the camp, a dental surgery, a dining hall with kitchens manned by our own cooks, a library, a hall for the big Sunday service and for theatrical productions, and a canteen where we could spend our 'lagergeld' for small requirements. We had a Czech doctor at first, but he was mysteriously removed from the camp and replaced by a British army doctor (a Scot who claimed to be a staunch Presbyterian). The dentist who was also from the British army attended to the teeth not only of prisoners but also of several German soldiers who came to him on the quiet. It would be interesting to know what their reaction would have been had they ever found out that he was a 'Jew'!

"As the war dragged on the quality of the guards deteriorated, for the best of them were taken away to help in resisting the pressure on various fronts. There was, for instance, an elderly guard attached to one of the huts who could hardly be called soldierly apart from his uniform He had been conscripted into the German army, though his home was in Luxembourg where he had had a civilian occupation.

"It was soon found that trading could be done with some of these guards, even with those who manned the machine guns in the corner towers. They were eager to obtain certain items that came in the Red Cross parcels, and gave in exchange eggs, vegetables, and other things wanted in the camp. This trading, which was usually carried on when no German officers were around, was the cause of a tragic incident. One of the prisoners had arranged to meet after dark for such a transaction with a guard who was then expected to be on duty in the compound; but it happened that a different guard was there that night and he, seeing someone approaching when all were supposed to be in their huts, took alarm, fired at the man and killed him.

"We had a bad time one winter when trains carrying our Red Cross parcels could not get through because of the weather, and even the German rations were affected. In normal times the parcels from the Red Cross were issued every week, one to each man. They were a great boon, especially those from Canada; and so also were the parcels from relations at home, and those received by seamen from their shipping companies. Cigarettes became so abundant at one time that they were used not only for trading but also in place of cash at gambling sessions.

"News about the war reached us in various ways. Some was received which was said to have been broadcast from England and picked up by a receiving set hidden somewhere in the camp. The source of this news could not be authenticated since the location of such a set would have to be a carefully guarded secret, but the presence among us of several wireless operators made it possible. The Germans certainly suspected the existence of a set, and for that reason the camp would sometimes be subjected to a rigorous search. On one occasion, all the thermos flasks we had bought from the canteen were impounded; apparently the Germans had somehow got the notion that a receiving set might be concealed in one of them.

"I remember a production of *The Student Prince* and also a superb presentation of *Snow White and the Seven Dwarfs*. Many others were involved in these productions, and much ingenuity was used in devising from limited resources appropriate scenery, properties, and costumes. I had the help one Good Friday of some actors and musicians, together with our Sunday choir. This was for a three-hour period of readings and music, which was attended by a large number of our fellow prisoners. There were outdoor activities for the young and energetic. The Australians, for instance, introduced their own style of rugby football, and some wild demonstrations of this game were enacted on a patch of ground on the edge of the camp. There was even a brief spell of swimming one summer in the two deep ponds inside the camp which had been made to provide a quick supply of water in case of fire; but this met with disapproval and was stopped.

"There were of course some attempts at escape. I know of one tunnel which was successfully completed, and several got away but not for long; they were all recaptured, and after a few days in the 'cooler' were brought back into the camp. It was not altogether a waste of time and effort, for it provided through several months a diverting occupation for those who made the tunnel and for those who protected the secrecy of the operation.

"Only one man achieved a successful escape. He was a third engineer of unadventurous appearance who made long and careful preparation for his solo venture. He was regarded as eccentric, and even condemned by some, for volunteering to work on a farm; since as an officer he was not obliged to do such work. At first a guard accompanied him on his daily journey to and from the farm; but he became so trusted that after a while the guard was withdrawn and he was allowed the use of a bicycle to get to his job. One day he failed to return to the camp. By the time his disappearance was confirmed he had cycled a long way from the camp presumably taking with him some suitable items of food saved from Red Cross parcels.

"After the war, I learnt from him that he had gone north, and after some narrow escapes from recapture had reached a port to which ships came from Sweden. There he got into touch with some Swedish sailors, having acquired in the camp some knowledge of their language. By promising a bribe, later honoured by the Consulate in Stockholm, he was smuggled on to their ship, and hidden in a coal bunker while the Germans made their usual search before allowing the ship to sail. His escape had a romantic ending, for his Norwegian fiancée also escaped into Sweden at about the same time. They were flown to England after their marriage, and he received the MBE."

There appears to be some evidence to suggest that Guy Hunter having returned home in 1942, similar to the above incident told by Reverend Ball, could have done so by some form of escape, legitimately or not. Alternatively, did Guy become one of the Milag [merchant navy] prisoners who were given early release? If so then having been captured on a Norwegian cargo vessel with other merchant seamen, including British, did he managed to keep the German authorities believing he was a merchant seaman, and not a Royal Navy – Able Seaman. Unlikely, I should think! Back of his mind must have been the possibility of his signed 'Declaration' becoming known.

However, there is another possibility that Guy was able to be repatriated early, which I will come to shortly.

Reverend Ball continues his memories. "Some cheering news came to us through a pamphlet raid; copies of the pamphlet were picked up in the camp and translated, and so we learnt about the conclusion of the fighting in North Africa. We also learnt indirectly about the bombing raid in which a dam was destroyed. It became known that some of our guards who came from the affected areas were granted leave to go to their homes to find out what had happened to their families and to render any help.

"Nearly all of us remained at Milag Nord until our release, which came for some of us in October 1943 and for the majority shortly before the end of the war. The camp probably compared favourably with others in Germany, for the naval command seemed to take some pride in the way it managed what was perhaps the only POW camp in its charge."

In the latter stage of the war POWs evacuated from other camps began to arrive, resulting in overcrowding, and a reduction in food rations. In February 1945, some 3,000 men evacuated from Stalag Luft III also arrived. In order to accommodate them the NCOs joined the Officers in their part of the camp.

On 2 April 1945, the POWs were confused about the enemy's decision making. First, the Commandant announced that he had received orders to leave the camp with most of his guards, leaving only a small detachment behind to hand over the camp to Allied forces, who were already in Bremen. However that afternoon a detachment of over a hundred German SS military police entered the camp and rounded up over 3,000 men and marched them out. They headed to the east but the next day, they were strafed by RAF aircraft, and several POWs were killed. The same type strafing happened over the next few days. Finally the Royal Naval officer in charge made a request to the Germans to allow the men to rest during the day and march at night, to which they agreed.

Returning back to the situation at Marlag and Milag, on the 9 April 1945 the guards having moved out, their place was taken by local older men, known as the 'People's Storm', who were German national military men, between the age of sixteen and sixty at the latter months of the war. The next day a Division of Panzer Grenadiers positioned their tanks and artillery next to Marlag and Milag camps. The prisoners left behind responded to the threat of a pitched battle on their doorstep by digging trenches. Although artillery was fired from the Panzer positions, fortunately they had left by the time the British Guards Armoured Division liberated the camps on 27 April 1945.

With regards to the marching men, they had crossed the River Elbe north of Hamburg, on the 18 April and finally arrived at Lubeck on the Baltic coast. They were finally liberated by the British 11th Armoured Division on 1 May 1945.

There is another interesting story from a sailor who was also incarcerated in various POW camps, but to hear it we must go back to the beginning of the war.

In early 1941, the German cruiser *Thor* was raiding in the mid-Atlantic; she had already confronted two Royal Navy armed merchant cruisers. So by the time she encountered the larger vessel HMS *Voltaire*, she was ready to be battle-tested and anxious to sink an enemy combatant.

One of the crewmembers on board *Voltaire* was Able Seaman 'Gunner' Thomas 'Tom' Barnham, who had been a professional boxer before joining the Royal Navy. Thomas begins his account, "Within three months of war breaking out I was on my first ship [...] We went to Malta where they put us on a 'contraband' patrol and we toured the Greek Islands for five months. Then we got word that we had to go to Canada to escort a convoy. This was in 1940 [...] we were doing convoys for nearly twelve months [...] We put in to Trinidad and started making our way to Freetown [East Africa]. Early on 4th April [1941] the alarm went off. We could see this ship coming and we kept signalling it, 'who are you, what are you doing in this area?' But it still kept coming and never signalled.

"All of a sudden up came her guns and they opened up. We all got to our guns but where our shots were falling short, hers were catching us. Within a few minutes, we had orders from the officer to split the crew and go down to man a gun in the well deck. When we got there we found everyone lying dead and when we got up on the gun we couldn't focus it round because it had had a direct hit. So we came back up on to our other gun and we just fired away but she kept hitting on us and all of a sudden we went over and the officer said 'Abandon Ship'. I didn't abandon ship, I went right through the ship to the stern. I had one or two mates there on other guns. On the way I saw mates of mine lying dead. I went up to the Captain who was at the stern, with about twenty other people. He asked me and another kid, a fellow called Ginger McInnes, to go in to the workshop and get some wood to use as floats.

"While we were in there a shell came in and Ginger was peppered with everything. I finished up with a nasty cut on the elbow. We came out and all of a sudden the ship just turned over and slung us all into the water. I'm in the water and I saw two boys struggling, trying to get on each other's backs. I got in between them. One of them was McInnes and the other a lad called Scott. Neither of them could swim and they were trying to hang onto this piece of wood, so I said, 'Now, cut it out, let me in the middle and we'll just hang on and see what happens.' Then McInnes says, 'Look, Tom,' and he held his arm up and his hand was gone. We were in the water about thirty minutes when the boy behind me drowned.

"Now all I've got is McInnes, myself and this boy that's drowned behind me. An officer had a life jacket on – you could see his head and shoulders above the water – and I shouted to him, 'Pardon me, sir, do you mind coming over here and giving me a hand with McInnes?' He said, 'I'm sorry Barnham but I can't swim'. That finished the boy. He kept putting his head on his plank and there was nothing I could do for him. Another lot of lads came on bits of wood so I went with the other boys and after about two hours the German ship, who'd sank us, came back.

"You could hear t-t-t-t like a machine-gun coming from the ship, and we thought they were shooting at us. We had been given to understand that the Germans were right villains and took no prisoners. One of the best swimmers, a boy from Wembley, just gave up and drowned when he heard the machine guns. But the Germans put boats down to pick up the survivors. They brought us back to their boat and bathed us because we were all covered in oil. They had an officer who spoke English, 'You were given to understand we were firing on you in the water but we weren't, we were keeping the sharks away from you'. Then they took us to the bottom of the boat, gave us a blanket and everybody went off to sleep. Everybody was woken up after a while, given soup and the wounded were attended to while we were there, I think we buried about three or four of our lads. Our officers conducted a burial ceremony but while they were doing that we had all the machine guns on us.

"The Germans worked hard on the wounded and we were well looked after on the ship, in fact Easter came round while we were on board and they sent a bit of chocolate and a bottle of beer to each of the prisoners. But we were dispirited. I'd lost all my friends on the Voltaire and there were quite a number of wounded amongst us.

"We were taken to Bremerhaven and then on to a German naval base. We were there roughly three to four months. They supplied us with a shirt, I had a woman's overall and they gave us a handkerchief-like holder for our socks and we had clogs. They had us all working in different parts of the barracks. About nine o'clock in the morning they'd put us in a room all day peeling potatoes.

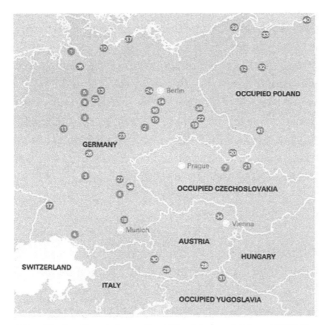

POW Europe Map ['Stolen Years'. Australian War Museum] These POW Camps would be:
Nos. 1 Marlag-Milag 2. IVC [Colditz] 18. V11A [Moosburg] 19. V11A
[Gorlitz] 20. V11B [344 – Lamsdorf] 21. V111B [Teschen]

"After we'd been there about a fortnight they would come in, call one of us out and take us to be interrogated. Once we'd finished they would put us back with the other boys. When I went up for interrogation the German officer offered me a cigarette (if you didn't want a cigarette he'd offer you an orange) and then all of a sudden he started on me – How long had I been in the Navy? Was I a conscript? How many brothers did I have in the services, what were they, naval men, Air Force or Army men. What part of the country did I come from – London? Then all of a sudden he finished up saying, 'Well, tell me who do you think is going to win this war?' Naturally I said, 'We are.' So his reply was, 'Tell me what makes you think you are going to win the war?' and then he goes on and says, 'Look, I'll tell you why you can't win the war. We've chased you out of France, we're chasing you through the desert.' Everything he said was correct but nevertheless I said, 'We're going to win the war.'

"After the interrogation, two cars would take you to another room where all those who had been interrogated were. They asked you what you'd said and they'd all been through the same procedure as I had. Then after everybody had been interrogated they drove us off to a naval camp, all naval

469

ratings and, on the other side of the camp, the Merchant Seamen's Camp. [Marlag und Milag] From there we got into shoes and English army uniform. We were there about five to six months. We used to play football to keep our spirits up and there was always something to do.

"In the morning they had us all out early on parade and a German officer came up and said, 'That lot over there, go back to your barracks and get all your belongings, you're leaving.' There must have been about two hundred of us. They put us in cattle wagons and we finished up in an Army camp, Stalag 344, [Stalag VIIIB] the biggest camp in Germany."

Stalag VIIIB

Stalag VIIIB was a notorious German Army prisoner of war camp located near the small town of Lamsdorf, now called Łambinowice in Silesia. The camp initially occupied barracks built to house British and French prisoners in World War I. At this same location there had been a prisoner camp during the Franco-Prussian War of 1870–71. Opened for Polish prisoners from a heavily populated industrial region, when after the September 1939 offensive the Roman Catholic sections of men were replaced by German settlers. Later 16,000 POWs from Britain and her dominions were housed at the camp. [94]

In the second issue of the camp magazine *The Clarion* in February 1943, the RC Chaplain Father John Berry says that, "[...] there are about 600 working parties and [...] you will be able to guess why so many of you will have not yet had a visit.

Shortly after Joe Murphy had been captured by the Germans, his family received a letter with a cryptic message. I leave it to his nephew Keiran Hosford to explain: "Whilst in Sweden, Joe had also befriended a Swedish girl called Evie Carlsson who subsequently wrote to my grandmother to let her know that she knew him. Evie's letter to my grandmother came subsequent to Joe being taken as a POW, because Evie's described the scuttling of the ship in her letter in broken English as "ship sink self which be good". We think this was Evie's way of saying that Joe had probably been taken as a POW rather than the ship having been sunk in battle.

---

94   In World War Two, Sosnowiec (Sosna is Polish for Pine Forests) was occupied by Nazi Germany. It had a large Jewish community who were deported to the concentration camp Auschwitz.

"My grandmother subsequently received a telegram (I think from the British Red Cross) confirming that Joe was a POW. We know that he was in a few different POW camps and my grandmother received a photograph of him in the form of a postcard that was postmarked Marlag U. Milag Nord and dated 17.8.43. On the back, it referred to Joe as POW No. 608 in Stammlager VIII B. (Stalag VIIIB).

Eight Hunter survivors, only five can be positively identified but the others could be Harris, Clayton and Ward. [Joe Murphy Family Collection]
Caton   Murphy   Ward   Harris
Hunter   Falzon   Clayton   Black

"Whilst Joe was a POW, my grandmother began sending regular parcels to him via the Red Cross. The Red Cross had instructed her to leave the parcel a few pounds light so that they could also pack chocolate and cigarettes into it. The cigarettes seemingly came in as a handy bartering tool, because Joe recalled that they used to get some sort of horrible dark or black bread to eat in the camps and some of the German guards used to sneak white bread in for them in exchange for cigarettes.

"Joe also recalled their camp being liberated by Russian troops at the end of the war and locals running into the camp trying to take refuge in the wake of the Russian advance. The Russians then helped the former POWs to get planes back to Britain."

Not only Joe Murphy, Fred Ward, Frank Caton, Charles Falzon but also Leslie Clayton and Anthony Bartolo were imprisoned in Stalag VIIIB [later to become known as Stalag 344].

In 1943, the Lamsdorf camp was split up, and many of the prisoners and Arbeitskommandos (labour camps) were transferred to two new base camps Stalag VIII-C [Sagan] Stalag VIII-D [Teschen]. There were more than 700 subsidiary Arbeitskommandos outside the main camp. [95]

I do not know if any of the *Hunter* crew men were detailed to work at these labour camps because these were the ones that the men would have been considered lucky to avoid. The Arbeitskommandos were set up to house lower ranks that were working in the quarries, factories and on railways. However, there were many camps for coal mining and the men initially worked as labourers for the Polish miners. They did the hardest tasks, and the conditions were not pleasant, due to the mines being damp from having water everywhere inside them.

Some of the mines were deep, going down four levels and as you would expect it was a frightening experience descending as the cage plummeted down the shafts. Each man was issued with an ID tag and a carbide lamp with a flint for lighting, which made gas that burnt when the water dripped onto it. There were three shifts, eight hours long. The morning and afternoon shifts dug out the coal and the evening shift moved equipment and supports into position for the next day. It was during this late shift that the work was the most dangerous. As you would expect, in order to delay the mining process, the prisoners considered sabotaging the mine. However, there were always men working on the lowest levels. On occasions the lift was damaged and the men in the lower levels had to escape by a complex system of ladders.

The men lived in huts just outside of the mines, ten to twelve in each. Men on different shifts were billeted together. Apart from their circumstances, this would have reminded the *Hunter* crew of life at sea. Although the food rations were a lot different; bread and coffee for breakfast and one meal of soup. Their only incentive and pleasure was the arrival of the Red Cross parcels, and many of the men later acknowledged that without them they would not have survived.

It is worth mentioning that when the International Committee of the Red

---

95   Because of the several reorganisations and number changes of camps there is considerable confusion in accounts of prisoners, even in official German records.

Cross completed their regular visits, the mine was closed down. (National Records Office at Kew – Ref WO 224/27) [96]

Able Seaman 'Gunner' Tom Barnham, as mentioned, was an ex-professional boxer before he joined up. "When we arrived at Stalag 344, in 1942, it was full of Army personnel except for one compound which had a few Air Force lads. Those that weren't NCOs had to go out to work, working on farms, all different jobs. Some were billeted out permanently, some of them worked in coal mines or brick works. At this camp we had a boy who was an Imperial Amateur champion boxer. Another camp asked for him to go and box at their camp, which the Germans agreed to. But he wouldn't have it, he said, 'I'm a regular in the Services and if I get beat I've got to live with it.' So one morning we got up early, I had a couple of mates with me, a British officer and three Germans. We set off and we travelled half a day and I boxed at this camp and won.

"The Germans had the front seats. After that I had it made. We had roll call at seven in the morning, but when they came and said '*Aufstanden*,' which means 'Get up everybody,' they said, 'Boxer, *bleiben*, you can lie in, stay,' so I never used to go on roll-call. Only a silly thing but I appreciated it, and that's what happened every morning after a boxing match. They'd never cry 'Well done,' but they'd always give me a lie-in, which was a real luxury. And I never lost a match.

"We were treated reasonably well. First thing in the morning you'd have either black coffee or mint tea. At 11.00 am you'd get four or five jacket potatoes and a black loaf between seven of us, with a bit of butter and a bit of meat; then about 12.30 you'd get a pea soup or sauerkraut. That was your lunch and at about half past two you'd either get your coffee or tea again, that was your meal. That was all you got, but fortunately we used to get one Red Cross parcel a week each from Britain. But if we ran out of them we could go probably two months before they'd come again.

"I was fortunate because of my boxing. A British army officer said to me, 'What food do you get, my friend?' I said, 'I get the same as you, sir', although I knew he was living a lot better than I was. So he says, 'You've no extras at all?' and I said, 'No, I get Red Cross parcels the same as the rest of them.' 'Oh,' he said, 'Something has got to be done about this,' so he gave me a chit so that I could get an extra Red Cross parcel a week. But there were a lot of hungry lads, so whatever I got went in the middle and was shared out, so it hardly meant much.

---

96   Extracts from the *Diary of Alan Forster* a British soldier, POW 3921, Stalag VIIIB at E7O2 Arbeitskommando. (Klimontow, outskirts of Sosnowiec in Silesia)

"Towards the end of the war the Germans brought thousands of Russian prisoners in and put them in a camp next to us. There was only barbed wire in between. We watched these people walking and they looked to us as though the wind was blowing through them. They were starving. Typhus broke out and a lot of them died. There was a Russian kid there who was about sixteen and whenever we threw any bread over to him, which we often did, before he could get it, all the other Russians had it. So I said, 'I want to get that kid and bring him into our camp.

"One day I cut the wire, brought the kid in and put him in British uniform. He stayed with us two months in our camp. Couldn't speak a word of English, but we used to sit him on our bunk and say, 'What's your name?' and we'd teach him to say, 'Monty Banks in English; 'Where have you come from?' 'London.' 'Where were you caught?' 'Arnhem.' Four or five little questions which he knew the answer to.

"A British officer came to me one day and he said, 'We'll toss him back, because if typhoid breaks out in this camp I'm going to hold you responsible and put you on a court martial.' But if you've been a prisoner for four-and-half years you don't care, so you can guess what I told him to do. I must have been at that camp about two-and-half years and then they shifted us to a camp in Obersilesien and while we were there the Russians came in." [Moved into Upper Silesia]

By 1943, the famous camp for Allied air force personnel at Stalag Luft III – had become so overcrowded that about 1,000, mostly non-commissioned aircrew, were transferred to Lamsdorf. A part of Stalag VIII-B was separated by building new barbed-wire fences. Thus a camp within a camp was created. However all food was provided from kitchens operated by army personnel in the camp proper.

The hospital facilities at Stalag VIII-B were among the best in all Stalags. The so-called Lazarett (hospital) was set up on a separate site within eleven concrete buildings. Six of these were self-contained wards, each with space for about a hundred patients. The others served as treatment blocks with operating theatres, X-ray and laboratory facilities, kitchens, and a morgue, as well as accommodations for the medical staff.

The Lazarett was headed by a German officer with the title Oberst Arzt (Colonel Doctor), but the staff was made up entirely of prisoners. They included general physicians and surgeons, even a neurosurgeon, psychiatrist, anaesthesiologist and radiologist.

The 500 or so prisoners who died at Lamsdorf whilst in captivity were first buried locally, but after the war their bodies were moved to Krakow where they were reburied in the Commonwealth War Cemetery.

In October 1943, Harold Siddall had arrived at Stalag VIIIB, it maybe that this was before or after some of the *Hunter* men had arrived. "My first impression when approaching Stalag VIIIB, was that it was in the middle of a moorland, with clear ground as far as the eye could see. There were endless rows of what appeared to be numerous potato clamps. What we did not know was these were the graves of hundreds of Russian POWs who had died of typhus in their Stalag, not very far from VIIIB."

German ration card for one day's supply in 1943. [Barbara Roche Collection]

After Harold had settled into his next abode and found his way around the camp and understood the regime system, it was time for him to start looking for ways to improve his and his companions' deplorable surroundings. Because of the shortage of civilian workers in the forest near the camps, volunteers were taken from the compounds daily to trim trees and cut down those that were selected to be used as pit-props in the coal mines.

Harold made the acquaintance of a Flight Sergeant, who hailed from Plymouth. "He was able to tell us about the state of the city after the decimating bombing it received in 1941. He described and named whole streets which had disappeared. This took a lot of believing, especially when he said that almost all of Fore Street had gone, together with the good old Royal Sailors' Rest. No more threepenny jugs of soup, games of snooker and hot water baths with a drop more hot water for a cigarette!"

As one would expect not all the POWs were physically fit as there would have been a considerable number for example who were severely wounded.

Therefore, as I have previously indicated, discussions between the opposing sides were ongoing regarding the repatriation on an exchange basis. This left a sense of excitement, not only for the disabled but also those chosen to escort them back home. With regards to these unfortunates, especially those who had lost limbs, all the residents of the camp had been lectured by a camp doctor to adhere to a policy of not assisting them unless really necessary. This was to allow them to become independent as they had to be encouraged to manage for themselves.

One day the medics decided to put on a cricket match between the one-arm and the one-leg men, which turned out to be a verbal and physical contest, involving both participants and audience. Harold Siddall explains, "There was no rule about eleven a side in those teams and there was much laughter and derision among them as they lost balance and fell when trying to perform the elementary movements of bowling and batting. We, the audience, were told to applaud and offer advice, which became barrack-room stuff and the players soon returned the compliments with expletives, cursing themselves, their rivals and us in particular. The game, such as it was, served to unleash much of their stored hates and anxieties as they unloaded all of that pent-up abuse. When talking to some of those who had lost an arm it was surprising to find they had difficulty in maintaining balance when turning rapidly or throwing a ball, due to the missing 'wing' – as they called the lost arm."

The repatriation arrangements were finally agreed and actioned. Returning back to Guy Hunter's arrival home early, could it be he was one of those repatriated, due to ill health? I say this because when I sent Granddaughter Shelley a copy of the picture of the eight *Hunter* survivors at Stalag VIIIB, she said "He doesn't look well!" I must agree when comparing him to his picture in the group at Gunnarn in April / May 1940.

In the meantime, back to life in Stalag VIIIB, where it appears the camps regime became harsher, with longer roll-calls and guard dogs in attendance and an increased censorship policy. Harold recounts, "During those despondent days, conditions deteriorated to such an extent that members of the Red Cross came to inspect the camp. The outcome was that Jerry agreed to change the camp. He did – he changed the name to Stalag 344, so Stalag VIIIB ceased to exist! And nobody seemed to notice; the Red Cross didn't make any more inspections."

The snow came early towards the end of 1944 with a cold northerly wind which made its presence felt. The huts cold concrete flooring made life very uncomfortable, so after morning roll-call those who were fit enough spent longer periods than usual tramping around the perimeter of the compound. The men had to be careful what they talked about to each other in case the Germans had slipped a 'mole' within their groups. This required an understanding that each member of a group had to be recognised.

The *Hunter* men would have been particularly interested in a news report on a covert wireless that the man who led the Alpine Troops into Narvik in 1940, now promoted to Colonel General, Eduard Dietl had been killed in an air crash. Ironically the accident occurred in Austria alongside him were two other Generals. Subsequent to Narvik he was a recipient of the Oak Leaves cluster to the Knight's Cross of the Iron Cross.

At the funeral his friend read the Eulogy: [not part of the broadcast].

On June 23, 1944, Colonel General Dietl died in a plane accident. As an outstanding soldier in the struggle for our National Socialist Greater Germany, Colonel General Dietl stood out for his fight in Norway and Finland. He led his men from victory to victory.

His battle for Narvik will remain unforgotten. He fought against a greatly superior enemy and under the harshest conditions [...]

Colonel General Dietl will remain an embodiment of the belief in our National Socialist Germany and its victory [...]

My personal friendship with him makes it especially painful for me to commemorate him. When I today take leave of this friend, I do so with the most bitter sentiments of a badly hit man, but, on the other hand, I do so with unbending zeal, so that this sacrifice on the altar of the fatherland will be a new obligation to all of us.

Adolf Hitler. [97]

---

97 Naturally there was controversy over Dietl death, as it was quite intriguing how many *Renown* soldiers died on aircraft accidents. For example, Hube, Mölders, Süssmann, Höring, Gablenz, Wever, and Grolig. An historian pointed out that a Finnish officer Erkki Ansa, who was liaison officer with Germans, [Russo-Finnish War 1939-40] says in article the *Kansa Taisteli* magazine (3/1966) that everyone thought it was murder.

In a book by Gustav-Gecrg Knabe, he also believed Dietl died when his Ju-52 crashed in Semmering. It has been claimed the pilot was inexperienced and the weather conditions were difficult [...] He also suggests that few weeks before his death Dietl had met an old friend who had tried to recruit Dietl to a resistance movement against Hitler. Dietl had declined to join. A few days after an assassination attempt on Hitler, Dietl crashed to his death.

Returning to Christmas 1944 there was a Red Cross issue of one parcel between two men. Subsequently after the air was filled with a loud droning sound. The men looking to the clear blue sky could see hundreds of silver bomber aircraft which seemed to be meeting high in the sky above. Harold remembered, "Somebody in the know said they had come from Italy and Britain to join up and proceed to somewhere like Breslau. Of course we all cheered our heads off, but there was a most depressing sight when a bomber began to fall out of formation; obviously shot down, the silver speck fell, twisting and turning, like a leaf in autumn." [98]

In the RAF compound a news bulletin over a covert wireless announced that the Russians had commenced their big push. From the reaction of the guards it became obvious that they were aware of these developments. Even before this the original guards had been replaced by elderly men with old fashioned long rifles and a long bayonet to match. However, the guards with dogs were still in evidence.

Then very early in 1945, a NCO guard came to tell them to pack their possessions as they were going to march westwards. [99]

---

98   Nearing the end of the war, some of the British servicemen who had managed to escape from the camps back to Britain, made it known to Senior Officers that they were concerned that as the Allied troops approached the POW camps, SS and Gestapo would conduct mass killings. It was taken seriously and measures were taken to make sure they were not given the opportunity.

99   Breslau was the German name for the city. It became part of Poland in 1945 as a result of the border changes after the Second World War and became known as Wroclaw.

Death March

In early 1940, the German authorities realised that POW camps, rather than remaining in the east or west, would be far safer within the German borders. This would allow the Germans to show they were abiding with 'Article Seven of the Geneva Convention', that "Prisoners of War be moved out of danger from a fighting zone." Therefore, POW camps in Poland and eastern Germany would be evacuated westwards if Russian forces appeared likely to reach them.

The movement of POWs would be on foot and the only means of travelling. It was acknowledged, that in adding the hundreds of thousands of POWs to the already large streams of evacuating civilians and troops it would place an added burden on the already chaotic food rationing system, causing immeasurable hardship and an increase in casualties.

Thereby, in early 1945, so began the vast trek of prisoners in Germany from east to west. Initially, the plans were reasonably well-organised where men from outlying work detachments were to be moved to nearby Stalag camps. Then these gatherings of men were to be moved west to other Stalag camps. However, the plans although well meaning, did not live up to expectations as Germany began to fall into increased chaos. Rather than lines of evacuees aiming for Stalag camps, when they came to the central parts of Germany the aim of the guards was to make for the main regions, for example, Hanover, Brunswick, Thuringia and Bavaria.

In January 1945, as the Soviet armies resumed their offensive and advanced into eastern Germany and Poland, many of the prisoners were marched westward in groups of 200 to 300 in the so-called 'Death March'. Many of them died from the bitter cold and exhaustion. The lucky ones got far enough to the west to be liberated by the American army. The unlucky ones got 'liberated' by the Soviets, who instead of turning them over quickly to the western allies, held them as virtual hostages for several more months. Many of them were finally repatriated towards the end of 1945 through the port of Odessa on the Black Sea.

By late February there were approximately 100,000 Allied prisoners moving along a northern route towards the general area of Bremen, Hamburg and Lubeck; another 60,000-odd were moving westward through a central region bounded by Leipzig, Dresden and Berlin; in the south approximately 80,000 were moving through northern Czechoslovakia, some destined for western Sudetenland, others for Bavaria and southern Württemberg.

The first large camps in Upper Silesia to be affected by the evacuation were Stalags 344 at Lamsdorf and VIIIB at Teschen. According to the original German plan Lamsdorf was to send as many as possible to Stalag VIIIA at Görlitz, in order to make way for prisoners from Teschen and the Upper Silesian Arbeitskommandos. In fact, Teschen was too far south for its occupants to outpace the Russian advance in a move north to Lamsdorf, and was forced, as were most of its detachments, to turn west into Czechoslovakia. All prisoners except the sick left Teschen in a snowstorm on 27 January. Extremely severe weather conditions in the first stages of their march caused many cases of frostbite, one hospital at Oberlangendorf having to treat twenty-five of them by amputation

The general route of the column from Stalag VIIIB and its work detachments, as well as many of those from Stalag 344, was west through the southern tip of Upper Silesia, across the mountain ranges of eastern Sudetenland to Königgraz. Thence they moved in a general westerly direction towards Karlsbad.

There was also a train provided for the sick prisoners leaving the Lamsdorf camp on 21st February 1945 travelling via central Germany. In each of the fifty trucks there was a medical orderly with a first-aid box. Another truck was used as a 'hospital', staffed by two medical orderlies and a medical officer. However, it was recorded that the supplies of satisfactory drinking water were apparently totally inadequate. They became dependent on various sources, from river streams, train station pumps and sometimes even railway engines. The latter source possibly causing severe diarrhoea to the prisoners on board. The journey took ten days, six of those days there was no food rations. Finally, they arrived at Stalag XIIIC in Hammelburg, northern Bavaria.

Unfortunately, for the newly arrived prisoners on the 2nd of March, their plight was not over. Some prisoners again became infested with lice, probably from the cattle trucks. Fortunately, at Stalag XIIIC there was a good delousing block, so it was a repeat of the system of reception huts, delousing and clean barracks. However, in the following weeks the food rations decreased, giving rise to concerns of 'famine oedema' [abnormal swelling].

Most sailors are known to have an aversion for marching drills, in fact the very word brings them out in spots and Tom Barnham was probably no different. "The Germans put the whole camp on a march, bar those that were sick. I suppose there were a few thousand on the march and there was thick snow. I pretended to be sick so I didn't have to go. About three weeks later they sent off everyone who remained on cattle wagons and we travelled for about five or six days and finished up near Munich."

As of yet I have been unable to find any of HMS *Hunter* crewmen's accounts of their experiences on the 'Death March'. I was unsure as to whether any had not been able to survive either their long term of captivity or later on the 'Marches'. This led me to contact the Commonwealth Graves Commission, pointing out that the list of men were POWs and could be buried in one of the CWGC memorial cemeteries in mainland Europe. I will give you the outcome later.

However, I have the ongoing accounts of Siddall, Barnham, and Harris who did manage to complete the ordeal. Here is the HMS *Glowworm* survivor, Stoker Bert Harris, whom you will remember was captured 9th April 1940. It is now February 1945. Having been transferred from camp to camp around Germany, Bert was now in a working party camp at Oderberg, near Stalag VIIIB in Poland.

Here Bert Harris begins the last part of his personal account to freedom. "Towards the end of the War we were woken up one night by the Germans in a terrible panic. 'Get up, get up, get your clothes.' When we asked why, they replied 'Russkies!' It appeared that the Russians weren't very far from our camp. We said we wouldn't leave without our large supply of Red Cross parcels. We managed to find some carts which we loaded up with them. I was glad we did as the parcels kept us alive in the following strenuous 'March'.

"We started picking up more prisoners from other camps, it was a Polish winter, snow and icy. We finished up with thousands, Jewish, Persians, Russian, British and French. Quite a lot died or were killed, especially the Russians and Jews. As some of them fell down they just shot them, even within earshot."

In Harold Siddall's *A Stoker's Story* he mentions having made the acquaintance of a number of naval colleagues. Perhaps he had also met some of the *Hunter* men whilst at the camp. Hence, Harold's summarised account of the march to freedom would have been similar to any that the *Hunter* crew had experienced. This is once more a summarised account of Harold and other Royal Naval men's experiences on the 'Death March'.

Harold begins his road to freedom, "I could see flashes in the sky and hear the rumbling of the guns in the far distance, but as my column moved along sounds and sights faded. Initially we passed through villages in the dead of night; dogs barked to warn the occupants. Because of the sharing of a Red Cross parcel between two I had chummed up with a young naval lad named Smart, curiously nicknamed 'Panic'."

The column passed through farm land where they were able to stop for the night in barns. However some of these turned out to be not such a good idea. Harold, "Tired and exhausted, I climbed up onto a huge mound covered in snow. With daybreak only to find that we had become social pariahs, the snow had covered a mound of pig manure; the warmth of our bodies had melted the snow and the essence of the muck clung to our greatcoats. The snow fell and the wind blew such that we had to keep moving to keep alive. At the end of our column was a horse-drawn cart, carrying the guards' packs. Should a *Kriegie* [German for POW] fall by the wayside he would be thrown up onto the cart, which would be fatal in the freezing cold; he could freeze to death, as some did. Soon nobody wanted to ride the cart."

It was a hard survival with marching from dawn to dusk and then dropping to the ground, cold, exhausted and hungry. With so many on the march from Stalag VIIIB plus those from working camps, the food resources in that winter would have slowly depleted. Each time they stopped for the night, they held on hoping 'lady luck' would help them out with any extras. Harold, "We very rarely moved onto main roads and were kept on country lanes, thus meandering like a wandering stream, hoping to stop in a village, to find a barn or doorway in which to sit for the night."

On occasions they were able to use some of their personal items in exchange for food from the locals. Harold knocked on a door, just about to give up when the door was opened by a lady. He showed her a cake of perfumed soap originally from his Red Cross parcel, asking if she could exchange it for bread. The occupants were frightened of Russians coming and were relieved when he told them, "Kriegsmarine – Englander." It worked and he even received a cup of coffee and what seemed to be Madeira cake. They wanted him to stay to help when the Russians came.

When late February arrived the snow began to thaw but whilst the impending rise in temperature was welcomed, the snow turned to slush. Harold: "Boots let in water and the ground was wet come bedtime." Those with sledges abandoned them but there remained piercing cold winds. "Their only relief was to curse Jerry and Hitler and all. We did strike an Autobahn and were all surprised to see the string of horse-drawn carts, loaded with men and material on the move. The obvious subject of talk amongst us was why the soldiers weren't marching on the move [...] We all hoped that they were going to the Russian Front, because they were travelling in the opposite direction to us. On one occasion we passed a contingent of uniformed youngsters of the Hitler Youth Movement, fully armed. Some so young and so small, seeing us they sang one of their morale-building songs: '*Wir fahren gegen Engeland*'. [100]

At dusk, it depended on luck as to whether they found a comfortable barn, especially one with hidden 'gifts' inside. For instance, half rotting onions or under the potential straw bed, grains of wheat, both providing a good source of nutrients and vital vitamins. One evening the column stopped for the night near an encampment of German soldiers. Harold describes the event, "On the outskirts of their camp was a cluster of buildings [...] Outside one of them was an armed guard and this building turned out to be the kitchen [...] I had nine cigarettes, but in exchange currency with the soldier racketeers, ten cigarettes were needed to acquire a loaf. Nothing ventured, nothing gained. I sort of drifted over to the guard and asked to see the 'Feldwebel'. [NCO in charge] To my surprise he allowed me to enter. It housed several cooking vats, each containing large pieces of pork, which could be seen boiling merrily away when the cooks lifted the lids. Upon reflection I could have been in dreamland, because none of those three cooks took the slightest notice of me and I could only stand in that kitchen like 'Ali Baba' in the cave.

"Someone must have told the 'Feldwebel' that a disreputable-looking specimen was in his clean kitchen, because he appeared shouting '*Was ist los hier? Was brauchen Sie?*' I told him I had nine English cigarettes for a loaf of

---

100 This is a patriotic German soldier or sailor poem written at the beginning of World War One. To hear the song, go to 'YouTube'.

bread. *'Neun englische Cigaretten fuer einen Brot.'* He became interested when I showed him the nine cigarettes in a round tin. Then he replied that he had a loaf of bread for ten cigarettes and shrugged his shoulders. So I asked him if I could have three quarters of a loaf for the nine. *'Drie viertel Stueck Brot fuer neum Cigaretten?'* But no dice, he was adamant about ten cigarettes or nothing and, what is more amazing, he just said: *'Los'*, meaning for me to leave the kitchen, whereupon he and the cooks went into a small room at the end of the building, leaving the place unattended. That was enough for me. As quick as a flash I lifted the cover of one of those vats, stuck my hand in, grabbed a large piece of pork and secured it inside my jacket. How I did not get scalded in the process I will never know. The guard outside saw the lump under my jacket and just asked; *'Geht's gut?'* Meaning was all well, thinking it was a loaf of bread. I answered that all was well and sped back to my billet, where 'Panic' [Smart] was minding the fort."

It seems it was Harold's lucky day, taking the rough with the smooth, he continues, "By chance there had been the issue of a small amount of bread to each person [...] When I found our bedding place my companion 'Panic' could hardly believe his eyes as I brought forth the hot pork."

Once more the men witnessed further visible signs of the enemy's desperation when another troop of 'Hitler Youth' came by armed ready for war. The men looked on and learnt the boys were heading for the Russian Front. Harold describes the moment: "Some of them seemed to be hidden in their over-large helmets and greatcoats, which touched the ground. There must have been some copious weeping among some mothers about them. Surprisingly enough, we stood in silence as they marched past. We felt an inward sense of sorrow for those poor young sods."

The column continued drearily along the country lanes, however the wider roads had deep drain ditches, which allowed them to find cover from an air attack. Harold recounts, "On one occasion we did have to dive into the trenches when an Allied aircraft machine-gunned a section in which I was at the time. In his efforts the pilot felled a large tree by gunning it [...] Once again the RAF was blamed and many choice epithets were hurled skywards. Plans were made for the leading group each day to be prepared to form the letters POW with bodies, but I don't recall that the plan was used [...] Once a large aircraft flew low over us and bundles fell from it. We all thought of food [...] But no they were bundles of front-line newspapers, which served two purposes. The first was to keep us up-to-date about the progress of the war, the second I will leave you to work out for yourself. At least we had the consolation of knowing that we had been recognised. Even the elderly guards were pleased at being under supervision of the Allies and far away from the Russians."

The column finally reached a town called Brunswick [now called Braunschweig] with only a few people left in it. The roads were empty, devastation was everywhere and buildings had turned to rubble. They continued back onto the country lanes, moving through villages that also appeared empty. There was not even barking dogs to greet them. Harold explains, "We each received a packet of 'Knackerbrot' biscuits and after that food seemed to be left off the agenda [...] All the conversations on the march at this time were about freedom: how we would be released, who would first make contact with us [...] Some bods were talking about self-heating tins of food; fantasy ran riot, but the staple joke to the married men was the old question: "What's the second thing you are going to do when you walk in the door?" And the stock answer was always; "Take off my pack." It still raised a laugh, although conditions then didn't give us much to chuckle about."

It was now the middle of March, Harold and his fellow travellers' sense of humour was probably becoming strained. Body weight loss became a problem and then the inevitable dysentery struck the men. "That seemed to be the end. I remember how we had to dig trenches and fix five bars across them as latrines. Came one occasion when, with nothing inside me, I still had to dash to a bar and, whilst sitting there, I just had to say: 'Please, God, help me.' As I am just pulling up my trousers a German soldier with a dog came and told me to accompany him to the block in which the soldiers were based. For now soldiers with dogs had taken over, there were no signs of the aged guards. Outside was another POW and we were to carry a milk churn which contained soup [...] Nearing the kitchen I saw the high entrance had a flat roof and – wonders of wonders – I could see a turnip on the roof [...] I lost no time in taking possession of that beauty. Someone up there was listening, and chewing pieces of that turnip so slowly was heavenly." [101]

The men were at this last stop for a number of days and strangely "were left to our own devices" but hanging around the cookhouse was out of

---

101 A little known tactic of the Germans was to send out leaflets to the Allied POWs on the marches inviting them to come on their side to fight the Russians. It appears that to my knowledge there were not many takes.

bounds. The guards and their dogs made sure of that. Then they were off again back to the same mundane procedure as before. A few days later they came across a town called Duderstadt where the men were taken into a church. An event that Harold would never forget. "We were packed tightly into wooden pews [...] I felt a delicious sense of warmth [...] Whether it was the warmth, the weakness or the coloured glass representation of the Lord holding out his hands to me, I shall never know, but I found myself quietly crying. Self-consciously looking around I found that many other weary, filthy fellows were crying as well."

They had been placed in the church to allow an enemy convoy to pass by and after their uplifting experience they were on their way again. Harold recounts, "Someone discovered it was the month of April; days were certainly warmer, but nights cold. Then we stopped on a farm. There were cows and hundreds of white feathered chickens, but we were hemmed in by the guards and the chickens were '*STRENGST VERFBORTEN*'. But at last we were told the Germans were no longer able to support us and that for the foreseeable future, we were surrounded by untouchable chickens. And that was on Thursday 12th April 1945."

Tom Barnham by now was somewhere near Munich, "The Yanks were coming towards us so then everybody had to march, sick or not. We marched all night and slept during the day. Our guards were old men, seventy or more and they kept falling asleep on the march and we had to wake them so they could take us on. After the first night I'd had enough – I had huge blisters on my feet. So I planned to escape with seven mates of mine, including 'Monty'. An officer came to me and said, 'I hear you're going to bugger off tonight,' and I said, 'Yeah, I'm not having any more of this.' He said, 'You're not taking the Russian, with you?' and I said 'he wants to come,' and so he said, 'Well look, do yourself a favour and the boy a favour, don't let him come because ninety-nine percent, you'll get caught and he's got no chance. You being English, you'll get away with it, but if they know he's Russian they'll shoot him.' So I left Monty behind with a mate of mine. He later told me Monty was taken off by some Yanks, but I don't know what happened to him after that."

Bert Harris the survivor on HMS *Glowworm* had gone full circle in POW camps and finally arrived at the Oderberg camp part of Stalag VIIIB in Poland. The rapid advance by the Russians took Bert and the other POWs completely by surprise. They were hustled out of bed by their guards in the middle of the night and were on the road immediately. One prisoner recalls, "It was pitch dark in the countryside and freezing cold as we trudged along narrow winding roads. In the next forty-eight hours, we stopped for two hours only, so desperate were the Germans to get away from the Russian advance. We were keen to keep on the move too because the Russians were just as likely to mistake us for Germans and shoot us. When they finally decided we were out of the immediate danger area, they allowed us to sleep. But by then we were lost. Apparently we should have rendezvoused with the main body of British prisoners from Teschen but we had missed them and we were on our own."

The column of New Zealand coalminers from Milowitz passed into eastern Sudetenland in late January, joining up with a group from Oderberg. At this moment in time was Bert Harris and any of the *Hunter* survivors in the same group? The POWs marched approximately twelve miles per day, and in early February they were climbing into the mountains on the Czechoslovakian border with no definite destination.

The march continued along country roads. In towns and villages along the way, it was noticeable that the local communities were concerned for their welfare. It was reported that the SS were shooting Russian prisoners of war and leaving their bodies to line the very roads that the Soviet tanks would soon be sweeping along. Hence the locals feared they would pay with their lives for this brutality. There had been an uprising by Ukrainian slave labourers when they been told that their Russian allies were closing in, with the result of them taking action against their guards. However, they had acted too early and now faced a firing squad.

This group continued their journey in the southwest direction towards the mountains of the Sudetenland. There they met deep snow and some suffered from frostbite. Once out of the mountains they found larger roads, where they were finally able to join up with the main column of prisoners. There were literally thousands of groups, many of whom were Russians, still being treated very badly by the German guards. The march then changed to travelling along minor roads, bypassing towns and negotiating the forests of Czechoslovakia. They were fed infrequently with watery dried vegetable soup and had to drink from cattle troughs. At the end of the day they were packed like sardines into large barns.

The New Zealand [and Australian] soldiers and possibly their Royal Navy chums were still bravely hanging on in there. Comments such as;

"Spring coming. Onwards, forever onwards. Barns and backache. Pinched a case of honey." They bypassed Prague, 100 km sign to Vienna heading towards Sudetenland [now the North Czech Republic]. Signs were displayed for Red Cross parcels but not found. Some of them ended up eating horse meat, finally they were issued with cigarettes, fourteen each. Later French parcel of nougat fruit bars. It was now 27th April they were now 140 km northeast of Munich when the POWs were set to work repairing a railway line.

There were air raids by the Allied air forces where they were subjected to strafing. They found a Red Cross wagons "nights of salvage and plunder – days of work, eating and strafing. Do they recognise us?" Wet and tired they finally reached a barn 70 km from Munich near Landshut where rumours began to go around. The march started to become a straggle and on the 1st May they crossed the River Isar to Freiberg. The next day there was snow everywhere around them and the POWs refused to march any further. At this point the German guards left them knowing the American army was nearby. "So the great day has arrived, just a recce patrol but 180 tanks are nearby, and all is quiet. We were sitting huddled in straw, miserable look-ing and cold but had a good breakfast. Who would have thought we'd finish POW life surrounded with Red Cross parcels."

On 3 May 1945, the ninety-sixth day since the trek had commenced, the 14th American Armored Division liberated the New Zealanders and their fellow marchers. Later that day they were trucked out, back over the river northward, and billeted in a grain store near Stalag VIIA at Moosburg. At some stage the POWs moved to a barn closer to Landshut to await their turn to fly out. On 10 May, they marched the 4 km to the 'Landshut 134' airfield, and the next day were on a plane to Brussels.

Now back to Bert Harris who continues on his road to freedom. "We were on the march till May 1945, at times you see we were in between the Russians and Americans [troops]. We ended up in Bavaria, Germany where the Russians were pushing forward. Then they [German guards] turned us around again, when our people were coming from the West. We went into part of Czechoslovakia then back into Bavaria. One evening the Germans came to a halt, the next thing we knew they had vanished. We were left on our own, so everybody dispersed as best they could. Me and my mate, and two Australians and two New Zealanders troops went and found a little farm, we slept in the loft of a barn.

"Next day we went searching for food. We were there for a few days, and we heard all this [commotion], tanks and vehicles up the road. We didn't know if it was Russians or Americans so we decided to draw straws. I think it was one of the Aussie's who went up, and came running back, saying it was the Americans. An American [in charge] told us to stay on the farm until told otherwise and take whatever food we wanted and to get out of the barn and go live in the farmhouse. Adding, 'Any Germans there, turf them out.'

"I don't remember where we were but it was not far from Munich. From what I recall, the Americans treated the locals pretty good. The place now was flooded with ex-POWs, we stayed in the farmhouse until the Americans said to get out and wait our turn to get on an aircraft. We were all [placed] in a field, just waiting, they took our name and numbers. As our turn came we had to get into an American transport plane, which flew us to Reims in France. When we arrived they could not do enough for us. They had everything, anything you wanted, tons of cigarettes, food and white bread which we thought was cake, we only had black bread [in the camp]."

The most probable airbase near Munich where Bert was flown out was München (e. Munich) which became occupied by U.S. forces on 1 May 1945. [Henry L. de Zeng IV. Luftwaffe Airfields 1935-45. 'www.ww2.dk/warfields.] [102]

Of those hundreds of thousands of British Commonwealth and American POWs in appalling winter conditions, force marched in different directions across central Europe, many died of disease, starvation and exhaustion. **Yet when the war was over those who survived found their extraordinary tale was largely ignored and forgotten, and this was not helped by the fact that many were unable to talk of their experience.**

---

102 Today a car journey from Wroclaw, Poland [Oderberg] to Munich via Dresden and Nuremburg is 450 miles. [Part motorways] But that is not taking into account the group march deviating into Czechoslovakia and back into Bavaria.

Repatriation Plans

Release came to prisoners of war in Germany in such a variety of ways that a description of what happened to those at main camps and to a few of the hundreds of smaller parties cannot do more than cover some of the more typical aspects of liberation. Evacuation was a much more uniform affair. For, although a few of our men commandeered transport, most were willing to wait for instructions from those officers of the Allied occupation forces whose task it was to cater for released prisoners.

A plan had been made by 'SHAEF' [Supreme Headquarters Allied Expeditionary Force] in the autumn of 1944 for this evacuation, and a central organisation known as PWX was set up at Supreme Allied Headquarters, with liaison groups at major headquarters which worked through contact officers. The latter were sent forward by every possible means to areas where prisoners were assembled. There were representatives from the Dominions and from all arms of the service in these contact teams.

They carried instructions to the prisoners in camps to remain there, and for those outside to report to the nearest transit centre, in order to simplify maintenance and documentation and to avoid any uncontrolled movements of prisoners which might hamper operations.

A chain of transit centres was set up on the lines of communication, and ad hoc units were formed to organise and maintain them. The latter were equipped with special disinfestation, bathing, clothing and medical facilities, Red Cross services, YMCA teams to organise amenities, and Army Education teams to give up-to-date information. The plan was to evacuate prisoners by air to the United Kingdom. In view of the bad physical condition of many prisoners resulting from the forced marches they had undergone, the air evacuation was pushed forward with all possible speed, and some of the services provided at transit centres on the Continent never had a chance to function fully.

Ex-prisoners either remained in their camps, or were taken to a transit centre, or were found billets until they could be evacuated from the nearest important airfield. Sometimes 'K' rations and other army rations were supplied to prisoners in billets. As soon as possible they were taken to the airfield by army lorries and organised into groups of thirty-odd ready for emplaning.

Almost as soon as the flights of Dakota transport aircraft arrived they loaded, took off, and headed back towards the west. Only the prisoners from a few camps in northwest Germany were evacuated direct to the United Kingdom in British aircraft; most were taken to France or Belgium, where they broke their journey and spent a night, or a few hours only, at a specially prepared transit centre before going on. Most of our men seem to have gone to either Rheims or Brussels.

The transit centre at Brussels, which was the one to which it had been intended that the majority of British ex-prisoners should go, received and sent on some 40,000 of them in three weeks at the end of April and early May. As the streams of Dakotas arrived from Germany and unloaded, lorries took the ex-prisoners to the transit centre; and at the same time streams of British four-engine bombers were taking on to England those who had already passed through.

At the centre they were given showers, new uniforms, and an advance on pay. They could stay a night in a hotel run by the Belgian Red Cross Society; they had full use of recreation rooms run by the YMCA; and they could go on leave to take advantage of private hospitality, or to buy presents in the city, or just to look around. A liaison officer speaks of the prisoners being 'all in rocketing spirits'. But most of our men's spirits did not reach their climax until they arrived in England, for not until then were they back among people and in an environment nearly the same as their own. There was in England the additional thrill of seeing again (or seeing for the first time) the country from which from which those from the Dominions had come during the last hundred years. had come during the last hundred years. [Quote from the 'Official History of New Zealand in the Second World War'.]

It is now 16th April 1945. Harold Siddall was almost at the last hurdle. If it had not been such an emotional experience it would have been laughable. He arrived at the airport controlled by the British Forces, and the men said their goodbyes. Here is a summarised version of his account. "In next to no time we were back in the arms of officialdom and naval discipline. Instead of wanting to discover our identities, we were paraded by officious British

Army sergeants and marched into a hut where we were deloused by having white DDT powder pumped down the backs of our necks, over our heads and up the legs of our trousers."

An Army corporal registered their identities and allocated an aircraft number. "He asked where I came from and when I answered: 'Plymouth', he remarked that he came from Taunton, saying we 'Westho's must look after one another. He would put my name against a low number flight so I wouldn't have to wait long. He also told me that there was another sailor, called Venning, from Plymouth to whom he had given the same flight number. The meal towards the end of the day was a mess tin of good thick stew, packet of biscuits and hot sweet tea and I had no complaints.

This card is to be handed to the server at the NAAFI Canteen, when purchasing your week's supply of Chocolate and Confectionery, Cigarettes or Tobacco, and Matches

Space for Ship's Stamp.   Form 578A—5.50

NAFFI Card (Navy, Army and Air Force Institution) – supplied
to the returning POWs. [Barbara Roch Collection.]

"During the next day planes came and left with bodies who filed on board according to the numbers on the notice board. And then the penny dropped; the numbers were increasing in numerical order and there was no sign of any lower numbers. Nor was there any sign of Mr Helpful [Corporal] to be told that my plane number had gone before I had registered! Then I met Venning, whom I recognised, but had not known his name. After commiserating with one another he told me that he had observed an aircraft standing apart from the runway with its engines running and a fellow with a clipboard who was obviously waiting for somebody. With nothing to lose, we ambled over to the aircraft and enquired as to the chances of a flight. He was an RAF officer who had once served on an aircraft carrier, so when we told him we were Navy, he told us to stick around [...] The waiting time was only to be a matter of minutes […] we waited hoping the two bods wouldn't turn up. Finally, with no sign of the missing pair, we were told to scramble on board."

The aircraft landed at a place called 'Wing' [RAF Wing – a bomber training base, Aylesbury Vale, Buckinghamshire] from where they were taken in an Air Force lorry to a large house in London.

"Venning and I said we were Navy and somebody in authority must have presumed that we were naval officers. A WAAF orderly came to tell me that she was my orderly and would show me to my room. She asked me if there was anything else I wanted. 'Yes please. A cup of tea and a hot bath.'"

Both stayed the night and were given hotel standard service. On leaving the RAF Club he gave the WAAF orderly several packets of his cigarettes but he remembers the emotional moment when the young orderly, thanking him was in tears but not because of her gift, she told Harold, "Hurry and put some weight on."

Arriving at Paddington station, they were met by a Master-of-Arms who began to laugh loudly, saying: "You pair of beauties have been putting one over on the RAF, pretending to be officers." He promptly gave them Meal Vouchers, so off they went to the station buffet. The lady assistant's first words were "My Gawd! Where have you two come from?" "Returning prisoners of war and could we please have something to eat?" So they were shown to the station staff's canteen, and proudly told everyone present, who they were and that they had to be looked after.

Harold recounts, "No sooner were we seated than an elderly lady came to us, stifling her tears, wanting to know why we were home and not her son. Did we know him and had we met him? What could have happened to him? Naturally we tried our best to placate her, telling her there was no reason why the lad wouldn't show up at any time."

In the meantime, their packs were taken from them, and when they removed their greatcoats there was an immediate 'gasp'. In no time the canteen was filled with staff wanting to look at them, and a collection was instigated of several pounds and silver coins. "We shook hands, received many kisses and 'God bless you-s' when we went back to our seat on the platform."

The two sailors were now on their way with the prospect of a long train journey back to Plymouth. Harold continues, "We arrived at North Road Station and one of us telephoned the Officer of the Day requesting transport – only to be told to hop on a bus. We were back in the Navy. I suppose if we had had no money for a bus fare we would have been told to walk."

On arrival at the Barracks they were told to report to the gymnasium. Harold had visions of being told "Top of the wall bars. Go!" at the tender mercies of the 'Muscle Bosun'. But no, somebody in authority had ordered that they be held incommunicado until debriefed. At the sight greeting his eyes: a Lieutenant said in disbelief, "What in bloody hell are you two?" "Venning and I just looked at one another, gave a shrug and I said, 'Just a couple of ex-Prisoners of War obeying orders, Sir.' He looked around at two Physical Training Instructors standing nearby and they shook their heads." The Lieutenant took them back to the Officer of the Day and said they should be allowed home and he would take responsibility. "He was the only one to shake hands with us, took us past the guard house, with instructions to report back to him next morning."

"Remarkably, my Dad arrived outside the barracks just as I was leaving – such a coincidence. Our eyes watered as we hugged one another and together in a taxi we went HOME."

I am glad to say that Harold's homecoming reception at the barracks was an improvement on his arrival the previous day. Although still bedraggled and long haired he was received with suspicion. Completing a medical the naval doctor "could hardly believe his eyes when I was stripped", weighing in at eight stones. He was then quickly put in front of the previous day's Lieutenant who was naturally concerned about whether Harold had been in contact with any newspapers. However, his fears were allayed, and whilst Harold's attire and personal appearance were not up to the standards for reporting directly to the Commodore of the barracks, this was disregarded under the circumstances.

The Commodore, as you would expect, wanted to know about Harold's ordeal in captivity. He must have been impressed because Harold was issued with a 'Commodore's Priority' card. This privilege allowed him to go straight to the front of the queues, first at the naval stores for new kit, then to the Pay Office and NAAFI canteen and then when the 'six bells' rang, to the rum ration issue.

Unfortunately, the new kit that he had been issued with provided a problem, as it was for New Entry ratings, hence there were no insignias on either arm. Having enjoyed their tot of rum, although the strength of it after being teetotal for so long, went straight to their heads, it still set them in good stead for their meal. However, at the dining hall door wearing his New Entry uniforms Harold was questioned by a Chief who demanded, "What

494

are you and where do you think you are going?" "Leading Stoker Siddall, going to have my dinner, Chief."

Harold continues, "Now a New Entry uniform is described thus; it fits where it touches; if it's on the small side it will stretch with the wash; if it's too big the wearer will grow into it. In addition, I sported no departmental badges or NCO's on the arm. 'Chiefy' was ready to perform his act of authority [...] until, like a music hall act, I produced my leave pass and priority card. 'Open Sesame.' All he could counter with was the time-honoured censure: 'Get your hair cut.'"

With one hundred and eight days' leave accrued and back pay from January 1941, Harold was on his way, "I had once more entered the realms of society."

As witnessed by Harold Siddall, on his own homecoming there was an immense amount of sympathy from the general public on learning they were returning prisoners of war, evidenced by their unkempt and physical appearance. However, this was because Harold and his fellow captives were early arrivals in mid-April. The bulk of the others returned in May, when by then the public had got used to the traumatic and newsworthy conditions of the prisoners.

I cannot go further without sharing this newspaper cutting dated around this time concerning another character in the book.

The Citizen, Thursday April 19 1945.
KING'S NEPHEW POW MOVED

"From a Diplomatic correspondent [...] Nephew of the King with two relations of Mr Churchill were moved according to some reports reaching London, at midnight, from various centres, some from camps which were on the point of being liberated [...] A member of the *Times* newspaper, who was taken prisoner at St Nazaire [...] gives some names of these special prisoners as follows:

Lieutenant – Lord Lascelles, nephew of the 'King'. Captain the Master of Elphinstone nephew of the 'Queen'. Captain Earl Haig, son of Field Marshall Captain Michael Alexander, a cousin of Field Marshall Alexander. A civilian **Giles. R. Romilly,** nephew of Mr Churchill. Mr John Winant, son of American Ambassador in London.

Also, the Polish General Bor Komorowski, who was Commander

of the Polish Home Army and a dozen other senior Polish officers, captured after the suppression of the Warsaw rising last autumn."

So those known as the 'Promintentes' were kept alive, irrespective of the Nazis knowing they were fast losing the war. Perhaps it was an attempt to improve the chances for their future fate, when finally they would be brought to justice.

It is said that Romilly lived in 'relative luxury' with other 'Promintentes' who over a period of time joined him. They were all guarded twenty-four hours a day to avoid any attempts to escape. Apparently, Romilly kept the prison staff busy by his apparent nuisance tactics, habitually complaining about every conceivable issue he could raise. It has been recorded that the guard was keeping him awake by the continuous sound of marching of boots. It seems this was rectified by placing a carpet outside his prison cell.

At the latter end of the war, Giles Romilly was finally successful in making an escape from 'OFLAG VII-D' [Tittmoning Castle]. This was with three Dutch officers by abseiling down the castle walls. The four had false identity papers showing they were French forced labourers. All the rest of 'Prominente' officers in the prison, played their part by hiding in the castle grounds, to give the impression that they had all escaped. It took four days before the German guards managed to account for all 'Prominente' officers.

In the meantime, Giles Romilly and the three Dutch officers made good their escape, mainly due to one of the Dutch officers being able to speak fluent German and French. When stopped and interrogated by German officials, the Dutch officer did the talking whilst Romilly pretended he was deaf and dumb.

Giles Romilly at Oflag ICV (Colditz Castle – Circa 1940-45). [Pegasus Archive.]

After the war Romilly returned to live at the family estate at Huntington Park in Kington. During the war much of the house was vacated and used by the Army for officers accommodation and the grounds used as a temporary war hospital complex. After derequisitioning, Romilly paid to remove all signs of the considerable number of hospital buildings on the estate. Saying, that he did not wish to be reminded of the war by continuing evidence of its presence on his doorstep.

He married Mary Ball-Dodd in 1949 but they were divorced in 1963. He died from an overdose of tranquilizers in 1967 in California. At the time he was researching for a new book. At a relatively young age of fifty-one, he had fitted in more interesting and brave experiences than most older men or his contemporaries.

Bert Harris, after five years and one month in France, is also able to taste freedom. "We were there a fortnight and we were transported to England in a Lancaster bomber and landed at Ford Airdrome, They kept us there for two days but we were well looked after. They gave us money, if you wanted to buy clothes. Then taken to Portsmouth and got a train to Weymouth. [103]

The IWM interviewer asked Bert whether there were any health repercussions after his experience. Bert replied, "I thought I was all right but when I returned off leave I had a medical and was sent to Cholmondeley Castle in Cheshire for 'psychosis', I was shaking all over. [Royal Navy Auxiliary Hospital, which treated serving men suffering from nervous breakdowns.] They said it was the reaction of all that had happened. I suppose when I got home I was all keyed up, then as I relaxed, it came on. I just needed rest. Then I was sent down to Bristol [convalescence], I was in hospital for six months, then invalided out and given a pension of twelve shillings a week. In those six months it had gone, it came back at times but not so bad."

Finally, Bert was asked, what was the worst time in captivity? "The first eighteen months in 1940 to 1941, when your life wasn't worth much over there in Germany. Where they had over run France and Europe, they thought they could do whatever they liked to you. There was not a lot of food until the Red Cross parcels started to deliver. Small working parties, miles away, were places that often missed out on then, if you were in the main

---

103 West Sussex – RAF Ford, Battle of Britain airfield and Royal Naval Air Station HMS *Peregrine*, both now HM Open Prison Ford.

camp you more or less got them regularly. The guards' attitudes changed and eased up in 1941 to 1944, when Rommel came out of North Africa. The Germans [guards] knew things were changing [becoming on the defensive against the Allied troops.]"

After the War, Bert retired from the Navy with the injuries he received on the *Glowworm*. But still managed to keep fit by joining a cycling club for many years'. Bert lived his retirement in Havant and became an accomplished photographer.

A sailor's intuition usually allows him to think of a novel way of getting out of a tricky situation and coming out smelling of roses. Tom Barnham provides the last part of his interesting account. "The rest of us got away and finished up in a barn. Some German farmers looked after us for a while, but we were getting a bit restless, so we went out and nicked two cars, a BMW and a Mercedes-Benz, and half of us went in one car and the other half in the other. We drove right through Germany and into France. Whenever we got low on petrol, British or American lorries would give us cans of petrol. We finished at a place called Nancy and when we got there the Yanks pulled us in and put us on a plane home.

"When we landed they put us on a train and we finished up at the naval base at Havant in Hampshire. They supplied us with a naval uniform, and gave us our back pay, which was about £200 or £300. Enough to buy a house with, in those days."

Maybe Able Seaman Tom Barnham spent some of his back pay on buying a big bunch of roses for either a girlfriend or his mother, who welcomed him home.

Sadly, not all the men returning as Prisoners of War had a smooth rehabilitation back into family life. Petty Officer Stoker Joseph 'Pat' Duffy as you will see from the list, was kept captive in the Marlag camp until the end of the war. His son Patrick recalls, "When Dad was eventually repatriated and returned home by then my Mother was in sole charge and we were well – established. I suppose we kids resented this 'stranger' who tried to change things, we didn't get on. He was perhaps hardened by his wartime experiences and his Dad had been killed in the First World War. In the Navy he was a Petty Officer and probably had a bit of authority but this carried no weight in Civvy Street." There is more from Patrick Duffy in a later chapter.

WHERE ARE THEY NOW?

I joined the British Army in Nineteen Thirty-Nine
I really did enjoy myself and thought that life was fine
But in France I was captured a Royal West Kent
Pride of the Army but to Deutschland I went.
Into a big Stalag they called it VIIIB
We had breakfast, no dinner and no blooming tea
They sent us out working we were just skin and bone
And Mittenbruck Silesia became our new home
There I met lots of pals t'was long, long ago
But where are they now that's what I'd like to know
Gerry Rush and Mick Dowling slept in the next bed
And a fellow called Andrews he slept overhead.
Sgt Don Eager or Edgar I'm never quite sure
He helped me a lot when conditions were poor
And young Ginger Kett with his mouth organ band
Called Kat and his Kit-Kats were really quite grand
And to all other chaps who were held by the "Hun"
In that little old camp called E91
If you remember ole Book and Benny his mate
Then let's get in touch before it's too late!

This is a poem written by my Father, Arthur Booker. Barbara Jutsum

It is worth noting, as pointed out in Fred Ward's account that he was initially sent to Marlag, then Milag until finally ending up at Stalag VIIIA. Patrick, son of Joseph Duffy mentions it's, "likely [Joseph] took the same route as your father [Fred]". Therefore, the above camps where the men were recorded to be imprisoned could have been only one of a number of different camps. [104]

---

104 The first 'Geneva Convention' was instigated in 1860s when an international agreement had been sought to offer assistance to wounded soldiers after a battle was over. Sixteen nations signed the treaty which stated, "In future wars they would care for all sick and wounded personnel, regardless of nationality. Medical personnel would also be considered neutral in war and they would be identified by a red cross on a white background".

A second 'Geneva Conference' led to the inclusion of those wounded at sea and enemy forces who are wounded, sick or shipwrecked must be treated and cared for. Those killed in battle, their bodies should be collected quickly and protected from robbery. Medical equipment must not be deliberately destroyed and medical vehicles should not be attacked or damaged or otherwise prevented from operating.

The third 'Geneva Convention', drawn up in 1929, covered military personnel who fall into enemy hands.

There were almost 100 Articles in the Treaty, too many to be mentioned here. However, there are numerous websites available for those interested in the subject

Whilst, almost fifty countries signed the 1929 Geneva Convention, interestingly two prominent countries that did not were USSR and Japan. The USSR only agreed to the terms of the Hague Convention of 1907. This did not allow prison camps to be inspected, prisoners to receive correspondence, or notification of prisoners taken. Whilst in 1942, Japan did promise to abide by its terms.

Both countries did not expect their armed forces to surrender, so their apparent excuse was, why consider a need for their wellbeing in camps? Subsequently, history has shown the appalling treatment handed out by these two countries to other nationalities. Although, as you will read below Germany was selective in her treatment of Prisoners of War.

Germany and Italy treated prisoners from the British Commonwealth, France, USA and other Western Allies in accordance with the 'Geneva Convention'. The main complaints of Western Allied prisoners of war in the German POW camps, especially during the last two years of war – concerned the lack of food. The comments of one POW: "The German plan was to keep us alive, yet weakened enough that we wouldn't escape."

As Soviet ground forces approached some POW camps in early 1945, German guards forced Western Allied POWs to walk long distances towards Central Germany, often in extreme winter weather conditions. It is estimated that, out of 257,000 POW's about 80,000 were subject to such marches and up to 3,500 of them died as a result.

The approximate reported percentage figures for those that died in camps show:

Russian POWs held by Germans 57%
German POWs held by Russians 36%
British POWs held by Germans 3.5%
German POWs held by British 0.03 %
British POWs held by Japanese 25%

It is not unexpected that whilst countries were signatories to the 'Geneva Convention', when they were at war their attitude changed in the worst possible ways.

I have provided you with a poem from a prisoner of war from the Army, I feel I should now give another from a sailor in the Royal Navy.

Home-Coming in 1945

Cliffs breaking thro' the haze and a narrowing sea,
Soon will my eager gaze have sight of thee.
England, the lovelier now for absence long,
Soon shall see your brow, hear a skylark's song.
Heart curb thy beating – there Channel cliffs grow.
Eddystone, Plymouth, where Drake mounts the Hoe.
Red of the Devon loam, green of the hills,
And I am home. God, my heart thrills.
Far have I travelled and great beauty seen.
But oh! Out of England is anywhere so green?
Thankful again as never before,
One of the Englishmen comes home to his shore.

Anon.

(A Prisoner of War on returning home to Devon. Probably from the Far East.)

Almost all Accounted

In addition to the previous list of the *Hunter* survivors, either returned home by other methods or who were Prisoners of War.

This is the list of those flown back to Britain, as kindly supplied by Trevor Baker

Signalman. Thomas Norton 29/08/41 age 43
Petty Officer. Will Barrett 31/08/41 age 36
Stoker Thomas King 06/12/41 age 22
Stoker George Lane 30/12/41 age 47
AB Norman Bowden 17/05/42 age 31
Telegraphist Rex Brown 17/05/42 age 23
AB Stanley Cook 08/10/42 age 29
AB James Renshaw 08/10/42 age 24
AB Harry Clark 12/11/42 age 29
Seaman Robert Hay 03/11/42 age 22
Stoker William Sim 14/11/42 age 23
Seaman Francis Youd 18 /11/42 age 24
Seaman Bill Parton 18/11/42 age 29
Cook Bill Wallis 18/11/42 age 24
Stoker Thomas Grady 18/11/42 age 37
CPO David Moore 26/11/42 age 45
Seaman James Watson 28/11/42 age 18
AB Charles Coutts 28/11.42 age 23
Stoker Desmond Broom 28/11/42 age 21
Leading Cook James Williams 03/12/42 age 34

The four who were flown out in a sequence of flights between 12th and 18th November 1942, were affected by poor weather conditions. Subsequently, not all returned to Leuchars but were diverted to other RAF bases.

These are the names of those for whose final return to Britain from Sweden I have so far been unable to account. Although I can confirm they did return at some time either by flights or other methods similar to Marshal Soult and Kershaw

AB Norman Stewart, Plymouth, aged 19.
AB Stanley Swales, Newport, Wales aged 23.
Seaman John Steel, Cambuslang, aged 20.
Stoker Stanley Hutton, Kidderminster, aged 23.
AB. David Johnson, Plymouth, aged 25.
Stoker John Hiscock, Kings Langley, aged 40.
Seaman Fredrick Butcher, Unknown, aged 19. [105]

As you have read it is mentioned by John Hague that Leading Seaman John Minstrell (Malta aged 30) was 'suffering in a bad way' on the march. It is possible Minstrell was initially hospitalised in Sweden and then for medical reasons sent back to Britain.

The list of POWs unaccounted for are in **bold** below, the remainder for various reasons were accounted, three of whom were on my father's list of members of the 2nd Destroyer Flotilla Association.

Stoker Frank Caton, Morecambe, aged 21.
Able Seaman Leslie **Clayton**, Leeds, aged 25.
Steward Anthony **Bartolo**, Malta, aged 18.
Mr Charles **Falzon**, Malta, aged 26.
Petty Officer Joseph Duffy, Plymouth aged 40.
Stoker John Harris, Plymouth, aged 23.
Petty Officer Andrew **Black**, Portsmouth aged 26.
Seaman Fred Ward, Cinderford, aged 20.
Stoker Daniel Murphy, Co Cork, aged 27.
Seaman Guy *Hunter*, Rosyth, aged 24.
Lt Eng. Alick Reid, Surrey. (Promoted during captivity to Lieutenant Commander)
Leading Seaman John **Minstrell**, Malta, aged 30.

---

105 The ages provided are those given when they were interned in Sweden.

The list of the five POWs I had not had confirmation of – whether they had survived during their time in captivity or on the 'March' to freedom – was sent to the Commonwealth Graves Commission. I was relieved to receive the following, "With the information provided I have been unable to find 'matching' casualties on our 'Casualty Database'."

I end with these words of sentiment from Able Seaman James 'Stormy' Renshaw. Unlike the rest of his account which may have been perceived as being 'tongue in cheek', here he is now very serious.

Kapitän z. S. Raeder und britische Gäste: Aus den Gegnern von einst wurden Freunde

Bremerhaven Reunion. Organised by Kapitan Raeder (at the microphone) himself a young officer on Erich Giese during the Battle of Narvik. To his left Cyril Cope, Ralph Brigginshaw and Dougy Bourton and right veterans from the Kriegsmarine Zerstörers at Narvik. [Cyril Cope Collection]

"I made a point with my own children, that if they go to foreign places, then they must learn a little language. My learning of a little of the language had stood me in jolly good stead, insomuch as they permitted me to leave the camp and go and live privately, 200 miles away with a little family. They fed and clothed me, in fact, the son of the family (they had sons and daughters), deferred his father's 'Will', he didn't want his father's property. Somewhere in the woods, they owned a portion of land, which they have turned over to me. They made it in my name, so somewhere in Sweden is a plot of land that I can legally claim. But, I'd rather not go back, no, I'd rather not go back."

There are two issues that I have not raised in this book concerning the awarding of the 'Norwegian Participation Medal' and 'Recollections of the Reunions' by the Royal Navy and Kriegsmarine veterans. Regarding the first, despite the bravery of all those involved in the Battles of Narvik, it would seem that not everyone received the recognition which they deserved. Secondly, between thirty to forty-five years after the battles, on these veterans meeting in a social environment, of the 2nd Destroyer Flotilla Association, as you can imagine some very interesting conversations were thrown up. In fact, information that has never previously been printed. These two additional chapters can be read in my first book.

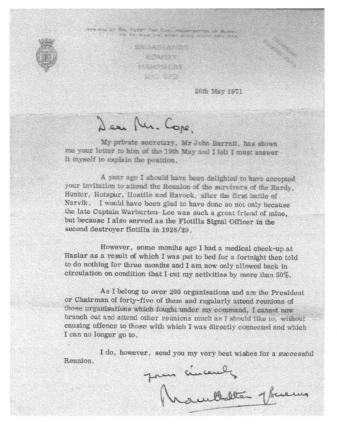

Letter from Lord Mountbatten of Burma to Cyril Cope. Honorary Secretary of the 2nd Destroyer Flotilla of Narvik Association. [May 1971]

Epilogue

I now return to Marshal Soult's meeting with Lucretia Kelly in 1968 [previously Miss Johns]. Lucretia was probably then about fifty years of age. It appears she had a premonition about 'Alan', the man she had met for a short while, before the *Hunter* left to go to Narvik.

Marshal begins, "There were 159 men on board and forty-eight were picked up, three being killed in action, the rest drowned. I felt sure the vision was a presentiment of Alan's death, and that our goodbye was really and truly forever. I didn't check any list of those who had died, but I saw a photograph taken in Sweden of the survivors, sent here to a mother and father of a local boy, and, of course Alan was not in the group."

Now, twenty-eight years later, Lucretia Kelly was sitting on the same seat in the same shelter on Falmouth seafront.

Lucretia, "It's the first time I've been back here. I've sat in other shelters but never this one. All because of what happened that night, I suppose. In a way, it's a strange sensation sitting here again after all those years.

In less than half an hour Lucretia Kelly was experiencing even a stranger sensation.

"Alan Clayton was his name, wasn't it?" Marshal Soult the manager of Brigg's shoe shop, in Church Street, who had served on HMS *Hunter*, looked thoughtful. I've got a suspicion he survived. I didn't know him all that well, mark you, but I've got an idea I saw him alive after *Hunter*'s sinking."

Lucretia Kelly sank into the nearest chair. Bewilderment creased her face. "Don't tell me he's alive after all these years."

Marshal Soult carefully studied a photograph, a snapshot of a group of survivors. "No, he's not among them." Lucretia Kelly studied the faces too. "Your mother showed me this soon after it had happened ..." Marshall Soult interrupted her. "But these aren't all the survivors. There must have been another twenty who weren't in this. Alan Clayton might be one of them ..."

Later, Lucretia Kelly and I continued our conversation over a cup of

506

tea at her home, Grove Cottage, in Swanpool Street, where she lives with her husband, twenty-six-year-old daughter, Marlene, and her Siamese cat, Pasha.

"I still think he's dead", was Lucretia opinion. "Just a feeling you know ..."

"There's only one way to find out," said Soult. "I'll write to Naval Records."

Marshal Soult continues, "Back in Tintagel, I wrote to the offices of the Commodore, HMS *Drake*, at Devonport. A Naval man had advised this as the best avenue of information. Four days later, I had a letter telling me my request for information regarding Able Seaman Alan Clayton had been forwarded to the Principle Director of Accounts (Naval), Branch 3D Enquiries, Warminster Road, Bath.

"The following week I was out of Cornwall. A brown 'On Her Majesty's Service' envelope was among the hillock of mail awaiting my return.

"'I have examined the ship's ledger of HMS *Hunter*,', the letter read, 'which was sunk during 1940, but an Able Seaman Alan Clayton does not appear as a member of the crew.'

"My line of enquiry now switched back to the starting point of Falmouth. Lucretia Kelly, for her part, stuck to her story; moreover, she insisted she had written to Alan Clayton during *Hunter*'s time in Plymouth, and received replies. Marshall Soult, on consulting other ex-*Hunter* sailors, confirmed that a 'Clayton' was aboard. Both though confessed they didn't know the man well, and could not be certain about his Christian name.

"Once more I contacted Bath. Again the same reply: Alan Clayton was not a member of the crew on HMS *Hunter*'s last voyage. But, by this stage official patience had worn thin: 'I regret to say that information relating to serving and ex-service naval personnel is considered as confidential and cannot be disclosed without the consent of the person concerned,' the Director replied. 'As you are unaware of Mr Clayton's correct details, I am unable to help further with your enquiry.'

"Was Alan Clayton aboard HMS *Hunter* on that final, doomed expedition? Or was the Clayton mentioned in the records another man? Was Lucretia Kelly given an assumed name? And, either way did Clayton survive?"

Marshal Soult.

Author Comments: After eight years of researching for this book and my previous one focused on HMS *Hardy* crew member's accounts, as you would imagine, I have collated a vast amount of information relating to the 'Battles of Narvik'.

Therefore, I am able to confirm, as you may now have noticed, that on board HMS *Hunter* there was an Able Seaman with name of 'Clayton'. He was on the cargo vessel *Buccaneer,* one of those apprehended by the Germans in the 'Blockade Busting' attempt from Gothenburg. Consequently, as shown he was one of those *Hunter* survivors who became a Prisoner of War No 607 at Camp Stalag, Lamsdorf.

It is now too late to inform Marshal Soult, after his thoughtful attempt to establish whether 'Clayton' was a survivor aboard *Hunter* or not; but he and his colleagues were close to the facts. In the photograph, as shown, of the forty-five interned in Sweden, only thirty-two were actually present, although Clayton's, name, date of birth and home town address, is on the register compiled for the handover from the German military to the Swedish authorities.

I estimate that Lucretia, at this time of writing, if still alive, would be well into her nineties. If not then her daughter Marlene would now be the age of seventy-two. Hopefully, both are still with us, and to know that Able Seaman Leslie Arthur Clayton [Service Number D/SSX 22615] from the 'Leeds' area survived the sinking of HMS *Hunter.* Before joining the Navy he was employed as a 'Cloth Finisher' and was aged twenty-six at the time of the Battle of Narvik

A little late in the day, but ironically, I know Leslie Clayton was repatriated back to Britain after the war because he was on my father's list of HMS *Hunter's* members in the 2nd Destroyer Flotilla Association of Narvik. As was Marshal Soult, maybe they never met at the same reunions or in Leslie's case he never actually attended, unlike Marshal who enjoyed the events.

Leslie Clayton, most probably along with most of the other *Hunter* POW's would have been in captivity for over three years before finally returning to his family; which would have been over five years since he and Lucretia met in Falmouth. It maybe that because Leslie preferred to use his second name Arthur, that Lucretia mistakenly thought it was Alan, or was his nickname. We will probably never know and I leave it to readers to make their own judgement. Suffice to say, like many war time short relationships, those were uncertain times but life went on after the War.

As previously pointed out, conditions in German POW camps were very harsh. So Lucretia's premonition of Alan being a skeleton could have been true. Although not death as she interpreted it, but he was probably exceedingly skeletal by the end of his incarceration.

Here is the last of Marshal Soult's account:

"I recall reading a poem some time ago, the last line of which was a row of question marks. Such an ending might be suitable for this chapter. But, inevitably, the last word must be Lucretia Kelly's: "I still insist I wrote and had replies. My one big regret now is that I did not keep his [service] number ... that would have been proof enough for anyone, but I never thought my story would be of interest in years to come."

The Sunken HMS Hunter Discovery

On the 5th March 2008, almost sixty-eight years after her sinking with the loss of 111 crewmembers, most going down with their ship, HMS *Hunter*'s resting position was discovered. The Royal Norwegian Navy 'Mine Control' vessel HNoMS Tyr [Royal Norwegian Mine Sweeper Tyr] is designed for deep water operations, and was testing new equipment which can reach depths of 1,000 meters below the surface. Lieutenant Tom Thorgrimsen explained, "We searched the area where HMS *Hunter* most likely was located and spent around fourteen hours before we found the vessel." The story became worldwide news:

Mon Mar 10, 2008 [Reuters]
British World War Two ship found in Norwegian fjord

A memorial service for HMS Hunter is conducted in the Ofotfjord, off Narvik, Northern Norway March 8, 2008. More than 1,000 British and Norwegian soldiers attended the memorial service. The wreck of the Royal Navy destroyer, sunk by the German Navy on April 10, 1940, was discovered in the Norwegian fjord.

The wreck of a British warship sunk by the Germans during World War Two, killing more than 100 men, has been discovered on the bottom of a deep fjord in the north of Norway, the Norwegian Navy said. HMS Hunter went down on April 10, 1940, in the Ofotfjord outside of the Arctic port of Narvik during the first of two battles between the British and the Nazis, during which several other ships were sunk and never seen again in the deep inlet.

The Memorial Service led by HMS Albion the Royal Naval Fleet Flagship, the five warships involved steamed in line past the spot, marked for the occasion by HNoMS Tyr, where the ship lies. HMS Hunter's final resting place was commemorated with wreaths cast into the sea. [Ends]

Ceremony on board HMS Albion's flight deck. Note the two survivors of the battles
on either side of the ship's padre. [2008 – Royal Navy Photography Department]

The procession of warships from the Royal Navy showed their respects by
laying wreaths and then the order on board the ships was well received by
their crews – 'Splice the Main Brace'. Also, to enable the toasting of the
fallen by the pouring of a tot of rum over the side.

Two of the youngest members of the ship's company aboard HMS *Albion*,
seventeen-year-olds Engineering Technician Joe George and Able Seaman
Warfare Specialist Yasmin Thornton, dropped the wreath over the side on
behalf of the ship's company.

In traditional form, with signal flags, HMS *Albion* flew the last order of Captain Warburton-Lee, the Commander of the 2nd Destroyer Flotilla who died leading the naval attack: "Continue engaging the enemy." [106]

As the Royal Navy sailed from the fjord for home, it signalled back by Morse "Farewell, we'll meet again."

[2008 – Royal Navy Photography Department.]

---

106 As you have already read, up until 1970 sailors were issued a daily 'rum-ration'. However, in the past when a ship came out of battle repairs needed to be made to the sails and rigging. The most difficult tasks was that of 'splicing the main brace', it not easy working high up. So as a reward the sailor would be awarded a double tot of rum. Returning back to the present day, is now only ordered for occasions of great significance, such as the birth of royalty, the Queen's Jubilee and 'Fleet Reviews'. Only the Queen or the Admiralty Board can order it.

Back in the UK, several survivors were notified of the discovery and have given their reactions to the find. Here a newspaper reporter writes, "John Hague, aged 87 from Manchester, was a 19-year-old Able Seaman serving in the shell room below [...] Regarding the discovery of the ship's wreck he said: 'I am so pleased and overwhelmed to know that after so many years HMS *Hunter* has been found and my fellow shipmates have a known resting place. I'm so sorry not to be able to go to the wreath-laying, but I will be spending a quiet time at home with my family and thoughts. Also my daughter in Cornwall will be laying flowers at sea for me dedicated to my shipmates.'

"Another survivor Seaman Fred Ward, aged 88, spoke of his great sense of relief that the wreck had been found: "I would like to thank the Norwegian people and the Royal Navy for their very kind tributes following the discovery of my old ship. I have mixed emotions about the events from over 68 years ago and the loss of so many of my fine friends. I now have a great sense of relief knowing the final resting place of my comrades and our ship."

In Memory

For your freedom, they gave their lives. *Daily Mail*, Friday, April 26th 1940

THE Admiralty, announcing to-day casualties in H.M.S. Hunter, give the names of eight officers, 147 ratings, and two men of the N.A.A.F.I. staff missing.

The communiqué was as follows:—

"The Secretary of the Admiralty regrets to announce the following casualties recently sustained in H.M.S. Hunter. There is a faint possibility that a very small number of these officers and ratings may be prisoners of war, but there is no confirmation of this as yet.

"Any information that may come to hand will immediately be communicated to the next-of-kin concerned."

OFFICERS

Missing: Lieutenant-Commander L. De Villiers, R.N. (in command); Mr J. H. Coombe, Acting Gunner (T), R.N.; Probationary Temporary Surgeon-Lieutenant R. G. Evans, R.N.V.R.; Probationary Sub-Lieutenant Peter Norman Lancaster, R.N.V.R.; Lieutenant H. R. M. Marlow, R.N.; Lieutenant K. B. P. Pearson, R.N.; Lieutenant (E) A. G. Reid, R.N.; Lieutenant H. A. Stuart-Menteth, R.N.

RATINGS

Missing: Armstrong, John L., able seaman; Bailey, Albert J., leading seaman; Bailey, Wilfred, able seaman; Ballard, Harry, leading stoker; Barrett, William H. J., supply petty officer; Bartlett, Leonard, able seaman; Bassett, Eric W., able seaman; Beavan, Francis, telegraphist; Beckford, Daniel P., stoker 1st class; Bennett, William C., able seaman, R.F.R.; Berry, John F., stoker 1st class; Bitters, Thomas, stoker 1st class, R.F.R.; Black, Albert, acting electrical artificer 3rd class; Bower, Robert W., able seaman; Bradeld, Nicholas, able seaman; Bowden, Norman W. G., Able Seaman; Bradfield, Wm. A., Stoker 1st Class; Bray, Frederick S., Able Seaman; Brickle, Gilbert G. C., Leading Stoker; Brooks, Desmond R., Stoker 1st Class; Brown, Rex, Telegraphist; Brown, Thomas, Signalman; Butcher, Frederick W., Ordinary Seaman; Carding, Douglas G., Ordinary Seaman; Carruthers, Cyril, Stoker 1st Class; Carruthers, William, Able Seaman; Caton, Francis D., Stoker 1st Class; Clark, Harry; Able Seaman; Clayton, Leslie A., Able Seaman; Collis, Sydney, Able Seaman; Cook, Stanley W. J., Able Seaman; Coults, Charles; Able Seaman; Cox, John, Able Seaman; Dorward, Fred P., Able Seaman; Duffy, Joseph, Stoker Petty Officer; Edwards, William H. J., Able Seaman; Eley, Thomas, Acting Leading Seaman; Evans, Leonard, Able Seaman; Cross, Robert, Ordinary Seaman; Cromer, Walter, Able Seaman; Cunningham, John, Petty Officer; Cusimie, Hector, Stoker 1st Class; Day, Edward F., Signalman; Davies, Walter F., Ordinary Seaman; Evans, Samuel E., Stoker Petty Officer; Farnell, John A., Engine-room Artificer 1st Class; Foster, Joseph G. J., Acting Leading Seaman; Flynn, John J., Able Seaman; Foot, George H., Leading Seaman; Fox, Thomas F., Stoker 1st Class; Gilbert, Ernest A., Stoker 1st Class; Gould, John, Supply Petty Officer, R.F.R.; Gould, Edward H., Acting Chief Engine-room Artificer 2nd Class; Gowers, Charles F., Able Seaman; Gray,

Thomas, Stoker 1st Class; Hague, John C., Able Seaman; Haket, John, Able Seaman; Harris, Edwin J., Stoker 1st Class; Hay, Robert P., Ordinary Seaman; Hay, Robert W., Ordinary Seaman; Hayes, Michael P., Acting Leading Seaman; Heasey, Harry, Able Seaman; Hill, Alfred, Able Seaman; Hiscock, Jack, Stoker 1st Class, R.F.R.; Holehouse, Cyril, Able Seaman; Holt, Alfred, Able Seaman, R.F.R.; Hooley, Alfred, Able Seaman; Hooper, Alfred F., Stoker 1st Class; Horne, Charles W., Acting Petty Officer; Howell, Tudor R., Ordinary Seaman; Hunter, Guy R., Able Seaman; Hunter, Thomas C., Able Seaman; Hutton, Stanley G., Stoker 1st Class; Irwin, Arthur D., Able Seaman; James, Gwilym I. G., Able Seaman; Johns, Robert G., Ordinary Seaman; Johnson, David, Able Seaman; Kerswell, Stanley W., Acting Petty Officer; Kessell, William J., Leading Signalman; King, Thomas T., Stoker 1st Class; Knight, William H. H., Able Seaman; Lane, George, Stoker 1st Class, R.F.R.; Lavson, Thomas A., Acting Leading Telegraphist; Lawton, Charles A. C., Leading Seaman; Macdonald, Alfred, Ordnance Artificer 2nd Class; McDonald, Robert, Able Seaman; Maddocks, Frank, Sick Berth Attendant; Mann, Samuel H., Able Seaman; Marck, Thomas C., Stoker Petty Officer; Marsh, Leonard P. G., Stoker 1st Class; Matthews, William G., Acting Leading Seaman; Minstrell, Charles J., Leading Seaman; Moore, David H., Chief Stoker; Morgan, Frederick A. N., Petty Officer; Muddie, William M., Stoker Petty Officer; Mulhall, John R., Petty Officer; Mulhall, Daniel R., Petty Officer; Murphy, Daniel, Stoker 1st Class; Murphy, Michael, Able Seaman; Nazzarrow, Ronald, Able Seaman; Norton, Thomas, Signalman, R.F.R.; Parton, William H. J. F., Ordinary Seaman; Paul, Maurice G., Able Seaman; Payne, Edward, Able Seaman; Pitt, Gordon D., Leading Seaman; Prescott, Samuel, Able Seaman; Radcliffe, David, Able Seaman; Regan, Patrick, Stoker 1st Class; Renshaw, James, Able Seaman; Richards, Frederick W., Leading Stoker; Roberts, Frank, T.I.S.A.; Robertson, William E., Telegraphist; Rothwell, Ernest, Able Seaman; Rowe, James S., Leading Steward; Ryman, Richard W. S., Stoker Petty Officer; Settle, Joseph, Stoker 1st Class; Sim, William S. R., Stoker 2nd Class; Small, James, Chief Petty Officer; Smart, Harold J., Stoker 1st Class, R.F.R.; Smith, Marshal G., Able Seaman; Steel, John R., Able seaman; Stevens, Bertie H., Stoker 1st Class, R.F.R.; Stewart, Norman J., Able Seaman; Stone, A. J., Engine-room Artificer 2nd Class; Stuttard, Roy, Stoker 1st Class; Sullivan, George A., Chief Petty Officer; Swales, Stanley G., Able Seaman; Taylor, Frederick J., Acting Engine-room Artificer 4th Class; Thomas, Ernest, Able Seaman; Tucker, Alfred C. J., Ordinary Seaman; Tucker, Nicholas J., Able Seaman; Wada, William H., Assistant Cook; Ward, Frederick H., Ordinary Seaman; Warren, Trevor L., Engine-room Artificer 3rd Class; Warrender, George, Ordinary Seaman; Watson, James, Ordinary Seaman; Webber, Harold C., Telegraphist; Westlake, Cyril G., Able Seaman; Williams, Francis, Ordinary Seaman; Williams, James O., Leading Cook; Worsdale, John H., Ordinary Seaman; Wranghain, Joseph S. T., Stoker 1st Class; Yate, Horace J., Able Seaman; Yeud, Francis H., Ordinary Seaman.

Maltese Ratings: Aquilina, Antonio, Officers' Cook 2nd Class; Bartolo, Anthony, Assistant Steward; Merceica, Anthony, Cook O.

N.A.A.F.I. Staff: Falzon, Charles, Canteen Manager; Mulligan, Joe, Canteen Assistant.

Daily Mail. Friday. April 26th 1940, newspaper cutting with list of full HMS Hunter crew.

What happened to the survivors after Narvik?

Stanley Cook

For quite some time after the war Stan Cook and 'Stormy' Renshaw remained good friends. I was finally able to make contact with Stan's son Jim Cook, who informed me that his father was "never much of a hoarder, but would dig out anything I have". Unfortunately, having searched the loft all Jim could find was 'Stormy' Renshaw's account. However, he did inform me that after returning back to Britain his father was stationed at Drake Barracks, Devonport. He remained there until the end of the war, due to the form he had signed to not take up arms against the enemy like the other *Hunter* survivors. It was an outcome he found hard to accept. They all just wanted to get back to sea again and do more for the cause.

Returning back to civilian life, Stan joined the merchant navy. His first ship was *Bullfinch* in 1946 then *Margaret*, both were cable-laying vessels. He continued to live in Plymouth and retired in 1979. Stan passed away at St Luke's Hospice in June 1990.

Percy. C. Danby

Percy Danby remained on the *Hotspur* after it was refitted and sent to Gibraltar. The ship was damaged again when it rammed and sank an Italian submarine. It went into dry dock for repairs. He and a friend, another artificer, were transferred to HMS *Sheffield*. He was on board the ship during the pursuit and destruction of the *Bismarck*.

Percy had married Marguerite, known as Peggy [*nee* Proctor] also from Doncaster in 1939 a month after the war began. They had two children, a son Laurence, and a daughter, Angela. Having signed for twelve years in 1938, Percy remained in the Royal Navy until 1950. Just when he began to think about the end of his service, he got a letter from the Navy telling him that he might be needed a bit longer – the Korean conflict was brewing. He stayed on in the RN for another six months, but arranged in the meantime to join the Royal Canadian Navy.

Percy retained his full rank of Chief Engine Room Artificer when he transferred to the RCN which was still expanding and no doubt they were glad to have such an experienced and highly decorated senior rate. He returned to England a few years later to do a ten-month naval engineering course and later was promoted to Commissioned Engineering Officer. He completed a number of positions at the RCN Headquarters.

After thirty years' service and loyalty to both countries, and at the age of fifty, Percy retired from the Navy.

Then he moved to Florida and took a job at Florida Power and Light, where he worked for eleven years. Sadly, Peggy passed away in 1999, leaving her two children, two grandchildren and three great-grandchildren.

Percy, aged eighty-three in 2001, married Mabel [*nee* Wallwork] in Ottawa. Her son Victor says, "She was seventy at the time and was astonished to learn Percy's age – he didn't look it. They are quite happy, still living independently and, against all odds, heading toward their sixteenth wedding anniversary!

"So, Percy is my stepfather, but he came into the role relatively recently. It is an unusual situation for all of us – I became a grandfather and got a new stepfather in the same year, at the age of 46. I am very fond of him, as are all my siblings and our children. Some of the step-great-grandchildren call him "Grand-Dan". [Dan being his nickname from his naval days.] He recently joked that we must all promise to start calling him 'Dad' if he lives to 100, then he chuckled and said: 'No, make that "Super dad!"'

"Percy's daughter, Angela, lives in Ottawa. She is very good to Dan and to my mother, driving them to appointments and for groceries. She and my mother have become great friends."

Percy C. Danby, a phenomenal family man who can still remember his involvement in the epic First Battle of Narvik seventy-seven years ago; is a credit to both the Royal Canadian and Royal Navy that he served so well. Percy may you have many more years of well-earned happiness.

Joseph 'Pat' Duffy.

Joseph's wife Mabel, on receiving news that *Hunter* had been sunk, had to carry on looking after their six children, not knowing whether Joseph had gone down with the ship. The two youngest daughters Hazel and Joyce made daily prayers in their 'little' church at Keyham, Devonport, "Please God, give us back our daddy". It was not until almost a month later that a telegram arrived to say he was alive and safe in Sweden. The Plymouth newspaper then recorded the emotional moment. **"Their Prayers for Daddy Were Answered.** For Petty Officer Stoker Joseph Duffy is among the *Hunter* men safe in Sweden."

Back in Joseph's home town the local newspaper reported;

SKELMERSDALE MAN IS SAFE
Was Reported Missing

"A telegram was received on Tuesday [7th May 1940] by Mrs Duffy, of Ashwall Street, Skelmersdale, that her son, Petty Officer Joseph Patrick Duffy, who had been reported missing, when HMS *Hunter* was damaged in Narvik Fjord, is now safe. 'Pat' Duffy, as he was called, is well known in Skelmersdale and district. He has been in the Navy for over 20 years and would have finished his service at Christmas. He is married and has six children living at Swithy, Plymouth. His father was killed in the in 1918 during the Great War. Mr John Watkinson, as Chairman of the Skelmersdale Urban District Council, has sent congratulations on behalf of the people of Skelmersdale to Mrs Duffy, who has also received other congratulations."

Joseph's son Patrick, takes up the story, "When Dad was taken prisoner and Devonport was bombed we were to be evacuated but Mother would not leave her children. So we all travelled 250 miles north to a place she had never been to before. The family was separated until a house could be found for us all to be together. I was two when the war started, so I cannot remember Dad prior to this and the same applied to a younger brother who had not yet been seen by my Dad. All I remember of that time was sending food parcels of tinned jam and my mother's cake to the 'Red Cross'. I think the heroes in this episode of our history were the mothers who had children to protect, feed and shelter.

As you have already read Joseph's homecoming was not smooth, his children resented "this stranger coming back into the family". Patrick continues, "Unfortunately Dad didn't have a lot of civilian skills and ended up as a storeman in a local military establishment". Sadly, Joseph Duffy died in a road traffic accident in 1959. He was aged fifty-nine.

Sam Evens.

There was an article in the Plymouth newspaper, *The Evening Herald*, dated the 17th of March 2008. This story was triggered by the recent discovery of the ship's remains 800 metres below the fjord where she sank. It inspired Sam's proud grandson Jason Evens to write to the newspaper about his grandfather's memoirs and stated. "In my eyes my Granddad's a part of a legend." I tried to make contact with Jason through friends in Plymouth but unfortunately to no avail. Hopefully, he will get to hear about this book and we can arrange to meet, especially because he and other family members may not be aware that Sam Evens is one of the few *Hunter* survivors who provided his audio recorded account with the Imperial War Museum.

Sam Evens passed away in 1990 aged 85.

John Arthur Farnell

Engine Room Artificer 1st Class John Farnell prior to Narvik was present in the action against the *Bismarck* and was called as an official witness to the enquiry for the loss of HMS *Hood*. Remaining with HMS *Prince of Wales* he was present on board during her engagement with the *Bismarck* and once again was forced to abandon ship when the *Prince of Wales* was sunk by Japanese dive bombers 1941. Surviving he went on to serve in Korea. Mentioned in Despatches published in the *London Gazette* on the 15th December 1942, his ship is given as HMS *Sultan*, this was the shore establishment at Singapore, which was lost following the capture by the Japanese. It is possible the 'MID' is a result of gallantry during his service with HMS *Prince of Wales* or during the Battle for Singapore.

He appears to have returned to the northwest area of operations, prior to the end of the War. Remaining with the Royal Navy after the war he was serving on board the frigate HMS *Crane* during the Malaya emergency and the Korean War. He was discharged from the Royal Navy in January 1958.

Highly decorated in WW2 His group represents the maximum WW2 Star allocation to one person (five stars), including Queen's Korea Medal and the UN Korea Medal. It is sad that his medals for whatever reason after an exemplary service to his country had to be put up for auction.

Surgeon Captain Alfred Flannery, OBE

Having left the 2nd Destroyer Flotilla, Alfred's final report written by the Flotilla Commander read, "This officer takes his professional duties seriously. He is an excellent officer, loyal and tactful. A pleasant personality and popular with officers and ratings. He has taken a keen interest in Ships' Companies games."

Alfred continued to serve in the Royal Navy until his retirement in August 1963, a total of thirty-two years. On his emotional departure from the 2nd Destroyer Flotilla in 1939, his next appointment was on the depot ship HMS *Greenwich* and a two-year term at the HMS *St George* training establishment on the Isle of Man. In April 1942 Alfred spent eighteen months on the cruiser HMS *Orion* and by now had achieved the rank of Surgeon Commander. His last two years of the war was spent as the Senior Medical Officer and Medical Specialist at HMS Royal Arthur the training establishment, then based at Skegness. It was here that he heard he had been awarded the King Haakon of Norway, 'Liberty Medal'.

Between 1945 and 1958, Alfred completed a further twelve appointments at various Royal Naval Hospitals. These include, Ceylon, Plymouth, Bermuda, (when he was awarded his OBE) and Portsmouth. He was promoted to Surgeon Captain in 1956. In 1958 to 1960 he was the Specialist Medical Officer at the Chatham Base. During the following years, Alfred and Liz's family expanded to seven children. The oldest, by 1960 was Hugh then twenty-one and the youngest Terence (Terry) aged thirteen. At which point their father's career went full circle and in 1961, Alfred was appointed back to Malta serving first at the Royal Naval Hospital Bighi and then as officer in charge of 'United Kingdom Families' Clinic. He and his family were popular and highly respected in both the naval fraternity and the general Maltese community. In 1962, nearing the end of his distinguished and loyal career to Britain he proudly became a 'Honorary Physician' to Her Majesty the Queen.

Surgeon Captain Alfred Flannery, OBE, was retired from the Royal Navy on the 23rd August 1963 aged fifty-seven. Sadly he passed away six and half months later and was buried at Kalkara Naval Cemetery on the island he loved, Malta. Subsequently, Liz and their children maintain contact with close friends in Malta, his three daughters still live there. Liz Flannery died in 1981, also a remarkable person, having qualified in her younger days as one of the first female lawyers in America.

John 'Albert' Hague, BEM

John Hague's mother died when he was a small child. So his Auntie Rosie became his surrogate mother and it was to her that he came home from Sweden in January 1941. Rosie informed John's old school headmaster about John's homecoming, so the headmaster asked John to give a talk about his exploits to the whole school. He was also requested to relate his experience to the local Oldham newspaper. As mentioned earlier, John was awarded the British Empire Medal for his part in bringing back the Norwegian cargo ships.

John renewed his relationship with May Chamberlain and found employment at the Ford's car engine plant for the duration of the war. In April 1944 he and May were married. John went onto work at Ciba Geigy Chemicals in Trafford Park.

However, having achieved well-earned recognition by his country, bureaucracy took over. John, similar to other survivors had signed the Germans form "To not take up arms ..." He was discharged from the Navy on the 14th of February 1942. Firstly, having left the *Ranja*, John received a payment account from the cargo ship. This was from the 21st of December 1940 when he moved on board to his leaving on the 4th of February 1941. This included such items as Hire Rate of Pay, Wartime Supplements, Travel Bonuses and overtime payments. It was still taxable leaving him with 612 Kroners equivalent to £34.11s.7d., paid on the day of leaving the ship.

Whilst John was interned in Sweden, he continued to receive his daily rate of pay for Stoker 1st Class which was approximately 17 Shillings a day (85p today). Then the second letter arrived on his door step. This time from the 'Director of Naval Accounts', almost to the day of the Second Anniversary of the sinking of *Hunter* and over a year since he had left the *Ranja*. The contents of which, due to his having now been decorated, rightly left a somewhat sour taste in the mouth.

"With reference to your representation of the 13th February last to the Commodore, R.N Barracks, Devonport, regarding Naval Pay drawn by you during internment in Sweden, the attached statement shows the amounts actually received by you from the Naval Attaché, Stockholm, during the period of your internment in that country.

"I have to inform you that, on your release from Royal Naval Service on the 14th February last, a debtor balance of £8.7s.7d was outstanding on your account due to the fact that the above advances of pay were in excess of your Naval earnings.

"I have, therefore, to request you to be good enough to refund this amount by remitting the sum, to the Director of Naval Accounts. An envelope is enclosed for your reply.

"I am, your obedient Servant."

John told me, he still hasn't paid the money back. Whilst, his daughter Carole Knowles, went onto explain, "If they still want it, there's going to be a lot of stink about it, in the newspapers."

Carole explained, that when she was eight she accompanied her father to London for the 2nd Destroyer Flotilla of Narvik Association's Reunion. She remembers the wreath laying ceremony on Horse Guards Parade and later that evening going to the German Embassy for dinner. Carole herself later joined the Services as a Nursing Sister. (Queen Alexandra's Royal Naval Service, QARNS.)

Although John loved his rugby, he could no longer play because he had suffered an ankle injury at Narvik, but he still enjoyed seeing it on TV. As well as watching cricket and football at local sports grounds, when taking his dog for a walk. Here daughter Carole provides additional insight into her father's life. "Dad did not talk about what happened in the war until later years. This was when my Auntie Annie gave Dad some newspapers and all of a sudden more papers came out. Dad spent his spare time walking his many dogs, riding his many push bikes and watching his grandchildren grow into adults. Mum and Dad loved their holidays either home or abroad. They loved musicals and would often be found singing around the house. Dad has never been a man to keep still.

"Mum and Dad had many happy years until Mum died in June 1999. They went on to have four daughters, Lillian, Jean, Susan and myself. There are now six grandchildren, seven great grandchildren and so far one great-great-grandchild.

"In a chance conversation with a friend, who happened to be a 'Medal Collector', we mentioned to him that we had heard Dad had been awarded another medal. The friend looked up Dad's name and found an article in the *London Gazette* stating he had been awarded the Norwegian War Medal. Subsequently, I emailed everybody 'below God', including the Queen. At first I was told he was not able to receive a Medal from another country, a rule brought about in 1952. I pointed out that Dad was awarded the medal before this ruling, so more emails were sent."

In November 2008, the Royal Navy made contact with John, then aged eighty-eight. Carole's determined hard work paid off, when Colonel Knut the Norwegian Military Attaché, arrived from London. So it was that John Hague, BEM, with his proud family in attendance, received the medal at the 'Trafford Branch' of the Royal Naval Association.

John Hague passed away on 20th December 2013.

Guy Hunter

Back to Guy Hunter's granddaughter, Shelley Hutton, "My Mum died four years ago and I've lost touch with my Uncle Guy – he's the one with all the photos and papers. So I am unable to get the details of the escape [or otherwise] from the POW camp. The only thing I remember was my Granddad was unable to eat fat when he got home because that's mostly what he ate at Marlag. I remember hearing he was friendly with one of the German guards and possibly escaped via Sweden. My second cousin Pat (Guy's niece) remembers being a really young girl when Guy showed up out of the blue at her Gran's house (Guy's Mum – Granny *Hunter*) in Rosyth. He just came in the back door.

"I do have a few photos of my Granddad post war with my Gran and with his children and at work. He's working on a car, so I guess he turned his hand to car mechanics after he came home. I am feeling very frustrated that I don't have further details. Granddad died in 1966 – aged just fifty."

David 'Jonno' Johnson

David and Ethel had three daughters, Irene born 1939 [mother in law of Nigel Sefton], Kathleen born 1942 and Linda born 1943. Irene, having looked at the Gunnarn group photograph believes her father was second from the left, 3rd row from the back.

Service papers confirmed David came back from Sweden with John Hague [and others] on M/V Ranja, returning to Devonport Barracks on 2rd February 1941.

Cruelly another of David's brother died in 1942 from an accident on board the trawler GY851 off Iceland.

Like many families, David and Irene's home was bombed during the Plymouth 'blitz'. But at least David arrived home after less than twelve months of the Battle of Narvik. David went on to serve in the RN until 1962. Perhaps somewhere in those early days the 'powers that be' had not been made aware of the form he had signed for the German's. Unfortunately, David continued to suffered from ill health caused by the amount of oil he swallowed whist in the fjord at Narvik. He sadly died in 1966 aged 52 from liver failure.

Stanley 'Jake' Kerswell.

As you have read, other than those who were wounded, Jake Kerswell was the first to take the opportunity to escape from Sweden, arriving home on Christmas Eve 1940. Much later after the war, his son, Peter had contact with Stormy Renshaw and John Hague. Both commented about his escape, "He just disappeared." This was probably because, being the first survivor allowed to be sent on his way by the Swedish authorities, it needed to be completed under strict secrecy.

Having been discharged from the Navy in 1943 Jake was able to get on with his life once more as a family man. However, I was informed by his son, Peter, that Jake's younger brother, whilst serving in the merchant navy, lost his life on board the *Canadian Star* which was sunk three months earlier. He was aged nineteen.

Jake quickly found work at Swansea Docks before securing long term employment with the Post Office. Subsequent to reaching retirement age, he continued in work as a car park attendant at his local hospital. From my father's documents, Jake became a founder member of the 2nd Destroyer Flotilla Association'.

Jake, a well-regarded Petty Officer by his subordinates on HMS *Hunter*, passed away at the age of seventy-two in 1974.

George Lane.

Chris Lane writes, "Thanks for the photograph, my Granddad died when I was about 5 years old and I am 52 now. I am certain the person in the second row up and third in is him (group photograph on arrival at Gunnarn). I have no other information on him other than he was a postman who took great pride in his job. But I do remember that he was held in high esteem by all the family, and my mother had nothing but the greatest praise for him. All my relatives are deceased including my father George Clifford Lane and his sister Nancy, so I can't offer any more information. Sadly, my elder sister can't remember anything either. Although we are certain he remained captive until the war was over and never escaped."

As you have read, George Lane was in fact flown out of Sweden on 20th

December 1941. I have since informed George's family and given them details of his escape.

Daniel Joseph Murphy

As you have read, Joe Murphy was one of a number of *Hunter* survivors who was taken to Germany as a 'Prisoner of War'. I have been unable to make contact with his nephew Kieran Hosford. At present the only additional information I have from Kieran is brief. "Joe spent another thirteen years in the Royal Naval and finally retired in 1958. He never really talked about his experiences during the war and the information we have is sketchy".

It appears that Joe, similarly to his fellow survivors, was grateful to the Swedish friends met on their long journey to freedom. In Joe's case, let us not forget the name of 'Evie Carlsson', who was brave enough to try to get a cryptic message back to his family to confirm he was alive.

Daniel Joseph Murphy died in 1985 shortly before his seventy-third birthday.

Thomas 'Daddy' Norton.

As you have read, Thomas Norton was a veteran of both World Wars and the first *Hunter* survivor to be flown back directly to Britain from Sweden on 29th of August 1941, then almost aged forty-three. It is uncertain as to why Thomas was the first to be flown home direct from Sweden, but as I have previously suggested, it may be that the forging of a close working relationship with Captain Denham was a 'God send'. From what I have read about the Captain, it appears he was loyal to those he trusted and would probably have known of Thomas' wife's ill health after hearing the news of HMS *Hunter*'s sinking.

The personal information on Thomas was provided by his two grand-daughters Jose Johnson and Ellen Siddall, both of whom still live in the part of Manchester, where their grandfather had lived.

Jose explains, "I am not sure that Granddad was told about Gran's illness, but his sister Florence may have wrote and told him. As she was with Gran during her illness, as Gran had three children to look after. I would imagine that if Granddad knew of Gran's illness he would have wanted to be back home, as they were very close. This is because when Granddad died, my Auntie Margaret said Gran was ill then."

After Thomas returned home from Sweden, similar to other *Hunter* survivors, he was given non-combatant duties. Apparently, he wanted to go back to sea but was not allowed, because of the document he had signed with his stamped fingerprint. Subsequently, he was discharged and went back to his job in the Post Office as a driver. He eventually rose to the position of 'Inspector'."

Ellen adds, "I know my Granddad never spoke about his war years very much. I think surviving three ships sinking during the two wars, as well as having marched over the mountains to Sweden by the Germans, had took its mark. I for one was proud of my Grandfather and others who fought for this country. I am pleased to think his part has not gone unnoticed. My Gran and Granddad had four granddaughters and four grandsons."

Jose reminisces, "I remember him as a quiet and placid man who never seemed to raise his voice. His daughter, my Auntie Margaret, has said much the same. He was once getting it 'in the ear' off my Gran for something when he stood in front of the fireplace, spread his arms out and burst into a song. Granddad used to sit in his armchair and quietly smoked his pipe and read his paper. If he fell asleep whilst reading the paper he always said that he was 'resting his eyes'. He always had a paper bag of boiled sweets. From what my Auntie Margaret said it was Gran who told her about what Granddad had gone through [...] I got to have my Granddad in my life for ten years until he unfortunately died of cancer."

Ellen goes on to say, "I actually did not know Granddad was the first one flown directly home and to have an actual date has just made me smile. I would love a copy of his flight details. I work in a school and when we do the topic on the World War this would be an interesting document to show the children; but more importantly it's something for my family to see."

Thomas 'Daddy' Norton a fond husband to Georgina Ellen, a father, a granddad and a great granddad to twenty great-grandchildren and six great-great-grandchildren passed away on the 2nd of July 1967 aged six-ty-nine. Georgina Ellen died on the 23rd February 1982, which was a few days after Ellen, named after her Gran, had celebrated her twenty-first birthday.

In the two 'World Wars', Thomas had given exceptional service to his country and thankfully on both occasions by the 'Grace of God' was able to return back to his family.

William Henry Parton.

Bill Parton was born in the South Wales town of Pontardawe, a young man beginning of his naval career, saw him going into battle, his ship sunk and having to survive in a freezing Norwegian fjord. Bill's daughter Christina (married name Tomkins) accompanied her father and mother in the 1970s to the 2nd Destroyer Flotilla Association of Narvik in London and later to the German veterans' reunion in Bremerhaven.

Here, Christina tells not only her own memories but those of other family members. "My father was twenty-one at the time of Narvik but didn't speak much about what had happened. My grandparents received the news that the '*Hunter*' had been sunk and that my father was missing. My grandmother was told by a 'spiritualist' that my father was still alive and she believed it was the case. My father told me there was little food and that is why they were sent to Sweden. When they got there my father worked on a farm. I remember him talking about Charlie Swales, also a seaman from Newport, South Wales, who met a Swedish girl and my father and Charlie kept in touch. My son Julian was told by his grandfather that he was repatriated to Scotland by plane and then travelled by train to report to the appropriate naval authorities. Another story my father told me is that immediately on arrival, when spoken to in English he replied in Welsh. He must have been really disorientated. Welsh was his first language and I think in his own mind he thought he was nearly home. I think he must have returned to UK in 1942, but I am not certain.

"He then went straight home to Pontardawe, there were no telephones in those days. He just walked in the back door. You can imagine my grandmother's reaction. Having contacted my eighty-nine-year-old Aunt, Lilwen Pezzelli, my late mother's sister, who now lives in Rhode Island USA, she tells me that on my father's return he worked in an ammunition factory in Bridgend. It was there that he met my mother Anne and later my brother and I were born.

"My parents went on holiday to Sweden in the 1980s and met up with Charlie Swales and his wife. I know he thought Sweden was a great place. They then went on to Narvik and visited the nearby graveyard where some who had died were buried.

"My father had a copy of the commemorative plaque produced in Devonport. He had it framed and it was displayed on the wall of my parent's living room until my father passed away in 1998. The other photograph you sent, I hadn't seen before. My father is in the group of *Hunter* survivors he is in the top row, first on the left, in the sweater. It was just fantastic to see them.

"I can believe that the lads were popular with local girls. My son now has the picture of his grandfather taken when interned in Sweden. He was on skis and looked very dashing. I often wondered whether he had a Swedish girlfriend."

Alick G. Reid, OBE
The only information I have which confirms Alick Reid returned in one piece from a POW camp is that he was on my father's 2nd Destroyer Flotilla Association's mailing list. In the 1970s, he had deservedly risen to the rank of Captain (Engineering) and lived at Oxshott, Surry.

James 'Stormy' Renshaw.
The Navy tries very hard to look after its own, especially as already mentioned, those *Hunter* survivors who had signed the form presented by the Germans. So it was, that Jim 'Stormy' Renshaw found employment in the Tug Section at Devonport Dockyard. Thereby continuing to have an ongoing connection with the Royal Navy, he served on all the tugs, 'shepherding' warships, both home and away in Plymouth Sound. Stormy explains, "I served there for forty-odd years, losing half my hand in the process". Subsequently, on his retirement he was awarded the 'Imperial Service Medal'.

Stormy married Audrey Williams or 'Little Auds' as Stormy used to call her, and they went onto have seven children.

I managed to make contact with Stormy's son Jim, in Plymouth. Jim was very helpful with providing additional information and trying to track down the family of Sam Evens in the Plymouth area. Jim takes over, "I notice you followed your Dad into the Navy. Just to let you know that coincidence is still alive and well, I also joined the RN in the same year as you. It is funny you should refer to him as 'Stormy', that was his password when he tried, with great difficulty, to master the computer.

"When Dad was first reported missing my Mum was a policewoman in Plymouth. It caused a bit of a stir at the time, as the local paper picked up on it, as my Mum was the daughter of a prominent local Alderman, by the name of Williams. After their marriage they stayed with the 'in-laws', until they were given one of the first prefabs to be built in Plymouth after the war. They later moved to a large three-bedroom house where they raised their four daughters and three sons. My Dad worked in the dockyard on the Tugs working his way up to 'Bosun' and earned the 'Imperial Service Medal'. Both achievements of which he was very proud.

"I well remember when I was in the RN, on more than one occasion going across to visit him on the 'Superman' tug. Only to find him having a quiet half hour: as he called it. These days it would be known as a 'power nap'. This was a ritual he enjoyed every day of his life from then on. My Mum passed away on the 27th of September 1999. Dad visually went downhill from there and he missed her terribly. He was a member of the Royal Maritime Auxiliary Service, and always called himself the 'Senior Hand'; which in a way he was as he was the oldest member right up until the day he passed away.

"Dad made me ensure he was known as "J. Renshaw, ISM" on the Order of Service sheet at the crematorium. My brothers and I placed the Union flag and a floral anchor on his coffin, and a great many 'Tuggies' and RMAS members turned up, to send him on to his final Anchorage."

Right up until Stormy's latter years he maintained his amusing forthright manner. Here is an example provided by a family member when she took Stormy to Henny Penny's Fish Restaurant in Yorkshire. "I remember going to a restaurant and him sending back the fish to the kitchen – declaring, "I have not spent 45 years at sea protecting the fishing fleets for them to treat it like that."

James 'Stormy' Renshaw, ISM, died on the 13th of January 2009. The Imperial Service Medal originates from 1902 by King Edward VII. It is awarded to selected 'Civil Servants' on completion of twenty-five years meritorious service, on their retirement.

Joseph Settle

Joe Settle the young man working at a colliery, who becoming restless had decided to join the Royal Navy, would never have imagined that within nineteen months, he would gain early promotion and then find himself swimming in freezing water to save his life. In his relatively short spell in the Navy, through no fault of his own, he would experience enough fear and excitement to last for the rest of his lifetime.

Joe having married Evelyn six months earlier was discharged from the Navy in January 1943. He had an exemplary service record being 'Mentioned in Dispatches' and awarded the Norwegian War Medal. For him, it was now, prematurely, back to 'civvy life', which saw Joe and Evelyn returning to Norton, Doncaster, to live with Joe's parents.

Joe found employment at the renowned locomotive works, where such famous train engines as the 'Flying Scotsman' and the 'Mallard' were built. Joe became a skilled tradesman in painting, decorating, French polishing and sign-writing; moving on to other factory work, until his retirement in 1983.

Between 1944 and 1956 Joe and Evelyn had two sons and a daughter. Here his daughter Sheila takes over, "We had a very happy childhood, with lots of fond memories. Mum and Dad enjoyed ballroom dancing throughout their lives. Dad finished his working days at a Shipyard in Selby, which was ironic really as he had returned to his love of ships. This he showed on numerous occasions by doing pencil drawings of ships and the sea.

"Just eight weeks after retiring, my Mum died very suddenly. She was sixty-three and it came as a great shock to everyone. Dad's experiences in the Navy during the war formed a great part of his character; as he was so grateful for life. As he said, on numerous occasions, 'every day is a bonus'. He was extremely tolerant and placid and showed no malice or animosity towards anyone. He was great to be around and great with the grandchildren, who thought his magic tricks really were magic."

Joe Settle passed away on the 23rd of July 1996, from prostate cancer. As Shelia points out just as he did during his time in the Royal Navy. "He dealt with his illness with dignity, bravely and without complaint. But that was Joe."

Regarding Joe's pal Thomas King, who was also awarded the Norwegian War Medal, I have little information. However, in my father's papers is a letter dated 1970 sent by Thomas' sister who had obviously been keeping up to date with her brother's membership in the Association; she mentions he had passed away and she was considering giving his papers and medals to the local Gainsborough Community Centre.

Harold Siddall

Less than two months after he returned home to Plymouth, Harold married his fiancée, Mabel Sheard, to whom he had been engaged since 1938. Mabel had been an Air Raid Precautions Warden in Devonport, and was awarded the British Empire Medal for her bravery and selflessness during the blitz on Plymouth in 1941. Subsequently, she was called up to the ATS, and worked as a 'listener' for the Bletchley Park team, scanning the airwaves for German military messages and transcribing them to be passed to the codebreakers.

Harold had joined the Royal Navy as a Stoker in 1937, intending it to be his career. After about three months' leave accrued in the prison camps, he continued that career in 1945, climbing the ladder until he was promoted to Chief Engineer Mechanical in the early 1950s. He served in the engine rooms on a variety of ships from the corvette HMS *Porchester Castle* to the Aircraft Carrier HMS *Eagle*. He did three stints as an engineering instructor at HMS *Raleigh*, and finally finished his twenty-two-year service in 1959.

Harold had enjoyed his time as an instructor, and two years after leaving the Navy he embarked on a teacher training course, specialising in Arts and Crafts, at St Luke's Teacher Training College in Exeter. On qualifying in 1963, he was appointed to Mount Street Primary School in Plymouth, where he spent the majority of his teaching career. He was well-liked by his pupils, who enjoyed the anecdotes he told them about when he was a sailor.

After retirement, Harold continued to teach pottery on a voluntary basis at the primary school he had attended as a boy.

An after-effect of his time as a POW was arthritis which plagued his joints that had been damaged due to malnourishment, so in 1994, Harold and Mabel moved from their house in Plymouth to a bungalow in Weston-super-Mare to be near their daughter, Barbara. In 1997 Harold was diagnosed with the cancer mesothelioma, which is caused by inhaling asbestos fibres, a legacy of all his years in ships' engine rooms where asbestos was freely used. He died later that year aged eighty, at his home in Weston-super-Mare. Mabel died in 2010 at the age of ninety-two, still missing him deeply. [107]

Norman. J. Stewart. DSM.
I have no information on Norman other than that his mother was contacted by the Admiralty. "Mrs B.A. Stewart of Risdon Avenue Plymouth has received the following, 'I am pleased to inform you that information has now been received that your son Norman. J. Stewart, Able Seaman of HMS *Hunter* is safe in Sweden. Letter follows.'"

---

107 From 1941 the ARP officially changed its title to Civil Defence Service to reflect the wider range of roles it then encompassed. During the war, almost 7,000 Civil Defence workers were killed. In all some 1.4 million men and women served as ARP wardens during World War Two. The Civil Defence Service was stood down after the end of the war in Europe on 2 May 1945.

Marshal Grant Soult.

On Marshal's eventual return to civilian life, "he honoured the undertaking [not to take up arms again] and went to work at the Climax plant Camborne," says Neville Davies a family friend. During the remainder of the war Marshal met Kay, a schoolteacher, and they were married in 1947. Whilst they did not have any children of their own, they enjoyed the company of their friend's offspring. Betty Bagley recalls, "Marshal was the favourite with us little ones. I was always hoping he would bring me a china dolly, as toys and dolls were unattainable during wartime."

Marshal found employment in a shoe shop where he eventually became manager. They bought a house on the Flushing Quay in Falmouth and had a sailing dingy. He enjoyed taking family and friends on tours of the Falmouth dockyard. "Marshal and Kay were great travellers, most summers heading across the channel with their camper van", says Betty. Apparently, during one trip the VW broke down in Germany. Subsequently, they were put up by friends and the van was taken to be sorted at the VW factory. It appears their German saviour was a contact they had made when they attended the London Reunion, which was also attended by the German veterans of Narvik.

Kay passed away in 1998 and Marshal became diabetic and sadly lost his legs. Barbara Wakeham, Kay's niece, living in St Austell, Cornwall became the carer for Marshal in his latter years and had kept his documents and photographs. She explained to me that Kay was the person who wrote down Marshal's account, called *The Hunter Story*.

Barbara also told me that Marshal had always thought the story of the battle and his and other seamen's accounts of their survival would make a great film for the cinema. I visited Barbara at her home in Boscoppa, St Austell, Cornwall in July 2012.

Here Barbara reminisces, "Kay was the village schoolteacher for several years and we know that she taught almost every child in the village to swim. I spent some happy holidays with them during those years, being about eleven years old. It was so exciting staying on the water's edge and as everyone would tell you they were such fun. Both keen swimmers themselves they encouraged me to improve my swimming. One day they took me out in their rowing boat into very deep waters, where tanker type vessels were berthed. Staying close at hand they were ready to fish me out if I floundered. The reward for doing this was, 'Now you can really say you can swim'.

"I think of how Marshal swam back in the fjord's icy waters, dragging the dinghy and rescued those who would have drowned had he not done so. His sterling qualities of patience and fortitude stayed with him until the end of his life."

I leave it for Betty to have the last words, "I do not imagine the information regarding Narvik will be new to you as Marshal knew your father, but I can tell you our lives especially childhood were certainly enriched by knowing him and Kay."

Marshal Soult died in 2006 at the age of 87.

Alexander Stuart-Menteth, DSC

Although Alexander Stuart-Menteth, because of his injuries, was not one of the survivors to be interned in Sweden, I felt it fitting, as the First Lieutenant on *Hunter* and for his exemplary service throughout the war, he should still be mentioned in this chapter.

As already outlined Alexander was fortunate to survive the sinking of *Hunter* by the bravery of Able Seaman Norman Stewart. However, shortly after the event his obituary was published in the *Times* newspaper, having been officially listed as 'Killed in Action'. Although initially considered a 'Prisoner of War', having been hospitalised in Narvik, once again his good fortune held fast. The Allies temporarily took control of Narvik and Alexander with other patients was brought back to Britain. After months of further treatment in hospital he was back at sea. In December 1940 he was appointed First Lieutenant to another destroyer HMS *Somali*.

In March 1941, *Somali* became involved in landing Commandos on the Lofoten Islands. The destroyer also confronted a German patrol trawler that was out of action and sinking. However, it appears that Alexander, remembering how he had been rescued by his adversaries at Narvik; with the trawler doomed, scrambling nets dispatched went down to help haul up the German sailors. Subsequently, Alexander led a landing party that was sent on board which resulted in the important seizure of German cryptographic equipment. These were passed onto the 'then secret' establishment Bletchley Park, greatly assisting in their attempts to decode the now well publicised 'Enigma' communications messages.

Alexander Stuart–Menteth went onto become involved in many eventful incidents during the Second World War, too many to recall here. However, during this period he finally had his own command of a destroyer, including

HMS *Aldenham,* amongst which he was 'Mentioned in Dispatches' and later awarded the DSC. On board *Aldenham* was Petty Officer Bert Mason, one of the main characters in my first book which focused on HMS Hardy at Narvik. Bert says, "A better Skipper you wouldn't find."

After the war Alexander was loaned to the Royal Australian Navy where he met Penelope Giles and in 1952 they were married. They had two sons and a daughter. Having had a distinguished career in the Royal Navy, on retirement in 1958 he became responsible for overseeing the 'Corps of Commissionaires' in Scotland. However, the war never quite left Commander Alexander Stuart-Menteth, because in early 1990 he was asked to make a contribution to the film *Seizing the Enigma.*

Alexander passed away in June 2000 at the age of eighty-seven.

Fred Henry Ward

As previously mentioned Fred Ward was taken as a Prisoner of War after his blockade busting cargo ship *Skyterren* was captured by the Germans. He and his Royal Naval shipmates were first sent to the 'Milag' camp and then onto the 'Marlag' camp. However, he finished his time in the war at Stalag VIIIB, another story in itself. In fact, Fred wrote a book which is with the Imperial War Museum in London. His son Robin says that his father could not publish it as he still had too much respect for his lost shipmates. In January 2008, as already outlined, HMS *Hunter* was found by the Royal Norwegian Navy over a thousand feet down below the fjord.

Robin describes his father's thoughts when told of the discovery of *Hunter.* "It took a while for it to sink in, he is now eighty-eight (2008). One thing he did say was that now he could let them go, knowing that they will be remembered forever and not forgotten. He said that 'They were lost and now they are found.' He lost a lot of mates on the 10th of April 1940. There have been a lot of tears over the last few days from all the family, but we are happy for him now."

Bibliography

The German Invasion of Norway – April 1940. Geirr Haarr. ISBN 9781 84832 0321

Death at Dawn: Captain Warburton-Lee V.C. and the Battle of Narvik. April 1940. Alf R. Jacobsen. History Press.

Narvik: Battles in the Fjords. Peter Dickens. ISBN 0 7110 0484 6

Commodore Per Askim's, 'Personal Report', Kampen om Narvik, April 1940, and Battles of Narvik April 1940 London. [more comprehensive July 1940]

Askim's Diaries 1950. Fars Erindringer [Father's Reminiscences]

Fra Narvik Till Washington. Signe Askim. Dr Ole Petter Bormer Collection.

Narvik. Donald Macintyre. Pans Books. ISBN 0330 02708 5.

Destroyer Actions. Harry Plevy ISBN 978-1-86227-483-9.

Jack's War. G.C. Connell. ISBN 0-7183-0565-5.

Fortress Malta: An Island Under Siege 1940 James Holland ISBN 978-0-3043-6654 -5

'Kvarstad Ships and Men'. www.warsailors.com/free fleet/ kvarstad.html

The Blockade Busters. 1976 Ralph Barker ISBN 1 84415 282 0

SOE's – Balls of Steel: Operation Rubble. Sophie Jackson. History Press. 2013.

A Stoker's Story – from Scapa to Crete, Stalag and Home. Harold Siddall 'www. naval-history.net/WW2Memoirs'

Zerstörer Z2 Georg Thiele: 1934–1940. Harnack and Sifferlinger. ISBN 978-3-936691-46-7

The Mountains Wait. Theodor Broch. Michael Joseph Ltd, London 1943.

The Privileged Nightmare. Michael Alexander and Giles Romilly. Weidenfeld and Nicholson, London, 1954.

Giles Romilly's Despatches. Daily Express from 5th April 1940 and the days immediately following.

Tag*Glowworm*,'admin@hms*Glowworm*.org.uk'

The Last Escape. John Nichol and Tony Rennell Penguin Books.

Lost Voices of the Royal Navy. Max Arthur. ISBN 978 0 340 838143.

'Warmemories.com'

The Author

Ron Cope was born in Salford in 1946 before his family moved to Flixton, Manchester. On joining the Royal Navy in 1964 in the radio and radar maintenance branch, his first ship was a new guided missile destroyer HMS *Devonshire*. He was then aged eighteen and this gave him not only his first experience of travelling the world but also involvement in a conflict zone.

In 1969 Ron joined the aircraft carrier *Eagle* where he was promoted to Petty Officer. During this period, he married Alison [*nee* Hooper], from Holsworthy, Devon. The daughter of another naval man who served in the Fleet Air Arm during World War Two and Korea, Lieutenant Commander Anthony Hooper. M in D.

On completing further professional training, Ron was sponsored by the Navy to participate on an Army 'free fall' parachute course at Netheravon on Salisbury Plain. His next draft to Singapore Communications Centre allowed him to be accompanied by Alison, where for the second year Ron was attached to the Australian Army 9th Signal Regiment. Returning to United Kingdom he served on the frigate *Keppel* followed by a return to aircraft carriers, this time *Ark Royal*.

In 1976, Ron had a spell on the staff of Dartmouth Naval College before being posted as a 'systems engineer' in the Gibraltar Communications Centre, once more accompanied by Alison. As a Chief Petty Officer he went on to serve on the frigates *Naiad* and *Galatea*, in charge of radar and communication systems and in the role of training officer. He retired from the Navy in 1986 to complete a full-time Home Office sponsored Probation Officers university qualifying course in Plymouth. This led to him gaining employment with the Shropshire Probation Service based at the Telford office.

Over the following twenty years Ron was a generic caseworker and lead facilitator for 'offending behaviour' groups. His last appointment was at a 'Young Offenders Institution' in Shropshire. He says that moving from a naval environment, where his training responsibilities were predominantly with junior ratings, gave him the necessary experience to work with other young men having social and lifestyle difficulties. Whilst presenting a different challenge, it was also very rewarding.

Ron retired from the Probation Service in 2008 moving to the private sector. This was with Telford Training Consultants (TTC 2000) in a part time role, counselling substance misuse offenders within the West Midlands Probation Area. During which time, having been given his father Cyril Cope's documents and memorabilia, he began researching for his two books.

Ron and Alison remain living in the village of Horsehay, just above the 'Ironbridge Gorge'. The have a son James and a granddaughter Naomi.

Ron is a supporter of the 'Royal Navy and Royal Marines Charity'.

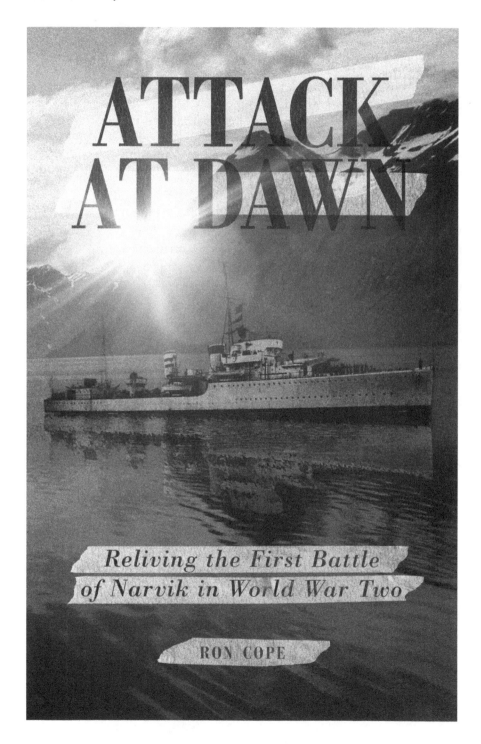

ATTACK
AT DAWN

*Reliving the First Battle
of Narvik in World War Two*

RON COPE

British 'Amazon' Readers.

Radish. 16 November 2016
This book in relating the experiences of many of the participants of the battle, gives a very human view of the fearful struggle to fight and survive in very difficult circumstances.

Peter. 2 October 2016
Well researched account particularly focused on those who fought so well in this classic. World War 2 naval action. Highly recommended.

Amazon Customer 21 August 2016
Ron has written a really engaging account of the events of the Battle of Narvik. The personal perspective really brings it to life.

Amazon Customer. 18 January 2017
Excellent well informed data, well written, the sort of information you cannot put down until you have finished the book.

Paul. 19 November 2016
What a very well-researched book. It was a very interesting read and a book I will not forget very quickly.

Kindle Customer 12 June 2015
As a crew members on a later HMS *Hardy* (F54) a Blackwood class frigate, we visited Narvik in 1960 and visited the graves of the crew mentioned in this book, we also met some of the Norwegians who had given aid and assistance to the crewmembers. This book really brings to life the momentous actions of all concerned both officers, crew members, civilians, British Norwegian and German. I could not put this book down.

Jessica Nightingale. 10 August 2015
I bought this book at a book signing by the author. Although I'm not a big reader, I read this book within a week while on holiday as I found it hard to put down. The book is written in such a way that you feel like you are right there witnessing the battle take place. It was also an interesting insight into the lives of the sailors leading up to and following the war. The second book has been ordered in advance.

Gaarghoile 19 November 2016

Some story this well researched and collated book covering many aspects of this battle. Yes this story is a very human story of a really nasty viciously fought battle of survival [...] literally page by page the story unfolds like a slow motion tragedy [...] the author tells their stories and gives us their thoughts of these cataclysmic events in their lives.

Sylvia Dinnage 28 August 2016

I would say that I was thrilled with your book but I was at times in tears. I had family in the navy in the Second World War (my father [...] My heart goes out to all of the *Hardy* men may god bless them all. Brian

Mrs M. Bieniasz 3 June 2016

A really well written account of the events. I enjoyed reading it, made me feel proud of our services, and also the Norwegian help they received. I have recommended this book to family and friends. Who are now reading it, well done to Ron Cope.

T. A. ORFORD 10 October 2015

My uncle was at the first battle of Narvik on HMS *Hotspur* this is a brilliant book about the battle. I thoroughly enjoyed reading it.

America / Canadian 'Amazon' readers

Christine Keown. February 17, 2016

Very well researched and gave a lot of detail about those involved and how it effected their lives.

Vincent Sebastiano. October 24, 2016

Author utilized his father's memoirs and his own naval perspective to portray battle scenes effectively. I enjoyed the book and it was worth retaining in my library.

Amazon Customer. November 22, 2016

Thorough, insightful and important about the naval effort in Narvik

CPSIA information can be obtained
at www.ICGtesting.com
Printed in the USA
LVHW111309231118
598057LV00001B/68/P